The Western Front

A History of the First World War

NICK LLOYD

PENGUIN BOOKS

UK | USA | Canada | Ireland | Australia
India | New Zealand | South Africa

Penguin Books is part of the Penguin Random House group of companies
whose addresses can be found at global.penguinrandomhouse.com.

First published by Viking 2021
Published in Penguin Books 2021

001

Copyright © Nick Lloyd, 2021

The moral right of the author has been asserted

All images reproduced courtesy of and © Alamy

Maps by BD Illustrations
Typeset by Jouve (UK), Milton Keynes
Printed and bound in Great Britain by Clays Ltd, Elcograf S.p.A.

The authorized representative in the EEA is Penguin Random House Ireland,
Morrison Chambers, 32 Nassau Street, Dublin D02 YH68

A CIP catalogue record for this book is available from the British Library

ISBN: 978-0-241-34718-8

For William

Contents

Illustrations

Maps

Glossary

A7V: German heavy tank introduced in 1918.

ADC: Aide-de-camp.

Amalgamation: Concept of placing American soldiers into British or French units.

Army: Formation containing between two and seven corps commanded by a General.

Army Group: Two or more armies commanded by a General.

Battalion: Unit of infantry (nominally up to 1,000 strong) commanded by a Lieutenant-Colonel.

Battery: Organization of artillery pieces (usually containing between four and six guns).

Boche: Slang for a German soldier.

Brigade: Major tactical formation commanded by a Brigadier-General. Three brigades made up a British division (each brigade containing four battalions). French, German and US brigades operated on a different system, each with two regiments.

Chasseurs: Elite French light infantry.

Chief of Staff: Principal staff officer of a military organization. In the German system, a Chief of Staff was usually a co-commander.

Corps: Collection of divisions (usually between two and five) commanded by a Lieutenant-General.

Counter-battery: Fire directed at an opposing side's artillery.

Creeping barrage: Moving wall of shellfire that advanced at a pre-determined pace. Designed to keep defenders' heads down and escort infantry on to their objectives.

Division: Basic tactical unit on the battlefield employing between 10,000 and 15,000 men with supporting medical, engineering and artillery arms, commanded by a Major-General. US divisions were significantly larger, with 28,000 men.

Doughboy: Slang for an American soldier. The moniker had originated in the Mexican War of 1846–8 when US troops had become so caked in dust that they looked as if they had been covered in unbaked dough.

Eingreif division: Literally 'intervention division'. Specially trained reserve unit kept out of range of enemy artillery and brought forward to counter-attack.

Escadrille: French Air Service squadron.

Groupement: Battalion-sized organization of tanks or at least two *escadrilles*.

Hindenburg Line: Major German defensive system constructed during 1916–17 that included a number of subsidiary positions, such as the Siegfried Line and the Drocourt–Quéant Line.

Jagdgeschwader: German Air Service fighter wing (containing four *Jagdstaffeln*).

Jagdstaffel: Fighter squadron (usually containing between nine and twelve aircraft).

Landwehr: German reserve units intended for garrison duties, often containing older men.

Materialschlacht: Literally 'material battle'. German term for the kind of industrialized, mass warfare that emerged on the Western Front in 1916.

Minenwerfer: German heavy trench mortar.

New Army: Wartime volunteers raised in the United Kingdom.

Pillbox: Reinforced concrete blockhouse.

Regiment: Organization of infantry battalions. French and German divisions contained four regiments (each of three battalions). The British regimental system differed from Continental use and regarded the regiment as a permanent organizational unit for its battalions.

U-boat: German submarine. Abbreviation of *Unterseeboot*.

Vollmacht: Authority given to a staff officer in the German Army to issue orders in his superior's name.

Zero Hour: Time that an attack would commence.

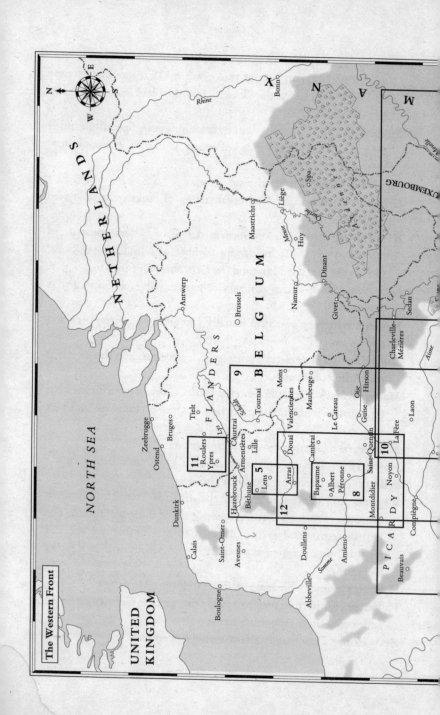

The Western Front

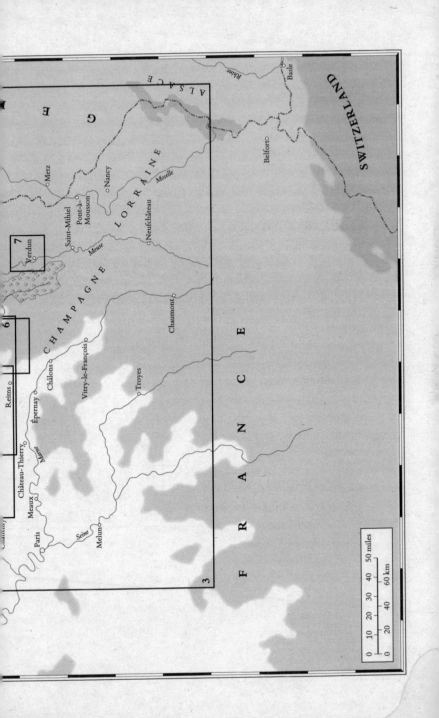

Paris
Melun
Seine
Meaux
Château-Thierry
Marne
Épernay
Châlons
Reims
Vitry-le-François
Épernay
Château-Thierry

6
7
Verdun
Meuse
Saint-Mihiel
Pont-à-Mousson
Metz
Nancy
Moselle
Neufchâteau

CHAMPAGNE
LORRAINE

Troyes
Chaumont

F R A N C E

G
A L S A C E

Belforto

Basle
Rhine

SWITZERLAND

3

| 0 | 10 | 20 | 30 | 40 | 50 miles |
| 0 | 20 | 40 | 60 km | | |

Preface

On 21 July 1916, Private Arthur Thomas, a soldier with 1st Australian Division, went into the trenches near Pozières on the Somme. 'We have reached the pit in the theatre of this great drama . . .' he recorded in his diary, 'and we are feeling fascinated by the terrific ordeal ahead of us. The sky for miles in a semi-circle round us, is a blaze, and the colours of the rainbow from star shells illuminate the heavens, and the earth rocks and trembles from the sickening concussion, nothing less than the average imagination of hell.'[1] After journeying from Melbourne, via Egypt, Thomas had arrived on the Western Front, the decisive theatre of the First World War, where the armies of four great powers – Germany, France, the United Kingdom and, from 1917, the United States – fought in some of the bloodiest battles of the twentieth century, including the Somme, Verdun, Ypres and the Meuse–Argonne.

Thomas's reaction to what he saw, terrified yet awestruck, was typical of those who witnessed, at first hand, that cauldron of war: a bubbling, fermenting experiment in killing that changed the world. The Western Front would become synonymous with stalemate and mass slaughter, with indecisive, attritional struggles amid a tortured landscape of barbed wire and mud, while inspiring some of the most important works of literature of the twentieth century, including Erich Maria Remarque's *All Quiet on the Western Front*, Ernst Jünger's *Storm of Steel* and the haunting poetry of Wilfred Owen, killed in November 1918. In Britain at least, the legend of the Western Front has become deeply embedded within the social fabric. Of the 764,000 British Great War dead, almost 85 per cent were lost in France and Belgium.[2] This enormous sacrifice, far greater than any previous (or subsequent) conflict, has never been forgotten and has formed the main component of a story of futility and folly that continues to influence social attitudes towards the war to this day.

This book is intended to be the first of a three-volume history of the First World War. Subsequent volumes will concentrate on the Eastern Front (including Italy and the Balkans) and the wider war (the struggle in Africa and the Middle East), but I have chosen to begin in France and Belgium. Although each theatre of war clearly influenced and impacted upon the others, being linked together by the movement of fleets or the pull of railways, the flow of people or the transfer of money, I wanted to focus on each part of the war in turn. Each had its own set of heroes and villains, rogues and knaves. They came with their own environmental challenges, whether it was the mud of Flanders or the mountains of the Carpathians, the deserts of Arabia or the tropical grasslands of East Africa. And each front had its own internal dynamics that were unique enough to warrant their own full narrative, unbroken by diversions into secondary theatres or subsidiary activity. It is this distinction that makes this history different, allowing the full course of the war to emerge as it appeared to those who fought it. Together the three volumes will tell the story of the Great War; that shattering, cataclysmic moment of the twentieth century, when an old order collapsed and a new age was born, terrifying in its possibilities.

My aim throughout has been to write a narrative history of those four and a half years; to tell the story as closely as possible, without burdening the text with abstract theorizing or lengthy commentaries on differing interpretations (of which there are many). Instead, I have tried to bring readers closer in so that they might see the war, sit beside the main characters, and form their own judgement. It has been written primarily through the lens of those senior commanders who fought the war at what modern militaries refer to as the 'operational level'. Politics clearly intruded on this domain, and the struggle on the home front to manage resources and maintain domestic content was crucial to the war effort, but my main focus has been on those fighting generals who were faced with the reality of modern warfare in all its horror and complexity. How they tried to deal with it, how they succeeded or (more likely) failed to do so, is at the heart of this book.

For years these men have been characterized as 'donkeys' or

'butchers': unfeeling military aristocrats fighting the wrong kind of war, unable to adapt or change to the new realities unfolding on the battlefield. The truth was a much messier picture of trial and error, success and failure, with each promising development followed by an equally effective counter-measure. On the Western Front, the onset of trench warfare in the autumn of 1914 meant that the Allied powers of Britain and France had little choice but to attack. So they mounted a series of major offensives, each bigger than the last, to break up the trench network and return to mobile warfare in the hope that, once it had been restarted, Germany could be defeated and France liberated. Into each offensive they poured their manpower and deployed their technology in ever-increasing amounts, only to see their efforts thwarted and the blood cost rise ever higher. In response, Germany dug deeper trenches, widened and expanded her defensive networks into ever more labyrinthine fortifications, and counter-attacked whenever possible. It was only in 1918 that maturing weapon systems, new tactics and fresh manpower allowed the front to be broken, manoeuvre restored and a decision finally reached.

All the commanders struggled in this maelstrom, trying to cope with a war that had shattered their lives as much as any other. They were not, as is so often portrayed today, unapproachable men of iron, devoid of humanity or warmth. They were human beings with families – some of whom would be terribly damaged by the battles they themselves directed. Ferdinand Foch, one of the great heroes of the war, would lose his only son in the first weeks of fighting. Another French general, Noël de Castelnau, had three sons killed in action. Erich Ludendorff, who led the German armies to their shattering defeat in 1918, found out that his stepson had sustained fatal injuries in a plane crash several days after launching a vast new offensive. Generals were not even safe themselves. Contrary to the myth of the 'chateau general', hundreds of general officers would be killed or wounded during the war; shot by snipers, caught by shellfire, or succumbing to disease and ill-health brought on by the effects of ceaseless campaigning. Few European families were untouched by the Great War, and its commanders were no different.

The armies that these soldiers had to lead were unprecedented in their size and possessed of weapon systems that were dazzling in their power and lethality. Although many of the most recognizable technologies of the First World War had their origins in earlier years (quick-firing field artillery had been pioneered in 1897; Hiram Maxim's machine-gun patented in 1883; and powered flight invented in 1903), it was the Western Front where they were refined and developed into brutally effective killing machines. They took their place alongside the wholly novel inventions of poison gas (first introduced in 1915) and tanks (debuted in September 1916), giving the war in the west a revolutionary quality that was not always true of other theatres of war, whether in Eastern Europe or the Middle East. It was in France, wrote Major-General Jonathan Bailey, former Director General, British Army Development and Doctrine (2002–5), where the 'modern style of warfare' was born. By 1917, battles were being fought in three dimensions with artillery and air power playing a central role in the planning and execution of operations. This 'indirect-fire revolution', which allowed for the targeting of enemy defences, command and control facilities, and reserves, in depth, transformed warfare into something entirely different to what it had been in 1914.[3]

It was crucial to be able to tell this story from the perspectives of all the main protagonists: Germany as well as France, Britain and the United States. Although I wanted to keep the text as neutral as possible, it soon became apparent that the efforts of the French Army had been consistently overlooked in much of the writing on this period. Apart from the legendary defence of Verdun in 1916, the role that France played in the war is still largely unfamiliar to English-language audiences. With the largest of the Allied armies (on the Western Front) from the first until the last days of the war, the French Army took on the lion's share of the fighting, often leading the way with many of the technological and tactical developments that created this 'modern style of warfare'. If this book can contribute to a wider recognition of France's sacrifices and the undoubted tenacity and inventiveness with which she fought, then a much more balanced and fair assessment of the respective contributions of the Allies to the victory of 1918 can be made.

Writing this interwoven narrative was dependent upon a wide range of sources, beginning with the official histories and collections of documents published after the war: the fifteen-volume *Der Weltkrieg* (compiled by the German Reichsarchiv between 1925 and 1944); Sir James Edmonds's *Military Operations. France and Belgium* (published in fourteen volumes between 1922 and 1947); and the multi-volume French official history, *Les Armées françaises dans la Grande guerre*. They have their flaws, but all contain an enormous amount of factual material that helps to provide some order and coherence to the almost non-stop fighting on the Western Front between 1914 and 1918. The appendices included with the French official history also contain thousands of pages of documents, letters and reports that can be mined by the historian. Although the United States never published an official history, a seventeen-volume collection of selected documents on the history of the American Expeditionary Force (*United States Army in the World War, 1917–1919*) ensured that the enormous contribution that the doughboys made towards ending the war has not been forgotten.

The Western Front has been the subject of a substantial and growing body of scholarship and I am indebted to the legions of historians who have studied crucial aspects of it. The works of Elizabeth Greenhalgh and Robert Doughty were constantly by my side as I navigated the experience of the French Army and its epic struggles at the Marne and Champagne, Verdun and the Aisne. I am indebted to Greenhalgh's detailed biography of Foch, her general account of the French Army at war and her scholarly investigations into the nature of the Allied coalition. Doughty's *Pyrrhic Victory. French Strategy and Operations in the Great War* also provided a thorough assessment of how France fought the war. For the opposing side, special mention should be made of Jonathan Boff's *Haig's Enemy. Crown Prince Rupprecht and Germany's War on the Western Front*; Holger Herwig's *The Marne, 1914*; and Robert Foley's *German Strategy and the Path to Verdun*, which I found to be essential in understanding German strategy and operations on the Western Front.

The staff of numerous archives and libraries, both in the United Kingdom and overseas, have never failed to produce what was requested of them, and I would like to thank the National Archives of the UK; Imperial War Museum; British Library; Bodleian Library; Canadian War Museum; Library and Archives Canada; Australian War Memorial; Bundesarchiv-Militärarchiv, Freiburg; Military History Institute, Carlisle, Pennsylvania; and the Library of Congress, Washington DC. Particular gratitude must go to the team at the Hobson Library in the Joint Services Command & Staff College, Defence Academy of the UK. I am also grateful to Dr Tim Gale and Dr Jonathan Boff for reading through the manuscript; to Daniel Crewe and all at Viking; Dan Gerstle at Liveright; Peter Robinson; and my literary agent, Jon Wood. Finally, to my family, thank you for providing me with all the love and support that I could ask for. This book is dedicated to my son, William, who was born shortly after the manuscript was completed and whose growing presence in our lives added an extra incentive to finish on time.

NL
Cheltenham, England
April 2020

Prologue

'An act of hostility'

Shortly before seven o'clock on the evening of 2 August 1914, there was a flurry of activity at the Belgian Foreign Ministry in Brussels. Herr von Below-Saleske, the German Ambassador, handed an envelope to the Minister for Foreign Affairs, Jean Davignon, marked 'Very Confidential'. Inside was a document that would shatter the peace of Europe: 'Reliable news has been received by the Imperial Government to the effect that French forces intend to march along the line of the Meuse by Givet and Namur. This information leaves no doubt as to the intention of France to march through Belgian territory against Germany . . . It is essential for the self-defence of Germany that she should anticipate any hostile attack.' Should Germany be forced 'for her own protection, to enter Belgian territory', this should not be considered 'an act of hostility'. On the contrary, if Belgium adopted an attitude of 'benevolent neutrality', then Germany would evacuate her territory as soon as peace was declared and would pay for any damages caused. If, however, Belgium attempted to obstruct German troops or deny them free passage, she would be left with no option but to consider her as an enemy. 'In this event, Germany can undertake no obligations towards Belgium, but the future regulation of the relations between the two states must be left to the decision of arms.'[1]

The dramatic events in Brussels were the result of an unparalleled crisis in European diplomacy that had been sparked off by a brutal assassination in Sarajevo five weeks earlier. On 28 June, the Archduke Franz Ferdinand, heir to the Austro-Hungarian throne, had travelled to Sarajevo to inspect the empire's restless southern dominions, but was shot and killed by a deranged Bosnian gunman, Gavrilo Princip, who had links to a Serbian nationalist organization, the Narodna Odbrana ('National Defence'). The murder brought to a head the rivalry between Austria and Serbia that had been festering for decades. An ultimatum had been delivered to Belgrade on 23 July, warning Serbia that unless she suppressed the 'subversive movement' that had carried out the assassination and engaged in various 'acts of terrorism' against Austria, then she would have no choice but to 'put an end to those intrigues, which constitute a standing menace to the peace of the Monarchy'. Serbia swiftly agreed to the majority of Austria's demands, only to baulk at the request for an inquiry to investigate the conspiracy, staffed by Austrian appointees, as being 'a violation of the Constitution and of the law of criminal procedure', which was enough for Austria to recall her Ambassador and begin preparations for war.[2]

The system of alliances that criss-crossed Europe now began to activate: the Central Powers of Austria–Hungary and Germany versus Serbia and her erstwhile protector, Russia, who, in turn, was allied to the Republic of France. As Austria readied herself to invade Serbia and settle the 'Balkan question' once and for all, her main ally, Germany, would march in support. For Germany, this meant following the 'Schlieffen Plan', the latest in a series of operational schemes that had been developed by Count Alfred von Schlieffen, Chief of the General Staff between 1891 and 1906. After examining Germany's situation at length, Schlieffen concluded that in the event of a European war, she must be prepared to concentrate almost her entire strength in the west, leaving just a handful of corps to stave off the expected invasion of East Prussia by the Russian Army. Fearing a two-front war, Schlieffen wanted to take advantage of a slow, lumbering Russian mobilization to defeat France within a matter of weeks. This would take the form of a wide sweep through Belgium and the Low Countries, outflanking the heavily defended Franco-German border and bringing about a decisive battle somewhere east of Paris. Once this had been completed, Germany could deal with Russia as she saw fit.

Albert I, King of the Belgians, knew what was at stake. Thirty-nine years old, with piercing blue eyes and a ruddy complexion, he had assumed the throne in December 1909 under the shadow of impending war. He assembled his Cabinet ministers at 9.30 p.m., just as the sun was going down, the buildings glowing pink in the twilight. He reminded them that the meeting 'was called together less with the object of decid-ing what reply should be given' than of 'impressing the responsible leaders of the nation with the gravity of the situation which would be brought about'. The war, he prophesied, would bring about 'a charac-ter of violence undreamed of by them' and be a 'terrible trial' for the country. With that they drafted their response, while appealing to Great Britain and France for help in resisting the invasion. The Ger-man note was a 'deep and painful surprise' and 'a flagrant violation of the law of nations' that could not possibly be justified. Belgium was, therefore, 'firmly resolved to repel with all means in its power every attempt against its rights'. There would be no 'free passage' for the Ger-man Army.[3]

War was now inevitable. Germany declared war on France on the evening of 3 August; France responded within hours. With Europe's cities becoming more restive – a combustible mix of cheering, patri-otic crowds and sullen bystanders – Europe's leaders scrambled to justify their positions. In Berlin, the Imperial Chancellor, Theobald von Bethmann Hollweg, addressed the Reichstag at three o'clock on the afternoon of 4 August and confirmed that Germany's troops had already occupied Luxembourg and 'perhaps' had entered Belgian ter-ritory. 'Gentlemen, this is contrary to international law', he admitted, rather candidly. 'Although the French Government declared in Brus-sels that it would respect Belgium's neutrality as long as the opponent did so, . . . we knew that France was ready for the advance.' Beth-mann Hollweg insisted that they had to move to forestall a French offensive on the lower Rhine. 'Thus we were forced to ignore the justified protests of the Governments of Luxembourg and Belgium. The wrong – I speak openly – the wrong that we are thus commit-ting we will try to make right again as soon as our military goal is reached.'[4]

At the French Parliament, the Prime Minister, René Viviani, read out an address by the President, Raymond Poincaré: 'France has just been the object of a violent and premeditated attack, which is an inso-lent defiance of the law of nations.' Expressing confidence in her army and navy, Poincaré insisted that France had 'Right on her side' in the coming struggle and would be 'heroically defended by all her sons; nothing will break their sacred union before the enemy; to-day they are joined together as brothers in a common indignation against the aggressor, and in a common patriotic faith'. France would march again, defending her soil while supporting the efforts of the Russian Army on what would soon become the Eastern Front. Poincaré then reminded his listeners that France would also be aided by the 'loyal friendship of England' – which alongside the other major powers of Europe had been a co-signatory to the 1839 Treaty of London that guaranteed the neutrality and independence of Belgium.[5]

The war may have originated in the Balkans, but a sense of unfinished business hung over the main participants in the west. Germany would use the war as an opportunity to knock out a dangerous and implacable rival, while France was committed to avenging the humiliation of 1870, when Prussian forces had defeated the armies of Napoleon III's Second Empire in a series of bloody set-piece battles. When the German Empire was proclaimed in the Hall of Mirrors in the Palace of Versailles in January 1871, uniting the German states under Prussian leadership, it marked a sea change in the European balance of power. France, now the Third Republic, lost the eastern province of Alsace and most of Lorraine and was forced to pay a vast indemnity of 5 billion francs – a sum reflective of her new, reduced status as the second power on the Continent. But France never forgot her 'lost provinces', and the call to recover them was a persistent refrain in the years leading up to 1914.

A strange restlessness was upon everyone as they waited for what would happen next; a feeling only heightened by a smothering summer heat that lay like a blanket over Europe. At the American Legation in Brussels, Brand Whitlock, the US Ambassador, met Herr von Strum, the Secretary of the German Legation, on the afternoon that war was declared. Strum was 'nervous, agitated, and unstrung', with dark rings around his eyes that revealed how little he had slept the past week. 'Tears were continually welling into his eyes, and suddenly he covered his face with his hands, leaned forward, his elbows on his knees, an attitude of despair.' And then finally, after what seemed like an eternity, he spoke:

"'Oh, these poor, stupid Belgians!' he said. 'Why don't they get out of the way! Why don't they get out of the way!'"

Whitlock, standing in front of him, said nothing. With that, Strum stood up and wiped away his tears, and they parted with a handshake. The German delegation left for Berlin that evening.[6]

PART I

'War is not like manoeuvres'

Liège to the Second Battle of Champagne
(August 1914–November 1915)

I. 'A vision of Attila'

The task of achieving German victory was the responsibility of Schlieffen's successor, the 66-year-old Colonel-General Helmuth Johannes Ludwig von Moltke. Moltke's name was an illustrious one (he was known as 'the younger', to distinguish him from his legendary uncle, who had led Prussia's armies to victory in 1866 and 1870), but his appointment had been received with little cheer, many critics putting it down to his close friendship with Kaiser Wilhelm II (whom he had served as aide-de-camp for many years). Too sensitive for a Prussian officer, there was always a strange, languid softness about Moltke. Balding, with a pronounced paunch, jowls hanging over the stiff collar of his uniform, he was a highly cultured individual who was an uneasy fit within the 'blood and iron' traditions of the Great German General Staff. A lover of music and fine art, spirituality and esoteric wisdom, Moltke lacked those essential qualities that truly great military commanders possess: robustness and an ability to think twice as fast as any opponent. His outlook was also darkened by a bleak pessimism about Germany's future – a belief that unless she fought now she would be crushed by Russia and France in a future war. 'We are ready, and the sooner it comes, the better for us', he wrote on 1 June 1914 – barely four weeks before the assassination of the archduke.[1]

If the German Army was to advance rapidly, then it would need to take the chain of frontier forts that lay along the eastern edge of Belgium. Whereas Schlieffen had planned to invade Holland as well as Belgium, giving his troops ample room to deploy, Moltke insisted that Holland should remain neutral as a kind of 'windpipe' through which Germany could access the outside world.[2] Because of this, the German right wing had to push through a narrow corridor around the city of Liège. Situated in a wooded valley along the River Meuse, it was at the centre of a complex web of roads and interlocking railways that served this part of Europe. As the gateway to the Belgian plain, Liège's strategic significance had long been recognized and a series of twelve forts had been constructed between 1888 and 1891 that ringed the city like the hours on a clock face. Each fort was an equilateral triangle, made of concrete, and defended by a wide ditch strung with barbed wire. Inside the fort were machine-guns and armoured cupolas, which housed howitzers that constituted their primary armament.

For King Albert and the Belgian people the situation seemed irretrievably gloomy. The country was in no shape to resist the oncoming invasion. Comprising fewer than 120,000 regulars in just five divisions, the Belgian Army was ill-trained, short of artillery, lacking in modern communications equipment, and all too reliant upon fortress troops of between thirty and thirty-five years of age that were, as one observer put it, 'of absolutely no military value'.[3] Together they could not hope to win any large-scale action against the might of the German forces then massing behind the border, but they could delay them, interfere with their plans and prove their mettle. Given the political necessity of neutrality, as late as 3 August Belgian forces had been scattered across the country to cover a variety of multiple invasion routes by the British, French or Germans (to be deployed against whoever should breach their neutrality first). With the expiration of the German note, Belgian troops were swiftly concentrated, with 3rd Division heading to Liège where it would soon encounter the six reinforced brigades of General Otto von Emmich's X Corps.

Emmich's task was simple. He had to seize the city in a lightning *coup de main*, allowing the German right wing to begin its long march towards Paris. His men reached the outskirts of Liège on the evening of 4 August and ran into Belgian troops barring their way; the defenders taking cover behind quickly improvised barricades, thickly forested with rifles. A proclamation was hastily read out, signed by Emmich, which repeated the German Government's claim that France had already entered Belgian territory. This was a lie – at that moment French troops had been ordered not to go within ten kilometres of the frontier – but it was an essential one if Germany was to try to justify her plan of campaign. Emmich demanded that German troops be allowed to pass. If they were given free passage, he promised that the Belgian people would be spared the 'horrors of war'.[4]

German planners had assumed that there would be no more than 6,000 defenders in the city, but instead they found a far more numerous and stubborn opponent than they had anticipated, which would cause the first and most crucial delay to Schlieffen's iron timetable.[5] The commander of the garrison at Liège was Lieutenant-General Gérard Leman, a 63-year-old former instructor at the Belgian War College. Stern-faced with deep-set eyes, and possessing an unbreakable sense of duty, Leman commanded about 30,000 troops and had been told by King Albert to 'hold to the end'. He ordered his men to dig in, throwing up lines of defences to link the forts together and hurrying up supplies and ammunition to withstand a siege. But there was little time. On the following morning, 5 August, a bearer waving a flag of truce took another message to Leman (who had set up his headquarters in the old citadel in the city centre) and, once again, requested that German troops be allowed to pass. But the Belgian dismissed it with a curt wave of his hand. He was not interested in parleying with the invader.[6]

German attacks were immediately ordered against the eastern ring of forts – Fort d'Évegnée, Fort de Fléron and Fort de Barchon – preceded by heavy artillery fire, but the first waves collapsed in a welter of blood and confusion. The attackers came on in thick columns, marching as if in peacetime, right under the muzzles of Belgian riflemen until they were cut down in droves. Although a party of German troops was able to infiltrate the city centre, led by an intrepid staff officer, Erich Ludendorff,[7] the fortresses held out for another ten days. The last telephone communication between Belgian HQ and the garrison was on the morning of 6 August, when a harassed telephone operator whispered, 'The Germans are here' before the line went dead.[8] The forts had not been designed for 360-degree defensive operations and were weaker on their interior sides. They were also no match for the super-heavy guns that Germany and Austria–Hungary had been building and which were being rushed up to the front. On 11 August, the components of four massive weapons had arrived in Belgium and were being readied for deployment. Two 420 mm M-Gerät howitzers (nicknamed 'Big Berthas'), capable of hurling a 2,000 lb shell up to nine kilometres, and two 305 mm Škoda siege mortars were brought within range of the forts and on the following morning, 12 August, they opened fire.[9]

The sound of these enormous weapons, with their high-angle fire plunging down upon their targets, was akin to an express train, an ominous rumbling, turning to a demented scream as it got closer, before ending with a shattering explosive crack. One by one the forts fell; their cupolas caving in with clouds of concrete and brick dust, snuffing out hundreds of lives in the choking darkness. At Fort de Loncin, Leman and his dwindling band of men held out until 15 August. Conditions inside the fort were almost indescribable. The cacophony of sounds – guns of all calibres, the thud of metal on concrete and brick, and the shuddering of high-explosive shells – went on hour after hour. Inside the crumbling walls, along dimly lit corridors stinking of dust and cordite, Leman did what he could. By then most of the other forts had either surrendered or been destroyed, leaving Leman's detachment desperately trying to keep resistance alive. The general's legs had been crushed by falling masonry, but he remained at his post, driven around on a makeshift automobile. A further bombardment by the much-feared 'Big Berthas' brought the matter to a swift conclusion, and by the morning of 16 August tattered white flags were seen waving from the last two emplacements still in Belgian hands.

As for General Leman, he was extremely fortunate to survive the bombardment. Most of his garrison had been consumed in a vast explosion that ripped through the walls of the fort after a shell had struck its magazine. 'It is impossible to describe the appalling results of that explosion', recorded a Belgian survivor; 'the entire middle-part of the fort collapsed in a stupendous cloud of flames, smoke and dust.'[10] When Leman regained consciousness, he was greeted by Emmich, who offered a few words on the gallantry of his men. Leman smiled and thanked the general, before muttering an old joke, 'War is not like manoeuvres.' Then, remembering something, he began to unbuckle his sword, which lay twisted by his side, to offer it to his conqueror. But Emmich refused to take it. He leant in close to the general and whispered in his ear:

'To have crossed swords with you has been an honour.'[11]

It might have taken slightly longer than anticipated, but the German war plan could now be unleashed. The road was open to the heart of Belgium.

The French Chief of the General Staff (who was appointed Commander-in-Chief on the outbreak of war) was Joseph Jacques Césaire Joffre, a 62-year-old engineer who had spent much of his career out in France's colonial empire. Joffre was a heavy-set and paunchy figure, with thick, wavy grey hair, broad-brimmed eyebrows and a *grande moustache*. A contemporary described him as 'more massive than elegant', adding that 'His short neck and broad shoulders give to his personality an appearance of greater strength than distinction, but his *bonhomie* and kindliness of manner add a real charm, an irresistible fascination, to the face of a clever, a strong, a kind, and, above all, an essentially manly man.'[12] He may not have been the most spectacular or flamboyant officer that the French Army ever produced, but in France's fraught political landscape, riven with class and anti-clerical prejudice, this pragmatic, strong-willed man seemed to fit. He was not political or religious enough to arouse suspicion, was competent, and had the gift of knowing when to speak and when to remain silent. He was appointed Chief of the General Staff in 1911.

The French war plan had been issued in February 1914 and was the product of multiple authors, multiple compromises and enduring strategic difficulties. France, with a smaller population than Germany, and a markedly inferior economic strength, had to find a way to win, or at least to do enough damage to the Kaiser's armies until her ally, Tsarist Russia, came to the rescue. The result was Plan XVII, the latest in a series of deployment schemes that provided for the concentration of France's armies along her eastern frontier. France deployed 1.3 million men in five armies: three along the Franco-German border, stretching all the way from Belfort to Longwy, and then another two to the northwest. Once they were in position, Joffre would 'develop' attacks in two directions: on the right between the Vosges and the Moselle below Toul (to recover the 'lost provinces' of Alsace and Lorraine); and the second, to the north of the line Verdun–Metz. These attacks were intended to seize the initiative, unbalance whatever German forces were nearby, and – particularly in the case of Alsace–Lorraine – 'assist the removal of that part of the population . . . that has remained faithful to the cause of France'.[13]

The left flank would be crucial. Holding the northernmost part of the line was General Charles Louis Lanrezac's Fifth Army, which lay between Hirson and Sedan along the wooded Franco-Belgian border. Lanrezac had once been darling of the French Army, a protégé of Joffre's who had lectured at the École Militaire and gained a reputation as a bright and original thinker. There his martial bearing and sparkling wit were perfectly at home; but now, in the white heat of command, he began to lose his nerve. After being alarmed by a stream of urgent intelligence reports from Belgium, he visited the French High Command – GQG (*Grand Quartier Général*) – on 14 August and told Joffre that he suspected the Germans were making a major flanking movement in the north. If this was the case, then he would need to redeploy immediately, shifting to the northwest, or risk leaving his flank wide open. After returning to his headquarters, Lanrezac was handed further evidence that the German right wing could comprise as many as eight corps and four cavalry divisions. 'This information,' he wrote to Joffre, 'which came to my knowledge after our interview, seems to indicate the threat of an enveloping movement carried out by very considerable forces on both banks of the Meuse.'[14]

The possibility of an attack through Belgium was hardly unsuspected by the French military, but the full scale of what the Germans were attempting was never truly grasped, either by Joffre or by his closest advisers. Germany would *not* violate Belgian neutrality. Schlieffen's plan was *probably no more* than elaborate disinformation to mask a thrust into France, and there was *simply no way* that Germany would have enough troops to deploy in strength north of the Meuse. But so what? Even if Germany wheeled right and placed the bulk of her combat power in Belgium, then it must surely leave her weak in other sectors? Joffre fired a short telegram back to Lanrezac dismissing his concerns: 'I only see advantages to the movement you are talking about. But the threat is remote and its certainty is far from absolute.'[15] Joffre's focus was elsewhere. He had issued 'General Instructions No. 1' on 8 August, outlining his intention to 'seek battle, with all his forces united'. He was planning two quick thrusts across the border to gain the initiative, give France an early victory, and coincide with a planned Russian offensive on the Eastern Front. First Army, on the extreme right, would push towards Sarrebourg, while on its left Second Army would head for Sarrebruck (Saarbrücken). Lanrezac would have to wait.[16]

The march began on 14 August. For five days two French armies advanced eastwards, cautiously at first, watching as the German rearguard melted away in front of them, leaving abandoned villages in flames, and using their artillery to harass and slow down the French columns. It was here that the French first came up against the impressive firepower that German corps could deploy, with 77 mm, 105 mm and 150 mm guns outranging French artillery and keeping the attackers at arm's length. By as early as the second day, the commander of Second Army, General Noël Édouard Curières de Castelnau, confirmed that his army was engaged in a 'battle of attrition' that required 'certain procedures similar to those in siege warfare'. Each position had to be conquered successively, with the 'widest use' of trenches, fortifications and shelters, although he was at pains to stress that this did not mean 'that we abandon the idea of an offensive'.[17] Yet even a few days' campaigning was enough to reveal the dangers of France's offensive war plan. 'The troops, infantry and artillery, have been sorely tested', reported Second Army on 15 August. 'Our artillery is held at a distance by the long-range artillery of our enemy; it cannot get close enough for counter-battery fire. Our infantry has attacked with élan, but they have been halted primarily by enemy artillery fire and by unseen enemy infantry hidden in trenches.'[18]

The German commander in this sector was Crown Prince Rupprecht of Bavaria, one of Germany's most senior royal generals. He commanded Sixth Army and had been instructed to draw the enemy into a 'net' before mounting flanking attacks that would devastate the French advance. This was in line with Germany's plan to concentrate her strength on her right wing, doing just enough to keep the French engaged until the main blow could be struck from the north. This was well understood, but the further the French pushed, the more anxious Rupprecht and his staff became, particularly when they began to suspect that they had the edge over their opponents. They were also concerned lest the war end before Bavarian troops had a chance to do more than just retreat. Rupprecht asked for permission to counter-attack, and after a series of heated discussions with Moltke he was finally given permission to do whatever he thought right, having been warned that he 'must bear the responsibility' for what happened.[19] His troops went forward on 20 August, stunning the French with the ferocity and vigour of their assault. The result was a rout. By 23 August, First and Second Armies were retiring, in bedraggled columns, back to their start line, having gained no ground, but with a lasting respect for the power of their opponents.

As the French war plan began to fragment, Joffre kept up a furious round of meetings. On Sunday, 16 August, he met Field Marshal Sir John French, the British Commander-in-Chief. French was sixty-one years old. A decorated cavalryman whose epic ride to relieve Ladysmith during the South African War had made him a hero throughout the empire, he was physically brave, but small in stature and possessed of a nervous, irritable temperament. When he was angry – which occurred all too often – his cheeks would redden, his eyes would narrow, before his fist would come banging down on the table, scattering attendants in its wake. The French President, Raymond Poincaré, who met Sir John in Paris, was unimpressed with the English commander. 'He is a small man, quiet in manner, with nothing particularly military in his appearance, except that he looks you straight in the face; his cheeks and chin are closely shaved, his moustache is grey and rather drooping.' He 'speaks our tongue with great difficulty'.[20]

Joffre did not share Poincaré's opinion of Sir John – having a more charitable assessment of his strengths as a commander – but it was a worrying example of how hard the British commander would have to work if he was going to operate closely with Britain's allies. At that moment, an expeditionary force of two infantry corps (each comprising two divisions) and a large cavalry division – about 100,000 men in total – was being ferried across the English Channel to take its place on the French left around the fortress city of Maubeuge. Joffre hoped to launch a major offensive on 22 August, but Sir John insisted that he could not deploy any earlier than 24 August. Joffre explained his campaign plan and urged Sir John to get his men into the line as quickly as possible. His knowledge of German deployments in Belgium was, he admitted, 'so lacking in precision that I could not give any exact form to my intentions'. He did, however, want to mount a 'general action' somewhere north of the Sambre, where the British would be able to attack 'the outer flanks of the German forces, taking them if possible in reverse'. Sir John promised to do what he could.[21]

Notwithstanding the frustration at GQG and in Paris at the seemingly unhurried pace of British mobilization, the despatch of the British Expeditionary Force (BEF) to the Continent had been a swift and smooth undertaking. On 6 August, two days after Britain declared war on Germany, a Council of War had been held at 10 Downing Street chaired by the Prime Minister, Herbert Asquith. It was decided to send the expeditionary force to France, although the newly appointed Secretary of State for War, Field Marshal Earl Kitchener of Khartoum ('K of K'), only agreed that four divisions (plus a cavalry division) would sail – leaving two remaining at home to protect against invasion.[22] Kitchener, a rigid, authoritarian figure infamous for his centralizing tendencies, suspected that a swift and decisive victory, by either side, was unlikely, so he had no desire to throw everything he had into the ring at the present moment, despite urgent appeals to do so from Paris. This caution was reflected in the instructions he gave to Sir John. While 'every effort must be made to coincide most sympathetically with the plans and wishes of our Ally', Kitchener made it clear that 'the numerical strength of the British Force and its contingent reinforcement' was to be 'strictly limited' and the 'greatest care' must be exercised over it.[23]

This delicate balancing act, of supporting his ally, but only up to a point, would constantly play on Sir John's mind as he readied his divisions to take their place in the line. He met Lanrezac on 17 August and found him to be an encouraging and impressive figure. 'Lanrezac appears a very capable soldier and struck me very much by his sense and decisiveness of character', French noted in his diary. Lanrezac also appeared uncharacteristically confident, professing that they were now on the brink of a great victory so close to the site of Waterloo! It was only later on, after they parted, that their relationship began to crumble. Under the pressure of the great retreat, each man accused the other of being unreliable and leaving them unsupported. Lanrezac was unimpressed by the sight of French stumbling over his language, while Sir John looked down upon Lanrezac's 'superior education' as a former War College professor, a position, he noted sourly, which had 'given him little idea of how to conduct war'. From this moment onwards, Anglo-French cooperation on the most crucial sector of the front would be dogged by mistrust and misunderstanding.[24]

The speed with which Joffre launched offensives may have surprised the German High Command, but any concerns had evaporated by the time the right wing was ready to begin its grand enveloping movement. Germany's armies had now concentrated. For the past two weeks, hundreds of trains had been rattling westwards every day, crossing over the Rhine and disgorging crowds of bewildered, excited and nervous young soldiers, newly clad in their grey woollen tunics and stiff leather boots. They were swiftly organized into companies and battalions, regiments and brigades, divisions and corps, to make up what was, by common consent, the most formidable military organization in the world. By 17 August seven vast armies had been formed, lined up from Strasbourg all the way to Düsseldorf, comprising thirty-four corps (including eleven reserve corps), ten cavalry divisions and seventeen reserve (*Landwehr*) brigades, with a total strength of 1.6 million men. Just 250,000 were left in East Prussia to guard against the imminent Russian invasion.[25]

Hopes were high that the decisive action of the war was now just weeks away. His spirits waxing as the moment drew nearer, Moltke wrote to his most senior officer in the field, General Karl von Bülow, the 68-year-old commander of Second Army. With his distinctive head of closely cropped white hair, Bülow was one of the most decorated soldiers in the empire, with Prussia's highest award, the Order of the Black Eagle, pinned on his chest. 'I am writing you just a few words to express my satisfaction that you will be the leader by whose hand the first major decisions will be made. As soon as our armies have completed their deployment, we can form up. The order for this will be decreed by His Majesty. It was thanks to God that the adventurous coup on Liège succeeded under the leadership of General Emmich. He carried it off well. The unanimity of our people is impressive . . . Now there is only one goal, victory!'[26]

Apart from Moltke, Bülow's most important relationship would be with General Alexander von Kluck, the commander of First Army, the largest (and arguably most important) of the German armies in 1914 – a 250,000-man battering ram that would deploy on the right wing and lead the attack. A fierce individual whose face would sometimes freeze into a terrible-looking scowl, Kluck had a habit of carrying numerous personal weapons, a sidearm or even a rifle, that he would wave in front of him, giving off an air of barely controlled aggression. 'No one seemed to dare approach him', wrote a terrified French civilian, Monsieur Fabre, whose house was requisitioned by the general during the campaign. 'He had a truly terrible air. I had a vision of Attila.'[27] On 10 August, Kluck issued his first orders, instructing his men to hold themselves in readiness to go forward. When the word came, they would cross the Meuse and then push past Liège towards Brussels. The concentration of so many troops in such a congested area required the tightest of discipline and the best of organization, so Kluck warned his officers: 'Great demands will be made on the marching power of the troops.'[28]

German military headquarters – including the Supreme Army Command, *Oberste Heeresleitung* (OHL) – departed Potsdam for Koblenz on the morning of 16 August, with the Kaiser and his entourage, including Moltke, seated in comfortable carriages as the German countryside slipped by. Everything passed off smoothly, apart from a momentary delay when Moltke's wife, Eliza, boarded the royal train with her maid after asking to accompany her husband. Such an unusual arrangement – Eliza and her maid were the only women on the train – caused consternation among the ranks of the General Staff and increased the mutterings against Moltke, who, it was said, had suffered a period of ill-health, perhaps even a breakdown. The truth was that he was already ailing and had clashed with the Kaiser on 1 August over whether the German war plan could be activated against Russia and *not* France. When Moltke told him that this was impossible, Wilhelm shot back: 'Your uncle would have given me a different answer!'[29]

It was not until 18 August – a day after OHL opened at Koblenz – that First, Second and Third Armies of the German right wing were able to go forward. In Kluck's First Army, four full-strength corps, followed by another three reserve corps, skirted past Liège and, in the blazing sunshine, marched west. To the south, Bülow's Second Army did likewise, heading for the fortified city of Namur, which was reached on 20 August and, like Liège, would require the attention of the super-heavy guns. Baron Max von Hausen's Third Army moved, in echelon, to the south through the Ardennes aiming for the Meuse between Givet and Namur. The sight of three German armies on the move was breathtaking. Endless grey columns of infantry, raising clouds of thick brown dust, followed by an enormous baggage train, crept across the landscape to the strange and unnerving sound of thousands of boots crunching over the roads and the continuous jangling and banging of rifles and bayonets, mess tins and helmets. 'Looking ahead and back the column stretched out of sight in both directions like some gigantic snake threading its way through the landscape', remembered one German soldier.[30]

The march made pressing demands on the men; endless miles under a burning August sky, passing villages that once teemed with life, now haunted by hushed groups of old men and women, those who could not flee, staring at their conquerors as they passed by. Moving such an enormous number of men, horses, guns and supplies required intricate organization. First Army used three main routes. Each would be used by two corps, placed under a commanding general who was responsible for making common arrangements for accommodation and food.[31] They made impressive progress and, apart from the occasional desperate rearguard action, the Belgian Army could only watch helplessly as its country was overrun. After the fall of Liège, King Albert's remaining divisions had withdrawn to the line of the River Gette (one division being sent to garrison Namur), before retreating behind the defences of Antwerp. Brussels was entered by German troops on 20 August – the day of Rupprecht's counter-attack in Lorraine – and soon afterwards Namur came under heavy bombardment, with howitzer and mortar shells screaming over the town. By 24 August most of the forts had been either disabled or destroyed and the garrison evacuated, luckily escaping to French lines before the city was engulfed by the seemingly irresistible tide of German forces.

In order to ensure close coordination between the three armies of the right wing, Moltke subordinated Kluck to the commander of Second Army, Bülow, whom he regarded as his most capable general. Kluck, who brimmed with aggression, found subordination to Second Army a tiresome distraction and he would increasingly come to see Bülow as a drag on his success. The command situation was further complicated by the poor communications that would bedevil Moltke's armies. Inexplicably, OHL had only one radio transmitter, with a range of just 300 kilometres, and although relay stations were opened as the armies advanced, delays were common and messages were often sent *en clair* because it took too long to encode them. Crucially, there was no radio communication between First and Second Armies, the result being that they tended to fight their own wars, with little reference to the other's plans.[32] It was another indication of how the 'friction' of war was beginning to affect Germany's attack, which was already showing signs of strain and frustration that would drive German soldiers to terrible acts of murder and desecration.

The march through Belgium was punctuated by shootings and burnings as rumours of guerrilla fighters – so-called *franc-tireurs* – spread through the German Army. Men, already exhausted after a week of long marches, easily became prone to thinking that behind every corner lay teams of snipers and arsonists, or inside every home awaited cruel Belgian housewives eager to mutilate their wounded. Men, of all ranks, were understandably nervous about marching so far through enemy territory, and the intense pressure to cover more and more miles meant that no delay could be tolerated. The centre of Louvain, the great medieval university town (which housed King Albert's headquarters before he left for Antwerp), was burnt on the evening of 25 August after shots were fired (although they seem to have come from German units). Over the following days, Kluck's men ransacked the city, rounding up suspects and shooting terrified civilians, the air full of scraps of burning paper; all that was left of one of the great libraries of Christian civilization, now just a sad collection of 'blackened walls, stone columns, and the glowing embers of books'.[33]

It was not just in Louvain where German soldiers lost control. Since the early days of August, there had been scattered incidents of violence against Belgian civilians and soldiers. Visé, one of the first towns to be occupied, was torched on 16 August after rumours swept through the streets that shots had been fired. Six hundred houses were burnt and twenty-three inhabitants killed in the ensuing reprisals. At Aarschot, where Belgian soldiers had held up the Germans for several hours, twenty captured soldiers were executed and their bodies thrown in the river. Other areas of Belgium also bore the brunt of a calculated desire to subdue and dominate. The city of Dinant, which was reached by troops from Hausen's Third Army on 23 August, was the scene of one of the worst massacres of the war when 674 Belgian civilians were murdered in a brutal series of outrages. After French battalions had made a fighting retreat through the town and blown up the bridges over the Meuse, German soldiers took their revenge, burning houses, deporting civilians and murdering about 10 per cent of the population in a matter of hours.[34] Schlieffen's clear road through Belgium was now becoming a slaughterhouse.

Undeterred by the setbacks in Lorraine, Joffre was now ready to unleash his main offensive. In the French centre, Third and Fourth Armies (commanded by Generals Pierre Ruffey and Fernand de Langle de Cary respectively) would push northeast towards Arlon and Neufchâteau, hoping to catch Germany's northern wing in the flank. GQG estimated that Germany had no more than six corps and a handful of cavalry divisions in the Ardennes region, and so assumed that French forces would enjoy a significant advantage. But French intelligence was mistaken. The Germans were not weak at all. On the contrary, there were two armies in this sector (Fourth and Fifth) that could boast ten corps plus a series of *Landwehr* brigades devoted to defensive duties. They were also backed up by forty-two batteries of 105 mm and 150 mm howitzers – 'twice the heavy artillery of the French' – which, in the words of one French officer, gave their infantry 'an armour of steel: they scarcely have to show themselves to walk into positions rendered untenable by their guns'.[35]

22 August dawned with a heavy grey mist that hugged the ground

and masked the thousands of troops, on either side, that were marching towards one another. By the time the fog had burnt off and the heat was rising through the tangled woods, a series of bitter and continuous battles began to spark into life right across the line; hundreds of confused, sometimes chaotic skirmishes that produced terrible carnage and left the peaceful, verdant Ardennes landscape shattered by heavy fire. 'From the unknown country beyond the hills came the terrific noise of battle', recorded an awestruck Frenchman; 'the rattle of musketry and the roar of machine-guns, like great rollers being sucked back on a pebbly shore, and the thunder of artillery enveloping and uniting all these noises into a single voice like that of a storm in mid-ocean, with heaving, crashing waves, deep, thudding undertones and the shrill whistle of the wind through the surf.'[36]

Joffre had placed great hopes in Langle de Cary's Fourth Army being able to deliver a thunderous blow at what he thought was the weakest part of the German line. Instead there was only a shattering defeat; a tragedy so awful that it resulted in the collapse of Plan XVII and the loss of thousands of soldiers, including some of France's best troops. The forests of the Ardennes were terrible places to fight. Hills and valleys rapidly exhausted marching infantry; thick woodland prevented proper observation and reconnaissance; and narrow roads resulted in units becoming strung out and vulnerable to ambush. Fourth Army was advancing north, with each corps marching forward in parallel, slightly in echelon of each other (like 'a staircase falling away to the south and east'), leaving their right flank exposed to attack.[37] With little coordination across the army and poor knowledge of the enemy, when French units met strong German forces, they quickly found themselves in trouble.

The price of these mistakes was ultimately paid for in French lives. In just four days – 20–23 August – perhaps as many as 40,000 Frenchmen were fatally wounded, most of them in the killing grounds of the Ardennes, which was littered with French dead, clad in their colourful red and blue uniforms. The worst day was 22 August with 27,000 dead. This was, as one authority later put it, 'the climax of the horrors of 1914'.[38] Some of the worst fighting was at Rossignol, where the elite Colonial Corps became engaged in a life-and-death struggle against

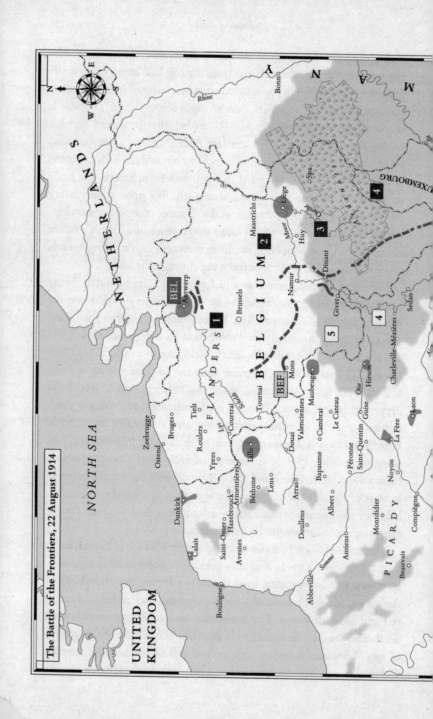

The Battle of the Frontiers, 22 August 1914

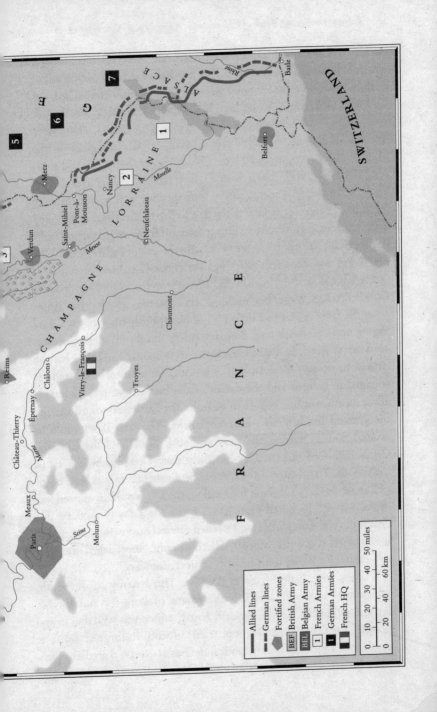

Allied lines
German lines
Fortified zones
BEF British Army
BEL Belgian Army
1 French Armies
1 German Armies
French HQ

| 0 | 10 | 20 | 30 | 40 | 50 miles |

| 0 | 20 | 40 | 60 km |

FRANCE

SWITZERLAND

ALSACE

LORRAINE

CHAMPAGNE

Paris
Meaux
Meulun
Seine
Marne
Château-Thierry
Épernay
Châlons
Reims
Vitry-le-François
Troyes
Chaumont
Verdun
Saint-Mihiel
Pont-à-Mousson
Neufchâteau
Meuse
Moselle
Nancy
Metz
Belfort
Basle
Rhine

5
6
7
E
G
J
1
2

the German VI Corps. The French commander, General Jules Lefèvre, was convinced that there were only a handful of cavalry patrols ahead of him. Instead he encountered German soldiers, well entrenched and deployed in strength, so he launched attack after attack, wave after wave, only to see his men mown down in huge numbers. There were 'swarms of bullets', recorded one account, 'mostly slaughtering the officers, easily recognizable by the gold stripes of their kepi, and stopping all charges with the bayonet . . . men fall by the dozen, under the blows of an invisible enemy, every time they try to throw themselves forward'.[39] Even worse, later in the day, Lefèvre's men were outflanked and, in places, surrounded – cutting them off from neighbouring units despite desperate efforts to break out. By the end of the day the Colonial Corps was shattered, suffering over 11,000 casualties.[40]

French commanders could do little to stop the unfolding disaster. Langle de Cary was at his headquarters at Stenay – over thirty miles from the front – and had little idea of how poorly his army was faring. In any case, with only despatch riders and the civilian telegraph network at hand, he had little chance to influence the battle had he chosen to do so. 'Modern battle, with its large number of soldiers engaged in combat and the extent of the battlefront, can no longer allow a commanding officer to go on to the battlefield, or go and see the ground for himself', he complained. The first news came in around noon. Progress was slow and both XVII and the Colonial Corps had been surprised by 'skilfully concealed' machine-guns in the woods. The nature of the terrain meant that there was little point in Langle de Cary's leaving his headquarters. 'I would have been lost in the woods!' he noted years later. 'But what a day of anxiety! . . . Given the constant bad news, I needed not only to maintain composure, but to show my officers, all those who approached me, this self-mastery a leader must have in critical moments.'[41]

Things were little better in Ruffey's Third Army to the south, which was advancing towards the towns of Longwy and Virton. Running into the German Fourth Army, which was well dug in and waiting for them, French troops tried, in vain, to forge ahead. The result was a series of heavy tactical defeats as German artillery punished French divisions badly, leaving fields strewn with dead, mangled bodies; battalions shattered under fierce fire; and thousands of wounded men streaming back from the front. That night Ruffey despatched a brief telegram to Joffre: 'The attacks yesterday failed solely because the ground in front of them had not been prepared first, neither by artillery nor infantry fire. It is essential that the infantry should never advance without the attack having been prepared first by the artillery, which should then be ready to back it up. Bayonet charges cannot be permitted in the conditions that have prevailed for most of the time until now.'[42] By 24 August both Third and Fourth Armies were in full retreat.

The acid test of combat had revealed a whole series of problems, at all levels, with the French Army. Although France could mobilize almost as many men as Germany, this was only because she conscripted a higher percentage of her manpower, who tended not to be as well trained or as well led. Germany had a deep pool of experienced NCOs, while French regiments had longstanding problems with the recruitment and retention of sufficient officers and other ranks, leaving many units lacking initiative and drive in combat. Moreover, Germany's General Staff had been lauded as the finest in the world for decades, but it was only in 1911 that France had something comparable when the position of Chief of the General Staff was given full authority to prepare the army in peacetime as well as in war. This was a welcome development that streamlined command in the French military, erasing an old law that had prevented the concentration of too much power under one individual, but whether it was introduced too late remained to be seen.[43]

Lower down the army, other problems were evident. French cavalry had an unfortunate habit of staying in the saddle too long, wearing out their mounts and frequently arriving on the battlefield exhausted and unfit for action. The infantry were brave but raw, often unable to accomplish relatively simple tasks and lacking in tactical sophistication. Reconnaissance was poor or non-existent, and when attacks were made, too often they were pressed without sufficient artillery support and in an uncoordinated, haphazard fashion that resulted in appalling losses. In terms of infantry weapons, the mainstay of the French Army was the 1886 Lebel bolt-action rifle, which compared poorly with the more reliable and quicker-firing Mauser Gewehr 98 issued to German infantry. While the Lebel held eight rounds in a tubular magazine (compared to the five-round magazine on the Mauser), it was cumbersome to reload and tended to result in varying accuracy as the rounds were fired off. Even the celebrated canon de 75 Modèle 1897 quick-firing field gun – the famous 'French 75' – had significant shortcomings. Although it could achieve remarkable rates of fire, up to six rounds per minute, showering enemy troops with a rain of lethal shrapnel, its flat trajectory was limited in hilly country and its shell was not heavy enough to destroy field fortifications or trenches. When the war solidified, France's chronic lack of heavy artillery proved a significant disadvantage and one that would take years to rectify.

As fighting raged in the Ardennes, attention switched to the French left wing. By 20 August, Lanrezac's Fifth Army had executed a swift, if exhausting, march north to meet the oncoming German advance and found itself occupying an exposed salient in the southwestern corner of Belgium. The commander of Fifth Army could not make up his mind whether to attack (as Joffre had ordered) or whether to await the oncoming storm. He waited for forty-eight hours, keeping his subordinates in the dark and weighing up the dangers of fighting on the north or south bank of the Sambre.[44] 'Up till now the sensation in General Lanrezac's entourage had been of sailing swiftly and strongly forward with a firm hand on the tiller', recorded one observer; 'but now it seemed as if the sails of the ship were flapping in the wind. There was a curious atmosphere of hesitation.'[45] In the absence of a firm French attack, it was left to Bülow to seize the initiative, which he did on 22 August, launching a series of thrusts across the river, hoping to coordinate them with an attack from Third Army, which was advancing on the Meuse. Suddenly coming to his senses, Lanrezac authorized counter-attacks to drive the Germans back, but it was too late. Unless something miraculous happened, there was no way that Fifth Army could hold.

Elsewhere, 23 August was a day of heavy fighting out to the west as Kluck's First Army crashed into Lieutenant-General Sir Horace Smith-Dorrien's II Corps of the BEF, which had taken up positions along the languid green waters of the Mons–Condé Canal the previous evening. Reports of German troops in the vicinity had been coming into GHQ (General Headquarters) with growing urgency, and Sir John French (who visited Smith-Dorrien's headquarters that morning) was unsure how to proceed, noting that II Corps was in an isolated position and had to be prepared 'for any kind of move, either in advance or retreat'.[46] In the end, the enemy settled the matter. By ten o'clock, Smith-Dorrien could hear the rumbling sound of small arms and artillery fire coming from the canal. At that moment, Lieutenant-General von Quast was moving his IX Corps up, assuming that there was nothing much in front of him, perhaps a thin screen of cavalry that would fire a few shots before galloping off. Instead his corps collided with regular British infantry who were in no mood to let them pass.

The Battle of Mons was an encounter battle – two armies colliding into one another – with one struggling to deploy in enough strength to maintain its momentum while the other hung on grimly against a numerically superior opponent. Fighting continued for most of the day as the German columns gradually forced their way over the canal against heavy fire. Smith-Dorrien's men gave a good account of themselves; pouring volley after volley into the attackers. 'The Germans came out of their trenches in mobs because their game was to rush up by their numbers, but we took steady aim and mowed them down . . . as soon as one line went down on came another like bees', reported one British soldier. 'Line after line kept coming on and taking cover behind their dead, but the nearest they got to our trenches was about 200 yards, yet that was near enough . . . Our officers told us to keep up a rapid fire and we did, it was poured into them.'[47] But as the day wore on, and the full power of the German attack began to be felt, the British were left with no choice but to break off contact as darkness fell. Their morale, however, burnt bright as they slipped away 'full of confidence in their superiority to the enemy', as Smith-Dorrien put it, and proud of the 'rapid and accurate rifle-fire' that had kept the enemy at bay. 'It was this rifle-fire, and the fog of war so thick on both sides, which were the outstanding features of the day', remembered the II Corps commander.[48]

As the British fought off the Germans at Mons, twenty miles to the east the position of the French Fifth Army was beginning to crumble. Lanrezac knew that the British were in action, but was little inclined to give them assistance, perhaps fearing that, if he did so, he would leave himself vulnerable to a counter-stroke. On the afternoon of 23 August, detachments of Hausen's Third Army finally crossed the Meuse and were making their way towards the village of Onhaye, which would have uncovered Lanrezac's right rear. Fortunately, a furious bayonet charge by men of 51st Reserve Division threw the Germans back. At his headquarters in Philippeville, Lanrezac decided that a retreat was now inevitable and drafted the order to withdraw. 'I am deeply worried', he wrote.

> It cannot be said that my fears are groundless, because, however great the danger may appear to me, it is still even greater, for the enemy is everywhere and far more numerous than I believed. Charleroi is not far from Sedan [the decisive French defeat in 1870] . . . To flee in the face of the enemy is not glorious, but to act in any other way would be to condemn my army to total annihilation, making it impossible for our French forces to recover from the general defeat they are now suffering all along the front from the Vosges to L'Escaut. An immediate retreat is vital; I am resolved to order it.[49]

The Allies were on the run. That was the impression at OHL as report after report came in of German victories right across the line on 23 and 24 August. In the Ardennes, Crown Prince Wilhelm's Fifth Army reported 'total victory' on the afternoon of 23 August, with the 'capture of thousands of prisoners among them generals and very many enemy guns'. Within hours Third Army wired that the enemy on its front were 'in complete retreat' and it was in pursuit of them. On 25 August, the Adjutant-General, Hans von Plessen, met with the Chief of the Operations Section at OHL, Lieutenant-Colonel Gerhard Tappen. After discussing the movement of the armies and digesting the latest reports, which once again predicted an imminent German triumph, Tappen was convinced that the end was near. Perusing the maps that were pinned to the walls, he turned to Plessen, took off his steel-rimmed glasses and smiled.

'The whole matter will be settled within six weeks.'[50]

2. 'To the last extremity'

'One must face the facts', wrote Joffre in his report to the War Ministry on the morning of 24 August. 'Our army corps, in spite of the numerical superiority which was assured to them, have not shown on the battlefield those offensive qualities which we had hoped for from the partial successes obtained at the beginning . . .' Given the reverses that they had suffered, French troops would now return to the defensive and wear out the enemy as best they could, while waiting for the moment to counter-attack.[1] The same day, Joffre sent a note to his army commanders bringing to their attention a number of worrying tactical problems that had been identified in recent operations, particularly the need for 'intimate combination' between infantry and artillery. Simply relying on the bayonet and high morale to take ground was no longer enough. Unless attacks were properly coordinated, French bravery would be in vain.[2]

Joffre spent the day at his headquarters sorting through the wreckage of Plan XVII. News of the defeat in Lorraine was particularly hard to bear. When Joffre received reports confirming that French troops had been driven back, his eyes seemed to dim slightly; for a moment it was as if his heavy frame would buckle under the weight it was bearing. But then a glint of light. A liaison officer arrived, still dusty from the road, and explained that the retreat had been conducted in good order, that the men's morale was still high and that they would be ready to fight again in a day or two. Instantly, Joffre recovered his sense of poise.

'Wel, now I am at peace', he told one of his staff officers later that night. 'I know that I shall have a good weapon to fight with.'[3]

Joffre, who at times seemed so stolid, so big and unimaginative, had one quality, above all others, that was now required. *He did not panic.* He kept going. He kept playing the game. 'General Instructions No. 2' was issued the following day (25 August) and marked his first major response to the disappointments of Plan XVII. 'Having been unable to carry out the offensive manoeuvre originally planned, future operations will be conducted in such a way as to reconstruct on our left a force capable of resuming the offensive by a combination of the Fourth and Fifth Armies, the British Army and new forces drawn from the east, while the other armies hold the enemy in check for such time as may be necessary.' Joffre had previously discounted the possibility of a major German move through Belgium, but now he could focus on little else. Like a chess player moving pieces across an enormous board, he began to redeploy his order of battle, taking corps from his right and moving them to his left, where they would form a new army massed around the city of Amiens and able to strike into the German flank.[4]

While Joffre's thoughts on a possible counter-attack (or what he called a 'general battle') began to coalesce, he needed enough time for his armies – particularly Lanrezac's embattled Fifth Army – to withdraw in one piece, without getting caught out or surrounded by the enveloping German right wing. Third, Fourth and Fifth Armies were ordered to continue their retreat, but ensure they remained in contact with each other and mount 'short and violent counter-attacks' to keep the enemy off balance. But as Joffre surveyed his maps and read the latest reports, one thought nagged at him: *Lanrezac*. The Fifth Army commander may have been right about the threat from the German right wing, but Joffre had detected more in his subordinate than just a prudent desire to safeguard his men. On the contrary, the French Commander-in-Chief smelt fear and indecision, and on the Western Front they could be fatal. He was also anxious about the state of the BEF and knew that he would need wholehearted British support in the next few weeks; something that might not be forthcoming if Lanrezac remained in post.

Day after day the retreat went on. After breaking contact at Mons, the BEF headed southwest, skirting either side of the forest of Mormal towards Le Cateau, while Fifth Army fought a series of running battles with Bülow's Second Army. Both British and French armies managed to avoid being encircled by their adversaries, but it was a perilously close affair for troops already exhausted by days of endless marching under a blazing sun. On the evening of 25 August, Major-General Edmund Allenby, the bull-headed commander of the British Cavalry Division, galloped up to see Smith-Dorrien and told him that unless he could resume his retreat early next morning, Kluck's men would be 'upon them before they could start'. The nightmare scenario of being caught by the enemy and destroyed in detail was a real possibility, and for Smith-Dorrien and his men, harassed beyond measure, tired and hot, coated with the dust of days of marching, an urgent decision was now required. Sir John had ordered the retreat to continue, but Smith-Dorrien was not sure it could be done. He spoke to one of his divisional commanders, Major-General Hubert Hamilton – a cheerful and brave old colonial soldier – who admitted that because many of his men were still straggling in they would be in no state to resume their march the following morning. Faced with disaster, Smith-Dorrien did what any natural soldier would do: he stood his ground and fought back.[5]

Once the early-morning mist had cleared away the following day, 26 August, Kluck found II Corps holding a line of shallow defences along the Le Cateau–Cambrai road. Without waiting, he pushed his divisions on, only to be met with the same heavy rifle fire, and this time British guns deployed forward, firing over open sights. The British held on until the late afternoon, but on this occasion casualties were heavier – 7,812 as opposed to 1,571 at Mons.[6] This was perhaps the closest the BEF would ever come to being overwhelmed. Yet somehow Smith-Dorrien's men escaped, eating the dust of miles of road, and leaving their opponents with a lasting respect for their skill as soldiers. 'The battle-field was a terrible sight', remembered a German NCO who stormed the village of Caudry that day; 'everywhere dead and wounded, and littered with equipment of every kind . . . The prisoners show that it was a well-tried adversary that disputed with us the honours of the day, veteran colonial troops, wearing the Egyptian medal, powerfully built men of splendid appearance and well-equipped.'[7]

Throughout those desperate days of retreat, much was revealed about the French Army and much of it had been disappointing. Yet there were signs of encouragement. First and Second Armies had made a fighting retreat from Lorraine, keeping the Germans at bay and holding a line of wooded hills known as the Grand Couronné outside the city of Nancy, from where they stubbornly refused to budge. With his right flank now more secure, Joffre began to move more and more units eastwards – taking advantage of the French railway network to shuttle troops across his front and give him the advantage where it mattered. Crucially, Joffre's left wing was now becoming stronger as Sixth Army, commanded by General Michel Joseph Maunoury, was forming in and around Paris. Joffre had originally intended to fight at Amiens, but the speed of the German advance meant that he had to deploy his reserves further south. Maunoury, a graduate of the École Polytechnique and a veteran of 1870, was now headquartered in the French capital trying to wield a collection of reserve divisions and North African troops scraped up from every possible direction. Joffre ordered him to 'act offensively on the enemy's right wing' and resume the offensive 'in the general direction of the north-east'.[8]

Through the test of battle began to emerge a cadre of competent officers, those who had shown a remarkable ability to get results against what seemed like fearful odds. Ferdinand Foch, a Gascon from Tarbes, was commander of XX 'Iron' Corps, which had fought in Lorraine, and was quickly gaining a reputation as a fierce, aggressive and capable general. He was promoted to take charge of a new army, the Ninth, which was formed from elements of Langle de Cary's battered command. Another rising star was Charles Mangin, a Brigadier-General from Lorraine, whose counter-attack at Onhaye on 23 August had swept the Germans back to the Meuse (and thus saved Fifth Army from a possible envelopment). The man who had ordered the attack was Louis Franchet d'Espèrey, commander of I Corps, who was deeply impressed by Mangin's irrepressible spirit: 'I arrived just as our foes were fleeing under cover of nightfall. The flames from the burning village lit up the dark and I saw Mangin waiting for me, smiling, victorious, impassive beneath the hail of bullets fired by the retreating enemy. I can see him still; the fiery glare of those deep-set eyes, that determined jaw struck by an iron bullet at Diena [part of French West Africa]; I can still hear that quiet yet

commanding voice which has launched so many irresistible attacks.'
Franchet d'Espèrey was adamant that Mangin's presence on the battlefield was irreplaceable. He had 'shown his worth and all the qualities
which made him an exceptional commander were evident – clear
understanding of the situation, swift decision-making, indomitable
courage and especially an indefinable charisma, that intangible power
which emanated from his very being and made lesser men bow down
before him'.[9] Joffre would need men like these in the coming weeks.

As if expecting an imminent end to hostilities – a hunter creeping in
closer for the kill – OHL relocated forward to Luxembourg on 29
August. German headquarters was now billeted in a drab school-
house, smelling of chalk dust and mothballs. 'We have neither gas nor
electric lighting, just dull kerosene lamps', wrote Moltke (in a letter
to his wife). 'So the report that arrived today from our armies bright-
ened things up for me all the more.' He went on:

> In the west, the Second Army under Bülow reports that a complete
> victory has been won against five and a half French corps. We are all
> living together, that is my men and me, in the Hotel de Cologne,
> which has a German proprietor. It is not very nice, but one has to
> make do when in the field. It's not a matter of whether one has it bet-
> ter or worse. I am glad to be here and not at the court. I feel quite ill
> when I hear the talk there. It is heart-breaking how clueless his lord-
> ship is about the gravity of the situation. There is already a certain
> sense of jubilation, which I will hate for as long as I live. Now, I will
> continue to work with my good people. For us there is only the ser-
> ious business of doing our duty and none of us is in any doubt about
> how much there is still to do and how difficult it will be.[10]

Moltke had issued a general directive several days earlier outlining
how he saw the rest of the campaign proceeding. All active French
corps had been engaged and had 'sustained heavy losses'; their reserve
divisions had likewise been 'severely shaken'; and the Belgian Army
was in 'a state of complete disintegration'. It was anticipated that the
French armies, now in 'full retreat', would try to buy time for the
Russians to advance further, while reconstituting as much manpower

as they could. Accordingly, the German armies were to 'advance in the direction of Paris', moving forward as rapidly as possible 'so as not to allow the French time to re-form and organize new resistance'.[11] Given that they were on the cusp of a historic triumph, Moltke authorized the transfer of two corps from his right wing to the Eastern Front. With East Prussia menaced by two Russian armies, OHL was increasingly nervous about the threat from the east, and with victory over France apparently imminent, they could probably be spared. It would prove to be a decision of enormous, and fatal, consequences.

At his headquarters, Moltke waged a lonely, almost monastic, struggle. He surveyed the maps that lay in piles on improvised tables. He read the situation reports. He chatted to his staff. Every evening he dined with his wife, when they were served plain, stolid food with an occasional glass of Rhenish wine. In sharp contrast to Joffre, who could rely on good interior lines and a host of fast drivers, Moltke was inactive and slow-witted, as if he was directing the war under water. The tradition of allowing subordinates freedom of action – what was known as 'directive command' – was deeply rooted within the German Army, and in 1914, with the distances involved, it left Moltke isolated and unsure if and when to intervene. It also left his army commanders to sort it out for themselves: Kluck, who bristled at his subordination under Bülow; Hausen, whose Third Army kept up a slow and cautious pace; and Rupprecht, champing at the bit to seize Nancy. Because, at this crucial moment in history, Germany's vast armies – now deep into France – were too far away to direct or recall.

The spectral figure of Count Alfred von Schlieffen loomed large over the German Army as it marched towards the Marne. The former Chief of the General Staff had died in January 1913 after serving as head of the German Army for almost fifteen years. His operational design had been based upon a massive flanking movement that would turn France's defences. 'The essential element of the entire operation', he had written in 1905, 'is a strong right wing, the formation of which will help to win the battles and allow the relentless pursuit of the enemy and bring defeat to him again and again.'[12] Yet Moltke always felt that amendments would need to be made to the plan, so as the campaign progressed he began to alter it. The decision to mount an offensive in Lorraine on 20 August was one of the first diversions from Schlieffen's emphasis on the right. Moreover, when a group of reserve brigades became available, Moltke sent them to strengthen Rupprecht's Sixth Army. Indeed, as the advance unfolded, Moltke began to fantasize about the prospect of a double envelopment, with the right wing pinning French forces, before his central armies snapped the French Army in two. The march through Belgium was, for Moltke, 'not an end in itself, but only a means to an end'.[13] Yet this crucial modification to Schlieffen's grand design was neither shared nor understood by the commanders who would have to carry it out.

At the tip of the right wing, Kluck constantly sought out the flank from where he could bring about the climactic battle that would scatter and destroy what remained of the armies of the Entente. By the time First Army reached the Marne river on 3 September, its men had been marching and fighting for thirty days and had covered 312 miles. It was a performance of almost superhuman endurance and willpower. Down the cobbled roads of Belgium and the endless tree-lined avenues of northern France, dusty and footsore, shoulders aching, heads bowed beneath the unblinking sun, Kluck's men trudged on. 'Marches and fights, battles and marches, followed one another without interval', Kluck admitted; a situation made even worse by the gradual erosion of German strength the further they advanced – having to detail more and more troops to guard their lines of communication and hold the large population centres they had overrun. For example, III Reserve Corps had been sent north to mask Antwerp, where King Albert's army was now dug in, and a reserve brigade remained in Brussels, holding the Belgian capital.[14]

There was now an urgent need to bring the campaign to a glorious conclusion. Schlieffen had originally tasked First Army with enveloping Paris from the north and west, which had been repeated in Moltke's 'general directive' of 27 August. Yet the further the armies of the right wing advanced, the more stretched they became and the more anxiety that built up inside General Bülow. To keep the German armies together, he asked Kluck (on 30 August) to make an 'inward wheel' to 'gain full advantages of the victory' that had been achieved over the French Fifth Army.[15] This meant that Kluck would shift the axis of his advance from southwest to south and then south-east; skirting to the east, instead of west, of Paris. This had occurred to Kluck several days earlier, so he quickly agreed. He believed that the British, like the Belgians before them, had almost certainly been destroyed and would be of no further consequence. Moreover, Paris would fall like a ripe apple once the French armies, now little more than a collection of debris, had been surrounded and eliminated. It was, therefore, essential that First Army should find the French left and outflank it, attacking in conjunction with Second and Third Armies to destroy one wing of the French forces. Once this was achieved, the front could then be rolled up and the war ended. Accordingly, on the morning of 31 August, Kluck's troops shifted their direction and headed for the Oise river.

Back at OHL, Moltke had approved of Bülow's 'inward wheel' (given the delays in communication, he probably had little choice but to rubber-stamp it), but his strategic vision remained crucially different to that of his army commanders in the field. By 2 September, Moltke was increasingly confident of crushing the French with his central armies, not those on his right. Therefore, the decision to forfeit Paris (for the time being) meant that Kluck's army would have to operate as his flank guard to prevent any sorties from the French capital. OHL confirmed this in a wireless message sent to First, Second and Third Armies on the night of 2/3 September. 'The intention is to drive the French in a south-easterly direction from Paris. The First Army will follow in echelon behind the Second Army and will be responsible for the flank protection of the Armies.'[16] But it was too late. IX Corps, the spearhead of First Army, had already crossed the Marne and was a day's march ahead of Bülow. They were not in echelon; they were ahead. If they were going to guard the flank, they would need to stop, turn around and then march back north.

Kluck was stunned. The order was not only confusing, but also totally inconsistent with Schlieffen's emphasis on the strength of the right wing. If he halted for a day or two to let Bülow catch up, then he would hand the initiative back to the enemy! Kluck was in no mood to do this, so he authorized the pursuit over the Marne to continue. IV Reserve Corps, bringing up the rear, was ordered to guard his flank, but the rest of his army would keep going. He radioed Moltke on 4 September explaining why the order to stay behind Second Army could not be carried out:

> The First Army asks for information on the location of the other armies; their messages about crucial victories have so far been followed by pleas for support on several occasions. Under continuous heavy fighting, the First Army has reached the limits of its capabilities in marching orders. Only in this way is it possible to open up the Marne crossing for the other armies and to force the enemy to retreat . . . Order of the Supreme Army Command 2220 that the First Army is to follow the Second Army in stages could not be followed in this situation. Planned pushing away of the enemy from Paris in a south-easterly direction will only be possible to carry out if the First Army proceeds. Necessary protection of the flanks weakens the offensive force. The speedy reinforcement of the right-hand flank . . . is urgently required.[17]

Kluck was unrepentant. His reconnaissance aircraft had spotted long columns of enemy troops retreating to the south, which confirmed his belief that if he could force the French over the Seine, the offensive could be finished. But he was unaware of how many troops Joffre was mustering around Paris and how open his own flank was becoming. The genie was out of the bottle. Moltke had lost control.

On 30 August, it was agreed, after much agonizing, that the French Government would head for Bordeaux. Joseph Galliéni, the newly appointed Military Governor of Paris, was told by the Minister of War, Alexandre Millerand, that he now had full authority to defend the city 'to the last extremity'. When Galliéni heard these words, he seemed to recoil momentarily, stopping the minister and asking him slowly and deliberately: Did he understand the full import of what he had said? Did he realize that Paris, or large sections of it, might have to be razed to the ground? Millerand nodded slowly:

'To the last extremity . . .'[18]

The ruthless attitude that characterized the defence of Paris was symptomatic of how France was now responding to the crisis. Joffre was never the most sentimental of men, but he acted swiftly to root out those whom he believed were weak or ineffectual. General Ruffey, whose Third Army had been shattered in the Ardennes, was relieved on 30 August after Joffre visited his headquarters. Finding him 'in a high condition of nervousness, giving vent to bitter reproaches against the majority of his subordinates', Joffre took him aside and told him to hand over to Maurice Sarrail, a corps commander who had performed well during the Battle of the Frontiers. Lanrezac did not last much longer. Joffre went to see him on 3 September and found him 'hesitating and timorous'; still possessed of his brilliant intellect, but now apt to criticize every order and unable to lift the depression in his headquarters.[19] Lanrezac went quietly, convinced that his order to retreat had saved the army, but relieved that someone else would now bear the terrible burden of command. Joffre replaced him with one of his more determined subordinates, Louis Franchet d'Espèrey.

It was eleven o'clock on the night of 1 September when French intelligence confirmed that Kluck's army had turned to the southeast. A German cavalry patrol had been shot up, losing one of their men, who slumped off his horse, leaving a bulging haversack lying on the ground. Inside, French staff officers discovered a map, smeared with blood, which showed Kluck's order of battle and the line of advance his army was taking. This confirmed information that had been gleaned from the breaking of German wireless codes several days earlier.[20] It was now clear that First Army was moving to the southeast, evidently still searching for the left flank of the French Army. This meant that a major plank of the Schlieffen Plan – that the right wing would drive to the west of Paris and envelop the French capital – had now been discarded, leaving the German flank wide open.

As Joffre steeled himself to mount his great counter-attack, his counterpart in the BEF, Sir John French, was beginning to come apart. French had been horrified by Smith-Dorrien's stand at Le Cateau, and the sight of some of the survivors stumbling along, puttees trailing in the dust, caused him to fear the worst. Like Lanrezac, a sense of pessimism was beginning to darken his outlook and convince him that defeat was inevitable. He wired Joffre on 30 August and warned him that the BEF would not 'be in a state to take its place in the line for ten days' and that he proposed to retire behind the River Seine.[21] This was, in part, an overreaction to the hardships that his men had endured, as well as a complete loss of faith in Lanrezac, whom he accused of leaving him exposed at Mons. He even wired Lord Kitchener the following day repeating his sense of disgust. 'If the French go on with their present tactics which are practically to fall back right and left of me, usually without notice, and to abandon all idea of offensive operations, of course then the gap in the French line will remain and the consequence must be borne by them.'[22]

The consequences of Britain pulling out of the line at such a crucial moment were not lost on Kitchener, who almost surrendered his legendary self-control when he read Sir John's telegram. He dashed off an urgent reply expressing 'surprise' at the proposal before calling an emergency meeting of the Cabinet. When the members had assembled, Kitchener demanded that French be instructed to remain where he was and that under no circumstances was he to make his planned retirement. This was agreed. Another telegram was then fired off ('The government are exceedingly anxious lest your force . . . not be able to co-operate closely with our allies . . .') before Kitchener returned to the War Office, where he found Sir John's subsequent letter in which he damned the French for falling back on either side of him.[23] Realizing that he would have to grasp the nettle to prevent a strategic catastrophe, Kitchener took the first train he could and crossed the Channel in a Royal Navy destroyer. He met with Sir John at the British Embassy in Paris on the afternoon of 1 September and made his feelings clear, telling French that the BEF was to act, at all times, in accordance with Joffre's wishes. The British Commander-in-Chief, his cheeks flushed with anger, his face contorted with frustration, found the meeting to be deeply insulting, and the sight of the Secretary of State for War dressed in the khaki serge uniform of a British Field Marshal only heightened his sense of humiliation. Yet it worked. The BEF stayed in the line.

Kitchener's urgent stiffening of Sir John's resolve was not a moment too soon. The final arrangements for Joffre's counter-attack were now being completed. GQG issued its operation orders on 4 September: 'The time has come to profit by the adventurous position of the German First Army and concentrate against that Army all the efforts of the Allied Armies on the extreme left.'[24] The counter-offensive would begin in two days' time, with Sixth Army debouching east from Paris towards Château-Thierry, while the BEF and Fifth Army turned around and faced the enemy, ready to drive north. Now that he had been assured of British support and had put Franchet d'Espèrey in command of Fifth Army (who told him that his men were ready), Joffre was happy to go ahead. He knew that a moment of supreme importance had arrived; one in which the fate of his country was in the balance, but he betrayed little sense of anxiety. His meals were always taken at the usual time and his appetite remained generous. Joffre's broad shoulders carried a weight that would have crushed lesser men.

Perhaps inevitably, there were some last-minute doubts. Henri Berthelot, one of Joffre's most trusted staff officers, would have preferred to wait a little longer to give the Germans more time to push further into the trap, but Joffre was concerned lest the opportunity slip away. On the morning of 6 September, the day of battle, he issued a staunch proclamation to his troops. It was a stark, unwavering demonstration of the gravity of the situation: 'We are about to engage in a battle on which the fate of our country depends and it is important to remind all ranks that the moment has passed for looking to the rear; all our efforts must be directed to attacking and driving back the enemy. Troops that can advance no farther must, at any price, hold on to the ground they have conquered and die on the spot rather than give way. Under the circumstances which face us, no act of weakness can be tolerated.'[25] Shortly after nine o'clock, Colonel Émile Herbillon, the High Command's liaison officer to the Government, arrived at Joffre's headquarters, which had moved to Châtillon-sur-Seine the previous evening. Joffre was now ensconced in the Château Marmont, 'an old castle in the woods', where he occupied a small, bright room with a desk and a few chairs. Herbillon made his way along 'great corridors, stairs with worn steps, old doors with huge latches' to see the Commander-in-Chief. 'As soon as I greet him, he beckons me to come closer to the map where the locations of the armies are marked. He shows me that von Kluck is turning towards the east, moving away from Paris and towards the British left wing. In these conditions, while the rest of the front would continue to withstand the German Army . . . Maunoury's army would come up against the German right wing and attack from the flank.' Herbillon was amazed at Joffre's incredible self-possession. 'I'll never forget that moment, and the wonderful calmness he possessed, having thrown the dice with a firm hand and peacefully awaiting the future; I felt an irresistible confidence and, as he shook my hand, he said, smiling kindly: "That's it now, my dear friend, and now heaven will decide the rest."'[26]

That was it; it was done. Joffre watched and waited, tilting his head to the window and listening to the rumble of guns out to the north; towards the shimmering battle line where two great armies fought to the death.

Joffre anticipated that the battle would begin on the morning of 6 September, but fighting had already broken out the previous afternoon when the lead corps of Maunoury's Sixth Army, marching out from Paris, collided with the German IV Reserve Corps around the village of Saint-Soupplets. Originally detached from Kluck's main body to guard his right flank as he continued his drive over the Marne, IV Reserve Corps were heavily outnumbered, with barely 22,000 troops against Sixth Army's 150,000.[27] But they did just enough to hold off Maunoury while urgently sending word for Kluck to come up at once. When a German pilot spotted long columns of French troops advancing towards the exposed flank that morning, he dashed off an urgent warning, only for it to be dismissed as 'by no means dangerous'. It was only later on, around midnight, that Lieutenant-General Alexander von Linsingen, commander of II Corps, put another call through to Kluck's headquarters and made it clear just how serious the situation was becoming, shouting down a crackling phone line: 'The ghost of Paris has acquired flesh and blood!'[28] Suddenly realizing the danger he was in, Kluck ordered two of his corps to march north as quickly as possible. This manoeuvre was essential to protect his rear, but it widened the already sizeable gap between

First and Second Armies and caused Bülow, who had long been suspicious of his fellow army commander, to explode in paroxysms of rage as his right flank, in turn, was uncovered.

The clash between Maunoury and Kluck on the Ourcq was only the first of a whole series of epic contests that took place between 6 and 10 September: between Franchet d'Espèrey and Bülow on the Petit Morin; between Foch and Hausen in the marshes of Saint-Gond; between Langle de Cary and the Duke of Württemberg around Vitry; between Sarrail and Crown Prince Wilhelm at Verdun; and between Castelnau and Rupprecht in front of Nancy. Each army fought its own war; desperately trying to keep in touch with units on either flank and jealously holding on to ground wherever possible. Everywhere the fighting was close and confusing, with most soldiers, from either side, having little sense of what was really happening. 'The struggle extended all around us, from one horizon to the other', remembered a French dragoon; 'and if it was incomprehensible to our officers it was still more so to us private soldiers . . . All around us the guns thundered. The horizon was, as it were, encircled with a moving line of bursting shells, and we knew nothing, absolutely nothing.'[29]

For four days German and French forces grappled with one another, gaining an advantage in one place, only to lose it in another. In most places, German troops fought with enormous courage, determination and tactical skill. Two of Kluck's corps executed a forced march of almost thirty miles on 6 September to get to the Ourcq, and then went straight into battle. Elsewhere, along the marshes of Saint-Gond, four German divisions mounted a ferocious night assault in the early hours of 8 September, sweeping away the startled defenders and almost causing the total collapse of Foch's newly formed Ninth Army, which was holding a precarious defensive line along the French centre. Despite the ferocity of the fighting, French battalions continued to show an almost unbreakable will to keep going and to keep taking terrible casualties; even Kluck – not one to wax lyrical about his adversary – found himself admiring the 'extraordinary and peculiar aptitude of the French soldier to recover quickly', no matter what they were subjected to.[30] One German officer watched a French counter-attack form up 'in thick lines' and observed how time seemed

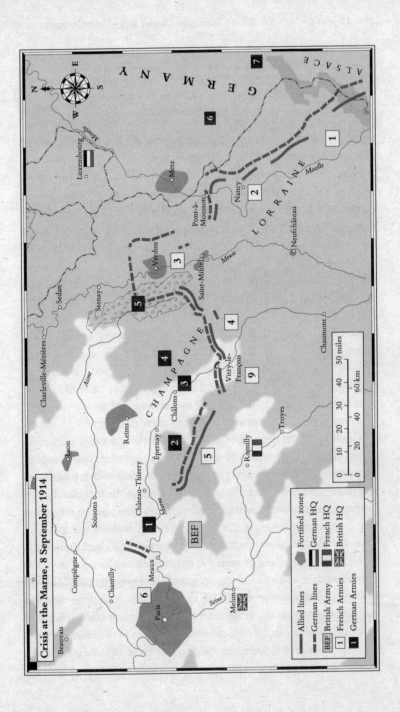

Crisis at the Marne, 8 September 1914

to slow and then stop: 'I can still see the French today, at their head a commanding officer with a gold-embroidered uniform, a sabre in his right hand, a pistol in his left, challenging us in pantomime fashion to lay down our weapons, Captain von Gerlach conversely demanding the same of him. When he shook his head, there followed the command: "Fire!" Then there was a loud salvo of gunfire, the first row of French soldiers toppled over, the others fled.'[31]

Notwithstanding the clumsy tactics that French units often employed, they could do fearsome damage in the right circumstances, particularly if they were defending good ground. Sixth Army tried repeatedly to break the French right around the fortress city of Nancy, but sustained up to 60 per cent casualties in fruitless frontal assaults on the wooded hills of the Grand Couronné between 3 and 10 September. Here German troops advanced across open ground and then tried to scramble up a series of rocky escarpments where the French were dug in. Even though Joffre had stripped most of the best troops from Second Army, the French line held, with their 75s doing terrible work, earning the nickname 'black butchers' after their characteristic black puff of shrapnel smoke. Rupprecht's army lost 35,000 casualties in August and another 29,000 the following month. Seventh Army, which also took part in the fighting in Lorraine, lost 64,000 casualties in the same period, yet proved unable to break the front.[32]

The hero of the defence of Nancy was the commander of Second Army, General Castelnau, a 62-year-old from Saint-Affrique, Langue-doc, tough mountainous country northwest of Montpellier. Castelnau's war had begun in disaster. He had overseen one of the first thrusts into Lorraine, only to be thrown back in less than a week, but he refused to be discouraged. Known as the 'fighting friar', Castelnau was a devout Catholic who was always accompanied by a personal chaplain to minister to him on the field of battle. A fervent believer in the élan of the French soldier and one of the architects of France's war plan that had been sunk at the Battle of the Frontiers, Castelnau adapted quickly, overseeing the stout defence of the French right flank and ensuring there would be no double envelopment of the French Army. 'He had the art of lighting up the faces of those he met by a single kindly word, and so making them his admirers in a flash', wrote a staff officer at GQG. 'This little man, so alert and cheerful, radiated honesty and trustworthiness.'[33]

But would the Allies be able to take advantage of the yawning gap now appearing between the German First and Second Armies? The position of the British was crucial. After his meeting with Kitchener on 1 September, Sir John had returned to GHQ and nursed his wounded pride, fretting over the damage to his army and waiting for further directions from Joffre. Although the BEF had now been boosted by the arrival of a third corps, the effects of the retreat from Mons were everywhere to see: mixed-up battalions; columns of walking wounded; piles of abandoned stores, discarded equipment and uniforms; and red-tabbed staff officers urgently sorting out the disorganization and muddle. Yet the British could still play an important role in the coming battle and Joffre had pleaded with Sir John on the evening of 5 September that the 'honour of England' was at stake if he did not take part. French instantly shrugged off his pessimism and promised that they would do all they could.[34] Unfortunately, owing to a mix-up with its orders, the BEF was over ten miles from its supposed jumping-off point by the morning of 6 September, having just completed another march to the south the day before.

When the BEF eventually turned around its advance was sluggish, delayed by aggressive and persistent enemy cavalry, which sprayed the attackers with machine-gun and shrapnel fire before galloping off. The British only gained eleven miles on the first day and less than eight the following day, before they finally crossed the Marne on 9 September with an average march of just seven miles.[35] But the British presence was magnified in the minds of the German High Command, who looked upon the gap between their leading armies with growing horror. Little by little, the BEF, alongside General Franchet d'Espèrey's Fifth Army, pressed further and further into Bülow's exposed flank and by the evening of 8 September, as reports were received of enemy columns marching northwards towards the Marne, Bülow was faced with imminent disaster. 'In these circumstances, there was a high probability that strong enemy forces would break through between First and Second Armies, unless First Army decided at the last moment to go back eastwards and join up with

Second Army again', he recorded in his memoirs. 'If this did not happen and the enemy followed First Army over the Marne, First Army faced the risk that they would be forced westwards.'[36]

Ensconced at his dreary headquarters in Luxembourg, Moltke began to suspect that the campaign was turning against him. 'I can hardly express how unimaginably heavy the burden of responsibility in recent days has weighed on me and continues to do so', he wrote to his wife on 8 September. 'It would be dreadful if all this blood had been spilt without any tangible success being achieved. The terrible tension of these days, the absence of news from the distant armies, the awareness of what is at stake is almost beyond the limit of human endurance. The dreadful difficulty of our situation often appears like a black wall before me that seems impenetrable.'[37] OHL had heard little from the right wing for two days. 'Still no decision', wrote Gerhard Tappen on 8 September. 'Situation at Second Army is critical.'[38] Moltke despatched messages to his commanders, trying to find out what was going on, but few replies were received, and even then they failed to pierce the fog of uncertainty that prevailed over the battlefield. On 8 September, he ordered his Head of Intelligence, Lieutenant-Colonel Richard Hentsch, to go to the front and, if necessary, authorize a retreat. One of the principles of 'directive command' was that staff officers could act in place of senior commanders, so Hentsch, although only a Lieutenant-Colonel, could issue orders in Moltke's name. Hentsch was one of the most highly regarded products of the Great General Staff, with a clear and sober mind, but he approached his mission with a sense of deep foreboding. He would have preferred a more senior officer to take his place or at the very least to receive his instructions in writing. But Moltke did neither, leaving Hentsch worried that 'in the event of failure, he would become the scapegoat'.[39] He visited the headquarters of Third, Fourth and Fifth Armies and satisfied himself that they were coping well. The problem, as he would find out, lay further west.

Second Army headquarters was located in the imposing Château de Montmort, a proud Renaissance castle noted for its four circular brick towers, which had once been home to Pierre de Rémond de Montmort, author of an obscure eighteenth-century manuscript, 'An

Attempt to Analyse Games of Chance'. The irony of the situation would probably have been lost on Hentsch, who met Bülow that evening. Bülow was concerned about the gap that existed between him and Kluck, and lamented the state of his army, which he believed was utterly burnt out by the efforts of the past month, even using the word 'Schlacke' ('cinders') to describe it.[40] There was a real danger that enemy columns moving up from the south would envelop First Army and break the German line, with perhaps untold consequences for the campaign. Hentsch – never the most optimistic of men – listened intently to Bülow's words as he realized the gravity of the situation. Crucially, he did little to counter Bülow's pessimism and accepted the general's stark assessment without question, sending a somewhat cryptic wire to OHL that the situation was 'serious but not hopeless'.[41] When aerial reconnaissance reports were received the following morning (9 September) confirming that British troops were crossing the Marne at La Ferté-sous-Jouarre, Bülow finally lost his nerve; pulling his right flank back north towards Épernay on the Marne and ordering a general retreat.

Hentsch, who had left Montmort as soon as it was light, eventually found Kluck's Chief of Staff, Hermann von Kuhl, outside First Army's headquarters at Mareuil. Kuhl said that they were endeavouring to crush Maunoury in front of Paris and were not concerned greatly by the BEF, knowing that they were likely to come up slowly and could be held off by his cavalry. Hentsch, who believed Bülow's Second Army to be in great danger, shook his head. Were First Army to remain in its current positions any longer, it would be enveloped by enemy forces moving north! Taking a piece of charcoal, he took Kuhl's map and traced the route he wanted First Army to follow. It was essential that it retreat northeast towards Soissons in order to support Bülow. When Kuhl objected once again, Hentsch revealed that he had been entrusted with 'full authority' from OHL – what was known as Vollmacht – to initiate a retreat if he deemed it necessary. 'The discussion lasted a long time', remembered Kuhl; 'I fervently opposed the call for retreat and repeatedly pointed out the favourable situation on our right flank. All options were considered in order to carry on fighting until the final victory.'[42] But it was no good. Reports came in that Bülow had already started moving back, so there it was. 'The army now stood isolated.' Kuhl went to see General Kluck and told him the news. 'With a heavy heart', the commander of First Army accepted the inevitability of retreat and ordered his men to pull back.

Whether Hentsch was right was a question that would linger on down the decades as German soldiers and historians picked over the remains of the 1914 campaign. Was Second Army as burnt out as Bülow believed? Could Kluck have defeated Maunoury had he been given more time? Was the order to retreat premature or even unnecessary? The questions would never be resolved, although it is clear that the balance of forces at the Marne was becoming increasingly unfavourable to Germany. The strength of the German right wing was now less than the combined British and French forces it opposed, and although German troops continued to perform well on the battlefield, they were fighting at the end of long, fragile supply lines and were becoming worn out. Victory also depended upon the nerve and willpower of their commanders. While Joffre and his generals kept theirs, the German High Command, from Moltke downwards (with the honourable exception of Kluck), became disorientated and unnerved by the intensity of combat and the difficulty of communication. Ever since its defeat in 1870 – often blamed upon too much emphasis on passive, defensive operations – the French Army had insisted that victory went to the side that lasted the longest, to those who simply refused to give in. In 1914, they were right.

A sense of exhausted euphoria washed over French commanders as they realized what had happened. General Maunoury, whose Sixth Army had fought Kluck's First Army to a standstill, telephoned Joffre on the evening of 9 September and told him that the enemy were in full retreat.

'*Mon général*,' he whispered, wiping tears from his eyes, 'I was sure then that victory was ours.'[43]

At Fifth Army, General Franchet d'Espèrey issued a dramatic proclamation, congratulating his men on their victory, but urging them to keep going. 'Held on his wings, his centre broken, the enemy is flying to the east and to the north by forced marches . . . This first success is but a preliminary. The enemy is shaken but not completely beaten. Great tests of your endurance lie ahead of you, you will have to carry out many long marches, to take part in many bitter fights.'[44] Foch also warned his men that there would be more fighting to come. 'The disorder rife among German troops is the portent of our victory; by carrying on, with the greatest vigour, the effort begun by our army is certain to stop the march of the enemy and drive them out of our beloved country. But it is very necessary that each of us be convinced that success will belong to him who holds out the longest.'[45]

Joffre maintained his usual *sangfroid*. 'This morning the German centre has begun to give way', he informed Poincaré on 10 September. 'Foch is moving towards the Marne and finding everywhere traces of the very hurried retreat of the enemy, whose Army Corps, and especially the Guards' Corps, have lost heavily. On our right we are vigorously withstanding violent attacks, and everything encourages us to hope that our success will be furthered.'[46] Joffre's mood had been tempered by the alarming news that a huge clash of arms had taken place on the Eastern Front, where the Russian invasion of East Prussia had been turned back at the Battle of Tannenberg. French intelligence had intercepted a German communiqué revealing how they had taken between 60,000 and 70,000 prisoners and that the Russian Second Army had been 'annihilated'.[47] For decades French strategy had been shaped by the assumption that Russia would play a major role in any war against Germany, forcing her to dilute her strength across two fronts, and providing the critical numerical superiority that would ensure victory. This calculation had now been thrown to the winds; scattered as the Russians being hunted like dogs in the marshes of East Prussia. If the Germans were ever going to be defeated, then it had to come on the Western Front.

Over the next four days, five German armies broke contact, retracing their steps back the way they had come, crossing the Petit Morin, the Marne, and then the Ourcq – river lines that had become like depth markers showing how far the German Army had gone into France – before finally coming to rest along the steeply wooded northern bank of the Aisne river, their bid for victory in ruins. 'I have rather given up since the French seem to be evading a decision', wrote General Bülow on 16 September. 'It is now likely to result in a certain pause in our operations. We are regrouping . . . the troops need replacements and to have a break.'[48] For those lower down the chain of command, there was a greater feeling of rage and confusion as they realized that their month-long ordeal would not end in a triumphant march along the Champs-Élysées, only more fighting and yet more marching. 'It must have been obvious now to the most dense what was happening', recalled one observer. 'We knew well what a victorious advance was like and the spirit that animated it; we had lived with it for a month; but this was very different. We did not understand, but we could see, and that sufficed.'[49] The euphoria and anticipation that had fuelled Germany's advance had now vanished; only a rigid, formal professionalism remained.

The German armies left a brutalized countryside in their wake, littered with empty wine bottles and the stinking remains of men and beasts blackening in the fly-tormented sunshine. 'Telegraph-poles were down, riddled with bullet-holes, the wires lying across the road in diabolical coils', remembered a British liaison officer who followed up the retreat. 'A broken rifle or a bayonet stuck in the earth marked a soldier's grave – red képis were scattered about amidst spent and unspent ammunition; shells had made deep gashes everywhere. Dead horses were lying about with most of their entrails protruding, infesting the air with a smell of putrefaction. Away in the fields solemn groups, identifying the dead, were moving among inert red and blue uniforms clinging to the ground.'[50] Casualty figures would not be finalized until some time later, but they revealed a terrible picture. French losses totalled over 18,000 dead, 111,000 wounded and 83,000 missing for September 1914. German losses seem to have been fewer, although no official figures were ever published. The ten-day casualty returns from 1 to 10 September totalled just shy of 100,000 dead, wounded and missing.[51]

Such a staggering bloodletting had only given Joffre a fleeting advantage, but he was determined to make the most of it. He wanted to push the Germans as hard as possible, so he ordered his armies to drive north, exploiting the enemy's withdrawal and turning it into a rout. But, much to his annoyance, his army commanders were unable to move up quickly enough. The cumulative effects of heavy losses and weeks of unceasing effort, combined with frequent storms of heavy rain, sapped the energy from France's troops and allowed the German Army to, as one report put it, 'detach from the enemy without losing guns and other noteworthy signs of victory'.[52] Despite hopes that the Germans would retreat all the way to the Rhine, by 12 September reports were crowding in to GQG that the Germans were slowing down and, in places, digging in. The German line now ran from Noyon on the Oise river (where Kluck's First Army had redeployed), along the Chemin des Dames Ridge north of the Aisne to Craonne (now occupied by the newly formed Seventh Army, which joined Bülow's Second Army), then on to Reims, before levelling out and running east for about seventy miles to the fortified city of Verdun, which was still in French hands. From there, the line hinged southeast, where it had been for most of August, down to the Swiss border.

As Allied commanders surveyed the new German positions, passing their binoculars around and cursing through their teeth, one thing was abundantly clear: the Aisne was a natural defensive perimeter. When the BEF tried to cross on 13 September, they were met with heavy fire raining down from the heights above the far bank, and the few bridges that were still standing (or the pontoons the British threw across) attracted much enemy attention, with flurries of shells crashing into the bank or landing in the water, sending great plumes of spray into the air. Further attacks over the next three days saw only slow, grinding progress, with battalions getting sucked into fierce close-quarter fighting up heavily forested hills and defiles, with frequent enemy counter-attacks, all amid ever-worsening weather. On 14 September, Sir John French ordered his men to dig in and on the following day Joffre recognized that his advance had come to a premature halt. It was evident that the German Army was 'going to accept battle, in prepared positions north of the Aisne. In consequence, it is no longer a question of pursuit', he admitted, 'but of a methodical attack, using every means at our disposal and consolidating each position in turn as it is gained.'[53] Whether Joffre realized it or not, trench warfare had begun.

The Aisne was a watershed in other ways too. For days, the Kaiser had been canvassing opinion on whether the Chief of the General Staff should remain, and on 14 September he ordered Moltke to report sick. Moltke initially refused to do so, claiming that he was fit and well, but his declining physical state was obvious to anyone who cared to look. Major Max Bauer, a staff officer at OHL, recalled how 'Moltke had completely fallen apart. He was sitting listlessly in front of the map – a broken man.'[54] No official announcement was ever made about his demotion, to avoid confirming suspicions that Germany had suffered a reverse on the Marne, so Moltke lingered on at OHL as a pitiful, tormented spirit; a symbol of the lost dreams of 1914. Germany's bid for a swift victory in the west was now over.

Fighting along the Aisne continued, on and off, for a fortnight as Allied attacks were replaced by a series of heavy German counter-punches. Little ground was gained by either side. The war had become stuck. Frequent downpours of rain reduced the roads to mud-splashed tracks, while shrouds of white mist lingered for hours, interfering with aerial observation and becoming a first, visible symbol of the hardening grasp of autumn. 'Day after day and night after night almost perpetual rifle-fire and guns thundering across the valley of the river and aeroplanes, though we hadn't many then, soaring aloft. Supplying, reinforcing, and relieving the trenches were serious diffi-culties, and had to be done at night, and through much of the time rain increased the hardships of war', was how Smith-Dorrien described the curious sense of anti-climax that followed the Marne. Within six days of combat on the Aisne, his corps had sustained 10,000 casualties, and although his men were in good spirits, the constant drain of losses was disheartening. 'At first it seemed extraordinary and impossible,' he lamented, 'but, as the war progressed, we learned that nothing was extraordinary or impossible, and that principles of war applicable to open warfare did not apply here.'[1]

Joffre's triumph on the Marne proved to be short-lived. 'Still no change in the overall situation', he noted in a letter to the Minister of War, Millerand, on 18 September:

> Violent counter-attacks have been repelled by units of the British Army and our Fifth Army which are occupying the high ground of Chemin des Dames to the north of the Aisne. Likewise, the enemy tried in vain to take the offensive against Reims. To the east of the city, as far as the Argonne and between the Argonne and the Meuse, we are making some slight progress. The Germans appear to be evacu-ating the southern Woëvre. This all leads us to believe that they are

reinforcing their right wing and their centre by moving and transporting troops. We are changing positions accordingly.[2]

With the German Army entrenched on the high ground, the only option available to the French High Command was to continue shuffling troops to their left to try to outflank them. Somewhat disappointed in General Maunoury (whose Sixth Army had opened the Battle of the Marne), Joffre decided to reconstitute a new force to do this. On 20 September, General Castelnau, whose stubborn defence of Nancy had made victory on the Marne possible, was given the task of re-forming his army on the French left. He would be given a collection of divisions and corps – as soon as they became available – and would use them to outflank the German right. Joffre also arranged for a new army, the Tenth, to assemble even further north, around Arras. This was to be commanded by another rising star, a paunchy-faced infantryman, Louis Ernest de Maud'huy, who had commanded a corps on the Marne. He was placed under Castelnau for the renewed offensive.

Joffre was hopeful of winning a decisive battle, but realized that this might not be possible. Shortages of ammunition were now becoming acute. Vast quantities of shells had been fired off (particularly by the ever-present 75s), leaving government stockpiles at dangerously low levels. Joffre hunted around for supplies, scouring depots from Dunkirk to Paris, while ordering his commanders to conserve shells wherever possible. He even wrote to Millerand again on 20 September, warning him that if shell production was not increased rapidly, they would run out of ammunition in just five weeks: 'It is therefore necessary for the government to see the reality of the situation; either the manufacture of artillery munitions will have to be considerably increased or we will no longer have the means to take an active part in the war from 1 November. I estimate that in order to continue operations the army's requirements would have to rise to at least 50,000 shells a day (around twelve shells per gun).'[3]

The unyielding pressure on resources was not unique to the French Army, and the situation facing Moltke's replacement at OHL, the Prussian Minister of War, Erich von Falkenhayn, was equally perilous.

Falkenhayn was fifty-three years old, young for a Lieutenant-General, with short greying hair, a thin moustache and a slight, mocking stare that betrayed a robust self-confidence. Moltke despised him, as did many other senior officers, but the Kaiser was convinced of his abilities and wanted him to take over, convinced that he was 'just the man' to restore the spirit of the army.[4] He even allowed him to remain as Minister of War – an unprecedented concentration of political and military power in a single individual. It was just as well that Falkenhayn had few friends and seemed to lack much human emotion, concentrating on the task in front of him with resolute precision. Whereas Moltke enjoyed music and literature, Falkenhayn had little time for such distractions and was known as an indefatigable worker who was calm, focused and thoroughly professional. He also had none of Moltke's fragility.

Falkenhayn surveyed Germany's situation and was not impressed. It was no secret that he had been sceptical of Moltke's handling of the campaign for some time. Even when OHL had been awash with news of victory after the Battle of the Frontiers, he had been studiously unimpressed. During a visit to the Supreme Command on 1 September he told Moltke's staff that they had achieved nothing.

'It isn't a battle won, it's an orderly retreat', he complained. 'Show me your trophies and your prisoners.' But nobody could.[5]

The German Army had undoubtedly been shaken by the fighting on the Marne, despite its commanders never publicly admitting what had happened. OHL even refused to tell the Austrian Commander-in-Chief, Franz Conrad von Hötzendorf, who had to draw his own conclusions about the strange reversal of fortune in the west. Yet the situation on the Eastern Front was hardly more encouraging. Despite the victory at Tannenberg, calls for a renewed commitment to the war against the Russians were growing. The Austro-Hungarian Army had performed poorly so far, mounting a disastrous invasion of Serbia (when it had been unceremoniously chased back across the Drina river by the end of August) and proving unable to stem the Russian advance into Galicia. Such a catalogue of errors had raised concerns at OHL that the Dual Monarchy would be unable to fight and win without a significant transfusion of German resources. Falkenhayn had little choice but to send what he could to the newly formed

Ninth Army in Silesia, authorizing a joint Austro-German counter-offensive that he hoped would attract Russian reserves and contain the situation long enough 'to gain time for the development of plans in the West'.[6] He was now trying to master that tortuous and unsatisfactory business of balancing resources and manpower – east or west – that would bedevil German commanders for the next three years.

Falkenhayn identified that the distance, both literal and figurative, between OHL and the fighting commands was a major problem, so he moved the Supreme Command to Charleville-Mézières in the Ardennes, which was closer to the front and would allow him to exercise a tighter grip on operations. He also did his best to remedy the shortages of ammunition and materiel that were beginning to bite, although it was not easy. In the west, the nearest railheads were five days' march behind the fighting line and there was only one main lateral railway line between Metz and his right flank. A lack of reserves was also hampering Germany's freedom of manoeuvre. Although the fortress town of Maubeuge surrendered on 8 September (bringing with it 45,000 French prisoners and 400 guns, and freeing up the besieging force of over 55,000 men),[7] Falkenhayn struggled to scrape together enough combat power for his plans. Most of the army commanders were reluctant to release troops from their sectors, so OHL had to look elsewhere, including back in Germany, where five reserve corps were being formed. Despite concerns that these units were not yet ready for battle, Falkenhayn was not interested. He needed them now.

With the failure of the Schlieffen Plan, Germany was faced with the unappetizing prospect of a war on two fronts that might conceivably last for years. But Falkenhayn had not given up hope of a decisive success in the west. The crucial ground now lay to the north between Noyon (where Kluck's right flank was 'in the air') and the Channel ports. If they could deprive the French of important industrial centres and cut the British off from the sea, then perhaps something could be recovered from the ruins of Moltke's war. Gerhard Tappen had returned from a lightning tour of the front on 15 September and reported that 'the main crisis seems to have been overcome' with the closure of the gap between First and Second Armies.[8] Moreover, the French were exhausted. If the German Army could launch a new offensive, Tappen was confident they would break. Falkenhayn knew that he needed to regain the initiative and move troops to his right as quickly as possible, so he ordered the redeployment of Rupprecht's Sixth Army from Lorraine. In the meantime, he authorized renewed attacks along the line, ordering Bülow (who was now an army group commander overseeing First, Second and Seventh Armies) to keep the French from reinforcing their left. Third, Fourth and Fifth Armies were also ordered to attack and fix the French centre.

Falkenhayn met Rupprecht on 18 September, with Tappen briefing him on his plans. The area as far as Amiens was free of enemy troops, but they knew that French cavalry were moving up, so they had to act quickly. Falkenhayn believed that a major opportunity now beckoned, so he issued new orders to Sixth Army, which would 'assume responsibility for protecting the right flank of the army' and aim to bring about 'a decisive end to the battle on the right flank as quickly as possible . . .'[9] German engineers and work gangs were frantically trying to repair the Belgian and French railway network, parts of which had been devastated by the fighting or blown up by Belgian or French saboteurs, and it was not until the night of 24/25 September that the first two of Rupprecht's corps were able to enter the line, driving the French out of Péronne on the Somme. Elsewhere, Falkenhayn was determined to wrap up any unfinished business left over from the opening phase of the campaign as the German Army settled down for a prolonged occupation of France and Belgium. Outside Antwerp, III Reserve Corps, commanded by General Hans von Beseler, had now encircled the city and was awaiting the arrival of the super-heavy howitzers that would allow it to take on its ring of protective forts. The focus of the war was now firmly in the north.

Siege operations at Antwerp began on 28 September with the familiar, horrifying sounds of 420 mm howitzer shells bombarding the outer forts. Within a day, two of the forts guarding the southern edge of the city had been reduced to smouldering ruins, and with them the

Belgian High Command's hopes that it could hold out as an Allied bastion in the north. It was clear now that Antwerp needed to be evacuated, saving as much of the army as possible, while holding off German attacks until the retirement had been completed. The garrison, outgunned but undeterred, continued to hold on, occupying a series of narrow trench lines and defensive works outside the city and repulsing regular German forays with heavy loss. But it was only a matter of time before the crushing power of Germany's siege artillery snuffed out all resistance. More worryingly, there was a danger that as Falkenhayn moved forces north, the Belgians would be cut off from linking up with the British and French. If Antwerp was to be held, it needed help.

Antwerp's would-be saviour came in the unlikely form of Winston Churchill, the First Lord of the Admiralty, whose war had hitherto been spent in London, waiting impatiently as the German High Seas Fleet refused to give battle to Britain's Royal Navy. Belgium had initially asked London to send 30,000 troops to keep the road open between Ostend and Antwerp, but this was not deemed possible and, instead, Churchill offered to send a brigade of Royal Marines to stiffen the resolve of the defenders.[10] He even proposed to lead this adventure himself. He arrived on 3 October, but found the situation far worse than he had anticipated. 'The outer forts were falling one by one', he wrote. 'Five or six shells from the enormous German howitzers were sufficient to smash them to their foundations . . . Material of every kind – guns, ammunition, searchlights, telephones, entrenching materials – was scanty.' Churchill realized that there was little chance that Antwerp could hold out long enough for the Allied forces to come up from the south, so after spending three days in the city, he endured an 'anxious drive over roads luckily infested with nothing worse than rumour' before reaching Ostend and boarding a warship back to England.[11]

By 7 October, the situation at Antwerp was critical. The inner line of forts was now coming under heavy fire, and increasing numbers of citizens were fleeing the city, carrying whatever they could gather and escaping in long, miserable columns out into the countryside. On 10 October, the governor had no choice but to raise the white flag as the defence finally began to give way. Fortunately, most of the Belgian Army – 75,000 men in total – had escaped and were hurrying west towards the Yser river, covered by French marines and the British 7th Division, which had been landed at Zeebrugge several days earlier. Once it had reached the Yser, the Belgians would hold the extreme left of the Allied line where the front disappeared into the grey, windswept dunes of Nieuport on the Channel coast. It was a desperately tired army, exhausted by the demands of constant combat and low on ammunition and supplies. Yet there would be no more retreats. As his men shuffled along, King Albert ordered that the position on the Yser must not be given up: 'The line of the Yser is our last line of defence in Belgium, and its retention is essential for the development of the general plan of operations. This line, therefore, must be held at all costs.'[12]

To the south, Castelnau's attempt to outflank the German positions on the Aisne progressed slowly. By 26 September, the Germans were in Bapaume on the Somme and were blocking his path. Whatever the reasons for Castelnau's failure to make progress – and there were many – the Second Army commander seemed to have lost something in the fighting in Lorraine. The death of his son, Second Lieutenant Charles de Curières de Castelnau, who was killed on 20 August, was a staggering blow. He was now tired and too easily discouraged, dwelling on his problems rather than trying to master them by his own force of will and personality. One witness who saw him at this time described him as being 'modest, grave, on his pale face an expression of inner sadness yet indomitable energy, he listened, silent, calm . . .'[13] On 4 October, his patience finally exhausted, Joffre asked Ferdinand Foch to coordinate the disparate Allied forces that were congregating in the north. In a letter to Millerand, Joffre admitted that (among his army commanders) Foch showed 'an incontestable superiority from the point of view of character and military ability'.[14] He had become one of Joffre's most important generals.

Foch was now the equivalent of an army group commander, Assistant to the Commander-in-Chief, and thus superior to his former head, Castelnau. 'Slim, elegant, a distinguished air about him, his dolman jacket fitting him like a glove, he was instantly striking . . .

full of energy, composure and honesty', was how a former student at the École de Guerre described him. 'A high forehead, a proud, straight nose; his grey-blue eyes looked one straight in the face. He spoke without gestures, with authority and conviction, in a serious, harsh, rather monotone voice, drawing out his sentences to demonstrate a rigorous reasoning power, an appeal to logic and even a ready recourse to mathematical expressions. His conversation was some-times difficult to follow because it was so rich in ideas but he kept one's attention as much by his note of sincerity as by the shrewdness of his views.'[15] Foch's rise had been remarkable; even more so given that, like Castelnau, he was dealing with a terrible personal grief. His only son, Germain, had been posted missing in August (his death would be confirmed the following year), and although Foch kept hoping for good news, it never affected his determination to fight on.

Foch wasted no time. He returned to his headquarters by motor car; the route 'lay along roads torn to pieces by artillery fire and still encumbered with convoys, across rivers where bridges had been destroyed and only summarily repaired, through villages disfigured by battle', was how he described it. He reached the village of Breteuil, south of Amiens, just after four o'clock on the morning of 5 October and spoke to Castelnau soon afterwards. The commander of Second Army was red-eyed with fatigue and told Foch that his men had run into heavy fighting. One of his corps had been held up outside Noyon and a group of territorial divisions were falling back on the Somme. Given the amount of ground he had to occupy, it was increasingly difficult to maintain contact with Tenth Army, which was assem-bling around Arras. Castelnau felt that he might need to withdraw, but Foch was having none of it. If they retreated they would risk the loss of much of the north, including the Channel ports, as well as ending any attempt to outflank the German right. So they would stand and fight. Second Army would hold 'no matter what might be the difficulties encountered or the sacrifices entailed'.[16]

By 1 October, German patrols were within sight of Arras, and over the next three days the coal-mining area of Douai and Lens came under German occupation. Attacks, followed by hurried counter-attacks, flared up across the front, sucking in battalions and regiments in a chaotic, swirling fight that was almost impossible to control. For the Allies, much now depended upon the commander of Tenth Army, General Louis de Maud'huy, a pipe-smoking native of Lorraine whose most fervent wish was to liberate his home city of Metz. He did his best to provide a semblance of order, but had little choice but to throw battalions into the line as soon as they arrived, often with little idea of what they were up against. There were no typewriters or telephones at his headquarters. The only way he could communicate with his units was to scribble down orders on scraps of paper and hand them to exhausted despatch riders. When liaison officers came back from the front, they always arrived with the same depressing story: 'We have been under violent enemy attack all day and are greatly outnumbered. We have no more reserves. We have no more munitions. Our troops are exhausted and strung out so thinly along the front that it is a miracle that they have the energy to hold the line. We demand reinforcements. We demand munitions.'[17]

In places the fighting was extremely close, with a kind of frantic unpredictability that demanded reserves of courage and steel. A French staff officer, Marcel Jauneaud, was sent to deliver an order to Victor d'Urbal (one of Maud'huy's corps commanders), whose command post was several kilometres southwest of Arras, situated in a ditch close to the front line. Jauneaud had just conveyed Maud'huy's orders when a 'whole line of enemy skirmishers' came up over a nearby ridge. 'Then General d'Urbal, perfectly calm and still smiling, said to me "Take a good look now." A burst of 75 gunfire from the batteries I had just seen drawn up in lines on the flat land on either side of the road, crashed down on the ridge. In the cloud of smoke from the explosions the spiked helmets jumped up, scattered, vanished. And we saw companies of our reinforcements, weapons at the ready, marching forward and climbing the ridge of La Chapelle to take it back again victoriously. It was a magnificent manoeuvre!'

Cowering in the ditch, Jauneaud looked up at d'Urbal, who was smiling broadly.

'Lieutenant,' he said, 'now go and tell General Maud'huy just how we carry out his orders.'[18]

Such was the chaotic situation that Foch inherited. He did his best to inject urgency into the Allied advance, but it won him few friends. Castelnau never forgave his former subordinate for overruling him and for refusing to listen to his entreaties about the difficulties he was facing. Even Maud'huy, about as unflappable as they came, found himself wilting under Foch's stern gaze when the latter turned up at his headquarters on the evening of 5 October, bursting into his chateau like 'a gust of wind'. At that moment, Maud'huy had been discussing with his Chief of Staff the possibility of abandoning Arras, which was then coming under fierce attack, but Foch refused to contemplate it. Embracing Maud'huy, he escorted the general into a side room and then closed the door. 'There was no need to listen intently to know what was going on', remembered one of the staff officers present. 'Now and again the shouting was so loud that the whole house shook.'

'I don't want to hear!' growled Foch. 'Do you understand? I don't want to hear! I am deaf! I know of only three ways of fighting. Attack! Resist! Fuck off! I forbid you to consider the last one – choose between the first two!' Then Foch's voice grew quieter. 'The entire XXI Corps? Manoeuvre? Hold the line? Leave? Have you done it? Echelons! We must find a line of resistance . . .'[19]

Fortunately for Foch, by 8 October the line at Arras had stabilized as the fighting flowed north towards Lille and, from there, on to the Channel coast. Maud'huy's left flank was also bolstered by the arrival of British forces, which had started to leave the Aisne in the first week of October. The idea to transfer the British north had come from Sir John French (prompted by the tireless Winston Churchill), who suggested to Joffre that it made sense for Britain to 'regain its position on the left of the line', where they were closer to their bases and lines of communication.[20] While this created a significant headache for Joffre – struggling as he was to move enough French units north – it was eventually signed off and Smith-Dorrien's II Corps was the first to leave, silently withdrawing from the Aisne on the night of 1/2 October and heading for the French left around Béthune. However, it took some time before all British forces could be concentrated, ready to take part in Joffre's general offensive, by which time the forces of

Crown Prince Rupprecht had secured important ground in the north; ground that would be the springboard for a new series of attacks.

A great clash of arms now loomed in the north. Much to Joffre's annoyance, Saxon troops entered Lille on 12 October, securing one of the most important industrial cities in France and snatching one of Joffre's principal objectives. Rupprecht was the first senior commander to visit on the morning of 13 October, making his way past crowds of refugees and grey-clad battalions marching along the wet, leaf-blown roads towards the city. 'Between Douai and Lille, hordes of Lille's inhabitants are fleeing the town', he wrote:

> Perhaps they are expecting a second bombardment of the town by the French and English. In Lille, the people are very nervous; no wonder as a part of the town has already been burnt down or is still in flames. I can indeed see firemen, but no work is being done to put out the fires because a grenade has destroyed the waterworks. Luckily there is no wind and a light fog is falling. There is debris everywhere on the streets. Bright flames are whipping out of the windows and roofs of some houses, others have already burnt down. The air is red hot in places, small clouds of smoke are drifting out of the side streets and there is the constant sound of crackling and banging.[21]

OHL issued orders for all German forces assembling between Lille and the Channel coast on 14 October. Rupprecht's Sixth Army would remain on the defensive, while the newly constituted Fourth Army marched forward to deliver a 'crushing blow' and break the Allied left. Commanded by Albrecht, Duke of Württemberg, Fourth Army had played a supporting role throughout much of the invasion of France, but it was now foremost in Falkenhayn's thoughts. Although it was a sizeable force, there were precious few veterans within its ranks. Of its five corps, four were reserve formations containing older men as well as large numbers of volunteers who had joined up since the outbreak of war, including many students, eager to play their part in the defence of the Fatherland. Falkenhayn had ordered them to be hurried to the front, convinced they could break the line. When one of Rupprecht's staff officers questioned whether such reserve corps could be effective, Falkenhayn told him that they would be given more heavy artillery than usual (much of it taken from the siege of Antwerp) and, moreover, that their spirit was 'brilliant'.[22]

Within days this grand movement was under way: five corps marching westwards, brushing away any cavalry patrols or groups of militia they encountered as they endeavoured to split the Allied line. Fighting broke out along the coastal sector as German troops, newly freed from Antwerp, attacked the Belgians along the Yser river, although they were unable to break through. Both sides had little idea of the other's strength, as well as an over-optimistic belief that some kind of victory could be achieved in the north. On 16 October, Foch received a telegram from Joffre confirming the deployment of two more French divisions, which he hoped would enable them to push on towards Courtrai.[23] But French intelligence had missed the movement of the new German army, with Foch thinking that he was faced with a gap in the line ('a region which was void of troops', as he put it), which meant that there was still an opportunity to outflank the German right if they could march swiftly towards Menin and Roulers. He visited the city of Ypres and climbed to the top of its great medieval Cloth Hall, looking out upon 'a sea of green, with little white islands marking the positions of the rich villages, with their fine churches and graceful steeples. To see open country in any direction was impossible.' This landscape would now become the location of what Foch later called 'a shock of supreme violence and brutality'.[24]

British troops from Lieutenant-General Sir Douglas Haig's I Corps marched through Ypres on 20 October, passing floods of refugees going the other way, soaked to the skin in the drizzling rain. I Corps was the last part of the BEF to move north and had been fortunate to escape the severe fighting at Mons and Le Cateau. It would now find itself directly in the path of the German Fourth Army, which was closing rapidly. Haig saw Sir John on 16 October, who told him that the enemy was 'falling back' and that we 'would soon be in a position to round them up'. He also 'estimated the Enemy's strength on the front Ostend to Menin, at about one corps, not more' and instructed him to capture Bruges.[25] Yet any hopes that the Allies would be able to make a sizeable advance soon broke down in the face of heavy and unrelenting German pressure. That day, Fourth Army finally made contact with the British and French forces arrayed against it, battering against the line and causing an urgent rethink about whether an Allied offensive was possible. By 21 October, in the face of what Haig called 'all this uncertainty, excitement and despairing messages', he was forced to call off his attacks and be content with holding a thin line around Ypres.[26]

None of the German commanders liked the ground. When he saw it, General Georg von der Marwitz (commander of II Cavalry Corps) complained that a decisive battle here was unlikely. 'We are certainly not thirsting for blood, but everyone realizes that there is nothing to be gained with barely half successes, and decisive successes will not be recorded for a long time yet. The terrain, with its thousand canals, its dense development featuring miles of villages, hedges, banks and ditches, and also even mining areas, really encourages the strategy of defending. One can only advance in a few sections, and this is of course slow.'[27] For infantry officers the problem in Flanders was the difficulty of observation. With little high ground, the flat farmland was intersected by drainage channels and small obstacles, which favoured the defence. Combat thus distilled down into separate struggles for each farmhouse or wood, trench line or field. Because they were deploying large numbers of new formations without the thorough training of pre-war soldiers, German commanders quickly found that their men were more likely to become lost or confused, or to panic once under fire, and required greater supervision from their officers. They did, however, have the advantage of numbers.[28]

Everywhere it was the same story: heavy German attacks flooding north and south of Ypres, supported by what seemed like monstrous amounts of artillery fire, booming across the front and pulverizing the shattered countryside. The British were now facing the full weight of the German Sixth Army, driving northwest over the Lys, and Fourth Army coming down from the north (from the direction of Roulers), placing the defenders in an ever-tightening vice around the city of Ypres. Heavy fighting continued over the next few days, with the British and French scratching thin trenches in the wet soil or punching out loopholes in the farms and villages they defended, struggling to hold on. German battalions marched forward with the shout of '*Vorwärts*' (Forward) on their lips, while the British fought with what a German officer called 'the courage of desperation' as both sides realized what was at stake.[29] Sir John French put it clearly in his memoirs: 'It was simply "up to us" to hold on like grim death to our positions by hard, resolute fighting, until relief in some shape could come.'[30]

At GHQ (now located at Saint-Omer), Sir John's mood seemed to fluctuate like the weather. He had good days and bad ones. There were times when he breathed out optimism and enthused about the coming Allied victory (usually after seeing Foch), but in other moments he struggled to contain a sense that he was being drowned by the war with all its immensity and suffering. When he had suggested transferring his command to the left of the French, he had been convinced that huge opportunities existed for the British to exploit the open German flank, but by 21 October, when he realized just how strong the enemy were, he began to look for a way out. He even suggested to Joffre that the British might withdraw to an entrenched camp in Boulogne, only for the French Commander-in-Chief to stamp on his proposal immediately, telling him bluntly that 'such a thing could not be allowed for a moment'.[31] So Sir John carried on, breezily insisting in his letters back to London that the situation was favourable, while privately breaking from the terrible strain he was under.

Still the Germans came on. 22 and 23 October were days of heavy combat as British soldiers, sometimes fighting in small groups, poured volley after volley into their tormentors. British infantry were armed with the Short Magazine Lee-Enfield, a tough and reliable weapon that could produce up to fifteen rounds of aimed rifle fire per minute in the right hands – often giving the Germans the impression they were up against many more defenders than was the case. With just three British divisions occupying a thin line around Ypres – facing more than double the number of attackers – there was a very real prospect that the line would break. Fortunately reinforcements, in the form of the French IX Corps, marched into Ypres on the evening of

22 October with orders to counter-attack the following day, causing spirits to rise among the Allies – confident that the decisive moment was at hand. 'As we stand now', reported a special Order of the Day issued by the French High Command, 'the tiniest rupture of equilibrium at any point may incline the balance definitely in our favour. The enemy troops which you have on your front . . . appear to belong for the most part to newly raised corps without great value. Take advantage of this to press your offensive on Roulers with the greatest vigour . . .'[32]

There would, however, be no grand march into Roulers. Coordinating the wide array of Allied units around Ypres was difficult enough, and although the Germans were pushed back in places, it was not possible for the British, Belgians and French to cooperate on more than a few local actions. Over the next week the situation remained critical, with fighting flaring up across the front from La Bassée to Nieuport, the Germans defending in some places, attacking in others. Throughout this period, casualties continued to spiral alarmingly. For example, Smith-Dorrien's II Corps (holding the front south of Ypres) sustained nearly 14,000 casualties during the month of October. Further north, the Belgians were equally hard hit. Between 15 and 25 October, the Belgian Army on the Yser evacuated over 9,000 wounded officers and men – not counting the dead and missing.[33] This was even more worrying when, on the evening of 25 October, British aircraft noticed ominous movements: long marching columns and heavy rail traffic heading for Flanders and signifying that more Germans were on their way. From now on the Allies would remain on the defensive.

The campaign reached a terrible climax in the last days of October when a new army group, consisting of two German corps, went into action. Lieutenant-General Max von Fabeck, a hard-bitten Berliner who had commanded XIII Württemberg Corps, was chosen to lead a renewed attack – Falkenhayn having lost faith that Rupprecht had the necessary drive to bring it to a successful conclusion. On the eve of the attack, Fabeck issued a bloodthirsty Order of the Day exhorting his men to achieve a breakthrough of 'decisive importance'. 'We must and will therefore conquer, settle for ever with the centuries-long struggle, end the war, and strike the decisive blow against our most detested enemy.' Enjoying a 2:1 numerical superiority, they would attack along the southeastern flank of Ypres, pushing up over the Messines Ridge (which lay to the south of the city) and driving the enemy towards the coast.[34] Fabeck brought up as much heavy artillery as he could, and at daybreak on 31 October his divisions swept forward, all under the watchful eye of the Kaiser, who had come to Sixth Army's headquarters to watch the assault take place.

The fighting that day was abnormally brutal. On the Germans came, sometimes in thick columns, only to meet unerringly accurate rifle and machine-gun fire from the defenders, as well as heavy shell-fire, causing clouds of dirty grey smoke to hang over the battlefield. 'The enemy met the first rush of the jaegers [light infantry] into an open beet field with a hail of infantry fire', was how one German officer remembered the attack. 'The stubborn English would not be ousted, yet with equal fortitude the Guard jaegers pushed their advance in total disregard of heavy losses. With the aid of accompanying engineers they succeeded in cutting and blowing up the wire defences . . . Through these gaps or over the wires the scanty remnants of both companies swept into the trenches . . .'[35] At times the combat was incredibly close, with hand-to-hand clashes breaking out across the line as men used shovels and clubs, rocks and stones, to batter their opponents. Yet the terrible pressure, particularly the heavy artillery fire, took its inevitable toll on the thin British line. Shortly after one o'clock, a flurry of shells exploded at Hooge Château, bursting in the room as a meeting of British divisional commanders and staff was taking place. Major-General Samuel Lomax, commanding 1st Division, was wounded and a score of staff officers were killed or badly injured. At that moment, the Germans were on the verge of breaking the line, having taken the village of Gheluvelt, and causing Haig to mount his horse and ride towards the line, convinced that there was nothing else to do but die with his men where they stood.

At his headquarters in Cassel, a small village perched on a hilltop about twenty miles west of Ypres, Foch did what he always did on such occasions: send reserves off to where they were needed and remain his usual, cheerful self. An ashen-faced Sir John French visited him shortly after Gheluvelt had fallen and relayed the bad news. Foch had refused to withdraw on past occasions and he was not going to do so now. As for the proposal that they should go to the fighting line, Foch brushed it off.

'We must stand firm first', he snapped. 'We can die afterwards.' He then went over to his desk and dashed off a directive: 'It is imperative not to retire, but to hold on to the ground where one is, and dig in.' He warned against any retreat that might cause a panic resulting in the wholesale loss of the position and sever contact between the British and French. 'The late time of day will allow for reorganization. It is useless to withdraw, and dangerous to do so in daylight.'[36]

Sir John left Foch's headquarters with the promise that French troops would attack to relieve the pressure on Haig. This was what the First Battle of Ypres was about for the Allies: a bewildering array of different units fighting together, sometimes organized, sometimes not. There were Belgians clad in their ragged black uniforms, French territorials and marines, dismounted British and French cavalry, interspersed with infantry of all kinds, mud-splattered, weary and decimated by casualties. Foch may have been an army group commander, but the Belgians and British were not in his chain of command and he was outranked by Sir John French – a *Field Marshal* to his *General*. Yet this seemed to matter little as the Allies fought on, plugging gaps wherever needed and sharing the terrible burden of holding the line. Foch was never the most diplomatic of men, but he understood the sensitivities of his position and always treated Sir John with the utmost respect. It was also fortunate that he was good friends with the British Sub-Chief of Staff, Henry Wilson; a man whom he had known for many years and who spoke his language with a rare fluency. When French and Wilson visited Foch at his headquarters one day, Foch shook Sir John's hand before throwing his arms wide when he saw Wilson, giving him 'a big smacking kiss on each cheek'.[37] Such matters smoothed the strains of war.

Somehow the line held. The crucial ridge at Gheluvelt, which overlooked Ypres, was retaken that afternoon by 2/Worcestershire Regiment, which executed a swift and decisive counter-attack across open ground. Rushing forward at the double, 'with fixed bayonets in one long irregular line', the Worcesters lost over a hundred men in the charge, but managed to restore the front.[38] The Germans tried again the following day, and would rush up the elite Prussian Guards for a final assault on 11 November, but they would never again get as close to a breakthrough as they had on 31 October. By then, the Belgians had opened the flood gates at Nieuport at high tide, flooding the low ground around the Yser Canal and closing off any further attempts to take the extreme left of the Allied line. The Germans had to be content with pinning their enemies into a narrow salient around Ypres while admitting to a grudging sense of mutual admiration across the scarred battle lines. Looking back years later, a General Staff Officer, Captain Otto Schwink, recorded that 'the fact that neither the enemy's commanders nor their troops gave way under the strong pressure we put on them . . . gives us the opportunity to acknowledge that there were men of real worth opposed to us who did their duty thoroughly'.[39]

The repulse of the attack on 11 November was Germany's final attempt to break the line in 1914 and its failure brought the battle to an end. As the weather gradually turned colder – by 20 November there was snow on the ground – both sides took stock of the carnage they had witnessed. The fighting in Flanders had been catastrophic for the reserve corps of Fourth Army. Battalions regularly fought on to extinction; others trudged out of the line a shadow of their former selves, just a handful of mud-splattered, hollow-eyed men. 'Yesterday we didn't feel sure that a single one of us would come through alive', wrote a German survivor. 'You can't possibly picture to yourselves what such a battlefield looks like . . . Every foot of ground contested; every hundred yards another trench; and everywhere bodies – rows of them! All the trees shot to pieces; the whole ground churned up a yard deep by the heaviest shells; dead animals; houses and churches so utterly destroyed by shell-fire that they can never be of the least use again.[40] It is possible that German casualties were as high as 134,000; certainly three of the reserve corps lost at least half their strength – laying the groundwork for a powerful myth of patriotic sacrifice in the '*Kindermord*': 'the massacre of the innocents at Ypres'.[41]

When the losses in Flanders were added to the grim total of German casualties since the beginning of the war, the figure was shocking. Germany had suffered at least 800,000 casualties, including 116,000 dead.[42] Such was the scale of losses that they became impossible to hide, biting deep into previously genteel, elite units. When the Adjutant-General, Hans von Plessen, accompanied the Kaiser to a 'lovely' Christmas Mass at the cathedral in Douai, he was stunned by the appearance of 1/Guards Fusilier Regiment, which formed up in the square outside. 'The first guard regiment has virtually no officers! My eyes started to fill with tears! On a large square, lining up in an open box formation. The address of the Supreme Majesty was moving. The troops gave a strapping good impression. But without officers. This is impossible!'[43]

For Britain and France, the fighting in October and November 1914 would never attain the kind of mythical status it possessed in Germany, but the memory of how close the line came to breaking was never forgotten. In later life, Sir John French would recall the days when 'no more than one thin and straggling line of tired-out British soldiers stood between the Empire and its practical ruin as an independent first-class power'.[44] The heroism of his men had never been in doubt, but the cost had been terrifying. Between 14 October and 30 November, the expeditionary force suffered over 58,000 casualties, including almost 8,000 men killed in action, which brought the total British casualties since the beginning of the war to 86,000 – more than the entire strength of the infantry at the opening of hostilities.[45] The BEF was now just a pale imitation of its original self, bolstered by whatever manpower could be scraped together from across the empire. The most notable addition was the Indian Corps (two divisions of colonial troops from Britain's *Raj*), which had played a gallant role in holding the line throughout October and November. Elsewhere, territorial battalions had been thrown into battle far earlier than anyone had anticipated, but Britain's crippling lack of trained manpower was impossible to hide. Reinforcements were desperately needed.

Gradually the fighting ebbed away. Although the crackle of rifle and machine-gun fire never left the flat Flanders landscape, the furies

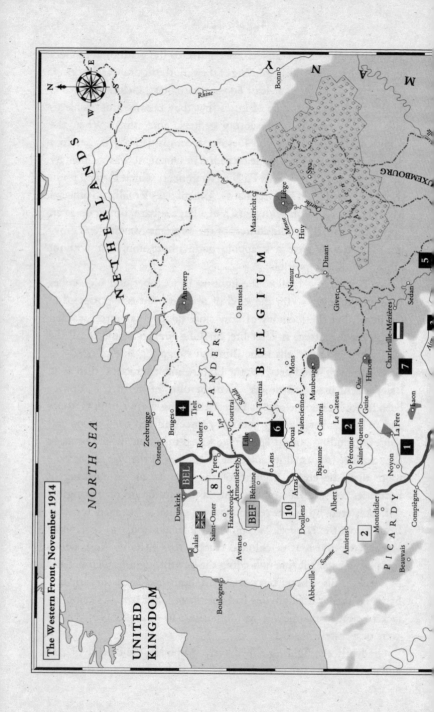

The Western Front, November 1914

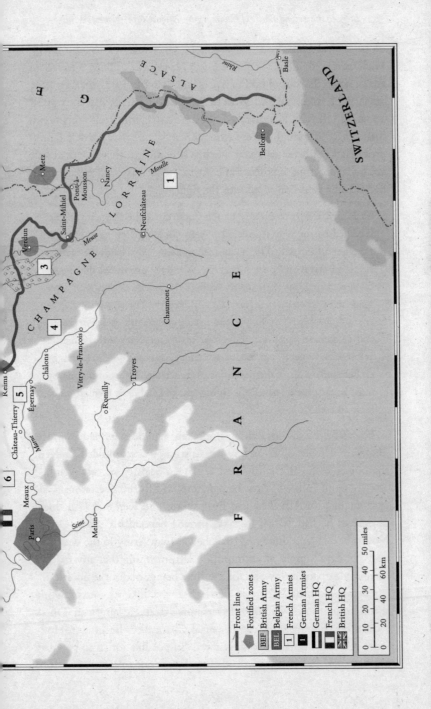

of battle had passed on. 'General, the enemy attacks have ceased', Foch wrote (in a letter to Joffre on 13 November): 'They seem to be abandoning the idea of taking Ypres and thereby giving up their plan to outflank us on our left. Most of the reinforcements you were good enough to send me have arrived; they are still landing without enemy disruption.' Although the enveloping manoeuvre that Joffre had proposed had not been achieved, Foch was confident that they had still secured something tangible in Flanders. He estimated that the enemy had thrown fourteen corps into the fighting:

> Such an effort is testimony to the importance the German officers attached to the Ypres position . . . As for us, if we have brought together all the Allied forces and secured our naval bases the tactical result gained is still purely negative. We have prevented the enemy from carrying out their plan whatever the sacrifices they may have made in order to carry it out. We will hold on. For, as a result of the enemy's weakness, in the present circumstances important decisions could be made which may be to our advantage. Such is the situation as it stands, General; our troops' resistance has been equal to the highest demands made of them; our losses are serious. Those of the enemy must be far greater, given the tightly packed and deep formations of their attacks.[46]

Foch's belief that something important had been gained from the desperate defence of Ypres was not as strange as it sounded. Indeed, the failure to break the line and achieve a decisive success weighed heavily upon Falkenhayn as he contemplated future operations. Calais remained in Allied hands. Even Ypres and Kemmel Hill, local objectives he had sworn to take, proved beyond his reach. On 12 November, he was informed that the German Army in the west had only six days' supply of ammunition left, meaning that any further large-scale operations were, for the time being, out of the question.[47] There was nothing left to do but let the war take its course, while trying to plot some way out of Germany's strategic labyrinth. On 18 November, he met with the Imperial Chancellor, Bethmann Hollweg, and told him bluntly that it was 'impossible for us to conquer our enemies' and that they needed to detach one major power from the Allied coalition, either Russia or France. Unless they did this they had no hope of defeating the combined forces of their opponents and would be condemned to a war of gradual strangulation. If they could come to a negotiated peace with Russia, perhaps demanding some 'small border adjustments' and a war indemnity, then it would almost certainly force France to come to terms.[48]

Falkenhayn's realization that the war could not be won without a dramatic alteration in strategy was met with stony silences and awkward glances. Bethmann Hollweg had already drafted a provisional list of war aims on 9 September that called for the 'security' of the German Reich 'for all imaginable time'. It included the possibility of territorial concessions from France (possibly a coastal strip from Dunkirk to Boulogne and the western slopes of the Vosges), the payment of a vast war indemnity, and the reduction of Belgium to a 'vassal state' under permanent German control.[49] Moreover, voices were increasingly being raised at OHL that Germany should reverse the main tenet of the Schlieffen Plan and seek victory in the east, not the west. This was an understandable reaction to the stalemate in France, but Falkenhayn's insight into the intractability of Germany's wider problems went unheeded as the war dragged on into its first winter.

'Where are we heading?' the Kaiser had asked on 1 December, as he waited on news from the front. 'Never a victory, always defeats', he muttered to himself.[50]

4. 'New conditions'

'He is a man of considerable height, with energy written on every line of his face, piercing eyes under well-defined eyebrows . . . He is clad in a simple khaki uniform without any decorations, and greets us cordially and with perfect simplicity.'[1] Such was how Raymond Poincaré remembered meeting Lord Kitchener, who arrived at Dunkirk on 1 November. With the fighting in Flanders reaching crisis point, the British Secretary of State for War had returned to France for a series of important meetings with his Allied counterparts as he urged them to provide more support for the embattled BEF. Everyone was there: Joffre, Millerand and Ribot (the French Finance Minister), while Foch was driven up from Cassel, his attention still fixed on events at the front.

'Well, so we are beaten!' Kitchener had muttered as he greeted Foch, whose stern face dropped when he heard the words. What was most important, Foch replied, recovering instantly, was that reinforcements be pressed into service as quickly as possible.

Kitchener was not to be moved. 'On July 1st, 1915, you will have one million trained English soldiers in France', he said – referring to the vast campaign of voluntary recruitment that had swept through Britain in the first months of the war. 'Before that date you will get none, or practically none.'

Several French delegates then burst in, almost in unison. 'We do not ask so many, but we would like to have them sooner – indeed at once.'

Kitchener growled before turning away. 'Before that date, do not count on anything.'[2]

As expected, Kitchener's firm refusal to commit his forces prematurely did not go down well with Britain's allies, who wanted to see as many British troops in France as quickly as possible.

'Two years,' Ribot had whispered to Poincaré, 'does he really think the war is going to last two years?'

Poincaré tried his best to warm Kitchener up; dining with the Field Marshal until midnight ('we seem to gain confidence with one another and to grow quite genial as the evening draws on'), but whenever he pressed too firmly, he would provoke the tell-tale stiffening in K's demeanour, the glint of steel in his blue eyes.[3] Kitchener was convinced that the war would be long and exhausting and that Britain must husband her resources as wisely as possible. Moreover, he was not struggling to create a brand-new volunteer army only to see it put into the field before it was ready. Kitchener's strategy was a sound one, if unpalatable to the French: Britain's 'New Army' would only be deployed once most of the fighting had been done. It would guarantee the peace after Germany and France had exhausted each other and thus uphold Britain's premier position in the world once the war was over.

The raising of the New Army was a chaotic business as hundreds of thousands of civilians – northern millworkers, London office clerks, bus drivers and everything in between – were turned into soldiers, or at least something resembling soldiers. With no tradition of conscription and little infrastructure in place, the early months of their training left much to be desired. There were weeks of sleeping rough in freezing church halls, long hours of drill in city parks, and the pretence (for there were no real weapons to spare) of loading and stacking arms. A territorial system of home defence had been organized before the war by the Secretary of State for War, Richard Haldane, but Kitchener opted to raise the armies himself. He would do it outside the territorial structure and under the direction of the War Office; a decision that was often criticized but which may have been unavoidable. Haldane had urged Kitchener to raise the new divisions through the county associations (as the territorials were), but K feared that if he did so, he would surrender too much power to local officials and distract them from their primary duty, that of home defence. Haldane would not be the last public official to realize that Kitchener would do things his way.[4]

The Secretary of State for War may have set his face against any premature deployment of his new armies, yet the winter of 1914–15 saw a gradual loosening of his position on the territorials as a trickle of battalions were sent overseas to bolster the thin, tired ranks of the

BEF. By February 1915, forty-eight territorial battalions had been pressed into overseas service and the first full division, 46th (North Midland), had arrived in France.[5] While this was a welcome and necessary reinforcement for Sir John French's command, it did little to improve the feeling between the two men. At Dunkirk, the French delegation had intimated that they still doubted Britain's commitment to the war effort, only for Kitchener to offer to dismiss Sir John if they were unhappy with him. Joffre would have grasped the chance to replace French with Wilson – a known Francophile who could be relied upon to support GQG loyally – but when Kitchener only offered up the name of General Sir Ian Hamilton, a 61-year-old former Commander-in-Chief of the Mediterranean, Joffre was nonplussed. He would rather keep French in place, assuring K that he worked 'well and cordially' with the Field Marshal.[6]

Inevitably word of the exchange leaked out to Sir John – from Foch via Wilson – who was furious, sending his ADC, Freddy Guest, to complain to the Prime Minister about Kitchener's duplicity. Soothing words were soon on their way to Saint-Omer, with Asquith privately reassuring Sir John that there was no truth to the rumours and Churchill urging him not to allow 'mischief makers [to] build a barrier before you and Kitchener'.[7] But Sir John took little comfort from these assurances and increasingly saw the occupant of the War Office as his mortal enemy – one who would stop at nothing to undermine him. This meant that he was now more dependent than ever upon the goodwill of the French. He visited Foch several days later, thanking him profusely for his support and loyalty. He wanted to see Joffre in person as soon as possible, but Foch calmed him down, suggesting that he 'wait a while until pressing events allowed us a little more liberty'.[8]

Joffre cast a cold eye upon the fractures within the British High Command, hoping to use them to his advantage. Unbeknown to Sir John, who laboured under the impression that he had been 'saved' by the French Commander-in-Chief, Joffre had spoken to Poincaré about the need to put pressure on the British Government to jettison the BEF's commander after his lacklustre showing throughout September and October, only to be unimpressed with the calibre of his potential replacement.[9] As for Kitchener's insistence on a long war, this was frustrating and, frankly, unwelcome, typical of an ally who seemed to revel in being as awkward as possible. Joffre issued another 'General Instruction' on 8 December, which revealed his intention to continue fighting through the winter. 'At the present time the re-forming of our units and the rebuilding of our stocks of munitions are nearing completion. Moreover, numerous signs have indicated that the Germans have begun to transport part of their forces towards Poland. Therefore the time has come to take up the offensive again in order to push the enemy towards the north-east and for us to prepare for subsequent action on their communications.' The offensive would take the form of two attacks: Maud'huy's Tenth Army pushing towards Cambrai and Douai, while, in Champagne, Langle de Cary's Fourth Army attacked north towards Attigny.[10] Joffre hoped that a renewed offensive – even if it was in mid-winter, across frozen fields and under white skies – would achieve significant results; if not, then at least it would offer an opportunity to test out a series of new tech-niques and tactics that the French Army had been working on.

In Artois, General Maud'huy proceeded cautiously. Foch saw him on 14 December and they agreed that the attack would 'take on the characteristics of siege warfare in terms of both its method and slow-ness'. The assault would 'only be launched when artillery superiority has been ensured by careful observation; when effective preparation has been made thanks to this superiority; and when it is possible to break the wire surrounding the trenches'. During the meeting Foch 'stressed the importance of not going in too quickly but rather of being sure about a successful outcome'.[11] The same day, Langle de Cary warned his commanders that he would not accept any failure to destroy the German defences, which was now recognized as one of the primary problems in any attack.[12] But this would prove more dif-ficult than anticipated and French guns could provide neither the weight nor the accuracy of fire to break up the German defences. The result was a failure; a bloody and futile demonstration of how diffi-cult it would be to make major advances in this strange new world of trench warfare.

In Artois, the day of the attack (17 December) was bitterly cold, with a biting wind blowing across the frozen battlefield. A preliminary bombardment crashed down upon the German lines, but it could not prevent the attackers from being cut down by rifle and machine-gun fire as soon as they left their trenches, which were soon filled with stiff corpses and shivering wounded. One French commander, Major-General Émile Fayolle, in charge of 70th Division, watched his men storm the village of Carency. The attack began at 10 a.m. after half an hour of intensive artillery fire 'with apparently devastating results'. But when the infantry clambered out of their forward positions, they were met by heavy fire and the attack broke down. The following day Fayolle was given another two battalions, which he again threw into the fray, but they encountered the same murderous fire and lost another 150 men. After the latest failure, he squelched up to the front line occupied by his dirty, haggard men and saw for himself the awful conditions in which they were fighting. 'The wounded spent all day and will spend all night laid out in the mud with icy rain coming down', he observed. 'Such unsung heroes! There is 50 cm of mud in the communication trenches. This war is terrible . . . We will win, ultimately, but why stubbornly persist in needless losses?'[13]

The second phase of the operation began three days later with Fourth Army attacking in Champagne. But the same sorry story was repeated, and although sections of the German line fell, including the shell-smashed village of Perthes – the scene of fierce fighting – the breakthrough never came close. 'The value of what was achieved needs to be weighed against the obstacles overcome', warned Langle de Cary in a letter to Joffre on 13 January. 'The attack was successful on 21 December following a long preparation preceding offensive operations, which have continued without interruption against different sections of the besieged area.' Langle de Cary believed that they should persist with these kinds of patient and methodical attacks ('any other tactic would risk endangering troop morale') and was hopeful that if they were 'implemented relentlessly' they could 'yield significant results'.[14] Joffre's response was both blunt and to the point, typical of a man who remained calm and unruffled during the most frantic of moments, and who still believed that a breakthrough was possible. The problem was that their attacks had been pressed along too narrow a front, perhaps no wider than 500–600 metres, and with too few men. 'An attack must be undertaken with all possible energy, surprise, and speed; if carried out under these conditions, the enemy is unable to regroup and call on reserves in good time. Attacks should also be carried out on as wide a front as possible with the available manpower. Broadside or enfilade attacks on narrow fronts are generally more easily countered; they allow the enemy to concentrate their forces on the point of attack . . .' Joffre also warned Langle de Cary that all commanders must be 'visible in the field' and 'personally engaged in the assaults', which 'with all due diligence, will result in total success'.[15] Such encouragement was typical of Joffre, offensively minded as always, but Langle de Cary correctly understood that the French Army did not possess the resources or wherewithal to attack on such wide fronts without sacrificing concentration of force. If they tried to break through everywhere, they ran the risk of breaking through nowhere.

The confused, somewhat frantic, search for answers that possessed the Allies was mirrored on the other side of the line. Falkenhayn's failure to restart Germany's campaign in the west unleashed a bitterly contested power struggle within the German High Command. The challenge to Falkenhayn was led by the imposing, corpulent figure of Field Marshal Paul von Hindenburg, the 67-year-old Commander-in-Chief of the Eastern Front (*Oberbefehlshaber Ost* or *OberOst*) and the nominal 'victor of Tannenberg'. Despising Falkenhayn as an upstart and distrustful of what he regarded as his excessive defeatism, Hindenburg repeatedly argued that a major effort should be made in the east. Writing to the Kaiser on 9 January, he claimed that if all reinforcements were sent to the Eastern Front, 'it will not be difficult to inflict a decisive, probably devastating, defeat on the adversary in Eastern Prussia'. Committing more troops to the west would 'merely result in the strengthening of our defensive power or, as with Ypres,' – and here he could not resist a swipe at Falkenhayn – 'lead to a frontal assault with high casualties and little chance of success'.[16]

Hindenburg came from an old Prussian family from Posen and was steeped in the traditions of German militarism, joining the Cadet

Corps as a twelve-year-old and seeing action during the wars of 1866 and 1870. Plucked out of retirement in August 1914, he was bundled on to a fast train for the east and given command of Eighth Army in time for the Battle of Tannenberg. En route he was introduced to his new Chief of Staff, Erich Ludendorff, fresh from his exploits at Liège. The two men quickly formed an unlikely, but close, partnership. Hindenburg was a font of pragmatism and solemnity, constantly projecting an aura of strength and almost imperturbable reserve, while Ludendorff, eighteen years his junior, was the engine room of the relationship, possessed of a ferocious work ethic and an unrelenting tactical aggression. Both had never accepted that the era of decisive victory had passed. Both believed that the Russians were beatable and, moreover, that, once Germany had settled matters in the east, a great reckoning could take place against France and Britain. But this could only happen, as Hindenburg put it, 'over the body of a Russia stricken to the ground'.[17] Now garlanded with the laurels of Tannenberg, Hindenburg and Ludendorff sought to reorient Germany's strategy. Their prestige made them formidable opponents.

As for Falkenhayn, he was never convinced by the promise of decisive operations against Russia. Haunted by Napoleon's doomed campaign of 1812, he believed that poor weather, the dire state of the roads and the enormous strategic depth into which Russia could retreat precluded any possibility of far-reaching results. In any case, it was 'a grave mistake to believe that our Western enemies would give way, if and because Russia was beaten', he later wrote. 'No decision in the East . . . could spare us from fighting to a conclusion in the West.'[18] When he visited *OberOst* on 12 January (headquartered in Hindenburg's home town of Posen), he was met with all the same arguments about the impossibility of success in France, as well as the uneasy, shuffled silences and whispers behind his back. He left Posen without giving any assurances on whether reinforcements would be sent east. It was only later, when he returned to Berlin and was, once again, faced with increasingly frantic telegrams from the Austrians, who were trying to hold on to the city of Przemyśl (in Galicia), that he agreed to deploy more troops on the southern front as part of the so-called *Südarmee*. *OberOst* could use them as they saw fit.

This was only the opening salvo in a fierce battle of wills. After authorizing the transfer of German units eastwards, Falkenhayn went one step further and ordered that Ludendorff report to the *Südarmee* – thus breaking up the increasingly powerful duo at *OberOst*. Hindenburg immediately realized what Falkenhayn was trying to do and determined to stop it. He wrote to the Kaiser demanding the removal of Falkenhayn, the return of Ludendorff and, once again, a pivot to the east. With just 'a few strokes of the pen, [he] could bring calm, security, and trust to the nation again through the reinstatement of Moltke to his previous position as Chief of the General Staff, through the return of Ludendorff to his position as Chief of Staff in Posen, and through the employment of the new corps in the east'. Moreover, unless Falkenhayn was sacked, he would resign, thus almost certainly provoking widespread public disbelief and concern about the fate of the one German commander who had achieved an unarguable victory during the war.[19]

But Moltke was not coming back. After his dismissal he had been sent off to direct siege operations at Antwerp. The fall of the Belgian fortress briefly raised his spirits, but there was no way back to supreme command (even if he continued to hope that he had only been temporarily moved aside). In late October, he fell ill with a serious gallbladder infection, which kept him bedridden for weeks. When Hans von Plessen visited him in hospital, Moltke struggled upright in his bed and said that he was feeling much better and 'wanted to take over the business again', only for Plessen to urge him to continue his convalescence, confiding in his diary that Moltke's return was 'impossible'.[20] Moltke did keep abreast of events, writing regularly to the Kaiser and, from January 1915, urging him to reorient Germany's strategy towards Russia. Should they be able to conclude a favourable peace on the Eastern Front, then 'the war would in my opinion be as good as won'.[21] But Moltke's advice was not sought out any more and he was left in a series of stale staff appointments in Berlin – brooding on his misfortune and joining in half-hearted manoeuvres against Falkenhayn.

At OHL, the Kaiser was a depressed figure, worrying about the constant bickering and infighting that was threatening to derail the German war effort and swearing to his aides that he was going to cashier Hindenburg for his insolence. Since the beginning of hostilities, Wilhelm II had struggled to find his place in the war. The downfall of Moltke – the man he had appointed to succeed the revered Schlieffen – was a great personal blow to the Kaiser, who now found himself marooned in his headquarters, plotting the progress of the war on maps, but strangely apart from it. He was regularly fed information from the front and enjoyed hearing bloodthirsty tales of German heroism, usually told after dinner by firelight, but this only whetted his appetite for the real thing. He visited the front in October, getting to within 1,000 yards of the trenches, which buoyed his spirits and made him 'full of lust for battle'.[22] Yet at other times his mood dropped and he found himself a passenger, blown along by events, while struggling to raise the courage to stand against them.

The Kaiser jealously guarded his right to appoint and dismiss the Chief of the General Staff and did not take kindly to the growing chorus of disapproval against Falkenhayn. Bethmann Hollweg wanted him to go, as did a host of senior officers, including Moltke and Rupprecht (the latter having lost faith in Falkenhayn during First Ypres). Although the Kaiser made it clear that Falkenhayn retained his confidence – at least for the time being – he did announce one compromise, with Major-General Wild von Hohenborn becoming War Minister. He also transferred Ludendorff back to Posen and authorized the deployment of Tenth Army (comprising four newly formed corps) to East Prussia. Yet the tensions within the German High Command remained unresolved as the war entered the New Year. There were now two poles of German strategic thought. At OHL, Falkenhayn tried to figure out a way of matching Germany's military position to her political goals, while in the east Hindenburg and Ludendorff sought to win the war in traditional fashion, through a great smashing blow by German arms. And the Kaiser, fidgeting nervously between them, remained an unreliable weather vane, pointing one way and then another.

Wilhelm II was nominally the commander of the greatest army in the field, yet since August 1914 he had allowed the Chief of the General Staff to issue orders in his name and had neither the temperament nor the command of detail that would have allowed him to interfere in the minutiae of military business. His relative impotence in the conduct of the war on land made him veer unsteadily towards action at sea. Grand Admiral Alfred von Tirpitz, the long-serving Secretary of State for the Imperial Navy and the man who had created Germany's great fleet (which remained, for the most part, bottled up at Wilhelmshaven), saw the Kaiser on 2 January and found the 'bastion' around him 'more than ever impenetrable'. When the Kaiser proclaimed that it was now time for the fleet to 'really do something', Tirpitz had tried to pin him down. 'It is just the Kaiser's peculiarity that he won't come to any resolve, or bear any responsibility', he complained; 'but he can't be induced to resolve what it is to do, and he simply evades me when I tackle and harangue him, which I never lose an opportunity of doing.'[23]

The problem for the Kaiser was the seeming invincibility of the Royal Navy, whose superiority in capital ships (a 3:2 ratio by the early months of 1915) meant that a conventional naval battle in the North Sea was unlikely to result in anything other than the annihilation of the German High Seas Fleet.[24] It was with this dilemma forefronted in his mind that he considered a proposal by the Chief of the Naval Staff, Admiral von Pohl, to use Germany's U-boats in a more aggressive fashion. The British blockade, which tightened every month, had effectively cut Germany off from international markets and prevented her from importing raw materials and food. Although Berlin protested that this was a breach of the Declaration of London (1909), which had made a distinction between various kinds of contraband (and theoretically allowed Germany to import food, oil and cotton), it made little difference; international opinion lay firmly with the British. Therefore, unless her submarines could counter this blockade with one of their own, Germany would eventually be starved into submission.

Both the Kaiser and the Chancellor, Bethmann Hollweg, were wary about escalating the naval war in such a dramatic way and worried about the effect of sinking neutral vessels, particularly in the United States. Tirpitz also needed convincing. He was unsure whether Germany had enough strength to strike decisively (she had only thirty-four U-boats currently operational) and would have preferred more time to plan such a campaign. Objections were also raised about the legality of sinking vessels without ascertaining their cargo or destination, but ultimately the need for a decisive victory, whether on land or at sea, settled the matter. On 4 February, the Kaiser inspected the fleet at Wilhelmshaven and afterwards signed the order warning 'all merchant vessels to avoid [the] north and west coast of France as Germany intends to employ all means of war at its disposal against English transports and shipments of ammunition to France'. The waters around the British Isles would henceforth be treated as a 'war zone'. Any merchant ship or neutral vessel found within this zone was liable to be destroyed and her crew lost at sea.[25]

The failure of the December offensives was the beginning of what would be a long season of disappointment for the Allies as the true strength of Germany's position on the Western Front became apparent. The rapidly hardening crust of defences was now everywhere to be seen: hundreds of miles of sandbags and wooden breastworks, interspersed with machine-gun nests, all covered by ever-lengthening tendrils of barbed wire, like some diabolical weed that grew wherever the armies settled. One French private recorded (in a letter back home in February 1915) how quickly the landscape had become deformed by the war into a horrifying spectacle where death hovered, ever close:

> When we arrived here in November this flat, open country was magnificent, with fields as far as the eye could see, filled with root crops, dotted with rich farms and stacks of corn. Now, it's the land of death, all the fields churned up, trampled, farms burnt-out or in ruins. This land has given birth to a different crop – small mounds topped with a cross or simply a bottle turned upside down in which have been placed the identity papers of the one who sleeps beneath. How often do death's wings brush past me as I gallop along ditches or sunken lanes to avoid enemy shrapnel and the rat-a-tat of their machine guns?

Some trenches were already in a terrible state; their walls propped up by corpses, flesh blackening in the cold air. In one godforsaken place, there were even two high boots sticking up, 'the tips in the air, just the right height', which inevitably brought out black humour about using the Boches as coat-racks.[26]

If and how this crust could be broken and movement restored was impossible to foresee, but recent disappointments had not dented Foch's belief that victory was within their grasp. He wrote to Joffre on New Year's Day, updating him on his plans to advance in Artois:

> For the moment we are confining ourselves to preparing attacks and we are pushing this preparation very far ahead; in fact, in front of and in particular to the north of Arras our situation can be summed up as follows: French artillery is very superior to that of the enemy, without doubt in numbers, but also by its positions; in every case asserting its superiority by silencing the enemy artillery every time it wishes to take action. All in all, the latter remains almost constantly silent. French infantry, numerous, is only stopped by the German infantry thanks to its shelters and obstacles of all kinds.

Foch explained that their field artillery was being moved as close as possible to the enemy's trenches (somewhere between 900 and 1,500 metres) and then dug in or covered over with shields. If the enemy's defences could be destroyed, he was confident his troops would be able to advance. Liaison officers ensured that close communication was maintained with the infantry battalions, which were deployed ready to go forward. 'This work is undertaken on the front of the Tenth Army with a view to launching several simultaneous attacks. As long as it keeps on raining, it's all we are able to do. When the weather improves we will reap the benefits of our preparations. This is still my firm belief.'[27]

France had little alternative to fighting on the Western Front. The proximity of the war, its real, physical intimacy, meant that wartime strategy was dominated by the central question of how to defeat the German Army. Nevertheless, as the war widened, the question of sending troops to other theatres became more pressing. This was of particular interest to French politicians, recently returned to Paris following their banishment to Bordeaux after 30 August, who were now eager to regain control of the war effort. At a special session on 22 December, French deputies voted to remain in Paris until the war had been successfully concluded, and opened a whole series of parliamentary investigations (so-called 'commissions') into every aspect of the war effort, from recruitment to munitions and medical care.[28] Joffre, who had enjoyed almost dictatorial powers since August, had little time for what he regarded as amateur meddling and did what he could to frustrate them. He stopped deputies from visiting the front and constantly fought back against the idea that the war was being run with anything less than superb efficiency.

Joffre's rearguard action was not helped by the renewal of heavy fighting along the north bank of the Aisne near Soissons. The French had originally launched a series of attacks across the river on 8 January and managed to seize the important position of Hill 132. Struggles for possession of the high ground continued for days, with French and German infantry toiling amid freezing rain and sleet and under heavy artillery fire. A major counter-attack on 12 January, with the French trenches 'inundated by shells', forced the evacuation of almost the entire north bank of the river and raised fears that the German advance on Paris was about to resume. Although this was not the case, the sudden and decisive nature of the defeat provoked unease back in Paris. In the days afterwards, Joffre even had to listen to a lecture by the War Minister, Millerand, about the need for better artillery concentration in French operations, which prompted a predictably spiky reaction. Joffre sent off a furious telegram the following day, threatening to resign if the Government lacked confidence in him, only for Millerand to back down and promise him unwavering support. Smarting from the embarrassment, Joffre hunted around for a scapegoat and eventually sacked General Henri Berthelot, a former under-Chief of Staff for operations and intelligence at GQG, who had commanded a group of reserve divisions at Soissons.[29]

The unhappy fallout from 'L'Affaire de Soissons' only heightened interest in the possibility of quick victories overseas. Hostilities against the Ottoman Empire opened at the end of October 1914, and although the British took the lead against Turkey, a number of senior French politicians, including the Justice Minister, Aristide Briand, were eager to intervene in the Balkans and the Mediterranean. When Joffre heard about this, he was determined to put a stop to any such speculation, which he believed would divert much-needed forces from the Western Front. On 8 January, he compiled a briefing note that laid out why French troops should not be sent to peripheral theatres (in this case there was a suggestion to send them to fight the Austrians). They did not have enough spare manpower to do so, but, crucially, the main drawback was one of strategy: 'Our object is to reach the enemy upon the principal theatre of operations. It is evident to all that this principal theatre lies in the region where Germany has massed the largest and best elements of her forces. It is not Austria we have to beat, it is Germany'.[30]

For Britain it was different, or at least it seemed so. At almost the exact moment that Joffre was trying to rein in his government's war plans, in London Kitchener was considering expanding them. 'The feeling here is gaining ground that, although it is essential to defend the line we hold, troops over and above what is necessary for that service could be better employed elsewhere', he wrote to Sir John French on 2 January. 'The question of *where* anything effective can be accomplished opens a large field and requires a good deal of study. What are the views of your staff?'[31] Kitchener's letter arrived at an opportune moment. Kitchener was considering a proposal to send a naval expedition to open up the Dardanelles Straits, hoping that a way could be found to knock the Ottoman Empire out of the war. As for the Western Front, Kitchener was dissatisfied and confused now that the fighting had gone to ground. In his lonely tower at the War Office, he paced the floors, struggling to find a solution.

'I don't know what is to be done,' he told the Foreign Secretary, Sir Edward Grey, 'this isn't war.'[32]

In France, Sir John responded to Kitchener's missive with a mixture of shock and disdain. The front *could* be broken if sufficient guns and ammunition were made available – a position he would maintain throughout the year. The best course of action would be to mount an offensive along the Flanders coast in conjunction with the fleet. If he was reinforced sufficiently, Sir John was confident that they could push on towards Ostend and Zeebrugge.[33] But his ideas went nowhere. After they were discussed at the War Council, Kitchener responded with a blunt letter informing him that 'the advantages to be obtained from such an advance at the present moment would not be commensurate with the heavy losses involved'. Moreover, the scale of reinforcements Sir John had requested 'could only be supplied at a considerable dislocation of the organisation of the future reinforcements to be sent to you', and there was, in any case, insufficient time to provide the ammunition he would need. 'You have pointed out that offensive operations under the new conditions created by this war require a vast expenditure of artillery ammunition, which may, for even 10 or 20 days, necessitate the supply of 50 to 100 rounds per gun per day being available, and that, unless the reserve can be accumulated to meet expenditure of this sort, it is unwise to embark on extensive offensive operations against the enemy in trenches.'[34]

Sir John and Joffre may have both shared a distrust of subsidiary fronts, but they could not always cooperate as fully as they would have liked. After meeting with Joffre in late January, Sir John had agreed to shift the British line north, relieving two French corps around Ypres and freeing them up for operations elsewhere. By now the BEF had been rationalized into two armies, First and Second (commanded by Haig and Smith-Dorrien respectively), and Sir John hoped to take the offensive with Haig's forces north of La Bassée alongside Maud'huy's Tenth Army. Yet when promised reinforcements from England failed to arrive (a regular division having been rerouted to the Dardanelles), Sir John had to admit that he could not, for the time being, relieve one of the French corps. Writing to Joffre on 18 February, he confirmed that he was being sent a territorial division instead, which would need 'some training before being sent to the trenches'. When Joffre was told, he tried to choke down his anger at this latest snub – yet another indication, as he saw it, of Britain's failure to take the war seriously. He wrote back on 19 February and told French that the forces he had received, 'although of a lesser quality', should not prevent him from relieving his troops, and, if this were not done, 'I would find myself unable to carry out the attacks I planned'.[35] He promptly cancelled Tenth Army's offensive and let the British attack on their own. Sir Douglas Haig's First Army would mount an independent operation on 10 March at the village of Neuve Chapelle.

The squabbles over trench frontage and how and where to attack would be a constant theme over the next three years and a point of often serious disagreement between the Allies. While Joffre and GQG wanted to harness as much British strength as possible for French war aims, London was wary of throwing everything into the Western Front and instinctively looked elsewhere, as much to retain strategic independence as to fulfil wider imperial objectives. For now, the British would try to manage a war on two fronts. Sir John was expected to do his best in France, while more and more resources were redirected to the Mediterranean, where the effort against Ottoman Turkey was about to begin. The naval operation to reach Constantinople opened in February and proceeded cautiously, with British and French ships coming under fire from shore batteries, while rows of mines, bobbing up and down in the narrow straits, proved fiendishly effective. After losing three ships and having another two severely damaged on 18 March, the Allies pulled back and began to plan for a major amphibious assault on the Gallipoli peninsula. The attack would eventually take place on 25 April 1915 – thus beginning the long-drawn-out agony of the Dardanelles.

In most wars, the arrival of cold weather almost invariably brought about a cessation of major combat operations, but not in 1914–15. On the Eastern Front, Germany's renewed offensive began on 7 February, with two armies battling through driving snowstorms to strike at the Russian Tenth Army around Grodno. Terrible casualties were inflicted upon the Russians – perhaps as high as 200,000, including 90,000 prisoners – but reinforcements were able to contain the situation and then launch counter-attacks.[36] As a tactical and operational spectacle the 'Winter Battle of Masuria' was highly impressive, but in a strategic sense it changed nothing. The Russians remained in the war and seemed no closer to outright defeat. At OHL, Falkenhayn could only bemoan his bad luck. As he had warned all along, deploying his reserves in the east had condemned them to a strict defensive role in the west for the foreseeable future, handing the initiative to the enemy, who were not slow to take it up. Moreover, regular reports revealed the growing power of the Entente. By the spring of 1915, it was estimated that the Allies would be able to field up to twenty-two new divisions, with German intelligence reporting that the first of Kitchener's New Armies would reach the front in February with another following in April.[37]

Across France and Belgium, the winter passed slowly. There had been brief moments of seasonal goodwill on Christmas Day, but in most sectors life at the front was an unedifying combination of cold and hunger, interspersed with occasional, seemingly random, moments of death and terror. Parts of the front had now become settled, with the opposing sides content to keep it that way, but other sections remained places of frenetic activity. In Champagne, which lay right in the middle of the Western Front, fighting never really ceased. This was Joffre's chosen battlefield and where the German line must surely break. If the French could push forward in this sector and sever the Charleville–Mézières railway line, which supplied hundreds of thousands of German troops, then it might be possible to restart the war of movement and achieve decisive results. The French Fourth Army had been steadily reinforced throughout the winter and, by the time it launched its attack in mid-February, it could boast 155,000 men from five corps, supported by 879 guns (of which 110 were heavy).[38] The plan was for two corps to make an initial breach in the German line (around the village of Perthes) and then roll up the front with a series of subsequent attacks. As he had done before the Marne, Joffre encouraged his generals to seize the coming moment. 'I count on you and have confidence in the Fourth Army', he wired Langle de Cary on the eve of the assault. 'In order that you may be able to exploit your success, you will be supported in good time by all the forces at my disposal.'[39]

Langle de Cary's task was a daunting one. German engineers were already turning their temporary defences of 1914 into well-prepared fieldworks, strongly supported by artillery, while the intensity of fighting had transformed the landscape into a forsaken, desolate place. The heights in Champagne were 'formed of white, brittle limestone, covered only with a thin layer of topsoil', remembered one German observer. 'Every bit of shrapnel, every action of the spade, exposes the glowing rock. The countryside has little water and only sparse vegetation. Ponderous pine trees, often crooked and stunted, coalesce to form wooded areas, most often in narrow, long strips, like iron bands that span over a bumpy shield ... Between the forests, there are wide stretches of meadows and fallow fields.[40] Across this barren landscape, now swept by a biting westerly wind, thousands of French soldiers and engineers toiled on the preparation for the great offensive: digging trenches, constructing roads, and bringing up tons of supplies, ammunition and food.

A sudden thaw in early February caused the snow and ice to melt, and the ground quickly turned treacherous. It was not until 16 February that the offensive went ahead, with the attackers once again struggling to make progress. Long lines of shivering, grey-faced French infantry attacked uphill into a series of German positions, only to face withering fire from their opponents. Ground was gained in places, but heavy counter-attacks were launched soon afterwards, which produced deadlock. The commander of the German Third Army, General Karl von Einem (who had taken over from Max von Hausen in September 1914), knew exactly what the French were attempting. 'In the afternoon, news spread of a major attack across a front of about nine to ten kilometres, and prisoners soon made it clear that the French I, IV and XVII corps were attacking', he wrote. 'The goal was to make a breakthrough towards Vouziers [where his headquarters was situated].' Heavy shelling continued throughout the day, with the German defences coming under a 'piercing hurricane' of artillery fire. OHL offered to send reinforcements, but as they were not immediately available, Einem tried to contact Falkenhayn to explain the enormity of what they were facing. When he eventually got through, the Chief of the General Staff was only able to offer him a single reserve division.

'Will you be able to hold with that?' Falkenhayn asked.

'Yes,' whispered Einem, knowing full well that he could not say no.

Einem was convinced that the German line in Champagne needed to be held at all costs. 'Our position here is currently the most important in the whole theatre of war', he wrote on 19 February. 'If the French succeed in breaking through, our whole front in France and Belgium will be in great danger, perhaps even untenable. But we will hold on, just as we have done so far.'[41] As the battle continued, he became increasingly concerned that this was not understood or appreciated by the High Command, which seemed to think that he was being alarmist. Gerhard Tappen, who saw most of the requests for reinforcements that landed at OHL, was unimpressed at having to deploy an extra division to Third Army: 'The Army is losing the feeling that it needs to hold its own . . .'[42]

In Champagne, the French attacks followed a similar pattern; one that would become the basis of trench operations for the next three years. There would be frantic activity for days, with the digging of trenches and saps closer to the German line, before the 75s (or whatever guns could be scraped together) opened up across the frontage of attack. This would then gradually increase into a furious bombardment, what the Germans called *Trommelfeuer* ('drumfire'), which was often likened to the sound of Chinese firecrackers, exploding one after another. Then the attacking infantry would try to cross no-man's-land; that frantic, heart-stopping moment of crisis when the troops had to expose themselves to the terrible fire-swept zone. Most attacks were beaten off by rifle and machine-gun fire, leaving the space between the opposing armies littered with growing piles of dead and wounded. Nevertheless, the unrelenting pressure on the defenders was not easy to deal with. Wet and cold weather, with its accompanying thick mud, caused trenches to collapse and require constant supervision. OHL even ordered the creation of a reserve line three kilometres to the rear; a sensible precaution, but one that sucked up precious manpower and engineering resources.[43]

Fighting would drag on until 17 March, when Joffre finally called it off. Division after division, French and German, had been drawn into a furious positional war along the scarred slopes of Champagne. Far from restoring a war of movement, the offensive had become concentrated on a small number of villages and outcrops – Perthes, Souain, Massiges – and produced rising casualties. French losses totalled some 43,000, and although German casualties were roughly the same, the failure to break through posed more difficult questions for the French High Command.[44] In the absence of significant gains, Langle de Cary stressed that an important moral ascendancy had been gained over the enemy: 'Once again, I must note that troops' morale is growing', he wrote to Joffre. 'They have a sense of victory and display an energy and drive in combat that increase this feeling day after day. The army's chief medical officer said to me today how much he had been struck by the excellent spirits of wounded soldiers returning to combat. I think I can say that the thirty-two days of the Fourth Army's offensive have had, in addition to undeniable material results, the benefit of boosting troops' morale and increasing their confidence in ultimate victory.'[45]

Whether Langle de Cary really believed this is unclear. Like all French officers, he knew the penalties for failure. But had he taken the time to see for himself the wretched condition of the front and the men and boys who emerged from the maelstrom, his view would have surely been different. They looked like the dead; plastered with the limestone and white chalk dust that came from the soil, giving them an unsettling, unearthly appearance, like pale ghosts newly emerged from the underworld. A German account recorded how:

> any progress through the sticky grey mud seemed almost impossible. The loose structure of the rock was smashed by bullets, and softened by constantly falling rain. The tough Champagne mud paralyses every movement, sticks and smears everywhere and leaves its white residue not only on uniforms and equipment, but also on faces and hands as a pale crust. It closes as an eerie, nameless grave over the bodies of the fallen – over friend and foe. No one returned from this Hell without having aged many years, in whose eyes there was nothing to read of this gruesome experience of human fervour being unleashed.[46]

These were the 'new conditions' of the Western Front. How long they could last was anyone's guess.

5. 'A real bad business'

By the spring of 1915, the pleasant city of Charleville-Mézières, capital of the Ardennes, had become firmly established as the second centre of the German Empire, now home to a bewildering array of nobles, politicians, attachés and soldiers from across the Central Powers. German Army officers rubbed shoulders with Turkish officials; press correspondents jostled in the streets with secret policemen and soldiers of every description; while each night the restaurants were filled with minor royalty from every corner of the Austro-Hungarian Empire, trying to get as close as possible to the seat of imperial power. Life in the town was centred upon the railway station and its adjoining square, the Place de la Gare, which had been cordoned off after the arrival of the imperial household. Kaiser Wilhelm II was based in the Villa Corneau, the former home of George Corneau, editor of the *Petit Ardennais*, where it was said he slept on an enamelled white iron bed (just like Napoleon). But that was where the similarities with the great French commander ended. The Kaiser's war consisted of regular rides out to the nearby battlefield of Sedan, scene of the great victory of 1870, or strolls around his villa, reviewing troops and visiting the sick in hospital, always accompanied by his favourite basset hound.[1]

Charleville had a mixed reputation with the German officers who lived and worked there. 'We are, naturally, regarded as robbers, murderers, and ravishers of women', complained Admiral Tirpitz, who was unimpressed by the place. 'Were I to compare it with any German town of the same size, the comparison would be altogether in favour of ours . . . Houses, streets, squares — somewhat dingy. And although the Place Carnot is evidently inhabited by well-to-do bourgeois families, it looks like a very badly kept parade ground.'[2] One staff officer, posted to OHL in January 1915, recalled spending what little spare time he had in the officers' mess in the prefecture, where they sat at small wooden tables, devoured pastries sent in by their wives, and tried to overhear what the senior officers were up to. Every evening, Erich von Falkenhayn would appear, with his face drawn and impassive, before sitting at his favourite table, flanked by his attendants, who were known as the 'whispering club' owing to their habit of keeping their voices as low as possible to prevent them from being overheard.[3]

Falkenhayn had much to preoccupy him. He resided in private apartments at the prefecture and like the Kaiser would take regular walks, swinging a cane as he strolled through the streets. A rumour went round that if he carried it in his right hand, it was generally good news from the front, but if the news was bad, he would grip it with his left hand and a scowl would darken his face.[4] Large stretches of the line were now quiet, which was fortunate given the number of changes that were forced on OHL in the spring of 1915. Alexander von Kluck had been badly wounded by shrapnel in March – predictably after getting too close to the firing line while out visiting III Corps. He was awarded the *Pour le Mérite* and replaced at First Army by General Max von Fabeck (who had led the bloody assaults at Ypres in the autumn of 1914). Kluck's nominal superior at the time, Karl von Bülow, lasted only a few weeks more and returned home in April after suffering a heart attack. A corps commander, Fritz von Below, took over at Second Army.

While Falkenhayn was largely unmoved by French efforts in Champagne and was confident that Third Army would hold, the question of whether Germany should attack on the Western Front remained unresolved. He agreed to a proposal by the Ministry of War to remove an infantry regiment from each division (from four down to three), using them to create new formations. These could then be employed in offensive operations, in either the east or the west. At the same time, he instructed his army commanders to explore the possibilities for offensive action in their sectors, which produced a number of different plans, although none were entirely satisfactory. On 4 March, Rupprecht's Sixth Army submitted a proposal for a major offensive to split the British and French around the city of Arras. A series of attacks would fix the enemy before a main assault broke the line and headed off for Boulogne and Calais. The problem was that such an operation would require a vast array of forces, upwards of thirteen corps and over 500 batteries of artillery.[5]

German commanders identified that it was essential to turn an initial breach into a wider, decisive offensive. According to the Chief of Staff at First Army, Hermann von Kuhl (who was working on how to cross the Aisne and renew the assault on Paris): 'The breakthrough operation must be prepared in such a manner and executed with the aid of such strong forces that its success – at least as far as is humanly calculable – will be assured. The breakthrough must come as an unexpected blow and must succeed.'[6] It was essential that the location for the breakout be carefully chosen, specifically that there were no major obstacles or good tactical features to hinder the attack. Furthermore, powerful diversions had to precede the main assault to draw the defenders' strength and make them vulnerable at the crucial point. Carefully targeted bombardments would then unlock the defences and allow the breakthrough to take place. But whether this could be done with the resources at Germany's disposal remained unclear. At the War Ministry, Wild von Hohenborn doubted whether any of the plans would work. The reorganization of divisional manpower had created only sixteen new divisions: helpful certainly but nowhere near enough for such large-scale operations. Any attacks now would probably just result in the acquisition of miles of 'worthless' ground, not a decisive victory; an opinion that Falkenhayn evidently shared.[7]

These deliberations were halted by the arrival of terrible news from the Eastern Front. The fall of the Austrian fortress of Przemyśl (in Galicia) on 22 March after a six-month siege was a disaster for the Dual Monarchy, with over 120,000 troops and 900 guns being captured by Russian forces, which were now poised to invade Hungary. Urgent, excited telegrams began issuing from the Austrian High Command, demanding a renewed commitment of German troops, and soon afterwards, during a stormy meeting in Berlin, Conrad von Hötzendorf even threatened to sue for peace if support was not given immediately.[8] Many officers at OHL were not minded to give in to Conrad's pleas, believing that he was exaggerating them for his own benefit, *just another case of the Austrian crying wolf*. In any case, the bad news from Galicia was surely balanced out by the repulse of Allied naval forces from the Dardanelles, which seemed to snuff out any immediate threat to the Ottoman Empire. Nevertheless, Falkenhayn was aware of the wider international situation and here storm clouds were appearing. Two powers that had stayed out of the war so far, Italy and Romania, were beginning to shift over to the Entente, causing alarm to Austria–Hungary, still reeling in the aftermath of Przemyśl.

Developments in the east forced Falkenhayn's hand. He now began to think seriously about an operation on the Eastern Front, a grand attack that would simultaneously stop the Russian advance and buoy the Austrians, as well as impressing Italy and Romania with a raw demonstration of German power. Accordingly, he wrote to Conrad on 13 April updating him on his plans. 'Your Excellency knows that I do not consider advisable a repetition of the attempt to surround the Russian extreme (right) wing [a reference to Hindenburg's and Ludendorff's Battle of Masuria].' Therefore, he proposed to send eight divisions to Gorlice, along the northern edge of the Carpathians, and then push them forward in a great drive to the northeast straight into the Russian flank. 'Apart from the strictest secrecy there remains a further preliminary condition for the execution of the operations,' he continued, 'and that is, that Italy is kept quiet by meeting her as far as possible, at least, until we have dealt the blow . . . no sacrifice seems to me too great if it keeps Italy out of the present war.' Conrad wrote back the same day expressing his hearty approval: 'The operations proposed by your Excellency coincide with those that I have so long desired, but which were hitherto impossible, owing to a lack of sufficient forces.'[9] The attack would go in on 2 May.

There only remained the question of what to do on the Western Front in the meantime. The attack at Gorlice would require troops to move east, with Germany taking advantage of her interior lines to shuttle troops to face the Russians. Falkenhayn wanted to distract or mislead the Allies as much as possible, so at the same time as planning a major attack on the Eastern Front, he wanted to conduct one in the west as well. It was at this point that he turned to top-secret plans that had been drawn up for the use of a new weapon: poison gas. Although the employment of 'poisoned weapons' and 'projectiles the sole object of which is the diffusion of asphyxiating or deleterious gases' had been banned by the Hague Convention of 1899 (to which Germany was a signatory),[10] senior German officers were largely unconcerned about the international ramifications of using such weapons. The French Army had already experimented with various chemical agents, including putting irritants in artillery shells, which offered enough justification for Germany to pursue chemical warfare; a decision that became increasingly necessary from the autumn of 1914 as stocks of conventional munitions began to dwindle. As Max Bauer (OHL's resident expert on heavy artillery) recorded, 'we only followed in the footsteps of our opponents'.[11]

By January 1915, limited stocks of gas shells had been made available, even if there were still doubts about whether they would have a significant effect on the battlefield. At this point, Fritz Haber, Director of the Kaiser Wilhelm Institute for Physical Chemistry in Berlin, suggested that chlorine gas be pumped into special tanks that could then be brought up to the front line and released when the wind was favourable. This use of cloud gas would have the advantage of being much more concentrated than anything that could be released from shells, as well as offering a way to break into heavily fortified positions or those that were too close to the German line for conventional bombardments to work. Soon afterwards Falkenhayn approved plans for the use of chlorine on the Western Front, despite unease from a number of his most senior commanders who saw it as dirty, underhand and not worthy of the great traditions of the Prussian Army. Karl von Einem, who had successfully held the front in Champagne, complained to his wife that it would 'produce a tremendous scandal in the world' and that it was yet another example of how 'War has nothing to do with chivalry any more.' Rupprecht, at Sixth Army, was similarly unenthused, writing that it would inevitably be copied by the Allies and used against German forces.[12]

Eventually Flanders was selected for the operation. It would be a limited attempt to break the enemy line and, if possible, take the city of Ypres. Duke Albrecht of Württemberg, commander of Fourth Army, agreed to do it, arranging for the gas attack to take place in Major-General Berthold von Deimling's XV Corps sector. Deimling was a hardened killer, notorious for the brutality he had shown as a commander in German South-West Africa before the war, and an ideal choice for the operation, even if he initially blanched at using such a weapon. What silenced his 'inner doubts' was the thought that 'using poison gas might perhaps lead to the fall of Ypres, perhaps even make the entire campaign victorious'.[13] By 11 April, 1,600 large and 4,130 small cylinders, containing almost 150 tons of chlorine, had been installed along the northern edge of the Ypres Salient, grouped in small batteries in shell-proof dugouts at the front.[14] Rudimentary protection, in the form of cotton pads soaked in anti-gas solution, was issued to German troops as they waited for the orders to go forward. It all depended on the wind. The operation was codenamed 'Disinfection'.

GQG was now based in the Hôtel du Grand Condé in Chantilly, about twenty-five miles north of Paris. Joffre had moved there after the Battle of the Marne in October 1914 and found it suited his needs well, although it was always a little too close to Paris for the Army's liking. Joffre lived close by, in the villa of Monsieur Poiré, director of the Nord Railway. Every day, after breakfast, he would walk to the Grand Condé, shuffling up the steps, past the liveried servants and plumed guards, his head bowed low, deep in thought. He usually wore a drab blue cloak, enlivened with red breeches, his features hidden beneath the peak of his kepi. Once inside, he would retire to his office (what had formerly been the library) and begin the day's work: hearing reports from the front; dealing with the mass of correspondence that came in every day; and meeting any foreign visitors that turned up. Lunch would be served at 11.30 sharp; hearty French food with few extravagances, which Joffre would usually eat in silence. In the afternoon, he would often take a walk in the woods that surrounded GQG, before working until nine-thirty or ten o'clock; a routine that continued day in, day out.[15]

Joffre's unbreakable confidence and stolidity had been essential in 1914, but now, as repeated attacks in Champagne brought nothing but lengthening casualty lists, the weight of years seemed to bear more heavily upon him. France's deputies did not know the full picture of the army's battlefield performances, but it was difficult to pretend that any great success had been achieved. As early as January 1915, Poincaré had been warned by a former War Minister, Adolphe Messimy, about the 'ivory tower' in which the officers of GQG were living. 'They order partial offensives so they have something to include in the communiqués,' he said, 'but these offensives are very bloody and are doomed to failure.'[16] This had been brutally revealed during the 'Soissons Affair' later that month, after which Millerand had questioned Joffre's tactics, only for this to prompt his threat of resignation. By the time the First Battle of Champagne had ground to a halt in March, Joffre's authority was slowly beginning to dissolve as it became apparent that France could not break the trench deadlock. 'I nibble them', he had said one day, referring to the process of slowly gnawing away at the German line; an answer that did little to silence his critics.

It was clear that the next offensive would take place in Artois. Joffre was mulling over an attack north of Arras by Tenth Army, which would require British support, and which Foch was determined to lead. But getting the British involved was easier said than done and Sir John French's refusal to relieve two corps around Ypres had resulted in Joffre pulling out of offering any meaningful support to Haig's planned attack at Neuve Chapelle – a decision that caused consternation both in Paris and in London and did little to improve the icy relationship between Sir John and Kitchener. When that 'old woman' in the War Office (as French called the Secretary of War) forwarded him some complaints from Joffre and expressed concern that 'having received reinforcements you are not prepared to carry out what Joffre requires of you', Sir John was furious. It would not be possible, he explained (in a short telegram several days later), to 'carry out, with a Territorial Division, what I had proposed with a regular one' and that his relations with Joffre were always 'most cordial'.[17] Nevertheless the failure to agree upon a joint offensive with the French meant that the British would fight alone in early March. He was unhappy about being unsupported by the French, but Sir John gave the go-ahead; keen to make the point that the British were capable of taking the offensive on their own if necessary.

Behind his usual veneer of bullish aggression, Sir John struggled to cope with the demands of war. The enormous scale and intensity of the Western Front had shocked most observers, not least British regulars whose careers had been shaped by years of imperial policing 'from palm to pine'. The heavy clash of arms in Europe was an abnormal, frightening spectacle and the horrific casualties (even for relatively small-scale engagements) were almost impossible to digest. The loss of Brigadier-General John Gough (Chief of Staff at First Army) in February 1915, mortally wounded by a sniper after getting too close to the front, was a particularly heavy blow. Aides noticed that Sir John began to drift away more often, gazing into the distance, thinking deeply about death and the soul. In a letter to a confidante, Mrs Winifred Bennett, he spoke of his office at Saint-Omer being 'thick with the spirits of my dead friends . . . I sometimes people my room with these glorious friends (all boys compared to me!), who have gone over. That "Silent Army". Alas, alas! The room is getting small to hold even my intimate friends.'[18]

Haig's First Army launched its offensive at 7.30 on the morning of 10 March. In itself, the battle did not amount to much. It was minute in comparison to French operations of the same period, yet it did seem to offer tangible hope that the Allies were on the right track. With careful preparation and concentration of force, Haig's troops achieved tactical surprise, making a 1,200-yard advance and capturing the village of Neuve Chapelle. Particularly novel was the use of aircraft to photograph the entire battlefield, which allowed British troops to go forward with a much better idea of what they were facing. Flushed with pride at what Haig had achieved, French wired his congratulations several days later. Although he blanched when he was shown the casualty figures (over 12,500 men killed, wounded or missing), he comforted himself with the thought that German losses were much higher. 'The enemy's trenches are said to be piled up with the dead.' Armed with this encouraging development, he sent for Wilson and told him to meet with Joffre as soon as possible 'to urge the absolute necessity for arriving at some conclusion as to our common action'.[19]

Important decisions now needed to be made about the direction of Allied strategy. On 24 March, Joffre wired Sir John: 'In a war such as we are now engaged in, where the enemy occupies defensive positions organized in the strongest manner, and, in addition, has sufficient men and material for an energetic defence, our offensive can only succeed under the following conditions'. The Allies needed 'numerical superiority' across a 'large front'; 'adequate material' to destroy the enemy's defences; and 'large reserves of ammunition'. Joffre was hopeful that within five or six weeks they would have built up the necessary combat power to do this. 'I am full of confidence that this offensive will inflict such a blow on the enemy that the greatest results may follow and that our movement may be an important step towards the final victory.'[20] Sir John signalled his willingness to take part, but he was still unclear whether this would be sanctioned by London or what reinforcements would be made available to him.

The scene was now set for a showdown of Allied leaders. On 29 March, Kitchener, French, Millerand and Joffre met at Chantilly to thrash out what the Allies would do next. Joffre wanted the attack in Artois to be fixed for the end of April, but before this date it was necessary to undertake a series of minor offensives, 'to prevent the Germans from taking troops from our front and, for example, sending them to the Carpathians'. Kitchener disagreed, claiming that partial offensives would only delay the moment when a large attack could take place. When Joffre reprised his regular calls that more British troops be sent to France, Kitchener was again unimpressed. The problem was not a lack of men, he shrugged, but getting enough ammunition and guns. Nevertheless, he did agree to send two divisions to France that would enable Sir John to relieve IX and XX Corps around Ypres, which produced a suitably warm reaction from the French Commander-in-Chief.[21]

Behind Kitchener's sphinx-like gaze lay a series of complex calculations. The French Government's thirst for more men and guns could never be sated, while British commitments to the Mediterranean were growing all the time. With landings on the Gallipoli peninsula pencilled in for late April, the British war effort was now split down the middle and Kitchener was struggling to pilot a safe course, hoping for something to turn up, either in Turkey or in France, that would illuminate the way forward. When Sir John breakfasted with K in London several days after the Chantilly meeting, the Secretary of War placed his cards clearly on the table. 'He then told me definitely', Sir John recorded in his diary, 'that he considered Joffre and I were "on our trial". That if we showed within the next month or six weeks that we could really make some "substantial advance" and "break the German line," he would, so far as he was concerned, always back us up with all the troops he could send. But that if we failed it would be essential that the Gov[ernmen]t. should look out for some other theatre of operations.'[22] Staying true to an old military maxim, Kitchener would only reinforce success.

The sun was beginning to set, burning away into the western horizon, when the cylinders were opened. After a few moments, a shrill sound of escaping vapour could be heard before a sinister yellowish-green cloud began to form in no-man's-land. 'The whole sky . . . turned yellow, all the fire from the enemy died down, our infantry marched forward and followed the cloud of mist in a noiseless advance without losses', was how one German observer described the terrible spectacle.[23] Within minutes German field guns barked into life and a rain of shrapnel began to explode over the Allied lines north of the battered city of Ypres. In the path of the ghastly cloud were two French divisions, holding a narrow line of breastworks and thinly scraped trenches, watching, terror-stricken, as the cloud flowed over their positions like a slow-moving wave. Men's eyes started to water and throats became tight; coughs and splutters turned to panic as the horrible realization that some kind of poison had been released. Those who did not succumb to the fumes broke in wild panic, spreading disorder in their wake. It was shortly after five o'clock on the afternoon of 22 April and the Second Battle of Ypres was about to begin.

Along a six-kilometre front, the men of two German corps stalked forward, staring in amazement at what remained of the old front trenches. They pushed the French back to the line of the Yser Canal, captured the villages of Langemarck and Pilckem, and were poised to roll up what remained of the Ypres Salient. 'From the side of the canal, we could see only patches of yellowish smoke', recalled one French colonel, who got to within 300 metres of Boesinghe before being 'overwhelmed by severe stinging in our noses and throats; our ears began to ring, breathing became laboured; an unbearable stench of chlorine was all around us'. They soon ran into the remnants of the two divisions; a scene of horror like something 'out of Dante's *Inferno*'. 'People were fleeing everywhere: territorials, *tirailleurs*, *zouaves*, unarmed artillerymen, all distressed and without their caps, with open shirts, running like mad, going in all directions, crying out for water, spitting up blood, some even rolling on the ground in desperate attempts to breathe.'[24]

A deep gouge had been torn in the Allied lines, but because there were no reserves at hand to exploit the victory (Falkenhayn having refused Duke Albrecht's request for follow-on troops), the German attack gradually lost momentum as daylight faded. When one of the corps commanders urged Albrecht to continue the attack by crossing the Yser Canal and taking Boesinghe, he had no choice but to refuse: 'It would result in great sacrifices while it would be difficult to hold that much ground on the western bank. The Corps should be satisfied with its present accomplishments.'[25] At the same time, orders were being hurriedly despatched for British and French reinforcements to move up as quickly as possible, some in buses and trains, others in long marching columns. On the right of what had been the front line was 1st Canadian Division, only recently arrived in Belgium, who now found their left flank completely 'in the air'. As darkness fell, a collection of Canadian battalions under the command of Brigadier-General Richard Turner VC launched a heroic counter-attack into a nearby wood – Kitchener's Wood – and although they took the position, the brigade suffered heavy losses and became disorganized in the frightening darkness of splintered trees, lit by fire. It was symptomatic of the chaos and confusion that would scar the fighting at Ypres.

News of the gas attack came as a 'sharp and short surprise' at Foch's headquarters in Cassell.[26] Although Allied intelligence had received word that the Germans were intending to use some kind of asphyxiating gas, most observers seemed to have dismissed the reports as rumours or untruths, which only added to the sense of anger and disgust in Allied capitals. Kitchener wrote to Sir John in the hours after the news broke, informing him that the 'use of asphyxiating

gases is, as you are aware, contrary to the rules and usages of war . . .
These methods show to what depth of infamy our enemies will go in
order to supplement their want of courage in facing our troops.'[27]
Kitchener urgently set in motion a detailed investigation into what
had happened, while within days the French War Ministry had issued
thousands of cotton mouth-pads to its troops. Doused in sodium thio-
sulphate, which neutralized chlorine, these pads offered only rudimentary protection, but they helped shore up morale in the dark days
after the attack.

Foch and Sir John met on the evening of 23 April and they both
agreed that it was vital to restore the Allied line – if it could not be
done quickly, then it might be impossible to hold on to Ypres. Before
the Allies could mount a major counter-attack, however, another gas
cloud was released the following morning (24 April). Duke Albrecht
had been ordered to roll up the Allied line, so he authorized a converging attack against the Canadian positions at Saint-Julien, which
would almost certainly force the abandonment of the salient. But this
time there would be no panic. The Canadians had been warned about
the possibility of further cloud attacks and had prepared as best they
could, wrapping wet cotton bandoliers around their mouths and
noses and standing on the parapets of their trenches, firing into the
oncoming waves. The bandoliers certainly helped, but the choking
effect of the gas quickly debilitated many of the defenders, and
allowed the Germans to enter their trenches, now lit by a strange
green gloom. 'It was impossible for me to give a real idea of the terror
and horror spread among us all by this filthy loathsome pestilence',
recalled a Canadian officer. 'The trench presented a weird spectacle,
men were coughing, spitting, cursing and grovelling on the ground
and trying to vomit.'[28]

The burning, shell-streaked village of Saint-Julien was evacuated
later that day as British and Canadian battalions streamed back from
the front. A series of hurried counter-attacks went in over the next
few days and managed to stem the German advance, although casualties were heavy and the situation remained highly confused.
Increasingly distraught, Sir John wired Kitchener and let loose a tirade against his allies. They had not been able to coordinate a proper

counter-attack 'as the French did nothing all day yesterday'.[29] The problem was that the French forces had retreated behind the Yser Canal at Boesinghe and it took time for them to reorganize. Most of their artillery had been lost on 22 April and reinforcements took longer to arrive than anticipated. When they were eventually ready to attack, coordination with the British and Canadians proved haphazard. Orders went missing, despatch riders got lost, and all the time German guns, which ringed the salient on three sides, bombarded their positions mercilessly.

Foch was preparing for the spring offensive in Artois, which was scheduled for the beginning of May (although poor weather would delay it until the 9th), so he had little spare manpower to send to Ypres. The responsibility would, therefore, fall to the BEF to restore the line. Accordingly, GHQ ordered a renewed series of attacks over the following week. Most of these did little more than increase British casualties and incur Sir John's growing wrath. He blamed the French for letting him down and lashed out at those he thought were undermining him. Smith-Dorrien, the man who had disobeyed his orders at Le Cateau, was sacked on 6 May, being summarily dismissed after suggesting a withdrawal to a more easily defendable rear position (known as the GHQ Line). Sir John objected to what he believed was Smith-Dorrien's 'pessimistic attitude', which 'has the worst effect on his commanders and their troops'.[30] Yet as soon as Smith-Dorrien departed, Sir John authorized the retirement, bringing British troops closer to Ypres, but on a line that was easier to defend. For Henry Wilson, who watched events unfold at GHQ, the fighting at Ypres was a mess: 'It is a real bad business', he wrote in his diary.[31]

From Falkenhayn's perspective, the gas attack had succeeded perfectly. A new weapon had been tested, while the enemy had been so preoccupied with regaining lost ground that they had been unable to react to the movement of German divisions to the Eastern Front. Yet a number of senior officers found the indecisive nature of the operation puzzling. Max Bauer, who had watched the gas attack with Fritz Haber, did little to hide his frustration as he paced the corridors of OHL, complaining about the lost opportunity presented by the use of chlorine. Falkenhayn 'did not recognise the possibility of quickly exploiting the new weapon on a large scale before the opponent found protection', he explained. 'The increase and use of gas troops was ordered only hesitantly and insufficiently. Instead of issuing orders, the armies were asked if they wanted to make use of it. If we had organized the gas attacks on a large scale at the beginning of 1915, there probably would have been great success in the same year . . .'[32] This might have been so, but Falkenhayn had other priorities.

At Charleville-Mézières, the first week of May saw a sudden and rapid movement of senior officers and their staff to the railway station, where they boarded trains for the east. In order to direct the counter-offensive against Russia, Falkenhayn had decamped, with most of OHL, to Pless in Silesia, leaving a skeleton staff to oversee things in his absence. He was confident that there was no imminent danger of an Allied breakthrough and that his armies could hold. With ninety-seven German divisions in the west against 112 French, British and Belgian divisions, the Entente had a slender, although not decisive, superiority. A senior staff officer, Fritz von Lossberg, was appointed as Falkenhayn's principal liaison officer with the authority (*Vollmacht*) to issue orders in his name, much as Richard Hentsch had done on the Marne. 'I trust you completely and you will do the right thing', was all Falkenhayn said before departing for the east.[33]

For the time being then, Lossberg would be on his own. A supremely gifted product of the Prussian War Academy, Lossberg had just celebrated his forty-seventh birthday when he was given the daunting responsibility for the Western Front. With just seven divisions in OHL reserve, there was precious little manpower available to reinforce the front in a crisis. Falkenhayn had ordered each army to construct a second defensive position about two kilometres to the rear, while also making it clear that there would be no voluntary retirements and the front line must be held at all costs. Lossberg kept in regular contact with Rupprecht's Sixth Army and made sure that two reserve divisions were within marching distance of the front in Artois, which was now coming under heavier and heavier bombardment. Falkenhayn and his staff departed on the morning of 7 May. Unbeknown to Lossberg, there was now less than forty-eight hours before the Allied spring offensive would be launched. If the French were ever going to break the line, it would be now.

The French High Command was in no mood to let the heavy fighting at Ypres derail plans for the spring offensive. As early as 14 February Foch had briefed GQG on his hopes for a new attack in the north, using short, staccato phrases that conveyed his fierce, unyielding will. The war could only be won by an *offensive*. This would always take the same form: a '*general action* across the whole front' and a '*decisive attack* to achieve the desired result of a breakthrough of the enemy line'.[34] Tenth Army would seize Vimy Ridge, the stretch of high ground that ran north of Arras and overlooked the Douai plain. Flank attacks on either side would seize the Notre-Dame-de-Lorette spur and the village of Neuville-Saint-Vaast, giving the French Army a commanding view of the flat mining country that lay beyond.[35] There would also be better coordination with the British. To the north, Haig's First Army would go into battle around Aubers, driving towards La Bassée, from where it could intercept German reinforcements moving south.

General Victor d'Urbal, the newly promoted commander of Tenth Army, was the man who would achieve this decisive blow. With six infantry corps, supported by over 1,000 guns with plentiful ammunition, there was now real hope that something tangible would be achieved. D'Urbal ordered the infantry attack to be conducted with 'the most extreme energy and speed' and be pursued 'without interruption day and night'. Every unit would push ahead at all costs, not worrying about units on their flanks, to maintain the momentum of the assault.[36] He also assigned the attack on Vimy Ridge, the most crucial sector of the front, to Lieutenant-General Henri Philippe Pétain, commander of XXXIII Corps, a blue-eyed infantryman from a small village in the Pas-de-Calais. Pétain had begun the war as a 58-year-old brigade commander, close to retirement, whose career had progressed all too slowly. He had been a Second Lieutenant for five years, a Lieutenant for seven and a Captain for ten.[37] But Pétain possessed striking qualities, ones that had been smothered in the numbing routine of garrison duty and regimental administration.

Senior officers noted his individuality and intelligence, as well as a cavalier disregard for higher authority, which had come to the fore when he was appointed instructor at the Army War College in 1900. There, Pétain had preached the importance of infantry–artillery cooperation and firepower – heresy in the pre-1914 French Army, which prized the offensive spirit and the need for troops to advance 'elbow to elbow' towards the enemy. For Pétain, no amount of ardour or personal courage could overcome strongly entrenched defenders armed with the latest weaponry: machine-guns and breech-loading rifles loaded with smokeless powder.

Pétain's heresies were rapidly reconsidered in the light of 1914. With French infantry often lacking coordination with artillery (something Joffre had noted as early as 24 August), attacks tended to be extremely costly and ill-prepared. As part of Lanrezac's Fifth Army, Pétain had seen for himself how vulnerable infantry were without fire support and how easily they could become demoralized as a result. By October, he had survived the regular culls of senior officers and been successively promoted, first to divisional and then to corps command. There, his care and attention to detail, combined with an insistence that his men must not be squandered in hare-brained ventures, won him a growing band of admirers. Reports noted 'his tenacity, steadiness under fire, unfailing foresight, [and] continual intervention at awkward moments'.[38] Unlike many infantrymen, Pétain familiarized himself with his artillery batteries, with each one having to fire a shot in his presence, which was checked for accuracy and technique.[39] He also visited the trenches when he could, passing through the dim corridors of earth like a ghost, as if he had seen it all before; a word of advice here, a word of command there. Soon rumours began to spread among the infantry: here was someone different; here was a man they could trust.

The detailed planning prior to the spring offensive was emblematic of the professionalism that was now coursing through the French Army. The attack would be supported by unprecedented artillery support, including the use of a so-called 'creeping barrage' to help the infantry on to their objectives. Hundreds of command posts, forward ammunition dumps and medical-aid posts were built in the weeks leading up to the attack, while saps were driven forward from the French lines to reduce the width of no-man's-land. As at Neuve Chapelle, the whole battlefield was photographed and mapped from the air. At the same time, the look of the French infantry was beginning to change. A new uniform, *horizon bleu*, began to be issued from the spring of 1915, replacing the characteristic dark-blue tunic and red trousers that had been highly visible on the battlefields of Lorraine and the Marne. The new version certainly lacked the dash of its predecessor, but it was a better fit on the Western Front, where its drab blue tended to fade into a dirty grey in the field. Even the kepi – France's iconic circular cap – fell victim to the remorseless industrialization of the war. It was gradually replaced during 1915 by the Adrian steel helmet, which provided protection from overhead shrapnel. Such detailed preparations produced a rising feeling of confidence. On the evening of 8 May, d'Urbal wired Foch: 'The infantry is ready and just waiting to march.'[40]

9 May dawned bright and warm, with a blood-red sun rising over the shattered expanse of no-man's-land. French artillery opened fire at 6 a.m., with a series of sharp cracks shattering the spring morning until they joined up into one roaring crescendo. The fire continued for four hours, covering the German defences in a shroud of boiling earth, dust, smoke and splinters. The spearhead of XXXIII Corps was the Moroccan Division, an elite formation recruited from native troops and French settlers from North Africa. The division was rested and its men were well trained. The first two waves, leaving their greatcoats and packs behind, would break the German line and advance as far as possible. 'My men left their packs so they could run faster', recalled one battalion commander; 'if their clothing got in their way, they would run naked . . .'[41] Reserve companies would then clear out the captured positions, hunt down surviving pockets of resistance and snuff them out. At 10 a.m., the artillery began to lengthen its fire and move on to targets further into the German position, and, right on cue, the infantry surged forward with a ragged cheer.

Within ninety minutes the Moroccan Division had broken the German centre and surged up over the crest of Vimy Ridge – an advance of four kilometres. 'The enemy was obviously in confusion', one officer remembered; 'we met with some localized resistance but . . . we no longer met with anything organized. Even the artillery seemed to have lost its axis; bursts of fire shot high in the air and at random mirrored the enemy's shambolic chaos.'[42] So swift was the advance of Pétain's divisions that Tenth Army was caught by surprise. Local supports were ordered forward as quickly as possible, but with army reserves more than seven miles away there was little chance they could intervene that day. Moreover, the furious assault in the centre could not be replicated across the front. On either flank lay the heavily defended villages of Ablain-Saint-Nazaire and Souchez on the left and Neuville-Saint-Vaast on the right. Here the German defences were deeper; consisting of multiple strongpoints, maze-like runs of trenches, and fortified cemeteries – which took time to clear. French infantry attacked with the same determination, but struggled to break through, fighting house-to-house, while supporting waves piled up behind, waiting to go forward.

With the French capture of Vimy Ridge, the German Army was faced with its most dangerous moment since the onset of trench warfare. Crown Prince Rupprecht had been woken at four o'clock in the morning by the 'tremendous noise' of an explosion, followed by the whine of a passing aircraft – piloted by an enterprising French flyer who had managed to locate his headquarters. Two hours later came news that the British were attacking in the north, although it was confirmed shortly afterwards that they had been unable to enter the German trenches. It soon became apparent that the chief danger was at Vimy, where a huge French attack was developing. Rupprecht marshalled his reserves as quickly as possible. He put a telephone call through to Lossberg and asked for the two divisions in OHL reserve, 58th and 115th, to be made available, which Lossberg agreed to, although it would be some time before they could be deployed on the battlefield. In the meantime, he authorized a counter-attack at Souchez, where the fighting was fiercest, while watching through his binoculars at the high ground around Notre-Dame-de-Lorette, which was now 'completely covered in explosions, as it was being fired upon so aggressively'.[43]

At Mézières, Lossberg watched the situation carefully. 'As soon as the initial reports started coming in', he remembered, 'I knew immediately from my own front-line experience that Sixth Army's situation was serious.' After Rupprecht had requested the deployment of the two OHL divisions, Lossberg tried to get in touch with Pless, but without success. Having been authorized to act in Falkenhayn's absence, he ordered the movement of the two divisions, while trying desperately to update the High Command on the seriousness of the attack. He eventually got through to his chief the following evening. 'The connection, however, was so bad that although General von Falkenhayn could understand my description of the situation and my directive, his words came back completely unrecognizable.' Lossberg had to ask the telephone operator (in Berlin) to relay his words on to Falkenhayn, who then approved the decision: 'General von Falkenhayn is in agreement with everything.'[44]

Fighting continued into the second day, although the crisis of the battle had passed. D'Urbal hoped that 10 May would produce the long-awaited collapse of the German position on either side of Vimy Ridge, so he ordered a series of renewed attacks, but they all failed. German artillery was now concentrating on pulverizing the French lines as well as intermittently shelling no-man's-land, which prevented the French from bringing up more supports. French batteries were also running so low on ammunition that d'Urbal had to remind his gunners to avoid 'unjustified consumption' of shells.[45] Although his natural impulse was to continue to feed men into the battle, this was unlikely to result in success; German reserves were now on the battlefield and digging in furiously. The Moroccan Division was relieved on 11 May after sustaining over 5,000 casualties.[46] Following a meeting with his corps commanders on 13 May, d'Urbal decided to concentrate on clearing their flanks, including the ruins of Neuville-Saint-Vaast, before trying again for the crest. It was now essential to reorganize his men, bring out the scores of wounded and restock ammunition supplies, which were almost exhausted.

The battle had also taken a heavy toll on the defenders. The three divisions that had borne the brunt of the assault had lost over 20,000 killed, wounded or missing.[47] 'For every ten dead there is one left living', recorded one survivor. 'There are hardly any officers left. The

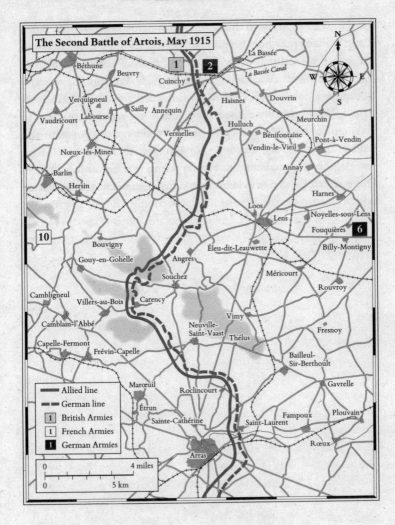

The Second Battle of Artois, May 1915

ammunition is gone, hunger makes itself heard in rumbling stomachs. The nerves, which have not known sleep for days, are in danger of being torn apart. Countless wounded, friend and foe, who nobody can help. The infantrymen and grenadiers lie exhausted in their holes, barely capable of any thought, just grasping one in moments of stupefying calm: one more such attack and the French can march towards

Souchez with shouldered rifles.'[48] At Sixth Army headquarters, Rupprecht realized how hard his men had been pushed, although he could not help thinking that if the Allies had coordinated their efforts a little better, more could have been achieved. 'Perhaps our enemies would have done better to wait until the full arrival of Kitchener's Army. They probably rushed their attack for political reasons, to make up for the defeat at Ypres and to encourage the Russians and Italians as a result of a success.'[49] Nevertheless, the fighting in Artois revealed how formidable the French Army was becoming, and, in Philippe Pétain, it was evident that it had a commander of unusual skill.

6.   'Only inaction is shameful'

On 15 June, the British Prime Minister, Herbert Asquith, addressed the House of Commons. 'The situation is without a parallel in our national history', he said, lifting his eyes from his notes to scan the rows of green benches packed with MPs. A new coalition government had been formed on 25 May, with the ruling Liberals bolstered by Unionist and Labour Party support. The aim of such an arrangement, said Asquith, was 'to pursue this War at any cost to a victorious issue'. What was required, he believed:

> was such a broadening of the basis of government as would take away from it even the semblance of a one-sided or party character; which would demonstrate beyond the possibility of doubt, not only to our people at home, and to our fellow subjects across the sea, but to the whole world – allies, enemies, and neutrals – that, after nearly a year of war, with all its fluctuations and vicissitudes, the British people were more resolute than ever, with one heart and with one purpose, to obliterate all distinctions and to unite every personal and political as well as every moral and material force in the prosecution of their cause.[1]

The formation of a coalition reflected a wider fear that the war was being lost. 'In the miscellaneous debate which followed his speech', reported *The Times*, 'there were many indications that the hard, unpleasant truths which we have been daily exposing in these columns, are becoming generally recognized at last. Out they come, one after another – the waste of public money in camps and ships, the gross injustice of the present methods of promiscuous recruiting, the refusal to face the truth about our various campaigns, above all the deplorable lack of foresight about munitions of war.'[2] Such introspection had been caused by the spectre of twin defeats: both in the Dardanelles and in France, as well as the deteriorating international situation. Instead of brushing Turkish troops off the rocky slopes of the Gallipoli peninsula,

British and Anzac divisions had run into tough resistance and faltered, encountering a ghastly repetition of trench warfare, only this time under a harsh Turkish sun. Although there were celebrations when Italy declared war on Austria–Hungary (though *not* Germany) on 24 May, the Italian Army was a fragile instrument, with severe shortages of machine-guns and artillery preventing it from striking a decisive blow against its hereditary enemy. On the seas, there was also growing concern about the impact of the U-boats. The Cunard liner *Lusitania* was sunk on 7 May, with over 1,000 people, including 128 US citizens, dying – the most famous victim of Germany's attempt to enforce a 'war zone' around the British Isles.

For Sir John French, the events of 9 May were a point of no return. Haig's First Army had been bloodily repulsed at Aubers Ridge when a forty-minute bombardment failed to clear a path for the infantry, who were slaughtered as they tried to cross no-man's-land. Eleven thousand casualties were sustained within just a few hours.[3] After watching the attack from a ruined church tower, Sir John had been driven back to Saint-Omer in silence, brooding upon the realization that he had now failed the 'trial' he had been set by Kitchener. His frustration was compounded when he strode up the steps of GHQ and was handed a telegram from the War Office demanding that he send 20,000 rounds of field artillery ammunition to Marseille, where a ship was waiting to take them to the Dardanelles. It would be quicker and easier, the telegram read, to move them from France. Sir John screwed up the telegram in disgust, his face darkening with anger. In the days that followed, he became convinced that Kitchener was at fault for everything; that his failure to adequately support the army in France was costing the lives of his men. He poured out his complaints to Charles à Court Repington, a former army officer turned war correspondent (who was staying at GHQ). As well as leaking information on the lack of shells to Repington, French also sent two of his aides to London to lay before the Government the 'vital need of high-explosive shells' for the army. It was a plot designed to bring down the Secretary of War.[4]

Repington's despatch ('A Lesson from France') was published in *The Times* on 14 May and alleged that the expeditionary force was 'suffering from certain disadvantages which make striking successes difficult to achieve'. Despite the attack being 'well planned and valiantly conducted . . . conditions were too hard. The want of an unlimited supply of high explosive was a fatal bar to our success.'[5] Combined with the setbacks in the Dardanelles, news of the 'shells scandal' proved too much for Asquith's embattled Liberal government and sparked off a dramatic political crisis. Although Kitchener's monumental prestige was enough to shield him from the storm, he was now a wounded figure, the subject of often furious complaint from members of the Government, alienated by his secrecy and high-handedness. Kitchener ignored it all. He had become used to the isolation of command in the Sudan and South Africa and saw little reason to change now. When a group of his subordinates at the War Office insisted that they publish a statement addressing the allegations, K waved them aside:

'Our job is to get on with the War – it will be quite time enough to answer these when we have won it.'[6]

Inevitably the political crisis caused a shuffling of personnel. Winston Churchill left the Admiralty, his reputation tarnished by the blood-soaked disaster that was unfolding in the Dardanelles. One of Kitchener's most forceful critics, the Liberal MP for Caernarvon, David Lloyd George, was given the Ministry of Munitions, a new government department that was charged with driving forward Britain's war production. As for Sir John French, the affair did him little good. Asquith was not yet convinced that he needed to go, but he was running out of time. While he had not exactly lied to Repington, the picture that had been revealed at Aubers Ridge was more complicated than Sir John realized. GHQ had not raised any specific concerns about high explosive prior to the attack and much of the failure was down to a combination of tough German defences (which had been strengthened after Neuve Chapelle), a lack of heavy guns, and poor-quality shells (a significant percentage of which failed to explode). This meant that German artillery batteries and their concealed machine-guns were able to stop the attack dead in a matter of minutes. Unless these deficiencies could be rectified in future attacks, the British would continue to struggle.[7]

In Paris the mood was equally sombre. 'A very gloomy Council meeting', recorded Poincaré on 29 May. 'The operations in Arras drag on and all the Ministers ask how soon we shall see the end of this siege warfare. They remember that when Joffre breakfasted here a few weeks ago, he led us to hope that the war might be ended in June; to-day that longed-for end seems further off than ever, and Parliament is becoming very restless.'[8] At that moment the President was still wondering how to respond to a scathing report by the parliamentary Army Committee, which outlined serious shortages of equipment for the Army in the field. Since August 1914, over 700,000 Lebel rifles had been lost or damaged beyond repair (out of a total stock of three million), and yet no replacements had been manufactured. The situation was even more critical with artillery. The French Army went to war with 4,700 field guns (primarily the 75), but 500 had already been lost and many more had suffered explosions owing to overuse or faulty ammunition. Although the War Minister, Millerand, dismissed the report, telling Poincaré that it was 'very prejudiced', it did little to still the growing chorus of disapproval against him.[9]

With every passing week complaints piled up in the French Parliament about how the war was being run. On 5 July, Abel Ferry, a former Under-Secretary for Foreign Affairs, who had been sent to the front in August 1914, presented a report to the Cabinet on operations in the Woëvre (the plain southeast of Verdun where there had been particularly heavy fighting). It chronicled a horrific story of futility and slaughter that left deputies reeling. On 18 March, his company of 250 men had gone into battle but within days there were only twenty-nine men left alive. Ferry was horrified by this bloody and futile 'war of attrition'. 'Launching human *grapeshot* without any warning on a set date is, it is said, taking the moral high ground. Thousands of French corpses in front of German trenches maintains this moral high ground . . . for the enemy.' If this continued, Ferry warned that the army's 'offensive value' would be 'destroyed'. What he had witnessed, he believed, was a common experience. 'There are tactical and geographical reasons for these small operations but there is a lack of strategic thinking behind them; *it looks like we are only fighting for newspapers or press releases*. We are improvising as we go along. With trench warfare, none of the specifics were expected or prepared for . . . *It will cause wonder in the future and perhaps in history to learn that the Government, which holds such authority among soldiers of all ranks, was so disinterested or silent.'*[10]

Such complaints inevitably fell at the feet of Alexandre Millerand. He was the mouthpiece of GQG, so it was said; unwilling to rein in Joffre or allow proper scrutiny of Army business (one deputy even contemptuously referred to him as 'a block of ice').[11] An experienced, patriotic and tough-minded politician, Millerand responded in the only way he knew; fighting off unwanted interference in military matters, while giving as little ground as possible. Fierce battles were fought over parliamentary access to the front (something Joffre was dead against) and the right of the Army Commission to inspect factories (which Millerand feared would prove a distraction). When he appeared before the Senate on 29 June, he defended his position forcefully, stating that in the ten months since the outbreak of war the production of war materiel had risen six-fold. Moreover, while he understood the demands for greater openness and scrutiny of the war effort, this should not come at the price of military effectiveness. Yet his calls only went so far and the Government was eventually forced to create four under-secretaryships in the War Ministry (armaments, medical service, supply and military aeronautics); an arrangement that curtailed Millerand's power and increased scrutiny on crucial components of the war effort.[12]

Millerand may have deflected much of the attention from the Commander-in-Chief, but Joffre was not immune from this growing frustration. He had formally split his command into three army groups in June; a move that had been pushed by Poincaré, who hoped that it would ease the burden on the Commander-in-Chief as well as ensuring that other senior commanders were involved in the formulation of strategy (something that had, more or less, been confined to Joffre since August 1914). The positions were occupied by three of his most senior generals: Augustin Dubail in the east; Castelnau in the centre, and Foch in the north (who also remained Joffre's de facto deputy). Unsurprisingly, when the French Government raised the possibility of having regular meetings at Chantilly with these senior officers, Joffre raised his hand. It would take his commanders away from their posts and interfere with the war effort, he grumbled, so there the matter was dropped. Yet Joffre needed a victory. He knew that pressure from the civilians would only increase as the war went on and the euphoria over the Marne was replaced by the depressing realization that he had only prevented France from being defeated, not won the war. Nibbling was not enough.

On the Eastern Front, Germany's counter-offensive exceeded Falkenhayn's wildest expectations, delivering a decisive blow against the Russians and turning the tide of the war in the east. At 6 a.m. on 2 May, a furious artillery bombardment shattered the spring morning around the Russian lines between Gorlice and Tarnow. Four hours later, German and Austro-Hungarian forces moved forward and met minimal resistance, breaking the Russian line and advancing into open territory. With no rear lines to fall back upon, the Russian Third Army collapsed amid scenes of panic and disorder. The Central Powers advanced sixteen miles within two days; by day six they had captured 140,000 prisoners and taken 200 guns. The great fortress of Przemyśl was recaptured on 3 June, and three weeks later Austro-Hungarian troops marched down the streets of Lemberg, the capital of Galicia, to scenes of 'indescribable joy' among the population.[13] Faced with the imminent destruction of his southwestern front, the Russian Commander-in-Chief, the Grand Duke Nicholas Nikolaevich, had to loosen his grip on the Carpathians and order his armies on a long, dusty march east. It would be the beginning of the greatest retreat of the war.

Falkenhayn returned to the Western Front on the evening of 7 June, visiting Duke Albrecht in Flanders before making his way to Rupprecht's Sixth Army. The success at Gorlice had done little to lighten his mood, at least according to Rupprecht, who found him 'much aged' in appearance, even if he still possessed his prodigious memory. 'He fully acknowledged that the army was in a difficult position,' remembered Rupprecht, 'and agreed that a division of III Corps would be sent in exchange for a spent one' in Sixth Army.[14] Despite Falkenhayn's helpful tone, there was little warmth between the two men. OHL had issued a strongly worded rebuke to Rupprecht on 14 May following his decision to call up the reserve divisions during the fighting in Artois, with Falkenhayn making it clear that it was 'out of the question to deploy the entire GHQ Reserve in order to supply relief to a sector of the front that is already well endowed'. This was combined with an unwelcome interference in Sixth Army business, with OHL sending its own liaison officer to communicate directly with two of Rupprecht's corps – a direct breach of the regular chain of command.

Rupprecht, the Crown Prince of Bavaria, was not used to being treated in such an abrupt manner and bridled at the suggestion that he had failed to manage the defensive battle properly. He stressed the scale of the French attack and the dangers that it posed. It was not his intention to 'deploy the last reserve on the Western Front unnecessarily, but it must be pointed out that only weak reserves are staged north of the La Bassée Canal, which would hardly be able to restore the situation in the event of another successful breakthrough attempt'. The situation was only smoothed over by the Kaiser, who (favouring Rupprecht) directed Falkenhayn to write a further letter confirming that he was responsible for supporting those 'whose intellectual, moral, and physical capacities are already severely tried' and that his intervention 'was apt to insult the commanders at the front who had without exception proved themselves up to the task'.[15] While Rupprecht now considered the matter closed, Falkenhayn could not resist one final swipe at the troublesome Bavarian. On the morning of 19 May, Rupprecht's trusted Chief of Staff, Krafft von Dellmensingen, was ordered to report immediately to the Alpine Corps (an elite group of mountain troops then assembling against the Italians); a parting gift from OHL.[16]

Falkenhayn had a masterful ability to annoy those who worked with him, and by the summer of 1915 most of the senior officers of the German Army were ranged against him, including Rupprecht, who had to get used to a new Chief of Staff, a gruff, unsympathetic Prussian called Gustav von Lambsdorff. But, however much fury was directed against Falkenhayn, the Kaiser remained a firm supporter. It helped that the Supreme War Lord lived a semi-detached lifestyle in

Pless, receiving Falkenhayn's daily briefing on the war, but remaining isolated from it. When Wilhelm Groener, head of the Railway Section at OHL, met the Kaiser, taking his daily stroll in the park at Pless, he was struck by how happy and contented he was. 'After lighting a cigarette for himself and for me, we chatted for almost an hour', he recalled. 'The Supreme Majesty was cheerful, amicable as always. We talked about the war and I thought I sensed a little concern . . . But the latest events in the East clearly filled him with pleasure. He is also relieved about the resistance of the Austrians on the Italian Front. When you talk to the Kaiser privately, he behaves quite differently to the way he does in his courtly environment. He talks man to man and does not feel like the Kaiser. His trust in Falkenhayn is unshaken and unshakeable. He believes in him, while he has no inner connections to the people of the East [Hindenburg and Ludendorff].'[17]

Notwithstanding the arguments over the reserve divisions, the German Army was adapting quickly to the ever-changing war in France and Belgium. OHL had already disseminated a series of reports on the fighting in Champagne that highlighted the challenges of both attacking and defending in the present conditions. Principally it found that the French had committed 'two indisputable mistakes': attacking on too narrow a front and not 'pressing home their offensive sufficiently'. Even though the French attacked in mass, they could not silence German artillery batteries, trench mortars or flanking fire, and lacked the combat power to keep advancing. It concluded that Germany must do better and recommended attacking on 'very considerable' frontages ('at least twenty kilometres') with the objective of capturing the enemy's artillery. The initial breakthrough was 'merely the means to an end' and the report stressed that the point of offensive operations was to 'fight a decisive engagement in the open field'.[18]

As for the methods to be adopted in future defensive battles, the picture was less clear. 'The main characteristic of the French attacks was an irresistible artillery preparation, defying all description, directed against that portion of the line which they intended to break . . . This preparation consists of deliberate preliminary ranging, followed by fire from massed artillery, like the roar of thunder in bursts of fire, sometimes lasting for hours without interruption'.

Because German trenches were usually situated on the forward slopes of any undulating ground – to gain a good field of fire – they were quickly reduced to 'little more than a mass of ruins'. Moreover, it was found almost impossible to hold ground with just a single trench line; what was required was 'not one or even several lines of fixed defences, but rather a fortified zone which permitted a certain liberty of action, so that the best use could be made of all the advantages offered by the configuration of the ground, and all the disadvantages could as far as possible be overcome'.[19]

Opinions differed on how this defensive battle was to be fought. Within the walls of the prefecture, many still favoured a strong forward defence in line with OHL's original exhortation that not a foot of ground must be given up ('Halten was zu halten ist').[20] Fritz von Lossberg argued that though it was necessary to construct a deep network of defences, the first line should be held in strength and recaptured as soon as possible if lost. The primary challenge to this idea came from Max Bauer, who argued that 'maintaining a rigid line in static warfare' was costly and unnecessary. 'The shocking victims of this process screamed to the heavens, but to no avail', he complained. 'The worst thing about it was that often commanders who lost a section of trench were dismissed instantly, which once again led to each commander occupying a really cramped section of trench. This caused the number of losses to grow again.'[21] Nevertheless much would depend upon whether the Entente would be able to modify and develop their methods of attack, and the answer to that could only be found on the battlefield.

On the scarred slopes of Notre-Dame-de-Lorette and Neuville-Saint-Vaast, the fighting went on. The skies were full of the screech of exploding shells, as thousands of Frenchmen toiled like ants across the blackened landscape, never ceasing their continuous movement to and from the front line. For the defenders, the days were fearful and wracked with pain, as men, worn down with tiredness, endured the horrors of seemingly endless trench warfare. 'Two days without intermission in a half-blown in trench, with every man keenly on the alert the whole time; bayonets fixed day and night', was how one German soldier remembered Souchez in the late spring of 1915:

Opposite, only about twenty yards away, the enemy, lying in wait. Between us saps run out, guarded by barricades. A mountain of bombs lies ready to hand beside them. Right on top of one such barricade, but out of our reach, lies a comrade, his dimmed eyes gazing westward; his trusty weapon in one hand, the other stretched out as he made ready to spring; his once fair hair dyed dark red with blood. Many are lying like that outside the trench, friend and foe. Nobody buries them; nobody has time.[22]

After the intensive fighting of 9–11 May, the front had settled down to a series of small-scale attacks, continuous bombardments and regular trench raids. On 19 May, General d'Urbal informed Joffre that under the present conditions 'the course of action that should be taken is to methodically take out, by means of heavy and overwhelming artillery fire, followed by a suitably prepared infantry assault, each of the spots identified as necessary to us as starting points'.[23]

A final effort was made on 16 June, with the French bringing up more guns and shells and plastering the German lines with torrents of fire, including the first use of gas shells – a mixture of carbon disulphide and phosphorus – which acted as both an asphyxiant and an incendiary and was targeted at enemy batteries, managing to silence them for an hour and a half.[24] French infantry made progress in places: the cemetery of Souchez was taken and the Moroccan Division again distinguished itself, gaining about a kilometre of ground, but then found itself in an exposed position, enfiladed on either flank. Eager to press on, d'Urbal offered to send reinforcements, but Pétain refused them, believing that unless his flanks could be cleared up, new units would simply suffer losses unnecessarily. Tenth Army was now reaching its limits. Reports from the front admitted that German guns were becoming more and more dominant, while French artillery was increasingly prone to accidents. Barrels would burst or swell from over-firing, sometimes injuring or killing the gun crews. On 16 June, XXI Corps lost seven guns after their barrels exploded; the following day Pétain's corps lost another nine, which led GQG to send a furious note complaining about a 'serious crisis' and ordering commanders to only fire when absolutely necessary.[25]

By mid-June, the Second Battle of Artois was over. It had been what one French general called the 'maximum effort' that the Allies had been capable of. On 9 May, the French had attacked with fifteen infantry divisions, supported by three cavalry divisions and 1,075 artillery pieces. On 16 June, almost twenty divisions were in place, with six reserve divisions and 1,160 guns – against just a dozen battered German divisions. Ammunition consumption was unprecedented. Nearly two million 75 mm and 350,000 heavy-artillery shells had been expended in five weeks' intensive combat. Yet it was still not enough. French casualties totalled over 2,200 officers and 100,000 men.[26] Afterwards one of Pétain's divisional commanders, Émile Fayolle, gloomily asked: 'What will be done after this abortive attempt? Should we conclude that any opening is impossible? This is definitely the case if the Hun have many defence lines that are spaced out from each other meaning that artillery cannot take them simultaneously under fire and that there are men to defend them. The fate of the war is now in the hands of the Romanians and the Bulgarians . . .'[27]

Joffre was not quite ready to rely upon dubious allies on the Eastern Front for deliverance. He wasted little time in planning another assault, on this occasion what he called a 'double action' that would be on a much greater scale than the attack in May. He visited the front when he could, often going to Reims, which lay close to the German line. Once there he would be chaperoned to a suitable observation point from where he would peer through binoculars at the enemy positions along the horizon that were now hidden by the long grass. His choice of battlefield was the same as it had been in December 1914: Champagne and Artois. On 12 July, he informed Foch and Castelnau of the outlines of the new operation. Foch would attack in the north, rupturing the German front, seizing Vimy Ridge, and, most importantly, drawing in enemy reserves and fixing them in place. The main assault would then be made by Castelnau's group of armies in Champagne, which would comprise the bulk of French strength, including Second Army, now commanded by France's rising star, Philippe Pétain. Once Castelnau's men had gone forward, this would be 'the signal to attack on the fronts of the other armies of the Republic'.[28]

In London, Britain's political and military leaders were increasingly preoccupied by operations in the Mediterranean. On 7 June, at the first meeting of the reorganized War Cabinet, now renamed the Dardanelles Committee, it was agreed to reinforce General Sir Ian Hamilton in Gallipoli so that a major offensive could be launched later in the summer, which would hopefully break through the Turkish defences. On 26 June, Kitchener authored an appreciation of the situation in which he stated bluntly that the only theatre in which the Allies could achieve a decisive victory in the near future was the Dardanelles. He was adamant that the French Army 'must not be exhausted by continuous offensive operations which lead to nothing, and which possibly cause the enemy fewer casualties than those incurred by us', with a policy of 'active defence' on the Western Front being the most sensible option.[29]

A meeting of Allied leaders was held on 6 July, with the British delegation, including Asquith, Kitchener and the new First Lord of the Admiralty, Arthur Balfour, travelling to Calais to discuss strategy for the remainder of the year. But as soon as they landed on foreign soil things began to go awry. The British had not been told the time of the main conference and, assuming that it was mid-morning, enjoyed a leisurely breakfast at their hotel, leaving the French Prime Minister, René Viviani (who was accompanied by Joffre and Millerand), 'ramping up and down the dismal Calais platform' waiting for their allies to turn up.[30] When things eventually got started, no clear agreement was reached. Kitchener, speaking fluent French, agreed to send six New Army divisions to France immediately, with more to follow, while at the same time calling for the cessation of major attacks in France.[31] Joffre was certainly glad to hear about the reinforcements, but he shrugged and mumbled when Kitchener talked about continuing what he called a 'war of attrition'. Although the French Commander-in-Chief made it clear that he favoured an offensive, he was careful enough not to promise too much, keeping the French delegation happy (who had been wary of over-committing to new operations) and leaving the British with the (incorrect) impression that he agreed with Kitchener.

The following day Asquith and Kitchener headed off to Ypres (where they reviewed troops), while Joffre hosted another meeting at

Chantilly with military representatives from Russia, Italy and Serbia. As he had done all year, Joffre argued that the Allies had to coordinate their attacks to put the enemy under as much pressure as possible. At the same time, they had to prevent the Central Powers from concentrating against one member of the alliance at a time. 'Under these conditions,' he explained, 'the basic principle for the Allied armies bearing the main brunt of enemy forces is that they are entitled to count on the support of a vigorous offensive by those friendly armies that are less keenly pressed.' Therefore, for reasons of military honour and national interest, it was necessary for the Franco-British armies to take the offensive as soon as possible. Sir John French, who was in attendance, gave his support to Joffre's proposals. Attacking not only made strategic sense, but it was also important from the perspective of morale. 'The French soldier, more than any other, has offensive qualities that must be used.'[32]

Russia's great retreat continued throughout the summer, darkening Allied council chambers and raising the horrifying spectacle that the Eastern Front might collapse entirely. Warsaw fell on 4 August; the northern fortress of Kovno surrendered two weeks later; and by the end of the month German and Austrian forces had cleared Poland, struck north into Courland, and even reached the town of Brest-Litovsk over 200 miles from where they had started out. The retreat was, however, finally coming to an end. Russian forces were now more concentrated than before, much nearer their lines of supply, and finally benefiting from an increased output of guns and shells as their industry geared up for a prolonged war. In contrast, Falkenhayn's troops were exhausted, far away from their railheads and coming up against impassable terrain along the western approaches to Russia: marshes and forests where there were few roads, no railways and little food.[33]

Falkenhayn spent most of his time in Pless, plotting his victories on increasingly large-scale maps and toasting his success with the Kaiser's favourite pink champagne. Although Hindenburg grumbled that they had not yet done enough, that their operations had 'not led to the annihilation of the enemy' (as he put it in a letter of 13 August),

Falkenhayn snapped back: 'The annihilation of the enemy has never been hoped for from the current operations in the East, but purely and simply a decisive victory in accordance with the aims of G.H.Q.'[34] Moreover, Falkenhayn's thoughts were increasingly focused on the Balkans, where negotiations with Bulgaria were at an advanced stage. Once this alliance was concluded, Germany would move south, opening up a land route to the Ottoman Empire and settling the 'Serbian question' once and for all. As for the Western Front, Falkenhayn was content to watch and wait. At a conference at Metz on 29 July, attended by army Chiefs of Staff, he reiterated that there was no indication the Entente would launch another attack in the near future. A large consignment of shells had left England for the Dardanelles, while it was unclear whether the French were preparing for another offensive after the cessation of fighting in Artois. It was therefore necessary for each army to gather intelligence on the enemy through raids or small-scale operations while preparing to hold the line for some time to come.[35]

The fear that Falkenhayn was underestimating Allied resolve only grew as the weeks passed. Fritz von Lossberg felt the General was being too optimistic and that it was surely not possible that France and Britain would leave Russia to be dismembered without doing everything they could. When OHL ordered another corps to move east the following month, Lossberg grew anxious. 'I was most uncomfortable with that decision, because I thought increasingly that our enemy in the west was marshalling new forces for a large-scale attack. If that happened, OHL had only three complete and two weak divisions in reserve on the Western Front.'[36] In Champagne – the probable site of any future French action – Karl von Einem was acutely aware of OHL's disinterest. When they met in early August, Falkenhayn told him how things were 'moving very slowly' on the Eastern Front and that he had no desire to be 'dragged further into the country'. Nevertheless, Einem worried that some of his infantry divisions were going to be 'siphoned off' and pleaded with Falkenhayn not to 'further weaken the army too soon . . .'[37]

Sir John French had initially pledged himself to Joffre's renewed offensive and met with Foch to arrange the finer details. Foch wanted the British to extend Tenth Army's attack up towards the La Bassée Canal, while also relieving French units south of Arras with Kitchener's Third Army, which was scheduled to arrive later in the year. Sir John agreed to these requests, but found himself backtracking rapidly once General Haig had been given an opportunity to look over the proposed site of the offensive. The area north of Lens was 'very difficult', Haig reported; littered with mining buildings, slag heaps and very well-sited defences that would require extensive siege operations. Although it might be possible 'to capture the enemy's first line of trenches . . . it would not be possible to advance beyond because our own artillery could not support us'.[38] Sir John, always volatile, now began to sink back into fits of depression and frustration that made his commanders uneasy. He fretted that he was being cornered into another disaster like the one at Aubers Ridge and struggled to find a way out. He visited the front, but came away more depressed than ever, his depression compounded by the realization that the BEF lacked the numbers of guns and munitions that would have given his troops a fighting chance of success.

Sir John refused to be hurried into committing to Joffre's proposals and explained, in a letter on 10 August, that he would prefer to fight north of the La Bassée Canal, which offered better opportunities for success. However, because he had promised to support Joffre, he would now reinforce Haig's First Army 'in accordance with the wishes, which you, as Generalissimo expressed'. This would allow him to aid French operations 'by neutralizing the enemy's artillery and by holding the infantry on its front'. Sir John's sleight of hand was obvious and Joffre spotted it immediately. French was proposing to conduct an artillery demonstration (*not* an infantry attack), which would hold the Germans on his front and shell their trenches, but not risk an all-out assault with the likelihood of tens of thousands of casualties. As might have been expected, Joffre refused to accept this and wrote back swiftly: 'You will certainly agree with me that this support can only be effective if it takes the form of a large and powerful attack, composed of the maximum force you have available, executed with the hope of success and carried through to the end.'[39]

Joffre's patience was almost exhausted. He followed his letter up with another strongly worded telegram to London (through Mille-rand), which arrived just as Kitchener was digesting news of the latest failure in the Dardanelles. General Hamilton's summer offensive had failed to break through, with New Army divisions getting bogged down amid the harsh scrubland of Suvla Bay. The Secretary of War had seen much in his long career, but this must have been one of his worst moments. He was confronted, once again, by serious com-plaints about the commander of the BEF at the same time as his faith in Hamilton was all but extinguished. With no choice but to return to France, Kitchener spent three days at the front between 16 and 19 August, talking to senior officers and coming under fierce pressure from both Joffre and Millerand. In the end, he gave in, telling Sir John that whatever his previous objections, he must now 'cooperate vigorously' with the French. This was confirmed at a meeting of the Dardanelles Committee on 20 August, when Kitchener explained, at length, that they could no longer avoid making 'a *real* serious offen-sive in the West'.[40]

No one liked it, but Asquith felt that he had little choice but to accept Kitchener's advice. While 'far from sanguine that any substan-tial military advantage will be achieved', Kitchener was (as Asquith wrote in a letter to the King), 'strongly of opinion that we cannot, without serious and perhaps fatal injury to the alliance refuse the cooperation which General Joffre invites and expects'.[41] The 'draw-backs and dangers' of such a course were pointed out 'with great force' by Winston Churchill, who continued to argue his case for weeks, but with little result. When the Dardanelles Committee reconvened on 3 September, Churchill implored the Secretary of War 'to discourage, by every means, the idea of the prosecution of a violent offensive in France'. K stared glassily at him, before taking off his cap, smoothing down his hair and shrugging his shoulders. If he did so, he replied, he would 'break the Anglo-French alliance', something that he was not prepared to do. Unfortunately, he added, 'we had to make war as we must, and not as we should like to'.[42]

Joffre had played his cards well, showing an agility and craftiness that belied his heavy frame. Now that he had enlisted Kitchener's support, he returned to the French Government and presented his case for an autumn offensive. Despite the news that there had been some sort of breakthrough in relations between the British and French, there was only lukewarm enthusiasm in Paris. We are 'going to be dragged into a new offensive, less in the hope of really helping the Russians than because we think we must justify ourselves in their eyes', was how Poincaré responded when he heard the news.[43] Nevertheless, there was little motivation to appeal against Joffre's judgement, even though his prestige was becoming increasingly tattered. He had got rid of another general, Maurice Sarrail, commander of Third Army, on 22 July, provoking a storm of protest in the French Parliament. Sarrail was one of the most powerful political generals in France, beloved of the left and a staunch republican, who – so it was whispered at the time – might be an ideal replacement for the current Commander-in-Chief. Joffre claimed that the decision was made because of poor performance in the field, but few believed him.

Joffre was now becoming an isolated figure, walking a lonely path where some of his closest allies began to waver in their support of him. Even his senior commanders were split upon the nature of the attack and what could reasonably be expected from it. At a meeting on 11 August, Foch and Castelnau had clashed over the outlines of the new offensive, with the former preferring a more limited siege-type operation, while the latter remained wedded to the decisive 'rupture'. When Foch said he needed ammunition for an extended series of attacks, taking place over many days, Joffre told him that 'siege war' was not what they wanted. Castelnau agreed: 'The aim is to create a flank in the enemy position, and then to manoeuvre from there. The first operation, therefore, is to breach the front – or at least to push it back enough in terms of breadth and depth to give us the necessary space for manoeuvre.' They should 'look to create this breach by a methodical attack rather than a rushed assault'. If this was done properly, they could gain ten or twelve kilometres within one or two days.

Foch was unimpressed. In Artois, he said, the enemy had brought up three reserve divisions almost immediately, which prevented them from breaking through. Their artillery could only be effective against the first enemy line, with the second and third each requiring separate attacks. In the discussions that followed, it was perhaps inevitable that Joffre would side with Castelnau.

'If we adopt your system of methodical attack,' Joffre said, looking at Foch, 'which would require a month of combat, with a maximum expenditure of ammunition, when would we be able to be ready to make the assault? Perhaps next year, perhaps never. We need to act, for our sake and the sake of our allies. Just as stated in our regulations: only inaction is shameful.'[44]

The main assault would, therefore, be made in Champagne and it would be decisive. Foch would have to be content with a subsidiary attack in Artois – a decision that he took with good grace, even if he now began to diverge from his Commander-in-Chief. They had to attack, of course, but the end would only come after a methodical series of operations, involving huge quantities of men and munitions, and slow, steady advances. 'General Foch, former swashbuckler, seemed bruised by his failure at Arras', remarked a staff officer who was in attendance at the meeting.[45]

What role the British would play gradually became clearer after Kitchener's visit. Sir John French was understandably furious at this latest intervention and rapidly lost interest in the forthcoming attack, brooding upon his situation and letting Haig get on with it as best he could. Although the First Army commander remained concerned about the state of the ground, his appetite for offensive action was whetted by the possibility of using poison gas. Within ten days of the attack at Ypres, Kitchener had ordered investigations into methods of retaliation, and an ambitious regular officer, Major Charles Foulkes, was put in charge of a new unit, the Special Brigade, which was tasked with organizing chemical warfare in the field. By June, the War Office had managed to put together a rough outline for a 'chlorine wave' attack that would follow what was known of German methods. Chlorine would be sealed in steel tanks, clustered together in batteries and dug into the front lines. From there pipes would be fitted to the cylinders, pushed out into no-man's-land and then opened.[46]

Haig became an immediate convert to gas. On 22 August, he had attended one of Foulkes's demonstrations of cylinder-released chlorine and was deeply impressed, rapidly incorporating it into his attack plans. He was convinced that it would unlock the trench stalemate and offer him the prospect of fighting a decisive battle. 'The moral effect of the gas on the foremost hostile troops', he told one of his corps commanders, 'may be such that the defenders of Loos may be affected as was the case North of Ypres after a distance of near five miles.'[47] Accordingly Haig began drawing up an attack of (for the British) unprecedented scale: two corps would make the main assault, capturing the villages of Loos and Hulluch and an enormous German defensive outpost known as the Hohenzollern Redoubt, before heading off east towards the Heute Deule Canal. If everything went to plan, they would make an advance of five miles and outflank the German positions north of Lens. As the Allied armies prepared for the attack, activity along the Western Front dropped off, like the drawing in of breath before a great exertion.

7. 'No getting through'

Tall, with short grey hair and a bristling moustache that almost covered his mouth, the new commander of the French Second Army possessed a striking figure. On 22 June, Lieutenant-General Philippe Pétain, commander of XXXIII Corps, had been notified of his promotion and transfer. In less than a year, he had gone from a passed-over colonel on the verge of retirement to commanding an army about to conduct the largest offensive of the war to date. Pétain accepted his latest promotion with little sense of celebration, visiting Castelnau in his headquarters at Château-Thierry in late July for his instructions. Watching the two men was Pétain's close aide, Bernard Serrigny, who stood in silence as the two generals thrashed out their plans: 'Pétain, a man from the Nord, unemotional, quiet, wrapped up in his own logic, never saying a word that was not needed, and the other one, from the sunny south, eloquent, exuberant, colourful, but sometimes drowning his ideas in a sea of words!' Castelnau explained that the attack was to be a repetition of 9 May on a larger scale, only for Pétain to register his disquiet. Conditions had changed profoundly since May, he explained. There was now a second enemy line, about four miles behind the first one and out of range of French artillery. It was, therefore, unlikely they could achieve anything more than a 'limited strategic success' given the amount of men and munitions that would be available.[1]

Castelnau's plan was for his armies to 'create a wing' that would 'rupture' the front and drive through the German position: 'Once this flank has been established, reserve forces would be ready to inflict a heavy defeat on a significant section of hostile forces operating on the Franco-Belgian front. Establishing a flank in the enemy's current position constitutes breaching its front and pushing back any remaining troops in terms of width and depth required for setting up a zone of free movement, a zone for manoeuvre for the forces tasked with attacking the enemy's entire position . . .'[2] Joffre originally wanted the offensive to begin in July, but frequent postponements meant that it was not until late September that everything was ready. The scale of the preparations was dizzying. In Champagne, two armies, comprising thirty-five infantry divisions and seven cavalry divisions, were massed against the German line, supported by 850 heavy guns and over 1,000 75s. In Artois, General d'Urbal would launch seventeen divisions along a twelve-mile front supported by 400 heavy and another 670 field guns. Along the British sector, the preparations were equally exhaustive. By the evening of 24 September, over 5,000 cylinders, comprising about 150 tons of chlorine gas, had been shipped across to France and dug in along the front of Haig's First Army between the outskirts of Lens and the La Bassée Canal. Haig's attack would also be supported by an unprecedented mass of artillery. Over 900 guns, including 110 super-heavy howitzers, would fire a four-day preliminary bombardment, raining over 250,000 shells on to the German lines and raising the possibility of a mass breakthrough right across the front.[3]

In reality, the Entente still had much to do. Although they outnumbered their opponents (forty-two divisions to seventeen in Champagne and twenty-nine to thirteen in Artois), they would have to fight their way through positions of unprecedented complexity. By the autumn of 1915, the German defences in Champagne had been reinforced and heavily fortified, consisting of multiple lines of trenches that incorporated a series of villages and natural fortifications. Then there was the second line, lying between three and five kilometres to the north. Because it was mostly unobservable from the French lines, it would be very difficult to shell.[4] Getting through all this would require meticulous attention to detail. Pétain issued final instructions on 5 September. His artillery would open up large gaps in the defences and destroy enemy batteries, while practice barrages and feints would tempt the defenders to man their trenches only to face renewed shellfire. Gas and incendiary shells would then be fired at specially selected locations, while the night before the attack, combat engineers would enter no-man's-land and open up any remaining breaches in the barbed wire. 'The aim of the preparations is to destroy all enemy positions in the attacking zone, and to weaken his resistance, so that the assault troops will only meet with a faltering and confused enemy.'[5]

The preliminary bombardment began on 22 September. Great stocks of ammunition were brought up to the front and the skies were full of French aircraft busily observing the fall of shell. Good weather allowed French guns to target systematically the belts of barbed wire that covered the German trenches, while smashing important crossroads and bivouacs behind the line, raising huge clouds of dust over the bare chalk hills. About 30–35 batteries were now engaged along each German divisional sector – row upon row of 75 mm field guns surrounded by stacks of smoking shell cases – bringing down an enormous weight of fire. The Saxons of 24th Reserve Division, holding the line at the village of Cernay-en-Dormois, counted 80,000 rounds as falling within just ten hours.[6] Unfortunately for the French, heavy rain on 24 September interfered with the bombardment and prevented observation of the German lines in the final few hours. The poor weather would continue, on and off, for the rest of the month. Yet there could be no thought of postponing the attack. The French Army had already fired off too much ammunition and brought up too many divisions to think of rescheduling the attack.

From his headquarters at Vouziers, General Karl von Einem watched the preparations with a sense of weary repetition. He had been warning OHL for weeks about the danger of a renewed offensive and now it was here in all its fury. 'The raging barrage has been going on for more than twenty-four hours, and the massive banging and crashing continues without a break', he wrote on 23 September. 'Twenty observation balloons hover in the sky on the French side, and countless planes buzz in front of our lines to watch everything and direct the fire. In the whole army we have only five balloons against the twenty of the French . . .' His main duty was 'collecting reserves, distributing them, and raising spirits'; while he pined to go nearer the front, which 'would be easier than being held here leading and waiting'. That day he spoke to Falkenhayn on the telephone, who – 'in a somewhat irritated tone' – gave him the delightful news that the Supreme War Lord, Kaiser Wilhelm II, would be visiting his headquarters the day after tomorrow, the afternoon of 25 September.[7]

The pressure of the looming attack preyed on everyone's nerves. Einem and his staff 'ate quietly' that evening. 'In terms of the temperature, the day had also been very sticky, and the situation was equally sticky. Everyone was mostly engrossed in their own thoughts, not much was said. I tried to start a conversation a number of times, but failed.' Despite the curtains of artillery fire that were falling right across the front of Third Army, Falkenhayn was still not convinced that the French were serious. In the days before the attack, he had accompanied the Kaiser on a tour of Colmar and Strasbourg, inspecting troops and handing out medals, while brushing Lossberg aside whenever he raised the issue of another attack. When Einem rang up on 24 September and alerted Falkenhayn to the 'very serious situation' in Champagne, he dismissed his request for reinforcements with a characteristic scowl:

'The French don't have any courage . . .'[8]

The early hours of 25 September were an anxious time, heavy with the sense of the immensity of what was about to happen. In the British sector, General Haig spent it at his advanced headquarters, the chateau at Hinges, pondering on whether to release the gas. He had been arguing with GHQ for the past few weeks about whether he could postpone his 'chlorine wave' if the weather conditions were unfavourable, with Sir John (and then Joffre) being insistent that all attacks must go in on 25 September regardless of the conditions. When Haig explained that his offensive was totally dependent upon the gas (and should not be launched without it), he would run into the same intransigence: that any postponement was 'highly undesirable'.[9] After being briefed by First Army's meteorological expert, Captain Ernest Gold, Haig eventually gave the order to go ahead shortly after five o'clock that morning. The wind was calm, with none of the bluster that was required to blow the gas over the German lines, but there was some hope that it would strengthen shortly before Zero Hour. Haig was also told by his gas expert, Foulkes, that if the conditions were completely unsuitable, his men would not release the gas.[10]

There was less sense of urgency in General d'Urbal's Tenth Army opposite the brooding rise of Vimy Ridge. Here the French attack would not go in until 1 p.m., giving their artillery at least four hours of daylight to observe the effects of fire on the German second line. Given his experience of previous battles, d'Urbal was cautious about pushing his infantry too far and wanted to mount a series of preliminary attacks before seizing the crest line, only for Foch, under pressure from Joffre, to insist that Tenth Army go further. In his loopy scrawl, Foch amended d'Urbal's plans, reminding him that the offensive was 'to pierce' or 'break through' the line and that his plans to take the ridgeline were 'too narrow'. Accordingly d'Urbal issued new instructions on 4 September which confirmed that the objective of Tenth Army's attack was to 'go beyond a tactical success' and achieve a 'strategic breakthrough' towards Douai.[11]

Foch knew that many of Tenth Army's officers were not keen to be attacking the ridge yet again. There were also, for the French, valid concerns about what the British were doing and whether they would really attack. They need not have worried. Haig's First Army was the first to go forward on 25 September: releasing the gas (interspersed with smoke) at 5.50 a.m. right across the front despite the wind conditions not being ideal. In places, the breeze was so weak that the gas hardly moved; in others it blew back on to the British lines and caused scenes of desperation and panic as harassed Special Brigade officers tried to stop the trenches filling with chlorine. Elsewhere, in the southern sector, opposite the village of Loos, the gas formed a dirty cloud out in no-man's-land, before rolling down the slope towards the German lines where it flushed out the garrison. 'It was a wonderful yet ghastly sight and one I shall never forget to my dying day', recalled an artillery officer who watched the attack go in. 'A hundred yards ahead the air was thick with reddish mist, thickened still more by every fresh shell-burst with its smoke and fumes . . . Into this red dimness, like daylight seen through the red panes of a coloured glass window, our men walked and stumbled forward in twos and threes, till they disappeared from our sight.'[12]

The preliminary bombardment had damaged, but not eliminated, the German defences, and large stretches of barbed wire were still intact across the front. As soon as the British crested their trenches, they were faced with vicious bursts of machine-gun fire sweeping no-man's-land. Wearing their gas helmets – a cloth hood saturated in anti-gas solution – which gave them the look of 'some horrible kind of demon or goblin',[13] British troops stumbled towards the German trenches under heavy fire. Relying on weight of numbers, alongside the stupefying effect of gas, they were able to break into the Hohenzollern Redoubt and crash through the village of Loos, even scrambling over the top of Hill 70, which overlooked the town of Lens. But they had become wildly disorganized. Battalions were led from the front by their officers, easily distinguishable from their men, and had suffered crippling losses. That day nine Lieutenant-Colonels (or acting battalion commanders) had been killed and twelve wounded. As one survivor later put it, 'becoming a casualty seemed only a matter of time'.[14]

At Rupprecht's headquarters, reports began crowding in of enemy attacks from about 10 a.m., including the horrifying news that some kind of poison gas had been used around Loos. 'What I had already feared for months has happened', Rupprecht noted. 'Our premature use of the latest weapon, the gas, should only have been used during a decisive attack . . .' He ordered a reserve brigade forward while also notifying OHL about the 'highly critical' situation. Falkenhayn shook off his earlier optimism and promised reinforcements in the form of the Guards Corps, which would begin to detrain at Lille the following morning. Although this was welcome news, the Guards had lost over 21,000 men on the Eastern Front, and Rupprecht worried that they would not be able to make much of an impact in an increasingly desperate situation.[15] At Loos, Major-General Kuntze, commanding 117th Division, had just three regiments to hold a front of nine kilometres against what seemed like overwhelming force. As the remnants of his division streamed back from the front, he hurriedly re-formed in the second line along the western edge of the village of Hulluch.[16]

It was still raining in Champagne, a thin, grey drizzle dripping off helmets and forming into puddles, when the preliminary barrage reached its furious climax at nine o'clock. Fifteen minutes later the assaulting battalions from eight French corps (including some of the best units in the French Army) went forward, clambering out into no-man's-land through the drifting smoke, as the guns pounded the defences in front of them. In contrast to earlier attacks, the barrage remained on the enemy position until almost the moment when the attackers were upon it; an incredible technical achievement that allowed the French to break into the first German line across most of the attacking frontage.[17] On the left, the attack of Langle de Cary's Fourth Army was led by General Blondlat's II Colonial Corps, with the Moroccan Division pushing north of the village of Souain towards a hilltop position called Navarin Farm. Although they were able to advance three kilometres in just forty-five minutes, losses were heavy and units became disorganized and mixed up. Major-General Marchand, commander of 10th Colonial Division, was seriously injured, a brigade commander was killed, and another was wounded. At 4 p.m., Blondlat telephoned Fourth Army headquarters and warned that the situation was 'very imprecise'. His men had 'given their all' but could not take the German second line. Exploitation of their 'partial success' was urgently required.[18]

A similar picture emerged in Pétain's Second Army. The high point of the advance was Lieutenant-General Baret's XIV Corps, which fought its way through four successive lines of trenches north of Perthes. 'The operation was carried out quickly; troops advanced in tight order', reported a French officer. 'They tackled the German first lines, swamped them, pushed forward without any delay, leaving the cleaning up of the trenches to designated units. It was too late for German artillery to counter with barrage fire on our front lines . . . by that point assault troops and their supports had already penetrated the line of fire, the dangerous zone', which meant that the reserve units were able to move up without hindrance. Elements of 27th Division even managed to reach the German second line, but its protective rows of barbed wire were uncut and heavy enfilade fire from either flank meant that the advance came to a halt. But it was an astounding feat. The division had gone four kilometres in just two hours.[19]

In Artois, Tenth Army had still not moved, despite British liaison officers sending urgent reports of what was happening at Loos to their French counterparts. Foch did manage to move Zero Hour forward to 12.25 p.m., but when the attacks eventually went in the results were

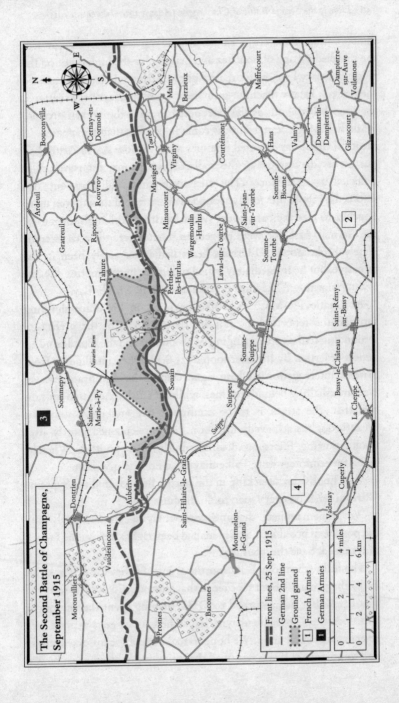

The Second Battle of Champagne, September 1915

Front lines, 25 Sept. 1915
German 2nd line
Ground gained
[1] French Armies
[1] German Armies

disappointing. Four corps launched heavy attacks, driving towards the smashed village of Souchez and making for the high point on the ridge, but elsewhere on d'Urbal's right recurring problems manifested themselves. Heavy machine-gun fire and plunging artillery shattered the French battalions as they struggled to cross the broken ground, while lightning counter-attacks came in quicker than anticipated. 'A dreadful time', remembered one survivor; 'the low sky in Artois had put on its darkest dress, the souls of our people sympathetically reflected its appearance.' The men were 'tired and worn-out'; reinforced by those previously wounded or unfit, and then driven up to Souchez to face the bare slopes swept by fire.[20] Although sections of the German first line were gained, in other places the attacks completely broke down. D'Urbal's heart had never really been in the offensive, but he immediately issued orders for its resumption the following morning: 'The most persistent side will win the day.'[21]

At Charleville-Mézières, Falkenhayn sat in his office shuffling through the reports that came in, the corridors of the prefecture resounding to the endless ringing of telephones and the sound of numberless orderlies. By the afternoon of 25 September, intelligence from prisoner interrogation in Champagne revealed that significant reserves were marshalling behind the lines, while a French officer told his captors that 'the attack is to be continued day and night until the breakthrough is achieved'. Karl von Einem telephoned shortly after noon reporting 'Enormous drumfire on the entire position'. When he asked for reinforcements, Falkenhayn had none to give him.

'The English are attacking in the north', he said, 'and the Supreme Warlord relies on every man to do his duty.'

'Yes', Einem replied, 'that goes without saying, but ultimately only the possible is possible.'[22] So Einem had been right after all; the French did, indeed, have the 'courage'.

The full realization of the enormous scale of the Allied attacks hit Falkenhayn hard. About six o'clock that afternoon, word was received that the Kaiser had returned to OHL (having spent the day out at Third Army), so Falkenhayn despatched an urgent report: 'All reserves are called upon. We hope to make good the losses overnight and tomorrow.'[23] It was not until the following morning that he was able to see the Kaiser and deliver his daily briefing in person. Falken-hayn (who was accompanied by Lossberg) admitted that the situation in Champagne was making him uneasy. The Chief of Staff at Third Army, Maximilian von Höhn, had 'recommended a general with-drawal of the front lines, which had been penetrated deeply in many places'. At this point, Lossberg broke in, stressing that 'the present position had to be held at all costs' and that they should 'fight for every inch of ground'. Suitably impressed, the Kaiser spoke to Fal-kenhayn and shortly afterwards it was announced that Lossberg would go to Champagne. He was now assigned as the new Chief of Staff to Third Army. Höhn was gone within the hour.

Lossberg ordered a car and drove to Vouziers straight away, strid-ing into General Einem's headquarters shortly after three o'clock that afternoon. Within minutes of his arrival, Lieutenant-General Paul Fleck, commanding officer of VIII Reserve Corps (which held the crucial part of the front at Tahure), rang up asking for guidance. He wanted to know whether his men should begin their planned evacu-ation because, if so, orders would need to be issued immediately. Lossberg put a stop to it in an instant:

'The withdrawal is cancelled. The VIII Reserve Corps will die in place exactly where it is now positioned.'

Fleck, taken aback by the tone of Lossberg's voice, asked to whom he was speaking.

'The new chief of staff of the Third Army', was Lossberg's firm reply.[24]

This iron refusal to retreat would be Third Army's new watch-word. When Lossberg saw General Einem later that afternoon, he 'appeared to be quite affected by the costly fighting and the difficult situation'. Recognizing that the eyes of OHL were now upon him, Einem had little choice but to let Lossberg have *Vollmacht*, giving him the authority to issue orders in his name. As the light faded, Lossberg made his way around the shelled roads and muddied tracks behind the line, glad now to return to the front, where, as he put it, he could 'breathe more easily'. The officers and headquarters staff he met along the way – their uniforms plastered with mud; their eyes ringed with exhaustion – told him the same thing. A major French effort around the town of Sommepy (north of Souain) was expected imminently, and more guns and ammunition, as well as any available reserves, were urgently needed. According to German intelligence, twenty-three French divisions (including five in reserve) were arrayed against just seven German ones, although Falkenhayn had ordered another division to be rerouted from Belgium to join the defence in Champagne, as well as despatching more heavy artillery and extra aircraft.[25] Snatching sleep when he could, Lossberg made sure they were sent to the threatened sectors, while energizing Third Army's tired staff by his intensity and persistence.

Getting through the German second line, whether in Artois or Champagne, would require more than just persistence. Because it was often situated on the reverse slope of any slight undulations in the ground, it was difficult to shell and, as Foch had warned prior to the battle, would require thorough and time-consuming preparation before it could be assaulted. At Loos, Haig's attack had lost much of its momentum during the afternoon of the first day, and without reserves at hand the defenders had been given just enough time to man a makeshift perimeter. Nevertheless, Haig was determined to continue and ordered two New Army divisions – the first to arrive in France – to push on through what remained of the German defences on the afternoon of 26 September. The result was a disaster. Executing a forced march to reach the front, the inexperienced battalions quickly became disorientated and confused on the battlefield. As one officer later put it, 'Nobody from the brigade commander downwards, had any idea of the situation at any stage of the proceedings.'[26]

Lacking artillery support and even the most rudimentary intelligence, battalion after battalion got caught in murderous enfilade fire as they tried to close with the enemy trenches around Hulluch. After receiving an order to attack 'written in indelible pencil and made almost illegible by the rain', one subaltern led his platoon forward, 'advancing in two lines at a walk', but came under 'very fierce' rifle and machine-gun fire from both flanks and only 'small groups of men' were able to reach the barbed-wire entanglements, which were 'still untouched, very strong', and partially hidden in the long grass.

'For some minutes we fired bursts of rapid fire at the enemy's parapet and at occasionally visible helmets' before the order to retreat was given.[27] Together the reserve divisions suffered over 8,000 casualties; their bodies littering the ground in front of the German second line that would later become known as the 'field of corpses'.[28]

While thousands of Britain's wartime volunteers were being slaughtered outside Loos, Joffre met Foch to discuss the future of the offensive. So much ammunition had been fired off in the last few days that there was little chance they could continue to support two major and simultaneous offensives. The French Commander-in-Chief, his usually placid features now furrowed by worry, told Foch that because it was not possible to force the crest of Vimy Ridge at the present time, he was ordering that every spare division and as much ammunition as possible be sent to Castelnau, who was marshalling his forces for a renewed push on the German reserve position. Foch was to economize as best he could while trying not to give the impression that operations in Artois were being wound down.[29]

In Champagne, it was not until late afternoon the following day (27 September), about four o'clock, that the assault on the second line took place. With a fading sun sending brilliant yellow rays across a scudded sky, Second Army's artillery opened fire and the familiar shriek of 75 shells heralded the advance. Once again, French infantry stumbled out of their trenches and pushed on, with fierce fighting breaking out across the front from Saint-Souplet and Sommepy to the blood-soaked village of Tahure. The German regiments in the line were able to beat back most of the attacks, while launching concentrated barrages against the French routes of approach, ensuring there would be no breakthrough. 'This has been a dreadful day', remembered an officer in the Foreign Legion, which had gone forward that afternoon. 'We're advancing slowly. Our opponent is tough, his well-served artillery is continually bombarding us with 140 mm gas shells. There's no respite, day or night. It's raining. Watery sun; we're shivering.'[30]

For Pétain, the failure of the attacks on 27 September confirmed what he had always suspected about the impossibility of breaking through on the Western Front. Although one report indicated that the second position had been breached, this was never the case. 'In reality the situation is different', he admitted (in a letter to Castelnau). 'The enemy's defensive line is continuous. Barbed wire positioned against the attacker is fully intact and can only be destroyed by scrupulously prepared artillery, carried out under the same conditions as the front line. All units engaged without this preparation will undoubtedly be crushed. This is my opinion and that of all front-line staff . . .' Pétain proposed to consolidate current positions, bring up heavy artillery and conduct photographic reconnaissance over the German lines. Any new attack, however, would have to be conducted by fresh troops. His divisions had suffered heavy casualties and their 'offensive value' was 'very much diminished'.[31]

At OHL, Falkenhayn was a moody presence, irritable and glowering at staff officers when they presented their reports to him. He remained 'greatly depressed', according to Gerhard Tappen, who saw him at the morning briefing on 27 September.[32] The mood did, however, gradually lighten when it became evident that the latest French attacks had failed. That evening – the air still full of the rumbling of artillery – a group of French prisoners were ushered in to see Lossberg at Vouziers. They had been 'sent into the infantry lines to reconnoitre the terrain for a breakthrough by major French cavalry formations that were in readiness'. Lossberg was glad to see that 'the French leadership had overrated significantly their current success'. That night he got his first good sleep since the first day of the battle; collapsing into his camp bed with his window wide open. He was so tired that he slept through an air raid when a French aircraft dropped a bomb about a hundred metres from his headquarters.[33]

On the other side of the line, the failure to achieve the longed-for breakout inevitably sparked off a search for scapegoats. In the BEF, the terrible carnage of 26 September was still raw. Haig had written to Kitchener on 29 September about GHQ's handling of the battle, particularly the decision to hold the reserve divisions too far back. 'No reserve was placed under me', he complained. 'My attack, as had been reported, was a complete success. The Enemy had no troops in his second line, which some of my plucky fellows reached and entered without opposition.'[34] The battle could have been a 'turning point',

Haig protested, but for Sir John's laggardness in bringing up re-inforcements. While Haig had a point, the subject of the reserves really boiled down to the scale of what First Army was attempting. French, who had given Haig a free hand, increasingly saw the plans for Loos as too risky and kept the reserve divisions under his own command as a way of reining Haig in. It was a messy solution that only contributed to the chaos and confusion encountered by the reserve divisions when they were rushed forward.[35]

Sir John French had only himself to blame. Frequently confined to his bed, suffering a series of recurring colds and fevers, the British Commander-in-Chief was now a melancholic shadow of his former self. 'He seemed tired of the war,' recalled Haig, when French went to see him on 28 September, 'and said that in his opinion we ought to take the first opportunity of concluding peace otherwise England would be ruined!'[36] Sir John spent whatever time he could riding around the lines; his ruddy features lighting up when he saw a face he recognized amid the long columns of officers and men marching up to the line. But the terrible cost of the offensive sapped what little deter-mination he had left. He wrote to Winifred Bennett about the experience of visiting casualty clearing stations; a terribly draining ordeal for a man already ailing in body and spirit. 'Dead, dying and badly wounded all mixed up together. Poor dear fellows they bear their pain gloriously and many of them gave me a smile of recogni-tion.' Particularly heart-wrenching was the news that Major-General Thompson Capper, a fire-eating former professor at the Army Staff College, had succumbed to his wounds on 27 September, having been hit while moving up a communication trench, trying to lead a counter-attack. 'My *Darling Darling*,' wrote Sir John, evidently in some distress; 'we've had such terrible losses which make me very depressed and sad.'[37]

Senior officers were never immune to the terrible costs of fighting on the Western Front. On 2 October, General Castelnau had been given the shattering news that another son, Hugues, had been killed in action and he almost collapsed with grief. Hugues had been deployed with his artillery battery in Artois, but had been working at headquarters, which kept him away from the front. When one of his fellow officers was wounded, Hugues asked to replace him in the line, only for his commanding officer to say no: 'Your father entrusted you to my care. I should refuse to give you permission.' Hugues accepted this, but pressed his case anyway. 'It is his paternal duty to take care of me, but it is my filial duty to ask this.' With that his commanding officer reluctantly agreed to let him go. When he was asked later on what he would do after the war, Castelnau replied gravely: 'I shall weep for my children.'[38]

After the frenetic pace of the first three days of the offensive, the week that followed was much quieter for the German command in Champagne. 'The French limited themselves to heavy artillery fire and local attacks conducted mostly in the dark', wrote Lossberg. 'These thrusts forced our purposely thinly manned forward lines to fall back initially, but then our hasty counterattacks launched immediately against the enemy's front and flanks always broke up their attacks and we regained our positions.'[39] Although the German Army continued to hold its ground and inflict grievous casualties on its opponents, the experience of such intensive combat was an enormous strain on the defenders. Reports from Third Army complained about heavy losses from artillery fire, exhaustion among the front-line garrisons, and 'trenches and obstacles [being] severely damaged'.[40] On 5 October, General Einem estimated his casualties at more than 40,000 since the beginning of the offensive. 'Because of the lack of dugouts, they grow daily in the front-lines; relief units are also suffering casualties because approach trenches to the [second line] have been lacking.'[41]

Champagne was now a byword for terrible carnage and slaughter. One German officer remembered marching up to the front line towards what he called 'the witches' kettle', where there was a 'constant wild howling of shells backwards and forwards'. After joining one of the main roads to the front, busy with trucks and horse-drawn guns, the troops' appearance soon 'blended with the background, as our shiny new Feldgrau [field grey] uniforms acquired a layer of grey-white chalk dust'. When they reached the front, the mood among the men dropped noticeably. 'The countless corpses and the sight of the plateau ploughed up by shells of all calibres could not fail to have an effect on the spirit and morale of our new comrades.[42] Indeed, Einem spent much of his time worrying about how green troops would cope with what he called the 'peculiarities' of 'positional warfare'. Third Army remained on the defensive, but the fighting of recent days had become a fierce tug-of-war, which demanded new tactics. Rushing across no-man's-land to take machine-gun positions was useless, Einem noted. 'They have to be sealed off and attacked with grenades from the flank. Or one cuts them off from their support. If this is not possible, the trench is cleared to the left and right and the area in question is then gassed. Even the most stubborn Frenchmen can't stand that.[43]

Joffre had hoped to launch the renewed attack on 5 October, but it was not until the following day that Castelnau's armies were ready. The attack went in at 5.20 a.m., with tendrils of mist clinging to the ground and dulling the sounds of great activity across the line. The reduced visibility meant that the bombardments that had been carried out over the previous forty-eight hours had not been properly observed, and, almost immediately, French troops found the enemy defences much more intact than they had been led to believe.[44] Langle de Cary's Fourth Army, which had been guarding Pétain's left flank, made little progress, with stubborn enemy defences holding them up, while Second Army ran into belts of uncut barbed wire that kept them from entering the German trenches. Small, grudging, hard-fought gains were made. French troops secured the village of Tahure and took the ruins of Navarin Farm, but were subjected to fierce counter-attacks up and down the line. On the evening of 6 October, Joffre finally bowed to the inevitable and authorized the cessation of the offensive. The Second Battle of Champagne was over.

Relations within the French High Command may not have been as broken as in the BEF, but support for Joffre inevitably waned as the disappointments of the autumn offensive became apparent. Millerand telephoned Poincaré on the evening of 6 October to inform him of the 'very poor results'. 'We have taken Tahur[e], we have moved forward near the Navarin farm, and secured a thousand prisoners, but there has been no "getting through".[45] The price that had been paid for such an inconclusive result was staggering. In two weeks of fighting, the French Army had fired off 4.1 million 75 mm shells, plus over 800,000 rounds of heavy artillery, which exhausted stocks across the country. The human cost had also been enormous. By 7 October, Pétain's Second Army had sustained over 62,000 casualties, with Langle de Cary's Fourth Army beating this with a tally of more than 75,000 dead, wounded or missing. In Artois, Tenth Army added 48,000 casualties, and Haig's attempt to break through at Loos had also been a horrific failure, with another 50,000 casualties added to the grim total of the Allied autumn offensive.[46]

The realization that the war was no closer to being ended snuffed out any lukewarm optimism that may have lingered on after the Battle of the Marne. In his report on Tenth Army's operations, General d'Urbal admitted that the Western Front had now mutated into a great siege, with one key difference. In a traditional siege, every position lost by the defender would bring his demise closer, but this was not necessarily the case in the present conditions. As Germany had shown in Champagne, she could build two or even three lines that required separate attacks to get through, thus preventing the attacker from gaining any kind of offensive momentum. Breakthroughs could, therefore, only be hoped for on fronts where the enemy had not been able to build such positions.[47] Pétain drew much the same conclusion. 'The Battle of Champagne has demonstrated *the difficulty, if not the impossibility, in our current state of armament, our method of preparation and opposing forces, of taking successive enemy positions in one wave.*' The only solution was to capture the second position in the same way that the first had been taken. 'These successive attacks involve a considerable use of manpower, an unprecedented expenditure of ammunition, and both the manpower and expenditure are only realistically able to permanently push back the enemy if, after the second strike, there are no fresh troops to oppose us.'[48]

For the German Army, to the contrary, there seemed little to learn. Falkenhayn crowed that the 'greatest battle of all time' (as some Allied commentators had christened it) had become 'a terrible defeat for the attackers. Tremendous sacrifices in men and material were made for a result which was nothing in comparison to the objectives

aimed at, and in itself amounted to but little, for it was of no importance from the general point of view whether a few narrow sectors of
the German position had to withdraw a few miles or not.[49] Sixth
Army even produced a printed document soon after the battle that
emphasized the basic soundness of German defensive doctrine.
Although the French had managed to make some gains, particularly
around Souchez, and the British had employed overwhelming masses
of troops to rush the German positions around Loos, elsewhere the
defence had proved remarkably resilient. Trenches on the reverse
slope of hills had been almost impossible for the Entente to take, and
well-executed counter-attacks helped to restore the situation on more
than one occasion.[50]

The German defenders may have beaten off the double offensive,
but the cost of doing so was considerable. In Champagne, 1,700 officers
and 80,000 other ranks had become casualties, while another 50,000
men had been killed or wounded or were missing in Artois. Artillery
consumption had also been unprecedented. Together, Sixth and Third
Armies had expended thousands of tons of ammunition in their desperate defensive action: 1.5 million field artillery shells in Champagne
and another 1.2 million in Artois, plus over 600,000 heavy-artillery
rounds.[51] Such a high expenditure of munitions was certainly impressive, but it raised fears that it was still not enough. The French and
British had fired off almost double that amount and, with plentiful supplies coming from overseas, there was every chance this would only
increase in the coming months. It was unlikely, however, that the
Allied blockade could be broken. Owing to growing protests, including strongly worded statements from the US Government, Germany
discontinued her campaign of unrestricted submarine warfare on 1
September, notifying Washington that liners would not be sunk without warning provided that they did not 'try to escape or offer
resistance'.[52] Two weeks later, the Imperial Navy modified the campaign even further, ending the policy of attacking merchant ships in
the English Channel and to the west of the British Isles. U-boats were
allowed to continue to operate in the North Sea, but they had to follow
standard rules on stopping and searching merchant vessels to ascertain
their cargos before they could be sunk.[53]

Falkenhayn shrugged off his disappointments over the U-boat war and focused on other battlefields. On 6 September, Bulgaria finally joined the Central Powers and set about carving up Serbia. A month later, as Joffre's attacks in Champagne were petering out, a combined Austro-German and Bulgarian army began to move south. It captured the smouldering ruins of Belgrade on 9 October, and then marched into the mountainous interior, while the Serbian Army, ragged, lacking basic supplies, began a long retreat southwards. French troops were swiftly landed at Salonika, breaching Greece's neutrality, but they were too late to save Serbia, which was rapidly overrun by the Central Powers. Such a turn of events marked a disaster for the Entente and yet another triumph for Falkenhayn, who had managed to end the year on a remarkable high. On 8 October, the *Frankfurter Zeitung* summed up a growing feeling that the tide was, finally, turning in Germany's favour. 'The danger of a break through our lines has been disposed of, our attack in the East is progressing, and our General Staff has spoken the decisive word – that we have men and strength enough to make Serbia and the Balkans the central point of the war. The stream of blood of the countless thousands whom our enemies have sacrificed on the battlefields of France, and are still throwing into the game of war, have been shed in vain.' All praise for this was due to the Chief of the General Staff, Falkenhayn, 'in whose hands all the threads meet'.[54]

For the man who had staked so much on the autumn offensive, the month of October 1915 was bitter and tasted of defeat, no matter how hard he tried to carry on as usual. Shortly after the battle had been called off, Mr Owen Johnson, an American writer for *Collier's Weekly*, was granted an audience with the French Commander-in-Chief at his well-appointed villa in Chantilly. 'An air of simplicity pervaded everything', wrote Johnson. 'No sentries were without, no bustle of officers thronging the garden . . . No one else was in the outer hall – absolute quiet and calm throughout the house, unbroken save for the low, continual murmur of officers at the telephone . . .' When Johnson met Joffre, the first and most striking thing about him was that he seemed to be 'the supreme court of common sense' and was 'the simplest and most approachable of men . . . His full-face, traditional photograph is fairly characteristic. The head is capacious and set with the massiveness of a block; the eyebrows and grey moustache heavy and overhanging. He is neither nervous nor electric. It is the mind, divorced from the tongue, that is ceaselessly at work.' When Johnson made some praiseworthy comment about the 'spirit of fraternity' within the French Army and how this might be vital to the outcome of the war, Joffre's face seemed to light up.

'Whatever happens, the French Army will never crack', he explained. 'It did not in the first unequal weeks; it never will.'[55]

Joffre may have exuded a warm and genial exterior, but the realization that France now faced a war of indeterminate duration weighed heavily upon him. Perhaps trying to pre-empt growing questions about his own authority, Joffre had written a note on 7 October acknowledging that despite 'considerable tactical successes, we have been unable to achieve the strategic breakthrough, which was the goal of our offensive'. There was now an urgent need for her allies to shoulder more of the burden. 'France has borne the brunt of the war from the start of the campaign. She has selflessly shed her own blood for the ultimate victory of our common cause. She cannot go on like this without permanent detriment to her own future. Her allies, who still have significant forces at their disposal, now must bear the main brunt of the war, which will ensure the final defeat of the enemy. France must keep its remaining troops for the final operational period leading to victory; she should not expend them needlessly.' Therefore, it was now up to the British to do more. 'During 1915, French forces were on the attack while British troops largely remained in defensive positions. This situation must be reversed during the coming winter.'[56]

PART 2

'Scales of fate'

Verdun to the Second Battle of the Aisne
(December 1915–May 1917)

8. 'A place of execution'

Precisely at noon on 19 December 1915, a bitterly cold day in France, General Sir Douglas Haig assumed command of the British Expeditionary Force. Haig had been appointed after the resignation of Sir John French following the escalation of a 'first-class squabble' over the handling of the reserve divisions at Loos.[1] Sir John argued that they had been transferred to First Army on the morning of 26 September and, therefore, that their unfortunate deployment was wholly Haig's fault. Haig presented documents to show that this was not the case and their tardy arrival at the front was because they were kept too long under GHQ control. When Sir John ordered Haig to let the matter drop, the commander of First Army held his ground, writing to a friend that not only was French 'very ignorant of the principles of the higher leading of a large Army but is also lacking in the necessary temperament! He is so hot and excitable – like a bottle of soda water in suddenness of explosion – that he is quite incapable of thinking over a serious situation and coming to a reasoned decision.'[2]

The question of who was right would rumble on for the next few years, but there was no doubt that Sir John had been outmanoeuvred by an increasingly strident Haig. French returned to London for an interview with the Prime Minister, who intimated that he felt a change was needed and that it was best if a younger man were appointed to succeed him. French was offered the command of Home Forces, which he accepted, but he would brood on his fate for the rest of his life. He was paid a generous farewell by Joffre on 20 December, the big Frenchman shaking his hand warmly – his eyes shining beneath the peak of his kepi – before pinning a *Croix de Guerre* on his chest, all under the watchful gaze of a battalion of zouaves that had been drawn up for the occasion.[3] Behind the smiles, however, there were few regrets that Sir John was going. For Joffre and the French High Command, the more pressing question was whether Haig would be more compliant than his predecessor had been and whether he would be able to bring Britain's growing forces to bear against the German Army and drive them out of France.

There was little shock at the choice of French's successor. As Winston Churchill later wrote, Haig's appointment 'created no surprise, aroused no heart-burnings, excited no jealousy'.[4] Douglas Haig was fifty-four years old and 'the first officer of the British Army'; a man who had risen steadily from his beginnings in the cavalry, through service in the Sudan, South Africa and India, until taking command at Aldershot in 1911. Haig was a taciturn man, intensely serious about his profession, 'his face set like a flint' as one of his closest aides would confirm. Several days earlier he had met the Military Secretary at GHQ, Brigadier-General Sir Henry Lowther, and told him that he had one idea, 'namely to do my utmost to win the war: that in my eyes only those who had proved their fitness for advancement should be promoted. I had no "friends" when it came to military promotion, and I would not tolerate a "job" being done.'[5]

Haig's instructions were largely the same as those which had been given to Sir John, although it was perhaps inevitable that Kitchener laid a greater emphasis upon working more closely with Britain's allies. Haig was 'to assist the French and Belgian Governments in driving the German Armies from French and Belgian territory, and eventually to restore the neutrality of Belgium'. His command was an independent one (and he would 'in no case come under the orders of any Allied General'), but the 'closest co-operation of French and British as a united Army' would be his 'governing policy'.[6] A fortnight earlier (between 6 and 8 December) a series of major conferences had been held in Chantilly, hosted by Joffre (and attended by Sir John), during which it was agreed that the Allies' main objective would remain the destruction of the armies of the Central Powers, with a resumption of coordinated offensives on the Western, Italian and Russian Fronts as soon as possible. This would place the enemy nations in a vice-like grip and prevent them from shuttling reserves to each threatened front in turn as they had done throughout 1915.[7]

In order to keep an eye on Haig, Joffre assigned a new liaison officer to GHQ, Pierre des Vallières, who was instructed to report back on what the British were thinking and do his best to 'bring them round' to French plans. Vallières, a cavalry officer noticeable for his tall, upright bearing and long moustache, met the British Commander-in-Chief on New Year's Day, when he was shown the instructions that Haig had received from London. Haig wished it to be known that 'there could not be two commanders-in-chief in one theatre of operations and that in the north-eastern theatre, the conduct of the war belonged to General Joffre under whose direction he placed himself'. Vallières did point out that Haig seemed to prefer an operation in the north to recover the Channel ports rather than fighting on the Somme (where a Franco-British offensive had been mooted), but he was pleased to report that he thought the Scotsman was 'prepared to give the French command more complete and more judicious help than the government directive indicates'.[8]

The clear decisions that had been made at Chantilly came at the end of a period of great turmoil in Allied politics. The Viviani government had fallen in October to be replaced with a ministry led by the veteran socialist Aristide Briand, who promptly installed General Galliéni as Minister of War (in place of the unpopular Millerand). Briand and Galliéni were both firm advocates of French intervention in the Balkans, believing that an eastern campaign could bring huge advantages (including swaying Greece and Romania to join the Allies), and even though Joffre had long been suspicious of such expeditions, he recognized the political necessity of that kind of commitment. The matter was further complicated by the presence of General Maurice Sarrail, who had been sent to Salonika to head France's grandly titled 'Army of the Orient'. Joffre had dismissed Sarrail from command of Third Army in July 1915, officially because of 'military considerations', but there were rumours that he had been openly critical of the High Command and had communicated with left-wing deputies in Parliament. Sarrail had powerful allies, and Joffre was only too aware of the need to tread carefully.[9]

Despite the dangerous political scene, Joffre's grip on the French war effort remained as tight as ever. In line with the broadening of the conflict, the French Government decreed (on 2 December) that Joffre was now 'Commander-in-Chief of the French Armies', including those forces outside France, which gave him responsibility for the landings in Salonika.[10] Briand also appointed General Castelnau, formerly in command of Army Group Centre, as Joffre's Chief of Staff in Chantilly (to help with these enlarged responsibilities). Joffre realized the danger that Castelnau posed as a potential successor, but the two men got on well enough and they would often be seen strolling side by side along the shaded paths around the Grand Condé: Joffre, 'powerful and heavily built', walking with 'his hands behind his back, his left leg dragging a little', while Castelnau, 'short, robust, and lively . . . hustled along a yard or so ahead, striking at the grass with his stick', before making a characteristic 'half-turn to bring himself back to a level with the Commander-in-Chief'.[11]

In London, Herbert Asquith's coalition government remained in place, even if its tenuous unity was beginning to fracture, the inevitable consequence of what Maurice Hankey (Secretary to the War Cabinet) called the 'persistent ill-success that dogged the Allies in every theatre of war except Mesopotamia'.[12] On 31 October, David Lloyd George, Minister of Munitions, and Andrew Bonar Law, Colonial Secretary, jointly threatened to resign if Kitchener remained in place, which finally forced Asquith's hand.[13] The Secretary of War was packed off on what was termed a 'fact finding' mission to the Dardanelles, which remained deadlocked after the failure of the summer offensives. K saw for himself the cramped, flyblown trenches and smelt the bitter stench of corpses decomposing outside the wire, but was unsure whether an evacuation was either feasible or necessary. When he returned to London in late November, he found, to his horror, that Asquith had moved swiftly in his absence, acting with a decisiveness that was uncharacteristic of the usually cautious and relaxed Prime Minister. He convened a new, slimmer War Cabinet (replacing the Dardanelles Committee), which recommended the immediate closure of the Gallipoli expedition. He had also transferred further powers from the War Office to the Ministry of Munitions and appointed Sir John French's former Chief of Staff, Sir William Robertson, as the new Chief of the Imperial General Staff (CIGS) in London, now armed with greater responsibility for advising the Government on military matters.

When Kitchener learnt of these changes, he drove straight to 10 Downing Street and offered his resignation, only for Asquith, pacing the room, to turn it down. He was very keen that Robertson should become the main source of military advice for the Government, but this did not mean that Kitchener was not needed. On the contrary, he told Kitchener to remember 'that he alone stood between the armies and political chaos; that he was the symbol of the nation's will to victory; and that he would betray his duty to the armies, to the public and to the King, if he refused to return to his post'.[14] K had no choice but to make the best of it. He worked smoothly with Robertson, a 55-year-old ex-ranker who was a professional and hard-working individual, but there was no doubting the direction of travel; Britain's strategy was now moving on without him. On 27 December, the War Cabinet (at the urging of Robertson) agreed to the evacuation of all remaining beachheads at Gallipoli (Suvla Bay and Anzac Cove having already been abandoned earlier in the month), thus bringing to an end one of the bloodiest and most frustrating episodes of the war. When the last troops left the peninsula on the night of 8/9 January 1916, Kitchener spent it sitting alone in his room at the War Office, grimly imagining what could be happening out on the dark waters of the Aegean: 'the boats fired at and capsizing, and the drowning men . . .'[15]

For once Kitchener was being overly pessimistic. The operation was conducted perfectly, and by morning over 35,000 men and thousands of horses had been evacuated without loss. Yet the failure of the Gallipoli expedition was a crushing blow to Britain's hopes of outflanking the fortress of the Western Front. Sir William Robertson, who now became, after Haig, the most important soldier in the British Empire, had few illusions that the war could be won in Turkey or the Balkans. Shortly before being appointed CIGS he had written a memorandum laying out the stark choice that now faced the Allies. 'The war may end either in the defeat of the Central Powers, in the defeat of the *Entente*, or in mutual exhaustion. The object of the *Entente* Powers is to bring about the first of these results, which can only be attained by the defeat or exhaustion of the predominant partner in the Central Alliance – Germany.' The campaign in the

Dardanelles 'can no longer help to the defeat of Germany', and any operation in the Balkans 'can, at most, assist very indirectly'. Therefore, 'France and Flanders must continue to be the principal theatre of war, and on it our main efforts must be concentrated.'[16]

On 18 January 1916, the Kaiser attended a royal banquet at Nish, Serbia, hosted by King Ferdinand of Bulgaria, to toast their recent successes in the Balkans and Poland. 'How did the Kaiser look?' asked an excited newspaper correspondent. 'Whether it be due to the fatigues of war, the effects of a two-days' journey, or ill-health I cannot say. So much is certain – the face is that of a tired and broken man.' Wearing a long grey coat, fur necklet and spiked helmet, the Supreme War Lord looked diminutive compared with the rotund figure of King Ferdinand. 'The hair is white, though the moustache is still suspiciously dark. There was an absence of the old activity of gesture, the quick, nervous wheeling about and unstable manner of the man.' Falkenhayn, who accompanied the Kaiser, looked better. 'Although a man well into the fifties, he looks as if he had not yet crossed the half-century mark. He is trim, alert of movement, has close-cropped grey hair, and seems the personification of vigour, vivacity, and virility. At any rate, he is bearing the strain of the war and his tremendous responsibilities well.'[17]

The German party said little to their hosts about their plans for the future. After the cessation of fighting in Artois and Champagne, Falkenhayn had spent weeks thinking about Germany's strategy for the coming year. He now recognized that a compromise peace was increasingly unlikely and that it was 'no longer a war as we previously understood it, but a fight for existence' (as he explained in a letter to Bethmann Hollweg on 29 November). 'The view that it is up to Germany to make peace soon, either through documenting conditions that are acceptable to our enemies, or to continue the war until the enemy's will to win is broken and therefore also its endurance of war, even at the risk of Germany needing to deploy its last man and last penny, is a false one . . . Any party who, in a fight with such high stakes, comes forward with a peace offering, without having a clear sign from any of the opponents that they are prepared to concede, shows ruinous weakness'. Such an act would 'automatically lead to a weakening of will on the part of one's own people to endure, the fighting power of the armies and the strengthening of the enemy's morale'.[18]

Falkenhayn was not short of advice on what Germany should do in 1916. Predictably, Conrad von Hötzendorf pressed for a strike against Italy, but Falkenhayn was unconvinced this would have far-reaching effects. In a letter to Conrad shortly after a meeting at the Austrian High Command at Teschen on 10 December, Falkenhayn complained that even if Italian forces along the border underwent a shattering defeat, Rome would not necessarily come to terms. 'Even if the blow was successful, it would not have a deadly impact on Italy . . . It cannot make peace without the agreement of the Entente, upon which it is fully dependent for its supply of money, food and coal.' Conrad replied on 18 December: 'A decisive defeat of the Italian Army in the north-east of the kingdom, with the abandonment of the region up to the Adige, would in all likelihood force Italy to make peace because the situation in the interior after such an event . . . would certainly be untenable'. Conrad believed that an offensive against Italy was a 'necessary introduction to the final decisive combat' in 1916, which was 'imperative' for the Dual Monarchy.[19]

Unimpressed by the possibility of operations against either Russia or Italy, Falkenhayn continued to believe, much as he had done in September 1914, that Germany would only be able to strike a decisive blow in the west. During December he authored a report to the Kaiser on Germany's situation, explaining what she had achieved and also what she must do to win outright victory. France had been 'weakened almost to the limits of endurance'; Russia's offensive power had been 'so shattered that she can never revive in anything like her old strength'; Serbia's forces had been 'destroyed'; while Italy had quickly understood she could not possibly achieve 'the realization of her brigand's ambitions within measurable time'. For Falkenhayn, England was Germany's most formidable opponent, whose 'enormous hold' over her allies had to be broken. Any attempt to reach an understanding with England would be taken as a sign that 'Germany's resolution was weakening'. On the contrary, Berlin had to convince

London that Germany could not be beaten in a war of exhaustion and there was no possibility of keeping the alliance together. Therefore, Germany could not simply remain on the defensive; if she did so there could come a point at which she would be overwhelmed by the resources massed against her.[20]

Turning to how and where an attack could be launched, Falkenhayn believed that the northern sector of the Western Front was unsuitable: the ground was boggy and would not be dry before late spring and, in any case, it would not be possible to concentrate enough forces to achieve a breakthrough. But even if the German Army managed to destroy the BEF, driving it into the sea, it might not end the war because England's 'real weapons' were 'the French, Russian and Italian Armies'. Falkenhayn continued in this vein a little further, twisting his arguments around to claim that because Britain was Germany's most implacable opponent, they must strike against France. Falkenhayn believed that France was weakening and that if she could be made to realize that the war was hopeless, then 'England's best sword' would be 'knocked out of her hand'. If Germany could seize a key point at the front, perhaps somewhere the French General Staff 'would be compelled to throw in every man they have', then France would 'bleed to death'. The operation was known by a suitably sinister codename: *Gericht* ('place of execution').

The phrase 'bleeding to death' slipped easily from Falkenhayn's lips as he completed his plans. He was fully aware of what this meant in practice, even if, over the coming weeks and months, it would be obscured or diluted as he tried to cover his tracks. At the beginning of December, he had spoken to the Kaiser about 'bleeding white' the French Army, a phrase that was overheard by Hans von Plessen, who included it in his diary entry for the day.[21] The Kaiser had responded positively to the proposal and the idea of forcing the French into a bloody and painful submission appealed to his sense of destiny and his unquenchable yearning for glory. At the same time, Falkenhayn was also keen to restart unrestricted submarine warfare, which would run in tandem with the ground campaign. But here he ran into difficulties. The spectre of American involvement had frightened off Germany before, while the nagging concern that she did not have

1. General Gérard Leman, commander of the Belgian garrison at Liège. Refusing to leave his command post, Leman was wounded and taken prisoner, muttering to his captors that 'War is not like manoeuvres.'

2. A destroyed gun cupola amid the ruins of Fort de Loncin, Liège. The destruction of the Belgian fortress system was an essential precursor to the German invasion of August 1914.

3. Colonel-General Helmuth von Moltke struggled to coordinate Germany's armies and suffered a nervous breakdown in September 1914. 'He was sitting listlessly in front of the map', remembered one officer; 'a broken man.'

4. Erich von Falkenhayn was Moltke's replacement at OHL. Cold and friendless, Falkenhayn struggled to commit fully to either Eastern or Western Fronts, provoking complaints about the 'gradual initiation of large undertakings … with inadequate resources'.

5. General Joseph Joffre, the French Chief of the General Staff, recovered from initial setbacks to execute the counter-attack on the Marne in September 1914.

6. German soldiers en route to the front, August 1914.

7. German dead on the battlefield at Fère-Champenoise on the Marne. By the end of 1914, Germany had suffered at least 800,000 casualties, including 116,000 dead.

8. Field Marshal Sir John French, Commander-in-Chief of the BEF (*second from left*), with his staff. French was quickly out of his depth in France and was removed after the ill-fated Battle of Loos in September 1915.

9. Field Marshal Horatio Herbert Kitchener. Appointed Secretary of War in August 1914, Kitchener raised a mass army of volunteers, only to see them committed prematurely to France. 'We had to make war as we must, and not as we should like to', he admitted.

10. French infantry on the march during the Battle of the Yser, October 1914. Often criticized for being brave but tactically inept, the French soldier showed an 'extraordinary and peculiar aptitude ... to recover quickly' throughout the war.

11. Sir John French *(left)* and Joffre, accompanied by a party of staff officers, inspect the front. Sir John's relationship with his French counterpart was often stormy as he struggled to provide support to Joffre's operations without exposing the expeditionary force to excessive risk.

12. Generals Joffre, Foch and d'Urbal inspecting troops. Despite repeated attempts to break the trench deadlock throughout 1915, the French Army could only achieve localized breakthroughs – what Joffre called 'nibbling'.

13. French zouaves charge across no-man's-land during an attack at Touvent, on the Oise, 7 June 1915.

14. Men of the German 106 Regiment wearing early-pattern gas masks. The first use of chlorine at Ypres in April 1915 ushered in a new age of chemical warfare, but failed to produce decisive victory.

15. French assault troops await the order to attack in a cramped trench somewhere in Champagne.

16. A Krupp 17 cm *Feldkanone* opens fire during the preliminary bombardment at Verdun, February 1916. The German attack was supported by the greatest array of artillery then assembled.

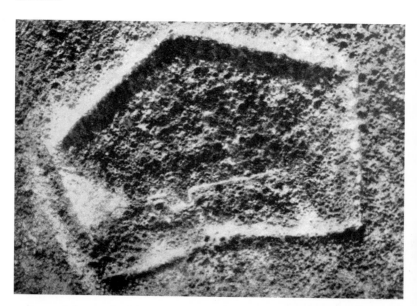

17. An aerial photograph of the battered facade of Fort Douaumont, which became the focal point of the Battle of Verdun.

enough U-boats to achieve lasting damage was another factor that had to be considered. Debate over the submarine war would go on for weeks, leaving Falkenhayn no choice but to get on with planning his main offensive.

The location selected for the 'execution' of the French Army was the moated city of Verdun, lying seventy miles east of Reims and nestled in the valley of the Meuse river, which snaked its way north towards the sea. It had traditionally been France's eastern gateway, bordered on the far side by a series of forested hills that rose up to 400 metres in height. Between 1885 and 1913, a series of powerful, mutually supporting fortresses had been constructed in a three-quarters circle around the city; built deep into the soil and covered over with brick, sand and concrete – a shield behind which France could be safe. Verdun had become the hinge of France's Western Front during 1914, anchoring the line in Champagne from where it turned south towards the Swiss frontier. Yet the fate of Belgium's shattered fortresses cast a dark shadow over Verdun. Many of its heavy guns had been removed on Joffre's orders in 1915 to try to remedy France's chronic shortage of howitzers, which left the forts themselves under-gunned and under-manned. They were also widely seen as a relic of nineteenth-century warfare; hollow shells in which the garrison would only become trapped and destroyed. As early as August 1915, General Dubail, commander of Army Group East, made it clear that such fortress complexes were valuable 'only to the extent that they can facilitate operations in the field' and that they were now to be placed under the orders of the Commander-in-Chief who could 'dispose of their resources without restrictions'.[22]

Falkenhayn entrusted the attack to the 33-year-old Crown Prince Wilhelm, the eldest son of the Kaiser and commander of Fifth Army. Wilhelm was a dilettante; a lover of women and cigarettes, whose thin, hollow-chested profile and unimpressive gait were a boon to Allied propagandists, who nicknamed him 'Little Willie'. He had been in charge of Fifth Army since the beginning of the war and had perhaps shown greater judgement than his critics allowed. He formed a tight-knit team with his Chief of Staff, the 55-year-old Schmidt von Knobelsdorf, a highly experienced guardsman who did most of the liaising with OHL. On 14 December, Knobelsdorf arrived in Berlin to brief Falkenhayn on an outline plan of the attack. Unfolding a map of the front, he explained that taking ground on both banks of the river north of Verdun would allow his artillery to overlook the city, forcing the French to vacate it. When Falkenhayn examined the plans, he explained that the scope of the attack was beyond their resources. They would only have five corps to employ in the operation, to take place sometime early in February, and they were only to attack on the east bank.[23]

Falkenhayn's insistence that the German Army had to approach Verdun along the east bank immediately presented problems. Knobelsdorf remembered how Falkenhayn pointed out on a map where the attack was to occur, sketching the route they were to take. 'I remember precisely how I looked at him hard and asked if that was everything and whether we shouldn't also attack on the western bank of the Meuse at the same time.' Falkenhayn shook his head. There were, he explained, not enough men or artillery to do this. When Knobelsdorf again protested, claiming that he might have to fight half the French Army along the eastern bank, Falkenhayn promised that he would have plenty of troops and ammunition. With that Knobelsdorf returned to the Crown Prince's headquarters at Stenay and completed his plans.[24]

Falkenhayn was deaf to the calls to widen the attacking frontage. OHL's heavy-artillery expert, Max Bauer, went to see the ground for himself and immediately came to the same conclusion – that unless they could strike along both banks, troops would come under fierce enfilade fire. When he protested that the attacking frontage was too narrow, he was ignored.[25] Falkenhayn's refusal to listen to the need for a wide-front attack came from a variety of sources. He was unconvinced that such an offensive, as the French had tried to do repeatedly throughout 1915, could succeed. The way to win was to use limited amounts of infantry and intensive artillery fire to inflict grievous losses on an opponent and draw them into an attritional struggle. He was also concerned about a lack of reserves and wanted to keep some divisions back in case the Allies launched a relief offensive elsewhere along the front. When Gerhard Tappen tried to press him on the matter, it provoked an uncharacteristic outburst of anger:

'I'll take the responsibility,' snapped Falkenhayn. 'I can't be bothered to get into a situation again like the one in the autumn . . . at the Battle of Champagne. I won't do it.'[26]

Falkenhayn, with the Kaiser in tow, shunted back into Charleville-Mézières on the morning of 11 February, ready to direct the imminent attack at Verdun. At a meeting of army Chiefs of Staff later that day, Falkenhayn explained that OHL would remain in the west for the time being. 'The decision in this war can only be achieved on the Western Front', he reiterated, explaining that the German Army was now 'moving into a phase of operations in the west that should bring about the decision'.[27] Whether Falkenhayn actually wanted to capture Verdun or not remained unclear. Both Knobelsdorf and the Crown Prince were convinced that the attack had to have a major objective and that it was essential to try to seize the city, or at least the fortress complex, while Falkenhayn's objective of destroying the French Army could be achieved just as well by taking the high ground and letting his artillery do the work. As for the Crown Prince, he seems to have shared the concerns of Falkenhayn's critics, being 'disquieted' by the idea of 'bleeding white' the French Army, only to swallow his fears and say little. He was only too well aware of how much his father still supported Falkenhayn and did not want to jeopardize the choice of Fifth Army to make the attack; a task that he approached with 'long-suppressed eagerness'.[28]

Artillery would be the key to the battle. Whereas the French offensive in Champagne had been supported by around 800 heavy guns, many of which were either worn out or obsolete, the German attack on Verdun relied upon a much more impressive array of artillery: over 1,200 guns were assembled, two thirds of which were classed as heavy or super-heavy, ranging from 150 mm howitzers to the 420 mm 'Big Berthas' that had been so effective at Liège and Maubeuge. At least two million shells were stockpiled for the opening assault, brought up on specially built narrow-gauge railway lines that threaded their way through the stark winter landscape. The operation would also make use of over 200 heavy trench mortars (*Minenwerfer*) brought up close to the front that would deluge the French line with fire at the moment of assault. Miles of telephone wire were connected up to the forward zones; battery positions were covered over with camouflage nets; while hundreds of supply depots and shell dumps were constructed, either in ravines and caves or under the cover of the tree canopy, which kept them from being spotted by French observers.[29]

Great emphasis was placed upon achieving surprise. Front-line units were forbidden from digging forming-up trenches or saps in no-man's-land (as would be usual before an attack) to avoid giving anything away, while squadrons of German fighters patrolled the skies above the battlefield, forming an aerial screen through which only a handful of French machines were able to penetrate. Hitherto, aircraft had only played a minor role in operations; useful for reconnaissance and artillery spotting, they were fragile and unreliable, with light, wooden frames vulnerable to the elements and prone to mechanical breakdown. It was only in the summer of 1915 that this began to change with the introduction of the Fokker E.I monoplane (*Eindecker*); built with steel tubing and fitted with synchronized interrupter gear that allowed a forward mounted belt-fed machine-gun to fire through the propeller. Aerial combat was still a rare occurrence, but by the closing months of the year, the slow-moving and (often) unarmed Allied machines found themselves under growing pressure from what was soon dubbed the 'Fokker Scourge'. Although the *Eindecker* were only produced in small numbers (and often kept behind German lines to preserve their technological secrets), the psychological impact of such a revolutionary device was profound.

Concentrating 168 aircraft in the Verdun sector, including twenty-one of the latest version of the Fokker (the E.III), the German Air Service swept their prey from the skies with devastating ease. Not only were the French outnumbered in the Verdun sector (where they could barely scrape together thirty machines), many of their aeroplanes were also 'pusher' types (with engines behind the pilot) that were vulnerable to the *Eindecker*. German aircraft conducted extensive observation over the battlefield, while targeting French observation balloons, which were shot out of the sky as soon as they were hauled up. By the time the offensive opened, French counter-battery fire had been severely impaired and her knowledge of enemy dispositions reduced to little more than what could be gleaned from scanning the horizon with binoculars. 'The first days of the attack came as a complete surprise to the enemy', recorded General Ernst von Hoeppner, commander of the German Air Service, 'and our flyers were almost complete masters of the air.'[30]

Anticipation rose as the attack drew nearer. On the evening of 11 February, the Crown Prince issued a proclamation to his men, urging them to 'show our foes that the iron will to victory is still alive in the hearts of Germany's sons' and that the 'Fatherland expects great things of us!'[31] The attack was originally to have commenced the following morning, but the arrival of more winter weather, squalls of snow and sleet, meant that a delay was necessary, causing consternation at OHL. Every day meteorological reports were eagerly digested for news of better weather and when it did not come, hopes for achieving surprise began to fade. 'Raining the whole day!' complained Wilhelm Groener in Charleville. 'If we don't get started in Verdun soon, then the element of surprise is going to be lost. The barometer is supposedly rising, but the rain is falling despite the waxing moon.'[32] Fifth Army had no choice but to wait under heavy blankets of cloud, its assault troops packed into underground bunkers that had been carved out of the hillsides (known as *Stollen*). And then on 20 February when reports indicated an improvement, orders went out that the attack would commence the following morning.

German fears were well-founded. The commander of what was known as the *Région Fortifée de Verdun* (RFV) was General Frédéric-Georges Herr, a 60-year-old from Alsace, who had been sent to Verdun in August 1915. Herr had been warning for months about the poor state of his defences, the lack of barbed wire and communication trenches, only to find GQG largely uninterested: France was committed to an offensive war and fortifications could only have a limited value in such circumstances. Yet enough intelligence filtered in to GQG that something was going on at Verdun to trigger a belated reinforcement of the front. By the time the offensive began, Herr had three corps in the RFV, although they were still heavily outnumbered and outgunned by the massive array of forces then assembling on the other side of the line. On the crucial northern face of the salient, Lieutenant-General Paul Chrétien's XXX Corps was strung out along a twenty-five-kilometre front, frantically trying to extend and strengthen their defences as the rain came down, praying that the skies would not clear.[33]

At exactly 7.12 on the morning of 21 February, Fifth Army's guns opened fire. 'In the clear winter air the thunder of the howitzers opened the chorus, which rapidly swelled to such a din as none of those who heard it had ever experienced hitherto', was how the Crown Prince described it.[34] He arrived at his advanced headquarters at Vitarville, about 18 miles north of Verdun, several hours later only to come under counter-battery fire from French guns. Although the shelling was spasmodic and somewhat wild, Wilhelm withdrew north to Stenay, out of range of enemy artillery, on advice from his staff, which allowed him to direct the battle without fear of being disturbed. The bombardment continued for most of the day, the forested hills echoing to the rumbling sound of gunfire. 'It was proper artillery fire!' recorded General Tappen, who accompanied the Kaiser to Stenay to see for himself.[35] It slowed somewhat around noon (to lull the enemy into a false sense of security) and then restarted again with the same furious intent; shattering trees into matchwood; blowing gaping holes in the ground; and obliterating anyone foolish enough to be in the open.

Under such an intensity of firepower, the defenders could only huddle in their trenches, cower under their helmets, and grip the earth with crazed, clawing hands. Communications between the forward positions and the rear had quickly been severed and those runners that tried to get through the smoke and dust were soon killed or incapacitated, leaving the defenders isolated and disorientated. When 'we left our shelters we no longer recognized the countryside where we'd lived for four months', remembered one Frenchman; 'there were hardly any trees left standing and it was very difficult to move around because of all the shell holes that had shattered the ground'.[36] At 4.30 p.m., as dusk began to fall, German assault teams picked their way forward, the air smelling of iron and gunpowder. Many of them were wearing the new M1916 *Stahlhelm* ('steel helmet') with its characteristic bowl shape, which provided excellent protection for the head and neck, and gave the German infantry the typical look they would have for the next three decades.

By the standards of French operations in Champagne, the first day at Verdun was relatively modest, with elements of just three corps going forward. They were not, in fact, making the main attack at all. Knobelsdorf had ordered a series of heavily armed patrols to assess the situation and, hopefully, mop up any surviving Frenchmen. As well as relying on its artillery, Fifth Army left nothing to chance, throwing gas shells into the mix and employing *Flammenwerfer* (flamethrowers) teams, whose terrifying jets of orange fire caused panic in the French ranks. In places, they advanced swiftly, finding the pitiful remains of the French lines blown to pieces, but in others, the defenders – maddened by the ferocity of the bombardment – held on. In the blasted woodland of the Bois des Caures, on the northern edge of the French lines, a Lieutenant-Colonel, Émile Driant, led two battalions of *chasseurs* (elite light infantry) into action despite being cut off by heavy artillery fire. Driant had made a name for himself as an author and parliamentary deputy, rousing the ire of the High Command for his criticisms of the state of the Verdun defences and the removal of the heavy guns from the forts. As he left his dugout to meet the oncoming storm, strapping on his helmet, he told his men: 'We're here. It's our position, and we're not moving from it.'[37]

Driant managed to hold on for the rest of the day, using his concealed machine-guns to inflict heavy casualties upon the attackers and counter-attacking whenever possible. Indeed, given the intensity of the preliminary bombardment, the initial German attack had been somewhat underwhelming. Parts of the French first line had been taken, but resistance had been fierce and hopes that the bombardment would destroy everything in its path had proved wide of the mark. The following morning, Knobelsdorf ordered the Bois des Caures to be taken at all costs, and once again a thunderous five-hour barrage would precede the attacks. On the German left, III Corps managed to take the Bois de Ville, but got caught up in the costly and time-consuming business of clearing out bunkers and dugouts that had somehow survived the initial bombardment. As before, the French fought valiantly, launching a series of counter-attacks, but the weight of numbers began to take its toll. VII Reserve Corps entered Haumont village (by then just a tumble of ruined farmhouses), taking 400 prisoners, while, in the Bois des Caures, Driant and his band of *chasseurs* were finally overrun, the colonel being shot in the head as he tried to organize a fighting retreat.

Despite the bitterly cold weather and frequent snowstorms, the German attack began to gain an ominous sense of momentum over the next few days. It was not as spectacular as the French attacks in the autumn, but Fifth Army, in its own remorseless, brutal fashion, gradually tightened its grip on Verdun, its attacks always preceded by heavy artillery fire. The village of Brabant, on the Meuse, fell on 23 February, and Samogneux, two miles further along the valley, was captured on 24 February (along with 900 prisoners).[38] Although German battalions were now coming under artillery fire from the opposite side of the river (something that Falkenhayn had been repeatedly warned about), the French defence on the east bank was beginning to crumble. Casualties in Chrétien's XXX Corps had been catastrophic. 72nd Division, which occupied the front from the Meuse to the Bois des Caures, had lost a staggering 192 officers and 9,636 men, while 51st Division, on its right flank, sustained over 6,000 casualties. Even 37th Division, which had been in support on 21 February, had lost almost 5,000 men after being fed piecemeal into the fighting, 'like clay shovelled into the cracks of a dyke'.[39]

Fortunately, reinforcements were on their way. General Maurice Balfourier's XX 'Iron' Corps (which Foch had once commanded) had been ordered to get to Verdun as soon as possible. Dripping steam in the cold air, long lines of footsore French soldiers marched through the sleet as the horizon flashed and rumbled to the interminable artillery fire. Refugees were streaming out of the city by every available road, while the terrifying sound of shells shrieking overhead, thudding into buildings or landing in the river and sending columns of spray into the air, only added to the sense of disorder. On 23 February, the commander of France's Army Group Centre (and Castelnau's successor), General Langle de Cary, put a telephone call through to

Herr and ordered him not to sanction any further retreats: 'The occupation of any spot . . . even if completely surrounded, must be maintained at all costs; this can, as hopeless as it might seem, have incalculable consequences in slowing down the progress of neighbouring enemy units or in facilitating our counter-attacks. *There's only one order to be followed: to hold on, to hold on whatever the cost . . .*'[40]

Even France's most senior commanders apparently became paralysed by a growing fear of disaster. From the moment that German guns began pounding Verdun, a curious lethargy seemed to creep upon Joffre. He was not, and never had been, known for swiftness of thought or action, but he could usually be counted upon to act when the time came. Yet for the first few days of the battle he seemed absented-minded and, for once, unsure of what to do. In recent weeks, French parliamentarians had been asking awkward questions about the defences at the front, particularly around Verdun, where the fortress system had been systematically plundered for spare artillery pieces and ammunition throughout 1915. When pointed remarks had been made by the War Minister, Galliéni, about whether the defences could hold, Joffre lost his temper and replied that nothing justified such concerns and that these practices (when subordinates complained about their chiefs) could only have 'a most serious effect on military discipline' and 'undermine the moral authority without which I cannot continue properly to exercise my command'.[41]

Joffre's titanic fury when dealing with the politicians in Paris contrasted sharply with his response to the unfolding crisis at Verdun. On the evening of 23 February, as news came in of renewed German advances, Langle de Cary telephoned GQG and informed Joffre that he intended to evacuate the Woëvre plain (the stretch of low-lying ground that lay due east of Verdun on the other side of the heights). Joffre said little, other than that he was 'free to take such decisions as he, who was on the spot, deemed necessary'.[42] Such a hands-off attitude did not sit well with Castelnau who was worried about the impact of successive withdrawals. He went to see Joffre the following day and, leaning on his walking stick, alert as ever, proposed to go to Verdun in person and make sure the east bank was held. Joffre had no objections, so Castelnau left at once, arriving at Langle de Cary's headquarters (situated in Avize, about twenty-five miles south of Reims) in the early hours of 25 February. The two men talked over the situation in Langle de Cary's small office, their grim faces lit by a flickering light bulb. Langle de Cary doubted whether the advanced positions on the far bank could be held, but Castelnau disagreed. He telephoned Herr and told him in no uncertain terms that the ground was 'to be held whatever the cost and by any means at your disposal'.[43]

Castelnau sensed that the French commanders in Verdun were shaky. Both Herr and Langle de Cary were exhausted and seemed nervy; their headquarters were scenes of frantic activity but, for Castelnau, lacking in organization and method. Before he left Chantilly, he had requested that a new commander be brought in and, thinking quickly, he suggested that General Pétain be given the opportunity to coordinate the defence. Pétain had been on leave in Paris (staying with one of his female acquaintances) and was hastily summoned to see Joffre at the Grand Condé on the morning of 25 February.

'Well! Pétain, you know it's not going that bad at all', was Joffre's rather cryptic greeting as he stood to receive the Second Army commander in his office.[44]

Joffre explained that Castelnau had been sent on to Verdun to relieve General Herr of his powers as regional governor and that he (Pétain) would now lead the defence. Pétain left soon afterwards, driving out to the embattled city, the still air petrified with frost, the ground covered with thick sheets of ice and snow. When he got to Herr's command post (situated just south of Verdun at the village of Dugny), they found a scene of disorder. Everyone was speaking at the same time – Langle de Cary, Herr, Castelnau, and assorted staff officers – so it was left to Colonel Claudel, Joffre's Assistant Chief of Staff, to try to bring some order to the proceedings. 'He managed to get some silence and set out the situation, which was bleak!' recorded one of Pétain's aides. 'Enemy columns, which had attacked on the right bank, were at the very walls of Fort Douaumont. The Woëvre pocket was being reduced. Reserves seemed to be annihilated. As for communicating with the rear, this seemed quite precarious: the railway line and road from Clermont to Verdun were cut off; we could only count on the highway from Bar-le-Duc for battle supplies. The only positive note in this flood of bad news: the enemy had not shown the slightest hint of an offensive on the left bank.[45]

As the French commanders tried to work out their next move, dramatic events were happening out on the east bank, where the German advance continued to creep forward, as one French staff officer put it, 'like a big grey carpet being unrolled over the country'.[46] That afternoon – 25 February – the centrepiece of Verdun's defences, Fort Douaumont, had fallen. Douaumont was one of the largest and most heavily protected fortifications in the world. Constructed at one of the highest points on the battlefield, it dominated its location, sitting squat upon the landscape 'like some incubus weighing upon the whole surrounding countryside'.[47] Yet by early 1916 Douaumont was in a sad state of disrepair, most of its garrison having been redeployed on other, more pressing duties and many of its guns removed on Joffre's orders the previous year. But it still possessed its main armament, an impressive 155 mm howitzer, manned by a group of ageing territorials, and it remained the lynchpin of the defences at Verdun, attracting shellfire and drawing German battalions towards it like a magnet. That afternoon, as flurries of sleet and snow swept over the battlefield, a small group of German pioneers from 24/Brandenburg Regiment managed to scramble into the fort, surprise the garrison, and take control of its dismal, echoing corridors without a shot being fired.

The presence of Pétain – big, imposing, unflappable – helped to calm nerves at Dugny as news spread about Douaumont, but the Second Army commander was not minded to stay in Herr's headquarters much longer. He decided to occupy the Town Hall at Souilly (a short drive to the southwest), where he would have the room and space to direct the battle without distraction. As soon as a telephone was installed, he put a call through to General Balfourier, whose corps was then moving into position on the east bank.

'Hello! This is General Pétain speaking. I am taking over command. Inform your troops. Keep up your courage. I know I can depend on you.'

'Very well, sir', replied Balfourier. 'We shall bear up. You can rely on us, as we rely on you.'

After speaking to several other commanders, Pétain had one of his staff officers hang up a large-scale map of Verdun on the wall, where he marked the position of each corps and then spent the rest of the night dictating orders. The following morning, he issued 'Operation Order No. 1', which outlined what they must do: repulse the enemy attacks and retake lost ground: 'Not a slip is to be made; not an inch of ground is to be yielded.'[48]

9. 'Costly and fatal toils'

The seizure of Fort Douaumont brought forth a rare burst of excitement at OHL. 'Excellency von Falkenhayn announced during our evening meal yesterday that Fort Douaumont had been stormed by the 24th Brandenburg Regiment', recorded Wilhelm Groener on 26 February. 'This is the capture of the allegedly strongest fortress in the world, and the rest of the French position on the right bank of the Meuse will, I most certainly hope, fall in a short time.'[1] But Groener was being too optimistic. Rain set in on 25 February and quickly turned the ground into thick mud, porridge-like in its consistency. There was also the disconcerting growth of French artillery fire, particularly batteries firing from the other side of the river. Hans von Zwehl's VII Reserve Corps tried to seize the crossings over the Meuse at Samogneux, but ran into heavy wire entanglements and made little progress, while fierce French resistance held up further attempts to push towards Verdun. Knobelsdorf ordered his guns to keep pace with the advance, but it was what the Crown Prince called 'a matter of endless time and difficulty' to redeploy them, such was the sodden state of the ground, which had already been churned up by the heavy shelling. By the end of the month the offensive had stalled.[2]

Fifth Army now urgently required a fresh infusion of troops and better weather, neither of which was likely to be forthcoming. Falkenhayn was not minded to let the Crown Prince have everything he wanted, even if he agreed that the 'discomfort' caused by French flanking fire 'had to be stopped' as soon as possible. He was also aware that there was some way to go before the French Army was exhausted. OHL's Intelligence Section estimated that the French had deployed somewhere between fifteen and eighteen divisions at Verdun by the end of February, but still had considerable reserves not yet engaged, so Falkenhayn agreed to send two more divisions to Knobelsdorf to enable him to extend the attack on to the western (left)

bank of the Meuse on 6 March.[3] But the weather remained uncooperative. The forested heights lay hidden in dark, heavy clouds,
while snowstorms rolled in across the battlefield, oblivious to the
life-and-death struggle taking place on the frozen ground, now littered with thousands of corpses, slowly decomposing in the thin air.

The morning of 6 March was murky with flurries of snow as Germany's massed batteries opened fire at 7 a.m., their muzzle flashes
flickering in the morning haze. For four hours they pounded French
positions along a series of villages and wide sweeping valleys on the
west bank, stripping away what little vegetation was left and blowing
away the rows of barbed wire that cloaked the French defences. The
'smoke rose to an incredible height,' remembered one French machine-
gunner, 'forming a curtain so thick not even the sun could pierce
through'.[4] The ground was more open on this side of the river, but
gradually swelled to two important tactical features: Hill 304 and the
Mort Homme ('dead man's hill'), upon which the main French line of
resistance had been dug. These hillocks commanded the battlefield,
providing a perfect shelter for French guns, while giving their observers a panoramic view of the German lines. General Heinrich von
Gossler, commander of a two-corps assault group, had been given the
task of breaking the French line, but could only make grudging progress. A few minutes before eleven o'clock, two divisions stormed
forward and captured the villages of Forges and Regneville, but came
to a halt on the slopes of Mort Homme, French artillery lacerating the
German columns with storms of shrapnel and high explosive.

Pétain had long been expecting a German attack on the left bank,
so when it happened he responded with an attitude of studied non-
chalance. His task as Second Army commander was not, as yet, to
plan a decisive offensive and win the war. It was more prosaic: to
allow his troops to fight and win a defensive battle; to hold on to their
ground and, if necessary, to take it back. After spending five days
recovering from a punishing bout of pneumonia (caught after a night
spent in the draughty bedroom of a local notary), he had begun the
process of organizing and managing what was becoming a battle of
enormous material appetites, consuming men, munitions and supplies at an alarming rate. Because Verdun was at the end of long and

congested supply routes, there was a danger that the defence might simply become unsustainable. The main rail lines from both the south and west (via Saint-Mihiel and Reims respectively) were out of action, either occupied by the enemy or vulnerable to shelling. Until a new connection could be completed to Revigny (from where it could access the main line to Paris), Second Army had to rely upon the road from Bar-le-Duc, about thirty miles to the south, which became a vital artery, the *Voie Sacrée*, or 'sacred way', that supplied the French defence with everything it needed.[5]

Every day, either from the window in his office or from the front steps, Pétain would stare at the long lines of French troops, now mostly clad in their *horizon-bleu* uniforms, marching past the Town Hall at Souilly. The sound was continuous; a cacophony of mess tins clanging and boots crunching over the gravel, interspersed with motor vehicles of all kinds, melding into a great jarring noise that continued night and day. 'Huddled into uncomfortable trucks, or bowed under the weight of their packs when they marched on foot, they encouraged each other with songs and banter to appear indifferent. I loved the confident glance with which they saluted me', was how Pétain described the scene. 'But the discouragement with which they returned! – either singly, maimed or wounded, or in the ranks of their companies thinned by their losses. Their eyes stared into space as if transfixed by a vision of terror.'[6] Between 27 February and 6 March, the *Voie Sacrée* delivered 23,000 tons of ammunition, 2,500 tons of supplies and 190,000 men to the city of Verdun; a prodigious effort that ensured the battle could be continued.[7]

Galvanizing his troops on the ground was only one element of Pétain's remarkable impact at Verdun. In the air, the *Eindecker* had ruled the skies since the battle had opened, with Germany's leading 'ace', Oswald Boelcke, amassing ten kills by the middle of March. Pétain quickly realized that something had to change, and within days of taking charge he had entrusted Major Charles Tricornot de Rose, a 39-year-old pilot and squadron commander, with organizing the French effort in the air. 'Clear the skies for me', Pétain is said to have told him, 'I'm blind!'[8] Rose began to concentrate fighter strength in the Verdun area, combining six fighter squadrons into a *groupement* under his own command, equipped with either Morane-Saulnier monoplanes or, if possible, Nieuport biplanes, and recruiting the best pilots, including an eccentric band of American volunteers who formed the Lafayette Escadrille. They were then ordered to mount aggressive patrols, usually in teams of four or five aircraft, which allowed them to overwhelm their opponents and ensure that their reconnaissance squadrons and balloons were able to observe the battlefield unimpeded.

During the course of the fighting above Verdun, a cadre of deadly flyers emerged that would become some of the most celebrated French 'aces' of the war. Georges Guynemer and Charles Nungesser were two of the most prominent members of de Rose's *groupement*. Guynemer was a delicate and sickly 21-year-old, convinced that he would not live long, who was dedicated to fighting as ruthlessly as possible, diving into combats with reckless abandon. He was killed in September 1917 after amassing over fifty victories. Nungesser was equally cavalier, a 'man of iron' who would be wounded seventeen times, but eventually reach a total of forty-three kills. In the early days of the battle, perhaps none were more impressive than the 20-year-old Jean Marie Dominique Navarre, 'an angular-faced, dark-eyed collection of nervous energy', who did his best to wrest control of the skies from Germany almost singlehandedly. Navarre shot down two enemy aircraft in a single day on 25 February – the day Douaumont had fallen – and continued to add to his tally throughout the spring. Flying a Nieuport XI Bébé, a fast and manoeuvrable little biplane introduced in January 1916, he pioneered an aggressive and merciless style of flying: firstly circling overhead until he spotted an appropriate victim, he would dive down, often right into the middle of an enemy formation, to find his kill.[9] Unlike the *Eindecker*, the Nieuports did not have a synchronized machine-gun, relying instead upon a Lewis gun mounted on the top wing, but they proved highly effective in the shell-tossed skies over Verdun and were soon in service with the British, thus helping to end the 'Fokker Scourge'.

On the ground, the fighting continued with undiminished violence. Heralded by a flurry of *Minenwerfer* fire, another German thrust was launched on the right bank on the morning of 8 March with the aim of taking Fort Vaux. Likened by one French authority to a cruiser (as compared to Douaumont's battleship), Vaux was one of the smaller forts at Verdun, but it was still a vital part of the defensive system and the French fought hard for it. A German officer from 19 Infantry Regiment recorded how he attempted to lead his platoon forward, but 'only a few followed'. With four men he managed to get within 150 metres of the fortress only to come under 'horrific' machine-gun fire.

> We sought refuge in a shell hole, but it was full of water. We lay flat on the ground behind the piles of earth created by the shells. No one dared stir or lift their head. The machine-gun fire was constant. A grenade exploded in front of us; a splinter shattered the thigh of the man to my left . . . We pressed even closer to the ground. It was impossible to bandage the wounded. We lay for five hours on the hard, cold ground in the face of this relentless fire. In the evening, one survivor and I managed to rejoin the battalion.[10]

With the Germans unable to push on through the thick wire entanglements that lay around Fort Vaux, the attack broke down. Knobelsdorf kept trying, ordering left and right hooks as often as he could, hoping to pull French reserves out of position, and allow his troops to push on through the fortress system, but the French defence was more organized now and better supplied, and its artillery was still causing German commanders huge problems from flanking fire.

On 14 March, General Gossler launched a renewed attack on Mort Homme, supported by the fire of fifteen heavy batteries, which allowed them to seize the northern part of the ridge. The battlefield now resembled an unearthly, smoking wasteland. Most of the trenches had been levelled by an artillery barrage, leaving a devastated, desolate zone where soldiers, either singly or in small groups, tried to find their way through the shell holes, carrying a rifle or clusters of grenades. Fighting was incredibly disorientating. 'What a sight this battlefield was,' recalled one French officer, 'sharing nothing in common with all the different theatres of war that we had seen until this point. There were small woods that only had one or two trees, the rest all knocked over; corpses were colliding everywhere,

an arm here, a leg there; in a corner a *turco* [Algerian sniper] was seated without any wounds: he had died of asphyxiation. Trenches are tunnels and only offer a little protection and you have to wait for the enemy and keep careful watch.'[11]

The deadlock on the west bank was deeply frustrating for German commanders raised on the spectacular operations of the past. Peering through his binoculars at the stormy front, trying to piece together what was happening amid the smoke and dust, the Crown Prince could only lament the terrible situation in which the Germans found themselves. 'We had now,' he noted, 'after the first victorious rush of the grand attack, been caught in the costly and fatal toils of fierce local fighting, and could only hope for the negative success of inflicting more losses than we suffered.'[12] He admitted that 'distant objectives' were now being given to his men in the hope that this would spur them on to a 'deep penetration', but this only tended to produce rising casualties and lowered morale when such objectives were not realized. It did not take much to work out that the fighting around Mort Homme was beginning to suck the life out of his army. VI Reserve Corps, which had spearheaded the attack, sustained nearly 10,000 casualties between 6 and 20 March. Officer losses had also been 'frighteningly high'. In the fighting around Forges, 82 Reserve Infantry Regiment lost its regimental commander and five battalion commanders. Losses were so heavy that both II and III Battalions were being led by lieutenants (who would normally have commanded platoons).[13]

The suspicion that the German Army was floundering around without a clear strategy was compounded by confusion and disagreement about Germany's wider war effort. Operation *Gericht* had originally been designed to run in parallel with a renewed campaign of U-boat sinkings, but no decision had yet been taken, which owed a great deal to Falkenhayn's main opponent, the Chancellor, Bethmann Hollweg. For him, there was little chance Germany could strangle Britain within an acceptable time frame. Moreover, if the United States entered the war, then it would be impossible for Germany to win a contest of attrition against the Entente. On 4 March, a Crown Council meeting was held at Charleville, where the arguments were repeated at length. Bethmann Hollweg had not moved from his earlier opposition and declined to support a renewed campaign. 'He was very nervous,' recalled the Chief of the Naval Cabinet, Alexander von Müller, 'smoked cigarette after cigarette and kept moving from one chair to the other. He is determined to avoid a break with America and almost as much determined to dismiss anyone who opposes his decisions.'[14] Falkenhayn, alternating between cold aloofness and his best courtier's smile, pushed for a new campaign as soon as possible. 'Submarine warfare strikes at the enemy's most sensitive spot,' he argued, 'because it aims at severing his overseas communications', and there was, therefore, 'no justification on military grounds for refusing any further to employ what promises to be our most effective weapon'.[15]

For the man who had to decide, the stakes could not have been higher. The Kaiser was now suffering from unwelcome waves of pessimism and defeatism, his nerves 'strained to breaking point'.[16] When he announced that a final decision would be postponed for another month, there was a furious response from those who wanted firmer action. On 10 March, Falkenhayn demanded 'the immediate launching of a ruthless U-boat campaign with an appeal to save the nation and dynasty', while Admiral von Tirpitz had already lost any lingering confidence in the Supreme War Lord. In a memorandum written in February 1916, he had called for the 'immediate and relentless recourse to the submarine weapon . . . Any further delay in the introduction of unrestricted warfare will give England time for further naval and economic defensive measures, cause us greater losses in the end, and endanger quick success . . . If we defeat England, we break the backbone of the hostile coalition.'[17] But he was ignored. Two days later (on 12 March) Tirpitz submitted his resignation (which was accepted). The 'bleeding white' would now only take place on land.

Falkenhayn may have decried the Kaiser's decision, but the halting U-boat campaign seemed to sum up his time in command of Germany's war effort and condemn him to further accusations that he was too indecisive and half-hearted to really fight and win the war. He consented to operations on the Eastern Front, but they were never meant to achieve decisive results, only limited ones. He ordered the first use of gas on the Western Front, but only as part of a small-scale attack that was soon called off. And now the U-boat campaign would continue in fits and starts, doing just enough to alienate neutral countries, but without being pressed to a definitive conclusion. Even Verdun was threatening to become a significant drain on resources without crippling the French Army. Falkenhayn had hoped to kill five Frenchmen for every two Germans, but as the winter weather faded away into warm, bright spring days, there was a bloody equivalence to the losses on either side. By the end of March, the French Army had suffered about 89,000 casualties at Verdun. German losses were almost the same. Every ten days, Fifth Army would send casualty reports back to OHL. By 31 March its total stood at 81,607.[18]

In London the British Government had emerged from what had seemed like a never-ending succession of political crises. The Military Service Act had been passed in January 1916, calling up all unmarried men, or widowers without dependants, between the ages of eighteen and forty-one (with certain exemptions).[19] Although it was opposed by elements of the Labour and Liberal Parties, Asquith's government was able to push it through over their objections, concerned that the war could not be won without another significant infusion of manpower into the armed forces. There still remained disagreements in the Cabinet over whether to press for universal conscription or hold off until the following year, but the Act was a powerful indication of the seriousness with which Britain was now taking the war. 'Victory springs, as history shows, from the preponderance of the sum of all physical and moral powers combined', wrote the military correspondent of *The Times* on 22 February, 'and we cannot afford to neglect any one of these factors for an instant. We have stayed the enemy, but we have not yet beaten him.'[20]

As for what to do with these forces, there was as yet no consensus. The basic outline for an Allied spring offensive had been agreed at Chantilly in December 1915, but its precise arrangements remained to be determined. Joffre and Haig had sketched out a rough plan for both British and French Armies to mount a combined attack on the Somme scheduled for 1 July, but after the Germans attacked Verdun, the question of bringing it forward became increasingly urgent. At an inter-Allied conference on 12 March, it was agreed that the coalition would 'undertake combined offensive operations at the earliest possible date', which finally forced the British Government into action.[21] While Sir William Robertson urged an attack, there remained considerable unease in the War Cabinet about the risks of such a vast undertaking. The chief dissenter was the Minister of Munitions, David Lloyd George. Like other so-called 'Easterners', Lloyd George was wary of deepening British commitments to the Western Front and cast furtive glances elsewhere, to either the Balkans or the Middle

East. Although the 'Easterners' had their fingers burnt by the abject failure of the Gallipoli expedition, they hung on tenaciously to their conviction that there must be an alternative to massive, endless offensives on the Western Front. Lloyd George had visited GHQ in January 1916, but found the Commander-in-Chief a difficult individual to gauge. Although he was keen to praise Haig as 'very keen and businesslike', his entreaties were rebuffed, Haig privately recording that the Welshman was 'shifty and unreliable'.[22]

As for Kitchener, he had been strongly against the offensive of the previous autumn, but had reluctantly accepted that the British could not avoid it without imperilling the Entente. He had once been a towering figure, able to dominate proceedings with just a wink or a slight nod of the head, but now he was a tortured individual, struggling to free himself from his bonds. By the early months of 1916, K was becoming isolated – half in, half out – wanting to support the French but queasy about the implications of mass offensives on the Western Front (in which he found an unlikely ally in Lloyd George). He would have preferred to wait until the autumn, giving the French Army more time to ready its divisions for battle and stock up on the vast quantities of shells that would almost certainly be required. But as this was becoming increasingly unlikely, he was left hoping that the armies he had raised would not be squandered in ill-fated and hasty attacks. He visited Haig on 29 March and warned him 'to beware of the French, and to husband the strength of the Army in France'.[23]

Because the Prime Minister was away on a trip to Italy, it was not until 7 April that the question of the offensive was considered by the War Cabinet. The subsequent discussion revolved around the nature of the planned offensive: how did it differ from previous attacks, would it succeed, and what did it mean for the coalition war effort? Differences of opinion were soon apparent.

'The question of what was really meant by the "General Offensive" was very difficult to understand', pondered Kitchener. 'We were on the offensive all along the line now. Did it mean that after Verdun, we were to push ahead, or was it to be something like the operations in Champagne?'

Robertson tried to smooth over any niggling doubts. 'Sir D. Haig would adjust the kind of fight which he intended to put up according to circumstances. If he was convinced that the French intended to leave all the fighting to him, then he would shut down at once. General Haig was perfectly alive to the situation, and would not do any foolish thing.'

'What would happen if the contemplated offensive failed?' asked Lloyd George, only for Asquith to brush the question aside.

'Any appearance of hanging back on our part would have a bad effect on the French.'[24]

The problem for the 'Easterners' was that there seemed no easy way to (in Lloyd George's words) 'smash the Turks'. At that moment, in Mesopotamia – the one theatre that had seemed immune from the series of reverses so far – concern was growing over the fate of 6th Indian Division, which had become besieged at the town of Kut on the Tigris river. Major-General Charles Townshend's force would eventually surrender on 29 April, condemning 8,000 men to the tender mercies of incarceration in the Ottoman Empire – fewer than half of whom would survive. The terrible news in the Middle East also coincided with another disaster nearer to home when Irish nationalists seized buildings and proclaimed an Irish republic from the steps of the General Post Office in central Dublin. Although the rising was quickly suppressed, such depressing events concentrated minds in London on the absolute need for a military success somewhere. The question revolved around the kind of operation that Haig wanted to undertake, whether it would be a grand breakthrough-style attack or something more limited. For Kitchener, any attempt to repeat the 'same line of action' as Champagne would be 'a great mistake', although it was clear that Haig had to be given authority to act as he saw fit. With no easy alternative available, there was an acceptance that they had to go ahead, but only on the understanding that Haig would be careful; that he would not, as Robertson assured them, 'make a fool of himself'.

Everything now depended upon Haig and the forces he commanded. The expeditionary force that Sir John French had led to war in August 1914 was no more. What few survivors there were left from the original four divisions had been subsumed into a wider, broader stream of manpower that was now flowing into France. By the beginning of 1916, the British Army on the Western Front had risen to almost forty infantry divisions (plus five cavalry divisions), about one million men in total, its ranks swollen by hundreds of thousands of Kitchener's volunteers, as well as reservists, territorials and two divisions of Canadians. Although its numerical strength was now, finally, able to compare with the mass armies on the Continent, the military effectiveness of this 'collection of divisions untrained for the field' (as Haig described it in his diary) was questionable.[25] Life in the New Armies had been long on physical activity and repetitive drill, but short on weapons training and tactical exercises. The men of 'Kitchener's Army' were enthusiastic, keen and physically fit; buoyed by a glowing sense of pride and moral certainty, but untested in combat.

By the spring of 1916, the British sector of the Western Front was extending quickly. General d'Urbal's Tenth Army, which had tried, time and again, to break the German line near Arras, had been relieved by troops of the British First and Third Armies, and Fourth Army, commanded by General Sir Henry Rawlinson, had gone into the line further south. The BEF was now stretched along a seventy-mile front from north of Ypres all the way down to Maricourt. This southern sector, astride the winding valley of the River Somme, would be the focus of the next Allied offensive. It was a region that had hitherto largely escaped serious fighting (apart from some scraps during September and October 1914) and was where the British and French sectors now met. Although it offered the best place for a joint Allied attack, the Germans had spent the intervening months fortifying it heavily, and what had once been a bucolic place of rolling fields and shimmering vistas had been transformed into a formidable defensive position, consisting of two separate lines of trenches, maze-like in their complexity.

On 27 March, Joffre wrote to Haig and updated him on how he saw the forthcoming attack now that Germany had revealed her hand at Verdun.

The question of whether there should be preliminary attacks by Franco-English forces no longer arises. In fact, the consumption of men and ammunition that we had to expend in the Battle of Verdun is such that I cannot, on the French forces' front, consider any other offensive action than a main attack south of the Somme . . . The other fact to be considered is that German forces on the Western Front are themselves severely weakened because of their prolonged offensive in the Verdun region and that, under these conditions, their reserves (or at least the reserves of men that they'll have at the time of our attacks) will be weaker than we thought.

The aim should be to break the German line between Hébuterne and Lassigny and then exploit out towards the east.[26] After receiving authorization from London, Haig replied on 10 April. 'If, as seems probable, we find that the enemy has used up his reserves in his unsuccessful efforts at Verdun, I agree that preparatory attacks will not be required and that better results are likely to be gained by devoting all the forces available to the main offensive.' He wanted the 'closest possible combination, both in space and time' with their respective attacks and urged a simultaneous push 'along the whole front'. He expected to employ about 20–23 divisions.[27]

The man who would lead the British part of the operation was Henry Rawlinson, the Fourth Army commander. Fifty-two years old in 1916, Rawlinson was tall and bald-headed, with a long, rangy stride. Educated at Eton and Sandhurst, 'Rawly' was an infantryman who, like most of his contemporaries, had served across the empire before the war, including in South Africa, where he was assigned a column to hunt Boers across the Veldt. In 1914, he was given command of a division, which he led during the 'Race to the Sea' (the frantic Allied dash towards the coast), before taking over IV Corps in time for the battles of 1915. He had enjoyed some success, breaking the German front line at Neuve Chapelle and Loos, but struggling to get through their reserve positions, an experience that gave him an appreciation of how important artillery fire was to any attack. His task would now be infinitely more complex: to prepare his unwieldy forces for a major assault on the Somme. It was 'capital country', he reckoned, with 'excellent observation' that would allow his artillery to batter the German defences and 'avoid the heavy losses which the infantry have always suffered on previous occasions'.[28]

By 3 April, Rawlinson and his Chief of Staff, Archibald Montgomery, had put together a plan for an attack on the Somme. Ten divisions would break the German line along a 20,000-yard front between the villages of Serre and Mametz. Although the German first line was formidable, with numerous fortified villages protected by plenty of barbed wire, Rawlinson was confident that his artillery could deal with it. The problem was how to break the second line, which lay about 4,000 yards further in. Because it had been constructed on the reverse slope, it was not observable from the British positions, which meant that Rawlinson could not guarantee its destruction. He did not think that a single attack could break through both lines and worried lest his inexperienced troops become disorganized if they tried to push on too far (as had happened at Loos). 'The troops are bound to become disorganised in a rush of this sort over 3,000 to 4,000 yards of broken ground . . .' Therefore, any attempt to go through the enemy's defences in one push 'will, under the conditions that obtain, involve very serious risks and will be in the nature of a gamble'.[29]

Given the strength of the German defences, Rawlinson felt that the attack should be split into two stages, conquering each line in turn after heavy bombardments, perhaps taking as long as two weeks. Although Rawlinson had much less combat experience than his French counterparts, he was already coming to a similar realization that it was useless to try to break through in one great surge forward. Instead they must concentrate on capturing each German position in turn, relying upon their guns to conquer what the infantry could then occupy.

> It does not appear to me that the gain of 2 or 3 more kilometres of ground is of much consequence, or that the existing situation is so urgent as to demand that we should incur very heavy losses in order to draw a large number of German reserves against this portion of our front. Our object rather seems to be to kill as many Germans as possible with the least loss to ourselves, and the best way to do this appears to me to be to seize points of tactical importance which will provide us with good observation and which we may feel quite certain the Germans will counter attack.

This was what he called 'bite and hold', but here Rawlinson sensed trouble with Haig. 'I daresay I shall have a tussle with him over the limited objective', he wrote in his diary; 'for I hear he is inclined to favour the unlimited with the chance of breaking the German line.'[30]

Rawlinson's concerns were well founded. Haig had a reputation as a thoughtful soldier, quiet and restrained, a man of method and reason, but his view of warfare remained staunchly traditional. A cavalryman by background, Haig never possessed the kind of flair and fury that had characterized the career of Sir John French, but he still believed deeply – much as Joffre had done in 1914 – that the fundamental factors in warfare were high morale and the offensive spirit. The debacle at Loos had not forced a reconsideration of these principles, which were reaffirmed in a note he authored in January 1916 that poured cold water on the idea that they should fight a limited series of preparatory battles to wear out the German Army. On the contrary, the best course of action was to launch simultaneous, decisive attacks that promised 'great results' if they could be conducted in 'sufficient force'. When Joffre explained that he no longer thought separate, preliminary 'wearing out battles' were needed, Haig swiftly cast aside any residual caution. There was no middle ground. If they were to go, they were to go all out.[31]

But going 'all out' was not what Rawlinson had in mind, and Haig was not impressed by Fourth Army's plan. 'I studied Sir H. Rawlinson's proposals for attack', he wrote in his diary. 'His intention is merely to take the enemy's first and second system of trenches and "kill Germans" . . . I think we can do better than this by aiming at getting as large a combined force of French and British across the Somme and fighting the enemy in the open!'[32] In a strange reversal of the situation that Falkenhayn had faced with the Crown Prince (with the former wanting a limited, attritional attack and the latter seeking a decisive objective), Haig complained that Rawlinson's attack was too cautious. 'It is, of course, inadvisable to push on isolated and disorganised bodies of troops beyond the reach of possible support . . . On the other hand, the importance of using every endeavour to surprise the enemy at the outset and to take full advantage of the confusion and disorganisation in his forces resulting from our first assault can scarcely be over-rated.' The risks that Rawlinson had highlighted were waved away. They could be 'foreseen and to a great extent guarded against by careful previous arrangement'. Therefore, Haig directed Rawlinson to give 'further consideration' to the 'possibility of pushing our first advance further than is contemplated in your plan'. He also raised the prospect of a much shorter, more intensive 'hurricane' bombardment (in place of the longer destructive bombardment that Fourth Army had specified) that would have a sharp, shattering effect on the enemy garrison.[33]

Rawlinson read Haig's letter with growing concern. He did his best to hold his ground, sending off an amended plan to GHQ on 19 April, which repeated the reasons for his caution, particularly the distance his troops would have to cover; the problem of cutting the wire in front of the second line; and the general inexperience of his men (and their likely disorganization). Moreover, he reiterated that a longer bombardment was still preferable because it would allow for greater destruction and prevent the enemy from bringing up ammunition and food. Haig's response, again, was lukewarm. When Rawlinson wrote that his operations would be 'sustained over a considerable period of time', Haig scrawled 'The enemy must be beaten!' on the document in blue pencil. Although Haig finally agreed to the nature of the bombardment, authorizing 'methodical' preparation until all obstacles had been destroyed, he reiterated that Fourth Army needed to prepare for a deeper advance and directed Rawlinson to include Serre, Pozières, Contalmaison and Montauban in the first day's objectives – villages that lay further away and, in places, right on the German second line; exactly the situation that Rawlinson wanted to avoid.[34] Thus the scene was set for one of the greatest mistakes of the war.

Throughout April and May, as Haig and Rawlinson jostled over the planning of the Somme, Verdun remained a simmering cauldron of activity. Every day fresh troops, from both sides, travelled to take their place on the amphitheatre of hills that surrounded the city, and every day the survivors returned, hollowed out by their experiences. The battle now seemed to have a life of its own, shorn of the guiding lights of strategy and policy, having descended into a brutal killing match driven on by its own logic. At the end of March, Falkenhayn had told the Crown Prince that the attack must be continued for as long as they were suffering fewer casualties than their opponents, but within days he was wavering in the face of rising casualties and negligible results on the ground. On 4 April, he wrote again: 'If we win the battle, then our prospects of ending the war soon will increase very much. If we do not win it, then after everything achieved so far, a victorious ending will be delayed but not adversely affected as long as we decide in good time not to get bogged down at Verdun but to dictate terms to the enemy elsewhere.'[35]

At OHL the question of what Germany should do seemed to have no answer. 'No one knows how to end Verdun', Groener admitted in early April. 'Falkenhayn seems to me to have serious doubts as to whether he will succeed in taking Verdun.'[36] Perhaps not realizing Falkenhayn's original purpose in attacking the city, Groener assumed that it was about seizing ground. As for Falkenhayn, he found himself increasingly hemmed in by the situation. Discussions had been ongoing with Rupprecht about the possibility of launching an offensive to take the city of Arras, which the British had recently occupied, but disagreements over how many troops would be available meant that the attack was never made. Rupprecht requested eight extra divisions, but OHL could only supply four, and with most of the heavy artillery on the Verdun front there was little appetite to make the attempt.[37] By the end of April, the possibility of the Arras offensive had been shelved, leaving Rupprecht wondering what was going on. 'What distresses me most', he wrote in his diary, 'is that General von Falkenhayn apparently no longer thinks a decisive victory can possibly be won. In that event, how must the war end for us?'[38]

Falkenhayn returned, once again, to the matter of submarine warfare. 'Long discussion with His Excellency about continuing operations and the U-boat question', Tappen recorded in his diary on 28 April. 'An end to the war with England is not foreseeable without an intensified U-boat campaign and the same applies to our other opponents.'[39] Falkenhayn tried to get the Kaiser to restart the sinkings, but the attempt foundered after the attack on a French steamer, *Sussex*, on 24 March, resulting in the loss of about eighty lives, including several Americans.

In response, Washington threatened to sever diplomatic relations with Berlin unless it immediately abandoned 'its present methods of submarine warfare against passenger and freight-carrying vessels', which it regarded as being 'utterly incompatible with the principles of humanity, the long-established and incontrovertible rights of neutrals, and the sacred immunities of non-combatants'. Immediately the Kaiser recoiled from this threat, and, on 4 May, Bethmann Hollweg announced that German naval forces would henceforth follow established principles of 'visit and search' and would no longer sink merchant vessels without warning (unless they tried to escape or fight back).[40]

Angry and disappointed, Falkenhayn went to see the Kaiser on 2 May and complained that as he had not been consulted on the note, he had no choice but to tender his resignation. The Supreme War Lord feigned surprise and shock, and attendants were soon on hand to try to bring Falkenhayn around, but their relationship was never the same. With no chance that Germany would try to win the war at sea, Falkenhayn was left with the operation at Verdun, which was now an unwanted battle, but one that could not be dispensed with given how much had been staked upon its success. So on it went. Falkenhayn allowed attacks to continue, but only in a limited fashion and on a small scale. He provided reinforcements but never enough to relieve sufficient front-line troops or allow for a major attack all along the line; a perfect reflection of his ambivalence: giving with one hand and taking away with the other.

The Germans continued to attack on the west bank throughout late spring, taking Mort Homme on 9 April, only for the weather to turn bad and prevent any exploitation for the next few weeks. A renewed attack on 3 May succeeded in wresting most of Hill 304 from French hands, but there was no sudden breakthrough or rapid decline in enemy fighting power. Progress was equally tortuous on the east bank, where, ever since Douaumont had fallen, the German Army had found itself fighting around prepared positions under terrible flanking fire. On 21 April, General Bruno von Mudra, commander of a combined assault group, wrote to the Crown Prince on the difficulties they were having and the mounting losses caused by the 'ever strengthening enemy artillery fire'. His men were subjected to 'constant heavy and field artillery fire in their positions, from multiple flanks, sometimes from behind; the supporting communications, the reserve camps and even the supply dumps are exposed in the same way to enemy fire of all calibres. Thus the advanced infantry positions are suffering heavy losses on a daily basis, and this is no less the case in their communications and in their camps; the transport of food supplies and other additional needs takes up a disproportionate amount of time and effort.[41]

The Crown Prince knew that it was too dangerous for his army to remain in their current positions, but it was equally evident that any attempt to continue attacking was fraught with risk. Decisive success, he believed, 'could only be assured at the price of heavy sacrifices, out of all proportion to the desired gains'. Matters were not helped by a growing estrangement with his Chief of Staff, Knobelsdorf, who remained wedded to the offensive and urged him to 'hold fast to the idea of attacking and wearing down the enemy'. Knobelsdorf had been assigned to Fifth Army as a safe pair of hands – someone to guide the impetuous young prince – but he was now carrying on as if Wilhelm were of no consequence. He urged Falkenhayn to keep going and dismissed the Crown Prince's pessimism, even conspiring to have one of his senior personal officers (Lieutenant-Colonel von Heymann) banished to a regiment of Foot Guards, which caused Wilhelm 'deep regret'.[42] When the Crown Prince complained to his father that he was being sidelined, he was ignored.

The squabbles in the German High Command over the purpose of the offensive were mirrored in the French Army. From his office at Souilly, Pétain instinctively understood how demanding the battle was becoming, so he rotated battalions regularly in and out of the line (rather than following the German practice of keeping units at the front until they became exhausted). This helped his troops to cope much better with the strains of combat, although it did require a continuous movement of divisions through the Verdun sector, which limited Joffre's freedom of manoeuvre elsewhere. By the beginning of April, Joffre was becoming alarmed at how Verdun was sucking in more and more divisions and warping his plans for the rest of the year. 'To be able to judge if it's necessary to send you some new divisions to replace XXI Corps, could you send me a telegram with how you intend to deploy III and XII Corps . . . ?' was Joffre's some-what schoolmasterly response to Pétain's demands for reinforcements on 2 April. 'You know the overall situation of the enemy and that of French forces. You should, therefore, do all you can to avoid me having to deploy the last completely fresh corps that I have available for the time being when having it in reserve is of obvious significance to our allies, as well as because of our future plans . . . This is the only way that the battle for Verdun will become a total defeat for the enemy without leading to a depletion in our forces, which would neutralize our army's unquestionable success.'[43]

Joffre had originally envisaged attacking on the Somme with thirty-nine divisions and 1,700 heavy guns, but as the long saga of Verdun dragged on, and as more and more units were embroiled in it, he was forced to downscale the French contribution. In late April, this was reduced to thirty divisions and 300 heavy guns, and a month later just twenty-six divisions. Even this assumption did not last very long, and on 27 May GQG was anticipating including only twenty divisions.[44] Foch, who as head of France's Northern Army Group was responsible for the French side of the battle, had never been particularly keen on Joffre's plans for 1916. He would have preferred to attack Vimy Ridge again, feeling that the Somme lacked a crucial tactical objective, and as Verdun consumed more manpower, he even raised the question of whether to attack at all.[45] But with Joffre unyielding on this point, Foch had no choice but to order Sixth Army, now commanded by General Émile Fayolle, to extend the British attack south of the Somme.

Joffre puzzled over how to handle Pétain. The man from the north was now one of the best-known generals in France, beloved of his men, which made him increasingly difficult to control. It was not just that Pétain's demands for manpower were (from Joffre's perspective) too lavish; it was also that the commander of Second Army seemed unenthusiastic about counter-attacking and driving the enemy away. Joffre was also feeling the heat of renewed scrutiny from Paris, where the Senate Army Commission, led by the eccentric Senator Georges Clemenceau, sat in judgement on the French war effort, with the Commander-in-Chief a regular target of abuse. A new Minister of War, General Pierre Roques, had been appointed in March 1916 (replacing the ailing Galliéni), and although he and Joffre were old friends, Roques was under unrelenting pressure to bring Joffre to heel. On 23 March, Joffre was told that two of his most senior officers, Generals Langle de Cary and Dubail, both army group commanders, should be retired and newer, younger men put in their places. With the walls now closing in, Joffre did as he was told, taking the opportunity to promote Pétain to Army Group Centre (a position he would take up on 1 May), thereby removing him – at least in theory – from day-to-day contact with the battle and allowing someone else to prosecute it with more aggression.[46]

Joffre inspected the Verdun front the day after the attack on Mort Homme (10 April) and was favourably impressed by the commander of III Corps, Lieutenant-General Robert Georges Nivelle, who he believed might just be the man he was looking for. Pétain, he felt, needed 'a more distant perspective' and 'a clearer view'. He was too pessimistic, obsessed with Verdun alone and perhaps not appreciative of the need to wage an offensive and aggressive war against the enemy.[47] Nivelle, on the contrary, possessed all the drive and optimism that Joffre could want. He came from a village in Corrèze in central France and had shown great promise since the beginning of the war with his courageous and imaginative leadership, rising from commander of a regiment of artillery in August 1914 to a Lieutenant-General just over a year later. Nivelle was a warm-blooded soldier who prided himself on his technical abilities and who was convinced that a more aggressive style of fighting could succeed at Verdun. When he took over command of Second Army, skipping up the steps of the Town Hall at Souilly with the spring of a much younger man (he was fifty-nine years old), he promised to make an impression, to give France something to cheer. That could only mean one thing: the recapture of Fort Douaumont – exactly what Joffre wanted to hear.

Nivelle knew that the attack had to be led by someone with an unquestioned faith in the offensive. He chose the commander of 5th Division, Major-General Charles Mangin, who was, as he put it, 'the only one who wants to attack'.[48] Mangin had formed a close relationship with Nivelle and was straining at the leash for promotion, convinced that Douaumont held the key to his personal advancement.

Working closely with Nivelle, who provided him with as much artillery and ammunition as could be spared, Mangin made sure that his officers were thoroughly familiar with the attack plan. They visited other French forts and were briefed by engineers who had worked on Douaumont. Aerial photographs were also distributed liberally to help familiarize them with its layout, and on 17 May the preliminary bombardment began. For five days, French guns battered the fortress and its approaches, while engineering companies laboured tirelessly to build saps and forward trenches to narrow the width of no-man's-land. And then, several days before the attack, Mangin addressed his men, urging them to seize their objective: 'In you the hearts of twelve thousand brave men rejoice, filled with the love of their country, with hatred for the barbarous invader, and with the thirst of just revenge. I salute your past successes and your future exploits, which will be even more illustrious. And I salute Victory that I see hovering over our heads and whose huge wings are making your glorious flags shake.'[49]

Zero Hour was timed for 11.50 a.m. on 22 May. At that precise moment, Mangin's men clambered out of their forming-up trenches and stormed towards the fort, accompanied by a lifting barrage that would 'jump' forward at precise moments to cover their advance. Some French batteries fired 1,200 rounds per gun in a single, furious twenty-four-hour period (about one shell a minute) and never ran out of ammunition.[50] The attacking battalions managed to reach the battered walls of Douaumont despite vicious German machine-gun fire sweeping no-man's-land. There they remained, huddling in small groups in whatever shelter could be found while trying to get inside the fort, which had been barred by the defenders. At two o'clock, a telephone message was received at Second Army headquarters. A reconnaissance aircraft, circling high above the battlefield, had seen 'a substantial number of foot soldiers at Fort Douaumont that he thought were French. A first group entered by the south-west corner . . . and went up to the middle of the fort. A second group was climbing up the moat along the western side. A third group was leaving the fort by the north angle.' Mangin was ecstatic, racing back to see Nivelle, who turned, half in surprise, as Mangin entered his office.

'Douaumont is ours!' he cried.[51]

The scarred, crumbling ruins of Douaumont were not in French hands for long. German counter-attacks were immediately launched, and by 24 May the few remaining French troops still around the fort, scrambling over its carapace like the hide of some great animal, had been killed or captured. Once again, the French were faced with disappointment. Out of 12,000 infantry of Mangin's 5th Division who made the assault, over 5,300 had been killed, wounded or posted missing – its bloodiest single engagement of the war.[1] Mangin put the failure down to the bombardment not being heavy enough and the late arrival of reinforcements, and was confident that, should he be given another opportunity, he would be able to retake the fort without difficulty. 'The 2,000 men of the 5th Infantry Division who have just come down from Douaumont carry the conviction that they have defeated the enemy and that if the conquered ground has not been retained, the cause is the inferiority of the troops who replaced them. They are convinced that with powerful preparation of artillery their attacks will always be successful.' Once the division had been re-formed, Mangin was confident its troops would 'again have the offensive value they have repeatedly demonstrated'.[2]

At Second Army headquarters, General Nivelle wanted to try again. Never one to become too disheartened, he wrote to Pétain on 31 May and urged him to sanction another attack, which would require 'at least two fresh divisions'.[3] Pétain looked upon the failure to retake Douaumont with a hollow feeling of sadness. The casualty figures were bad enough, but what made it worse was the recklessness of the whole affair, pushing a lone division forward into a heavily defended salient, overlooked by the enemy on three sides, and simply assuming that French élan would be enough. Such attacks could never succeed and would only result in straining the Army's already battered morale. Moreover, it was becoming increasingly difficult to keep Second Army up to strength. Joffre had warned Pétain in April that he would have to be content with holding his divisions in the line for longer, and, as the battle dragged on, the problem of properly supplying and manning the front grew rapidly; a situation worsened by the renewal of heavy German attacks and the loss of Fort Vaux on 7 June.

Plans for a new, bigger offensive at Verdun had been circulating at OHL for weeks. Whatever the failures of the battle so far, most senior German officers recognized that there might just be enough time for a big success before the Allied offensive on the Somme got under way. During one of his buoyant, victorious moods, the Kaiser had even stated, his fists clenched, that the German flag would fly atop Verdun by mid-June. Schmidt von Knobelsdorf, whose silver-tongued sermons had convinced Falkenhayn to try again, remained upbeat about finally breaking the French line on the east bank. The aim was to push on from Douaumont and drive through the remaining defences, crippling the French ability to hold on to the city. Guns and men were gradually transferred from the west bank and two corps attacked on the morning of 1 June; the Germans swarming forward 'like ants after someone has kicked over an anthill'.[4] Special teams of pioneers, equipped with flamethrowers, had been brought up to lead the advance. A 'gushing sea of fire poured down on the French, who were crowded into the front trench', recalled one German officer. 'The enemy saw blazing darting jets of flame from immense black clouds of smoke approaching . . . like a natural event of immense size, the unknown phenomenon bore down on him.'[5]

Initially, all went well. 'The first stretch to the French trenches cannot be described', remembered one attacker as he sprang forward. 'We saw only yellow, red and white flashes around us. Through the steam and smoke one sometimes saw the figure of a comrade crumple and fall. The gap was immediately filled by others.' There was little machine-gun fire and, stopping now and again in shell holes to catch their breath, the Germans continued to push on, clearing out bunkers and trenches with grenades or flamethrowers until they reached their objective, a wood known as the Bois de la Caillette, which lay half-way between Douaumont and Vaux. 'About us, half buried in the sand, lay masses of dead French soldiers. Here and there could be seen a piece of a human body . . . Clothing, uniforms, weapons, wagons and ammunition lay everywhere.' Yet the attackers had sustained heavy losses. Flanking fire from Fort Vaux and regular salvos of shell-fire gradually reduced the attacking companies and slowed down the advance, while every attempt to push on to the fortress failed.[6]

There was no thought of stopping the attack. By 2 June, Fort Vaux was under continuous bombardment. Perhaps as many as 1,000 shells an hour struck its thick walls, knocking out the machine-guns and preventing the garrison, 600-strong, from keeping the enemy at bay. Ordered to renew the assault, elements of two German divisions were able to break into the fort and begin clearing out the upper corridors, while the garrison retreated further inside. For the next five days, everything was tried to root them out. Flamethrowers, poison gas, grenades and machine-guns were all used, but still the French held on, fighting behind piles of sandbags and fallen masonry; the air choked with fumes and dust and the dead and wounded forming heaps on the ground. The garrison commander, Major Sylvain-Eugène Raynal, tried to get word to the French lines, releasing all his carrier pigeons, but when no relief came, and with the water supply having failed days' before, he had no choice but to surrender. 'I heard the most astonishing stories of heroism in the fighting around this fort', observed the Crown Prince, who was so impressed with the defenders' bravery that he allowed Raynal to keep his sword.[7]

The loss of Fort Vaux hit the French High Command hard. At Bar-le-Duc, Pétain believed that the 'increasing number of units engaged by the enemy and the increasing intensity of their artillery fire prove without doubt that they seek a quick decision on our part and that they will not rule out any sacrifice in order to get it'. He was concerned that the positions on the east bank were becoming increasingly cramped. Unless the French could maintain an inner defensive line (running from the fort at Froideterre along to Fort Souville and Fort Tavannes), the Germans would be close enough to shell the bridges over the Meuse and thus make Verdun impossible to hold. 'Verdun is threatened, and Verdun must not fall', Pétain wrote to Joffre. 'The occupation of this city would be an invaluable success for the Germans, which would greatly increase their morale and, at the same time, reduce ours. A tactical success of the English, however great, would not compensate the public for the loss of this city, and public opinion currently has a level of importance that cannot be ignored.' Therefore, he asked whether it might be possible to begin the relief offensive sooner. 'The reduction of effect that could result from a premature operation is incomparable to the risk of Verdun falling into the hands of the enemy.'[8]

Joffre was not impressed by Pétain's cries, throwing his hands up in the air when he read the letter, complaining that Pétain had 'once more scared everybody'.[9] He replied the following day (12 June), explaining that there was no choice but to hold on at all costs. 'This is a particularly serious time. The prolonged and victorious defence of Verdun, which has already allowed the successful offensives of our allies in Russia, constitutes the indispensable guarantee and the inescapable condition for the success of the coalition during the current campaign. Nothing has been or must be neglected in order to achieve this result. I count on your action and energy to convey to all your subordinates, officers and soldiers, the same flame of self-sacrifice, passion and confidence that inspires you.'[10] Fortunately, the crisis seemed to pass as quickly as it had arrived. Between 8 and 20 June no new German units were identified at Verdun and the level of artillery fire on the west bank, usually terrific, began to slacken off.

In Paris, the seemingly endless cycle of bad news from Verdun finally forced Aristide Briand, the Prime Minister, to address the growing calls for a parliamentary secret session on the conduct of the war. Calls for such a debate, which would allow French deputies to openly question aspects of the war effort (without the presence of the press), had been voted down on three previous occasions (by conservatives wary of allowing criticism of the High Command), but by June 1916 Briand could put it off no longer. Often compared to David Lloyd George ('the same prominent nose, the same long hair combed back, the same active eyes'),[11] Briand found himself in a curiously similar position, struggling to regain parliamentary control over the military, while also believing strongly in the strategic wisdom of the expedition to Salonika. He had shown himself to be a strong protector of

Joffre throughout 1916, but he was an astute and wily tactician, aware of growing restiveness in the French Parliament and anxious not to be tied too closely to the embattled Commander-in-Chief.

The deputies assembled on 16 June, with the opening speech from André Maginot, a 39-year-old from Paris. Like Abel Ferry, Maginot had gained a reputation as an outspoken and courageous critic of the High Command and he railed against what he claimed were lies told by GQG about the true scale of the losses they were suffering. Comparing French and German casualty statistics, he explained how French losses were proportionally greater than Germany's; something that, he argued, was due to their poor defensive positions and flimsy shelters as well as offensives that produced no significant gains, only 'very deadly losses'. Verdun was another sore point. Maginot read out a letter sent from Galliéni to Joffre in December 1915, in which the Minister of War had drawn attention to the deficiencies in the French defences and the urgent need for them to be refurbished.

> The case of Verdun, gentlemen, in fact illustrates in a striking way everything I have just said. As mentioned the other day . . . it is really quite symbolic; it is proof, without any possible dispute, of the improvidence, the insufficiency of our high command . . . It is painful for me, who would be so happy to be able to say that the losses of our enemies are far superior to those that we suffer, to assume this role of relentless criticism, but you really must know. The interest of the country, its fate itself, requires that the truth be known to you.[12]

The hearings continued for six days; six days of arguments and counter-arguments, accusations and assertions, pages of evidence and testimony, as French politicians poured out their frustration while Joffre's defenders rallied to his cause. Briand himself appeared on day four (19 June) to defend the Government's handling of the war, the role of the Army Commissions and the defence of Verdun.

> The commissioners of the House and Senate Army Commissions have been able to go everywhere at the front to make assessments. They have returned, and they have brought their conclusions. We spoke with them; I have been before the Senate's Committee perhaps fifteen

times, and before the House five or six times. I have not refused to meet with your commissions and they can say that on all points where it was in my power to inform them, I have not hesitated to inform them of the resolutions of the Government. It is possible that this control seems insufficient to you; that you would like to make it more efficient within the limits of your prerogatives. Whatever the procedure you adopt, I can say that the Government will facilitate it.

As for his handling of Verdun, Briand believed there was no case to answer. The policy of rotating divisions through the Meuse had attracted criticism, but the enemy, who had not imitated it, 'had seen entire units destroyed'. 'Now we find on German corpses letters to their families, prepared letters have been found on prisoners, on officers, and even on a divisional general. What do these letters say? They speak of the almost complete annihilation of certain German units, and of the appalling state of fatigue and wear into which the men had fallen.'[13]

Briand did enough. It was a 'very personal' performance noted one onlooker. 'He extolled the government's role to the detriment of Joffre and, while defending the general-in-chief, complacently recalled the comments he had received and the steps he had taken to limit his powers.' A vote of confidence was held on 22 June, which the Government won – 440 votes to 97 – although there was little sense that the critics of the Government had been reconciled.[14] The secret session may have been yet another round in the struggle for control of the French war effort, but it also signified something deeper. It was a cry of frustration and pain from the French deputies who looked upon the carnage all around them, the endless parade of wounded, broken countrymen, and wondered how long could this go on? How many more Frenchmen would have to die before victory would come?

The dramatic events in Paris coincided with an ominous, unsettling lull at Verdun as the German attacks tailed off. For once, France had Russia to thank for her deliverance. On 4 June, the Eastern Front – long dormant since the great retreat of Russian forces the previous summer – burst into life with an enormous attack against the Austro-Hungarians in Galicia. General Aleksei Brusilov, commander of the

Russian Southwest Front, launched a surprise assault which employed many of the latest techniques that had been pioneered on the Western Front, and within a week two Austro-Hungarian armies had broken apart and over 190,000 prisoners were being shepherded to the rear – almost bringing the empire to a sudden and catastrophic collapse.[15] Falkenhayn thus found himself, once again, torn between east and west. The Austrian High Command immediately requested reinforcements, sending streams of urgent telegrams to OHL. Although four divisions were eventually put on trains and transferred to the east, Falkenhayn would part with no more and forced Conrad von Hötzendorf to redeploy troops from the Italian Front. In a tense letter to Conrad, Falkenhayn made it clear that 'Another redeployment to the east is not feasible.' Moreover, Russian gains in the east had not 'shaken the conviction that the war will be decided on the Western Front. On the contrary, it is to be assumed that events will be hastened and made more acute by these operations in so far as the long-prepared Anglo-French offensive will soon begin. The forces present in the West will, as I certainly hope, suffice to ward it off, and then to act according to the circumstances.'[16]

At Verdun the battle was approaching its climax. The Brusilov offensive may have forced Germany to move troops east, but reserves were being accumulated for one last, massive blow on the Meuse. It would be a different kind of offensive: French artillery would now be targeted. The village of Fleury, Fort Souville and the Belleville Ridge, places where French guns were clustered, would be saturated with gas, and once they were knocked out, the infantry would go forward. Early on the morning of 21 June, the summer air without a breath of wind, French battery positions on the east bank were deluged with 'green cross': the codename for phosgene, which was much more toxic than chlorine and could penetrate French gas masks. The response was fitful. German bombardments would usually be answered by a swift, violent burst of counter-battery fire, but that day French artillery officers and their men were struggling to survive; either knocked out on the grass or clawing at mouths and throats and in no condition to service their guns.

Over the next two days the bombardments continued, pulverizing

the French positions and preparing the ground for a powerful infantry thrust led by the Alpine Corps. Once more, the Kaiser made his
way to the front in expectation that the city would fall, and on the
morning of 23 June four corps pushed towards the French defences on
the Thiaumont Ridge, meeting only dazed survivors and regiments
whose fight had already left them. I Bavarian Corps took Thiaumont
(a feat that would later be regarded as 'one of the greatest achievements of the entire Verdun offensive'), while the Alpine Corps
advanced over a mile, reaching Fleury, the air black with smoke and
flame. 'At first everything went well', recorded the Crown Prince,
'but the heavy hostile artillery and machine-gun fire everywhere
checked it before the final objectives could be reached. On the whole
front the ground in rear of our advancing waves was swept by an
impassable belt of fire . . .'[17]

Throughout the day, reports had been coming into Second Army
headquarters of heavy shelling across the front, followed by strong
infantry attacks. General Nivelle remained calm. A staff officer was
impressed by his composed bearing: 'his face a little pale, his profile
regular, sculptural, his eyes slightly veiled, his build solid; physically,
he seemed more reflective than daring; he spoke little, in a low voice
with sober gestures'.[18] He authorized counter-attacks as soon as possible and Mangin, now a corps commander, executed them with his
usual verve. French gunners were also able to pour fire at the breach
in the line (the attack having been pushed along too narrow a front)
and play havoc with German attempts at moving up supplies and
reinforcements, but the French line had become perilously thin –
along one 1,500-yard stretch of front was only a single battered
regiment of *chasseurs*.[19] It all hinged on the availability of reserves,
and here the French held the advantage. Reinforcements were hurrying forward, moving up in long blue-grey columns, flinching as
shells whined close by. One officer, on his way to the Thiaumont sector, described 'the vision of the battlefield' as he ascended 'a ridge
before dark': '[A]n avalanche of shells, bursts, fumes, observation
points and aeroplanes, over an incredible length and depth. This was
really a great sadness. The soul is far from the earth in such moments.
How many prayers went up to the sky, how much contrition, we feel

so small on earth at such a moment . . . All the dead were in piles, it was absolutely necessary to step on them on the way out, and the Germans, having spotted us, opened a barrage of shells; we lay against the slope facing the enemy that formed a blind spot.'[20]

Eventually the German advance slowed and then stopped as units became mixed up and confused. 'It was no longer possible to speak of unified leadership', one account read, 'and maintaining painstakingly precise individual formations proved completely impossible in the churned-up terrain, which had very few reference points left for orientation. In addition, enemy artillery fire was rapidly gaining in strength, increasing at midday to a ferocious intensity, so that even the reserves, who were mostly only deployed in small numbers, reached the battle line cut to pieces and confused. It was mainly small groups of fearless men who carried the attack forward.'[21] When it mattered most, Fifth Army had run out of reserves. Yet again Falkenhayn had launched an attack and let it wither on the vine, providing enough forces to open a way, only to let it fail because of a lack of follow-on troops. Even worse, the nearer it got to Verdun, the stiffer French resistance became. 'It is a decisive time', stated Nivelle in his Order of the Day on 23 June. 'Feeling hunted on all sides, the Germans launch furious and desperate attacks on our front, hoping to reach the gates of Verdun before being attacked themselves by the combined forces of the Allied armies . . . You will not let them pass, comrades!'[22]

At Bar-le-Duc, Pétain, for so long the embodiment of coolness and courage, seemed to lose his legendary poise. Not realizing how few German reserves were available and haunted by the sight of those shattered French regiments whose morale had failed them, he could only dwell upon how close their line had come to collapse. He telephoned Castelnau that evening: 'You must hurry the English attack.'[23]

Pétain's prayers were about to be answered. The following day, 24 June, General Rawlinson's guns began their preliminary bombardment on the Somme, which ratcheted up the pressure at OHL. Falkenhayn had no choice but to telegraph the Crown Prince at Verdun to hold firm: 'The general situation makes it appear urgently desirable to firmly limit the expenditure of men, materials and munitions by the Army Group.' Falkenhayn hoped that French positions around Thiaumont and Fleury would soon be captured, but left the matter open-ended. While the Crown Prince assumed that this meant an end to the offensive, Knobelsdorf – 'strong-willed as ever' – was not listening. He wired Falkenhayn to explain that because French defenders on the east bank were now crowded into a narrow area, with their backs to Verdun, he intended to continue to press them. Ammunition consumption would not exceed 'approved daily rates' and they would use their own troops, but the attack would carry on.[24] Yet the moment for decisive action had now passed. Reinforcements were urgently pouring into the Somme and, by as early as 2 July, Falkenhayn had transferred seven divisions to the new front, squeezing OHL's reserve almost empty. A week later, 150 modern heavy guns left Verdun, never to return. The fortress city was no longer a priority.[25]

At 7 p.m. on 2 June, the Admiralty in London announced that a 'naval engagement' had taken place in the North Sea, off the coast of Jutland, between the Royal Navy's Grand Fleet and the German High Seas Fleet.[26] The Battle of Jutland (as it became known) was the largest battle of the war at sea; a furious series of clashes that took place in failing light in the late afternoon and evening of 31 May. With both sides trying to trap and eliminate the other, the action was confusing and quick-moving, long lines of dreadnoughts glimpsed at long range, through passing smoke and spray. When the German High Seas Fleet realized that it might be caught and destroyed by the numerically superior Royal Navy, it turned away, escaping into the mist, thus eluding complete annihilation. It had, however, taken a heavy toll on the British fleet, which lost three battlecruisers after shells struck their turrets and ignited their magazines. The German fleet escaped with fewer losses, including only a single battlecruiser, but many of its ships had sustained such heavy damage that it would never venture out as far again, fearing that a repeat would only result in catastrophic defeat.

While the Royal Navy pondered why its ships had been unable to deliver a second Trafalgar, further bad news arrived the following week when the armoured cruiser HMS *Hampshire* was sunk off the west coast of Orkney. Over 600 men died when the *Hampshire* struck a mine, including Lord Kitchener, who was on his way to Russia for talks with her General Staff. With the British Government becoming uneasy about future Russian participation in the war (and having loaned large sums to the Tsar), it was hoped that a visit by a leading member of the Cabinet would help clarify the situation and impress upon Russia the need for reform. Kitchener agreed to go, hoping that it would give him some time away from the exhausting paper war in Whitehall; and, in any case, with Robertson taking over many of his responsibilities as CIGS, there was less for him to do. At four o'clock on 5 June, Kitchener boarded the *Hampshire*, which then set off amid a roaring gale, only to founder off Marwick Head several hours later. K was last seen pacing back and forth on the quarterdeck, little emotion upon his face, as the lifeboats were lowered, only to be smashed against the sides of the ship or splintered on the jagged rocks that lay off the coastline. The cruiser sank within minutes. His body was never found.[27]

The death of Britain's great war hero (combined with the ongoing fallout over Jutland) cast a profound gloom over the nation as the Army prepared to make its 'big push' on the Somme. In a fulsome tribute in *The Times*, Charles Repington called K 'an extraordinary figure' who 'towered over all his contemporaries in individuality as he did in inches, and, though often he stood alone, his personality was enough to carry him triumphantly through difficulties which would have ruined many a more brilliant man'.[28] When the Commander-in-Chief of the Grand Fleet, Admiral Sir John Jellicoe, was given the news, he broke down, sobbing at his desk. But it was in the Army where the news was felt the deepest. 'How shall we get on without him?' was all that Sir Douglas Haig said to his Head of Intelligence, John Charteris, who was convinced that there was 'literally no one who can take his place'.[29] Notwithstanding the tragedy of the loss, there was, for some at least, a sense that the Secretary of War had fulfilled his purpose. At Fourth Army headquarters, Rawlinson lamented the passing of 'one of the great landmarks of my life', but was buoyed by the thought that 'K had completed his task of raising the new armies . . . for I feel sure they would have made him proud of them'.[30]

The New Armies were now being readied to take their place in the line, providing what Kitchener had hoped would be the crucial advantage in manpower on the Western Front. On the Somme, work had been going on feverishly to establish the intricate network of support facilities that would be required to back up the offensive. Railways and roads were extended and improved. Wells were dug. Water pumps were installed. Telephone cables were strung along the roads and buried up to the front. Extra temporary accommodation was erected to house the thousands of troops that were moving up, while space was made for sufficient ammunition dumps and casualty clearing stations. In terms of artillery, Fourth Army managed to amass an impressive array of pieces, including 800 18-pounders (the standard British quick-firing field gun), over 200 4.5-inch howitzers and 128 60-pounders, significantly more guns than had been employed at Loos the previous year. There were also unheard-of numbers of shells, stocked in huge piles, including 2.6 million 18-pounder and 260,000 4.5-inch howitzer shells.[31]

Air support was crucial to the coming attack. Following the lead taken by the French Air Service, the Royal Flying Corps was now employing formation flying, with three fighters escorting each observation aircraft as it photographed and mapped the battlefield. Alongside the Nieuport, the British flew the DH.2 and the two-seat F.E.2, both 'pusher' types (with the engine behind the pilot), which allowed for the mounting of forward-firing machine-guns and gave them a much better chance of shooting down enemy aircraft. The British also had their own 'aces'. Major Lanoe Hawker VC, commanding 24 Squadron, who had shot down three aircraft in a single day in 1915, was, by the following year, the most prominent of this new breed of aerial heroes. His order to his pilots to 'attack everything' over the Somme epitomized the offensive attitude of the RFC as it undertook a sustained effort to take down German observation balloons and keep its opponents' fighters at bay. With enemy strength concentrated in the Verdun sector, the British enjoyed a period of dominance throughout the summer.[32]

The preliminary bombardment lasted for a long, punishing week. Huge clouds of dust and smoke covered the German positions as a never-ending stream of shells passed overhead. Yet the amount of wire that needed to be cut and strongpoints demolished strained Fourth Army's resources and produced an uneven effect, with wire being cleared in some places, but left untouched in others. Many of the shells were also faulty, the result of hasty industrial expansion, falling to the ground without exploding, while the reliance on shrapnel (and the corresponding lack of high explosive) meant that the British found it almost impossible to destroy the bunkers that lay deep within the German line and were resistant to everything but a direct hit from the heaviest calibres. At GHQ, Haig was deaf to the shortcomings of the bombardment, just as he had been deaf to Rawlinson's argument about the difficulty of cutting the wire on the second line. 'The men are in splendid spirits,' he wrote the evening before the assault; 'several have said that they have never before been so instructed and informed of the nature of the operations before them. The wire has never been so well cut, nor the artillery preparation so thorough.'[33]

One of the other problems was the timing of Zero Hour: 7.30 a.m. was much too late. Rawlinson wanted to go earlier, at sunrise, but he accepted French proposals to commence the attack in daylight, to allow for a final observation of the enemy's defences (as was standard French practice). By the time British troops were ready to go 'over the top' on the morning of 1 July, the sun was burning brightly in the azure sky; the air fizzing with the sound of skylarks. And then, at the right moment, whistles blew across the line and the first waves of British troops clambered out of their trenches, navigated carefully cleared paths through their own barbed wire, and headed for the German trenches, all but obscured in a haze of dust, smoke and gas. Whereas the French Army had long since abandoned overburdening their men when making attacks, Fourth Army made little allowance for this and provided the infantry with everything they would need to take and then consolidate their gains, in line with the assumption that nothing could possibly survive such a formidable bombardment. The British went forward in 'fighting order', taking with them a steel helmet, entrenching tool, haversack and rolled groundsheet; as well as two gas masks, 220 rounds of small arms ammunition, a rifle and two grenades, which made for a total weight of around 66 lbs., making anything more than a stumbling walk practically impossible.[34]

Beset by nagging doubts, Rawlinson rode over to a patch of high ground near the town of Albert known as the 'Grandstand' to watch the infantry go over. He could see little apart from a 'mass of bursting shells', so he returned to his headquarters, the Château de Querrieu, six miles to the southwest, to await news.[35] Initially hopes were raised that Fourth Army was on the cusp of a great triumph, with reports coming in that the attacking divisions had swept over the first line, but the mood gradually soured as the morning wore on and by noon it was definitely known that a number of strongpoints were still resisting stoutly and there would be little opportunity for the cavalry to move up. All the way down from Serre to Fricourt – the northern and central sectors of the front – four entire corps were repulsed by vicious bursts of machine-gun and shellfire that left no-man's-land strewn with clumps of the dead and dying. Almost everywhere the same horrifying story was replayed: attacking waves coming under fire as soon as they left their trenches, officers and men being cut down with sickening thuds as machine-gun and rifle bullets found their mark. More troops would then be moved up, ordered to attack, and suffer the same horrifying fate. 'We were supporting another company and were able to see how gallantly they leaped to it. But they got nowhere', reported one officer. 'The German machine-guns had not been eliminated and at once they opened up accurate fire on our parapets. The men simply got up and fell back into the trench, either killed outright or badly wounded. Those who did get further were never seen or heard of again, as far as I know.'[36]

In places, small lodgements were made in the German line. At Thiepval, the imposing strongpoint of the Schwaben Redoubt was taken by men of 36th (Ulster) Division, but the advance parties were soon cut off and surrounded, stranded amid flurries of hand grenades. Further north, at Gommecourt, a diversionary attack by Third Army also collapsed. As one survivor remembered:

A perfect hurricane of high explosive and shrapnel met the assaulting waves; added to this was the confusion caused by our own smoke barrage, the chocked [sic] communication trenches and the terrible casualties, and yet in spite of all this, the attack was pressed home with great determination and the objective reached. That the ground gained could not be held was due to the cutting off of help and ammunition by the furious and sustained shelling. Stunned[,] exhausted and bitter, the survivors at the end of the day straggled back to their own reserve line, too dazed to wonder how they had come through too tired to care, and worst of all with the cruel sense of failure.[37]

It was only in the southern sector, occupied by Lieutenant-General Walter Congreve's XIII Corps, that the day went as planned. His three divisions took the villages of Montauban and Mametz, aided by good observation (unusually the British held the high ground in this sector) and help from French batteries, which dominated the German defence. Congreve was a born soldier, 'a characteristically English combination of soldier and the country gentleman',[38] who had won a Victoria Cross in South Africa. He ensured that his artillery gave a high priority to counter-battery fire, taking on enemy batteries and either destroying or driving them away. His attacking divisions also employed a form of creeping barrage that forced the defenders to keep their heads down. This helped his men to cross no-man's-land without facing a typhoon of fire and then break into the German trenches, which had been badly damaged by the bombardment: 'every inch of ground was churned up and pitted with shell holes', remembered one member of the Manchester Regiment, 'all craters and newly turned earth'.[39]

Continuing the attack to the south was General Fayolle's Sixth Army, which gained about 3,000 yards and captured the villages of Dompierre, Becquincourt and Curlu with little loss. 'All the German first position has been removed', wrote Fayolle. 'Thanks to Joffre. He is radiant.'[40] Joffre was less impressed with his allies' performance, which judging from his liaison officers had been deeply disappointing. Major Héring, an artillery expert attached to Fourth Army, reported that 'The British infantry moved forward brilliantly and carried its first objectives. Unfortunately, at certain points, the British troops did not hold on under the German barrages . . .' British artillery was another cause for concern. Batteries of field artillery 'raked the ground in front of the infantry systematically and well', but it was almost entirely shrapnel, as opposed to high explosive, which would have been more effective. Crucially there was also 'completely inadequate' preparation for counter-battery fire (excepting XIII Corps). Héring believed that the failure ultimately stemmed from 'lack of firmness in command'. 'Much calmness and methodical action, in general a great deal of common sense, but not the slightest sign of decisiveness. Every decision, painfully arrived at, is followed by discussion with those who are to carry it out. Efforts are made to leave them as much initiative as possible.' Another observer blamed the 'causes of failure' on 'poor artillery preparation' and the 'neglect of mopping-up enemy trenches after the first assault waves'. 'The British', they concluded, 'have not yet got the "knack".'[41]

The magnitude of the disaster was not realized at GHQ for several days, leaving Haig with the impression that, although casualties had been heavy, the offensive had got off to a good start. His Adjutant-General reported on 2 July that total casualties were somewhere over 40,000, which, according to Haig, could not be 'considered severe in view of the numbers engaged, and the length of front attacked'. It was not until 5 July that more details emerged. Total losses so far reached 2,266 officers and 68,609 other ranks; a figure that Haig again believed was acceptable. 'A very large number are very slight wounds', he wrote. 'In no other Army would they be evacuated, but it is thought better policy to send them away for a short time . . .'[42] Despite Haig's ironclad optimism, there was little doubt that Fourth Army had suffered a serious setback, and within days rumours were swirling around London that something had gone wrong. Lloyd George even grumpily told Maurice Hankey that the offensive had 'utterly failed' and he had always known it was 'utter folly' to attack on the Western Front.[43]

By nightfall on 1 July, the men of the German Second Army had won a remarkable victory. With just a handful of divisions in the line, they had been heavily outnumbered, yet inflicted terrible casualties on their opponent, testament to their superb fighting skill as well as to the shortcomings of the British attack, which had been riddled with serious errors. Despite having been under ceaseless bombardment for seven days and nights, the forward garrisons had refused to leave their trenches, but fought on, rushing up to the parapets and manning their weapons in the frantic moments after the barrage lifted. Then, quickly opening fire, they decimated wave after wave of attacking troops; the air echoing to the *tap-tap-tap* sound of heavy machine-gun fire. The effects were devastating. Long after the firing had ceased, German veterans would recall the macabre sight of rows of dead bodies, interlinked with writhing wounded, that covered the fields that day.

In the southern sector, the picture was much less positive. There, the front lines had been overrun and their defenders mixed up and thoroughly exhausted. 6th Bavarian Regiment, which had been hurried forward to stem the British advance towards Montauban, had been 'completely wiped out', with only 500 mud-stained survivors out of a total strength of 3,500 men. In the French sector, the situation was even more serious. The preliminary bombardment had been at its most effective on this corner of the battlefield, with Lieutenant-General Hermann von Stein, commander of XIV Reserve Corps, reporting that he had lost 109 guns and that the entire artillery component of 121st Division had been 'incapacitated' by the heavy shelling.[44] South of the Somme the German defence had given way almost entirely, with Fayolle's men pushing on towards the second line. There, the local corps commander, Lieutenant-General Günther von Pannewitz, authorized a short retreat to improve his position, only to incur the furious wrath of OHL, which was determined to hold the line whatever the cost.

Falkenhayn was driven out to Saint-Quentin on the morning of 2 July, arriving at Second Army headquarters with a black scowl upon his face. He was in no mood for pleasantries and told the army commander, General Fritz von Below, that he was relieving his Chief of Staff, Paul Grünert, for sanctioning Pannewitz's retreat. Below protested at once, his mouth tightening as he defended his subordinate, only for Falkenhayn to wave him away and tell him that the decision had already been made and that Fritz von Lossberg, OHL's ever-reliable defensive expert, would now take his place. Although it later turned out that Falkenhayn had known about the retirement in time to rescind the order, he let it happen anyway, characteristically using it as an opportunity to stamp his authority on Second Army and remind them of who was in charge: 'The first principle in position warfare must be to yield not one foot of ground', he lectured the assembled officers; 'and if it be lost to retake it by immediate counter-attack, even to the use of the last man.'[45]

Lossberg arrived at Saint-Quentin the following morning and took off on a long drive to familiarize himself with Second Army's dispositions. What he saw convinced him they had 'to fight for every foot of ground and under no circumstances withdraw'. Such an order 'had worked well during the battle in Champagne the previous autumn' and he was convinced it needed to be done again. The ground was promising; there were numerous villages and tactical features that could be held, although he worried about the aerial superiority of Allied forces, which had aircraft constantly droning up and down the front observing German positions and directing fire upon them.[46] That evening General Below – suitably stiffened by Falkenhayn's instructions – issued a new order expressing his determination to stand and fight: 'The outcome of the war depends on Second Army being victorious on the Somme', it read. 'Despite the current enemy superiority in artillery we have got to win this battle . . . I forbid the voluntary relinquishment of positions. Every commander is responsible for making each man in the Army aware about his determination to fight it out. The enemy must be made to pick his way forward over corpses.'[47]

The true scale of the Allied offensive was a sobering reminder of all that Falkenhayn had warned about in September 1914: that Germany could not hope to win a war of exhaustion against so many powers. Yet it also brought into sharp relief the failure of his strategy for 1916 and the questionable nature of his decision to attack Verdun. Instead of bleeding France to death, Germany was now engaged in two enormous battles and it remained to be seen how her army would cope. On 8 July, Falkenhayn met the Kaiser and briefed him on his war strategy, trying to justify what had been done:

Our overall warfare has so far been guided by the following simple ideas: in the East it seemed sufficient, with the internal situation in Russia, if the gains made during the previous year were generally maintained. In the West, we were determined to bring France to its senses by drawing blood. This would force the English into taking offensive action, which we hoped would result in heavy casualties for them, but no decisive success, and would later give us the opportunity for a counter-offensive. In this way, we expected that, by winter, we would have damaged the will of our three main adversaries to continue the war so thoroughly that out of this mood a victorious peace of some kind would have to develop.[48]

On the Somme, there was little sign of imminent moves for peace. The British had suffered a terrible setback on 1 July, but already Rawlinson's forces were ready to try again. Another major operation was launched on 14 July, with two corps pushing north towards the German second line on the Bazentin Ridge. The plan had been approved against the better judgement of Haig, who had objected to Rawlinson's novel idea, claiming that a dawn assault 'over an open plateau for 1,000 yards' distance, after forming up 2 divisions in mass *in the dark*', presented too great a chance of failure and would be 'unsound'.[49] But Rawlinson kept his nerve and impressed upon Haig that his men were capable of it and, moreover, that the artillery would clear the way. He was right. Four divisions were able to move up in the mist-wreathed dawn, marching in silence along taped routes to within 500 yards of the German line. And then, at 3.20 a.m., a furious five-minute bombardment flared into life, and in its wake the infantry sprang forward. Escorted by a creeping barrage, they were able to secure the German second line along a 6,000-yard front against only spasmodic resistance.[50]

The attack on the Bazentin Ridge indicated that while the British may not have been on a par with either the Germans or the French, they were learning quickly. On 15 July, the Minister of War, Wild von Hohenborn, recorded that the mood at OHL was 'very serious'. 'It is still incomprehensible to us that our troops are crumbling away like this and losing village after village, forest after forest . . . Falkenhayn is very downhearted and was ready to throw in the towel last night.'[51] As if in response to the heavy fighting, the German defence was reorganized on 19 July. Below was given command of a re-formed First Army north of the Somme, while General Max von Gallwitz (who commanded one of the assault groups at Verdun) was brought in to take charge of both Second Army (south of the river) and a new army group tasked with coordinating the entire defence. On 17 July, Gallwitz reported to OHL, where he met Falkenhayn, finding him 'quite serious' with worry stitched across his face. Gallwitz adopted his usual bullish tone, arguing for a counter-attack against the French, only for Falkenhayn to interrupt him:

'Hold on, hold on,' was all he could say, his fingers pressed deep into his temple, 'that's the only thing that matters!'[52]

Sixty-four years old in 1916, with short grey-white hair and a goatee beard, which was trimmed carefully every day, Max von Gallwitz exuded an alert, professional exterior. He came to the Somme with a high reputation. A devout Catholic from Breslau, he had commanded a corps on the Eastern Front under Hindenburg before taking charge of Eleventh Army during the invasion of Serbia. After his meeting with Falkenhayn, he travelled to Saint-Quentin, where he found General Below in an agitated mood, pacing up and down his office, blaming OHL for everything. Below had repeatedly remonstrated with Falkenhayn about the urgency of the situation, only to be told that there was nothing he could do. 'It seemed to me that Falkenhayn underestimated the seriousness of the danger that threatened us here,' he recalled, 'and probably did not want to undermine the attack on Verdun with redeployments unless it was absolutely necessary.'[1]

Gallwitz was not impressed by what he found. 'No orderly liaison had been set up between the artillery and infantry. The troops were often thrown into battle tired from marching and without food; well-secured points were given up too early.' It was evident that things needed to change, so he issued new orders that afternoon. Current positions would be 'strengthened and maintained'. Aerial observation of enemy batteries would be increased. There would be 'precise regulation' of barrage fire and, given the limited supply of ammunition, 'so-called harassing, punishment and retaliatory fire was to be avoided' at all costs. If the enemy took ground, immediate counter-attacks were to be launched.[2] Although the new German command arrangements were not particularly smooth (Gallwitz was both an army commander with a specific section of the front to defend and also head of an army group responsible for the whole battle), the new commander was determined to reshape the defensive battle and give it more structure and order. After a few hours with Below, Gallwitz felt much happier: 'I understood the setbacks better now.'

Even though the British still remained somewhat unsophisticated in their operations, tending to lapse into numerous and more or less continuous small-scale attacks (unlike the well-planned dawn assault on the Bazentin Ridge), the toll that it took on the German Army was clear. By the end of July, German losses on the Somme amounted to over 120,000 men, including 18,000 dead.[3] Gallwitz recognized that one of the major problems the Germans faced was the growing materiel strength of their opponents. Both British and French Armies were now able to fire off thousands and thousands of shells and to do so with increasing effectiveness – the result of an impressive industrial mobilization (as well as unrestricted access to American arms producers). British shells remained somewhat unreliable, with duds still littering parts of the battlefield, but the enormous amount of firepower being thrown at the German lines proved terribly difficult for the defenders to deal with. This was combined with a worrying dominance in the air. When the battle opened, the Entente had 310 aircraft in the Somme sector against just 104 German machines. OHL diverted extra squadrons to the Somme, but they could never match what the British and French could put into the air, and by August First and Second Armies could only muster 251 aircraft to their opponents' 500.[4]

The result of this inferiority was most keenly felt by the German infantrymen. No longer did they hold clearly defined trenches and deep shelters bolstered by concrete and steel. The battlefield now resembled a storm-tossed sea, pockmarked by shell holes and strewn with bodies. Because of the ferocity of Allied bombardments, flickering across the front like summer thunderstorms, units at the front increasingly took up their positions in the turbulent grey zone between the two sets of trenches, what they called the *Trichterfeld* (or 'crater field'), which made it more difficult for them to be targeted by British and French guns, but inevitably increased their problems with supplies of food and water. The resulting breakdown in communication frequently resulted 'in the total isolation of the Higher Command and in the absence of all co-operation between the various arms', noted General Below in a report on the battle. 'The infantry, heavily engaged, were often left to their own devices for hours and days at a time', a situation aggravated by 'incontestable' Allied air supremacy. 'Not only did the enemy's airmen direct the artillery fire undisturbed, but by day and night they harassed our infantry with bombs and machine guns, in their trenches and shell holes, as well as on the march to and from the trenches.'[5]

Notwithstanding the changing demands of the battle, German commanders retained faith in the qualities of their men as the Somme continued. '*Our infantry is superior to that of the enemy*', stated General Below, who was convinced that the enemy was only able to 'gain the upper hand' because of the 'perfected application of technical means, in particular to the employment of guns and ammunition in quantities which had been hitherto inconceivable'. He also noted the 'exemplary manner in which [enemy] infantry, artillery and aeroplanes co-operated' – a development that had also been remarked on by the Entente.[6] Surveying the battle in mid-July, General Fayolle was convinced that the 'art of war' had essentially 'disappeared' on the Somme, replaced by technology and firepower: 'Mechanical means. The importance of aviation. The beginning of air warfare. Dazzling German artillery. The current lack of manoeuvrability by troops. They are stiffened by trench warfare and their mentality is distorted, especially for artillery, which cannot be done without small steps. Since the first day of preparation (26 June), 5,000 shells were fired per piece, compared to 140 on the Marne . . .'[7]

Nowhere was this character more evident than at Pozières, a hamlet that lay astride the Albert–Bapaume Road, which would become one of the most intensely fought-over sections of the front. Although the main weight of the British effort had shifted to the right, where Rawlinson tried to push on from the Bazentin Ridge, Pozières remained in German hands, where it blocked any further advance to the north. By mid-July several attacks on the village had been repulsed and it was evident that well-prepared siege operations, liberally supplied with artillery and manpower, would be required. On 17 July, Haig saw Rawlinson and told him that he was transferring that sector to Lieutenant-General Sir Hubert Gough's Reserve Army. Two of Rawlinson's northernmost corps, X and VIII – both of which had been shattered on the first day – were placed under Reserve Army control and ordered to secure the left flank, 'sapping' forward wherever possible through a maze of sandbags, widening the gap in the enemy's line, and keeping as many divisions engaged as they could.[8]

The attack on Pozières took place in the early hours of 23 July, the men of 1st Australian Division springing forward across no-man's-land under the glare of German signal flares, before crashing into the enemy trenches, which had been reduced to a crater-strewn shambles after a heavy four-day bombardment. Fighting was close and confusing and it took days to properly consolidate their gains: joining up their forward positions to the original front line; clearing out any remaining snipers; and enduring regular counter-attacks. Although most of the German attempts to retake Pozières were shot down in no-man's-land, General Below was not minded to lose the position so easily and ordered the village to be kept under intensive artillery fire, which turned it into a pulverized rubble of red-brick dust, the fields strewn with chalk spoil and bodies. 'Nothing can describe a bombardment by heavy artillery', remembered one veteran. 'You cannot do anything – just stand in your trenches and take it . . . When you see our own heavies smashing up the Germans [sic] line, preparing it for an attack, you almost feel sorry for Fritz – it is so hellish. I have seen a German blown high in the air amongst the debris – arms and legs flying.'[9]

In Fourth Army's sector, the chief obstacles to an advance lay in the twin positions of Longueval and Delville Wood, and the imposing rise of High Wood. After the dawn assault on 14 July, Rawlinson's operations had broken down, with German reinforcements pouring in to prevent further exploitation. Delville Wood was now just a tangle of upturned earth and shattered tree stumps. The South African Brigade took it on 15 July, only to find itself surrounded on three sides and subjected to repeated counter-attacks. The earth, thick with roots, was difficult to dig into and gain the kind of shelter that would have protected men from the heavy shelling. The fighting reached a terrible climax on the afternoon of 18 July, when a major counter-attack was delivered by elements of two German divisions, led by specially trained assault troops, pushing forward into the wood, supported by flamethrower teams. 'Grenades flew incessantly over the assault positions', observed one witness. 'Violent roars accompanied the explosions, with lumps of stone, beams, trees, branches whirling through the air, which was soon filled with a dense cloud of dust and smoke.'[10]

The result was a costly stalemate. German units entered the wood and came under heavy sniper and machine-gun fire, and the attack melted away in a series of confusing skirmishes, brutal bayonet fighting and counter-charges. 'None of the officers, as far as there were any, knew their people, and very few people knew their commanders', remembered one German survivor. 'All order was lost on the chaotic battlefield, especially in the dense, battle-scarred forests.'[11] When the South Africans were finally relieved on 20 July, just 780 men answered the roll call – out of a total strength of 121 officers and 3,032 other ranks.[12] This was what the Somme had become, in all its blood-soaked fury. Attack and counter-attack under an iron rain, fought in ever more desperate circumstances and amid a landscape that no longer resembled the pleasant farmland of northern France, just a pale, broken wasteland littered with the dead.

Rawlinson may have been a more conscientious commander than Gough, but he still struggled to coordinate his forces effectively; caught between the desire for decisive operations and the requirement to secure suitable jumping-off positions for future attacks. British units would move up to the front, make small-scale attacks and often meet with failure, and the following day more battalions would try again. Rawlinson authorized six separate attacks on the Longueval sector between 15 and 22 July, while at the same time failing to coordinate any meaningful activity with the French, leaving Foch growing increasingly frustrated. The Somme had never been his choice of battlefield and the halting inconsistency that characterized British operations in July 1916 so exasperated him that he sent a note to Haig on 19 July stating that 'an overall attack' (what he called '*l'attaque d'ensemble*') was the 'best way to obtain wide and lasting results, avoid losses and conserve the results gained by making it impossible for the enemy to concentrate his artillery fire'.[13]

Still the British attacked. To the northwest of Longueval stood the brooding darkness of High Wood, situated on one of the highest points of the battlefield. There the same horrific story seemed to play out time and again. It was first reached on 14 July by a collection of Indian cavalry squadrons, which galloped up through the cornfields, pennants streaming, only for a swift counter-attack to send them reeling back to the British lines. Over the next two months attack after attack, battalion after battalion, went up the sloping fields towards the wood, managing to secure a tenuous grip on its south-eastern edge, before being counter-attacked or bombarded in turn. A renewed attack was launched on the morning of 23 July, but ran into fierce resistance amid the tangle of splintered trees, now honey-combed with trenches. One defender recalled how 'wave after wave' of British soldiers came on 'against our shot-up trenches. Then red flares soared into the sky, and all at once the curtain of a deadly barrage descended in front of our entire position, cutting down the enemy by whole ranks . . . But the British are persistent!'[14] Afterwards Lieutenant-General Henry Horne, commander of XV Corps, which was tasked with taking the wood, was almost ready to admit defeat. 'We have got a portion of High Wood but not all of it,' he reported, 'and as things are now it is very difficult to get on any further. I puzzle my brains how to do it.'[15]

'The scales of fate have long wavered. Now that is over. One of the scales keeps on going up, the other going steadily down, laden with a weight which nothing can henceforth lighten.' The words of Monsieur Poincaré, President of France, were part of a series of stirring proclamations published in the Allied press on 1 August 1916 – the second anniversary of the outbreak of the war. Joffre, Haig and Lloyd George all added their thoughts as the war entered its third year and the populations of Europe began to face the daunting prospect of another winter with no sign of peace. Yet Poincaré believed that there was hope; the Allies were now, he wrote, 'beginning to gather the fruits of [their] perseverance'. 'The Russian Army is pursuing the routed Austrians. The Germans, attacked on the Eastern and Western fronts, are throwing in their reserves. British, Russian, and French

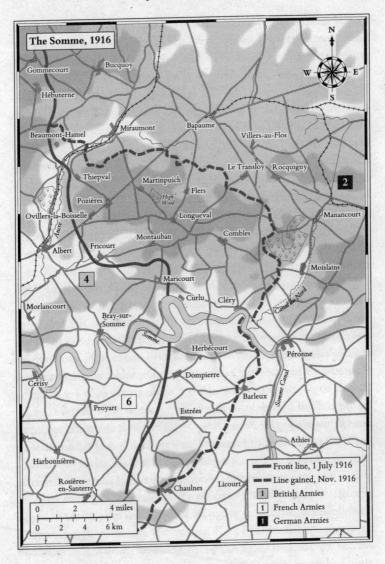

The Somme, 1916

Gommecourt
Bucquoy
Hébuterne
Miraumont
Bapaume
Beaumont-Hamel
Villers-au-Flos
Le Transloy
Rocquigny
Thiepval
Martinpuich
Flers
Pozières
High Wood
Manancourt
Ovillers-la-Boisselle
Longueval
Combles
Moislains
Montauban
Albert
Fricourt
Maricourt
Morlancourt
Curlu
Cléry
Bray-sur-Somme
Somme
Herbécourt
Péronne
Cerisy
Dompierre
Proyart
Barleux
Estrées
Athies
Harbonnières
Rosières-en-Santerre
Chaulnes
Licourt

Front line, 1 July 1916
Line gained, Nov. 1916
1 British Armies
1 French Armies
1 German Armies

0   2   4 miles
0   2   4   6 km

battalions are cooperating for the liberation of our territory. The sky is clearing, the sun is rising.'[16]

Despite growing disillusionment with his leadership, Joseph Joffre carried on, his bulky frame haunting the corridors of the Grand

Condé as he strained every muscle to keep the Allies united, their forces concentrated. In a report he had written on 20 August for his senior commanders, he expressed his belief that the pressure they had placed upon the German Army was beginning to tell. 'Whatever the extent of our success on the Western Front, the Anglo-French offensives, by the mere fact of their power and duration, will have a decisive influence on the end of the war. They retain and absorb the largest and best part of the German forces and, thus limiting the aid that Germany can give to her faltering ally, they are, with the victorious resistance of Verdun, the inevitable condition of the successful development of the manoeuvre of the Russian and Italian armies . . .' It was, therefore, not unreasonable to think that 'the campaign of 1917 will mark the final decay of the enemy powers if the Entente members remain faithful to unified effort, which is one of the essential elements of their strength and the most valuable pledge of their victory.'[17]

Joffre continued to worry about what the British were doing. Vallières kept him up to date with British progress, and he occasionally went to see Haig, but it proved difficult to coordinate the actions of their forces as closely as he would have liked. He had been unhappy at Haig's decision to concentrate his attacks on his right flank (where Rawlinson had made the most gains) and would have preferred the British to continue pushing along a wide front, only for Haig to refuse and tell him that he was '*solely responsible to the British Government for the action of the British Army*'.[18] Joffre tried, again and again, to get Haig to conform to French plans – preferably a broad advance to the east (rather than the northward push that Haig was now attempting) – but with little success. Poor weather, inexperience, differing priorities and logistical problems all condemned the two allies to muddle along, advancing when they could, and only rarely doing so in a concerted fashion. The British attack was now 'dying away in secondary and local actions', he complained, 'which are costly and slow and do no more than give an illusion of activity'. Instead, Joffre (like Foch) wanted to organize an '*action d'ensemble*' – a big attack like 1 July that would concentrate their forces and restart the offensive – hopefully to take place at the beginning of September to coincide with Romania's entry into the war.[19]

Despite Haig's oft-professed wish to cooperate closely with the French, it did not prove possible to attack on Joffre's preferred date, and a series of postponements eventually spoilt any prospect of a joint attack. Haig was determined to fight only when he was ready and, with the prospect of using a new weapon in the forthcoming attack, he would not be rushed. He had first heard about the development of armoured vehicles, or 'caterpillars' – what would become known as the 'tank' – in December 1915 and had been kept informed of their progress throughout the year. The first six machines left England on 15 August and Haig was able to inform Rawlinson the following day that he was to begin planning for a grand offensive in which tanks would be used to 'secure the enemy's last line of prepared defences between Morval and Le Sars with a view to opening the way for cavalry' – an attack projected for some time in mid-September.[20]

Sir Douglas Haig – 'lithe, active and firmly knit, always immaculately dressed in khaki service kit, with field boots shining like a mirror' – remained bullishly confident of victory as the Somme offensive continued into August. His attempt to break the line and push his army through the deep belt of German defences may have failed in July, but he never wavered from his belief that, sooner or later, the enemy would crack. He was buoyed by intelligence reports of the 'great confusion' that German units had encountered upon arriving on the battlefield and was confident that many battalions had been reduced to fewer than 100 men, with some regiments able to muster only about a third of their full strength.[21] Yet the cost of the offensive had been heavier than anyone had anticipated, and as early as 29 July Robertson had warned Haig that 'the Powers that be' were 'beginning to get a little uneasy in regard to the situation'. He was concerned that casualties were rising and the chief object of the offensive – 'relief of pressure on Verdun' – had largely been achieved. Therefore, he wanted Haig to consider 'Whether a loss of say 300,000 men will lead to really great results, because if not, we ought to be content with something less than what we are now doing.'[22]

Robertson was always keen to support Haig, even if the note revealed a niggling concern about the progress of the battle. The CIGS saw his primary role at the War Office as keeping Britain's

War Cabinet on the straight and narrow strategic path that had been laid out in the winter of 1915–16 – the main focus being on the Western Front – and avoiding (or minimizing) any risky adventures that resulted in British strength being dissipated. He also knew that any criticism of Haig and his performance might imperil Britain's concentration in France. Yet he recoiled from the over-sanguine acceptance of the offensive that Haig epitomized and on 5 July, just days after the great breakthrough attempt had failed so disastrously, he had written to Sir Launcelot Kiggell, Haig's Chief of Staff, that 'the road to success lies in deliberation'. While Haig always veered towards the breakthrough, Robertson – like Rawlinson, Foch and others – advocated cautious, siege-like advances that would rely on artillery to batter down the defences without risking mass infantry assaults. 'The thing is to advance along a wide front step by step to very limited and moderate objectives, and to forbid going beyond those objectives until all have been reached by the troops engaged.'[23]

What Robertson hoped to achieve by writing such a letter is unclear. He specifically requested that Kiggell not show this 'to *anyone*', but he may have been hoping that it trickled through to the Commander-in-Chief and caused him to modify his ambitions. His note on 29 July about casualties was probably written with a similar idea in mind; that by delicately offering advice couched in such a way as not to offend Haig's *amour propre*, he could help Haig avoid some of the fallout from promising too much without delivering. But Haig was thick-skinned, brushing off Robertson's warnings with a blunt restatement of the rationale behind the offensive. Verdun had been relieved. Moreover, it was unlikely that Brusilov would have had so much success had there not been such heavy fighting on the Western Front. Regarding the Somme, Haig was sure that he had 'inflicted very heavy losses on the Enemy' and it was his intention to carry on. He would 'maintain a steady pressure' and 'push my attack strongly whenever and wherever the state of my preparations and the general situation make success sufficiently probable'.[24]

Haig did, however, recognize that perhaps now was *not* the right moment for a decisive attack. In an appreciation of the situation written on 2 August, he sketched out what he called the 'general principles' on which operations were now to be conducted. 'The present situation is that the enemy has brought up considerable reinforcements of men and guns, and can continue for some time still to replace tired troops.' With German forces having recovered from the inevitable disorganization that followed the opening of the offensive, Haig admitted that they were 'still too formidable to be rushed without careful and methodical preparation'. Therefore, it was necessary to prepare fresh assaults while also strengthening defensive positions to guard against enemy counter-attacks. To bring this phase (what he dubbed a 'wearing out battle') to a 'successful termination', it was necessary to 'practise such economy of men and material as will ensure our having the "last reserves" at our disposal when the crisis of the fight is reached', which he believed would be some time in the second half of September.[25]

With the climax of the battle not expected for several weeks, a succession of royalty and senior politicians made their way to France, drawn to the titanic struggle taking place on the Somme. After being shown the enormous preparations behind the lines, the long rows of guns, their muzzles pointing skywards, alongside small mountains of spent shell cases, the visitors would inevitably stop by Haig and his staff. GHQ was now based at Montreuil-sur-Mer, a pleasant walled town a short drive from Le Touquet on the coast. On 12 August, His Majesty King George V came to lunch, posing for photographs outside Haig's chateau with Poincaré, Joffre and Foch, before heading inside to pore over a large map of the front. A waiting journalist confirmed that the meal 'was of the most friendly and intimate character'.[26] Another notable visitor was the Prime Minister, Asquith, who was escorted to the outskirts of Fricourt – one of the fortified villages that had resisted repeated attacks on 1 July – where he was met by his son, Raymond, an officer with the Grenadier Guards. They walked up a short rise, only for a German 'whizz-bang' to explode nearby, showering them in dirt. They hurried into a nearby dugout and there, under the flickering electric lamps, waited for the shelling to pass. Asquith dined with Haig that evening and, over a bottle of his finest brandy, expressed complete confidence in the offensive and offered to help in any way he could. 'Haig is I think doing very well', he wrote to a friend; 'sticking to his original plan and not allowing himself to be hustled'.[27]

David Lloyd George was of a different opinion. The new Secretary of War (who had been appointed after the death of Lord Kitchener) had long doubted the wisdom of attacking on the Western Front, and the heavy losses and inevitable obfuscation from Robertson did little to change his mind. When he received word of Romania's declaration of war upon the Central Powers, he dashed off an urgent note to Sir Frederick Maurice, Director of Military Operations, on the supreme importance of doing everything they could. 'We cannot afford another Serbian tragedy', he wrote – recalling the events of the previous year when the Allied landings at Salonika had been too slow to prevent Serbia from being overrun. 'I therefore once more urge that the General Staff should consider what action we could in conjunction with France and Italy take immediately to relieve the pressure on Roumania if a formidable attack developed against her.' But Lloyd George's entreaties went nowhere. At a meeting of the War Committee on 12 September, it was agreed to maintain the offensive on the Somme for the foreseeable future, with the CIGS arguing that the best method of aiding Romania was to stay the course in the west.[28]

Lloyd George could have interrogated Robertson's position at the War Committee had he not been in France, where he was touring Verdun and meeting with a host of senior French officials, including Foch. Lloyd George was keen to quiz Foch on the performance of the expeditionary force, particularly 'why the British who had gained no more ground than the French[,] if as much, had suffered such heavy casualties'. Foch was noncommittal and talked about how the French infantry had 'learnt their lesson in 1914', only for Lloyd George to press him again on the ability of British commanders. Once more Foch did not take the bait, replying 'that he had no means of forming an opinion'. Lloyd George went away unsatisfied, but within days word reached Haig of what had transpired, leaving him seething with anger and disbelief. 'Unless I had been told of this conversation personally by Gen. Foch, I would not have believed that a British minister could have been so ungentlemanly as to go to a foreigner and put such questions regarding his own subordinates.'[29]

The spiralling costs of both Verdun and the Somme finally began to have their effect on the German High Command. Offensive activity at Verdun was formally curtailed on 12 July, and although fighting on the Meuse continued throughout the late summer and autumn, the Crown Prince's forces would increasingly find themselves on the defensive as a series of powerful French counter-thrusts took place. Fleury and Thiaumont were recaptured on 3 August and a week later Falkenhayn addressed his senior commanders on future strategy. It was of 'great importance', he wrote, to convince 'both the enemy and our own troops that the offensive on the Meuse has not entirely come to an end . . . Moreover, the present position of our first lines on the right bank of the Meuse is such as to necessitate that all means should be employed to improve it before the coming of the autumn rains. On the other hand, the present military situation, strained as it is, compels us to economize men and munitions wherever possible.'[30]

Falkenhayn asked for his commanders' views on the situation, but there was no easy answer. He had perfectly encapsulated the bind that Germany had become locked into, having lost the initiative and been caught in two brutal battles that would only end with the onset of winter. Knobelsdorf and the Crown Prince were still at odds with each other. Wilhelm believed that without significant additional reserves of men and munitions there was no possibility of 'real gain', while Knobelsdorf took a different approach, following the logic of a Macbeth, who was so deep 'in blood' that to return would be as tedious as to continue. Pushing on would be difficult, but if they did not take the remaining high ground around Fleury and Fort Souville, then they would still be under French artillery fire throughout the winter. Falkenhayn could only issue a blithe reply on 21 August leaving it up to them to decide how to carry on: keeping the enemy under the impression that they still intended to attack, but without employing masses of new troops or shells. Knobelsdorf had, however, finally lost Falkenhayn's support and he was relieved later that day.[31]

Such concerns took their toll on Falkenhayn. By August he was suffering from lack of sleep and overwork, his temper aggravated by persistent toothache and neuralgia. Every night he would sit at his desk, which was covered with large maps, and struggle to think of some way to, as he put it, 'free his troops'. Falkenhayn's enemies – Hindenburg, Ludendorff, Bethmann Hollweg and Rupprecht among others – were growing more assertive in their criticisms. Even those who had been supportive of Falkenhayn in the past, including General von Lyncker (head of the Kaiser's Military Cabinet), had now come to the conclusion that he had lost the confidence of the army. On 16 August, Bethmann Hollweg told the Kaiser that Falkenhayn's strategy had failed because of 'the unexpected resilience of France, the surprising power of Russia and the collapse of Austria', with the decision lying 'more than ever in the East'. From his stronghold at *OberOst*, Hindenburg also regularly composed furious telegrams against the Chief of the General Staff, blaming him for Germany's bleak outlook and recommending transfers of troops to the Eastern Front. 'General Falkenhayn looks bad', wrote Wilhelm Groener; 'the dispute with *Oberost* is taking him to Hell.'[32]

The Kaiser remained supportive, privately reassuring Falkenhayn that 'we will stay together until the end of the war'. Moltke had died of a stroke on 18 June, news which affected the Kaiser deeply, and he was in no mood to lose another chief so soon afterwards. Yet the depressing news from the front and the intractable nature of Germany's situation gradually wore down Wilhelm's faith in Falkenhayn. When news broke that Romania had joined the Allies and declared war on Austria–Hungary on 28 August, the Kaiser finally bowed to the inevitable, consulting with Hindenburg about the latest developments. Falkenhayn found out soon afterwards and wasted no time in informing the Kaiser that 'he could only regard this summoning of a subordinate commander, without previous reference to him, in his province alone, as a breach of authority that he could not accept and as a sign that he no longer possessed the absolute confidence of the Supreme War Lord'. He was invited to OHL and relieved of his position on the morning of 29 August.[33]

The decision was not an unpopular one. Views among senior members of the German Army were broadly similar: that Falkenhayn lacked the necessary vigour and aggression to succeed and fought the wrong kind of war – halting and uncommitted. Max von Gallwitz spoke of 'the always missing two corps!' and reproached Falkenhayn for the 'gradual initiation of large undertakings . . . with inadequate resources'.[34] According to Groener:

> As the leader of a large working team like the Supreme Headquarters, he probably had exemplary qualities, but he hid behind an opaque wall which no one penetrated completely. He thus created for himself a self-imposed isolation, but this was not the isolation of a great man who commands reverence. He lacked the gift of inspiring trust and confidence. Therefore, very soon after his first failures, voices arose from his immediate environment wanting to remove him, and this explains why young officers offered to help overthrow him, despite the fact that scheming was not normally the order of the day in the German Army.[35]

Falkenhayn left Pless soon after his audience with the Kaiser. With 'iron restraint', he spoke to the headquarters staff, the department heads, and thanked them for their service, before departing with his adjutant, Captain Hans Henning von Pentz. As they boarded their train, Pentz tried to encourage Falkenhayn with talk of future endeavours (they were being sent to head Ninth Army for the campaign against Romania), but the general was incapable of being cheered up.

'Dear Pentz,' he said, 'You, with your healthy ambition, will surely understand that once you have had the wreath in your hand, no other task can satisfy you any more.'[36]

As Falkenhayn's star fell, that of his replacement, Field Marshal Paul von Hindenburg, was in the ascendant – even if the Kaiser remained sunk in depression. When an aide offered consoling words about the 'great jubilation' in the press over the appointment of Hindenburg, he snapped back, 'I do not care!'[37] He had only agreed to Falkenhayn's removal with reluctance, with his allies concerned that the immense prestige of Hindenburg would inevitably overshadow the Supreme War Lord. Hindenburg's totemic appearance – his big six-foot-tall frame and square head, with heavy-lidded eyes and a long grey moustache that flared up at the ends – had, by 1916, come to symbolize the strength of the German Empire at war. He was always dressed smartly in a general officer's field-grey uniform, littered with decorations, a pair of binoculars around his neck, with his hands in his pockets or holding a short cane. While Hindenburg projected a sense of imperturbability, even in the most frantic of moments, his friend and ally, Erich Ludendorff (who was appointed First Quartermaster-General), was a tightly bound core of nervous, unspent energy. His portraits, always taken with extreme reluctance, show a flabby, jowled face, with small black eyes and a curious, quizzical stare.

The two men inherited a difficult situation; one they knew was laced with uncertainty. 'The future is darker than ever' were the words that Hindenburg muttered upon being appointed Chief of the General Staff, a comment that was symptomatic of the profound depression that settled upon OHL in the late summer of 1916.[38] Although there was no imminent danger of a collapse on the Western Front, the heavy fighting consumed German resources at a steady rate. In the east, Brusilov's armies had, by late September, closed with the Carpathian Mountains and brought Romania into the war, while, along the Isonzo, Italian forces had won their biggest victory so far, taking the town of Gorizia and prompting the ringing of church bells across Italy. With Austria–Hungary beginning to crumble, Germany tightened her grip on decision-making within the Central Powers. The Kaiser was appointed head of a 'United Supreme Command' in the east on 6 September, which extended German control of key positions in the Austro-Hungarian Army (including the placement of veteran German officers and NCOs into Austrian units). 'I have the firm conviction', Hindenburg wrote to Conrad, 'that the fate of the Allies is so closely interlinked that the senior leadership can only take this into account in their action and must only act based on military considerations.'[39]

Despite their success on the Eastern Front, Hindenburg and Ludendorff men were largely unfamiliar with the situation in France. Hindenburg had long been retired when the war broke out and Ludendorff had left after the fall of Liège. Yet they acted with a clarity and ruthlessness that would become their hallmark. Hindenburg wasted no time in writing to Wild von Hohenborn on what would be called the 'Hindenburg Programme': 'Our supply of personnel is limited compared to the enemy's human resources. This terrible state of affairs can only be offset, to some extent, by the fact that all the people who are fit for military action will go to the front. Their jobs must be replaced behind the lines and at home by people who are fit to serve in a garrison – the number of which should be limited as far as possible . . .' But even if these measures were implemented, Hindenburg still feared that they would be ineffective. 'People – as well as horses – must increasingly be replaced by machines. This is becoming all the more difficult as the enemy has also recognized this principle.' Hindenburg asked for a doubling of current ammunition production by the spring of 1917 as well as a significant increase in the number of field artillery, machine-guns and aircraft. Such a programme would require an unprecedented mobilization of German industry, but Hindenburg believed that nothing should be overlooked, including an expansion of military service and the transfer of workers to those companies directly involved in war production. 'The principle of "anyone who does not work should not eat" is more justified than ever in our situation, even for women . . .'[40]

Within days of their appointment, the duo headed west, holding a major conference on strategy at Rupprecht's headquarters in Cambrai on 5 September. A host of senior officers were in attendance, including Below, Gallwitz, Lossberg and the Crown Prince. Hindenburg began by outlining that Falkenhayn's strategy of attrition would be abandoned; instead there would be a return to the principles of the past: decisive operations that would end in the ultimate supremacy of German arms. Firstly, Romania would be dismembered. An army group was being formed in Bulgaria, ready to strike north. While on the Western Front new defensive tactics would be introduced to save manpower and ensure that Germany was equipped with enough weaponry and ammunition to rival the Entente. They would also begin the construction of a new reserve position in France, built by forced labour and Russian prisoners of war, which would allow them to shorten the front and conserve manpower.

The effect of Hindenburg's and Ludendorff's appearance at Cambrai was striking. Lossberg noted how Hindenburg's 'calmness, serenity, and confidence made a big impression on all of us'.[41] Rupprecht was equally pleased by the performance of the two men. 'Hindenburg creates a good impression', he wrote. 'His forehead is strikingly broad, his eyes are blue and create an open and kind effect. His bearing is composed and determined. He loves hunting and is a joker but very approachable . . . Ludendorff has a well-defined, smart head. His face is very pale and I had the impression that he ought to take better care of himself. What he said was all spot on.'[42] Max Bauer, a veteran staff officer who had been progressively disappointed at Falkenhayn's indecision, was also thrilled by the new sense of direction now coursing through OHL and became an ardent admirer of the new commander. 'Hindenburg was the plain old Prussian general type. A big, proud-looking man, surprisingly young and sprightly for his age, he made an imposing impression on the outside. He saw everything through the eyes of a soldier.'[43]

While the German Army readied itself to strike against Romania, the problem of how to hold its positions in the west remained. Rupprecht, who had been promoted to Field Marshal, was given command of a new army group, which ran from Arras to Noyon, comprising Sixth, First, Second and Seventh Armies, almost 700,000 men, making him the most important German operational commander. Hermann von Kuhl, General von Kluck's old Chief of Staff, would accompany him (Rupprecht having managed to get the despised Gustav von Lambsdorff shunted sideways) and the two men formed a strong partnership. Rupprecht had been overjoyed at Falkenhayn's dismissal, but found his mood sinking when he contemplated the position on the Somme, where German troops were becoming worn down by heavy fighting, yet committed to counter-attack whenever possible. 'The veteran officers and other ranks become fewer every day and the replacements, however plentiful, have not had the benefit of the same military instruction and training', he noted on 4 September. The sheer weight of Entente combat power they were facing was daunting. In Below's First Army, twenty-one German divisions were ranged against thirty-two British and four French divisions. South of the river it was even worse. Second Army had only eleven divisions against twice the number of French divisions.[44]

This disparity was even more marked in the air. By early August the Allies had maintained their 2:1 superiority in aircraft over the Somme, which had an increasingly damaging effect on the artillery struggle.[45] German batteries had hitherto enjoyed a significant advantage, occupying the high ground, from which they had been able to pour fire down upon their adversaries, but gradually the British were conquering more ground, seizing higher points from which to continue the struggle, as well as using their aircraft to direct fire upon those locations where German guns were clustered. Between the opening of the preliminary bombardment on 24 June and late August, 1,068 field guns had been destroyed, lost or become unusable (out of a total of just 1,208) along with 371 heavy guns. The first two weeks of September was one of the worst periods of the year for Germany, with the defenders on the Somme suffering a succession of heavy blows. The French renewed their attacks on 3 September, taking the village of Cléry, while there was heavy fighting at Guillemont and High Wood in the British sector. In the first ten days of September, Second Army lost 520 officers and 23,000 other ranks killed, wounded or missing – 'painful numbers', as Max von Gallwitz himself admitted.[46]

For Gallwitz, now demoted to command solely of Second Army, the situation they faced was becoming intolerable and he was not alone in thinking that a tipping point had now been reached. 'So many losses!' he lamented. 'If this game lasts much longer, we will not be able to get replacements of suitable people and equipment in sufficient numbers. The only hope is that our enemies use their infantry even earlier in the ongoing attacks – we no longer have the advantage over them in terms of ammunition and equipment. But their reserves are too large, not just local Frenchmen, but also the English, Russians, colonial forces and the many other people who are providing assistance.'[47] Yet it was not only the races of the world that faced the German Army on the Somme. In the next attack, just days away, a new weapon would be used that ushered in the age of armoured warfare.

12. 'The face of a general in victory'

'The object of the tank is to help the infantry forward, and especially to deal with enemy machine guns.' The opening sentence of 'Preliminary Notes on Tactical Employment of Tanks', issued by GHQ in August 1916, provided the initial guidance for General Rawlinson on how to use these 'novel engines of war'.[1] A total of forty-eight Mark I tanks would be available for the forthcoming attack (including six machines deployed with Reserve Army), parcelled out across the front against selected strongpoints and brought up the night before the assault in strictest secrecy. They were split into two types: the more heavily armed 'male' (with a 6-pounder housed in each side sponson) and the 'female', with its array of machine-guns. The two types looked similar, with their rhomboidal shape and rough exterior made of boilerplate, which protected its crew of eight from small arms fire if little else. Weighing almost 28 tons and with a top speed of just 3.7 mph, the vehicles were noisy and slow, emitting a coughing, grinding sound as they slithered by. When he first saw them in late August, Rawlinson knew they were unlikely to lead to a major breakthrough, but he hoped they would help his infantry make progress. 'On the whole . . . rather favourably impressed', was his initial verdict.[2]

The attack on 15 September would be the biggest British operation since 1 July. Fourth Army orders called for three corps to make the main assault towards the villages of Martinpuich and Flers and then, if everything went well, exploit out towards the German third line to the north. As usual there was a predictable tussle between Haig and Rawlinson over the scope of the attack, with Haig being concerned that the Fourth Army commander was not appreciating the need to push on to the German gun line in one bold advance. Rawlinson, who was concerned that, as he put it, 'if we attempt too much we run the risk of doing nothing', wanted a more considered, step-by-step advance that would deal with each trench system in turn, allowing him to concentrate his artillery. Haig ordered Rawlinson to spread his gunfire across the whole German position on the assumption that it would help a wider breakout, but this was a risky tactic, potentially imperilling the initial assault if the bombardment was not heavy enough. With Rawlinson's caution again being thrown to the wind, he simply assembled as many guns and shells as he could and hoped for the best.[3]

The attack commenced at 6.20 a.m. at the end of a long cool night, with mist in the air and mud on the ground. The defenders knew something was up. The increased activity behind the British lines had not gone unnoticed and rumours were even circulating that some kind of 'land cruiser' had been spotted, which was invulnerable to everything but the heaviest artillery.[4] This was not so, but Rawlinson, keenly aware of the vulnerability of tanks, had ordered special 'lanes' to be left in the creeping barrage for them to go through (to avoid being shelled by their own guns); a sensible idea on paper, but one that produced terrible results on the battlefield. Only thirty-six machines (out of forty-eight) were able to reach the front by Zero Hour, leaving gaps in the line where there would be no tanks and no artillery.[5] As the infantry marched forward, quickly outpacing the tanks, numerous German strongpoints came to life and began pouring enfilade fire into the attackers. Those few tanks that did manage to avoid mechanical problems and cross no-man's-land soon attracted terrific fire, bullets zipping through the air and clattering on their boilerplate like a hailstorm, causing their terrified crews to huddle on the floor as white-hot fragments of metal ricocheted around the interior.

Yet the bombardment worked. Despite Haig's entreaties to spread his fire, Rawlinson managed to bring up a field gun or howitzer for every ten yards of front – twice the density of fire that had been achieved on 1 July – which pulverized the enemy front line and left it a cratered, smoking ruin.[6] Because of this, the attacking infantry were able to break into their initial objectives and begin mopping up the German trenches: throwing grenades down dugouts and sending dazed prisoners to the rear. In the centre of the attack, fourteen tanks helped capture the village of Flers, and one even drove up the main street, firing at German machine-gun positions as it did so. By mid-afternoon, Rawlinson knew that they had cleared High Wood and seized three villages (Flers, Martinpuich and Courcelette), although casualties had been heavy and many of the attacking units were spent. Machine-gun fire had proved particularly devastating in certain sectors; for example, the Guards Division, which was advancing towards Lesbœufs, found no-man's-land swept by fire from the Quadrilateral, a German strongpoint on its right flank that had escaped the preliminary bombardment. Although the Guards took their first objective, bayonetting scattered groups of Germans holding a thin shell hole defence, it could go no further. Losses were high: over 4,700 officers and men of the division had fallen, including Lieutenant Raymond Asquith, mortally wounded while leading his company forward.[7]

German commanders were predictably dismayed when scattered reports of the fighting reached them through the maelstrom. Rupprecht clambered up to the top floor of a house overlooking the battlefield and stared ruefully at the 'clouds of smoke' that obscured the horizon. The sound of the shellfire was terrible, 'resounding like the noise of some great waterfall, every now and then abating, then swelling violently up again'.[8] In First Army, which had taken the brunt of the assault, General Below considered withdrawing his forces to a rear line, then being constructed, only for Lossberg to veto it with his familiar argument about what they had done in the past. 'During the previous year's battle in Champagne,' he reminded Below, 'I had advocated conducting an unrestricted fight to hold every inch of ground. I was convinced that was the correct course of action here too.'[9] But staying and holding on was hardly ideal either, as German front-line soldiers found their morale wilting under the sustained pressure of what seemed like an increasingly unequal struggle. 'You could not imagine it', one veteran admitted after the attack on 15 September. 'They surprised us in a manner never seen before. They came on unstoppably in front of us. Behind came numerous armoured automobiles armed with machineguns [sic], flamethrowers etc. In addition, the greatest part of the trench garrison was certainly killed or buried alive by the preceding bombardment. What remained wanted to surrender but was mostly killed.'[10]

At Fourth Army headquarters, Rawlinson was pleased by the results of the day's fighting, even though (as he had expected) it had not been possible to exploit British gains to any significant degree. He issued orders for the resumption of the attack the following day 'to enable the Cavalry Corps to push through to its objectives and complete the enemy's defeat', but rain fell that evening, softening the already spongy ground and adding to the difficulties of moving up guns and consolidating their positions.[11] With more wet weather on the way, it was decided to postpone another major attempt until a joint attack could be properly coordinated with the French. Further attacks towards Morval and Lesbœufs were undertaken on 25 September; again noticeable for the concentration of firepower Rawlinson was able to throw at the German defences – over 400,000 shells – and this time alongside significant support from Fayolle's Sixth Army.[12] By the evening of 26 September, Rawlinson had cleared most of the German third line, with Reserve Army, on his left, orchestrating the capture of Thiepval – a strongpoint that had resisted repeated attacks since 1 July. Finally it seemed the British were getting 'the knack'.

Haig was well pleased with what had been accomplished. He wrote to the King on 5 October telling him about the 'highly satisfactory' results of recent operations. 'The troops see that they are slowly but surely destroying the German Armies in their front, and that their enemy is much less capable of defence than he was even a few weeks ago.'[13] Prisoner examination seemed to show that something had broken in the morale of the German forces facing the British, a claim that struck Haig as significant: 'Officers have no trench maps and are ignorant of the ground', he noted in his diary. 'Artillery is handicapped by the general confusion prevailing and want of good observation posts . . . [The] only arm in which Germans appear still to have confidence is [the] machine gun, but machine gunners are handicapped by lack of proper emplacements . . . The 1916 recruits are not seasoned or steady under fire.'[14] Yet the disappointing debut of the tanks and the lack of any obvious strategic results increased the pressure on Haig. New attacks were mounted on 1 and 7 October, but the onset of poor weather – mist that prevented aircraft from operating, heavier rainfall, and the accompanying mud that grew slippier and deeper every day – condemned British attacks to bloody failure. With intelligence revealing a fourth and fifth defensive position being constructed behind enemy lines, it seemed that the battle was reaching its final, concluding stages.

Haig was not yet ready to admit the 'great push' was over. In a letter to Sir William Robertson (dated 7 October), he reiterated the good results and explained how he was keen to continue operations into October and, if necessary, through the winter.[15] Accordingly, orders were issued for the renewal of the offensive, with Fourth Army launching new attacks towards the villages of Ligny-Thilloy, Beaulencourt and Le Transloy on the afternoon of 12 October. Rainfall fell most of the day, worsening the already precarious ground conditions, and sapping the morale of the battalions in the line, many of which were already under-strength and exhausted. The result was another bloody repulse. Little air cover could be provided because of the poor weather, which left German gunners free to pound British trenches. Artillery support was also too weak to batter down the defences, which inevitably meant that battalions found themselves under sustained machine-gun fire as soon as they tried to cross no-man's-land. The following day, as he flicked through the grim casualty returns, Rawlinson's Chief of Staff, Archibald Montgomery, penned a short but insightful note on why success had been elusive, including the 'absence of surprise'; 'difficulty of observation'; a lack of 'sufficient Assembly Trenches'; distant machine-gun fire; and, more ominously, 'the Moral[e] of the Enemy appeared to have improved, as his troops fought with greater stubbornness'.[16]

The attacks on the Somme may have been contained, but the effect on the German Army was stark. September was the worst month of the battle for the defenders: a terrible period of endurance that, in hindsight, would come to be seen as the tipping point, the moment that marked the great slide towards defeat. Together First and Second Armies sustained 135,000 casualties, a high percentage of which were prisoners, raising serious concerns at OHL about the Army's morale. On 26 September – the day that Thiepval finally fell to Gough's Reserve Army – Ludendorff wrote to Rupprecht about the difficulty they were having in providing enough reinforcements and reserves for the battle:

> The relief schedule of the army group of Crown Prince Rupprecht said that it 'provides for a regular changeover of the divisions after fourteen days'. This cannot be carried out in the long run. The army group will, therefore, have to change its relief process so that only at the fighting hotspots will the divisions be replaced every fourteen days; in all other places they will have to stay longer in the front. A fairer changeover should also be sought within First and Second Armies so that troops from quiet sections are posted to the places under threat and vice versa.[17]

For Rupprecht, the problem of reserves was only one of many. An honest man, lacking the supreme ambition or lust for power that characterized other senior German officers, Rupprecht had long been concerned about the deterioration in the army caused by 'continued, prolonged and exhausting fighting'. While he recognized that German infantry were 'inferior to that of the enemy in terms of size', they had always been 'far superior in terms of quality'. However, over recent months 'this qualitative superiority has been significantly diminished due to the large losses, especially of officers and NCOs', which was also combined with a worrying expansion in the number of enemy artillery batteries.[18] He also had to deal with the growing falling out between his senior commanders. Max von Gallwitz had not taken his demotion from army group lightly and accused Rupprecht of prioritizing the defence north of the Somme, leaving him without enough forces to defend against the French. When Rupprecht and his Chief of Staff, Hermann von Kuhl, paid Second Army a visit in late September, Gallwitz did not even deign to send an officer to meet them, leaving them to make their way to his office unescorted.[19]

The meeting was predictably stormy. Gallwitz pointed out 'the unequal distribution of forces in the two armies'. In First Army, each division held a frontage of 2.5 kilometres, but in Second Army it was 4.5 kilometres. While Gallwitz had a point about the comparative number of troops north and south of the river, both Rupprecht and Below understood that the British sector posed the more dangerous threat. Rupprecht found Gallwitz 'very temperamental'; while Kuhl complained that Second Army did not send enough reports and orders to the army group, leaving them in the dark about his operations. Gallwitz shrugged off their questions and warned them about a major attack that he believed was imminent along the French sector.[20] All Rupprecht could do was explain how he was issuing a directive on the construction of a rear defensive position between Arras and Laon, which would begin immediately. Until that was completed, Gallwitz simply had to hold on whatever the cost.

The strain on the German High Command was understandable. They had all been impressed by the intensity of the fighting; the huge array of resources that the French and British could now deploy, and the arrival of tanks, only hardened a belief that the Somme fighting was becoming deeply unbalanced. They had all seen the shattered remnants of battalions march back from the line: the thin files of muddied men, faces drawn with glassy eyes – a picture of total exhaustion that unnerved them. Casualties in those units sent to the front could be shockingly high. When 86 Fusilier Regiment assembled southeast of Saint-Quentin in early September, the regimental historian recorded that there was nothing left but 'debris'. Total casualties on the Somme had been seventy-eight officers and over 3,300 men. In just two months of fighting, the regiment had lost more men than its entire regular combat strength had been at the beginning of the battle. This was not an unusual occurrence. 26th Reserve Division fought valiantly at Ovillers and Beaumont Hamel throughout July, but sustained over 10,000 casualties. Even elite divisions found the Somme a terrible ordeal. 1st Guards Division lost over 5,000 men in just two days of brutal combat in mid-August. Likewise 2nd Guards Division was heavily engaged at Pozières and Thiepval, losing half its strength.[21]

The losses, as bad as they were, were only part of what made the Somme such an ordeal for the German Army. Surviving in a sea of craters, under almost non-stop artillery fire, German infantry were reduced to a kind of savage desperation in their struggle for survival. Chaplains reported that attendance at religious services had dropped, while regimental officers duly noted a growth in sickness and rates of desertion, with incidents of self-inflicted wounds rising throughout the battle. 'This is no longer war, but mutual annihilation', complained one sergeant after weeks in the line.[22] Gallwitz blamed the policy of 'pure defence', which had 'an erosive and crippling effect', and was concerned that junior officers were not impressing upon their men the importance of digging in. 'Sweat saves blood. A leader who does not rigorously encourage his troops to dig trenches is negligent with the lives of his men.' Even Rupprecht, not one prone to unnecessary defeatism, admitted in early October that 'The large number of prisoners that we have lost recently is a bad sign. Generally there is so much to be depressed about!'[23]

As for Ludendorff's complaints about reliefs, Rupprecht understood the dilemma he was facing, but could offer little comfort. In a reply written on 29 September, Rupprecht noted that 'The army group strongly believes that full replacements must be provided if at any point a company fails. However, such a possibility must be anticipated because experience already shows that units deployed on the Somme for the second time do not have the same fighting power as on the first tour. The reason for this is the lack of experienced officers and a sufficiently trained team . . .'[24] Kuhl described the process of managing the movement of divisions in and out of the line as like 'living from hand to mouth'. The original aim was to have sufficient reserves available so that no division would have to be deployed at the front for longer than two weeks. However, this soon proved impossible to manage. 'The divisions often had to be sent urgently to the Somme front without enough rest and were expended too quickly.' Therefore, local commanders had to have 'nerves of steel not to lose their heads and to deploy the incoming reinforcements' prematurely. It was only through the intervention of the Supreme Command, which provided extra reinforcements, that the front was held.[25]

Fortunately the pace of the battle slowed during October and allowed the German Army enough time to relieve worn-out units and replace them with fresh divisions taken from across the Western Front. At Verdun, the Crown Prince was ordered to maintain a strict defensive and provide as many troops as possible (to be replaced by exhausted ones from the Somme). The defence was also bolstered by the arrival of new aircraft – particularly the fast and sturdy Albatros D.II – that were formed into 'pursuit squadrons' (*Jagdstaffeln*) and made an immediate impact upon the air war. Very quickly it became apparent that the British and French would no longer have free rein over the German lines. The Albatros outclassed their fighters and proved lethal against the slower-moving reconnaissance aircraft that were crucial to the counter-battery effort. German infantry, who had long complained about the dominance of British and French aeroplanes over their trenches, now looked up to see silhouettes of 'silver-grey, short, stubby' aircraft 'in a compact battle array', chasing off their enemies or swooping down upon them, their twin forward-firing machine-guns chattering away. The obvious superiority of German fighters produced an immediate surge in morale.[26]

The changing balance of power in the air was revealed on 17 September, a warm Sunday with fine, clear skies, when Jagdstaffel 2, the first squadron to be equipped with the Albatros, was out in force. In a series of chaotic dogfights over Cambrai, the German squadron scored six victories, including an F.E.2, which was shot down by one of its newest pilots, Manfred von Richthofen, who had joined the squadron the previous month. It was only the beginning of a remarkable rise as Jagdstaffel 2 rapidly chalked up victories in the closing months of 1916. By the end of October, it had fifty kills to its credit – striking fear into the British and French and sparking an urgent search for answers.[27] On 29 September, Major-General Hugh Trenchard, commander of the RFC, wrote to Haig requesting an urgent increase in the 'numbers and efficiency of the fighting aeroplanes' at his disposal. 'Throughout the last three months the Royal Flying Corps in France has maintained such a measure of superiority over the enemy in the air that it has been enabled to render services of incalculable value. The result is that the enemy has made extraordinary efforts to increase the number, and develop the speed and power, of his fighting machines.' With the arrival of the Albatros, Trenchard warned that they were now in serious danger of losing their 'present predominance in the air'.[28]

*

At GQG, Joffre could only look upon the gradual petering out of the offensive with a feeling of sadness. His frustrations with Haig occasionally bubbled over into a cross word, or an unkind aside that the British were hanging back, but never into a real break in relations. Haig liked 'old Joffre', but (privately at least) never placed much stock in his ideas, preferring instead to stand his ground whenever the French demanded too much. On 18 October, Joffre asked Haig again to consider a return to wide-front operations, only to spark a spiky response from the British Commander-in-Chief, who reminded Joffre that he, and only he, would judge when attacks should be mounted.[29] Vallières immediately sensed the tension when he saw Haig several days later. 'It's the first time that Sir Douglas Haig receives me coldly, stating that he needs lessons from no-one, that he knows as much about the art of war as General Joffre, and that he does not accept the terms of his note.' Vallières managed to arrange a 'reconciliation' lunch between the two men, but was horrified by Joffre's 'abdication' of responsibility after he told Haig to disregard any future letters from Chantilly. 'He makes quite a poor picture', wrote Vallières; 'very tired, having put on an extraordinary amount of weight, taking little painful steps as though walking on eggs . . .'[30]

With the British not proving as pliable an ally as the French would have liked, Joffre had little choice but to relent. He was now increasingly besieged, with deputies in the French Parliament becoming more restive over the conduct of the war. The War Minister, Roques, had already informed him in August that parliamentarians would be free to inspect 'all the army services' and allow the Government to be kept 'constantly informed', which provoked another threat of resignation.[31] Joffre now felt himself to be surrounded by enemies, and even his chief lieutenants – men who had been with him since the opening days of the war – were not above suspicion: Foch, condemned to fight a battle he never believed in; Pétain, unsympathetic to Joffre's calls to attack; and Castelnau, ever genial, but a constant rival at GQG. Instead, Joffre looked to Nivelle, the pleasant and easy-going commander of Second Army. On 13 September – two days before Haig would launch the tanks at Flers – Joffre visited Verdun to attend a ceremony in the citadel and, taking Nivelle aside, told him that he must retake Fort Douaumont. If the British would not make the decisive push on the Somme, then maybe it would have to be done at Verdun. 'Don't count on the English,' he had told members of the Superior Council of National Defence several days earlier, 'just count on ourselves, count only on ourselves.'[32]

It took over a month to prepare the operation, but by late October the combined talents of Pétain, Nivelle and Mangin had produced a plan that seemed likely to succeed. 24 October was an overcast and dismal day, the air saturated with a thick white fog. It was not the most auspicious weather for the long-awaited attempt to retake Douaumont, but the French High Command was not minded to postpone it any longer. For the last three days, French gunners had been firing off salvo after salvo, both heavy and light shells, gas and smoke, into the German-held ridges along the east bank of the Meuse. Consumption of ammunition had been prodigious. Over half a million 75 mm shells had been expended, plus as many rounds as could be fired from a group of refurbished coastal artillery batteries and super-heavy mortars that had been hurriedly converted for use in the field. Pétain also insisted that the French employ two 400 mm railway howitzers – similar to the 'Big Berthas' that had cracked Liège – to batter the fort itself, its concrete facade now obscured by dust and smoke.[33] A day before the assault went in, a terrific fire swept through its corridors, forcing the garrison to withdraw apart from a few brave observers who were left to watch over it. Germany's great prize of February 1916, which had seemed to herald the impending collapse of the French defence, was now a curious relic: increasingly difficult to hold, yet impossible to abandon.

The French Army's method of attack was becoming ever more sophisticated. As well as pounding the German trenches and lines of approach, it systematically targeted enemy batteries in the weeks before the attack, while French fighter squadrons (*escadrilles*) photographed the front and engaged in perilous missions to bomb headquarters and billets, road junctions and railway yards behind the line. Three divisions had prepared meticulously for the attack, rehearsing their advance over specially constructed replicas of the battlefield after being given the latest intelligence on the state of the enemy and the layout of the fort. General Nivelle had never been more sure of success: 'Twenty-seven months of war and eight months of fighting at Verdun have shown and increasingly confirm every day the superiority of French over German soldiers. This superiority, that everyone should be aware of, is further increased by the gradual reduction in the quality of the troops we have in front of us, many of whom were at the Somme, and very weakened in terms of equipment and morale . . .' He now had 'exceptionally powerful' artillery support (over 700 guns), which would 'overpower the enemy's artillery and open up the way for assault forces'. Preparations were 'as perfect as possible'.[34]

The attack began at 11.40 a.m. with the infantry moving forward behind a creeping barrage advancing 100 yards every four minutes – a pace that could be maintained over shell-torn ground. Against the French were seven German divisions, an impressive order of battle, albeit most had been in the line for weeks and were exhausted and under-strength. Over 110 guns had also left Fifth Army's artillery component since August (bound for the Somme), while all its remaining batteries had been placed on severely reduced ammunition rates, which limited their response to the bombardment.[35] When the French attacked, German squads in the forward positions fired off a series of flares (to alert their supporting artillery), but these went unnoticed in the murk, leaving them alone to face the black barrage of fizzing shrapnel that surged over their positions. A German captain, caught up in the horror, scribbled a message for one of his carrier pigeons, which then fluttered into the smoky air, only to fall into the hands of the enemy: 'All of the battle position in Sector A has been completely flattened by violent "Trommelfeuer" shelling of all sizes that has continued incessantly since 8 a.m. Men who escaped the shelling state that they were overwhelmed with gunfire and hand grenades and that anyone who is still alive in the garrison is unable to fight.'[36]

The 'honour' of seizing Douaumont had been given to the men of 38th Division, mainly composed of colonial troops from North Africa, including the Moroccan Regiment, which would take the fortress. The battlefield was a terrible spectacle. The 'waterlogged clay was as greasy as butter', recorded one officer, 'battered by shells to the point of looking like it was blistered with foam with the consistency of soap lather and not unlike the bubbling white crests of a rough sea'. After taking and consolidating their first objective, the troops continued on to the fort around three o'clock. 'The enemy, even though in disarray, offered strong resistance', noted an after-action report. 'There were many bursts of machine-gun fire. Machine-guns, grenades and flamethrowers overpowered the resistance and the fort ended up with all its surface area occupied, despite some losses.'[37]

Joffre spent the day at Souilly chatting with his aides and waiting for news to come in. When it was confirmed that Douaumont was in French hands, he broke into a broad smile. 'That day . . .' he later wrote, 'was one of the happiest I spent during the war.'[38] In just four hours they had captured two miles of ground – what the Germans had taken months to wrest from French hands – vindicating the methods that Second Army had employed in planning and directing the battle. 'Victory at Verdun', screamed the headline of *Le Matin* as it contemplated the 'brilliant' operation in which Generals Nivelle and Mangin had taken the starring role.[39] For Charles Mangin, who commanded the assaulting sector, news of Douaumont's recapture was a moment of great personal redemption. A friend who saw him in the hours afterwards described him as being 'radiant and happy; younger than ever with his bright, smiling eyes, little wrinkled dimples, a smile not quite as crooked as before. The face of a general in victory is indeed a handsome one.'[40]

The fighting at Verdun and the Somme was not yet over. On the Meuse, Nivelle, now feted wherever he went, was authorized to continue attacking, which he did, utilizing his standard method of limited objectives and creeping barrages that took advantage of the weakness of the German forces now at Verdun to strike again and again. Fort Vaux was recaptured on 2 November, with French troops jubilantly celebrating on top of its battered, shell-gouged roof. Although some French officers felt that they had done enough, that they should be content with what they had just achieved, Nivelle wanted to do more. He wrote to Joffre on 11 November confirming that he intended to maintain an 'offensive attitude' over the coming months. Because Douaumont was still under direct enemy observation, it was necessary to push on further, out towards Hardaumont and Bezonvaux, which would give the French defences greater depth and ensure the safety of Douaumont, the preservation of which was of 'the first importance from a tactical and moral point of view'.[41]

On the Somme, Gough's Reserve Army continued to push north after the fall of Thiepval, although progress was now becoming more and more difficult. It was a similar story along Fourth Army's sector. By mid-October, Rawlinson's drive towards Le Transloy had stalled badly. Another push was launched on 18 October, this time in conjunction with French forces south of the river, but, once again, no ground was gained. The poor weather and lack of air support reduced the effectiveness of British guns, while the sodden ground meant that many of the shells buried themselves in the mud before exploding. When the infantry went forward, splashing across the ooze of no-man's-land, they encountered heavy machine-gun fire and their advance bogged down into fierce and ultimately inconclusive bombing fights. In what would become a typical, depressing experience, 4th Division, attacking on the extreme right of the British line, found that 'No organized line held by the enemy was met, but heavy machine gun fire and rifle fire was directed on to our waves from front and flanks . . . The ground was terribly torn up by shellfire, and as slippery as ice. The men kept on slipping and falling into the holes in the dark. The few who returned were one mass of mud from head to foot, and completely exhausted.'[42]

The continuation of attacks so late in the season strained the already fragile relationship between Haig and Rawlinson, whose natural impulses differed so dramatically: Haig never lost his stubborn, optimistic streak; while Rawlinson worried constantly about what he was putting his men through. When Haig told his army commanders (on 29 October) that both Fourth and Fifth Armies should prepare to continue operations through the winter, Rawlinson protested in the strongest terms he could muster. He would be failing in his duty as an army commander, he replied, 'if I did not represent the difficulties which this policy appears to me to involve'. All his divisions had taken part in the Somme twice, some up to four

times. 'They have had very heavy losses amounting in some cases
from 7,000 to 10,000 men, and have suffered very severely in officers,
N[on] C[ommissioned] officers and specialists.' Given such losses, it
would take time for these formations to recover. 'It is not exaggerating to say that in most units now, even in the best Divisions like the
Guards, the nucleus [of experienced officers and NCOs] on which we
must depend for preparing the general offensive in the spring has
almost reached breaking point.' He therefore believed it would be
unwise to 'engage in any extended enterprise' as there was a 'grave
risk' that 'by attempting too much during the winter we may fail in
matters of far greater importance next spring'.[43]

With Rawlinson proving stubborn, Haig turned to Hubert Gough,
the commander of the renamed Fifth Army (the old Reserve Army),
who had been planning an operation on the British left, astride the line
of the Ancre river for some time, only for it to be continually postponed because of the heavy rain. Haig was keen for the offensive to be
mounted and felt that a success would strengthen his position at an
inter-Allied conference, scheduled for mid-November. Gough's divisions went over the top at 5.45 on the morning of 13 November, when
it was still dark, the air frosty and thin. For the past week a heavy bombardment had been pounding the German positions between Beaucourt
and Beaumont Hamel, turning the villages into splattered brick dust
and destroying the nests of machine-guns that had proved so deadly on
1 July. The German High Command had long been expecting an
attack on the British left, but shortages of troops meant that they could
not hold up the advance when it came. Utilizing more artillery than
had previously been employed and a slower than usual creeping barrage (moving at a rate of 100 yards every five minutes), seven British
divisions were able to secure most of their objectives despite awful
mud, gaining about 2,000 yards, including the capture of Beaumont
Hamel, Beaucourt and Saint-Pierre-Divion. When confirmation was
received later that morning, Haig rode over to Gough's headquarters
and congratulated him and his staff on their achievements. 'The result
was good because, in spite of the wet ground, our troops took the position without much difficulty and the enemy surrendered much more
readily than on any previous occasion', he noted in his diary. Haig

believed that more guns had been firing on Gough's small sector than had been used along the whole of the battle line on 1 July 1916. 'The success has come at a most opportune moment.'[44]

The inter-Allied conference was duly held at Chantilly two days later, with Joffre presiding over a meeting of Allied General Staffs, including Haig and Robertson. Their conclusions were strikingly similar to those recorded in December 1915: that operations would continue, as far as possible, throughout the winter, and that the coalition would be ready to resume 'comprehensive offensives' by the first half of February 1917.[45] With Allied commanders now looking towards the spring of the following year, Haig finally relented and agreed to shut down operations on the Somme. Despite not gaining his objectives, the British Commander-in-Chief was bullish about what had been achieved and did not reproach himself for any setbacks. On the contrary, he believed that the offensive had been a success and that the results of the fighting augured well for the future. 'The enemy's power has not yet been broken,' he wrote in his despatch, 'nor is it yet possible to form an estimate of the time the war may last before the objects for which the Allies are fighting have been attained. But the Somme battle has placed beyond doubt the ability of the Allies to gain those objects.'[46]

Haig's confidence remained unshaken despite the heavy losses the New Armies had sustained in the course of the year. In the spring of 1916, Lord Kitchener had warned him not to squander the armies that he had raised, but to husband them jealously. At the same time, Robertson had told the War Cabinet that Haig would 'not do anything foolish' during the coming year. Yet by the time Gough's attacks on the Ancre had tailed off in mid-November, British losses on the Somme amounted to some 419,000.[47] It was a staggering figure; a blood cost of almost unimaginable proportions that raised profound questions about whether the war could possibly be continued. On 13 November, the Fifth Marquis of Lansdowne, a bewhiskered former Viceroy of India and Minister Without Portfolio in Asquith's government, circulated a paper to the War Cabinet on the danger of prolonging the war unnecessarily. Nobody could tell 'what our plight, and the plight of the civilised world will be after another year, or, as we are sometimes told, two or three more years of a struggle as exhausting as that in which we are engaged. No one for a moment believes that we are going to lose the war; but what is our chance of winning it in such a manner, and within such limits of time, as will enable us to beat our enemy to the ground and impose upon him the kind of terms which we so freely discuss?'[48]

As would become apparent over the coming months, there was little appetite for peace on either side. In Germany, the appointment of Hindenburg and Ludendorff had signalled a new determination to make whatever sacrifices were necessary to win the war, even if the Somme had been a terrible ordeal. German losses were slightly higher than the British figure: just shy of 430,000 if gas casualties and psychiatric disorders are added to the numbers of dead, wounded and missing in action.[49] While this might have seemed to indicate a favourable result in the grim stakes of attrition, Entente losses also had to account for 204,000 French casualties, which indicated just how expensive wearing down the German Army was; a business that might never bear fruit. Rupprecht even felt that the morale of his men in the final weeks of the battle was higher than it had been for some time. 'While the English previously moved forward in thin lines, they have recently advanced in company columns, as in the strong partial attacks of 6 and 8 [November], which were quickly stifled in some places just by our artillery fire, causing them to suffer very heavy losses. Presumably the English infantry can only be put forward in close formations. This may be due to the lack of skill of the troops and their officers, but also because they distrust the troops and therefore want to keep a firm grip on them.'[50]

As 1916 came to its inglorious end, bathed in blood, conditions at the front were deteriorating rapidly. Those who were there had to operate in a ghostly, frozen wilderness that seemed to suck the life out of them: trees and vegetation stripped from the land or shattered into pieces; rotting bodies in varying states of decomposition, their limbs stiffened into extreme angles; and all amid a landscape of barbed wire and corrugated iron; a Hell walled in by sandbags. 'The field drainage system had been utterly destroyed,' remembered one British officer, 'the metal surface of the roads completely blown away, so that now, in November, men and animals moved through a pale yellow-whitish slime, seldom less than knee deep and very often waist-deep in every trench or valley . . . our struggle was as much against the elements as it was against the Germans.'[51] The skies were now growing colder and the air thinner, while the scarred front lines were softened under a freshly laid coat of white snow on the morning of 18 November. The Somme was over.

13. 'A very serious decision'

Bucharest was abandoned on 3 December, with German and Austrian troops marching along snow-lined roads into the Romanian capital three days later. Romania, which had only joined the Entente on 27 August, had been occupied in less than four months, providing the Central Powers with a timely and decisive victory that revived hopes at OHL that Germany was still capable of winning the war. With most of Romania occupied, Germany now had access to her vast stocks of grain, which would help keep the German people fed over the coming winter. There were joyful scenes across the empire when news was relayed of this remarkable triumph. The Kaiser ordered church bells to be rung and toasted his 'victorious army' at Pless, while on the Somme the entire staff of First Army, led by Fritz von Lossberg, spent the evening celebrating by 'emptying a considerable number of bottles that only recently had arrived from a vineyard on the Moselle'.[1]

The victory in Romania came not a moment too soon. Already there were signs that the effects of war, including the vice-like grip of the Allied naval blockade, were having a deleterious effect on the home front, with long queues forming in German and Austrian cities by the spring of 1916 as staple foods began to run out – to be replaced by a lengthening and unappetizing list of substitute (*ersatz*) products. Food prices were already twice their pre-war level in Germany, while in Austria soaring inflation meant that the cost of living was six times higher by December 1916. The season would forever be known as the 'turnip winter', when starving citizens had to resort to eating the unfashionable root vegetable after an unusually cold spell caused shortages of coal, leaving many potatoes to rot in transit on Germany's overworked railway network. Soup kitchens began opening across the country, serving a thin stew that never seemed to hold off the pangs of hunger for long or the dissatisfaction with the war effort that grew week by week. As one German politician noted ruefully, 'People think most of revolution when they are hungry.'[2]

Eager to capitalize upon the victory in Romania, Bethmann Hollweg addressed the German Parliament on 12 December. Speaking before a packed assembly, with large crowds gathered outside, he declared that a note had been transmitted to neutral powers calling for peace negotiations. Germany and her allies, Austria–Hungary, Bulgaria and Turkey, 'have given proof of their indestructible strength in winning considerable successes at war. Their unshakable lines resist ceaseless attacks of their enemies' arms . . . The latest events have demonstrated that a continuation of the war can not break their resisting power.' Therefore, the Central Powers now desired to enter into peace negotiations, 'which would aim to assure the existence, honor, and free development of their peoples' as a basis for 'a lasting peace'. This was followed five days later by an intervention from the US President, Woodrow Wilson, who addressed each belligerent directly, calling for them to state 'the terms upon which the war might be concluded'.[3]

A formal reply from the governments of Belgium, France, Great Britain, Italy, Japan, Montenegro, Portugal, Romania, Russia and Serbia was transmitted on 29 December, with the Entente refusing 'to entertain a proposal without sincerity and without import'.[4] Whether the German High Command actually believed anything would come of the note was unclear, but its swift rejection by Allied governments – being bound together not to sign a separate peace – caused little surprise in Berlin and cleared the way for a further intensification of the war. The submarine campaign had never been far from the minds of Germany's leaders, and now, as operations in Romania drew down, the matter resurfaced. Her U-boats were still nominally following the 'Sussex Pledge' of May 1916, which consigned her vessels to standard cruiser rules on 'visit and search', but calls for this to be dropped grew each month, with both the Kaiser and Bethmann Hollweg attracting criticism for not pursuing victory with all the weapons at their disposal; a charge that pained the insecure Wilhelm II more than most.

Bolstering OHL's case was Admiral Henning von Holtzendorff,

Chief of the Admiralty Staff at the Imperial German Navy, who lobbied hard for the unleashing of its U-boats. In a memorandum circulated in late December, he argued for 'the commencement of unrestricted submarine warfare at the earliest opportunity'. If Germany could sink 600,000 tons of shipping each month – a figure that Holtzendorff believed was achievable – then this would devastate Britain's merchant shipping fleet and so interfere with her seaborne trade that she might be forced to sue for peace by the summer of 1917. 'If we succeed in breaking England's backbone,' he wrote, 'the war will immediately be decided in our favour.' The issue of American belligerence – the spectre that so worried Bethmann Hollweg – was waved away. Certainly, Holtzendorff admitted that war with the United States 'should by all means be avoided'; however, it 'should not lead us to recoil from making use at the decisive moment of a weapon that promises victory for us'.[5]

Holtzendorff's memorandum was heady stuff. The promise of decisive victory within a matter of months seemed to offer Germany another route out of the strategic impasse on the Western Front. Both Hindenburg and Ludendorff had no scruples about using whatever weapons they possessed and believed that now was the moment for the scrapping of any restrictions on German vessels. Writing on 23 December, Hindenburg urged the Chancellor to 'lose no time in adopting the measure of torpedoing armed enemy merchantmen without notice'. He was not convinced that President Wilson was an honest broker and felt that 'no further interest' be spared on him for the moment. He also warned that morale might be affected by not adopting a more forceful maritime strategy. 'The army now at grips with the enemy would regard this matter in the same light. Officers and men expect us to employ all our resources and ignore secondary matters. It is impossible to guarantee the *moral[e]* of the army if its resolution is to be undermined.'[6]

Bethmann Hollweg replied the following day, reminding Hindenburg that, as it was a matter of foreign policy, he had the final say on this campaign, which would, inevitably, be aimed as much at neutral shipping as at enemy vessels. Moreover, with Germany yet to receive a formal reply to her peace note (which would come on 29 December), the Chancellor was wary of moving too quickly. 'No one to-day is in a position to say what the answer will be', he wrote. 'Probabilities seem to show that it will mainly be a refusal, though it may leave some back door open. We must not close that door.' With rumours about the possible reopening of submarine warfare rampant in the German press, Bethmann Hollweg wanted to avoid giving the impression that Germany was not serious in her overtures and reminded Hindenburg that it was 'absolutely essential that Main Headquarters should take the sharpest measures to secure that such discussions should not take place in the Press'.[7]

OHL was unconvinced. 'Unfortunately our military situation makes it impossible that negotiations of any kind should be allowed to postpone military measures which have once been recognized as essential, and thus paralyse the energy of our operations', replied Hindenburg on 26 December. Furthermore, he would also do what he could to correct the widespread impression that it was OHL and *not* the Chancellor that was preventing Germany from employing submarine warfare.[8] When the rejection of the German terms was received several days later, both Hindenburg and Ludendorff maintained their aggressive stance, boxing Bethmann Hollweg into a corner during a meeting on strategy at Pless on New Year's Day. The Chancellor tried to hold his ground, telling the two officers that 'We must be quite clear that, judging by the military situation, great military blows are scarcely likely to bring us final victory' and that they must realize the U-boat campaign was their 'last card' – 'A very serious decision!' But Hindenburg was unmoved. 'The submarine operations in cruiser form have hitherto brought us only a slightly greater measure of success', he admitted. 'We need the most energetic and ruthless action possible.' Ludendorff agreed. 'The U-boat war will improve the situation even of our armies. The ammunition supply [of our enemies] will suffer from the shortage of timber and coal. That means a relief for the troops on the western front. We must spare the troops a second Somme battle.'[9]

The Kaiser would make the final decision. He had hitherto followed a cautious path, listening to his Chancellor and being wary of committing too much to a campaign that had always promised so much, yet seemed barren of result. At a Crown Council meeting at Pless on 9 January, the arguments were revisited once more: Holtzendorff urging them to take the opportunity to strike, while Bethmann Hollweg, outmanoeuvred and isolated, admitted that if the military authorities believed the time was right, he could not oppose it. The Allies' rejection of Germany's note had stung the Kaiser, and he knew that any further vacillation might have a demoralizing effect back home. By the autumn of 1916 there was a majority in the Reichstag for a change of policy, with even the Catholic Centre Party joining the chorus for a more intensive submarine campaign. So, when the order was placed before him, the Kaiser sat down and signed it. As he did so, he looked up at the assembled officers and told them that he now expected a declaration of war from the United States. 'If it came . . .' he added, 'so much the better.'[10] The campaign would begin on 1 February 1917. Germany had played her 'last card'.

The Somme may have petered out in the snows of mid-November, but at Verdun the front continued to smoulder and burn. At ten o'clock on the bitterly cold morning of 15 December, the white air like a shroud, the 155 mm howitzer on top of Fort Douaumont fired a single shot – the signal for the final attack of the battle. At that moment, Mangin's group of four divisions swept forward beneath a rain of shellfire: a double creeping barrage that would lead them on to their objectives. Firstly, high-explosive shells would clear the way, to be followed up by another line of shrapnel bursts, behind which came the French infantry, stumbling over the shell holes and smashing through the frozen pools of water. Five German divisions were in the line, although the effects of a six-day long preliminary bombardment had reduced their defences to a series of shambolic ditches. They fought with their usual courage, but they were unable to arrest the French advance, which reached three kilometres into their lines, seizing the twin objectives of Louvemont and Bezonvaux and taking back the shattered woodland of the Bois des Caurrières, which had been lost back in February. Eleven thousand prisoners were taken.[11]

The speed with which the defences collapsed shocked the German High Command, with Hans von Zwehl, a corps commander who had served on the Meuse since February, being sacked for his part in the debacle. For the French, the attack seemed further proof that Nivelle had what he called 'the formula'. On the evening of 18 December, Mangin issued an order to his soldiers; a defiant response to the German peace note, promising them the 'certainty of an ultimate victory'. The recent fighting ('fought on ground that offered exceptional defensive conditions') had proved that it was 'possible to defeat an enemy in greater numbers' and that 'with the careful use of artillery, the suitable layout of the land, and the support of an alert air force, a valiant and well-briefed infantry can break through, and then manoeuvre, under General Nivelle's command. We have both strategy and leadership. That's the key to success.'[12]

Despite the euphoria over Nivelle's victories, the mood in the French Army – as Pétain had long warned – was fragile. At the end of October, liaison officers had told President Poincaré that an 'evil spirit' was manifesting itself among soldiers at the front. After the Ministry of Finance began distributing pamphlets advertising a new war loan, Poincaré received 'dozens of letters from the front filled with insults and threats'. Although he felt the people were 'very calm and collected in the midst of sadness', French patience was running out.[13] In Paris, the parliamentary struggles over control of the war effort only intensified as Verdun came to an end. Two secret sessions were held in November, with deputies quizzing Briand on the disaster in Romania and whether France could have done more to prevent her from being overrun so quickly. 'I am afraid that the Ministry is nearly sick unto death', wrote Lord Bertie, the British Ambassador. 'The Government majority in the Chamber is in a shrinking state. Their enemies and rivals are out for blood, and the combination against them is formidable.'[14] Although Briand survived a vote of confidence, he knew that changes would have to be made if he was to continue in office. He devised a plan that would answer his critics, yet avoid the fallout from a messy and protracted divorce with France's most senior soldier. He told Joffre that he was about to be promoted, becoming a Marshal of France, where he would 'continue to direct the war' – albeit in a more removed role as 'technical advisor' to the Government. The French armies on the Western Front would henceforth come under the orders of another officer, who would be appointed as soon as Joffre's views had been taken into account.[15]

When Joffre was told about these plans, he shrugged his broad shoulders, saying that he had always followed the orders of the Government and that 'the project appeared entirely logical'. It was only later on, when the decrees were published, that he realized he was being neutered, pushed into a high-sounding position with little power and even less responsibility. Joffre requested clarification from Briand, only to find that the Government had no intention of listening to his recommendations, so accordingly, on 26 December, he sent in his resignation, which was finally accepted. Joffre's authority had now passed to his successor, General Robert Nivelle, who was the clear choice of the French Government. The decision to appoint Nivelle over the heads of more senior candidates, including the army group commanders – Pétain, Foch and Franchet d'Espèrey (who had replaced Augustin Dubail at Eastern Army Group in March 1916), as well as Joffre's Chief of Staff, Castelnau – aroused surprisingly little concern. For one reason or another each of the major figures in the French Army had ruled himself out: Pétain was too pessimistic; Foch too closely associated with Joffre; Franchet d'Espèrey largely unknown; Castelnau too devout. Nivelle was none of those things. 'He was good-looking, smart, plausible and cool', wrote an English admirer. 'He was a man of medium height, judged by our standards, with regular well-drawn features, thoughtful brown eyes, a slightly greying well-brushed moustache, dark hair showing white at the temples, and a *mouche* or tuft of hair, also turned grey, under the lower lip. He gave an impression of vigour, strength and energy.'[16]

At a time when the French people were wearying of the struggle and when France's politicians were unhappy about committing themselves to another series of indecisive Somme-like battles, Nivelle's 'formula' was a seductive alternative. 'The experience is conclusive', he had told his staff before he left for GQG; 'our method has proved itself. Once again the Second Army has displayed more clearly than before its *moral* and material ascendancy over the enemy. Victory is certain: of that I can assure you. Germany will learn this to her cost.'[17] Those who came into contact with the new commander were struck by his confident bearing, as if he were carrying a remarkable secret that no one else possessed. 'We bowed before his fortune,' remembered a staff officer, 'saw in it the sign of a destiny more powerful than the slow process of promotion, and we trusted in his good luck.' He would even be acceptable to the British. Speaking fluent English – his mother was the daughter of an Indian Army officer – Nivelle seemed to personify the close links between the two allies on the Western Front. In his person, so wrote the *Écho de Paris*, 'the Entente Cordiale is indeed incarnate'.[18]

As well as promoting Nivelle, the French Government made a number of other appointments. Pierre Roques was given an army command and replaced as Minister of War by Louis Hubert Lyautey, a 62-year-old colonial soldier who had spent the last four years as Resident-General of Morocco. Castelnau was appointed commander of the Eastern Army Group, while Mangin was also given an army (Sixth) and General Fayolle was transferred to First Army. Apart from Joffre, the main casualty of these manoeuvres was Ferdinand Foch, who was replaced as Northern Army Group commander by Franchet d'Espèrey. Foch had endured a difficult year, suffering a motor car accident in May, when his vehicle collided with a tree, leaving him battered and bruised. He also found his efforts on the Somme overshadowed by the enormous struggle under way at Verdun, where Pétain and Nivelle vied with one another for control of the French defence. Foch had never wanted to fight on the Somme, but chivvied Fayolle along, while being continually frustrated by the attitudes of both Rawlinson and Haig towards making coordinated attacks. Yet the meagre results of the battle unnerved French politicians, who were not slow to notice that Foch had formed a close relationship with Georges Clemenceau, the 75-year-old senator and arch-critic of the Government, who saw in Foch something of himself: a restless soul who burnt for France.

Joffre had fallen out with Foch over his lukewarm enthusiasm for the Somme as well as his penchant for preferring his own 'methodical battle' to the breakthrough style of operation that Joffre always favoured. When Foch's name was brought up as a possible future Commander-in-Chief, Joffre was nonplussed, saying that he did not want Foch to lead any renewal of the Somme battle, and nor would he be a suitable replacement for him at GQG. Foch, who had been an invaluable fighting general in 1914, was evidently now surplus to requirements. On 16 December, he received a telegram stating that he was being removed from command of his army group, and, shortly afterwards, it was confirmed that he was being placed 'at the disposition of the Minister of War'; a firm indication that he was being sacked.[19] Foch exploded, firing out invectives and storming off to see Joffre, who was staying in his villa in Chantilly. Getting up to greet his visitor, he placed his hand on Foch's shoulder and tried to calm him down.

'You are *limogé*,' he said – referring to the town in central France where French generals went to be reassigned – 'I shall be *limogé*, we shall all be *limogé*.'[20]

Joffre finally left the Grand Condé on the morning of 28 December. All those who worked at GQG, including many staff officers, were assembled outside waiting for him to depart. A company of territorials had lined up and when he appeared with his characteristic rotund shape, wearing his dark jacket, red trousers and kepi, they presented arms with well-drilled smartness. He inspected them briefly – a sad, distant look on his face – before saluting and then climbing into his car to be driven away.[21] Watching him leave was Pierre des Vallières, his liaison officer with GHQ, who was disappointed at how the 'victor of the Marne' had been treated and pondered on what the future held. 'We know what is being lost along with him: rare self-control, solid judgement, continuity of effort which has never failed, and very bold plans tempered by prudence. Whose fault is it if he was unable to deliver on the Somme the wide-ranging and powerfully exploited battle that he had prepared?'[22]

The urgent questions that were now being asked about the French war effort were mirrored in London, where a political storm that had been brewing for months finally broke over the weekend of 2–3 December. Herbert Asquith's authority had steadily diminished during 1916 and the regular toll of setbacks, from Loos and Gallipoli to Mesopotamia and the Somme, sapped the energy from his government. David Lloyd George, who had long railed against the misdirection and lethargy that were holding back Britain's war effort, finally threw his hat into the ring on Friday, 1 December; threatening to resign unless he was placed at the head of a new, slimmer War Committee, which did *not* include the Prime Minister and had 'full power . . . to direct all questions connected with the War'. Asquith could never accept such terms without becoming a mere figurehead and he wrote back to Lloyd George complaining that the Prime Minister must chair such a committee and not be 'relegated to the position of an arbiter in the background'.[23]

Asquith spent a frantic few days lobbying for support, only to find that he had misjudged the situation, with most of the senior members of his government – including Lord Curzon and Andrew Bonar Law – pledging their support to Lloyd George. Whatever Lloyd George's flaws, and there were many, the 53-year-old Welshman was an energetic and determined figure. With thick grey-white hair, brushed over to the right, his black eyes flashing with schemes and plots, he was full of fight, whereas by the close of 1916 Asquith was visibly ailing: 'his eyes were watery and his features kept moving about in [a] nervous twitching fashion', as one member of the Cabinet recorded.[24] He had never recovered from the loss of his eldest son, Raymond, mortally wounded on the Somme. The dreadful news had arrived when Asquith and his family were enjoying a weekend party at their home in Sutton Courtenay, Oxfordshire. After the telephone rang, Margot, Asquith's wife, got up to answer it, while the men – Asquith, Sir John Cowans (the Quartermaster-General) and Major-General Sir Tom Bridges (commanding 19th Division) – were 'lingering over port and brandy in the dining room'. When Asquith was told, he burst into tears; his hands shaking as he tried to choke down the grief, before staggering over to an armchair and collapsing. 'Our boy Raymond was killed on Friday' was all he could say to his guests.[25]

Asquith struggled on through the rest of the year, but could do little to stem the growing sense of impatience and frustration that consumed his ministers. When it became clear that he no longer commanded the support of the House of Commons, he resigned, allowing Lloyd George to form a new coalition, which depended, as before, upon substantial Conservative support. Andrew Bonar Law, leader of the Conservatives, recognized that the only man capable of drawing enough support from across the political spectrum, and who possessed the will to victory, was the acerbic Welshman. The new Prime Minister acted quickly. He formed a War Cabinet composed of just five members: himself, Lord Curzon (Lord President and Leader of the House of Lords), Bonar Law (Chancellor), Viscount Milner and Arthur Henderson (Ministers Without Portfolio). He also appointed Sir Maurice Hankey as Secretary to the War Cabinet, meeting him on the evening of 7 December and telling him that he was now Prime Minister, 'though he didn't much like it'.[26]

Lloyd George realized how heavy the burden of office would be. In his first address to the House of Commons as Prime Minister on 19 December, he admitted that he had now assumed 'the most terrible responsibility that can fall upon the shoulders of any living man, as the chief adviser of the Crown, in the most gigantic War in which the country has ever been engaged – a war upon the event of which its destiny depends'. He dismissed the German peace note as a dishonest and outrageous document 'delivered ostentatiously from the triumphant chariot of Prussian militarism' and stated, as clearly as he could, the tasks of the Government: 'To complete and make even more effective the mobilisation of all our national resources, a mobilisation which has been going on since the commencement of the War, so as to enable the nation to bear the strain, however prolonged, and to march through to victory, however lengthy, and however exhausting may be the journey.'[27]

Lloyd George had strong ideas about how he wanted Britain to fight the war, but found himself more restricted than he would have liked. In order to secure Conservative support for his premiership, he had agreed not to make any changes at the top of the Army, leaving both Robertson and Haig in place – a promise that he would soon come to regret.[28] His war strategy also struggled to gain wide acceptance. In a memorandum circulated on 5 January, he urged that action be taken to support an Italian offensive. 'The object of the Allies is to kill Germans. We can put them out of action just as well on the Italian as on the Western Front . . . Would it not be possible to make a great and sudden stroke against the enemy by a concentration of British and French artillery on the Isonzo front, so as not only to ensure the safety of Italy against any enemy concentration, but what is more important, to shatter the enemy's forces, to inflict a decisive defeat on him, and to press forward to Trieste and to get astride the Istrian Peninsula?'[29] The new Prime Minister blanched at the terrible casualties that the Entente had sustained and could not understand why such slaughter could be countenanced for another year. It was essential, he felt, to try something different, to smash the Austrians and break up the weakest part of the Central Powers. Only then, after a clear victory, would they be in a position to finish off Germany.

Lloyd George's wish to shift the focus of British efforts away from the Western Front found little support outside the confines of his own office. By the end of 1916, the Royal Navy was becoming increasingly nervous about the amount of U-boat activity along the Belgian coast and informed the War Committee that any operation to eliminate the German submarine bases at Zeebrugge and Ostend would be extremely welcome. Haig had long wanted an offensive in the north, to drive the Germans out of Flanders and roll up the coast, and the decision to unleash unrestricted submarine warfare only strengthened his case.[30] But when Haig and Robertson were received by Lloyd George at 10 Downing Street, they immediately realized that he would not be moved from his strategic assessments very easily. 'He had a bad throat and a slight cold, but he talked a great deal to start with', remembered Haig. The Prime Minister was anxious for a victory, possibly in Palestine, and he also wanted 200 heavy guns sent to the Italians, which Haig objected to, arguing that there was little time to do so and there would be no chance of getting them returned before the spring. 'To obtain great successes,' Haig added, in his own ponderous way, 'we must endure "minor ills"'.[31]

The discussions in London were soon overtaken by events in France, where the Government was keen for the British to rubber-stamp their plans for the coming year. The inter-Allied conference in November had agreed to a continuation of the Somme campaign into 1917, only for this to be abandoned as soon as Nivelle was installed at GQG. Nivelle immediately tore up Joffre's existing plan and substituted something more ambitious for it. 'In the offensive of 1917 the Franco-British Armies must strive to destroy the main body of the enemy's Armies on the Western Front' was how he explained it in a letter to Haig on 21 December. Nivelle proposed that a shaping attack would go in along the British sector, in order to fix as many German reserves as possible, before an *'attaque brusquée'* was carried out on another part of the front. This would bring about the break-through, after which an 'army of manoeuvre' would drive through the gap in the German lines.[32]

Nivelle had a chance to explain himself during a visit to London in mid-January, when he was invited to attend the War Cabinet. Lloyd George was wary of committing himself to such ambitious proposals, but found Nivelle's charm and eloquence a striking contrast to the usually monosyllabic generals he was used to dealing with. Nivelle restated the official French position that decisive operations would take place on the Western Front in the coming year. 'That is where the enemy has concentrated its main forces both in quantity and quality.' He did, however, accept that an 'indefinite continuation' of the Somme offensive was undesirable and unlikely to gain the Entente any kind of result commensurate with the 'efforts and sacrifices' it would demand. But this did not mean that they should stand on the defensive. On the contrary, he expressed his 'absolute conviction that we must attack as soon as possible' to achieve 'a decisive result'. The recent operations at Verdun were 'grounds for this hope and show us the direction to go in'.[33]

Such an offensive could only succeed if it was pressed early in the year, ideally as soon as possible. Germany had fifteen divisions on the Danube with another three in the Balkans; forces that could be brought back to the Western Front by the late spring or early summer of 1917, leading Nivelle to warn that they had to act now. *'On our side, we do not have anything similar to hope for: France cannot create new divisions and the men in existing units are starting to wear out.'* Nivelle was at pains to stress that these plans were not a counsel of despair, but founded upon a practical and realistic assessment of the developments within the French Army and its new weaponry, particularly the growing numbers of 155 mm howitzers that could pulverize the German defences. These guns would allow them to 'prepare the ground up to at least eight kilometres, beating the enemy's first line, second line, and artillery line' – opening the way to a breakthrough. Just six months ago French gunners would have required five or six days to move their batteries forward to attack a new defensive position. 'Now it is possible to carry out an attack, in one stroke and with minimal losses, because as soon as the infantry makes contact, the enemy's artillery fire ceases.'[34] This was what had happened at Verdun on 15 December. What had once required weeks or even a month to achieve could now be done in just twenty-four hours.

The British remained sceptical. Lloyd George asked about the weather in February, Arthur Balfour pondered on whether they had enough artillery, and Lord Curzon quizzed Nivelle on why his attacks would succeed when previous ones had failed. Haig, who had been asked to relieve the French Tenth Army south of the Somme (which would help Nivelle to create his 'mass of manoeuvre'), worried about having to take over more trench frontage and, at the same time, train and prepare his divisions for a subsidiary offensive to precede Nivelle's main attack. He would have preferred to wait, perhaps until the drier weather in April and May. This would coincide with Italian and Russian plans and allow his own divisions to be better trained and equipped with new tanks and aircraft. But Nivelle brushed off his concerns. Haig's reasons were 'good', he said, but 'we should not allow ourselves to be guided by these alone or we run the risk, once again, of giving the enemy the upper hand. The advantages offered by a longer delay cannot be compared to what we gain by taking the initiative.'[35]

Notwithstanding doubts about what Nivelle was proposing, the War Cabinet agreed to support him, promising to relieve French troops by the first week of March and then begin a joint offensive no later than 1 April. The attack would be pressed to a decisive result, but if it did not quickly gain the level of success that was expected, the battle would be stopped and then British forces, should they so choose, would be free to 'engage in further operations' around the Belgian coast.[36] Although Haig remained unhappy about having to take over so much extra frontage, Lloyd George was firmly of the opinion that it was better to do that than play a more prominent role in the offensive. 'If we take over that line, it means that the French will have four more divisions to put into their manoeuvring army. If we do not, we shall simply take a trench or two with these four divisions and the French will not be able to complete their manoeuvre.' When Haig disagreed, Lloyd George snapped back. 'If we lend them the men, they will take twice as much ground with half the loss.'

Lloyd George was still angry when he retired that evening, telling his secretary, Frances Stevenson, about his arguments with Haig.

'You rubbed it in well,' she said.

'Yes and I mean to', he replied. 'Haig does not care how many men he loses. He just squanders the lives of these boys. I mean to save some of them in the future. He seems to think they are his property. I am their trustee. I will never let him rest . . .'[37]

In the opening months of 1916, Falkenhayn had tried to crush the Entente on land by a punishing series of attacks at Verdun that would 'bleed white' the French Army. Now, a year later, Germany put its faith in strangulation at sea. On 31 January, Johann von Bernstorff, the German Ambassador in Washington, delivered a fateful letter to Robert Lansing, the US Secretary of State, informing him that because the Entente had now rejected the German note and wished to 'dismember and dishonour' the Central Powers, the German Empire had no choice but to respond 'with the full employment of all the weapons which are at its disposal'. With the British maintaining their 'war of starvation', Germany would now 'forcibly prevent' all navigation, including that of neutrals, within a zone around the United Kingdom, France, Italy and the eastern Mediterranean. 'All ships met within that zone will be sunk.'[38]

While Germany's U-boat fleet slipped out to sea, Hindenburg and Ludendorff weighed up the situation on the Western Front. Ever since their hurried despatch to Eighth Army on the eve of Tannenberg in August 1914, both men had believed most fervently that a German victory could only be found in the east. Their exposure to the true extent and violence of the war in France and Belgium produced an inevitable change of direction. On 17 January, a day after the British and French had agreed plans for the coming year, Ludendorff briefed the army group commanders and their Chiefs of Staff in Cambrai, telling them that the west was now the 'decisive theatre of war'. He regretted that insufficient reserves were available to launch a series of limited attacks (as proposed by Hermann von Kuhl), but he was hopeful that more troops could be brought back from Romania, as well as raising up to thirteen new divisions in Germany over the coming months.[39]

Everyone suspected that a major new enemy offensive was only weeks away. German aircraft scoured the cold skies looking for the telltale signs of the build-up of rolling stock and ammunition dumps, while trying to distinguish between old sites and new ones and always being alive to the possibility of deception and camouflage. German intelligence estimated that, by the spring, the British would be able to field over 1,200 tanks and the French another 800. This was a significant over-estimation, but other information was more reliable, with agents reporting that a Portuguese contingent of about 10,000 men were being shipped to the Western Front (although OHL was unimpressed by their probable combat value).[40] As to when and where the Entente would attack, Ludendorff believed that it would probably be in Champagne or in Upper Alsace, although there were rumours that a big push would begin on the Somme in March to be followed by British operations in Flanders. 'If the enemy attacks fail again,' he told Rupprecht, 'the war may end in the summer'.[41]

Given the wider strategic context, it was inevitable that the German Army would remain on the defensive in 1917 – a stand that did not sit naturally with commanders as offensively minded as the duo at OHL, but which was, nevertheless, a sensible and pragmatic decision. But to do so effectively required some method by which the German Army could defend its lines with fewer troops and avoid the heavy and sustained losses that 'Somme fighting' had produced throughout the previous year. While the Allies placed their faith in more and more firepower, German tactics had begun to change, emphasizing both defence-in-depth and also timely counter-attacks, rather than the static holding of front-line positions that had condemned battalion after battalion to destruction on the Somme under Falkenhayn's bloodthirsty exhortation that they must not yield 'one foot of ground'. Accordingly, two documents were issued over the winter that outlined the new approach: 'Conduct of the Defensive Battle' and 'Instructions for a Counter-Attack Organized in Depth'. The first confirmed that the purpose of defending units was not to 'rigidly cling on to territory' but 'to exhaust and drain the attackers while conserving one's own strength', primarily through the use of artillery, machine-guns and mortars. The second identified that the key to successful defensive operations was to counter-attack 'in depth' by stationing reserves three to five miles behind the line and then throwing them in at the right moment, ideally when the attackers were exhausted, had run low on ammunition and had not been able to consolidate their gains.[42]

New tactics would certainly help the German Army, or at least pose unfamiliar challenges for the Entente, but bringing as many units out of the line as possible, to rest, refit or constitute a strategic reserve, posed a more difficult problem. In France, the rear position that Hindenburg had called for in August 1916 was now nearing completion, offering a potential solution to the ongoing concerns over a lack of reserves. Under the supervision of German engineers, who selected the best ground and most lethal fields of fire, a series of strong defensive positions were constructed behind the Western Front: the most important was the 'Siegfried Line', which ran from Arras, west of Cambrai, and then down to Saint-Quentin and La Fère, before terminating east of Soissons at Vailly-sur-Aisne – thus eliminating the great bulge in the German line. Thousands of French and Belgian civilians, bolstered by Russian prisoners of war corralled into labour companies, toiled on the series of massive works: two trenches, 200 yards apart from each other, sprinkled with dugouts where the infantry and reserves could shelter while being protected by concrete machine-gun emplacements and thick belts of barbed wire – sometimes up to 100 yards in depth.[43]

If and when the German Army would occupy the Siegfried Line now became a matter of the greatest importance. Crown Prince Rupprecht, whose armies held the most exposed part of the front along the great Noyon bulge, was keen to bring his men out of their waterlogged, shattered positions on the Somme on to drier ground.

On 28 January, he wired OHL pointing out the 'bad condition' of the trenches on the fronts of Sixth and First Armies and the heavy losses and lowered morale caused by 'rigid defensive action' across the front. 'The troops are becoming exhausted and it is very doubtful if they are still capable of enduring such defensive battles as that of the Somme in 1916.' Retreating to the Hindenburg Line was a 'difficult decision', but Rupprecht was convinced that it was the 'proper one'.[44]

Debate continued over the next few days, with Georg Wetzell, Chief of Operations at OHL, who had replaced Tappen, noting on 2 February that any move into the Siegfried Position would free up thirteen divisions and considerable amounts of artillery, while also offering 'over two to three weeks, an opportunity that will never be repeated for offensive action against an enemy that has not dug itself in'. As for Ludendorff, he spoke to Kuhl and discussed the pros and cons of any decision, before penning a memorandum on the choices that faced Germany. With the U-boat war needing some time before it (presumably) forced the Entente to surrender, the Army would have to hold on against multiple Allied offensives, on both the Western and Eastern Fronts, as well as against the Italians along the Isonzo, while also remaining 'operationally free' to pursue other opportunities if necessary. 'We will repel the attacks,' Ludendorff noted, 'but we have few reserves to compensate for any setbacks or to conduct an attack ourselves, which is what we must aim to do . . .' In order to preserve as much manpower and ammunition as possible, they needed to shorten their front. Moreover, any move into the rear lines would have to be completed by March. There were 'political disadvantages' in doing so, Ludendorff admitted, but 'the English retreated from Gallipoli and we retreated from Warsaw' and 'it did us no harm'.[45] Accordingly, on the afternoon of 4 February, Rupprecht was ordered to begin preparations for Operation *Alberich* – the withdrawal of his four armies into the Siegfried Position. That evening news arrived that President Wilson had announced before Congress that there was 'no alternative consistent with the dignity and honour of the United States' than to sever all diplomatic relations with the German Empire.[46]

14. 'An entirely new situation'

Both sides entered 1917 with a sense of steely determination, having fixed upon strategies that they believed gave them a fighting chance of striking the decisive blow over the coming months. For the moment, however, the front was frozen solid. The winter of 1916–17 was the coldest of the war; a bitter spell of weather that brought polar conditions to the front, with trenches encased in thick, lying snow, whipped up into curls by fierce prevailing winds. GQG had now moved to Beauvais, forty miles north of Paris; a change demanded by French deputies who were eager to bury the memories of Chantilly and make a new start. The Agricultural Institute was chosen as its new home, a 'rambling and venerable old barrack' with no central heating which lay at the end of a series of twisting alleyways.[1] Nivelle would have preferred to remain in Chantilly – as would have most of his staff – but the decision had been taken, and long columns of trucks, buzzing with despatch riders, made the journey north, transporting the hundreds of tons of furniture, signalling equipment and paperwork that were required for a modern military headquarters and which, it was hoped, would mark a new start for France.

As well as organizing his new base of operations, Nivelle found himself trying to pin down the details of the forthcoming offensive. His 'guiding idea' – which he explained in a plan of operations issued in late January – was to destroy the German armies on the Western Front; an act that would take place in three main phases. Firstly, the British would attack towards Cambrai, some time around 15 March, followed four or five days later by Franchet d'Espèrey's Northern Army Group attacking in the direction of Saint-Quentin. Then, after another short pause, the main group of French armies would push north from the Aisne and bring about the crisis of the battle.[2] These plans bore a striking similarity to the offensives of 1915, when Joffre had launched preliminary attacks in the north before trying to break through in the centre (albeit in Champagne, not the Aisne), but Nivelle hoped that they would enjoy more success this time. The French Army of 1917 was undoubtedly a more powerful instrument than it had been two years earlier. It had a much heavier array of artillery, with an almost unlimited supply of shells to throw at the German lines. Nivelle would also be able to deploy 130 tanks that had been under top-secret development for months.[3] But his army was facing a stronger and deeper series of defences than had been attacked in 1915, and an opponent that was learning quickly. Nivelle believed that it would be possible to replicate the October and December attacks at Verdun on a much grander scale, employing not just a handful of divisions, but *whole armies* to create the conditions for a mass breakout. Such a dazzling plan of action, breathtaking in its ambition, should have raised serious concerns in Paris, but there was only a curious willingness to let Nivelle get on with it; to see what he could do. France had tried everything else; now she would place her trust in an officer who had been a mere colonel of artillery in 1914.

For all his affable confidence, Nivelle found his astonishing rise hard to comprehend. When he first heard rumours that the Government had 'mentioned his name' in connection with becoming Commander-in-Chief (as early as July 1916), he had written to his wife expressing his dismay. 'That would be sheer madness on the part of high command and I would never agree to replace General J[offre], who gives me increasing accolades, grants me more power, and has every confidence in me.'[4] Throughout the winter he remained his usual breezy self, reassuring his staff that everything was in order and that his methods were sound, even if those closest to him detected a growing unease. When Edward Spears, a British liaison officer with Tenth Army, interviewed Nivelle after his trip to London, he noted the weariness with which the French general approached the coming operation. He believed that British plans to attack in Flanders were unsound and that they could not have a decisive result. 'To drive the Germans a little way off is no good', he said. 'You must destroy them, smash their strength.' Moreover, if they were going to do it, then it must be now, for 'the French could not last another twelve months'.[5]

Nivelle's mood was not helped when Haig started to drag his heels.

By late January, Haig had informed GQG about the difficulties he was having in moving enough supplies from the Channel ports along the congested French railway network and how this might require him to revisit their plan of operations. Nivelle bristled at Haig's letter and (in a reply several days later) stated that he did not see why anything should change because 'the preparations for such a large offensive . . . are made gradually, in order to be carried out before they are fully completed, if the general situation so required'.[6] Nivelle was also growing concerned that the British were using difficulties on the railways to either limit the scope of their preliminary attack or delay it until late spring. Vallières, who remained as liaison officer at GHQ, warned Nivelle that he had 'reservations' about British commitment and suspected that the 'current transport crisis' was just 'an excuse for delay about which the British General Staff are pretending to be concerned'.[7]

The disagreements rumbled on for the next few weeks and it was not until 26 February that a conference was held to try to end the impasse, with the British delegation – led by Lloyd George, Haig and Robertson – meeting Briand, Nivelle and Lyautey at the somewhat dreary Station Hotel in Calais. After discussing British supply needs, the French delegation agreed to increase the amount of rolling stock available to Haig towards the end of March, by which time further upgrades to the railway network would have been completed. Haig believed that once the transport situation had been resolved, he would need three weeks, only for Nivelle to say that this must be reduced to no more than fifteen days. It was at this point that David Lloyd George sprang his trap. He dismissed the group of British and French supply experts with a wave of his hand, saying that it was up to them, 'the specialists', to study the question in detail. The most important thing, from the Allied perspective, was unity of command. 'The enemy has only one army', he said. 'The Allies must ensure that they have the same advantage, particularly in battle; without this complete success cannot be guaranteed.' Everyone, he added, must speak 'openly and frankly' about the 'joint effort'. He urged Nivelle to explain his plans again, which he did, and when suitably prompted the French general asked for 'a precise and formal agreement' to settle the relationship between the two Armies and the two commanders. Lloyd George quickly agreed to this, asking Nivelle to elaborate on his ideas for unity of command and a document, apparently drafted beforehand, was soon being circulated among the delegates. From 1 March, the French General-in-Chief (Nivelle) would have 'authority' over the British forces in France and Belgium 'in all concerns', including the planning and execution of operations. A senior British staff officer would reside at GQG and remain under French orders.[8]

The idea of putting Haig under French command had emerged a week earlier during a conversation between Lloyd George and Bertier de Sauvigny, the French Military Attaché in London. The British Prime Minister explained that he had complete faith in Nivelle, but that he needed to be able to call upon *all* the forces on the Western Front. Now Sir Douglas Haig, newly promoted to Field Marshal, could not be openly subordinated to a foreign general, but Lloyd George would, if it was deemed necessary, secretly order Haig to obey Nivelle.[9] At a meeting of the War Cabinet on 24 February (at which Robertson had been told that he need *not* attend), a strong argument was made in favour of Nivelle. The French had 'practically twice the number of troops in the field that we had'; they were 'fighting on French soil'; French commanders were 'without question . . . superior'; and Nivelle 'made a much greater impression' upon the War Cabinet than Haig. Therefore, in the words of Lord Curzon, he was 'the right man to have supreme command'. Lloyd George was thus authorized 'to ensure unity of command both in the preparatory stages of and during the operations' that Nivelle had planned.[10]

The conference had now broken up for dinner and Sir William Robertson, who had said little, returned to his room. When he was handed a copy of the document, his face darkened with suppressed anger and disbelief. He could, under no circumstances, agree to these proposals and went to see Haig, who was equally perturbed, muttering that his men 'wouldn't stand being under a Frenchman'. The matter was not resolved until the following morning, when Hankey, who had attended the conference in an administrative capacity, saw Robertson. 'He was in a terrible state', he remembered, 'and ramped up and down the room, talking about the horrible idea of putting the "wonderful army" under a Frenchman, swearing he would never serve under one . . .' He told Hankey that it was the only time in the war that he had not slept through the night and he was now considering handing in his resignation. It would not, however, come to that. Lloyd George quickly grasped how outraged his commanders were and began to backtrack. Hankey was tasked with coming up with what he called 'his formula', whereby Haig would be placed under Nivelle's orders for the forthcoming offensive only and also allowed to report back to London if he felt French demands would 'endanger the safety of his army'.[11]

The amended agreement was eventually signed on 27 February (with Haig adding a marginal note in his copy: 'Signed by me as a correct statement, but not as approving the arrangement'). What Lloyd George had exactly won at Calais was unclear. He had lost the trust of his two most senior commanders and only gained a temporary arrangement that was far from his cherished unity of command. He also set off vicious rumours that he had placed the army under French control as a first step towards the introduction of a republic in Britain.[12] As for Haig and Robertson, they both left Calais under a cloud, furious about the actions of the Prime Minister and smarting from their perceived humiliation. On 2 March, Robertson dashed off a note warning the War Cabinet that Calais 'might prove to be the thin end of the wedge which the French have for long desired to obtain for bringing the British Armies in France under definite French control'. Officers and men 'could not be expected to fight nearly as well' under a French general; there might be objections from the Dominions; and, moreover, 'that entirely to entrust the fortunes of this great battle to a foreign Commander, who as yet has had no opportunity of proving his fitness for the position, was a serious step viewed from the standpoint of the Empire'.[13]

As the Entente struggled to coordinate its forces for the spring offensive, the international situation suddenly began to shift, propelled by twin crises that had been brewing for months. In Russia, the strains of war were becoming unendurable. On 8 March, a sudden improvement in the weather brought huge crowds out on to the streets of

Petrograd, with thousands of people joining large demonstrations over working conditions, as well as familiar complaints about the poor quality of bread. Over the next few days the situation grew darker, with strikes spreading across the city and provoking a violent response from the authorities. The garrison was called out, agitators were arrested, and about forty people were killed when crowds were fired upon. But far from putting down the disturbances, the shootings only provoked further anger and sparked off a mutiny in the Petrograd garrison, which refused to follow orders. Within days, the Tsar's authority in the city had collapsed and a hastily drafted abdication manifesto had been signed, which handed the throne to Nicholas II's brother, the Grand Duke Michael. Although it was hoped that this would head off any further disturbances in this 'grave hour of national trial', the abdication of the Tsar was a mortal blow to Russia's war effort and intensely disorientating to her armies still in the field.[14]

As Russia was beginning to falter, America was taking the necessary steps to shed her neutrality and enter the Great War. Walter Hines Page, the US Ambassador in London, regularly cabled Washington with news of the latest sinkings around the United Kingdom, but on 24 February the 61-year-old native of North Carolina was given information of an entirely greater magnitude. That day, Arthur Balfour, the Foreign Secretary, handed Page a cipher telegram that had been intercepted by British Naval Intelligence between Dr Arthur Zimmermann, Germany's Secretary of State for Foreign Affairs, and her minister in Mexico, Heinrich von Eckhardt: 'We intend to begin on the 1st of February unrestricted submarine warfare. We shall endeavour in spite of this to keep the United States of America neutral. In the event of this not succeeding, we make Mexico a proposal of alliance on the following basis: make war together, make peace together, generous financial support and an understanding on our part that Mexico is to reconquer the lost territory in Texas, New Mexico, and Arizona.'[15] When President Wilson was informed of the 'Zimmermann Telegram', he reluctantly began to move in the direction of war. Within days he had proposed a state of 'armed neutrality', whereby US vessels could do whatever was necessary to protect 'our people in their legitimate and peaceful pursuits on the seas'.[16]

The United States was not yet at war, but the feeling that America was girding herself for a looming conflict was becoming inescapable. The Armed Ship Bill was defeated in the Senate (when a small group of senators filibustered for two days), but the publication of the German note in the press on 1 March caused a sensation and emboldened those who wanted to meet the challenge of Germany head on. Even Wilson, who had campaigned as the man who 'kept us out of the war', recognized that Germany's constant provocations could not go unanswered. After he was inaugurated for his second term on 5 March, he directly addressed the coming storm. Wearing a top hat, with a thick black coat around his shoulders to ward off a chilly wind, a sheath of notes in his hand, Wilson delivered his address with deep solemnity and sadness. 'We have been deeply wronged upon the seas, but we have not wished to wrong or injure in return; have retained throughout the consciousness of standing in some sort apart, intent upon an interest that transcended the immediate issues of the war itself. As some of the injuries done us have become intolerable we have still been clear that we wished nothing for ourselves that we were not ready to demand for all mankind – fair dealing, justice, the freedom to live and be at ease against organized wrong.' The 'tragic events' of the last thirty months of war had, he believed, 'made us citizens of the world'.[17]

For the time being, overseas developments had little impact on the German High Command, which was preoccupied with its impending transfer to Bad Kreuznach in the Rhineland. Given what Ludendorff had called the 'supreme importance' of the Western Front, OHL had moved to the agreeable spa town to be closer to its armies in France over the coming months. A third army group was also created, commanded by Crown Prince Wilhelm (with three armies), while Duke Albrecht of Württemberg took over the southern sector of the Western Front from Metz down to the Swiss border. An Allied attack was still awaited keenly, and with 154 divisions in the west, ranged against 190 British, French and Belgian ones, the Germans were faced with a sizeable numerical disadvantage, which only added greater urgency to the need to re-equip their men with more guns and ammunition.[18] A Supreme War Ministry had been created in November 1916, headed by Wilhelm Groener and tasked with driving forward war production, but it struggled to meet the ambitious targets set by OHL. Bureaucratic infighting, trade union resistance and political disagreements all conspired to water down Hindenburg's demands for the radical remobilization of Germany's war effort, leaving the generals fuming that they were being denied the tools of victory by politicians who did not realize 'that the war meant life or death to Germany'.[19]

In a letter to Freiherr von Lyncker, Chief of the Kaiser's Military Cabinet, Hindenburg bemoaned the failures of the production programme. 'The weapons industry was and is inadequate. In September 1916, for example, field gun production was at the same level as in February, and that is simply inadequate.' German forces were now being 'paralysed' because munitions production was 'way below promised figures'. Hindenburg admitted that they now had greater stocks of shells than at the beginning of the Somme offensive, but this had been achieved not through increased production, but 'solely through the greatest economy on the part of the armies, to whom I had to give very precise instructions . . . We will "survive", I have never doubted that. But it must happen with the minimum loss of human lives, and to achieve this goal I am still firmly in favour of a continuously expanding armaments programme and a healthy nutrition and workers policy, which, alone, will enable this programme to be realized.'[20]

Out at the front, the mood of the German Army dipped as the 'turnip winter' dragged on and food supplies, meagre at best, became increasingly scarce. 'The turnips we receive almost every day are usually frozen', remembered one soldier. Their meals consisted of small amounts of meat – no bread could be found – with lard or some kind of fat substitute, and supplies in their local canteens were scant: 'there is absolutely nothing edible to buy'.[21] Indeed, things were so bad that Hindenburg issued a decree in March warning that savings needed to be found because the army consumed 70 per cent of Germany's total food. 'Nothing superfluous must be consumed and not even the smallest amount must be allowed to perish. I urge all commanding officers to explain to their subordinates the seriousness of the domestic economic situation and the significance of the economic battle between our enemies and ourselves, which is becoming more difficult every day, and to repeat these instructions from time to time. We can hold out – but only if everyone makes the utmost savings', until such time as their enemies succumbed to the submarine war.[22]

For the time being, then, the only relief for Germany's armies would come from the retreat to the Siegfried Line. Ever since Rupprecht had been authorized to begin planning the withdrawal in early February, demolition teams had been hard at work turning the ground in front of the new defences into a wasteland, stripped of anything that might be of value to the enemy. The devastated zone was a pitiful sight: between six and eight miles deep and grim testimony to the fiendish and spiteful ingenuity that was brought to bear on some of the most fertile agricultural land in France. Trees were felled. Bridges were blown up. Telegraph wires were cut. Railway tracks and roads were torn up or booby-trapped. Water supplies were poisoned. Arsenic was leaked into the River Somme at Barleux, while wells were routinely blocked up with piles of stinking manure and the carcasses of slaughtered livestock. Banks were looted. Shops were burnt to the ground. Civilians were deported and those who could not work – 'useless mouths' – were left to greet their liberators, starving and bewildered by the destruction around them. 'They came in singing in 1914', said one woman in the town of Nesle, 'but they left in silence.'[23]

None of the senior German commanders were proud of what had been done in their name. Rupprecht made it known that he disapproved of the orders, but was told that he must carry them through. He argued with OHL, claiming that the destruction would harm Germany's international reputation and alienate neutral powers. He even suggested that they should incorporate large population centres into their defensive lines, perhaps Lille or Cambrai, and leave it up to the Allies to destroy them if they dared. But none of this went very far. Hindenburg and Ludendorff blamed a lack of manpower, but it was evident that they were already set on their path of destruction. 'Up until the last moment, I hoped that the orders would be changed,' Rupprecht admitted, 'but all I could achieve was that some larger towns, such as Nesle, Ham and Noyon, were spared. I would have preferred to take my leave, but it was indicated to me that this would not help and I was also not allowed to leave for political reasons, as the events abroad would be interpreted as a quarrel between Bavaria and the Reich. So I had to limit myself to refusing to put my signature to the implementation specifications.'[24]

Closer to the front, the mood was little different. General Georg von der Marwitz, who had taken over command of Second Army after Max von Gallwitz's reassignment to Verdun (the inevitable result of his falling out with Rupprecht and Kuhl), was given sealed instructions to evacuate his troops from the Somme – while destroying everything in their path, an order that the old-fashioned cavalryman did not like. 'Over a width of fifteen kilometres in front of this position, all towns and villages are to be burnt and blown up, and the wells are to be filled . . . Inhabitants who are able to work will be taken away to the east; those who cannot work, on the other hand, will be crowded together in a number of towns around Noyon, to be left for the French.' Marwitz knew that it was a 'bad plan', which 'once it becomes known, will turn public opinion strongly against us', but he was satisfied that it could not be avoided. 'The Military Command is too much in need of divisions and we must begin with the burning and scorching.'[25]

A local redeployment had begun on the mud-soaked Ancre on 24 February, but it was not until 14 March that elements of First and Second Armies, astride the Somme, began their main withdrawal to their rearward positions. The retreat was conducted with clockwork-like efficiency. Specially selected rearguards held the front lines as long as they dared and then slipped away at night, while German aircraft kept the skies clear of enemy fighters and continued to display the dominance that had been increasingly evident from the autumn of 1916. Once his armies were safely behind their new defences, Rupprecht issued an Order of the Day, commending his men on their 'skilful and timely' redeployment: 'The operations have been carried

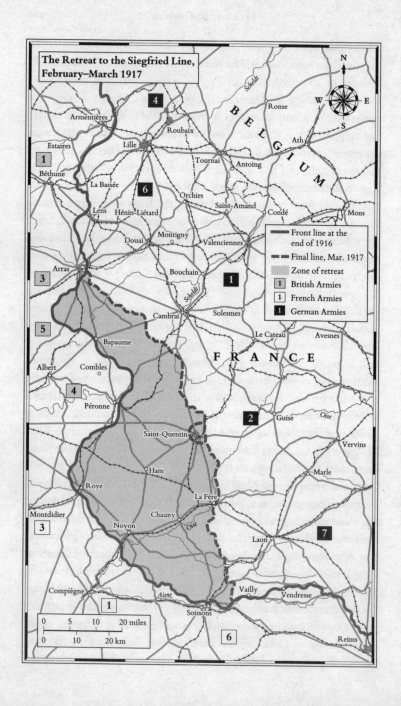

The Retreat to the Siegfried Line,
February–March 1917

BELGIUM

FRANCE

Front line at the
end of 1916

Final line, Mar. 1917

Zone of retreat

1 British Armies

1 French Armies

1 German Armies

Scheldt
Ronse
Armentières
Roubaix
Lille
Ath
Estaires
Tournai
Antoing
Béthune
Mons
La Bassée
Orchies
Saint-Amand
Condé
Lens
Hénin-Liétard
Montigny
Valenciennes
Douai
Bouchain
Arras
Cambrai
Solesmes
Scheldt
Bapaume
Le Cateau
Avesnes
Albert
Combles
Péronne
Guise
Oise
Saint-Quentin
Vervins
Ham
Marle
Roye
La Fère
Montdidier
Chauny
Noyon
Oise
Laon
Compiègne
Aisne
Vailly
Vendresse
Soissons
Reims

0 5 10   20 miles
0   10   20 km

out perfectly according to plan and undisturbed by the enemy, which only followed cautiously. Where enemy attacks were imminent before our departure, we were able to deceive the enemy and prepare our smooth disengagement, by means of skilful and timely evasion into our rearward positions. We went from muddy "craterfields" to good, well-prepared positions. It will take a lot of time and require major efforts by the enemy to be able to attack our new front.'[26]

The German withdrawal took the Entente totally by surprise. Rumours had been coming into British and French intelligence since the autumn that something was happening behind the German lines, but much was still unconfirmed. Reconnaissance flights had detected evidence of construction activity around Saint-Quentin, and intelligence from prisoners and refugees told of large numbers of civilians being corralled into building defensive works, but Allied commanders did not believe the Germans would willingly give up positions they had fought so hard to maintain throughout 1915 and 1916. Ludendorff had been clear on the need to mislead the enemy wherever possible and mounted an extensive deception campaign, with stories being planted of a possible major naval raid or a sudden descent through Switzerland, which did enough to throw the British and French High Commands off the scent. Indeed, so concerned did GHQ become about a possible attack at Ypres that an extra division and plenty of heavy artillery were sent to reinforce the front in Flanders in late January.[27]

By the beginning of March the extent of the German withdrawal could no longer be denied. Reports were flooding into both Montreuil and Beauvais that a major redeployment was under way in front of Rawlinson's Fourth Army and spreading southwards along France's Northern Army Group – from Péronne down to Noyon and Soissons. Nivelle hoped that his painfully worked-out plans would not be affected, but concerns were growing that, as in 1916, the Germans had stolen a march on the Entente and seized the initiative. Émile Fayolle, the newly appointed commander of the French First Army, could only shake his head in disbelief when reports came in of the German withdrawal. 'The situation is certainly very embarrassing and highly delicate. This is a very good manoeuvre by the Hun. If we follow them then we play their game by entering a devastated area without supplies and with our communications cut off. If we do not follow them, we will lose contact and they will remain at liberty. In any case, our offensive is now fruitless. Their plan is obvious: save up thirty or so divisions and attack us in one or two months' time.'[28]

Franchet d'Espèrey, commander of the Northern Army Group, was equally astounded. On 4 March, he cabled Nivelle and urged him to act quickly. If he was given some tanks, he could launch a sudden assault, throwing the Germans off balance and reaching deep into their rear zones. 'The sooner we attack', he wrote, 'the more chance we shall have of surprising the enemy and of capturing that portion of his artillery which has not yet been withdrawn.' Yet the French Commander-in-Chief had no intention of changing his plans and remained focused on moving all his pieces into position for his main attack. 'There seems little likelihood that the enemy will abandon without fighting, and indeed without resisting to the utmost, one of the principal pledges he holds on our soil, that is to say the line nearest Paris, which includes Roye, Noyon and Soissons . . . I decide therefore not to change in its general lines the plan of operations for 1917.'[29]

The sands were now shifting beneath Nivelle's feet as another political crisis broke out in Paris. General Lyautey, the Minister of War, suddenly announced his resignation on 14 March. Used to sole political and military authority in Morocco, Lyautey found the fraught diplomatic and political atmosphere at the War Ministry tiresome and confusing and wanted to return to the field. He regularly drove out to the front, chatted with officers, and soon came to the conclusion that Nivelle's plans were wildly optimistic. He was also deeply unpopular with parliamentary deputies and, during a debate on military aviation, he had made it clear that he disapproved of such a discussion, warning that it might 'expose national defence to risks', insinuating that there were some in the Chamber with less than loyal intentions. When the deputies shouted him down and accused him of 'insulting Parliament', Lyautey could only retreat in bewilderment. 'I can't understand a thing about it', he told a friend. 'I'd hardly begun when they started shouting – I don't even know why . . .' With the Government in chaos, Briand offered his resignation four days later.[30]

At the Élysée Palace, President Poincaré was left to pick up the pieces. 'Lyautey's resignation means that we need a man who can ensure harmonious relations between Parliament and the Army', he noted. 'A man is needed who will inspire confidence at home and with the Allies, a young, energetic man with a strong personality, someone who can easily forge patriotic unity.' But far from appointing a young man, vivid in life and spirit, Poincaré chose the 75-year-old Alexandre Ribot, a senator from the Pas-de-Calais who had been Briand's Finance Minister with a reputation as an 'excellent patriot, committed to all-out war, a decent man who is not caught up in intrigue or suspicious behaviour'.[31] As for who would replace Lyautey, the choice came down to two men: Albert Thomas, the socialist Minister of Armaments who had done much to reorganize French war production; or Paul Painlevé, an eminent mathematician who had been the former head of the Inventions Committee at the Ministry of War. With Thomas showing little interest, Ribot gave it to Painlevé.

At the front, British and French forces probed forward, somewhat unsteadily, unsure of what was going on and wary of booby-traps that lay strewn across their path. Hastily formed battalions of cyclists, together with whatever cavalry could be scraped together, were put in the vanguard and ordered to advance as quickly as they could, up the long, straight French roads, the only colour in the thin white sky being the plumes of smoke from burning villages. Haig held an army commanders' conference on 17 March and warned about the possibility of a major enemy counter-attack, but nothing happened – the Germans had vanished. Bapaume was entered by British troops that day. 'In the Bapaume country the villages are deserted', recorded a journalist who accompanied the forward patrols. 'All is looted and burnt out. On the night of our entrance into that city I saw from Bapaume the sky north and east lurid with the fires of towns and hamlets. On those roads yesterday our men, grimy, tousled, sweating, but whistling in what was a veritable blizzard, were getting forward fast, in spite of all hindrances.'[32]

Even among a generation of commanders hardened by their experience of war, the sight of the devastated French countryside was hard to bear. 'All that was productive or memorable has been destroyed', lamented Charles Mangin as he urged his troops to follow the enemy as quickly as they could. When General Fayolle was driven up to the Crozat Canal, which had been crossed on 21 March, he noted the 'systematic destruction' all around. Nothing had been left standing in Noyon, which was just a sinister maze of ruined houses and felled bridges; echoing to the sound of crows. 'It is not only lines of communication that have been destroyed but also houses have been burnt down or partially demolished, all in a very methodical manner. Many fruit trees have also been chopped down.'³³ Only Nivelle remained unmoved. The new War Minister, Painlevé, met the General on 22 March and told him that the 'new situation calls for new eyes'. Considering the almost certain entry of America into the war, as well as the growing concerns over Russian participation, should his plans not be 'profoundly modified'? Nivelle thought not. The German retreat had 'freed up more French divisions than German ones' and, indeed, 'he could not have done better if he had been in charge of enemy movements. The enemy front was broken, in a manner of speaking, without any losses'. Moreover, the crucial objective of the Craonne Plateau along the Chemin des Dames was now 'within reach'.³⁴

Doubts about Nivelle's plans were spreading rapidly. A new Reserve Army Group had been formed under the command of General Joseph Alfred Micheler, comprising Fifth, Sixth and Tenth Armies, tasked with breaking through the heavily defended Chemin des Dames Ridge. Micheler, darkly bearded, recognizable by the *pince-nez* he always wore, even in the trenches, had led a division at the start of the war before rising to command Tenth Army in the summer of 1916. With Nivelle nervous about entrusting the attack to Pétain (who lacked enthusiasm), Micheler was seen as a more reliable choice, albeit less experienced than other candidates. Yet Micheler quickly recognized the danger that the Germans would now be able to put more divisions into reserve, making his task on the Aisne even harder. He wrote to Nivelle on 22 March warning him that the 'German concentration on our front has definitely increased, though I cannot be specific about statistics: probably three new divisions, perhaps four or five . . .' Progress would now be slower, as the troops had to fight their way through more units holding the third and fourth positions. This meant that the situation highlighted in Nivelle's previous operation orders had 'drastically changed'.[35]

Leaving the chilly corridors of the Agricultural Institute for his advanced headquarters at the Palace of Compiègne, Nivelle continued to insist that all was well. With the main offensive scheduled to go in on 16 April and Haig mounting his preliminary operation around Arras a week earlier, on 9 April, there was little time for a wholesale revision of the attack plans. In a directive written on 4 April, he admitted that the missions of his various armies had been 'somewhat modified' by the German withdrawal, but their objective remained the same, namely 'the destruction of the bulk of the enemy forces on the Western Front'. This would now take the form of a 'prolonged battle' after which an 'exploitation phase' would occur when British and French forces converged: the BEF driving towards Cambrai and Douai, the Northern Army Group to Valenciennes and Maubeuge, and the Reserve Army Group conquering 'the entire loop of the Aisne'. 'It is through sudden advances with all our available forces, and *by the rapid conquest of the most vulnerable points*', that they would 'reap complete disarray'.[36]

Such confident predictions were greeted with growing scepticism in Paris. On 5 April, Adolphe Messimy, a former War Minister, handed a report to the Prime Minister, Ribot, urging him to call off the attack. Messimy had sounded out a number of senior officers, including Micheler, who all told him the same thing: 'The GQG, faced with an entirely new situation, has only made the minimum alterations in its plan . . . It is now about to commit a grave error which may have irreparable consequences for France.' While the French would certainly 'capture guns and prisoners', it would only be 'at the price of the heaviest sacrifices'.[37] After Painlevé had read the report, finding it painful in its direct criticisms of Nivelle, he immediately drove out to see Poincaré and presented it to him. The French President had seen for himself the great destruction caused by the German retreat and had found Nivelle more nervous than ever before. When they had met in the town square at Soissons on 2 April, Nivelle had complained that his cavalry was 'rusty' and that he had had to 'hit' some of his generals 'that he judged to be too weak'.[38] Now it was evident that there was a major split in military opinion, so Poincaré ordered an urgent Council of War to take place in Compiègne the following morning, 6 April 1917.

The mood at the council was subdued and dark with an uneasy sense of foreboding. When the presidential train pulled into a siding at Compiègne at 10 a.m., the most senior French generals were waiting: the 'stony and suspicious faces' of Nivelle, Castelnau, Pétain, Franchet d'Espèrey and Micheler, stamping their feet on the snowy ground and rubbing their hands to keep warm. When they had all assembled inside, Poincaré (flanked by Ribot, Painlevé and Albert Thomas) began by talking about the changed circumstances they were facing: the revolution in Russia and the entry of the United States into the war (which had been declared that very day). 'Does this justify changing our plans?' Painlevé explained that they did not wish to interfere with military operations, but it was essential to assess the situation clearly before the attack went ahead. 'The gathering was very uncomfortable', he remembered. 'General Nivelle was resentful and smug . . . Franchet d'Espèrey tried to remain calm; Pétain was impassive and cold; Micheler seemed anxious and in turmoil.'[39]

Nivelle must have found the proceedings deeply wounding, but he stood his ground. He 'pointed out the dangers of waiting' and warned that if they did not strike quickly, the enemy would regain the initiative. Micheler was then asked what he thought. He was 'pale and nervous', mumbling something about the need to attack as soon as possible, which created an immediate sensation, as it had been assumed that he was critical of the plan. Pétain then spoke. He did not think the attack would succeed and, in his level voice, without a hint of emotion, he began to dissect Nivelle's plans, arguing that there was little chance of a breakthrough. At that point, Nivelle, 'with his hand on his uniform, declared that since he did not agree with the government nor with his subordinates, the only thing left for him to do was to tender his resignation'. As the general delivered his concluding line, Poincaré and Painlevé seemed to wince in pain.

Others then joined in, arguing that now was not the time for a change in command and that it was necessary for Nivelle to remain at his post. However, his attack should proceed cautiously. 'If the desired results are not attained after a brief period,' warned Poincaré, 'we will not stubbornly continue the battle indefinitely as we did on the Somme.'[40]

The Council of War had failed to resolve anything. Nivelle was given authorization to mount his assault, even if Poincaré's words seemed to indicate a more careful prosecution of the offensive than had been envisaged. It had also done little to draw the poison that now coursed between France's most senior commanders. As the politicians headed back to Paris, the generals went their separate ways, returning to their headquarters to make the final arrangements for the assault. Sixty miles to the north, around the city of Arras, Haig's guns were already thundering away, covering the German lines in columns of smoke, dust and high-explosive. What Painlevé called the 'young school of Verdun', the 'method of Vaux–Douaumont', would now undergo its 'supreme test'.[41]

15. 'Tortured ground'

Almost totally bald, apart from a short strip of hair around the back of his head, General Sir Edmund Allenby, commander of the British Third Army, was fifty-five years old with a reputation as a short-tempered martinet quick to pounce on any minor indiscretion. He had been on the Western Front since 1914, commanding the Cavalry Division during the retreat from Mons before taking over Third Army in October 1915. With Rawlinson's Fourth Army shifting southwards to relieve French units bound for the Nivelle offensive, Haig assigned his part of the coming operations to Third Army, which held the front from Arras to Croisilles on the Sensée river. Allenby was ordered to break the German line along a ten-mile front, outflank the northern edge of the Hindenburg Line and then push on towards Cambrai. His left flank would be secured by the Canadian Corps (part of First Army), which would attack Vimy Ridge. Finally, Allenby was able to lead what he called 'a big battle'.[1]

Despite his reputation as a gruff firebrand, Allenby was keen on new ideas and filled his attack plans with the latest innovations, showing a willingness to take advantage of everything that had been learnt from the Somme. With Arras lying barely 2,000 yards from the German front line (and thus under regular bombardment), Allenby agreed to use the network of cellars and tunnels under the city to house the thousands of assault troops he would need, allowing them to get into action much quicker and without a long-drawn-out approach march under direct enemy observation. Above them, air-craft of the Royal Flying Corps also conducted an ambitious effort to isolate the battlefield and drive away the German balloons that ringed the sky. Despite suffering heavy losses from German aircraft, which, in many cases, outclassed the older British models, particularly the DH.2s and B.E.2s that were due for retirement, constant patrols were conducted over the lines in the days leading up to the attack.[2]

18. General Henri Philippe Pétain in his railway carriage in the autumn of 1915. Combining patience and tenacity with a sober recognition of the dominance of firepower on the modern battlefield, Pétain led the defence of Verdun and became a national hero.

19. French infantry prepare to move up towards Fort Douaumont, 25 February 1916. Officers would frequently contrast the confident bearing of troops going into battle with those that returned from the line: 'Their eyes stared into space as if transfixed by a vision of terror.'

20. Men of the Wiltshire Regiment advancing towards Thiepval, 7 August 1916. Attacks on the Somme were frequently clumsy and costly, with one French liaison officer complaining that 'The British have not yet got the "knack".'

21. An aerial photograph taken from about 600 feet above Vermandovillers, showing the enclosed, troglodyte world of the trenches. One French commander ruefully noted that the 'art of war' had essentially 'disappeared' on the Somme.

22. General Sir Douglas Haig, Commander-in-Chief of the BEF (*centre*), with Joffre (*left*) and Foch (*right*) at his headquarters at Beauquesne, August 1916. Despite outward appearances of cordiality, the Allied commanders struggled to coordinate operations on the Somme.

23. Field Marshal Paul von Hindenburg, Chief of the General Staff (*left*), and First Quartermaster-General Erich Ludendorff (*right*). After taking over from Falkenhayn in August 1916, the duo pursued a ruthless policy of total war.

24. From 1916, Crown Prince Rupprecht was Germany's senior army group commander on the Western Front, responsible for defensive operations at the Somme, Arras, Ypres and Cambrai.

25. Albatros D.III fighters of Jagdstaffel 2 at Douai, France. Germany dominated the skies during the winter of 1916–17 with a new generation of aircraft that outclassed Allied machines.

26. The tragic figure of General Robert Nivelle, architect of the failed Nivelle Offensive of April–May 1917. Eloquent, charming and a gifted artillery commander, he was unable to translate his successes at Verdun on a larger scale and brought the French Army to the brink of collapse.

27. An advance party of French infantry moves forward cautiously during the Nivelle Offensive, April 1917.

28. An 8-inch howitzer in full recoil during the Battle of Messines Ridge, June 1917. The seizure of the ridge was the high point of mine warfare on the Western Front, but was also dependent upon powerful artillery support.

The most crucial part of the plan was the artillery support, with Third Army being able to call upon one gun for every twelve yards of front, including almost 900 18-pounders, another 276 4.5-inch howitzers, and over 500 heavy guns liberally supplied with shells – a significant improvement on the Somme.[3] For five days, they saturated the German lines with a heavy and sustained bombardment, while an intensive counter-battery effort searched out gun positions and pummelled them mercilessly. Central to this effort was the development of effective ways to record and track enemy artillery. The principle of 'sound-ranging', whereby the location of a gun would be established by measuring the time interval between the arrival of a sound wave at different recording stations, had been established before the war, but it was not until the invention of a reliable microphone in the summer of 1916 that the system was perfected. Likewise, the expansion of 'flash-spotting' sections across the Western Front was another crucial development. Working in small teams, observers would record the bearing of muzzle flashes, the location of which could then be found by a straightforward process of triangulation. When these techniques were combined with improved mapping and tireless aerial reconnaissance, First and Third Armies were able to locate most of the enemy batteries they faced, recording their movements with remarkable precision. By the time the battle opened, Canadian staff officers knew the locations of 176 out of the roughly 212 German guns on Vimy Ridge – an astonishing success rate of 83 per cent.[4] As soon as Zero Hour came, they would be deluged with high explosive and gas, thus preventing them from either supporting their own infantry or interfering with the attack.

The British would strike the German Sixth Army. Its commander, General Ludwig von Falkenhausen, was, at seventy-two years of age, one of the oldest senior officers in the army and a veteran of the wars of 1866 and 1870. Known for his traditional approach to soldiering, Falkenhausen refused to implement OHL's new doctrine of defence-in-depth and, instead, ordered his men to hold the front line in strength. This was sensible at Vimy Ridge, where the layout of the ground meant that a more 'elastic' form of defence was impracticable – with the eastern edge of the ridge falling away sharply into the Douai plain – but elsewhere it proved less suitable. Falkenhausen's orders meant that German divisions further to the south, on either side of the River Scarpe, had little chance. Their counter-attack divisions, which should have been close in support, ready to drive the enemy back, were still a full day's march to the east when the attack came in. Although this was noted at army group, with Falkenhausen receiving repeated instructions to bring his reserve divisions closer in, he ignored them all.[5]

The attack was launched at 5.30 a.m. on 9 April – Easter Monday – an unseasonably cold day of biting winds and flurries of snow and sleet. At Vimy Ridge, four Canadian divisions moved forward under a heavy creeping barrage, thickened up at Zero Hour with a fusillade of mortar bombs and overhead machine-gun fire, which created a moving, clattering wall of metal. The bombardment was 'a hailstorm of iron such as nobody had ever experienced', remembered Lieutenant-General Alfred Dieterich, commanding 79th Reserve Division, which held the central and northern sections of the ridge. 'Its racket equalled the roaring and raging of a hurricane-lashed sea. Everywhere rose huge fountains of earth.'[6] Behind this came the Canadians, picking their way across the broken ground, before dealing with pockets of resistance: machine-gunners who continued firing to the end, isolated snipers, or dugouts and bunkers that had somehow survived the shelling.[7] Then, after pausing on each objective and allowing time to mop up their newly won positions, they continued their advance. By 11 a.m. most of the ridge was in Canadian hands.

A similar story unfolded to the south. Third Army had three objectives, each marked as a coloured line on their maps, which would be taken precisely on schedule: black (after thirty-six minutes); blue (two hours and forty-four minutes); and brown (eight hours). A fourth (green) would be taken before nightfall if possible, with two reserve divisions being 'leapfrogged' forward to take the final positions.[8] Although not all objectives were secured, almost everywhere the attacks met with remarkable success. 'The barrage kept a wonderfully even line', recalled a British officer; 'a curtain of continuous fire about a hundred yards ahead of us, creeping forward at walking pace. The smoke and the fountains of earth helped to conceal our advance a little as well as tending to diminish any fire from snipers, machine guns or any entrenched infantry that might be in front of us . . . A few of the Germans who resisted with small arms were bayonetted, the rest had their hands up in surrender.'[9]

Casualties inevitably increased the further the advance went and the British encountered defenders in positions that had not been subjected to such a fierce pounding, but it seemed for a moment that a great gap had been opened in the German defences. Elements of one British division even breached the third line – a march of three and a half miles – making it the furthest advance in one day, by either side, since the onset of trench warfare.[10] Allenby had massed three divisions of cavalry ready to go forward if a breakthrough seemed likely, but they struggled to make much of an impact. A few squadrons were able to mount up and push on, but most of the barbed wire was still intact along the German third line, which prevented any further exploitation. The tanks had also been disappointing. Forty Mark I's had been assigned to the attack, but uneven ground, mechanical breakdown and the predictably heavy losses from shells, grenades and mortars prevented them from making more than small, local impacts.

The cavalry and tanks may have been frustrated, but it was clear that the German defensive plan had failed badly. At Vimy Ridge, the intensity of the bombardment had wrecked the defences and thoroughly demoralized its garrison, who had been overrun with surprising speed. Elsewhere, Falkenhausen's deployments left his front-line garrisons fighting for their lives against heavy odds. Local counter-attacks were thrown in, but they all failed, German regiments marching forward into heavy machine-gun and artillery fire. OHL's response was predictably swift. On the morning of 11 April, Ludendorff telephoned Fritz von Lossberg (who was still serving on the Somme) and told him that he was being reassigned to Sixth Army and that 'I trust you will master the situation.' Lossberg did what he always did. He asked whether he would have *Vollmacht*, and when this was granted, he travelled to Sixth Army's area of operations and acquainted himself with the positions of each corps and the ground they occupied. 'I realized very quickly that the enemy had unrestricted fields of observation into our defensive sector, having seized

Vimy Ridge and the high ground on both sides of the Scarpe River.' Working out the probable maximum ranges of enemy artillery, Lossberg decided that, contrary to his usual maxim of fighting for each foot of ground, he had to deploy a light defensive screen amid the shell holes. Once the British mounted an attack, he would then stage a 'deliberate counterattack' from their rear positions.[11]

The crisis of the battle had, however, already passed and the British gradually lost momentum over the coming days. The initial attack had been well prepared and executed, but Haig and Allenby could not, as yet, work out what to do next and how to exploit an initial break-in. Moving forward over churned-up ground was a time-consuming process, and, with the weather showing no signs of improvement, the roads and tracks remained slippery and, in places, waterlogged – which allowed enough time for German reinforcements to pour into the breach. On 12 April, Haig admitted, in a letter to Nivelle, that he still hoped to push on to Cambrai, but 'owing to the bad weather and the consequent state of the ground, my troops have not been able to follow up the successes already gained as rapidly as would have been possible under better conditions'. Because the Germans had been able to bring in reinforcements and thicken up their artillery batteries, further advances would now require them to move up their own guns – 'a slow and difficult task' as Haig admitted.[12]

Haig had still fulfilled his part of the bargain. A heavy punch had been delivered against the German defences in the north and one of the most important pieces of terrain on the entire Western Front had been seized. With Vimy Ridge now in Allied possession, the BEF had secured invaluable views over the Douai plain and avenged the Moroccans who had almost reached its summit in May 1915 and whose remains were still scattered amid the smoking sea of no-man's-land. 'The marching and the joy of operating in the open at last and above all, the fact that the Army was *advancing* made everyone happy!' Haig wrote to the King. 'Our success is already the largest obtained on this front in *one* day.'[13] Despite Haig's understandable pleasure at seeing ground being taken, he was under no illusion that his operation would achieve decisive results. That was down to the hundreds of thousands of French troops who were now moving into position along a forty-kilometre front northwest of Reims. The fate of the spring offensive would be settled on the Aisne.

The artillery of General Micheler's Reserve Army Group began its preliminary bombardment on 6 April, the day of President Poincaré's ill-fated Council of War. With over 5,000 guns, including 2,000 75s and 1,650 heavy pieces, it was the greatest array of firepower ever seen, with the shelling going on day and night, ploughing up the ground and sending great clouds of smoke and dust over the heights above the Aisne river, still clad in a white veil of snow.[14] But the weather remained uncooperative. 9 April was wet with rain turning to heavy snow in the afternoon; 10 and 11 April saw more strong winds and ice; and conditions remained stormy over the next week, with low clouds bringing more freezing rain and sleet. Nivelle could only stare out of the high windows at the Palace of Compiègne and watch as the white-grey sky, laden with snow, refused to clear. Unlike Verdun, which was thoroughly mapped and where the French occupied the higher ground, the Aisne was much less favourable to offensive operations. German observers enjoyed wide vistas over the French lines, while their own positions were sheltered behind the heights.[15] When French aircraft struggled into the sky, often for only an hour or two, they could not gain control of the air and German fighters took a heavy toll on their opponents.

The task facing Micheler's army group was a formidable one. They had to breach three successive positions to a depth of about ten kilometres, each one containing up to three lines of trenches, often dug on the reverse slope and protected by double belts of barbed wire. They were also well served by railways and metalled roads that would allow for quick reinforcement in time of crisis. North of the Aisne was the plateau of the Chemin des Dames, which rose to a height of 800 metres, before dropping down steeply to the Ailette river. A French staff officer gloomily concluded that the ground was, therefore, 'impractical for the artillery' and 'often difficult for the infantry'. The steep slopes 'meant there were many blind spots in the valleys, which could only be destroyed by shelling'. It was this low ground, marshy and criss-crossed by drainage ditches and thickets, which was almost impassable once off the roads.[16]

Enormous quantities of ammunition were fired off in the days before the attack – over five million 75 mm shells and another million heavy shells – but the effect almost everywhere was disappointing. 'Artillerymen, faced with a considerable task and under time pressure, made the most of the rare occasions when observation was possible,' noted one report, 'but wind, snow and gusts increased the spread of gunfire and reduced its accuracy and therefore its effectiveness.'[17] Greater numbers of guns were assigned to each corps than had been the case on the Somme, but they were spread out over a much wider frontage, which diluted their effect. Moreover, because significant parts of the defensive system lay at the extreme range of French artillery, batteries had to be deployed further forward, which left them vulnerable to vicious counter-battery fire. By 16 April, VI Corps in Sixth Army had lost almost a third of its complement of a hundred 155 mm howitzers – vital weapons that Nivelle relied upon to break through the German lines.

The bulk of French strength would be directed against General Max von Boehn's Seventh Army, which was dug in from La Fère to Juvincourt and guarded the right flank of Crown Prince Wilhelm's army group. Boehn – an old Prussian general who had been brought back from retirement on the outbreak of war – grimly recorded the increase in artillery fire across his whole position, including regular gas bombardments, interspersed with heavy 'drumfire', which turned the forward positions into a pockmarked wasteland. On 12 April, he ordered his divisions to assume 'full combat readiness' and warned them to expect an attack imminently. OHL had already issued guidance on what to expect and how to avoid the fate of Falkenhausen's troops at Arras: 'front divisions, whose fighting strength had already suffered, were not replaced in a timely manner, artillery was not used adequately in the days when there were enemy bombardments, and battle reserves, as well as divisions located behind the front, were held too far back for timely counter-attacks'. Boehn gave 'strict instructions' to keep up heavy fire against enemy positions, particularly at night, while making sure his trench-holding divisions brought their reserves close enough forward to get into the fight at the earliest opportunity.[18]

Despite the mounting tension, German morale held up well enough. An emissary from Supreme Command, Major Bramsch, toured Seventh Army and reported that the mood of the troops was 'good' and the divisions 'battle-ready'.[19] Morale was strengthened by a sense that the defenders were as well prepared as they could be for the coming storm. German intelligence could not have been unaware of the scale of the French preparations, but Nivelle had been careless and operational secrecy had been uncharacteristically lax. Copies of orders were being circulated far too freely and even ended up in the front-line trenches. On the night of 4/5 April, a German raiding party stumbled upon a French sergeant and dragged him back to their lines. He was found to be carrying orders revealing the details of what three neighbouring corps were preparing. Yet, after being told of what had happened, Nivelle did nothing. The orders would remain unchanged.[20]

Nivelle was also loath to settle a furious row that had broken out between two of his most senior commanders. On the left of the attacking frontage was General Charles Mangin's Sixth Army. Its commander, now recognized as one of the fiercest generals in the French Army, had lost none of his fire. He had finally been given command of an army on the eve of the biggest offensive of the war and was entrusted with its most crucial sector. His beloved colonial troops – including both I and II Colonial Corps – were in the vanguard, tasked with opening a way for Tenth Army to exploit northwards. While other senior officers blanched at Nivelle's plans and urged caution, Mangin did not, finding himself rowing with Micheler over the nature of the offensive. Mangin opted to follow the techniques that had been pioneered at Verdun, including a fast-moving creeping barrage, only for Micheler – his nominal superior – to urge caution. Advancing 100 metres every three minutes was impossible, Micheler warned, particularly if you took into account losses and fatigue. But Mangin would not budge, leaving Micheler to grow increasingly exasperated at a subordinate who was now acting as his equal. A meeting with Nivelle failed to resolve the matter, with

Micheler storming out, complaining that he was being undermined and that he would no longer accept any responsibility for what happened to Mangin's attack.[21]

The first waves of Fifth and Sixth Armies – just under 200,000 men – went over the top at six o'clock on the morning of 16 April. It had rained heavily the day before, and all night, causing many of the trenches to flood and coat the assault troops, clad in their blue cloaks and steel helmets, with a cloying layer of mud and freezing water. Ahead of them the bombardment surged and crashed upon the German positions with furious intensity. One witness remembered the 'whipping, ripping sound of the shells tearing through the air', which competed with the rumble of 'distant explosions' and left the air swirling and buffeting in its wake.[22] Although the German counter-barrage was sporadic, which seemed to bode well, the rattle of machine-gun fire, which broke out soon after the leading lines left their trenches, was the first indication that something was wrong and that Nivelle would struggle to repeat the experience of Fort Douaumont.

Mangin's troops attacked with courage beyond measure, storming forward towards Chavignon and Pargny, only to find the German defences much tougher than expected and columns of German infantry emerging from the tunnels and mineshafts that honeycombed the hills and which protected them from the worst of the shelling. Once their defences had been manned, they opened fire and quickly blunted the attack. Colonial regiments managed to reach the crest of the Chemin des Dames, but once they pushed further on, down towards the Ailette, they came under enfilade machine-gun fire and lost their creeping barrage. Without it, progress was slow and costly. Mangin tried to push the attack on and fired off furious orders to the forward units: 'If the barbed wire is not destroyed, it must be cut by the infantry; you have to gain ground.'[23] But it did little good. One French officer went forward in the second wave, only to run into the corpses of the leading companies bunched up in awful clumps across no-man's-land. Two thirds of the first wave had been 'mowed down by enemy machine-gun fire coming from small reinforced concrete bunkers', with the survivors 'huddled together in the German front line'. Then, as he put it, 'everything slowed down'. They remained where they were, sheltered by the ridgelines, but under 'merciless' artillery fire until nightfall.[24]

On the right was General Olivier Mazel's Fifth Army, whose five corps could only make minor gains. The same problems were again evident. The bombardment had not been able to clear enough of the German defences and the infantry struggled to progress against fierce machine-gun and artillery fire. One corps complained about 'vigorous counter-attacks' that came in quicker than expected, causing heavy losses and breaking the momentum of the attacking waves.[25] Particularly disappointing was the experience of two tank battalions (*groupements*) – about 128 vehicles in total – that had been brought up to the front and ordered to help the infantry gain their final objectives (which, it was assumed, would have been much less damaged by the shelling). The tanks were Schneider CA1s, box-shaped armoured vehicles based upon the US-designed Holt tractor and carrying a crew of seven. Armament was a short-barrelled 75 mm with two machine-guns, more powerful than the British Mark I; but the CA1s had a similar set of problems: mechanical unreliability, a slow top speed and cramped, unhealthy conditions for the crews.

Early on the morning of 16 April, two columns of Schneiders tried to move towards the German lines near Berry-au-Bac, crawling over muddy tracks and struggling over the storm-tossed battlefield. One *groupement* was spotted by enemy aircraft and soon attracted heavy shellfire, with the vehicles coming up against the first trench line, which had been deliberately widened after the British had used tanks on the Somme. This slowed them down and made them vulnerable to the plunging fire that was shrieking down from the heights. Although French infantry heroically tried to help them get past these obstacles, they could make little progress and were gradually knocked out one by one. The second *groupement* got further, reaching the third line, but they proved terribly vulnerable to breakdown and enemy action and suffered heavy losses. Within a matter of hours, fifty-seven tanks had been destroyed by German guns (over 40 per cent of all those engaged), many shells igniting the petrol tanks that were stored on the exterior of the vehicle and turning them into flaming torches. It was a brutal, dispiriting debut for France's tanks. Vehicles

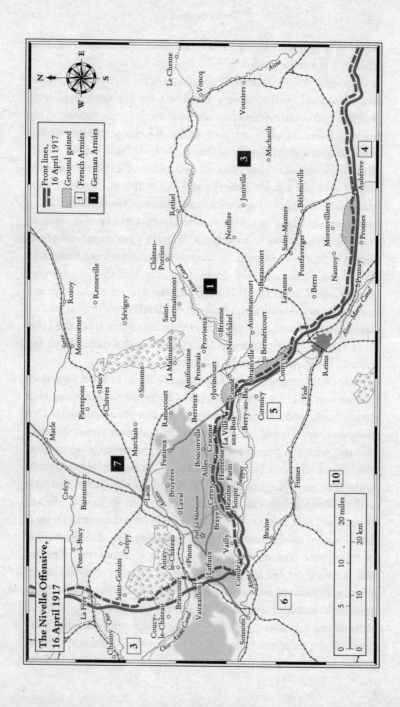

The Nivelle Offensive, 16 April 1917

Legend:
- Front lines, 16 April 1917
- Ground gained
- 1 French Armies
- 1 German Armies

that had been in development for over two years were now burning fiercely in the twilight; a perfect symbol of Nivelle's fading vision.[26]

As night fell, the realization that France's great gamble had failed began to sink in. At Compiègne, Nivelle sat at his desk, as if in a daze, glassily staring into space as aide after aide brought him despatches from the front. He was 'anxious', one wrote. 'His height seemed to grow less and swellings marred the strong lines of his face.'[27] 'Today did not give us the results that we were hoping for from the Sixth Army', read one report. An array of problems were identified, most of which had already been foreseen but ignored: 'the very significant reinforcement of the front by an enemy who anticipated our assaults'; 'robust defensive structures (caves, ridges, very deep underground shelters)'; faulty artillery preparation; bad weather (that hindered photographic reconnaissance); and what it called the 'tortured ground', made worse by the rain, which prevented the infantry from following the creeping barrage closely enough.[28]

France's colonial troops had suffered particularly badly and parts of the battlefield were now littered with their corpses. That evening, General Jean-Baptiste Marchand, commanding 10th Division, reported on the state of his division. 'Losses, whose total is still not yet confirmed, were heavy', he admitted. 'Colonels Quérette, Petitdemange and Garnier were put out of action as brigade and regimental commanders . . . The 52 and 53/Colonial Infantry no longer had a commanding officer. The 52/Colonial Infantry Regiment lost, so to speak, all its officers.' 15th Colonial Infantry Division had also been shattered. Major-General Maurice Guérin, its commanding officer, admitted that his regiments could no longer undertake any kind of offensive activity because of 'very high losses'. 'I ordered that the units be restructured and to hold their ground at all costs. In view of the casualties suffered by the officers, I found it difficult to ask for more.'[29]

A Council of Ministers was held on 18 April. 'Painlevé gave an account of the military operations of yesterday and the day before', recorded Poincaré. 'He presented them in quite a serious light. Ribot did not hide how disappointed he was. We did not even attain what Pétain hoped for and he had been the least optimistic of us all.' French losses were 'serious', estimated at 35,000. When Nivelle was summoned to Poincaré's office several days later, he was 'disappointed', but remained 'calm and confident', stressing that German losses were much higher than their own and that he was preparing to bring Tenth Army into the fight as soon as possible. Poincaré then shook his head sadly. They must 'look to the future' and do whatever they could to 'prolong the war'. Nivelle, who seemed not to hear him, replied that he was looking at a series of 'small operations', including the 'occupation of the Craonne plateau and the neighbouring heights'. For the moment, that was all he could do.[30]

Whereas previous French assaults had been the cause of acute anxiety at OHL, 16 April 1917 was not one of them, and Ludendorff wasted no time in releasing a communiqué to the press crowing over the failure of France's latest effort: 'The great French attempt to break through, which was very ambitious in its aim, had failed.' Their losses were 'very heavy' and German forces had taken more than 2,100 prisoners.[31] That such an enormous offensive could have failed may have been down to Nivelle's mistakes, but it also illustrated how strong the German lines in the west remained and how effective German defensive tactics had been. Indeed, apart from the local collapse around Arras (which could be put down to the non-implementation of the new doctrine), Germany's defence-in-depth had proved a highly adaptable system and fiendishly difficult to break down.

This is not to say that there were no lessons to learn. The fighting on the Aisne was quickly analysed, with the Crown Prince issuing a report on 25 April that reaffirmed the basic soundness of German defensive tactics. The 'flexible conduct of the defence proved a complete success', it noted, and 'the principle that the battle should be conducted around the first position must be upheld'. Each division could hold about 4–5 kilometres of front, as long as they were rested and supported by reserve divisions able to move forward when needed. They required good maps, previous orientation in the sectors where they would fight (particularly for the divisions that were expected to counter-attack), and a strong awareness of the need for deception and camouflage. 'Through photographs, prisoner statements and espionage, the enemy knows the details of our positions far behind the front.'[32]

Rupprecht's army group came to similar conclusions: that defence-in-depth was an effective response to enemy tactics. Even the growing menace of tanks was not something to be feared as long as they were dealt with resolutely. 'It has little to fear from the tanks if it remains quiet, and artillery as well as light mortars and machine-guns commence the battle. On the other hand, it must be made obligatory for these weapons to be used to fight off every approaching tank immediately.' The most important finding concerned the counter-attacking divisions, which had to be closer to the front, ready to intervene at the correct moment. 'As soon as the approach of enemy infantry is anticipated, all reserves must be made available to the divisional commander and brought forward. Only then can an immediate engagement be ensured.'[33] This had been the main criticism of General Falkenhausen's deployments: that his reserves had been too far back. Although Falkenhausen was still regarded favourably by OHL ('a particularly striking personality' according to Ludendorff), the setback on 9 April could not go unpunished, and when the Governor-General of Belgium, Moritz von Bissing, passed away on 18 April, Falkenhausen was chosen as his replacement. He was succeeded at Sixth Army by Otto von Below (the cousin of Fritz von Below).[34]

Notwithstanding the buoyant mood at OHL, a sinister feeling of unease, niggling at first but strengthening each month, began to haunt a number of senior German commanders from the spring of 1917. Reflecting on the loss of Vimy Ridge, Rupprecht believed that the situation was 'undoubtedly serious'. He knew that he did not have the manpower to retake the heights, so he had to be content with holding his line with whatever units could be scraped together. 'For the moment, we will certainly stop the enemy's attack', he wrote; 'it is doubtful, however, how further attacks will be stopped with such massively increased artillery fire. This raises a further question: is it, in fact, worth continuing the war in such circumstances?' Rupprecht could only look eastwards. 'If we are not successful in achieving peace with Russia within a few months, we will have to declare ourselves defeated; for if we hesitate too long, the peace terms of our opponents will only be harder.'[35]

The prospect of remaining on the defensive indefinitely was a difficult one. General Gallwitz wrote to the Crown Prince on 12 April criticizing the 'system of pure defence' that the German Army was now condemned to. The attack had 'always been the morally stronger form' of warfare. 'An attack is easier to conduct, brings visible success and strengthens the troops by increasing their self-assurance.' Defensive fighting, on the contrary, 'costs more men and ammunition than an attack that is carried out according to plan'. Moreover, 'our resources will, with a high degree of certainty, be consumed by a continuous defensive battle'. Gallwitz petitioned OHL in the same vein, but got nowhere. Ludendorff explained that in the present situation they could not go on to the offensive, although the army group would, of course, 'seize every opportunity' to inflict losses on the enemy.[36]

The possibility that the Allied attacks would simply go on, like the Somme, was a grim prospect. German losses had been significantly fewer than the British and French had sustained but still bit deep into the strength of the *Westheer*. Between April and May, Sixth Army recorded somewhere between 79,000 and 85,000 casualties. On the Aisne, where fighting was heavier, German totals were only tallied up by the end of June, by which time 163,000 casualties had been recorded. Munitions were also being expended at an unprecedented rate. The German Army had fired off ten million shells in April 1917, and such high consumption could not be maintained indefinitely.[37] Moreover, fears that Germany was bound to lose a *Materialschlacht* ('material battle') with the Entente (and now America) were sharpened by the upsurge of domestic unrest back in Germany. On Monday, 16 April – the day of Nivelle's great attack on the Aisne – up to 200,000 metalworkers went on strike in Berlin, forcing the closure of over 300 factories. While strikes were not unusual in Wilhelmine Germany, workers were now more strident in their demands, complaining about food distribution and worrying that strikers would be pressed into military service. More dangerous was the copycat strike that broke out in Leipzig at the same time, which had more political demands, including universal suffrage and the signing of a peace treaty without annexations.[38]

For the Chancellor, Bethmann Hollweg, the growth of popular discontent was a perennial concern, now sharpened by fears that revolutionary activity in Russia was spreading west. By the spring of 1917, he was hopeful of strengthening support for the war by enlarging the franchise in Prussia. He believed that by ending the three-class voting system that had been in place since 1848, the people would be bound more closely to the regime, thus pre-empting any attempt to change Prussian politics by force.[39] The Kaiser looked on in horror at what was happening in Russia, but could not be moved further than his 'Easter Message' of 7 April, which was greeted with widespread disappointment. His Imperial Majesty was 'determined to put into action the development of our inner political, economic, and social life', including the 'transformation of the Prussian Parliament' and the expansion of suffrage, but this would only take place once 'our warriors have returned home'.[40]

Predictably, Hindenburg and Ludendorff did not respond warmly to Bethmann Hollweg's latest initiative and, in the wake of the 'Easter Message', redoubled their efforts to move the Chancellor on. The pronouncement was just 'kowtowing to the Russian revolution', Ludendorff complained, and he would have nothing to do with it. Hindenburg saw it the same way, believing that it gave the impression that Germany's commitment to the war was weakening.[41] When German war aims were discussed at a meeting at the Supreme Command on 23 April, the duo won out, securing the Kaiser's agreement for a renewed series of annexationist demands, including the occupation of vast swathes of the Baltics and Poland, the incorporation of Belgium into a long-term alliance with Germany, and numerous other territorial prizes, such as Liège, the Flanders coast and the Longwy–Briey iron region. The meeting itself was 'a critical day of the first order' according to Alexander von Müller, the Chief of the Naval Cabinet. Bethmann Hollweg was a resigned figure throughout, shrugging his shoulders as OHL set out its plans for reordering Europe under German control. 'It will do no harm if we ask for the maximum', he was overheard saying as he left the meeting. 'We shan't get it.'[42]

The possibility of redrawing the map of Europe would ultimately depend upon what happened in the west. While Germany's armies held their ground in France, her U-boats tried to land the fatal blow against Britain. German submarines sank an impressive number of ships, sparking panic in the British Admiralty, which seemed, for the moment, completely at a loss as to how to stop it. 499,430 tons were sunk in February; 548,917 in March; 841,118 in April; and 590,729 in May – almost reaching the figures that Admiral von Holtzendorff believed would be enough to force British capitulation.[43] Hindenburg and Ludendorff both remained confident that the U-boats would continue to inflict terrible wounds on the Allied war effort, but the wider situation was still so full of uncertainty that further predictions were impossible.

At OHL, Georg Wetzell authored a note on 12 May that attempted to set out Germany's strategic options if the 'world war' did not end in 1917. For Wetzell, Germany had to make a 'worst case' assessment of her situation, namely that the submarine campaign would not achieve decisive successes. 'If the U-boat war does not result in a decision in late summer and we, up to that time, continue to operate defensively everywhere on land, the world war will not finish in 1917. If our opponents succeed in holding out until the autumn of 17, we will have to expect – after America's entry – a winter campaign and the continuation of the war into 1918. Our situation will then become considerably more difficult because, in the winter of 17/18, or at any rate in the spring of 1918, fresh American forces with strong artillery will engage in action on the Western Front.' Wetzell also speculated that a Russian collapse would not, at least for the foreseeable future, allow significant reserves to be moved west. 'The whole picture will look quite different, however, if we manage, despite all our opponents, to achieve a resounding success on land, at a decisive point, and destroy all our opponents before the winter. Is this possible?' For Wetzell the choice was clear. The decisive blow could only fall on Germany's weakest enemy: Italy.[44]

Ludendorff's response to Wetzell's note is not recorded, but he was not, as yet, thinking of offensive activity. His focus remained on the Western Front, where fighting went on. Nivelle may have told the politicians that the battle would be called off within forty-eight hours if it did not succeed, but on it continued – just like the Somme – week after week. Allenby renewed his offensive on either side of the Scarpe on 23 April and kept hammering away over the next seven days, while fighting continued on the Chemin des Dames as the French inched forward. There were no notable successes on either side, just continuous shelling, regular aerial battles, and a rising toll of dead and wounded. By 25 April, the French had sustained 134,000 casualties on the Aisne, including 30,000 killed in action.[45] This was bad enough, but worse was to come. The 'evil spirit' that Poincaré had been warned about in the autumn of 1916 had now returned and was spreading through the army with frightening speed. Morale had long been fragile, but scattered units began to display signs of an alarming deterioration of discipline, criticizing their officers and refusing to go into the line. Some, when they were told that they were returning to the Chemin des Dames, even cut loose entirely; surging back from the front, wild-eyed and dangerous, looting and burning.

May 1917 was a curious month: a time of endings and beginnings; a parting of the ways. Sir Douglas Haig had supported Nivelle loyally throughout April, but he now began to look elsewhere, conscious of the waxing strength of his army: 1.8 million men strong and becoming more powerful with every passing month. He met his army commanders on 7 May and told them that their focus would now be in the north. Already plans were well advanced for an attack on Messines Ridge, the swell of high ground to the south of Ypres, but this would only be the first stage of a climactic battle – a 'northern operation' – that, Haig hoped, would 'secure the Belgian coast' and bring the end of the war much closer.[46] Although there was as yet no authorization from the War Cabinet in London, which remained deeply split on what strategy to adopt, there was a sense that the British were now going their own way. Nivelle demanded that his main offensive on the Aisne continue for the time being, but Haig was uninterested. 'The situation has turned in his favour', recalled Vallières. 'Chewing over a solid resentment against General Nivelle, who had caused difficulties for him, he thinks now only of paying him back in the same coin.'[47]

Nivelle staggered on, although his authority, worn with such a lightness of touch since December 1916, was gone; shattered on the bleak slopes of the Aisne. With his future now the subject of almost constant discussion in Paris, Poincaré, Ribot and Painlevé had to weigh up the effects of sacking him with the costs of allowing him to continue. On 29 April, Poincaré decided to appoint Pétain as Army Chief of Staff – a position that had been mothballed since 1914 – where, it was hoped, he would contain Nivelle and begin to pick up the pieces of the armies broken since 16 April.[48] As for Nivelle, he suddenly seemed to come to his senses, realizing how close he was to losing everything. On the same day that he received the news about Pétain, he wrote to Micheler and asked him for his opinion on how Mangin had 'exercised command' during recent operations. Micheler had never got on with Mangin, but he would not be hustled into providing Nivelle with a convenient scapegoat: 'During the operation, and faced with a difficult situation, General Mangin remained the dynamic performer you know.'[49]

Blaming Mangin would not save Nivelle. Although Mangin was eventually removed from command and ordered to remain outside Paris (where he continued to agitate in his defence), the mood was now turning decisively against the Commander-in-Chief. Micheler had remained tight-lipped about Nivelle's plans at Poincaré's War Council, but he was now almost beside himself with grief and despair. Neither he 'nor his subordinate commanders had ever thought they could get to the distant objectives laid down', he told a British liaison officer in the days afterwards. He had repeatedly warned Nivelle 'that he could not "prepare" 3 positions for attack; but he was told[:] "You will go straight through, *there are no Germans there*." This was the underlying idea of the whole conception of the attack.'[50] On 15 May, with the bickering between senior officers threatening to get out of hand, the Council of Ministers decided to replace Nivelle with Pétain while also appointing Foch as Army Chief of Staff. To the end, Nivelle remained defiant.

'I am a soldier', he told Poincaré after being asked to resign. 'I have nothing to do with political or parliamentary policy. For three years I have thought about only two things: France and the enemy. I believe what has been proposed is bad for France and should be rejected in the alarmist campaign that has now settled down, and is advantageous to Germany, which will sing joyfully in triumph.'[51]

On 17 May, Pétain travelled to Compiègne and met Nivelle in his office – in the room where Marie Antoinette had once resided – and they shared a brief, silent meal before Nivelle left for North Africa, never to be heard of again. Nivelle's departure from the war came as swiftly as his arrival. War was more than a tactical method, but a brutal struggle of nations that was fundamentally about morale and strategy. For Bernard Serrigny, who served on Pétain's staff, Nivelle was always a limited soldier who could never see what was truly important. 'War was for him a scientific matter', he wrote; 'he claimed to treat it like an equation to find the final formula for victory. A technician above all, never having had any high-level role, neither in general staff nor in the forces, he must have been quickly overwhelmed in his position of authority.' Serrigny would always remember going into Nivelle's office in Compiègne on the day he left and perusing the maps that still lay strewn across the desk. He noticed that Nivelle only used 1:5000 scale master plans to direct operations 'as he did not have any maps of the entire front. That sums up his character.'[52]

On 19 May, a morning bright with the promise of spring, Pétain issued new orders to his army commanders. 'The equilibrium between the opposing forces facing each other on the north and north-east front does not permit us, for the time being, to contemplate a break-through of the front followed by strategic exploitation. Therefore, what is important at the present time is to bend our efforts to wear down the opponent with a minimum of losses.' Pétain was unambiguous that major operations – those 'with distant objectives' – would no longer be attempted; instead attacks would be conducted as 'economically' as possible with the greatest use of artillery.[53] The document, written in Pétain's clear, sober style, was a perfect distillation of what the new Commander-in-Chief had always believed: that all but the most carefully prepared offensives were impossible. Nivelle's dreams of a 'rapid conquest' were no more. All that mattered now was survival. The Entente had reached its darkest hour. Only a dim light across the Atlantic, where the greatest power on earth was beginning to mobilize, gave cause to hope that all was not lost.

'A matter of command'

Messines Ridge to Compiègne
(June 1917–November 1918)

16. 'Patience and tenacity'

'Up at about 4 a.m., and left at 5.40 a.m. on [a] special train for Folke-stone, where [I] embarked for Boulogne, arriving at latter port at about 10 o'clock.'[1] So began General John J. Pershing's diary entry for 13 June 1917, in which he narrated his first day in France, when he stepped upon French soil, escorted by Royal Navy destroyers and ser-enaded by a French military band. After inspecting a local barracks, he gave a short statement: 'I am very happy to act as a representative for my government here in France. I can say that I bring to the French people the best wishes for the future. The reception that I've received here this morning was extremely meaningful. It has left a strong impression on us all. It shows that we will have common objectives from now on.' Afterwards he boarded another train, which would take him to the capital for an evening reception with the US Ambas-sador. *Le Matin* was clear on the importance of the occasion: 'We are certain that 13 June 1917 will be considered one of the most celebrated dates of the Great War.'[2]

Pershing's train pulled into the Gare du Nord shortly before 6.30 p.m., where large crowds, waving American flags and breathless with anticipation, had gathered to see him. Dressed in a drab olive jacket with high collar, breeches and shiny brown riding boots, his cap pulled down low over his eyes, Pershing looked business-like and stern. He was met on the platform by Monsieur Painlevé, Marshal Joffre (who had been appointed head of the French Military Mission to the United States), René Viviani and Foch, as well as the Ambas-sador, W. G. Sharp. After a brief exchange of pleasantries, Pershing was escorted outside and then driven to the Hotel Crillon. 'Dense masses of people lined the boulevards and filled the squares', he recalled. 'Men, women, and children absolutely packed every foot of space, even to the windows and housetops. Cheers and tears were mingled together and shouts of enthusiasm fairly rent the air. Women climbed into our automobiles screaming, "Vive l'Amérique," and threw flowers until we were literally buried.'³

Pershing was clearly surprised by the enthusiastic reception he received on the streets of Paris, but he remained as impassive as ever. His face was an expressionless mask; 'tailor-made for monuments' as one authority later put it.⁴ It was as if nothing could possibly disturb the soul that lay behind the warm brown eyes and sloping nose with a tightly drawn mouth that gave nothing away. After enrolling as a cadet at West Point in 1882, he spent years out in the American prairie, riding for days at a time, chasing Sioux war parties and learning how to survive in the lawless expanses of the American West. Although not especially loved, he was trusted by his men, who saw him as more of a 'hard-boiled, super-drill sergeant' than a father.⁵ A difficult man to know, he was often accused of being cold and aloof; a distance that became more pronounced after a terrible fire had swept through his family's apartment in San Francisco in August 1915, killing his wife, Helen Frances, and their three daughters, with his son, six-year-old Warren, being the only survivor.

Ravaged by grief, his hair now turned completely white, Pershing threw himself into his work with an even more noticeable devotion. In March 1916, he had been placed in command of a punitive expedition to hunt the Mexican bandit Pancho Villa across the Rio Grande, and although he failed to capture his quarry, he had come to the attention of President Wilson, who was impressed by his application to duty as well as his obvious (and welcome) disinterest in holding political office. On 7 May 1917 – a month after America had declared war – Pershing was at the headquarters of the Southern Department at Fort Sam Houston, San Antonio, Texas, when he received a telegram from the Secretary of War, Newton D. Baker, ordering him to report to Washington with all possible speed. When he arrived in the capital, he was told that he had been selected to command the expeditionary force that was being readied to go to Europe.

'I will give you only two orders', Baker told him; 'one to go to France and the other to come home. In the meantime your authority in France will be supreme.'⁶

The US Navy was already one of the strongest navies in the world (and its destroyers were already committed to the campaign against Germany's submarines), but American ground forces were not yet capable of taking to the field. Comprising only 133,000 men and 5,800 officers, the US Army was tiny by Continental standards. Even if the (approximately) 70,000 men of the National Guard were added to this total, there was no chance that America would be able to play a decisive role in the conflict unless she undertook a huge mobilization of manpower.[7] This was combined with a crippling lack of equipment to fight a modern war. The Army had been the victim of a succession of parsimonious governments since the Civil War and lacked almost everything that modern warfare required, from aircraft and tanks, gas and quick-firing artillery, to machine-guns, hand grenades and trench mortars. Soon after America had joined the war, Joffre warned that it was vital the US Government, which was 'very inexperienced in the matter of military organization', should not encounter any 'disillusionment' that might discourage it and that a French task force should be appointed to advise it on such matters.[8]

Pershing formally assumed command of the American Expeditionary Force (AEF) on 26 May and was handed a brief set of instructions from Baker confirming that America was not, and never would be, formally allied to the Entente powers: 'In military operations against the Imperial German Government you are directed to cooperate with the forces of the other countries employed against the enemy; but in so doing the underlying idea must be kept in view that the forces of the United States are a separate and distinct component of the combined forces, the identity of which must be preserved.'[9] Already it was known that both the French and British were eager to incorporate US troops into their divisions – what was soon termed 'amalgamation' – as a kind of direct injection of manpower into the Western Front, but Pershing, in line with his instructions, made it clear that this was not what he wanted. Nevertheless, the Americans did lean heavily on the expertise of the French Army, agreeing to send a division overseas as soon as possible to be trained by the French, who undertook to supply it with everything it needed. The Americans would send the raw materials, steel and manpower; the French would turn them into a fighting division, equipped with French guns and ammunition, and trained in their methods.

Pershing met the new French Commander-in-Chief on 16 June. Wearing his kepi, dressed in a plain horizon-blue tunic and matching trousers, Pétain cut an austere figure; his face heavy with worry. 'Pétain is above medium height and weight, he wore a full mustache [sic], slightly gray, and was then about sixty', noted Pershing. 'He has a kindly expression, is most agreeable, but not especially talkative.'[10] Brigadier-General James Harbord, Pershing's Chief of Staff, was impressed by the knowledge and natural charisma that Pétain possessed and, as they sat down to lunch together, felt that this was a man who could be trusted. 'Pétain is easily the strong man in authority over here now. He knows what France can do; probably what Germany can do; what the temper of his own people is; what their need of coal will be in the next cold winter; what their need of certain foodstuffs will be . . .' Like Pershing, Harbord noted Pétain's reluctance to make conversation. He had said little during the meeting, only to 'break his silence' when he said that he was very glad America was now in the war and 'that he hoped it was not too late'.[11]

The officers who accompanied Pershing had all noticed the same thing: France was exhausted. 'The fact is that France is very tired of this war', Pershing wrote to Newton Baker on 9 July, after he had been in the country just under a month. 'The common people openly complain of heavy taxes, and protest that they are being ground down to enrich government contractors . . .' More worryingly, Pétain had told him that he feared 'something bordering on revolution' might break out, hence why Pershing had 'taken advantage of an occasional opportunity, without appearing to meddle and without talking too much, to speak encouragingly of the splendid stamina of the French people and of the army, and have endeavoured to inspire confidence among them in their military organization and its commander'. His own view was that the French could hold out until the spring against 'any probable effort of the enemy, but that poverty and discontent, magnified by the socialistic press, especially should the government fail to continue to back up the army, may so dishearten the people and the army that the latter will lose its morale and disaster follow'.[12]

The situation was even more dangerous than Pershing suspected. There were rumours of French divisions refusing to go into the line, but the Americans had little idea of the true extent of the disciplinary problems then affecting the French Army, which had almost been broken by Nivelle's gamble on the Aisne. The first outbreaks of disorder occurred in late April, as Nivelle ordered continued assaults on the Chemin des Dames. Grievances were both general and specific. War-weariness, news about the revolution in Russia and the unsettling outbreak of strikes on the home front, combined with the shattering disappointment of operations in April, sapped the already fragile cohesion of French regiments. When units were returned to the front line without sufficient rest and training, their long-term complaints about lack of leave, bad food and poor conditions reached breaking point. Between late May and early June, a spate of 'collective acts of indiscipline' took place, from refusing to enter the trenches, to the singing of revolutionary songs, desertions, vandalism and looting behind the lines.[13]

In total, fifty-four divisions – almost half the army – would be affected by poor discipline, with Sixth Army, now commanded by General Paul Maistre, being particularly susceptible. At the beginning of May, troops of 2nd Colonial Division had been sent back into the trenches and ordered to mount a renewed attack on the Laffaux Mill, a blood-soaked position on the heights above the Aisne, which caused a swift breakdown in discipline. Leaflets denouncing the war were found in their barracks, with the men refusing to fight while their compatriots were earning a fortune back home (industrial workers could earn 15–20 francs a day compared to the miserly 0.25 francs that the lowest ranks were paid in the army).[14] In 69th Division, one regiment rampaged through their depot singing 'The Internationale' and refused to go on exercise. A detachment of military police had to be deployed when a group of deserters from one battalion tried to prevent their fellow soldiers from boarding trains to go up to the line, shouting anti-war slogans and firing into the air. In 158th Division, widespread protests about leave, which the men insisted they had been promised, were eventually resolved when the officers got them to stand down, but Maistre had the division returned to the rear anyway, complaining that its morale left 'something to be desired'.[15]

For Pétain, good morale was ultimately 'a matter of command' and he was determined to restore the army's discipline and self-confidence.[16] On 8 June he made it clear that some officers had not shown the 'initiative and energy' required to deal with the 'evil spirit' that reigned in the worst units: 'Inertia is equivalent to complicity.' Therefore, 'all necessary sanctions' would be taken against those involved in the disorder, while those officers who showed 'vigour' in repressing them would be supported by the High Command.[17] 112 death sentences were passed for mutineers, although only twenty-five executions were carried out, Pétain insisting that only the most heinous acts of mutiny be punished in this manner. He also sweetened the pill by increasing the amount of leave (from seven to ten days every four months) and ordering improvements in the facilities behind the line, particularly at railway stations, where refreshment areas were specially set aside for soldiers, now stocked with better food and staffed by the Red Cross.[18]

Pétain went about rebuilding the morale of the French Army with a single-minded focus that came from deep within himself. He understood the limits of what men could stand and the suffering they had undergone. For a whole month, the new Commander-in-Chief visited division after division, ninety in total, meeting with the men and listening to their grievances. He did not hide the gravity of the situation or the seriousness of the task that lay ahead. In an article entitled 'Why We Fight', which was published in *L'Écho de Paris* on 27 June (after much debate in government over whether it should be censored), he explained why they should continue to keep going, why they had no choice but to go on: 'We rarely know or often forget why we fight. We fight because we have been assailed by Germany; we fight to chase the enemy from our territory and, through stable and complete peace, to stop such an attack from happening again. We fight because it would be a crime to betray, by shameful defeat, both our dead and our children; we fight for peace to re-establish our country's prosperity . . . we fight with tenacity, we fight with discipline, because these are the essential conditions for victory.'[19]

As the flames of revolt were being doused, Pétain started to rebuild the Army in his own image. In a series of short notes, he laid out how they would fight in future. In 'Directive No. 2', issued on 20 June, he established a number of training schools devoted to the instruction of all branches of the Army, including the infantry, artillery, engineers, cavalry and air force. Divisions were now directed to undergo intensive training in offensive operations for at least two weeks, which would focus on how to take an enemy position, including artillery preparation and consolidation. Objectives would be limited to only what the artillery could prepare, and extensive effort was placed on improving liaison between the different arms. Pétain also recommended that training schools for different weapons be grouped together. Infantry battalions would now train as they would fight: working intimately with artillery and aircraft to forge a common bond for what Pétain hoped would become an irresistible offensive weapon.[20]

This was followed by 'Directive No. 3', published on 4 July. Gone was the naïve reliance upon the offensive spirit and raw courage that had characterized the French Army of earlier years; instead the Army was to be rebuilt in a methodical manner, beholden to the gods of technology and firepower. The immediate aim was to allow for a period of rest and instruction, waiting until such time as the Army was re-equipped and readied to undertake a series of limited offensives. With French industry now concentrating on producing bigger, more powerful artillery, a heavy-artillery reserve was created and each corps was equipped with two groups of 105 mm howitzers and two groups of 155 mm Schneiders (each group containing twelve guns). Divisions would also be bolstered by two groups of short-barrelled 155 mm howitzers – a significant improvement on what had been prescribed in 1914 (when French divisions had gone into battle with just one regiment, or three groups, of 75 mm field guns).[21]

Not content with increasing the artillery's firepower, Pétain placed extensive orders for new tanks. The Schneider CAIs had been unsuccessful on 16 April, but the French High Command had not lost faith in them and signed off on an ambitious programme of vehicle production, including pushing forward the prototype of a light vehicle (what would become the Renault FT-17). Pétain was also convinced of the need to secure absolute control of the air in future operations and wanted aircraft capable of bombing German positions on the battlefield as well as conducting missions deep into the enemy rear against the industrial areas of Lorraine and the Saar. He was now confident the tide had turned: 'Here the weapons are being fully manufactured, the armies of our allies are continuously increasing, the life of the nation will finally be organized, the experience of war gained through great difficulty is beginning to be understood by all. France may await with reasonable confidence the victorious peace it needs and has earned through such great sacrifices. Patience and tenacity!'[22]

Sir Douglas Haig was not minded to wait until either the French or the Americans were ready. He wanted to strike quickly and had been lobbying London for weeks about mounting his so-called 'northern operation' now that Nivelle's attack had self-evidently failed. At 3.10 on the morning of 7 June, General Sir Herbert Plumer's Second Army launched its assault on the Messines–Wytschaete Ridge, the attack heralded by the blowing of nineteen mines under the German line. The idea for a mine attack had originated with a former engineering contractor, Major John Norton Griffiths, who had suggested that it would be possible to undermine the German lines by tunnelling through a layer of blue clay that lay between sixty and ninety feet under the surface. These galleries could then be packed with explosives and detonated at the right moment. Coordinating the excavation of so many tunnels (twenty-four were eventually built) and keeping them secret was challenging, as the efforts of small teams of miners, sweating their way through hundreds of feet of damp earth, were combined with razor-sharp staff work to move the spoil out at night and ensure that little was suspected.[23]

When the mines were detonated, a tremendous shockwave was created, carrying away most of the garrison and leaving the front line an unrecognizable series of smoking shell craters and collapsed dugouts. One German witness was horrified by what looked like 'nineteen gigantic roses with carmine petals, or . . . enormous mushrooms, which rose up slowly and majestically out of the ground and then split into pieces with a mighty roar, sending up multi-coloured columns of flame mixed with a mass of earth and splinters high into the sky'.[24] As the debris began to rain down, the infantry launched their attack.

'The sky was lit up by continuous flashes from the massed artillery barrage all along the length of the ridge', recalled one British soldier.[25] As was becoming standard practice in the BEF, the advance was split into a series of short bounds all covered by a precisely engineered creeping barrage that flared out in front of the assaulting waves. Behind it came long lines of British and Dominion soldiers, spread out in artillery formation, bayonets fixed. In places the clanking sound of heavy armour could also be heard as seventy-two Mark IVs, the latest version of the British tank, moved forward. With better armour and improved transmission, the Mark IVs were more resilient on the battlefield, rolling over no-man's-land like ships in a heavy swell. As an oily-grey dawn broke, the air thick with dust, small groups of stumbling Germans came in from their lines, wild-eyed with horror. Seven thousand prisoners were taken that day; and the ridge – long seen as impregnable – was in British hands.

Messages of congratulation were soon flooding into GHQ. 'Tell General Plumer and the Second Army how proud we are of this achievement by which, in a few hours, the enemy was driven out of strongly entrenched position held by him for two-and-a-half years' was how His Majesty King George V described it in a letter to Haig on 9 June. Haig responded warmly, issuing an Order of the Day that hailed Plumer's victory: 'Following on the great successes already gained it affords final and conclusive proof that neither strength of position nor knowledge of and timely preparation to meet impending assault can save the enemy from complete defeat, and that, brave and tenacious as the German troops are, it is only a question of how much longer they can endure the repetition of such blows.'[26] Even the French – normally critical observers of the British – were impressed. A liaison officer attached to GHQ reported on the 'great success' of the attack in which the first objective had been carried within just two hours. 'The British troops have lost few men; their morale is very high and it is important that we show how our troops have been very much motivated by the affection that all, from the generals to soldiers, have for General Sir Herbert Plumer, and how much they admire his character.'[27]

A tubby, overweight figure with white hair and a thick moustache,

Plumer had taken charge of Second Army after Smith-Dorrien had been sent home in May 1915 and prided himself on doing everything possible to safeguard the lives of his men. 'Nothing whatever was left to chance', remembered his Chief of Staff, Charles Harington. 'He kept his finger on every pulse and the whole army knew it.'[28] The attack plans were put together with supreme care. In the weeks before the attack, a large-scale model of the ridge was constructed behind the lines ('about the size of two croquet lawns') and officers from every battalion were ushered in to help familiarize themselves with the ground. Second Army also benefited from the growing power of British artillery, which Plumer wielded with great skill. The attack was supported by over 2,000 guns, which hurled 3.5 million shells at the German line, blasting away the belts of barbed wire and collapsing dugouts and trenches with terrific effect. Moreover, a full third of all British guns were allotted to counter-battery fire, which prevented German artillery from being able to interfere with the attacking waves when they went over the top.[29]

Messines was certainly impressive, but, away from the front, the situation facing Britain and her empire was less certain. The economy was now suffering from labour shortages and rising inflation, while a decline in imports was the inevitable result of a steady loss of merchant shipping. The Government responded to the U-boat campaign with a series of new measures: reducing non-essential imports; ordering a comprehensive programme of shipbuilding; and adopting a convoy system that would ensure merchant ships could be brought across the Atlantic more safely. Although the Admiralty dragged its feet and continued to express concerns that convoying might not work, the tonnage lost to the U-boats began to decline steadily throughout the second half of the year – from a peak in April down to 268,813 tons in October, by which time convoying had been more widely adopted.[30]

On 8 June the Prime Minister formed the War Policy Committee, a body composed of himself, Milner, Curzon and Jan Smuts (the former Boer commander who had come to London as part of the South African delegation), which was tasked with reporting to the War Cabinet on the 'naval, military and political situation'.[31] The CIGS,

Sir William Robertson (who was pointedly *not* on the new committee), could only watch from afar, languishing behind his desk,
frustrated that his advice was no longer sought. 'There is trouble in
the land just now', he wrote to Haig on 13 June. 'The War Cabinet,
under the influence of L.G., have started, quite amongst themselves
plus Smuts, to review the whole policy and strategy of the war and to
"get at facts." They are interviewing different people singly, and
sending out to Departments various specific questions to be answered.
All this instead of first settling on the policy and then telling me and
Jellicoe to carry it out, if we can.' With Haig due in London the following week, Robertson warned the Field Marshal to be careful in
how he set out his plans. 'Don't argue that you can finish the war this
year, or that the German is already beaten. Argue that your plan is
the best plan – as it is – that no other would even be *safe* let alone
decisive, and then leave them to reject your advice and mine. They
dare not do that.'[32]

Haig appeared before the War Policy Committee on Tuesday, 19
June – his fifty-sixth birthday. They 'asked me numerous questions',
he remembered, 'all tending to show that each of them was more pessimistic than the other'. Haig presented his 'Appreciation of the
Military Situation', which warned against any 'relaxation of pressure'
on the Western Front. 'Waning hope in Germany would be revived,
and time would be gained to replenish food, ammunition and other
requirements. In fact, many of the advantages already gained by us
would be lost and this would certainly be realised by, and would have
a depressing effect on our armies in the field, which have made such
great efforts to gain them.' Therefore he wanted to concentrate all
British resources in France for an attack that would bring 'great
results this summer – results which will make final victory more
assured and which may even bring it within reach this year'. He was,
therefore, hoping to clear the Belgian coast over the coming months,
winning a series of battles against the enemy, which 'might quite possibly lead to their collapse'.[33]

Haig was playing for high stakes, making a great pitch for his offensive that flew in the face of Robertson's caution. For Lloyd George,
who listened to Haig with obvious discomfort, another major

commitment on the Western Front was not what he wanted and he was not slow in challenging the thinking behind the new attack. Haig's memorandum was 'a very powerful statement' and his plans were certainly 'a splendid conception', but were they 'practicable'? The United States 'had not yet developed their resources' and might only have 150,000 or 160,000 men in France by the end of the year, which meant that the United Kingdom was still 'sustaining the whole burden of the war'. Therefore, the committee had a duty 'not to break the country' with an offensive that would put an enormous strain on their manpower reserves. 'We were now reduced to the point where we had to scrape up men where we could', he added. 'He wanted the country to be able to last.'[34]

A further meeting was held on 21 June, but the distance between Lloyd George and his generals remained unbridgeable. The Prime Minister pointed out that they had to advance fifteen miles before they would really begin to clear the Belgian coast; that for an advance on such a scale they needed an 'overwhelming force of men and guns' and a diversionary attack which would draw off enemy reserves; and that 'the enemy's *moral* should be so broken that he could no longer put up a fight'. Yet he did not believe that any of these conditions were close to being fulfilled. The numerical superiority of the Allies was barely 15 per cent, and this included 25,000 Portuguese, 18,000 Russians (brigaded with the French) and 131,000 Belgians, 'who were not first-class troops'. Moreover, he reminded the committee that 'he had never known an offensive to be undertaken without sure predictions of success'. He had always been told that by applying the lessons of the past, each new attack would succeed – an experience that 'had not unnaturally made him feel sceptical'. Why should they 'anticipate a greater measure of success on this occasion than in the Battle of the Somme where we had only succeeded in making a dent of five or six miles?'[35]

The showdown in London seemed not to have settled anything. Haig was permitted to continue preparations for his attack, with the final decision still remaining with the War Cabinet, which waited on events. There was no doubt that clearing the Belgian coast was a worthy prize, fitting neatly into British strategic thinking and now given greater urgency by the presence of U-boats and destroyers operating out of Zeebrugge and Ostend. If these bases could be seized, or even just shelled by heavy artillery, then it would push German ships further away and make it more difficult for them to interfere with British cross-Channel traffic. During the meetings in London, Admiral Jellicoe, the First Sea Lord, had struck a depressed note, warning that it might not be possible to continue the war into 1918 'for lack of shipping'. Moreover, if peace were to come before the Germans had been pushed out of the Belgian ports, they would never surrender them. When Lloyd George heard what Jellicoe was saying, he immediately shot back that if this was true, 'then we should have far more important decisions to consider than our plans of operations for this year, namely, the best method of making tracks for peace'.[36] But Lloyd George was not ready for peace – at least, not yet.

The early summer of 1917 was ripe with possibilities for Germany, and she seemed closer to victory than at any point since September 1914. In Russia, a Provisional Government had been formed in March, comprising moderate deputies with support from workers' councils across Petrograd, which was authorized to rule until a constituent assembly could be elected later in the year. Although the Entente hoped that this would produce a renewed determination on behalf of the Russian people to continue the struggle, Russia was crippled by mounting strikes and disaffection, growing violence in the countryside, and loud demands for land reform and peace. The War Minister, Alexander Kerensky, managed to launch another offensive in July, striking against Austrian positions in Galicia, but it rapidly ran out of steam, and within days German counter-attacks had restored the situation and caused another galling retreat, which provoked further unrest in the capital.

On the Western Front, reports from the French Army indicated that Germany's most formidable opponent was teetering on the brink of collapse. On 8 June, the day after the attack on Messines Ridge, Major Witte, an intelligence officer with the Crown Prince's army group, reported on the mood of the French Army, which he believed was 'unrecognizable' since the failure of the attacks on the Aisne:

No doubt the statements by prisoners, which are taking place under the effects of enormous emotional shock and also with a view to appeasing their captors, should be accepted with caution, but the interrogations of the last week showed uniformly consistent details about certain instances of loss of discipline, mutiny etc., such that the moral fighting power of the French Army can, without exaggeration, be viewed as severely shaken. It consistently shows: 1. War weariness and a reluctance to fight. 2. A lack of trust in higher leadership and even more in political leadership. 3. The conviction that a decisive victory against the Germans will never be achieved. 4. Hatred and anger towards England.[37]

The possibility that France, like Russia, would fall to revolution was eagerly discussed at OHL, with every scrap of intelligence being pored over for evidence that the end was near. Ludendorff's mood had been radiant since word had been received about the abdication of the Tsar, and even the news about America's entry into the war did little to dampen his belief that the situation had now fundamentally changed in Germany's favour. Ludendorff was confident that the arrival of a US Army on the Western Front, large and fully equipped, was simply not possible before 1918. He estimated that the transfer of half a million men would require 3–4 million tons of shipping space, with yet more needed to keep them supplied. 'America's involvement in the war changes little', he thought. With a gradual decrease in the shipping tonnage available to the Allies, Ludendorff predicted a slow but inevitable strangulation. 'The entire wartime economy of our enemies will drop to such an extent that a decision against us can no longer be forced. In addition to this, there is an increased risk for England that, with such a reduced tonnage, her peacetime economy could not function. This means the collapse of naval prestige, which relies upon a strong merchant navy.' Therefore the 'prerequisite for victory is merely that we remain united and keep our nerve'.[38]

Hindenburg agreed. 'In a military sense our position is secure and will remain so', he wrote to the Chancellor on 19 June.[39] The main danger came from the threat of revolution at home, or at least a growth of feeling against the war, which became increasingly apparent during the summer. In a letter to the Kaiser, Hindenburg warned that the popular mood had to be lifted, 'otherwise we will lose the war'.[40] In Berlin, where shortages of food and basic supplies were now impossible to hide, the German Parliament was becoming increasingly restive. Matthias Erzberger, a prominent member of the Catholic Centre Party, was the first to break ranks, speaking on 6 July about the urgent need for 'far-reaching reforms' in Germany and a peace 'without annexations or indemnities'. The effectiveness of the submarine war, he suggested, had been over-exaggerated and there was no doubt that the sounds of 'something creaking, cracking, collapsing' could now be heard in Germany. Erzberger's speech was electrifying, bringing together a majority in the Reichstag (when the Catholic Centre Party voted with the Social Democrats) to pass a 'Peace Resolution' on 19 July calling for 'mutual understanding and lasting reconciliation among the nations' without 'forced acquisitions of territory' and based upon 'international political organizations'.[41]

The resolution may not have been binding, but it served to annoy the High Command and brought to a head the crisis between Bethmann Hollweg and the Supreme Command that had been brewing for months. Hindenburg offered 'the most serious objections' to the declaration, while Ludendorff even threatened to resign. 'In the most serious crisis which Germany and Prussia have ever known', he wrote to the Kaiser, 'Your Majesty has decided to retain in office the present political head, the Chancellor.'[42] Although the Kaiser summoned both men to Berlin and told them 'fairly harshly' not to 'meddle in politics', Bethmann Hollweg had run out of time. Both wings of the Parliament were now united in their antipathy to him. For those on the left, the Chancellor had failed to achieve the political changes that were deemed necessary to win the war – particularly the thorny issue of voting reform – and the right had long seen him as an obstacle to a more ruthless prosecution of military operations. With the duo showing no appetite to back down, Bethmann Hollweg fell on his sword, drafting his resignation letter several days before the 'Peace Resolution' was delivered. The Kaiser, nervously shuffling around the Bellevue Palace in Berlin, accepted it with little fanfare and appointed Georg Michaelis, a former Prussian Food Controller, as Bethmann-Hollweg's replacement. OHL was delighted.[43]

No sooner had Bethmann gone than a new crisis emerged on the Western Front, where storm clouds were gathering. German commanders had been largely unimpressed with British battlefield performance in 1915 and 1916, but the failure to hold Messines, on top of the loss of Vimy Ridge earlier in the year, was worrying. Rupprecht had watched the British build-up of troops and guns in the north and did his best to disrupt them, but the furious display of firepower on 7 June was a terrible reminder of all that Germany was now up against. In the first ten days of June, Fourth Army in Flanders lost 10,374 men killed in action with another 12,624 wounded.[44] Moreover, the reliance upon counter-attacks to throw back the British had, once again, proved difficult to execute. General von Laffert, commanding a corps-sized group of divisions that held Messines Ridge, had assumed his front-line divisions would be able to hold on for at least twelve hours, which would give his reserve units plenty of time to move into position.[45] But with most of the ridge in British hands by as early as 9 a.m., the counter-attack divisions (known as *Eingreif* divisions) were still miles away. A scattered series of counter-attacks were eventually launched in the early afternoon, but they were broken apart by a standing barrage falling in front of the newly won British positions; and those few survivors who managed to pass through it were soon repulsed by bursts of machine-gun fire.

Even the air war, which Germany had dominated since the autumn of 1916, was now shifting over to the Entente. Germany had enjoyed a period of unparalleled success throughout the early months of the year and April 1917 had been the bloodiest month of the war for the Royal Flying Corps, with 275 aircraft shot down and over 421 pilots or observers killed, wounded or missing.[46] Much of this was down to the dominance of the Albatros, both the D.II and an improved variant, the D.III, which entered service in December 1916. Fast, manoeuvrable and lethal in the right hands, the D.III would become the mainstay of the German Air Force for the remainder of the war. German pilots were also better trained and prepared for combat than their counterparts across the line. With British flyers frequently getting to front-line squadrons with only a handful of hours' training, they were easy prey for a band of veteran German pilots who racked up impressive scores over the winter and spring, with Manfred von Richthofen, now commanding Jagdstaffel 2, reaching an astonishing tally of forty-three confirmed kills by 13 April.[47]

It was only later in the year that the Allies began to recover with the arrival of a new generation of aircraft: the SE.5 and Sopwith Camel in the RFC and the SPAD XIII in the French Air Service. Despite suffering from a range of teething problems, the SE.5 proved a highly dependable and capable aircraft once it was fitted with a powerful 200-horsepower engine: easy to fly, stable and a powerful gun platform. More manoeuvrable was the Camel, probably the best British fighter of the war, 'a wonderful machine in a scrap', as one pilot put it.[48] Both aircraft were in service by the summer of 1917 and helped to swing the aerial balance back in the Allies' favour. They were joined by the SPAD XIII, a tough single-seater with two forward-firing machine-guns, which quickly became a favourite of both French (and later American) pilots. First introduced in May, the SPAD underwent a series of production problems and delays, but would eventually become one of the most formidable fighters of the war.

The significant improvement in Allied fighter strength forced Germany to deploy her own machines in larger and larger groups. On 23 June, four *Jagdstaffeln* were combined into Jagdgeschwader I, based at Courtrai, under Richthofen's command, which was soon dubbed the 'Flying Circus' after its pilots began painting their aircraft a series of vibrant colour schemes. Although Germany was still able to achieve local air superiority by massing her aircraft, she struggled to match the amount of machines that the Allies could produce. In a letter to the Prussian War Minister, Hermann von Stein, on 25 June, Ludendorff demanded 'a considerable strengthening of the air force by 1 March 1918'. He wanted to form up to forty new *Jagdstaffeln* and demanded monthly production of 2,000 aircraft and 1,500 machine-guns – an ambitious set of targets that would be known as the 'Amerika Programme'. But it was not just numbers of aircraft that mattered. Germany was struggling to produce machines that were as technically proficient as her enemies' ones, and the latest version of the Albatros, the D.V, entered service in May 1917 to widespread disappointment, being only a lightened version of the D.III with little improvement in performance. As Richthofen wrote shortly after being shot down on 6 July (when he was wounded in the head), 'The English single-seater [presumably the Sopwith Camel] is faster and climbs better than our planes . . . Beside better quality aircraft they have quantity . . . No one wants to be a fighter pilot anymore.'[49]

Germany would have to be patient. It would be months before the 'Amerika Programme' could get under way, which meant that the defensive operations in Flanders took on an even greater importance. Fritz von Lossberg was ordered to Courtrai a week after the attack at Messines, driving in a staff car from Tournai to Fourth Army headquarters. After meeting the commanding officer, Friedrich Sixt von Armin, Lossberg was briefed on the situation. Another attack was expected imminently, with German officers worrying that a further push from Messines along the high ground towards the area known as Tower Hamlets (a mile west of Gheluvelt) would unlock the defences and make holding on to the Ypres Salient all but impossible. Lossberg reported to OHL on the numbers of divisions, both trench holding and counter-attack, that he would need, while also making arrangements for the defence. Despite the scale of the British preparations, the mood at Rupprecht's army group was one of growing confidence as the long-awaited attack drew nearer. 'I await the attack with all the more confidence,' Rupprecht wrote in late July, 'as we have never had such strong and well-prepared reserves . . .'[50]

17. 'Terrible butchery'

It took another month before Haig was given the green light for his offensive. On 18 July, Robertson confirmed that no official approval had yet been given, the main fear being that 'you might endeavour to push on further than you were justified'. The CIGS went on to explain that the War Cabinet wanted a much more cautious type of attack than Haig was proposing: a 'step by step system of advance' limited to what could be covered by artillery. As might have been predicted, Haig did not take kindly to what he deemed to be unnecessary interference in his affairs. 'It is somewhat startling at this advanced stage of preparations to learn that the War Cabinet had not then yet determined whether my attack was to be permitted to proceed', he replied. 'The Members of the Cabinet evidently do not understand what is entailed by preparation for an attack under existing conditions, or what the effect – material and moral – would be of altering plans once preparations are in full swing.' The importance of operating along the Belgian coast had been communicated to him months earlier and, as for the kind of operation that he was planning, 'such matters should be left to the Commander on the spot'.[1]

Robertson found himself in the awkward space between a Prime Minister and a GHQ that saw things very differently. 'The fact is that the Prime Minister is still very averse from your offensive and talks as though he is hoping to switch off to Italy within a day or two after you begin', he told Haig on 21 July. Robertson explained how he had told Lloyd George that 'unless there were very great miscalculations on your part . . . I did not think it would be possible to pronounce a verdict on the success of your operations for several weeks'.[2] It was only on 25 July, just days before the attack was scheduled to begin, that Haig got his way. Robertson and Lloyd George were attending a meeting on Allied strategy in Paris, and when the CIGS pressed for the approval (or not) of Haig's plans, he was allowed to give it, Lloyd George finally relenting when presented with Haig's *fait accompli*. Just before the French Army had launched its great attack on the Aisne, Robertson had warned the British Commander-in-Chief that 'Nivelle is going into action with a rope round his neck'. Now Haig was doing the same.[3]

Regiments from every corner of the British Isles were now concentrating in Flanders, hitching a ride on the winding narrow-gauge railway lines that brought them to the front. Billets, tented encampments and casualty clearing stations began springing up everywhere, producing a rising sense of anticipation. There would be an unprecedented amount of artillery to support the attack: 3,000 guns (including almost 1,000 medium or heavy pieces) and over four million shells. At night, hundreds of howitzers were brought up in long, trundling columns and spread out across the countryside, wherever space could be found. The flat ground was devoid of much cover, which left many batteries in the open, covered over with netting or behind camouflage screens to try to hide their muzzle flashes. And in the air the Entente had massed over 800 aircraft (including 200 French fighters), which were ordered to mount aggressive patrols over the enemy lines, while selected bombing squadrons were tasked with attacking known aerodromes and supply depots, billets and headquarters.[4]

The attack had been entrusted to General Sir Hubert Gough's Fifth Army. Imperious, a long broad nose his most recognizable feature, Gough took several weeks to sketch out a plan in line with Haig's directions to capture the Passchendaele–Staden Ridge and the railway junction at Roulers, which would then facilitate future operations to 'gain possession of the Belgian coast'. Despite Plumer's success at Messines, Haig did not trust him with the main component of his 'northern operation' – considering him too cautious – so he went for Gough, who could be relied upon to execute the attack with the offensive spirit that was demanded. Deploying four corps along an eight-mile section of the front, Gough hoped to gain about two miles on the first day, while also making a final advance up to the village of Broodseinde if everything went well – a march of almost three miles.[5] His left flank would be covered by General Paul Anthoine's French First Army, a force of six divisions, lavishly supplied with artillery, which Pétain had agreed to send north (even if the French Commander-in-Chief had long been sceptical about Haig's 'northern operation').

Bad weather delayed the attack until the morning of 31 July, a damp night with low cloud and thick mist. The battlefield was already wet. No-man's-land was a morass of shell craters, touching end to end; the inevitable result of a two-week preliminary bombardment. 'The whole horizon to the north east, east and south east, was lit up by one continuous dancing flame composed of jagged flashes of busting shells' was how one British officer described the awe-inspiring spectacle of massed artillery fire at Zero Hour.[6] When the infantry went over the top, scrambling up behind the creeping barrage, they found that most of the German garrison had been evacuated from their forward positions (in line with the doctrine of defence-in-depth). Because of this, they made good progress, crossing the Yser Canal and passing through the village of Pilckem, dealing with any pockets of resistance with the help of three brigades of tanks, which crept forward over the soft ground. French troops also secured their objectives on time, helped by a heavy bombardment that cleared the way. 'Never had we seen such artillery work', reported one French NCO, impressed at the sight of the German trenches torn to pieces by the shelling.[7]

It was on the southern rim of the battlefield, where the ground sloped up towards the Gheluvelt Plateau, that the Germans held firm. Here the defenders were deployed in fortified positions, concrete dugouts and blockhouses, many of which had survived the bombardment and greeted the attackers with heavy fire. The advance 'was slow from the outset owing to the very heavy ground which had to be traversed', noted one observer. 'The enemy's machine-guns appear to have fired through our creeping barrage and this, combined with the difficulty of getting over the bad ground', caused the attack to break down.[8] By the time the leading waves had taken the first line, they were behind schedule, missing the creeping barrage that was supposed to escort them on to their second objective. As had been predicted at Tank Corps headquarters, this sector of the front, containing numerous copses and small woods, was unsuitable for armoured vehicles, only for Fifth Army to insist that they be deployed anyway. 'To start with we had putrid weather and worse ground', recalled one crewman. 'We went slowly on and eventually reached a ridge on which our front line was and here struck an awful barrage and came under machine gun fire . . . Two minutes after, the bus sank half its weight into the ground and stopped.'[9]

Even in the northern and central sectors of the front, where progress had been good, the advance slowed by midday as more and more German troops were fed into the battle. The defensive plan, as written by Lossberg, was to let the British come forward, gradually exhaust them as they fought their way through the lethal, fire-swept maze of machine-gun positions, and then counter-attack. Six *Eingreif* divisions were ordered forward at midday, and although they were much closer to the battlefield than on previous occasions, they had to make their way across a landscape devoid of features and now under almost continuous artillery fire. Battalions became confused and lost; maps disintegrated in the rain; and columns were scattered when predatory aircraft zoomed low over the battlefield strafing anything they could see. 'There were endless halts to keep everyone together', remembered one German captain. The divisions worked their way forward 'through a great swampy expanse of ground that had been drenched with gas. There was not a sign of the enemy, just this endless torrent of fire of all calibres hammering down from the right.' Soon, sharp cracks of rifle fire could be heard snapping overhead as they went into battle.[10]

The *Eingreif* divisions struggled forward, sometimes finding themselves in the wrong location, but they did enough to blunt Gough's main advance and, in places, push it back. It started raining about four o'clock that afternoon and, as daylight faded, the fighting gradually tailed off, leaving the British in possession of their first and second objectives, having made an advance of about 3,000 yards, but still short of the major breakthrough that had been anticipated. Casualties had been correspondingly heavy. Fifth Army's dead, wounded and missing totalled somewhere around 27,000, including almost 4,000 killed in action. Tank losses were equally costly. Of the 117 fighting tanks, principally Mark IVs, that had gone into action on 31 July, about half had broken down, ditched or been knocked out.[11] While much of this could be blamed on the nature of the ground, which had been softened by heavy rain, Ypres was the first time that the British had encountered a specially prepared and interlocking anti-tank defence consisting of direct fire from artillery, machine-guns and rifles (the defenders having been issued with armour-piercing 'K' ammunition), and support from aircraft dropping flares to signal the location of tanks, which would then be shelled by batteries in the rear.

Gough remained upbeat, insisting that the day had been 'decidedly successful', although he did admit that the arrival of heavy rain was 'particularly galling'.[12] Even Haig, who normally took an optimistic slant on things, grew worried as the storm continued. 'A terrible day of rain', he recorded in his diary on 1 August. 'The ground is like a bog in this low-lying country! The light railways and roads are steadily being pushed forward. Still, in view of this terrible wet, I judge that we are fortunate not to have advanced to the extreme "Red line," [Gough's final objective] because it would not have been possible to supply our guns with ammunition. Our troops would thus have been at the mercy of a hostile counter-attack!' He visited Fifth Army's headquarters and spoke to Major-General Herbert Uniacke, head of artillery, who told him that he needed 'two days of good observation' before they could restart operations.[13] But it rained steadily for a week, with torrents of water falling from the sky, filling the shell craters to the brim and depressing the mood of the British Army, which toiled amid the mud. Already the battlefield had taken on the appearance of a sodden moonscape: flat lands blasted clear of farm buildings or hedgerows; the occasional blackened stalk where a tree had once flowered; and endless lines of British 'Tommies', faces blank beneath the rims of their helmets, their khaki uniforms splattered with mud, making their way up and down the line. While this was not an unusual sight in such a war – both Verdun and the Somme were deeply dispiriting places – the scenes from Ypres seemed uniquely depressing.

At Bad Kreuznach, the opening of Britain's long-awaited attack in Flanders marked 'a period of tremendous anxiety' for the German Supreme Command as it struggled to balance the demands of both Eastern and Western Fronts. The Kerensky Offensive had been blunted by the first week of July, and every subsequent day revealed, a little more clearly, just how far the rot had set in to the Russian Army. Never satisfied, Ludendorff was hoping to mount an offensive at Riga ('to keep on hammering at Russia in order to bring about the fall of the Colossus'), but it would be some time before sufficient divisions could be redeployed from Galicia.[14] In the meantime, he needed the lines in France and Belgium to hold, and he was not minded to sanction any significant reinforcement unless it was imperative. This would allow Germany to finish off Russia and then, perhaps in the spring of 1918, mount a final, decisive effort on the Western Front.

More than anything else, Ludendorff worried about the domestic situation. On 31 July, he issued an instruction to his higher commanders, warning them of how the mood of the people had 'fallen deeply': 'In the interior, in addition to crass egotism and hedonism, scaremongering, pessimism and neglected duty are becoming widespread, which can put the outcome of the war at risk.' Ludendorff admitted that 'such phenomena' were partially driven by 'genuine states of emergency', including 'monetary worries', the length of the war and heavy losses, but he also blamed the 'deliberate agitation of certain elements' bent on exploiting the difficulties to instigate discontent, strikes and so on. Such a worrying decline in morale could not be ignored and he urged his commanders to 'raise and strengthen the spirits' of their men. 'In the army, it is necessary to strongly preserve the fighting spirit and, with it, confidence in victory, which is absolutely justifiable in our situation'. They also must instil 'love of the Kaiser and the sovereign and a strong German sense of fatherland', which would ensure that the 'agitators, scaremongers and weaklings at home' would be confronted and defeated.[15]

OHL may have cheered the resignation of Bethmann Hollweg, but finding a Chancellor who would command the support of a Parliament that, as Hindenburg put it, 'inclined more and more to the Left' proved difficult.[16] Despite being hailed as Germany's version of David Lloyd George, Georg Michaelis possessed none of the British Prime Minister's drive and ambition. He was 'a little, insecure scared rabbit', in the words of Hans von Beseler, Governor of Warsaw, who briefed him soon after his appointment. Michaelis admitted to knowing little about how the war was run (after occupying an administrative post in the War Food Office), and within days of his appointment had declared that he would act in 'constant agreement' with OHL, which was received with predictable dismay in the Reichstag. After the 'Peace Resolution' had been passed, Michaelis distanced himself from it, announcing that 'If we make peace we must in the first line make sure that the frontiers of the German Empire are made secure for all time'. If some kind of agreement were to be made, then there must be guarantees that 'the league in arms of our opponents does not develop into an economic offensive alliance against us'.[17]

But peace remained elusive. On 1 August, Pope Benedict XV called for 'a just and lasting' settlement based upon mutual disarmament, 'the true freedom and community of the seas', and 'entire and reciprocal condonations'. This would be combined with the evacuation of Belgium and all occupied French territory as well as the return of Germany's colonies, which had been seized soon after war broke out.[18] That day Michaelis paid a visit to Vienna, where the Austro-Hungarian Foreign Minister, Count Ottokar Czernin, pressed him on the urgent need for an end to the war before the winter, and stated that if Germany would signal some kind of compromise over Alsace–Lorraine, Austria would forgo her claims on Poland. But Hindenburg and Ludendorff showed little appetite for a wholesale revision of German war aims, and when Michaelis visited Kreuznach on 9 August, he found the duo insistent that Belgium had to 'remain in German hands' and that the Longwy–Briey iron region was 'indispensable' (although they did accept that some French-speaking areas of Upper Alsace could be returned to France). In the east, Courland and Lithuania had to be brought into a close economic relationship with Germany, and Poland must be under 'German military, political and economic supremacy'.[19]

Michaelis had little room for manoeuvre. The Entente was unconvinced that much would come of the papal peace note, with Painlevé only issuing a statement in mid-September, in which he reasserted France's 'unshakeable determination' to continue the war until she achieved a 'just peace'. The British requested a formal statement on German war aims, including Germany's position on Belgium, before committing themselves any further. But this was not forthcoming, and Michaelis rejected any kind of 'public statement' that could only 'have a confusing effect and injure German interests'.[20] While the Pope's efforts to broker a compromise peace fizzled out, Richard von Kühlmann, the new Foreign Secretary, was authorized to try to split the Entente by asking whether Britain would enter into talks about the possible restoration of Belgium, while returning Germany's colonies and giving her a free hand in Russia. Although Lloyd George was sorely tempted by the chance of making peace with Germany, even if it meant abandoning Russia to her fate, the War Cabinet were concerned lest this leave Germany in a stronger position in which to wage a future war. When the other ambassadors were informed of Kühlmann's approach, they made it clear that no compromise peace could possibly be considered until they had achieved their main war aims.[21]

With no end to the war in sight, the remaining Allied powers continued to fight on – each in its own way convinced that attacking was the only route out of its difficulties. On 18 August, the Italian Army launched the Eleventh Battle of the Isonzo – employing a staggering 3,750 guns to shell the Austrian positions along the entire Isonzo front. The Italians threw everything into the offensive, breaking the line in the first few days and seizing the key objective of the Bainsizza Plateau, only to see subsequent attacks falter after outrunning their artillery.[22] Verdun also witnessed heavy fighting as Pétain mounted the second of his limited offensives (the first being in Flanders). Second Army, now commanded by General Adolphe Guillaumat, would push northwards between one and two kilometres, seizing the old bloodied heights of Hill 304 and Mort Homme on the west bank while moving towards Beaumont on the eastern side. This would improve its own positions as well as offering an opportunity to test the morale of the Army – to see what kind of result it could produce after months of turmoil and dissatisfaction.

Artillery preparation began on 11 August, and over the next nine days heavy shelling shook the bare hills, interspersed with regular bombardments of poison gas. The commander of the German Fifth Army, General Gallwitz, mounted a number of spoiling attacks and raids to try to dislocate French preparations, but could only watch helplessly as his forward positions were systematically torn apart. 'At midnight on 18/19 August, the firing became quite frenzied', he reported. 'There was the incessant rattling of windows and flashes of fire in the sky.' He spoke to his Chief of Staff and authorized the deployment of his *Eingreif* divisions closer to the front, while the artillery storm 'carried on incessantly'.[23] The attack began before dawn on 20 August. Four French corps went into battle, supported by 3,000 guns, which had fired over three million shells in the days before the attack. With only six divisions in the line (against eight French ones) and half as many guns as the French, Gallwitz's men were outnumbered and outgunned.[24] About two thirds of the German artillery had already been either destroyed outright or neutralized by gas, and most of the machine-guns that dotted the front were quickly put out of action by a thunderous creeping barrage which flayed the ground in front of the attacking infantry, rolling forward at a set pace of one hundred yards every three minutes. The French objective, Mort Homme, looked like 'a gigantic crater' or a 'dug out, abandoned quarry'. 'There are holes everywhere you look, heaps of wires, rags, abandoned weapons, large pieces of clay piled in different places . . .'[25]

Finding and keeping direction in such a landscape, like a moon pelted with numberless asteroids, could only be achieved by following the line of the 'intensifying, rumbling, striking, troubling, deafening' barrage.[26] Behind its shield, French infantry were able to take their objectives on time, seizing Mort Homme and encircling Hill 304 (which fell several days later). Fighting was fierce: 'terrible butchery' in Gallwitz's words. The defenders put up a staunch effort, throwing grenades and firing into the attacking waves until the last moment. Then bloody combat broke out along the trenches that ringed the slopes. Those who resisted were killed: bayonetted, strangled or shot at close range. Bodies soon clogged up the trenches, now just thin ditches strewn with the detritus of war. Counter-attacks were launched, but made little headway as French soldiers stood on their parapets and fired at the advancing enemy. Casualties had been remarkably light. With just over 4,000 dead, the attack seemed to vindicate the methods of Pétain, who was awarded the Grand Cross of the *Légion d'honneur* in the days afterwards.[27]

On 21 August, Gallwitz recommended a short retreat east of the Meuse between Brabant and Beaumont, only for OHL to veto it on the grounds that this would mean 'a lost battle'. Ludendorff was eventually persuaded (by an apoplectic Gallwitz) that a withdrawal was necessary, although he wired that any 'impression of voluntary retreat' should be avoided and that he 'attached great importance to giving up as little ground as possible'. The reasons for the failure were essentially the same as those encountered on 24 October 1916 when Douaumont had been lost, and it proved the difficulty of holding on to tactically unfavourable ground in the face of such artillery supremacy.[28] There was only so much that could be done; if Pétain wanted to attack with such force, then there was little to stop him.

In Flanders, it was a different matter; there the mood of German commanders was more positive and it was widely assumed that the battle was now over. 'The British target was clear', noted Hermann von Kuhl. 'It was their intention to take the high ground east and north of Ypres as a spring-board for a break-through into the Flanders plain. So far their efforts had been contained.'[29] Indeed, German defensive tactics seemed to have (finally) been vindicated. The *Eingreif* divisions had been able to intervene on the afternoon of the first day, engage the enemy at the right moment and push them back. Moreover, they still held on to the crucial high ground, and fierce fighting throughout August had not dislodged them from it. OHL had also been pleased with a new weapon, dichlorodiethyl sulphide, which had been introduced in July 1917. Known as 'yellow cross', it had been developed by the same German chemists who had introduced chlorine to the war and was soon christened 'mustard gas' after its distinctive, pungent smell, akin to garlic, mustard or horseradish. It was not especially toxic, but it caused painful blisters on the skin and irritated the lungs and eyes, producing symptoms similar to bronchitis or conjunctivitis. With a propensity to remain in the ground for weeks, mustard gas was a particularly effective defensive weapon, and within three weeks of its introduction the BEF had recorded 14,000 gas cases – more than in the whole of the previous year.[30]

Yet the Ypres offensive gradually sucked in more resources as it dragged on. General Gough continued to attack throughout August, launching a succession of relatively small-scale assaults as he desperately tried to secure the high ground around Gheluvelt. By 20 August, seventeen German divisions had been worn out at Ypres, with Kuhl complaining that the 'provision of new divisions could only be maintained by sending the exhausted divisions to quieter sectors of the Western Front, thus releasing units for Flanders'.[31] There was little chance of more significant reinforcement. Ludendorff visited Rupprecht's headquarters on 19 August to update the army group on his plans for an attack at Riga on the Eastern Front (which was scheduled to begin on 1 September). He warned his commanders that French attacks at Verdun showed that they were 'not as exhausted as we had once thought' and it was, therefore, necessary to 'manage with our own resources in Flanders' for as long as possible.[32]

Lloyd George had only consented to the 'northern operation' with grave misgivings, and it took all Robertson's powers to keep the War Cabinet from bringing it to a premature end. Haig completed a despatch on the battle on 21 August in which he blamed bad weather for the 'unavoidable delay' in operations, while also crediting the German Army with impressive powers of resistance. 'The strongest opposition of all was experienced on the main ridge', he wrote. 'Appreciating the tactical value of this ground, the enemy has concentrated his efforts on retaining it, and every foot of our advance there is bitterly contested and will doubtless continue to be so until the enemy's power of resistance is beaten down.' Nevertheless, the results of the offensive were 'very considerable'. The defenders had sustained about 100,000 casualties and the 'fighting value of these boys' was low. 'Conclusive evidence is now available that all, or practically all, his 1918 class are in the ranks and have already suffered severe casualties.' The 'right course to pursue', therefore, was 'to continue to press the enemy in Flanders without interruption and to the full extent of our power'.[33]

Lloyd George should have snapped the book shut on Haig's campaign in Flanders. He had been promised a breakthrough, but all he had was increasingly bloody and indecisive combat under an unrelenting downpour of rain. But the British Prime Minister let the battle go on, distracted by other pressing matters and 'obviously puzzled', as Hankey put it, as to 'how far the Government is justified in interfering with a military operation'.[34] News of the fighting on the Italian Front also dazzled the Prime Minister as he urged Robertson to reinforce the (initial) success of Italian arms on the Isonzo. 'It would indeed be a severe reflection upon us all', he wrote on 26 August, 'if later on it were discovered that we missed a great chance of achieving a signal and far-reaching military success for the allied cause, through lack of readiness to take advantage of an opening made for us by the Italian Army.' But Robertson was unimpressed and (during a meeting in Downing Street several days later) reiterated the previously agreed concentration on the Western Front. If the War Cabinet believed that more support should be given to the Italians, then it would 'entail breaking off the great battle now in progress in Flanders'. This would have a 'very grave' effect on the morale of the Army and, moreover, he doubted whether sufficient guns could be redeployed to the Isonzo in time to make a difference. But Lloyd George shrank from an open split in Cabinet and, for the time being, a decision was shelved.[35]

In France, Haig sensed that things were moving against him. On 25 August, he drove out to Second Army's headquarters at Cassel and told General Plumer that he would now have responsibility for the main effort at Ypres. Gough's Fifth Army would guard his left flank, but he would be given the opportunity – should he want it – to restart the offensive and get them up and over Gheluvelt Ridge. Plumer, who had been snubbed earlier in the year when Haig had chosen Gough to lead the Flanders breakout, made it clear that he needed time to prepare and, moreover, that he wanted to do it his way. Already Second Army had identified that the 'new system of defence' adopted by the enemy, namely 'lines of shell holes in depth' and significant reserves 'disposed in readiness for counter-attack', meant that British tactics had to change. Plumer understood that the 'farther we penetrate his line the stronger and more organized we find him' and 'the weaker and more disorganized we are liable to become'.[36] Therefore he wanted to move on to his objectives in a series of 'steps', each limited to about 1,500 yards and taking place every six days.

Plumer took his time. He had asked for three weeks to prepare his attack and he employed the methods that were now becoming routine in the BEF. Divisions underwent extensive training in offensive tactics, pillbox clearing, and fire and movement; a large-scale model of the ground was constructed and battalions were bussed in to see it; extensive aerial reconnaissance took place; and a thorough counter-battery effort was mounted to prevent German guns from interfering with the attack. Plumer had requested (and received) almost double the number of medium and heavy guns that Gough had employed on 31 July: 1,295 pieces in total, comprising 575 heavy and medium and 720 field guns and howitzers – supported by 3.5 million shells.[37] Just as importantly, the weather now began to improve and warm sunshine replaced the rainfall of August, allowing the battlefield to dry up and the ground to harden. A preliminary bombardment began on 13 September, and over the next week British guns systematically targeted the pillboxes and machine-gun nests that lay in wait, while sparing no effort to destroy the German batteries that had proved so deadly in earlier attacks.

When Plumer's mass of artillery opened fire at 5.40 a.m. on 20 September, it marked a new stage in the struggle for Flanders. Known as the Battle of Menin Road, it was on a scale not seen since 31 July. Eleven divisions from six corps went over the top, supported by a barrage of awe-inspiring power: five separate lines of shellfire, about 1,000 yards in depth, creating 'a wall of dust and fumes, intermingled with shell bursts', according to an officer with I ANZAC Corps, which spearheaded the assault:

> For a while all was confusion in the gloom. You could just hear yourself shout. There was a continual roll in the rear – the drumfire of our artillery. You could see only a few yards. Troops pressed on in sections broken often by the burst of shells of the Hun counter barrage . . . In this way, keeping close to the barrage we advanced steadily to each objective, where each unit proceeded to dig in and consolidate the ground won, as well as to 'mop up' the Huns still to be found scattered in shell holes etc., in front of their position.[38]

Fighting around numerous pillboxes was both brutal and merciless, but the defenders were unable to stem the advance, and even the

The Offensive in Flanders, June–November 1917

Front line, June 1917
Front line, Nov. 1917
Line gained
during the Battle
of Messines,
7–14 June 1917

1	British Armies
1	French Armies
1	German Armies

Zonnebeke
Beelaere
Polygon Wood
Gheluvelt
Geluwe
Glencorse Wood
Zandvoorde
Frezenberg
Chateau Wood
Dumbarton Wood
Hooge
Sanctuary Wood
Shrewsbury Forest
Wieltje
Zillebeke
Hollebeke
Ypres
Voormezeele
Messines
Dickebusch
Wytschaete
Kemmel
Wulverghem
Wervicq
Bousbecque
Comines

5
6
2

0   1,000 2,000 3,000 4,000 5,000 yards
0   1,000   2,000   3,000   4,000 m

counter-attack divisions, of which so much had been expected, comprehensively failed to push the British back. When Lossberg authorized the deployment of the *Eingreif* divisions, they marched forward into a hail of machine-gun and mortar fire, while British aircraft, circling overhead, notified their artillery of the Germans' arrival and down came another storm of shells.[39]

Within days, another blow was landed. The Battle of Polygon Wood began on 26 September with Anzac troops again leading the advance, striking eastwards through the shattered remains of the wood and reaching the outskirts of Zonnebeke. 'The advance itself was the finest we had ever experienced', recalled one of the Australians in the first wave. 'The artillery barrage was so perfect and we followed it so close, that it was simply a matter of walking into the positions and commencing to dig in. The men were never in such spirits. Everything went just as planned. The enemy had no fight left in him!' Again the *Eingreif* divisions were moved forward, only to struggle to get through the wall of fire Plumer had put down:

> From a sunken road about a mile away Fritz was first seen debouching and advancing upon our position. Soon thousands were scattered over the open fields in no apparent order . . . like a flock of playful sheep in the distance. Then a sudden transformation took place. What was a minute before a line of men digging, throwing, building, now became one of ugly looking bayonets waving but gradually settling into a line pointed at the enemy and jumping with life . . . Then the roar of the guns increased into deafening noise as the barrage again descended. As we looked the ground beyond seemed to break into convulsions, and this and the enemy disappeared in the rising smoke. Another counter attack had been repulsed.[40]

It was in the days after Polygon Wood that the German High Command began to realize the depth of their predicament in Flanders. The British were now inching their way up the ridge, chewing through more and more German units as they did so. Between 11 and 30 September, 38,000 men had been killed or wounded or were missing at Ypres, increasing the pressure on Rupprecht and his staff.[41] Even Kuhl, who usually provided the optimism at army group headquarters,

admitted that there was little they could do against such properly executed limited attacks. 'Our "*counter-attack divisions*" kept in close
proximity to the front did not move quickly enough in the cratered
area through the heavy artillery fire, and often arrived too late. Their
thrust came against a defence already deeply echeloned with a curtain
barrage . . .' He also recognized that, whatever tactics were used, the
battle was taking a frightening toll on the morale of the army. 'The
suffering, privation and exertions which the soldiers had to bear was
inexpressible', he wrote. 'Terrible was the spiritual burden on the
lonely man in the shell hole, and terrible the strain on the nerves during the bombardments which continued day and night.'[42]

When Ludendorff returned to Courtrai on 29 September, there
was a growing atmosphere of anxiety. The Germans had long since
got used to the British Army's 'famous penetration tactics' (as one
officer called them),[43] which suited their defensive doctrine perfectly,
but Plumer's approach – closely resembling what Pétain had done at
Mort Homme – was almost impossible to parry. Lossberg proposed
that they revert to a more traditional style of defensive battle: placing
more men in the front trenches to try to resist the initial 'bite', while
saving their reserve divisions for more thoroughly prepared counter-
attacks at a later date (instead of rushing them up to the front
prematurely). This was agreed and Fourth Army issued orders on 30
September confirming that they had to 'fight decisively for even the
smallest piece of ground'. The trick was forcing the enemy to place
more men in their forward positions, which could be achieved by
mounting spoiling attacks at regular intervals.[44]

The idea of making each 'bite' harder to achieve was a logical
response to Menin Road and Polygon Wood, but it failed abysmally
during Plumer's third 'step' on 4 October: the Battle of Broodseinde.
Once again, Second Army's infantry sprang forward behind a furious
barrage, catching a German division in the process of mounting one
of Lossberg's spoiling attacks, and causing carnage. In the words of
Major Prager, a staff officer attached to Army Group Rupprecht,
Broodseinde was 'surely the heaviest slaughter there has been so far.
Suffocating drumfire of the heaviest calibres.'[45] British, Australian
and New Zealand divisions attacked that morning over fields

carpeted with German dead, clearing the whole of Polygon Wood, taking the villages of Poelcappelle, Gravenstafel and Broodseinde, and seizing the Zonnebeke and Gravenstafel spurs, the final ramparts of high ground before the Passchendaele Ridge, which crowned the Ypres Salient. For so long, British operations in Flanders seemed to have been cursed, fought in a swamp amid unrelenting rain. Yet autumnal sunshine had broken through in September and given Haig a second chance at achieving something. The Allies were still far away from their final objectives – and the railway junction at Roulers remained over seven miles away – but a renewed sense of optimism surged through GHQ on the evening of 4 October. It was 'a very important success', Haig wrote, 'and we had great good fortune in that the Enemy had concentrated such a large number of divisions just at the moment of our attack with the very intense artillery barrage'. Over 3,000 prisoners had been taken.[46]

Haig's mood was only tempered by the arrival of rain, which began to fall during the afternoon, and a letter from Robertson reporting that the British Government had 'approved in principle' the idea of taking over more line from the French – a decision that left him shaking his head in frustration. 'Robertson comes badly out of this, in my opinion – especially as it was definitely stated (with the War Cabinet's approval) that no discussion re: operations on the Western Front would be held with the French without my being present.'[47] Haig dashed off an urgent report on the military situation on 8 October that confirmed his opposition to 'any of the various indirect means' of attacking Germany and reiterated that he was making good progress at Ypres. 'The enemy is undoubtedly considerably shaken and the ground we have already gained gives us considerable advantages and renders us less dependent on weather in following up our successes . . . In these circumstances it is beyond question that our offensive must be pursued as long as possible.'[48]

The War Cabinet remained as split as ever. When Jan Smuts brought attention to the poor weather that had hampered operations in Flanders, Lloyd George was unimpressed. 'In considering the present offensive, they had been guided by the very confident Paper they had received from General Haig, and he (the Prime Minister) thought that no-one would have voted for that offensive if they had not been considerably influenced by his optimism.' It was, therefore, 'imperative . . . that action should be taken in some theatre of war during the coming winter' and that they 'should not look to an offensive on the Western Front before next May'. Switching his focus from Italy, Lloyd George now wanted to send divisions to Egypt for a renewed offensive in Palestine, which would begin the process of detaching Germany's allies from her one by one.[49] He had no intention of letting the British Army bleed itself white in futile offensives in Belgium, only to see the Americans win the war a year or two later. 'If our army were spent in a succession of shattering attacks in 1918, it would not be in a condition to renew the offensive in 1919', he told Hankey. 'It would, indeed, be in exactly the condition that the French Army was in at this moment, with its numbers reduced and its *moral* weakened.'[50]

All Robertson saw was an array of difficulties and he tried, in vain, to dissuade the War Cabinet from reinforcing Palestine, arguing that it would be 'unwise to weaken our efforts on the West front'.[51] When Lloyd George invited Henry Wilson and Sir John French to express their opinions at a meeting of the War Cabinet on 10 October – a clear breach of Robertson's role as the sole provider of strategic advice to the Cabinet – he tendered his resignation, but the Minister of War, Edward Stanley (Lord Derby), refused to accept it. So Robertson was left to carry on as before, and he could often be seen strolling between the War Office and Downing Street, his expression grim, his mouth tight-lipped. 'You are getting on splendidly, and your forecasts as to the cumulative effect of your efforts are proving well founded', he wrote to Haig. 'One would think that the fine successes you are winning would suffice to satisfy even the people with whom I live, but it is not so apparently or they would drop the Palestine rot . . . It is a hard war – not because of the Boche, but because of these people here.'[52]

18. 'Nothing but the war'

'Waiting for troops to come was weary work three thousand miles from home', remembered General Pershing's Chief of Staff, James Harbord, as he looked back on the late summer and autumn of 1917. 1st (Regular) Division had arrived in France in Pershing's wake in late June – where it was promptly attached to an elite French division to undergo extensive training – but it would not be until late September that it was joined by a second division, 26th (National Guard). It took months for America to organize the raising of her vast armies – projected to be over twenty large divisions by the summer of 1918 – leaving Pershing and his staff waiting anxiously for units to arrive and fending off the inevitable questions from the French about how quickly they would be able to take to the field. After initially being based at the Hotel Crillon in Paris, American headquarters was formally transferred to the small walled town of Chaumont, fifty miles east of Troyes, on 1 September. A ceremony was held in the Town Hall a day after they arrived, with the Mayor clasping the general's hand warmly and telling him that this was the moment they had prayed for. A marble tablet was then unveiled and a delegation of local women gave Pershing an American flag 'made by their own fair hands'.[1]

American headquarters occupied the Caserne Damrémont, a regimental barracks that had plenty of space and was close to American lines of communication. From there, in a draughty office ('heated only by the old-fashioned base-burner stove common in his native State of Missouri'), Pershing began to sketch out how and where his armies would fight. Soon after the United States had entered the war, it had been agreed that the expeditionary force would occupy part of the French sector in Lorraine, southeast of Verdun between Saint-Mihiel and the Vosges Mountains. The decision to place the American Expeditionary Force along the eastern border of France was a logical one. In the north, the Channel ports, and their associated railways, were heavily burdened with British traffic, while further south the cream of the French Army sat athwart the route to Paris. Pershing feared that if the AEF occupied a section of the front between the two, then it would 'restrict its sphere of activity' and make it more difficult 'to avoid amalgamation and service under a foreign flag' – difficult questions that had already been raised. Moreover, fighting in Lorraine would allow the AEF to utilize the Atlantic ports of Saint-Nazaire, Bassens and La Pallice and then draw supplies along the main double-track railways that ran from the coast to the interior. But Pershing was also attracted to Lorraine because of its strategic significance and the possibility of landing a decisive blow. On a large map of the Western Front that was pinned up on the wall of his office, Pershing worked out how to end the war. If the AEF could strike north into the Ardennes towards Metz, it would simultaneously threaten the Longwy–Briey iron region and the crucial lateral rail line between Strasbourg, Metz and Sedan that supplied Germany's armies in the west.[2]

Pershing may not yet have had an army to lead – he was what Harbord called a 'symbol without substance'[3] – but detailed planning for the expeditionary force was already under way. Because the standard size of a European division was about 15,000 men full strength (although admittedly most British and French divisions struggled to reach this tally by late 1917), it was initially assumed that America would follow suit. But after discussions with the War Department it was agreed that US divisions would go to war with a much bigger total, just over 28,000 men. Concerns about a shortage of officers (and how by having fewer, larger divisions this could be mitigated) were an important consideration, but Pershing also recognized that bigger divisions would suit the kind of war he expected to encounter in France. With the enormous casualties and wastage that offensive operations could produce, large US divisions would have the strength and power to keep going and fight on for a number of days – allowing them to break through into the open, whereas standard divisions would have to be replaced.[4]

For Pershing, the 'most important question' that he faced when preparing the forces of the United States for 'efficient service' was 'training'.[5] He was committed to the creation of an army based upon what he deemed were the 'standards of West Point': 'The rigid attention, upright bearing, attention to detail, uncomplaining obedience to instructions required of the cadet will be required of every officer and soldier of our armies in France.' Maintaining offensive spirit was of crucial importance. In a directive published in October 1917, he laid down a marker for how the US Army would fight in France. 'The general principles governing combat remain unchanged in their essence', he wrote. 'The rifle and the bayonet are the principle weapons of the infantry soldier. He will be trained to a high degree of skill as a marksman, both on the target range and in field firing. An aggressive spirit must be developed until the soldier feels himself, as a bayonet fighter, invincible in battle.'[6]

Central to this vision of warfare was the 1903 Springfield, effective up to 1,000 yards and regarded as one of the best rifles of its day. With his men armed with the Springfield, Pershing was convinced that they would overwhelm the defences they faced and restart mobile warfare. But because the Springfield could not be manufactured in sufficient numbers (it was only produced by two factories in the US), it was decided to modify the existing British Lee Enfield by rechambering it to take the 0.30-calibre round fired by the Springfield. Other weaponry was almost entirely adopted from the French, including the Hotchkiss heavy machine-gun, the Chauchat automatic rifle, the French 75 field gun and the 155 mm Schneider howitzer.[7] Just how much firepower the Americans should use remained a source of debate. Pershing wanted his troops to prepare for 'open warfare', able to move and think quickly on the battlefield, but this ran contrary to the methods now being employed in the French Army, which would only attack after painstaking preparation and artillery supremacy.

Pershing kept a close watch upon 1st Division, which had spent the summer at Gondrecourt (a village about thirty-five miles northeast of Chaumont) undergoing instruction from 47th Division, an elite unit of *Chasseurs Alpins* known as the 'Blue Devils'. The Americans were put to work building a series of practice trenches, including support and rear positions, before being instructed in weapons handling and tactical drills: how to use bombs and rifle grenades, as well as how to survive the perils they were likely to encounter in the trenches such as enemy bombardments and gas attacks. Relations between the 'dough-boys' (as the Americans were affectionately called) and their 'professors' was generally good; the French were respected for their intimate knowledge of modern warfare, while American eagerness and fight-ing spirit were widely commented upon. But Pershing was concerned that too much emphasis was being placed on 'trench weapons' and artillery fire, and was dismayed to learn that at Gondrecourt targets on the rifle range were being placed at between fifty and a hundred yards' distance, which surprised American officers, who were used to hitting targets at over 500 yards. Their instructors would just shrug and explain that such fleeting targets were highly unlikely in the enclosed, troglodyte world of the trenches.[8]

The reality of what the Americans were now up against was read-ily apparent to the four battalions of 1st Division that went into the line on the evening of 21 October, entering a quiet sector at Einville, backed up by a French division. After several days of routine activity – the usual dawn stand-to and the occasional sniper – their presence was picked up by the Germans, who had been planning a trench raid for months and were eager to test American mettle. At 3 a.m. on 3 November, they pounced, unleashing a furious box barrage that cut off a section of the line occupied by 16 Infantry Regiment before pounding it with mortar and artillery fire. Under a heavy bombard-ment, as sparks and explosions flashed into the night air, an elite group of raiders from 1st Bavarian *Landwehr* Division, about 200 strong, scrambled across no-man's-land and entered the trenches. In a furious fifteen minutes of cutting, slashing and firing, three Ameri-cans lay dead, five were wounded and another twelve taken prisoner. In a very real, visceral way, the United States was now in the war.

Elsewhere on the Western Front there seemed little else but costly stalemate. By mid-October, Haig's push in Flanders had, once again, ground to a halt. Despite the success at Broodseinde, which had pro-duced near panic in the German High Command, the return of heavy rain on 7 October inundated the battlefield and made it more difficult than ever to bring up the artillery and conduct the aerial reconnaissance that was vital to Plumer's attacks. It was 'practically impossible to tell where one is on the map in daylight', recalled a British officer, 'as every single feature has been absolutely blotted out, trees and hedges are just splinters scattered about, farms and cottages can sometimes be identified by bits of broken brick. Everywhere is just the same dreary waste of pockmarked country, shell hole touching shell hole and all full of dirty yellow water.'[9] Further attacks on 9 and 12 October ended in disaster: the supporting barrage was weak; the ground was a swamp; and heavy rifle and machine-gun fire cut bloody swathes in the attacking battalions, leaving British troops about a mile short of Passchendaele Ridge.

At a meeting of army commanders on 13 October, Haig admitted that they had to wait for better weather before trying again: '*When the ground is dry* no opposition which the enemy has put up has been able to stop our men.' But continuing in the face of stiffening resistance inevitably raised questions about the future of Allied strategy, and when Haig met Pétain several days later, he was presented with wearily familiar demands to take over more line. 'Pétain's main arguments were that since Russia might go out of the war entirely, we ought to make our defensive arrangements accordingly', Haig wrote. Pétain estimated that up to forty-five enemy divisions might be brought back from Russia while, at the same time, some of his own divisions were being broken up. Painlevé and Foch had travelled to London and, apparently, already settled this question with Lloyd George. Haig resisted as best he could. Pétain's arguments 'seemed to me to be quite unsound'. He disputed the figures of possible reinforcements from the Eastern Front ('we had worked out 32 as the maximum number of divisions') and explained that the best way to hold off German pressure was to continue to attack. If, however, the British Government insisted on taking over more line, then he would make the necessary arrangements.[10]

Haig and Pétain did not enjoy the warmest of relationships and this encounter merely reinforced the distance between them. Both men were alternately puzzled by or annoyed at the other and struggled to find common ground. In one of their first meetings, Pétain had pointedly said that he had 'reached the top of the Vimy Ridge before Haig did, and that he had conducted in Champagne and at Verdun much more difficult battles' than the Somme. According to GQG's former liaison officer, Vallières, 'Pétain's dry and cutting tone' grated with Haig. 'Never had a commander-in-chief spoken to him with such energy and clarity.' As for Haig, he frequently damned the French Commander-in-Chief with faint praise. After one of their initial exchanges, he wrote that Pétain was 'businesslike, knowledge-able, and brief of speech. The latter a rare quality in Frenchmen!'[11]

The disagreements between the two men were sharpened by what seemed like irredeemably bad news from other fronts. The German offensive at Riga, which opened on 1 September, had showcased a ser-ies of new offensive tactics, including short hurricane bombardments, interspersed with heavy gas shelling, aimed at neutralizing, *not* destroy-ing enemy positions, before stormtroopers went forward, bypassing any strongpoints, which were then isolated and mopped up by subse-quent waves. The result was devastating. By noon on the first day, a breach twelve kilometres wide and six deep had been made in the Rus-sian lines, with the defenders surrendering freely. Russian Army morale, which had long been fragile, now began to fail entirely. An army intelligence report, transmitted to the Russian High Command in the final week of September, admitted that 'general war weariness' was now endemic, combined with 'an intense defeatist agitation accom-panied by refusals to carry out orders, threats to the commanding personnel, and attempts to fraternize with the Germans'.[12]

Italy also seemed to be tottering on the edge of total collapse. On 24 October, a sudden Austro-German attack around the town of Capo-retto sent the Italian Second Army reeling back towards the Venetian plain. After the breakthrough on the Bainsizza Plateau in August, which had triggered desperate appeals from the Austrian High Com-mand, Ludendorff sent a detachment of six divisions, including elite mountain troops, under the command of General Otto von Below, to mount a counter-offensive. The attack began under heavy cloud cover and utilized the tactics that had been pioneered at Riga. Counter-battery fire silenced Italian guns while thousands of phosgene shells were directed at command and control facilities, producing paralysis.

With German and Austrian units racing along the valley floors – in complete contrast to the usual practice in mountain warfare – the defenders were outflanked and surrounded. The result was a calamity as Italian troops abandoned their guns and left their positions *en masse*. Within a month over 300,000 soldiers had surrendered, with entire corps being disbanded.[13]

For the time being the British and French carried on, fighting their own wars. Pétain's third and final limited attack had opened on 23 October, a day before Caporetto. The objective was La Malmaison, a ruined fortress that occupied one of the best vantage points on the entire Chemin des Dames. Originally constructed in the late 1870s, Malmaison had long been obsolete – and had been abandoned in 1914 as the Germans swept through northern France – but it had been incorporated into the German defensive system because of its excellent views. Pétain instructed General Paul Maistre's Sixth Army to get his troops up and over the ridge – hopefully completing the task that had started, in such difficulty, back in April. A preliminary bombardment opened on 17 October, and over the next six days the German defences were subjected to a tornado of fire – about five times the intensity of shellfire that had been unleashed in Champagne in September 1915. Forward positions were razed to the ground, while German batteries were deluged with 'special shells' (including phosgene and phosphorus) as part of a concerted effort to neutralize German defences prior to the attack, rather than having to physically destroy them.[14]

The attack went in before sunrise at 5.15 a.m. – the air crackling with gunfire, the rumble of shells on the wind. Once again Moroccan troops (from 38th Division) were in the vanguard, moving towards the fort, which was all but obscured in the misty darkness. 'No man's land has not seen too much devastation; the soil is dry, and by increasing the speed, one can regain one's place in the plan', remembered one veteran. 'But as we move forward, [there is] no precise landmark: only tracer shells, phosphorescent and fantastic fireworks illuminate the battlefield with a network of distant flashes'.[15] Sixty tanks were also in action, but only about half were able to cross the first German line, the rest either being destroyed or ditching in no-man's-land, which had been softened by morning rainfall. This would be a recurring problem. French tanks were underpowered and prone to mechanical breakdown, while inherent design flaws were now becoming increasingly apparent. The larger Saint-Chamond, which had been designed in competition with the Schneider, was nicknamed the 'elephant on the legs of a gazelle', and was notorious for the 75 mm gun that protruded from its hull; with tracks only slightly longer than the Schneider, it was unstable and susceptible to tipping over.[16]

Notwithstanding these weaknesses, about twenty machines were able to play a role in the advance, helping to mop up the German positions after the first wave had passed as well as ward off any counter-attacks. In one celebrated incident, forty Germans even surrendered to a single tank, having been horrified by its appearance, covered in mud, as it squealed over no-man's-land. While this was encouraging, and much would be made of the improved morale in the French Tank Corps (the 'Artillerie Spéciale') after the battle, the weight of artillery that the French could employ, and the fact that it was being used more imaginatively, to neutralize or interfere with the defenders, was of greater importance. 'It's frightful,' recalled one attacker; 'everything is devastated, we stumble into huge craters, German corpses everywhere, blown to pieces, others overcome by gas, dying. It's dreadful, but superb.'[17] La Malmaison was taken and the Sixth Army made an advance of several kilometres on to the ridge, forcing the German High Command to sanction a retreat northwards off the high ground that it had held with such tenacity since 1914. Over 11,000 Germans were taken prisoner and Sixth Army captured a sizeable haul of weaponry: 200 guns, 200 mortars and 700 machine-guns – all for a loss of 14,000 men put out of action, which, as was noted later, 'did not appear excessive'.[18]

Whether such operations could ever be exploited fully remained unclear, and some critics of Pétain were not slow to remind him of how many similar operations would have to be conducted if they were ever to liberate all of France. But Pétain would not be rushed and he had no desire to endanger his success with risky attempts to move forward. 'I do not want the moral benefit, from a perfectly successful mission, to be diminished.'[19] Malmaison was exactly the kind of operation that he had wanted to mount since taking over from Nivelle, aimed at restoring his army's confidence and spirit in the attack. Even *The Times* understood what Pétain was doing. The battle would 'surely form a classic example of General Pétain's theory of the limited offensive, delivered at the right moment with apparently absolute certainty, inflicting heavy losses on the enemy, and resulting in the acquisition of new positions of the highest value'.[20] Although Pétain rarely displayed his emotion – with his thoughts remaining hidden behind an ice-cold *froideur* – news of the success of his troops on 23 October visibly affected him. When a staff officer drafted a communiqué reporting 'progress on the whole front of the attack', Pétain insisted on correcting it by hand to read: 'Made great progress.'[21]

In Flanders, things were not so positive. With Haig's troops still short of the highest part of Passchendaele Ridge, there could be no thought of stopping the offensive. But any new attacks would require fresh troops. Haig chose the Canadian Corps after it became evident that I and II ANZAC Corps, which had spearheaded the attacks since mid-September, were exhausted. The Canadians' commander, Lieutenant-General Sir Arthur Currie, was not keen on taking the ridge, but Haig insisted, telling him that it was absolutely essential to do it and that he would have '*an unprecedented amount of artillery*' to support the attack.[22] Roads and bridges needed to be repaired and light railways pushed forward. There was little cover, save for a few battered pillboxes, leaving guns in the open, covered over with tarpaulins or sheets of corrugated iron. Infantry had to march along wobbly plank roads and duckboard tracks that were frequently blown to pieces or sunk in slime. Every gun had to be brought up along a tortuous route strewn with broken-down lorries and dead horses, while shells were usually strapped to mules, which were then led up to the line in long, stumbling columns after dark. When Currie first saw the wilderness of mud and standing water all he noted was 'Battlefield looks bad – No salvaging has been done and very few of the dead [are] buried.'[23]

Gradually the Canadians fought their way on to the ridge. On 26 October, two divisions moved off into the mist and rain, attacking uphill into a hellish landscape of half-submerged pillboxes and barbed-wire entanglements. They gained about 500 yards, following it up four days later with another advance, which brought them to the outskirts of Passchendaele. It took all Currie's ingenuity to keep the attack going. For the final attack on 6 November, the Canadians managed to bring up a field gun for every eight metres of front and a howitzer for every thirty-two metres – a remarkable concentration of fire given the terrible ground conditions.[24] But wresting the ridge from German hands was about more than weight of metal, and the Canadian attack bore all the hallmarks of aggressive, well-led infantry, eager to close with the enemy and strike hard with the bayonet. Opposition was dealt with mercilessly, crushed by the barrage, scythed down by rifle fire, or run through with muddy bayonets. Finally, at a cost of just under 16,000 casualties, the ridge was theirs.

On 7 November, the day after Passchendaele had fallen, the Bolsheviks seized power in Petrograd. The effect of the *coup d'état*, and the days of street fighting that followed, was fatal to the Russian war effort as the Provisional Government was overthrown. On the Eastern Front, Russia's armies now began melting away like ice in the sun. Thousands of peasants, hungry and tired of the war, were deserting their units and beginning the long journey home. The leader of the Bolsheviks, Vladimir Lenin (who had been transported to Russia from Switzerland with German connivance, his pockets bulging with German gold), vowed to take Russia out of the war, and soon decrees were being sent across the empire abolishing private property, encouraging further agitation and demanding that peace negotiations begin immediately. On 21 November, a radio message was broadcast to all Russian troops announcing the end of the war: 'Soldiers! Peace is in your hands . . . Let the regiments holding the line immediately select delegates for formal negotiations with the enemy looking to an armistice.'[25]

News of the seizure of power was greeted with a curious mixture of relief, happiness and confusion within the German High Command. Both Hindenburg and Ludendorff had always believed that the way to victory pointed east and now they seemed vindicated. Harry Graf Kessler, a German diplomat, visited OHL at this time and was struck by its mood of sunny optimism and confidence.

Ludendorff 'has become stouter, but just as pink, fresh, and energetic as a year ago. He has the blond skin complexion and healthy blood supply of a northern German.' He believed that the French were 'truly getting tired', while he was 'not afraid' of the Americans. 'Up to now they have sent, in total, thirty thousand men [this was an underestimation], so two divisions. That is as good as nothing on the Western Front.' Hindenburg was also beaming with pride at German successes. 'He sits in the middle of his enormous frame without vanity, with a kind of grandfatherly good humour that he expresses in short sentences. His voice sounds like hoarse thunder, like that of some old thunder god Wotan, but with laughter underneath.' Kessler noticed the differences in the two men: Hindenburg, a 'huge packet of healthy nerves and force, a kind of boxer'; while Ludendorff was 'more intellectual, a constantly mobile intellect'. Together they were the focal point of Germany's war: 'the tiny, powerfully tense feather spring driving and ordering the entire affair'.[26]

The turmoil in Russia offered Germany a unique opportunity – to throw all her weight into a one-front war that she could fight and win. It would not be until 22 December that peace negotiations with the Bolsheviks opened at Brest-Litovsk (the location of Germany's eastern headquarters), but already the duo were thinking ahead about striking back on the Western Front as soon as possible. Ludendorff was adamant that a defensive posture could not be considered for the forthcoming campaign and most of his senior commanders agreed with him. Attacking, on the contrary, seemed to be the only option; a last great act of will that would cut the 'Gordian Knot' tying up Germany and allow her to dictate terms to her enemies. A conference on future strategy was held at Mons on 11 November with Ludendorff asking his most trusted officers to be present, including Rupprecht, Wetzell, Bauer and the army group Chiefs of Staff (Kuhl and Count Friedrich von der Schulenburg). No civilians were in attendance. Ludendorff had not seen any reason to invite the new Imperial Chancellor, Georg von Hertling, who had replaced Georg Michaelis on 1 November.

Michaelis had lasted just three months in office. After a clash with the Majority Socialists over the treatment of a group of sailors who had tried (and failed) to provoke a mutiny in the High Seas Fleet, Friedrich Ebert, the Socialists' leader, indicated that they had no confidence in him and wanted a new Chancellor. Although the Kaiser cared little for what Parliament thought, he recognized the need to calm the Reichstag and eventually settled on Hertling, a 74-year-old Catholic politician from Bavaria with a long and distinguished career, including as a professor of philosophy at the University of Munich.[27] Despite being almost blind, with a calm and accommodating nature Hertling worked assiduously to manage the Reichstag, but struggled to forge a good relationship with Ludendorff, who proceeded to sideline him during the negotiations with the Bolsheviks and over the plans for the spring offensive – both of which would now determine the fate of the German Empire.

But where was this offensive to be directed and against whom? Hermann von Kuhl had drawn up plans for an attack in the north via Bailleul and Hazebrouck with the aim of cutting off the British sector of the front. 'To the north and west is the sea, the worst possible operational position. The decisive operation!' he noted. 'Do not swing north too early, but conduct deeply staggered left flanking attacks to cut off the English. Just keep in mind: the Lys lowlands are flooded in winter and need to be crossed.' Such an attack would not be feasible before April and would require thirty-five divisions and 400 heavy batteries. Georg Wetzell, who had drafted a memorandum on 9 November, looked elsewhere. Dismissing the prospect of an attack in the north because of the swampy, wet ground and close proximity of reserves, Wetzell stated that the best option – as Falkenhayn had believed in 1916 – would be to go after the French. 'In my view, on the French sector, or more generally on the entire Western Front, there is only one really generous opportunity for an offensive with the most wide-ranging consequences for its success.' Wetzell proposed to attack on either side of the French positions at Verdun, pinching off the fortress city without attacking it directly. He argued that France could not withstand such an attack and that Verdun remained 'crucial' to the outcome of the war.[28]

Ludendorff was unconvinced by either plan. The difficulty with attacking across the Lys was that an attack had to be mounted early in the year to forestall any enemy movement, but would the ground be dry enough? As for Wetzell's suggestion, it might be possible to mount a diversionary offensive at Verdun, but Ludendorff doubted whether they had enough men and ammunition to do anything more. The 'promising' alternative was an attack from Saint-Quentin, breaking the front along the Somme and driving northwest to roll up the British front. Ludendorff was convinced that for both 'political and military reasons' they should attack the British sector of the Western Front. The British were a less formidable adversary – 'easier and safer' as he put it – who were likely to sue for peace if they suffered 'a crushing defeat on French soil'. After three hours of discussion on 11 November, no final decision was reached, but Ludendorff made it clear that it was now or never:

'The situation in Russia and Italy is likely to make it possible to strike on the Western theatre of war in the New Year. The balance of power on both sides will be roughly equal. Around 35 divisions and 1,000 heavy guns can be made available for an offensive. They will be sufficient for one offensive; a second, major attack, perhaps as a diversion, will not be possible. Our overall situation requires that we attack as early as possible, possibly at the end of February or the beginning of March before the Americans are able to contribute strong forces. We have to beat the English.'[29]

Time was running out. Even OHL, which had placed its faith in the success of Germany's U-boats, became increasingly resigned to their failure by the autumn. With the introduction of the convoy system across the Atlantic in September, losses of Allied shipping had fallen steadily. Just under 200,000 tons had been sunk that month, and although the figure rose again in October, much of this was down to sinkings in the Mediterranean, where convoying had only just been introduced.[30] Overall the trend was progressively downwards, which meant that unless Germany could find some way to break the deadlock in the west, she might find herself ground down beyond any possibility of recovery. At home, the Central Powers had already endured years of shortages and a thin, hollowed-out population haunted the main cities, desperate for news about the possibility of peace, but increasingly resigned to yet more sacrifices. Flour had been rationed in Berlin from as early as January 1915, and over the next two years more and more foodstuffs were brought under government control: potatoes (from the spring of 1916) and fats and milk (from the summer and autumn of 1916). There was now an elaborate array of substitutes for cheese, sugar, jam and coffee, and although vegetables could still be had – if one was prepared to queue for hours – civilians were now surviving on about 1,400 calories per day (compared to 3,000 before the war), with only soldiers receiving the recommended 2,500 calories required to maintain their weight.[31]

At 6.10 on the morning of 20 November, without any warning, a thousand guns opened a fearful barrage along a seven-mile section of the front southwest of Cambrai, and 378 fighting tanks, supported by infantry, went forward. This was Haig's surprise tank attack, which had been approved on 13 October, a day after the first push towards Passchendaele had failed. Three brigades of tanks, supported by six divisions from General Sir Julian Byng's Third Army, would break the Hindenburg Line, take the city of Cambrai, and prevent German reinforcements from moving against the Italians. The attack would offer a welcome opportunity to employ tanks *en masse* on good, dry ground – something officers of the Tank Corps had been pleading for since the summer – as well as allow the Royal Artillery to attempt 'shooting off the map', whereby guns would be calibrated beforehand without the need for ranging shots. With readings being taken of air pressure, wind direction and temperature, each barrel could be individually registered to ensure that its fire was as accurate as possible, negating the need for a long preliminary bombardment and allowing surprise to return to the battlefield.

Along the German trench lines, frenzied shouts of 'Tanks!' could be heard as the machines crawled towards them, tearing up the thickets of barbed wire with their tracks. A counter-barrage was immediately put down, but it was insignificant compared with the British fire, 'weak music in contrast to a powerful concert', as one defender noted.[32] With only three divisions in the line, the German outpost positions were quickly overrun, and the British were able to liberate the town of Marcoing and reach the Saint-Quentin Canal at Masnières – an advance of between three and four miles. In the skies, British aircraft gained control of the air, despite thick mist, which had grounded the few enemy aeroplanes in this sector, and they took full advantage, with Sopwith Camels of No. 3 Squadron launching a series of daring raids on German aerodromes. One pilot remembered flying through the smoke and mist over the battlefield: 'One retains vivid pictures of little groups of infantry behind each tank, trudging forward with cigarettes alight, of flames leaping from disabled tanks with small helpless groups of infantry standing around, of the ludicrous expressions of amazement on the upturned faces of German troops as we passed a few feet above their trenches.'[33]

Haig desperately tried to exploit these gains. He visited General Byng and they discussed striking north towards Bourlon Wood and trying to secure the crossings over the canal to open a way for the cavalry. Yet exploiting the initial breach would not be easy. Tank losses had been heavy: 179 machines had been put out of action (sixty-five suffering direct hits and the rest either breaking down or getting ditched), which left precious few available to repeat the success of the first day.[34] There were also only limited infantry reserves near the battlefield, which caused Haig considerable anguish and left him scrambling around for reinforcements. He received permission to deploy two divisions that had been earmarked for service in Italy, but it would be some time before they could come into action. In the meantime, Byng's troops kept pushing on. Cavalry clattered through the village of Noyelles – just three miles from Cambrai – on 21 November, while over the next few days, most of Bourlon Wood (a key tactical feature that overlooked the approaches to Cambrai) was secured after fierce hand-to-hand fighting.

It did not take long for German reserves to appear on the battlefield. By 24 November, British intelligence was aware that three divisions had arrived and more were expected over the coming days. There were also greater numbers of fighter aircraft in the skies. Richthofen's 'Flying Circus' had flown down from Flanders – trebling German fighter strength and evening up the odds in the air.[35] On 27 November, Ludendorff drove out to Second Army's headquarters at Le Cateau and authorized a counter-attack to strike the British right flank and roll it up northwards like a vicious sickle cut. This would then be joined by an attack around Bourlon pushing southwards. The weather had turned wintry, with falling snow and heavy mist that concealed German plans, now based upon the methods that had been so successful at Riga and Caporetto: short, hurricane bombardments of gas and smoke, followed by fast-moving infantry ordered to bypass centres of resistance. It was straight out of their textbooks, someone said, quoting the Prussian military thinker, Carl von Clausewitz: 'A sudden powerful transition to the offensive – the flashing sword of vengeance – is the greatest moment for the defence.'[36]

By the eve of the German counter-attack, the momentum of the battle had swung sharply away from Haig's forces. Lacking reinforcements and complacent about enemy movements, Haig hoped that the battle would now die down – perhaps with a sizeable German retreat. British troops were also worn out and lacking the manpower to convert their sketchy defences into something more substantial. When the German attack opened just before dawn on 30 November, it hit the British hard, like a blow to the kidneys. Out of the cold white skies, swarms of aircraft swooped down, some flying as low as 100 feet, strafing British positions and causing panic. The main attack struck against the weakest part of the line, driving towards the village of Metz-en-Couture and threatening to cut Third Army off from its rear. British battalions struggled to coordinate the defence and found themselves outflanked and surrounded, while hurried counter-attacks were thrown in. The situation was only restored with a desperate action by the Guards Division at Gouzeaucourt. Philip Gibbs, a journalist, remembered watching the Guards march forward into the line, 'munching apples and whistling'; only to see the remnants of the division a day later 'lying under tarpaulins, all dirty and bloody'.[37]

Fighting continued for another week as the weather closed in. The British were able to hold off the threatened pincer movement in the north, around Bourlon, where their positions were stronger and an interlocking machine-gun and artillery defence did fearful execution to German columns, but the main thrust on the right put a significant dent in the gains of the preceding week and left Byng with little choice but to withdraw to more easily defended lines around Flesquières – thus bringing the battle to an inconclusive, unsatisfactory end. British casualties were around 44,000, including 6,000 prisoners and 150 guns lost on 30 November, while German figures were roughly equal: 41,000 casualties, with 14,000 men being taken prisoner – testament to the brutal nature of the fighting in the closing weeks of 1917.[38]

The Battle of Cambrai would later be interpreted as a kind of messy draw, but it provided vital hints about how the war would be fought in 1918. On the German side, there was initially a sense of disappointment that the results of the counter-attack were, as Rupprecht put it, 'not so great as we hoped'. The tactical success on 30 November would have probably achieved greater results had more preparation been allowed, but despite 'gruelling defensive battles and shortages of food', German troops were 'still animated by an exemplary attacking spirit'.[39] Rupprecht and Kuhl fired off a whole series of reports about the lessons from the battle as they prepared to strike again in 1918. Kuhl noted in his diary on 19 December that it was 'necessary to be flexible and agile, not just obstinately wanting to penetrate at one location'. Speed was clearly the essence of success: to be able to quickly regroup and then attack elsewhere along the front. For Kuhl, the reason why British 'breakthroughs' had always failed was that 'they brought everything to one location and then hammered away incessantly with their superior material and personnel'. If Germany did the same, the result would be a costly 'material battle'. 'This is not an option for us.'[40]

As for Haig, he emerged from Cambrai in a more vulnerable position than ever before, and confidence in his leadership was seriously shaken for the first time. When rumours about Cambrai began to spread in the British press (including the question of whether Haig had been surprised by the counter-attack), Lloyd George pressed his claims for a fundamental rethink about British strategy and suggested promoting Haig and Robertson into high-sounding but impotent positions – much like what had happened to Joffre – only to find the Minister of War, Lord Derby, reluctant to do so. Nevertheless, Derby did write to Haig about the need to freshen up his headquarters staff, particularly his Head of Intelligence, John Charteris, who was accused of providing Haig with assessments of enemy strength that bore little resemblance to reality. 'The War Cabinet are constantly saying that the statements and views you have put forward at different times regarding the moral and numerical weakening of the enemy are not borne out by the opposition your troops encounter,' he wrote in a letter dated 7 December, 'and so it appears to me and to the General Staff here.'[41] Haig protested, but in the end agreed to let Charteris go. By January 1918, his long-serving Chief of Staff, Launcelot Kiggell, had also been moved on.

Not satisfied with clipping Haig's wings, Lloyd George pressed ahead with plans for a unified command structure, or at least some kind of permanent military staff that would help to coordinate coalition strategy. Proposals for such a 'high council' had been circulating for years, although the unhappy results of the last time it was tried, under General Nivelle in the spring of 1917, boded ill for any attempt to resurrect it. Yet the danger that Italy would exit the war was a prime mover in the decision to hold a conference at Rapallo, on the Italian Riviera, in early November, from where it was agreed to push forward plans for what became known as the Supreme War Council. Based at Versailles, the council consisted of a Permanent Military Representative from each of the Allied powers, including Major-General Maxime Weygand for France, General Luigi Cadorna for Italy, and Sir Henry Wilson for Britain. General Tasker Bliss, Chief of Staff of the US Army, was appointed the American representative. After settling into the Hotel Trianon, the military representatives and their staffs were instructed to 'report immediately on the present situation on the Italian Front' as part of a 'general review of the military situation in all theatres', which would examine what assistance was required and how it could be furnished.[42]

Matters were complicated by the fall of Painlevé's ministry on 13 November. The former Minister of War had taken over a short-lived government in September, but struggled through a series of political scandals, which sapped public confidence, already battered by the heavy losses of the spring. When Painlevé lost a vote of confidence – the only French ministry to do so during the war – President Poincaré decided to ask the senator Georges Clemenceau to form a government. Clemenceau had first been elected to the Chamber of Deputies in 1876 and, in a long career in and outside Parliament, aroused hostility from across the political spectrum, from both left and right, for the causes he championed. Short of stature, with bald head and small eyes, sunken beneath thick eyebrows, he was instantly recognizable as he shuffled along, his hands clad in grey silk gloves, clasped firmly behind his back. Winston Churchill, appointed Minister of Munitions in July 1917, got to know the new premier at this time and watched his opening speech in the Chamber of Deputies. Clemenceau 'ranged from one side of the tribune to the other, without a note or book of reference or scrap of paper, barking out sharp, staccato sentences as the thought broke upon his mind. He looked like a wild animal pacing to and fro behind bars, growling and glaring; and all around him was an assembly which would have done anything to avoid having him there, but having put him there, felt they must obey.'[43]

Clemenceau was a man in a hurry; someone who knew what needed to be done and was determined to do it. He appointed himself Minister of War and brought in a decorated soldier, Jean Mordacq, to act as his personal military adviser, while making it clear that he would visit the front as often as he could. He also requested that a former Prime Minister, Joseph Caillaux, be stripped of his parliamentary immunity over accusations that he was trying to strike a compromise peace with the enemy – a firm indication that France was no longer interested in bartering over her war aims. In his first prime ministerial statement, delivered on 20 November – the day of Haig's attack at Cambrai – Clemenceau laid down a marker for the coming struggle and warned the French people that henceforth there would be no distinction between the 'zone of the army' and the interior. 'No more pacifist campaigns, no more German intrigues. Neither treason, nor semi-treason: the war. Nothing but the war. Our armies will not be caught between fire from two sides. Justice will be done. The country will know that it is defended.'[44] France would see the war through, Clemenceau promised; whatever the cost.

Before Germany could mass all her strength in the west, peace had to be signed with Russia. Negotiations with the Bolsheviks at Brest-Litovsk had dragged on throughout December and into January, with the Bolsheviks sending the loquacious radical Leon Trotsky to haggle for as much time as possible, hoping that if he dallied long enough revolution would break out across the Central Powers. He stormed out of the conference on 18 January, only returning before the end of the month, which left Ludendorff 'burning with impatience' to get moving, eager to settle matters in the east that would allow for the wholesale transfer of divisions to the Western Front.[1] Unwilling to spend long hours jousting with Trotsky over the meaning of self-determination for the peoples of Eastern Europe, Hindenburg and Ludendorff quickly ran out of patience and launched renewed operations in mid-February, with German troops overrunning large areas of Ukraine and the Crimea and forcing the Bolsheviks to the wall.

Humiliated and subdued, the Bolsheviks returned to the table on 3 March and signed whatever was put in front of them: a peace treaty so vicious that it would long be remembered. At a stroke, Russia lost half her industrial production, about 90 per cent of her coal mines and 30 per cent of her pre-war population. Finland and the Baltic States, Poland and Ukraine would (nominally) become independent, leaving Germany the masters of a vast new empire stretching from the Baltics to the Don. The Kaiser, with his usual hyperbole, announced that it was 'one of the greatest successes in world history', the significance of which would only be understood by people's grandchildren.[2] But even this failed to satisfy the duo at OHL, who had been horrified by the way in which the German negotiating team, led by the Foreign Secretary, Richard von Kühlmann, had resisted their demands for even further territorial gains, with Ludendorff arguing for the outright annexation of conquered territory, including land deep in Russia.

Kühlmann, backed by Hertling and the Kaiser, refused to agree to this, claiming that Germany would be weakened by the creation of a 'protective belt' of land in the east and that the addition of several million Poles into the Reich would be dangerous.[3]

Kühlmann's refusal to bow to these demands inevitably provoked another threat of resignation from Hindenburg, who used the impending offensive in France as an opportunity to cleanse the Imperial Government of all those he suspected of being unreliable. In a letter to the Kaiser on 7 January, he acknowledged the 'difficult situation' that had emerged between the Foreign Secretary and OHL and warned about the consequences of 'disregarding' his advice. The heavy burden that was placed upon those who had to 'prepare and conduct' operations in the west – what he called 'the greatest effort we have made in the entire war' – meant that they had to be assured of the 'unqualified personal support' of the monarch. 'They and the army must be bolstered by the feeling that political success will correspond to military success. Most humbly, I ask Your Majesty to make a fundamental decision.'[4]

The Kaiser resisted as strongly as he dared. Although he had backed the generals on the decision to restart operations on the Eastern Front, he would not support Hindenburg's demands on annexations. Thanking the Field Marshal for his 'soldierly frankness' and 'extreme lucidity', he heaped praise on Germany's two leading soldiers. 'In this matter both you and General Ludendorff who, you say, identifies himself with your views, have shown yourselves to be men whose utter devotion and energy are indispensable to me for the further prosecution of the war.' His confidence in them could not be 'shaken' by the fact that both he and the Imperial Chancellor took a different view. 'It is in the very nature of things – and an ancient phenomenon which has often appeared in history and in no way surprises me now – that in the course of the greatest coalition war which the world has ever seen the soldier and the statesman should look at affairs from a different angle in individual questions of war aims and the method by which they are attained.' Therefore, he wanted Hindenburg to withdraw any further objections he may have had and work 'without regrets' on the forthcoming campaign.[5]

Behind the warm words, the Kaiser fumed, impotent and angry. On one occasion, 'beside himself with rage', he slammed the door in Hindenburg's face, shouting 'I don't need your paternal advice!' On another occasion he swore that Ludendorff was 'a malefactor' and vowed that he would never shake hands with him again.[6] But the Kaiser's rage tailed off almost as soon as it erupted, leaving him a more shrunken figure than ever before. He stood by Kühlmann, who remained Foreign Secretary, but crumbled when rumours began circulating about Rudolf von Valentini, the chief of his Privy Cabinet, who was regarded with suspicion by OHL. Valentini, a conservative, aristocratic Prussian, who had been close to Bethmann Hollweg, resigned on 16 January, with Hindenburg making it clear that Friedrich von Berg-Markienen, head of the province of East Prussia, would be an ideal replacement. Bald with a thin moustache, and small eyes peering out from behind steel-rimmed glasses, Berg was all the generals wanted in a politician: a radical conservative who agreed with them on everything and who worked ceaselessly to keep Wilhelm on the straight and narrow path that OHL laid out for him.[7]

The purging of suspect officials and their replacement with more reliable, hard-line characters was an essential element in Hindenburg's and Ludendorff's vision for 1918 – a necessary strengthening of the home front before the enormous demands of the coming year. No one at the German High Command was under any illusion about the scale of the undertaking, and a renewed seriousness settled upon its senior officers as they contemplated the future. 'In order to secure our political and economic world position, we need to beat the Western powers', was Hindenburg's blunt assessment, which he predicted would demand the 'greatest sacrifices'.[8] Ludendorff called it 'the most formidable task ever faced by an army', and approached it with his characteristic hyperactivity, ordering a whole series of plans to be drawn up for a range of operations by both main army groups. Each was given a specific sector of the front to consider as well as a code-name: Armentières (*Georg I*); Ypres (*Georg II*); Arras (*Mars*); Bapaume (*Michael I*); Péronne (*Michael II*); La Fère (*Michael III*); Reims (*Achilles*); Argonne (*Hector*); and Verdun (*Castor und Pollux*).[9]

Terrain and weather were crucial factors in the choice of any battlefield, as were the strength of the enemy and the objectives that might be secured. Ludendorff spent hours poring over maps of the front, his fingers tracing river lines and areas of high ground, while speaking almost daily to the Chiefs of Staff of the two army groups, Kuhl and Schulenburg, who became his main planning aides. In mid-January, he toured the front, working his way from top to bottom and, wherever possible, peering through binoculars at the front lines, those thin scars of chalk spoil and dirt that zigzagged across the landscape, seemingly absent of life and activity. Ludendorff was unconvinced by calls to attack the French, either at Verdun or at the Chemin des Dames, and remained clear in his own mind that the heaviest blow must land against the British, ideally in the north. The danger that the Channel ports would fall was a recurrent British nightmare, but a host of difficulties seemed to prevent a decisive strike from taking place there. The British were too strong and well dug in and Ludendorff conceded that attacking on the right, whether at Arras or Ypres, was not feasible in the time they had available: *Georg* was too dependent on the weather, while *Mars* was tactically too difficult.[10]

The matter was settled at a planning conference at Avesnes on 21 January. Both army group commanders and their Chiefs of Staff were present as Ludendorff briefed them on the forces that would likely be available and the direction that any attack would take. At the present moment, sixty-three divisions were in reserve on the Western Front ready to take part in any offensive. It might be possible to draw upon another twenty-four divisions that were currently stationed either in Italy or in Russia, giving them between eighty-five and ninety divisions available for operations by the beginning of March.[11] With these considerations in mind, Ludendorff found his attention being drawn to the central part of the front. Intelligence had revealed that the BEF was extending its line to the south as part of a series of reliefs that Pétain had been asking for since October, which would bring British troops south of the Somme and down past the Oise river. An attack here had the advantage of good ground. It could be undertaken earlier in the year and would offer the chance to strike at what was traditionally the weakest point of a coalition, where its forces joined. Therefore Operation *Michael* would now become the main focus of their efforts, with German forces attacking between Croisilles (southeast of Arras) and Saint-Quentin. Ludendorff admitted that such an attack lacked 'any definite limit', but he was confident that 'If this blow succeeded the strategic result might indeed be enormous, as we should separate the bulk of the English Army from the French and crowd it up with its back to the sea.'[12]

Two new armies were being created for this manoeuvre: Seventeenth Army would come into the line between Rupprecht's Sixth and Second Armies, and Eighteenth was scheduled to hold the line around Saint-Quentin. Each would be commanded by men with proven experience of breakthrough operations. Otto von Below, the balding, white-haired commander of Seventeenth Army, had masterminded the decisive attack at Caporetto and would have the most crucial role in the offensive, breaking the front at Arras and then wheeling northwest to roll up the British line. General Oskar von Hutier, whose attack at Riga in the autumn of 1917 had shown how effective infiltration tactics could be when they were combined with short, hurricane bombardments, was given Eighteenth Army, charged with safeguarding Below's left flank as far as Péronne. Although both armies were originally placed under Rupprecht's command, Ludendorff confirmed that he was now transferring Eighteenth Army to Crown Prince Wilhelm's army group, which meant that there would be no single commander in charge of the attack.[13]

Rupprecht, always cautious, grew concerned as Ludendorff's plan of operations was revealed. Coordinating a single offensive across two army groups was problematic enough, but the real danger was that Operation *Michael* would not lead, as he put it, in a 'favourable direction'. He understood Ludendorff's focus on achieving tactical success, but warned that larger, operational matters needed to be thoroughly worked out, and the direction of an offensive was crucial to its outcome. 'This may have been all the same to the unwieldy Russians, but not to the English and, in particular, not to the agile and deft French, where operations are concerned.'

When he pressed for specific ground phases in the attack, Ludendorff just shrugged:

'In Russia, we always set ourselves a very close objective and then see how we can progress.'[14]

A flurry of orders were issued in the days afterwards, but the great hole in Ludendorff's plans – the key objective that was the focus of their efforts – remained unfilled. The decision to split the attack across army groups allowed OHL and Ludendorff to remain in control, while (as it was whispered) also giving the Crown Prince an opportunity to resurrect a reputation that had never recovered from Verdun. But Ludendorff was fundamentally concerned with breaking through and instinctively focused on where the front line was weakest, showing a remarkable lack of interest in anything else. Fritz von Lossberg, who had fought in most of the major defensives battles of the German Army since 1915, also had doubts about what Ludendorff was attempting. He wrote a 'position paper' on the options available to Germany, arguing that 'it seems too risky to me to base all on a single massive offensive', but rather they should mount a series of 'smaller scale attacks' to exhaust enemy reserves and only then 'can our large-scale operational attack be launched on a broad front'. He recommended attacking towards Lens, thus outflanking the strong British defences around Arras (including Vimy Ridge), while avoiding, at all costs, fighting over the old Somme battlefield, which 'consisted of shell crater fields that were almost impossible to get across'. He handed the paper to Ludendorff, but found his warnings ignored, his input unwanted.[15]

The offensive was gradually refined over the next six weeks. *Michael* remained the main focus of effort, but it would be supported by strong flanking attacks around Arras (*Mars*) and south of the Oise (*Archangel*). If these failed, new operations would be mounted either in Champagne (*Roland*) or in Flanders (*Georg*) as soon as the long trains of heavy artillery could be redeployed. Ludendorff immersed himself in the details: the nature of the enemy's defences; the speed of the creeping barrage; the amount of aerial activity; the routes that German guns would need to take through the forward zones; and a thousand other things, pouring his energy and determination into perfecting the offensive as if he could, almost single-handedly, overturn the great weight that pressed down upon Germany. 'The battle in the West is the greatest military task that has ever been imposed upon an army', he told the Kaiser on 13 February. 'We must not imagine that this offensive will be like those in Galicia or Italy; it will be an immense struggle that will begin at one point, continue at another, and take a long time; it is difficult, but it will be victorious . . .'[16]

As the German Army returned to the offensive, the Allied powers contemplated a grim New Year, full of forebodings. On 5 January, David Lloyd George addressed a gathering of trade union delegates at the Central Hall, Westminster, and asked, with his usual rhetorical flourishes, 'what cause or causes' they were fighting for. He was at pains to insist that they were *not* fighting 'a war of aggression against the German people' and had no wish to 'disrupt or destroy' Germany. Nor were they fighting to overthrow her 'military autocratic constitution' – any change in Germany's political structure was 'a question for the German people to decide'. On the contrary, 'we were forced to join in this war in self-defence, in defence of the violated public law of Europe, and in vindication of the most solemn treaty obligations on which the public system of Europe rested, and on which Germany had ruthlessly trampled in her invasion of Belgium'. Any peace settlement must restore the independence and liberty of Belgium and secure the withdrawal of the armies of the Central Powers from all occupied territories, including Alsace–Lorraine, with sufficient 'reparation for injuries done in violation of international law'. The British Empire wanted 'a just and lasting peace' that could only be founded upon three conditions: 'the sanctity of treaties'; a 'territorial settlement' based upon 'the right of self-determination or the consent of the governed'; and 'the creation of some international organization to . . . diminish the probability of war'.[17]

Lloyd George's words, which seemed to mirror those of President Wilson, who had called for a 'League of Nations', reflected a growing acknowledgement of just how exhausted Britain had become. Manpower was now the most critical issue. Haig's armies had lost 822,000 men during 1917, which left them well below establishment, fuelling rising criticism of the British Commander-in-Chief.[18] Lloyd George was not minded to provide any more reinforcements than absolutely necessary and fought his corner staunchly, instituting a Cabinet Committee on Manpower to investigate how the empire's resources should be managed in the coming year. It reported on 9 January that 'absolute priority' should be given to the Royal Navy and the air force, after which came shipbuilding, the construction of tanks and aircraft, and finally food production and timber felling. Moreover, it acknowledged that Britain, France and Italy would be forced on to the defensive in 1918 and that the enemy 'will be so strong on the Western and Italian fronts as to preclude any reasonable probability of a decision on those fronts' in the Allies' favour. Therefore, it was essential to 'safeguard' the 'staying power' of the Allies for as long as possible, particularly the United Kingdom's, which was primarily responsible for keeping open the sea lanes, supplying coal, munitions and food to her partners, and transporting troops across the Atlantic.[19]

Haig and Robertson found themselves outmanoeuvred and under harsher scrutiny than ever before. When Haig travelled to London in the first week of January (when he was presented with his Field Marshal's baton), he explained that the next four months would be '*the critical period* of the war' and that it was highly likely 'the enemy would attack both the French and ourselves, and that he would hold Reserves in hand ready to exploit wherever he might have gained a success'. Moreover, he doubted whether the French could withstand 'a resolute and continued offensive' and the 'best defence' would be to continue the offensive in Flanders in order to 'retain the initiative and attract the German Reserves against us'.[20] But new offensives were not on the Prime Minister's agenda; nor were sizeable reinforcements. A day after the Committee on Manpower reported to the War Cabinet, Haig was ordered to reorganize his divisions by disbanding one infantry battalion from every brigade, thus reducing the number of battalions in each division from twelve to nine. 115 battalions would be disbanded over the winter, the men being reassigned to other units to keep their numbers up to strength, although the contingents from the Dominions of Australia, New Zealand and Canada retained their original order of battle, keeping four battalions in each brigade – and giving them a sizeable manpower advantage over their cousins from the old country.[21]

The travails in the French Army were, if anything, even worse than those in the BEF. Pétain had already 'dissolved' three divisions in November and would soon follow the British example of reducing the number of battalions across the Army. The following month a detailed assessment of personnel requirements gloomily reported that unless there was a significant increase in recruiting, there would be a deficit of 328,000 men by 1 October 1918 – the equivalent of twenty-five divisions.[22] Unlike Haig, who entertained hopes of renewing offensive operations in the spring, Pétain believed that the Russian collapse had transformed their fortunes and they must respond accordingly. 'Directive No. 4' was issued on 22 December: 'The Entente will not recover a superiority in combat strength until the American Army can put a number of large units into the line: until then we have to, despite irreparable damage, maintain an expectant attitude, with the idea of resuming the offensive as soon as we can – this alone will give us the final victory.'[23]

Worryingly, America was still a long way from being able to provide this superiority. By the end of 1917 only four US combat divisions had been transported to France, just 176,655 men, causing growing alarm in Paris and London that the American build-up was simply too slow and laborious to counteract their own diminishing reserves.[24] During a visit to GQG in December, General Pershing was presented with renewed demands from Pétain to 'amalgamate' his divisions into the French Army. 'Instead of following the plan then in operation as to training step by step, beginning with smaller units,' Pershing recalled, 'he wanted a quicker method and have each of the four infantry regiments of each of our divisions, together with the proper proportion of the artillery, engineers and other troops, assigned to a French division at once.' After several months, his divisions would be reassembled as whole units, but until that point American regiments would be used 'for whatever service might fall to the lot of the French divisions to which they were assigned'.[25]

The request to 'amalgamate' US manpower into the French Army had already been rejected in May 1917 and was no more popular now than it had been before. Pershing was against the proposal and, in his formal reply to Pétain on 6 January, explained that there were 'many real obstacles' in the way of placing his regiments in French divisions for service in the field. 'The differences of language, military methods, and national characteristics . . . would seriously hinder complete cooperation necessary in combat. Moreover, the American people would not approve of giving up the integrity of our organization and scattering it among French and British units.' Such a plan, he believed, 'would eliminate the possibility of training higher commanders and their staffs and would prevent the final building up of a cohesive, aggressive, self-reliant American force which must be depended upon to deliver the final blows necessary to end this war'.[26]

Privately, Pershing was growing tired of these endless demands and worried that the French were using the excuse of the looming offensive to scupper the chances of an autonomous US Army. He was even more upset when he found out that the new French premier, Clemenceau, had been extending feelers out to Washington on the urgency of resolving the 'misunderstanding' that had arisen between himself and Pétain. Working through the French Ambassador (who had met with Newton Baker), Clemenceau had urged that it would be 'safer' for US troops to be attached to French divisions than to be given 'an independent place in the line'. General Tasker Bliss, the US Chief of Staff, communicated these conversations to Pershing, but made it known that Baker was content to 'leave the matter wholly within your discretion'. Relieved at such vocal support, Pershing held his ground. He cabled Bliss on 8 January:

> French have not been entirely frank, as unofficial information indicates they really want to incorporate our regiments into their divisions for such service in the trenches as they desire . . . Our men are working hard and instruction is progressing favourably. Have expressed a willingness to aid in any way in an emergency but do not think good reason yet exists for us to break up our own divisions and scatter regiments for service among French and British, especially

under the guise of instruction. As we are now at war ourselves the integrity of our own forces should be preserved as far as possible.[27]

Pershing was also coming under pressure from the British. On 10 January, Robertson wrote on the question of 'supplying some American battalions for temporary employment with British infantry brigades'. With Entente manpower 'rapidly diminishing' and Germany moving forces west, Robertson admitted that it was 'with considerable anxiety that the British and French authorities look forward to the summer', and he warned that unless they received 'substantial' military assistance, it might be too late. The main problem was a lack of shipping. However, His Majesty's Government was prepared to reduce stocks of food and war materiel, on a temporary basis, to make room for an additional 150,000 US soldiers to be shipped across the Atlantic and placed, either as individual battalions or as brigades, in British divisions. Pershing trusted the British even less than he did the French, but he agreed to Robertson's request, with the caveat that it would be regarded 'as a temporary measure to meet a probable emergency' and that they would be reorganized as full US divisions 'as soon as practicable'.[28]

With Robertson and Lloyd George congratulating themselves on an unexpected coup, Pershing got cold feet. When a joint Anglo-American conference was held at Versailles on 29 January, the British delegation were surprised to learn that the plan had not been approved by Pershing and that both he and General Bliss (who had travelled to Paris) now had severe reservations about it. Instead, Pershing wanted six *whole* divisions (including their supporting units) transported instead, which would mean seventy-two battalions (not the 150 that the British were counting upon). Lloyd George did not take long to state his objections, raising the spectre of a disaster should they not 'amalgamate' these battalions into British divisions. 'We must consider what a terrible thing might happen on this front if Germany with all her resources should turn upon us and should bring the Austrian divisions which might become available; that if Sir Douglas Haig should report to him that a military emergency existed for putting British battalions in French divisions, he would, himself, understand that Haig looked upon it as something that must be done and that he, himself, would be protected by Haig's statement of the necessity for such action.' But Pershing was not budging. There might be a 'general upheaval' against the war if these measures were adopted, which would 'expose the President to considerable criticism', not to mention the concerns among the Irish population in the United States 'if America gave her troops to serve in the British army'.

'The battalions would be under American officers', said Lloyd George.

'The brigade and division commanders would be British', replied Pershing.[29]

If the Americans were standing firm, there was little the British could do about it and Lloyd George knew well enough when to relent. The extra transport would be provided and the US units would train alongside British divisions, but they would come across intact, infantry as well as auxiliary and support troops, not as individual battalions. A similar compromise was hammered out with the French. American divisions would continue to train alongside their French counterparts, including going into the line for acclimatization, but with the view that, once ready, they would be formed into full divisions and put into a dedicated sector of the front. Pershing did, however, offer to send Pétain four regiments of African-American soldiers that had been raised, but which were still awaiting full organization into a division (93rd). Pétain was delighted and said that he would be 'very glad' to have them.[30] Each regiment was assigned to a French division and would become the only elements of the US Army to formally 'amalgamate' with the French.

On 30 January, a full meeting of the Supreme War Council took place in the palatial surroundings of the Hotel Trianon. Everyone was there: Clemenceau, Pétain, Foch, Pershing, Bliss, Lloyd George, Haig and Robertson. The military representatives had already produced a range of studies on the Allies' situation, and a paper, 'Joint Note No. 12', had been circulated, which argued that because neither side was likely to achieve 'a final, or even a far-reaching decision' in the western theatre during the year, the Allies should look to mount a 'decisive offensive against Turkey with a view to the annihilation of the Turkish Armies and the collapse of Turkish resistance'.[31] 'Joint Note No. 12' had Lloyd George's fingerprints all over it. The British Prime Minister was keen to focus efforts on Palestine, which he argued was the most viable theatre for success. General Allenby had been sent to command the Egyptian Expeditionary Force in June 1917 and had pushed forward operations with predictable impatience, capturing Jerusalem on 9 December and raising hopes that the war in the Middle East could be brought to an end quickly.

Clemenceau, in a foul mood, immediately signalled his disquiet with a curious look upon his face as if he was suffering from indigestion. As a strong supporter of Pétain, he knew that remaining on the defensive in France was essential, but he would not agree to the drawing down of forces on the Western Front when 'the enemy were practically knocking at the doors of Paris'. Objections were raised to attacking Turkey from most of the senior commanders present, predictably from Haig and Robertson, but also from Foch and Pétain, who wanted all available resources concentrated in France for the coming battle, leaving Lloyd George 'very badly mauled and I never saw him look more knocked out' (as Robertson noted in a letter to Lord Derby).[32] When the council assembled the following day – tempers having cooled somewhat overnight – 'Joint Note No. 12' was accepted with the important proviso that no forces would be taken from the Western Front and that an offensive against Turkey would not begin for two months (to wait and see what Germany would do).

The other subject was that of a general reserve, a collection of divisions – British, French and Italian – that would be used to react to any German offensive. The idea was widely accepted, although where the divisions would come from, and who would command them, was unclear. Having just extended their line to the south, the British had no troops to spare; the French were already exhausted; and when it was proposed to bring Italian divisions over to France, the Italian delegation protested in the strongest terms. Who would command the reserve and what relationship they would have to the Commanders-in-Chief was similarly controversial. Robertson wanted the Chiefs of Staff of each nation to have joint command, but both Lloyd George and Henry Wilson (Britain's military representative) had no intention of letting Robertson anywhere near them and argued that they must be commanded from Versailles.[33] With this in mind, Lloyd George proposed that they form an Executive War Board consisting of the Permanent Military Representatives of the council with Ferdinand Foch as president – someone who was acceptable both to the French and to the Americans. Foch was 'loyal not only to France but also to the Allies', said Lloyd George as he announced the decision of the council. 'When the British Army in Flanders was in difficulties he threw all his weight into rendering it assistance. So prompt and generous was that assistance that General Foch might almost have been an Englishman himself . . . We can be quite sure that as President of the Committee General Foch would be quite unbiased.'[34]

Robertson, as he usually did, scented trouble. 'Long after the Supreme War Council had risen . . .', recalled a junior assistant at the conference, 'and only a few secretaries being left in the room, Robertson still remained sitting alone in his place, motionless, his head resting on his hand, glaring silently in front of him.'[35] Distrusting Wilson and haunted by the ambush at Calais a year earlier, he saw the council and the push for a general reserve as a dangerous gamble – 'damned rot', as he told Haig. After the meetings in Versailles had wound up in early February, Robertson reported to Lord Derby that the 'real question' over the general reserve was 'one of command' and that they now had a 'French Generalissimo' for 'all practical purposes'. Moreover, 'I do not know how or by whom powers are to be delegated to an officer, not on the Army Council and not directly under you, to issue orders to a Commander-in-Chief of about two million men.'[36] He refused to be bullied into supporting Lloyd George's schemes, and over the next fortnight a furious row broke out in London over the formation of the general reserve and the position of Haig's armies in France. When the Prime Minister offered Robertson the choice of going to Versailles as part of the Executive Committee, with Wilson becoming CIGS in his place, or remaining in London with reduced powers, he would not budge and resigned on 16 February.

The need for greater cohesion within the alliance – a Generalissimo perhaps – had been identified since Joffre's time, but for one reason or another, had always fallen through. But now, darkened by the twin shadows of the Russian collapse and the impending German offensive, the Allies were gradually, gingerly, moving towards the idea of unified command. 'Had the heads of governments been able to exercise their full power, guided solely by their individual judgements, it is possible that the position of Commander-in-Chief, in some form, might have been created at the meeting of the Supreme War Council, January 30–February 2, 1918', wrote Tasker Bliss as he reflected on the long struggle over the general reserve:

> They knew its importance. They knew that it had to be a Frenchman. And they knew General Foch . . . He had impressed them all by his indomitable energy, and the rapidity and accuracy of his decisions, but the heads of governments were not free. They had behind them peoples who had already overturned governments on lesser questions than this. There was no unity of view among the military men – neither as to the need of a Commander-in-Chief nor as to who he should be. And all of these – civilian and military – had first to eat the bitter bread of despair before their governments could act.[37]

★

The crucial part of the front, where Ludendorff would strike, was now occupied by General Sir Hubert Gough's Fifth Army, which had been redeployed from Flanders as part of Haig's promise to relieve the French Sixth Army around Saint-Quentin. Gough had arrived in December and noted, in some dismay, the amount of work that needed to be done. Telephone wires had not been buried and his men, filtering into their new trenches, were quick to complain about the state in which they had been left. The front-line positions were strong enough, but behind them were few reserve positions and fortified strongpoints. Matters were worsened by the state of the ground – alternately muddy or covered over with snow – which had been devastated in the spring of 1917 and had not yet fully recovered. 'There was no life about;' recorded one of Gough's staff officers, 'civilians were not allowed to return to their homes, although they implored us to let them; there were no homes left for them to go to.

Labour battalions lived in the ruins, isolated from the world like men living in caves. We had days of grey leaden skies when the roads shone from the rain and telegraph poles stood out darkly. Here and there were patches of acid-green grass; the country looked drenched and hopeless.'[38]

Infantry battalions, bolstered by Chinese labourers and whatever other units could be scraped together, toiled on Fifth Army's defensive positions throughout the winter as Gough looked on nervously. On 1 February, he warned GHQ that he was likely to be faced with 'a heavy hostile offensive' and urgently required extra companies of Royal Engineers to help in the construction of defences, accommodation and communications. His worst fears were confirmed when he found out that his opposite number was General Hutier, the conqueror of Riga. 'The more recent German attacks . . .', he added, 'have been characterised by a short bombardment up to about 6 hours, and the most strenuous efforts to obtain surprise. These efforts I cannot be sure of defeating . . .' Herbert Lawrence, Haig's new Chief of Staff, replied a week later, confirming that 'in the event of a serious attack being made on your Army on a wide front, your policy should be to secure and protect at all costs the important centre of Péronne and the River Somme'.[39]

In theory, Gough's defences should have consisted of three zones: Forward, Battle and Rear. Troops in the Forward Zone would hold on for as long as possible, inflicting losses on the enemy before the crucial fight for the Battle Zone took place. Fifth Army would then counter-attack and drive the enemy back – a mirror image of the kind of defensive tactics that the German Army had adopted since 1916. But with a front of forty-two miles – the longest in the BEF – Gough worried about how long he would be able to hold. The Forward Zone was satisfactory, with numerous well-wired strongpoints, but his Battle Zone was patchy and his Rear Zone almost non-existent. He had twelve infantry divisions (plus three cavalry divisions), which meant that each one was strung out across three miles of front. To the north, Sir Julian Byng's Third Army was more concentrated, along just twenty-eight miles, with each of his divisions being responsible for a two-mile sector. But Haig remained surprisingly relaxed. At a meeting of his army commanders on 2 March, he noted how 'very pleased' he was with their preparations. 'Plans were sound and thorough, and much work had already been done. I was only afraid that the Enemy would find our front so very strong that he will hesitate to commit his Army to the attack with the almost certainty of losing very heavily.'[40]

There was no danger of that. Things were now slotting into place, moved by what seemed like an irresistible will, impossible to stop. OHL transferred to the resort town of Spa in Belgium on 8 March and an advanced headquarters was also set up at Avesnes, twelve miles south of Maubeuge, where Ludendorff spent most of his time, while the Kaiser shuttled up and down the front on his personal armoured train. The final operation orders for the attack were signed off by Hindenburg on 10 March. With a swift scribble of his pen, he set in motion Germany's final roll of the dice; a last, desperate attempt to appeal against the verdict of the Marne and the failure of the Schlieffen Plan. Reflecting years later, the Field Marshal had no regrets. Remaining on the defensive throughout 1918 was inconceivable. 'A slow death from exhaustion, unless our enemies succumbed to it first, would unquestionably have been our fate.' With her allies beseeching her to act, Germany had to bring the war to an end as soon as possible. 'It cannot be urged against us that even our opponents had come to the extreme limits of their material and moral efforts. If we did not attack they might prolong the war for years, and if any among them had been unwilling to go on he would simply have been compelled to do so by the others.'[41]

By mid-March, Ludendorff had assembled a mass of enormous striking power along the crucial Arras–Saint-Quentin sector. In total, forty-eight divisions were transported from the Eastern Front. Although only six took part in the opening day of the offensive, the rest were able to take over sections of the front and free up divisions for training.[42] Ludendorff's three main armies, Seventeenth, Second and Eighteenth, comprised seventy-seven divisions, over a million men, supported by 6,400 guns, both field and heavy, alongside thousands of trench mortars and almost unlimited shells. An array of elaborate measures were taken to keep the build-up as secret as possible. Plans were only circulated among a 'narrow circle' of senior officers and all movement by troops and vehicles in daylight was forbidden throughout a vast zone stretching between sixty and seventy kilometres from the front. The mass of guns, ammunition, building materials and supplies were either camouflaged as carefully as possible or only brought into position in the final hours before the attack. 'Not a single man in the army must have any doubt in his mind that the fight has already begun, the fight for secrecy and for concealment of our preparations', read a Second Army security order issued in the weeks before the assault. 'Everyone must realize that he himself stands in the midst of this battle and that he must employ the weapons of caution and reticence in order to win out.'[43]

Operation *Michael* would begin at 4.40 a.m. on 21 March. Following the tactical model that had been tested at Riga and Caporetto (as well as in the counter-attack at Cambrai), a five-hour bombardment would clear the way for the infantry to advance. Specially trained teams of stormtroopers, heavily armed with light machine-guns, grenades and flamethrowers, would push on quickly, bypassing centres of resistance and driving as far as possible into the enemy's positions. The 'first great tactical object' of Rupprecht's armies would be 'to cut off the British in the Cambrai Salient' and move rapidly on to Bapaume and Péronne. After holding the line of the Somme, the attackers would then sweep west towards Albert before pivoting north and rolling up the British front. On the left, the armies of the Crown Prince would seize the passages over the Somme and the Crozat Canal, securing the left flank, while holding off any French attempts to counter, leaving Rupprecht to deal with the British unimpeded. What would happen afterwards was impossible to foresee. Subsequent attacks – *Mars* and *Archangel* – 'must depend upon the progress of the operations'.[44]

There was nothing else to do. Morale was high among the German troops now converging on the front, crunching over the metalled roads in long columns and filling up the barracks behind the line. There was an intensity to them that had not been seen since 1914. Across all ranks a steely determination was evident that this would be their final vindication and triumph. One junior officer, waiting to go forward, pondered on what it meant. 'The decisive battle, the last charge, was here. Here the fates of nations would be decided, what was at stake was the future of the world. I sensed the weight of the hour, and I think everyone felt the individual in them dissolve, and fear depart.' He remembered that the 'mood was curious, brimming with tension and a kind of exaltation'.[45] Everyone felt it; when time seemed to slow and freeze as if the planets were themselves hanging in the balance. A staff officer, Albrecht von Thaer, could barely write the entry in his diary the night before the assault, so bad was the tremor in his hands: 'Here in the west we stand before the future as before a dark curtain.'[46]

20.   'I fear it means disaster'

The morning of 21 March – '*der Tag*' as it was known in the German Army – dawned with a thick white-grey fog that covered everything, grounding aeroplanes, blinding observers and playing havoc with the carefully calculated schedules for the preliminary bombardment. Ludendorff had spent the previous day closeted with his meteorologist, Dr Schmaus, who kept him updated on the latest atmospheric conditions, particularly the strength and direction of the wind. Because German planners were relying heavily upon gas to neutralize the enemy's defences, it was essential that the wind was not too strong or blowing in the wrong direction. There was also the problem of fog, which would interfere with the movement of men across the battle-field. Ludendorff had no intention of calling off the attack; that 'would have been very hard to do', as he noted years later.[1] With his staff officers frantically trying to make the necessary adjustments, the army groups were notified at noon that the programme would go ahead as planned. Although the wind died down during the night, the fog was heavier than expected, blanketing the battlefield in a strange, ominous mist, broken only by the occasional flare.

The bombardment opened at 4.40 a.m. with a series of heavy thuds, before the mass of field batteries and trench mortars joined in, producing a thunderous roar that echoed around the landscape, dipping and rolling. Along a fifty-mile front – from the River Scarpe to La Fère – the British forward positions came under a rain of gas and steel, which pulverized trenches and sent great geysers of earth surging into the air. 'The dense wall of fog is filled with sulphurous flashes, and the noise is so monstrous that it obliterates everything', wrote a German eyewitness. 'Only a natural disaster or the end of the world comes close to such force.'[2] It continued for five hours, alternating between trench destruction and counter-battery fire, severing communications and shrouding artillery batteries in clouds of gas.

First the Germans released 'blue cross' (chloropicrin or diphenyl chloroarsine); a fine dust that was designed to cause fits of sneezing and vomiting, making those affected unable to wear their gas masks. This was then followed up by repeated doses of phosgene, combined with bombardments of mustard gas on selected locations, particularly the Flesquières Salient near Cambrai, which was going to be pinched off, not attacked directly. Finally, after being subjected to years of repeated attacks, the horrors of tanks, endless 'drumfire' and week-long bombardments, the German Army would have its revenge.

General Otto von Below's Seventeenth Army had what was, by common consent, the most difficult task: pivoting to the southwest of Arras before heading for Bapaume. In his operation orders (dated 27 February), Below stated that 'With the first overwhelming blow, as many English divisions as possible, including reserves, must be destroyed in order to create the conditions for further operations.'[3] His troops faced General Sir Julian Byng's Third Army, which was in well-established defensive positions and, unlike Gough's Fifth Army to the south, had reserves much closer to hand. The attack was finally launched at 9.40 a.m., with Below's assaulting divisions springing forward behind a *Feuerwalze* ('fire roller') that crept towards their objectives, still partially hidden in the gloom. 'The first waves rush into the cratered field of no-man's-land, above which thick smoke is settling', recorded one account. 'The first waves advance quickly and with a loud cheer, paying no attention to their casualties, caused initially by the short-rounds of their own artillery and mortar fire, they break into the English lines.' Within twenty minutes most of Byng's Forward Zone had been captured with 'strikingly little resistance'.[4]

The left flank of Operation *Michael* had been entrusted to Eighteenth Army, which had been ordered 'to throw the enemy back over the Somme and the Crozat Canal', and to do so in 'an unstoppable manner', which reflected the aggression and self-confidence of its commander, General Oskar von Hutier.[5] They would strike the southern half of Gough's Fifth Army, a nineteen-mile sector of the front from Saint-Quentin down to the Oise river, and with thirteen divisions in the first wave (against just six defending ones), they enjoyed a sizeable numerical advantage. The fog lay particularly thick along this part of the line, masking the approach of the attacking battalions. It was only in the final moments before the collision, when British sentries, peering out into the unnatural murk, saw the ghostly figures of stormtroopers almost upon them, helmeted, wearing gas masks that gave them an unearthly, goggled-eyed appearance. Stunned by the bombardment and cut off from their supporting artillery, the defenders were quickly overwhelmed, either annihilated where they stood or taken prisoner. In a matter of hours, about a third of Gough's entire force had been swallowed up – leaving an enormous gap in the line.[6]

Gough was not a soldier who enjoyed waiting around for news, so he drove out to see his corps commanders, finding them sanguine and cheerful in spite of the darkening scene. He told them that 'our policy was to fight a delaying action, holding up the enemy as long as possible, without involving the troops in a decisive struggle to hold any position'.[7] But already his army was fighting for its life. The loss of most of the Forward Zone in the first few hours of the attack was catastrophic. Perhaps as many as 21,000 British soldiers were taken prisoner that day, rounded up in their redoubts as the German tide washed over them. Some resisted for hours, surrounded by smoking spent cartridges, while others quickly realized there was no hope against such overwhelming odds and surrendered *en masse*. Such a startling collapse of resistance revealed how sapping and demoralizing the war had become. Of the twenty-one British divisions involved that day, nineteen had seen action at Passchendaele and many senior officers were not slow to blame the heavy fighting of the previous year, as well as the reduction in the size of British divisions, for much of what happened.[8]

Fighting was as brutal in the air as it was on the ground. Above the smoke-blackened battlefield, a thick aerial screen of German fighters was out in force, patrolling over the advancing armies. The 'Amerika Programme' had resulted in a surge of aircraft production, and in the opening days of the offensive Germany concentrated over 800 aircraft (against 600 British and French machines).[9] Those few Allied pilots who managed to get airborne reported seeing long columns of infantry and cavalry, even a smattering of German tanks in action. As well as a handful of refurbished Mark IVs, the German Army had also sent into battle four of its own vehicles, the A7V *Sturmpanzerwagen*, which was based on the Holt tractor and had a crew of eighteen. Although it was relatively fast (with a top speed over even ground of 8 mph) and bristled with machine-guns, it was a clumsy design, akin to a moving pillbox that presented an inviting target. Four machines were deployed around Saint-Quentin, but they made only a modest impact, being relegated to mopping up positions rather than leading the charge forward – reflecting OHL's rather ambivalent attitude to mechanical warfare. The breakthrough would come from German infantry that were now spreading out towards the main line of British defences – the Battle Zone – like hounds scenting prey.

At GHQ, Haig was, as yet, unaware of the extent of the disaster engulfing his southern flank. He was informed of the German bombardment at eight o'clock that morning, just as he was getting dressed, but it was not until three hours later that telephone calls were received from Third and Fifth Armies reporting a massive infantry assault. In spite of the unnerving news, he remained upbeat. 'Very severe fighting on the Third and Fifth Army fronts continued well into the evening', he wrote. 'Our men seemed to be fighting magnificently.'[10] Gough was authorized to withdraw his right flank back to the Crozat Canal while two divisions from GHQ reserve were ordered to move to Noyon. An official communiqué was also sent to Pétain after midnight alerting him to the serious situation unfolding along the British sector. It had been agreed to concentrate up to six divisions (of the French Third Army) around Montdidier and Noyon by the fourth day of any offensive and now Haig wanted them brought up 'as soon as possible'.[11]

Pétain spent 21 March at his desk at Compiègne, listening to the long rumbling of artillery fire and studiously ignoring the rumours that swept through the corridors of GQG as staff officers looked at each other nervously. He knew that the German attack was extremely dangerous, possibly the great offensive they had been expecting, but he worried about Champagne – where there had been unusually heavy artillery fire – and wondered whether it might precede an imminent attack. But as the situation in Fifth Army worsened, and before he had even heard from Haig, he ordered three divisions to move north the following day.[12] Coincidentally, both Poincaré and Clemenceau were visiting and met with Pétain to discuss the situation. 'The President of France and Clemenceau are calm,' reported a government liaison officer; 'General Pétain is too, but everyone is solemn because we can sense the seriousness of the hour.'[13]

By nightfall the German attack had gained about four and a half kilometres; a solid feat by the standards of trench warfare, but well short of their objectives for the day. The British had been able to make more of a stand in the Battle Zone, where they held a series of sandbagged redoubts, fortified farms or hills. By the time the attackers were upon them, the fog had burnt off, presenting their machine-gunners with excellent targets as masses of *Feldgrau* jogged across the long, open fields. Resistance was toughest in the north, where Below's troops struggled to bring up enough firepower to overwhelm the defences. The narrow roads behind the line were clogged with infantry, and batteries of field artillery took hours to get into position, struggling over cratered ground softened by the rain. At his headquarters in Cambrai, Rupprecht worried that not enough had been achieved. The target had been to seize the mass of the enemy's guns on the first day, but Équancourt, where the link-up between the Second and Seventeenth Armies would take place, was still almost six kilometres away and Second Army had only captured fifty guns.[14] For once Ludendorff shared Rupprecht's pessimism: 'According to reports . . . the result of the first day of battle could by no means be considered fully satisfactory.' Nevertheless, there could be no thought of stopping the offensive, so evening orders were issued for the continuation of the attack. Ludendorff also alerted six reserve divisions to begin moving up behind Eighteenth Army, deciding that his only course of action was to reinforce its success.[15]

Fighting was resumed on the morning of the second day, with Ludendorff continuing to feed divisions into the battle, widening the breakthrough and letting his commanders probe for any weaknesses in the increasingly ragged British line. With most of the forward positions having been overrun, a series of running battles were fought as both Third and Fifth Armies fell back, holding on in places or retreating as quickly as possible in others. Years later the Crown Prince would still remember vividly the frantic first days of Operation *Michael*. 'As if shaking off some horrible nightmare my infantry had risen from its trenches and crushing all resistance with unexampled vigour had broken through the enemy's defensive system.' That morning, 22 March, he had driven through the streets of Saint-Quentin (nothing but 'a dead heap of stones'), which were crowded with 'waves of interminable columns and marching troops'. 'All around me cheerful faces,' he wrote, 'cheers and shouts at my car, which had great difficulty in threading its way forward, an irresistible onward march, the beating pulse of a victorious army . . .'[16]

Ludendorff's disappointment at the opening day of the offensive remained, but Saturday, 23 March, finally saw the kinds of gains that he had been waiting for, and that morning he excitedly telephoned General Georg von der Marwitz at Second Army to tell him that 'it's going great'.[17] The Flesquières Salient, which had remained a thorn in the side of the German line since the Cambrai fighting of the previous autumn, was abandoned, with General Byng ordering his troops to pull out lest they be outflanked and surrounded, while, to the south, Hutier was given the all-clear to cross the Crozat Canal and push further eastwards. By the evening his men had even reached the line of the Somme and marched into Péronne – packs of German troops, grenades in hand, fighting British rearguards through the burning streets. That afternoon (23 March), Haig ordered the line of the Somme Canal, from Ham to Péronne, to be held at all costs: 'There must be no withdrawal from this line. It is of the greatest importance that the Fifth Army should effect a junction with the French on their right without delay.'[18]

Ludendorff now sensed an opportunity. On the afternoon of 23 March, he held a conference at Avesnes (at which Kuhl and Schulenburg were present) to explain a significant change to his plans. A 'considerable part' of the BEF had now been defeated and it was highly unlikely that the French would be capable of a relief offensive. The aim of German operations was, therefore, to separate the Allies 'by a rapid advance either side of the Somme' and then 'throw the British into the sea'. Seventeenth Army would push northwest in a wide sweep towards Doullens and Saint-Pol, Second Army would make for Amiens, while Eighteenth Army crossed the Somme in the direction of Noyon, trying to force the French Army back over the Aisne.[19] Instead of focusing all their efforts in a single direction, Ludendorff was now proposing that the offensive should diverge along three different routes, aiming to strike the British and French at the same time.

Kuhl was confused. 'Thus the High Command had decided to change its plan completely', he was to write years later. 'Hitherto the attack of the Second and Seventeenth Armies on the British had constituted the main effort. It had been the task of the Eighteenth Army to cover this attack against [any] action of the French. Now it was proposed to separate the French and British from each other and to attack both simultaneously.' Whether they could achieve such an enormous task with the forces available was not mentioned. 'The danger of dispersion was undoubtedly present.' But Ludendorff had little choice and, upon reflection, even Kuhl admitted as much. It had not been possible to attack further north because of the strong defences in the Arras sector, including the old Vimy battlefield, and even if troops could have been redeployed from Eighteenth Army and sent north to reinforce the main effort, they might have arrived too late and Germany would then have been faced with deadlock on both wings. Ludendorff *had* to strike out in as many directions as possible. Eighteenth Army had hit a weak point and so it would continue in the hope that once on the run their enemies would never stop.[20]

For a moment it seemed that the German advance, like a great river in full flow, would burst its banks and become unstoppable. Bapaume fell on 25 March. Eighteenth Army had now taken Noyon and Nesle and was closing in on Chaulnes, while Albert was abandoned on the afternoon of 26 March with German troops marching past the ruined basilica that had been such a beacon to the troops of 1916. 'We dug ourselves in, time after time, with almost incredible labour and just as we were getting the enemy where we wanted them, i.e., in the V of our rifle sights, the order to retire came' was a familiar complaint from one British officer.[21] Gough's Fifth Army was now falling apart. What had formerly been a proud, disciplined fighting force was disintegrating into a collection of broken units, dead-eyed and exhausted, stumbling on in dust-caked columns towards the setting sun. Gough tried to maintain morale, motoring up and down the front, but behind the lines a feeling of panic was rising as a major withdrawal got under way. 'Camps and canteens had already cleared away', noted one observer; 'trains at railway sidings were being loaded up. Chinese and all other available labour was working at the dumps – what could not be shifted was being blown up. Forward casualty clearing-stations had folded and packed up their tents; bonfires were clearing up the rubbish.'[22]

The first note of uncertainty could also be detected at GHQ. Haig had hitherto struck a determined attitude, confident that the enemy was being dealt a series of stopping blows, but the widening hole in the British sector was impossible to hide, causing him to look anxiously to the south for French support. The two Commanders-in-Chief met on Sunday, 24 March, at Dury, a sleepy village three miles south of Amiens where Haig had set up his advanced headquarters. Ever since the beginning of the offensive, Pétain had sent a steady stream of divisions north, while also placing the two northernmost French armies, Third and First, under General Fayolle as part of a reactivated Reserve Army Group to coordinate the defensive effort and ensure that their forces kept in touch. But when Haig asked Pétain to 'concentrate as large a force as he could, and as soon as possible, astride the Somme about Amiens to support the British right', *say twenty divisions*, Pétain was horrified. This was a far greater level of support than had been agreed beforehand and, moreover, there were 'definite signs' that he was going to be attacked in Champagne (where an impressive German deceptive effort was under way) and he worried lest his precious reserve divisions, carefully hoarded, would be spent, leaving him with few troops to react to a second enemy blow. He would give Fayolle 'all the troops he could', but if a retirement was ordered, then his men were to fall back south towards Paris.[23]

Haig was now suffering the same torments that had gripped Sir John French in the dark days of October 1914. He found himself struggling to react to a battle that was moving far quicker than he had anticipated and, uncharacteristically, discovered his nerves beginning to trouble him. Sir Henry Wilson – Robertson's replacement as CIGS – saw Haig on 25 March and could not help recording his 'cowed' appearance after he told Wilson that the 'whole French Army' needed to move up, otherwise they should 'make peace on any terms we could'.[24] Gough was relieved of command on 27 March, with Haig putting Henry Rawlinson in his place as part of a reconstituted Fourth Army (Rawlinson's headquarters having been disbanded in 1917); a move that he hoped would bolster his increasingly precarious position. Already a quickening of pace was evident in Allied governments as the scale of the offensive began to sink in. In London, Lloyd George – always fearing disaster where Haig was concerned – quickly resolved to meet the crisis head on. He despatched Lord Milner to act as his emissary for a series of high-level discussions with the French, which had been hurriedly put together – with not even the Americans being invited. 'Things look very bad. I fear it means disaster', he told the newspaper proprietor, Lord Riddell. 'They have broken through, and the question is what there is behind to stop them . . . The French are now bringing up their reserves, but it may be too late.'[25]

The Town Hall at Doullens – eighteen miles north of Amiens – was the unlikely setting for an emergency gathering of Allied leaders on 26 March. Haig held a series of meetings with his army commanders that morning, but it was not until noon that the French delegation – Poincaré and Clemenceau with Pétain and Foch – arrived. The British Commander-in-Chief took the lead, urging 'the absolute necessity of the French hurrying forward as large reinforcements as possible from the south to support General Gough's Army which had been in the battle since the 21st without a pause'. Pétain then pointedly reminded Haig that Fifth Army 'was no longer a fighting force' and that nine of his divisions were already engaged in the battle with fifteen more being detrained as he was speaking. The discussion ranged back and forth for some time. Everyone was in agreement that '*Amiens must be covered at all costs*', but how were they to relieve Gough's shattered divisions? Pétain said that 'he was moving everything as fast as possible', while Foch gave his usual bromide about 'the necessity of instant action and of impressing on all troops that they must give up no ground'.[26]

Haig was not the only one worried about Pétain's mood. During a brief stroll around the grounds of the Town Hall shortly before the meeting had started – 'beneath a pure sky and quite a sharp cold' – Pétain told Clemenceau that he had issued orders for his troops to cover Paris if they were forced to retreat.

'The Germans will defeat the British in open country', he told him; 'after which they will beat us as well.'

Clemenceau, who had never lost his fighting spirit, found such a defeatist attitude inexcusable. He hurried off to see Poincaré and told him that Pétain's pessimism was 'irritating': 'Should a general speak or even think this way?'

Foch – hovering nearby, his hands clasped behind his back – soon confirmed these suspicions, but added that the situation was not as bleak as Pétain seemed to think. 'Common sense shows that when the enemy wants to open a hole, you don't make it any bigger. You close it, or you try to close it. We only have to try and to want to; the rest will be easy. We cling to the ground, and we defend it step by step. We did it in Ypres, we did it in Verdun.'[27]

Evidently Pétain did not have the confidence of either Foch or Haig to command the coming battle. After the meeting had broken up into small groups, Clemenceau spoke with Lord Milner and then called Haig over. It was agreed that the British would accept the direction of Foch, who would be 'charged by the British and French Governments with the co-ordination of the action of the British and French Armies in front of Amiens'. This was agreed, only for Haig to say that authority was required over the whole Western Front and Pétain, sitting in silence, nodded in acquiescence. With that the meeting ended and the generals strolled outside into the bright spring air, feeling that a great burden had been lifted from their shoulders. Foch, who had now completed his rehabilitation to the front ranks of Allied command after being '*limogé*' following the Somme, was undaunted by the task he faced. A plan of action was swiftly pulled together: 'The French and British troops must keep close together in order to cover Amiens'; 'the forces already in action must maintain their positions at all costs'; and French reinforcements would firstly 'consolidate' Fifth Army and then 'constitute a mass of manoeuvre' for future operations. Pétain's orders to retire to the southwest were swiftly cancelled.[28]

Haig would later claim that Pétain was 'very much upset, almost unbalanced and most anxious' at this time, his nerve breaking under the terrible strain, convinced that the end was near. But Pétain held up well enough, a staff officer at GQG noting the 'undisturbed look and careful speech he assumed at critical times', with the only concern being visible in 'a movement of his eyelids'.[29] But, crucially, Pétain's very calmness, his refusal to be flustered or make sweeping changes to his arrangements, militated against him in March 1918. He had spent the war trying to protect his men from the full fury of modern war, assuming the mantle of high command at a time when the French Army had almost been broken by overzealous leaders eager to drive it forward. He would, therefore, not commit his divisions to the furnace lightly; if Foch wanted them, then so be it. He was not yet convinced that Germany was spent; all his soldierly instincts told him that somewhere out there new reserves were being mustered and that he must be alive to it.

As the Allies underwent their own moment of reckoning, Ludendorff's offensive began to run out of steam. Exhaustion now began to act as a drag on Germany's soldiers; a headwind they could never escape. The days were wintry and cold, with grey-blown skies hinting at snow. Slogging forward across the old Somme battlefield, a topsy-turvy 'crater field' still littered with mouldering bodies and crumbling trenches, depressed the spirits and made men long for 'the first breath of the Atlantic in Amiens', as one German officer put it: 'No desert of salt is more desolate.'[30] When General Marwitz first drove through it, he could only marvel at the destruction around him:

> What changes this land has had to endure; it is now a desert, terrible to behold, mournful in the grey of endless dust that covers everything along the treeless avenues. Many tanks, England's hope, stand around; they occasionally held up troops, usually they do not work . . . Yesterday's journey through the warzone of the Battle of the Somme was the saddest sight so far: places could only be found

with difficulty, conspicuous crater fields covered with sparse, dead grass and scattered, in between, small English crosses. The journey like this continues for hours, often on wagonways. That is northern France! Overcoming this zone is also hard for us; if it were not for the English barracks standing all over the place, it would be virtually impossible. The troops are showing a superhuman performance and their morale is nevertheless good.[31]

On 24 March, Marwitz was driven out to Gouzeaucourt, a ruined village that had been devastated during the fighting at Cambrai, where he met the Kaiser and Hindenburg. The Supreme War Lord's mood had been 'sluggish' since the beginning of the offensive, but he comforted himself with the thought that the 'territorial gains were consistently larger than anything the French and English had achieved'.[32] Wilhelm was having breakfast when Marwitz turned up, and he was promptly handed a bowl of soup and a medal (the Commander's Cross of the Order of Hohenzollern).

'But, Your Majesty, the battle is not yet over.'

'The first part of the great battle is . . .', replied the Kaiser.

Marwitz accepted the award with thanks as the Kaiser went over to Hindenburg, pointing to a star on his chest – the Blücher Star – that had been awarded because he 'had gained a victory against the English'. Hindenburg did not flinch; 'he stood like a wall', saying nothing.[33]

As so often in the past, the Kaiser's optimism was premature. It was true that within barely a week the German Army had taken 90,000 prisoners and conquered vast amounts of ground – far exceeding anything the Allies had achieved since 1914 – but, crucially, they had not dealt a mortal blow to their enemies.[34] The British and French forces had been battered but not separated, and with Foch now charged with coordinating the defence of Amiens, they were beginning to show a greater degree of cohesion than ever before. Germany had also suffered heavy and irreplaceable losses. Between 21 March and 10 April, the three attacking armies sustained 239,800 casualties, the brunt in the elite storm divisions that had led the attack. These were now increasingly being replaced by lesser units, those drawn

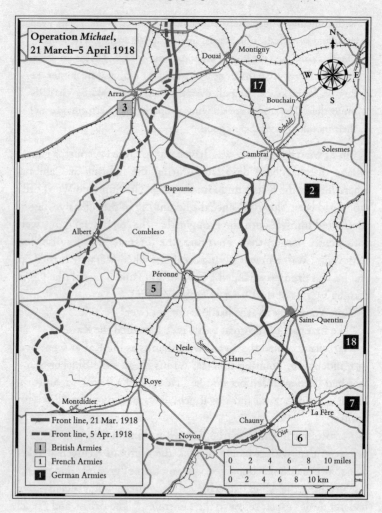

**Operation *Michael*,
21 March–5 April 1918**

Front line, 21 Mar. 1918
Front line, 5 Apr. 1918
| 1 | British Armies
| 1 | French Armies
| 1 | German Armies

from the east, lacking in aggression and skill. The *Westheer* thus found itself in a vulnerable position, stretched out along a 150-kilometre front (compared to ninety kilometres at the beginning of Operation *Michael*) from the Scarpe down to Montdidier and then back through Noyon to La Fère. It was now in the open, having left the comfort and protection of the Hindenburg Line far behind.[35]

The momentum of the assault was quickly draining away, an inevitable result of moving so far so fast. No matter how many miles had been covered, there always seemed many more to go. By late March, Eighteenth Army was over fifty kilometres from its railheads and its supply columns were falling behind.[36] Hutier pushed his men as hard as he could, but his troops were being stretched out across an ever widening front and they inevitably began to follow Napoleon's dictum of living off the land, only this time scavenging whatever could be found from the British supply dumps that had been overrun – filled with tinned meat and stew, bread and whisky. German soldiers found the sheer abundance of Allied supplies both wondrous and demoralizing – shattering any illusions they might have had about the extent to which the submarine war had starved their enemies into submission. One battalion commander in Seventeenth Army, Major Holthausen, recalled how their advance began to stall soon after his men found an abandoned British supply depot, 'stuffed with good things, the like of which had not for many a long day passed their lips, and it was by no means easy for us officers to tear them from the feast thus spread before them so temptingly'.[37]

As Germany's offensive power waned, that of her opponents grew. French fighter squadrons were over the Somme by the third day of the battle, and with each succeeding day more and more Allied aircraft were in action, sweeping down upon German columns, machine-gunning and bombing them with everything they had. One German bugler reported how his company lost twelve men killed and another eight wounded by enemy flyers during their advance through the Somme. Suddenly there 'appeared before us some twenty British aeroplanes which dived to a height of about 100 to 200 metres, and then, continuing to within 2–3 metres of the ground, attacked us with their machine-guns. At first we thought they intended to land; but we speedily saw the danger, and opened a vigorous fire upon them.'[38] That day his battalion shot down five machines, but other units were not so fortunate and a weary sense of unease grew in German hearts as they looked up towards the skies, their ears pricked for the whine of engines roaring down upon them.

Both Seventeenth and Second Armies had made little progress for days, with General Byng's Third Army fighting hard for every piece of ground. French divisions were also moving up quickly, having taken over the front up to Roye on the Avre river. In their haste to push on, German units were increasingly throwing caution to the wind, abandoning the carefully prepared infiltration tactics that had worked so well on 21 March and attacking in large numbers without enough time to prepare properly. But Ludendorff would tolerate no delay and issued orders that the attacks were to go on. When reports came in that the advance was slowing down, he grew increasingly exasperated, prone to telephoning his subordinates at all hours. 'He was quite beside himself', remembered Rupprecht after Ludendorff had rung up one evening, complaining that Seventeenth Army was 'doing nothing'. Afterwards Rupprecht spoke to his Chief of Staff and they discussed how best to help General Below; he was, they said, 'not to shy away from losses' if necessary.[39]

As so many other general officers had found out, sooner or later the war would consume you. Ludendorff's stepson, Erich, was reported missing on 23 March. His body was eventually found in a shallow grave near Nesle, close to where his aircraft had crash-landed. From this moment a raggedness and shortness of temper, a barely concealed frustration, became noticeable in Ludendorff's demeanour. His nerves 'have completely gone', noted one of Rupprecht's staff officers. 'It is a crime to leave him in charge of commanding the armies. All our divisions will be placed in an operationally impossible position, facing stronger resistance in tactically disadvantageous conditions. So our divisions will be rendered useless. We could have forced a decision, if we'd been handled properly!'[40] Ludendorff cared little for what his subordinates thought of him and gambled that he could continue attacking on either flank, widening the frontage in the hope that the line could be broken and the offensive resumed.

Operation *Mars* was launched on 28 March with three corps attacking Arras and trying to roll up Vimy Ridge from the southeast. A heavy *Feuerwalze* preceded the attack and seven divisions were able to overrun the front trenches, but stalled against the 'virtually undamaged' second position. German losses were 'particularly heavy' – about 5,000 casualties, including over 1,000 missing in action. For once, everything had gone right for the defenders. A subsequent post-mortem concluded that the enemy's defences had simply been too strong. Particularly disappointing was the failure to silence British artillery batteries, which joined the fight with 'great violence' soon after the attacking divisions went over the top.[41] The abject failure of *Mars* was a turning point, a day that revealed how the balance of forces was now slipping against Germany. Attacking one of the most heavily fortified sectors of the front had produced deadlock and wasted yet more precious time. Ludendorff's plans for 1918 had been predicated on the need to strike quickly before the Americans could deploy in strength, but with each passing day his numerical advantage eroded.

General Pershing may not have been present at Doullens, but he threw his full support behind Foch's leadership. On 28 March, the day that Ludendorff's divisions had been repulsed at Arras, he drove out to the headquarters of the French Third Army at Clermont-sur-Oise, threading his way past 'continuous columns of motor trucks', before he found Foch, Pétain and Clemenceau in a small farmhouse, 'intently studying a map spread on the table'. Foch took Pershing aside and explained that the British had already deployed about thirty divisions, the French another seventeen, and that seventy-eight enemy divisions had been identified in action. Pershing assured him that 'the Americans were ready and anxious to do their part' and he would send whatever troops were available. 'He was evidently very much touched', Pershing observed, 'and in his enthusiasm took me by the arm and without hesitation rushed me out across the lawn to where the others stood and asked me to repeat what I had said to him.' Very quickly orders were drafted for five US divisions (then undergoing training) to move immediately into the line, each relieving two French ones. 'As our divisions were more than twice as large as theirs,' Pershing noted, 'it amounted to [an] almost immediate reinforcement of ten divisions.'[42]

On 3 April, another meeting of Allied leaders was held at Beauvais, this time with US participation, where the powers that had been conferred on Foch at Doullens were confirmed and enlarged. Foch was entrusted formally with the 'strategic direction of military operations' on the Western Front. Each national commander would have 'full control of the tactical action of their respective armies' and were given a right of appeal to their own governments if they felt Foch's orders 'endangered' their armies.[43] It was an arrangement that finally brought about unified command in France – a long, tortuous process had now come to an end – although it remained to be seen how well it would work in practice. Foch issued a general directive later that day setting out his intention to drive the enemy away from the railway junction at Amiens by a joint Franco-British offensive astride the Somme. Almost immediately, Foch's presence – his character and will – made itself felt. 'Pétain is in thrall to Foch, who always has the same audacious and stern temperament', wrote Fayolle.[44]

The failure of *Mars* left the German High Command in a quandary, stuck in suspended animation, struggling to work out what to do next. Their three attacking armies had now come to a standstill, their offensive power spent. On 3 April, the day that Foch had been crowned Generalissimo, 'general directions' were issued for the conduct of future operations. *Saint-George*, an attack between the La Bassée Canal and Armentières, which had originally been conceived as a 'second act' to Operation *Michael*, was now dusted off and renamed *Georgette*, with the right wing of Sixth Army crossing the Lys in a northwesterly direction, while Fourth Army continued the attack to the north towards Messines if the British line showed signs of crumbling. But now the certainty of success was replaced by a gnawing sense of unease. 'So the second act of the mighty operation begins', noted Kuhl. 'Hopefully it will lead to a decisive victory over the English because we cannot continue to operate in this way (replacements, munitions, horses etc.) . . .'[45]

Once again, German forces were gathered. Huge stocks of ammunition were brought forward to feed the guns and almost 500 aircraft were massed overhead. The terrain was hardly ideal for a breakthrough attempt, but Ludendorff hoped that the unusually dry spring would offer his men the best chance of making progress across the flat, marshy ground. The shelling began at 4.15 a.m. on 9 April with a four-and-a-half-hour bombardment, high explosive mixed with phosgene, targeting roads and bivouacs, trenches and the few buildings still left standing. Eight divisions, none of which had been involved in the March fighting, were massed to go forward, half of which were concentrated against 2nd Portuguese Division, which held the front around the village of Neuve Chapelle – the scene of Haig's first trench battle three years earlier. The Portuguese had joined the war in March 1916 after seizing German vessels in their ports, and eventually sent an expeditionary force of two divisions to France a year later, but they were an uneasy fit alongside the BEF. The British suspected the Portuguese were a weak point, and the local corps commander had warned of unrest in the division, but before the Portuguese could be taken out of the line the Germans struck.

Under a 'constant shower of shrapnel', the Portuguese line melted away. German gun batteries hit everything they could find – roads and tracks; communication trenches and headquarters; casualty clearing stations and reserve positions – causing a thick black smoke to spread out across the whole Lys plain. It was 'diabolical', recorded one witness, 'an infernal rain of red-hot iron'.[46] Soon groups of defenders were streaming back from their forward positions, impervious to their officers and the desperate attempts to rally them. A British divisional staff officer, Captain Harry Graham, managed to find their commander, Major-General Manuel Gomes da Costa, who remained in his 'half-shattered chateau . . . sitting by himself in an attitude of a captain refusing to leave his sinking ship'.[47] That day the Portuguese Expeditionary Force would lose over 7,000 casualties and leave a gaping hole in the British line.

Haig's mood had lifted markedly since Doullens, but the violence of the German assault over the Lys revived all his old fears for the Channel ports. The southern sector of the attack held firm, where 55th Division defended the ruins of Givenchy, but in the centre the Germans were able to punch through the thin Portuguese screen and reach the line of the Lys at Estaires, threatening to turn Armentières from the south. Foch was visiting GHQ that day and found Haig sunk in depression. This proved that the Germans were aiming 'at the destruction of the British Army', Haig said, arguing that his front should be reduced immediately, allowing him to form a reserve 'to keep the battle going', while giving the enemy 'a smaller target to strike at'. But Foch was unyielding. He refused to part with any more French divisions, which were needed elsewhere, and expected Haig to get on with it. Moreover, he reminded Haig that 'maintaining absolute control of the current front in Flanders is just as important as in the region of Arras'; and that 'all voluntary evacuation such as that from the Passchendaele Ridge, can only be interpreted by the enemy as a sign of weakness and a prompting to take the offensive, and as a result should be avoided unless under direct attack from the enemy'.[48]

The British Commander-in-Chief had little choice but to scramble around for manpower, only to find that his reserves were now all but gone. Between 21 March and 5 April the expeditionary force had sustained 178,000 casualties – almost the strength of an entire army.[49] He went to see General Plumer, who offered two of his reserve divisions, which provided a welcome reinforcement of his line against an attack that showed little sign of ending. Ludendorff pressed the attack on succeeding days, throwing in more divisions, taking Armentières and advancing towards the crucial road and rail junction at Hazebrouck. Whereas Operation *Michael* had thrust wildly into miles of open ground, the advance over the Lys was closing in on multiple valuable objectives: Ypres and Kemmel Hill (a crucial high point), as well as the Bruay coal mines (from where most of the fuel powering France's armaments production came). It also threatened to cut the entire British sector in two, like a knife to Haig's throat. On 11 April, Haig – by now at his wits' end – issued a 'Special Order of the Day', asking his men to stand and fight where they were: 'There is no other course open to us but to fight it out. Every position must be held to the last man: there must be no retirement. With our backs to the wall and believing in the justice of our cause each one of us must fight on to the end.'[50]

Haig's words were deeply uncharacteristic of the usually undemonstrative and dour Scotsman. The mood at GHQ was depressed, possibly at one of its lowest ebbs during the war, as defeat seemed close. Ignoring Foch's advice not to make voluntary withdrawals, Plumer ordered his men off the Passchendaele Ridge on 12 April, shortening his line and providing much-needed forces to hold on to the battered front. But, yet again, the advance congealed and then stopped. German troops had taken Bailleul and managed to get within six miles of Hazebrouck, but then *Georgette* stalled. The ground was difficult and there were few roads, and most of them ran across the line of advance (north–south not east–west), which made it difficult to bring up enough manpower and artillery to support subsequent attacks. With enemy machine-guns seemingly concealed in every fold of ground, farmhouse or shell hole, German troops took heavy losses trying to push on, while the overcast skies interfered with aerial observation and artillery spotting. But there was something else as well. The fighting spirit of the attackers, so noticeable in March, had vanished. Hermann von Kuhl's verdict was stark. 'The troops appear finished', was all he would say when asked what had gone wrong.[51]

21. 'Hold the line at all hazards'

Finding Beauvais too crowded for his liking, the new Allied supreme commander moved out to the village of Sarcus (about twenty miles to the northwest) on 7 April, accompanied by his close friend and Chief of Staff, Maxime Weygand. Foch's headquarters was modelled on the arrangements of his former army group and never contained more than twenty members of staff – with the general preferring a quiet, stable routine. The main problem was finding suitable accommodation. 'The general was housed at a chateau located in the centre of the village, on one side of a large fairground, the other side being occupied by the church', noted Weygand. 'Mrs B—, his hostess, whose husband was in the army, waited for him on the threshold surrounded by her five, still very young children. She asked him if she could continue to live at home without fear. The general reassured her in marked terms with such good grace and confidence that as I heard it I wished that all of France could hear it too.'[1]

Lieutenant-General Sir John Du Cane, a former corps commander, went to Sarcus on 12 April to act as Haig's liaison officer. Haig had pulled Du Cane out of the front line and told him that there had been problems with 'unity of command' and that he was being sent to do 'something with Foch'. Much like the situation that had faced Vallières when he arrived at GHQ in December 1915, Du Cane was an outsider, treated with suspicion until he had been able to prove his worth. He initially found Foch to be 'difficult to follow' (as he wrote in a letter to Sir Henry Wilson). 'He repeats certain phrases constantly without explaining what he means by them . . . Only those who have been with him for some time and have been in his confidence are able readily to interpret his ideas.' Du Cane, therefore, found himself relying upon Weygand, who had worked with Foch for years and had 'imbibed his military education from him'. Notwithstanding these observations, Du Cane was deeply impressed by

Foch. 'In spite of his age he appears to me to be exceptionally alert in body and mind, and to be of a masterful and determined character. He knows what he wants and gets it done.'[2]

Every day the number and location of enemy divisions were tracked closely. Foch estimated that Germany still had up to forty-eight divisions in reserve, ready to go into battle, which forced him to husband his own resources jealously.[3] Foch's initial instructions to Haig and Pétain had been to draw up a strong defensive position north of the Somme and, at the same time, begin preparations for an offensive to 'disengage' Amiens – with its crucial rail junction – from enemy interference.[4] But gathering enough forces for a timely counter-attack was, at the present moment, not possible, and both Haig and Pétain looked to their own lines with growing anxiety. Haig, in particular, had been deeply annoyed by Foch's refusal either to reduce the British sector of the front or to send sufficient divisions north to help fend off renewed attacks over the Lys and he was not slow to enlist high-level support in his quest for French reserves.

Foch and Haig met at Abbeville on 14 April, with the British Commander-in-Chief (who was accompanied by Lord Milner) pressing for action. The enemy were aiming to destroy the expeditionary force and, therefore, it was necessary for the French to 'take a more active share in the battle'. But Foch refused to countenance relieving troops while a battle was in progress and 'at a moment when the Allied reserves were hardly sufficient in number'. He did order a single division of General Maistre's Tenth Army to be ready to march north if necessary, but would part with no more. It would be, in his opinion, a 'wrong employment' of French reserves to commit any more troops to the British sector, as it would leave them unable to react to any subsequent German offensive.[5] Du Cane remembered how Foch continually used the same phrases over and again: 'never withdraw' and 'never relieve tired troops during the battle'. When Haig pointed out the importance of the Channel ports, Foch retorted:

'I know all about that. I fought for the Channel Ports in 1914 and I will fight for them again.'[6]

The British Commander-in-Chief left Abbeville in a furious, black mood. 'Foch seems to me unmethodical and takes a "short-view" of the situation', he recorded in his diary. 'For instance, he does not look ahead and make a forecast of what may be required in a week in a certain area, and arrange accordingly . . . Also, as at Ypres in 1914, he is very disinclined to engage French troops in the battle.'[7] Haig had been asked to put his thoughts in writing, so he did, firing off a letter reminding Foch of the 'very heavy losses' his men had suffered 'during the engagements of the last ten days' and warning him that 'serious reductions' in the strength of his units would make the reorganization of his divisions 'much more difficult or even impossible'. Therefore, to help the expeditionary force 'continue its role in the war', he wanted reserve divisions sent as quickly as possible 'to assure the situation'.[8]

For all Foch's stubbornness (and it was the same ferocity and unwillingness to yield that had so annoyed Castelnau in 1914), he was always able to reconsider a situation if necessary. Sir Henry Wilson visited Sarcus on 17 April and explained that without extra support, it might be necessary for the Allied armies in Flanders to make a further withdrawal, inundating part of the coast and pulling back from Ypres towards Saint-Omer, perhaps even giving up Dunkirk. Coming from Wilson (who had been sent to France by Milner because he alone could 'bridge the gap') perhaps made it easier for Foch, who still believed that Haig was exaggerating the threat. Nevertheless he accepted that the British must have more support, so agreed to send reinforcements, ordering five infantry and three cavalry divisions north as part of a special army detachment under a distinguished cavalryman, General Antoine de Mitry, which began filtering into the line over the following week.[9]

Moving divisions north inevitably aroused the ire of the French Commander-in-Chief. Pétain's sole focus remained the survival of the French Army and he complained to Foch (in a letter dated 24 April) about 'certain dispositions taken or contemplated by the British High Command', which 'to my mind, appear to augur badly for the future'. Pétain alleged that the British were not putting all their manpower into the fight and that they were standing by while France used up her dwindling resources. 'They lose sight of the fact that the battle will last a long time, a very long time and they tend toward lessening the effort of the British army, prematurely drawing available French forces into the British fight when these forces will be so necessary for the development of subsequent operations.' Up to forty-seven French divisions had already been engaged in the British sector since the opening of the great offensive, and all Pétain had received back were four worn-out British divisions that had been sent to the Chemin des Dames to recuperate: 'It seems indeed as if we were the debtors!' Pétain noted, with obvious irritation. The French Army, he added, 'will fight tomorrow on the British front, the day after tomorrow on the Belgian front perhaps, later on the French front, as yesterday on the Italian front, as everywhere on the one and only front. But it must have the certitude that the British army and the British Empire, the same as the French army and France, are determined to put forth their maximum effort.'[10]

Foch understood the pressures on both men, but was determined not to give in to either. These 'two fine fellows', he told his wife, needed to be 'held, sustained, maintained'. On 19 April, he warned that retreats could no longer be allowed and 'what must be achieved is a *foot by foot* defence of the ground' based upon 'a *series of defensive organizations*' (at least two positions), '*numerous and powerful artillery*', and 'counter-attacks' that must be '*foreseen, prepared and settled*' with the officers and men detailed to carry them out.[11] With each passing day, he grew more comfortable in the position of supreme commander, motoring up and down the front smoothing over problems, encouraging and haranguing where necessary. When Poincaré visited Sarcus in mid-April, he found Foch 'in very good form'. 'He is satisfied to be recognized as Commander-in-Chief of the Allied armies, but he would like to have an official investiture and a letter of command, and he is right.' Foch was confident that the 'march on Hazebrouck' had been stopped and that the Germans were going to try again at Arras. The French President also noticed how Foch complained much less about the British than his other generals. 'He says that he has a good rapport with Pétain, that Pétain is perfect as a subordinate working in the background, but that he shrinks when given responsibility and cannot command as a leader.'[12]

As Allied operations became more coherent, German strategy was rapidly unravelling into a series of unconnected, spasmodic bursts.

Operation *Georgette* had originally been designed to secure the crucial junction at Hazebrouck, but Ludendorff became increasingly
nervous as progress stalled and casualties began to rise. He now
switched focus, firstly ordering Sixth Army to seize the town of Bailleul and, when it was taken, redirecting Fourth Army to push on
towards Kemmel Hill.[13] The high ground at Kemmel, which rose to
over 150 metres and commanded the surrounding area to the southwest of Ypres, was an obvious objective, but the danger that German
troops would get bogged down in tough fighting, preventing them
from breaking through, worried Rupprecht: 'If the attack does not
produce decisive progress in the first few days, it must be discontinued, as we cannot allow our forces to be squandered in an unfruitful
"material-battle".'[14] Ludendorff dismissed these concerns and ordered
an attack to begin as soon as possible, while also authorizing another
thrust to be made by General Marwitz's Second Army towards
Amiens.

The first of these attacks took place on 24 April, with four divisions striking towards Villers-Bretonneux, which was situated on
a wide-open plateau about ten miles east of Amiens. Thirteen
A7Vs had been assembled for the attack and they were able to overrun the sketchy British defences around the village, their approach
having been covered by the thick morning mist and the roar of the
bombardment. The sight of these vehicles ('an enormous and terrifying iron pill-box' was how a witness described one) caught the
defenders totally by surprise and, with no anti-tank rifles or field
guns nearby, there was little they could do to stop them. When a
British divisional commander heard that German tanks had been
sighted, he ordered forward all four of his vehicles, two male and
two female Mark IVs that had been in reserve around the village
of Cachy. Rumbling forward, they engaged in a swirling fight
with one of the German vehicles, which scored direct hits on both
females, knocking them out with its 57 mm cannon, only to be hit
by a 6-pounder shell from the male Mark IV, which killed three
crewmen and caused the rest to flee.[15]

The action at Villers-Bretonneux was notable for the first tank-on-
tank battle, but it changed little in a larger sense. A swiftly executed

counter-attack by two Australian brigades restored the situation and left German forces still some way from Amiens. More dangerous was the renewal of heavy fighting in the north. The bombardment on Kemmel Hill opened at 2.30 a.m. on 25 April, with thousands of muzzle flashes lighting up the darkened sky. Gas shells were fired at British and French battery positions and rear areas, drenching them in mustard gas, while the front trenches were systematically bombarded with mortar fire. 'One can see the foot of Kemmel,' recorded a Bavarian waiting to go forward, 'but the view is then stopped by a dense black curtain of smoke only lit up by the bursts of flame from the high-explosive shell. Some three or four hundred yards ahead the sight is terrible, great heaps of earth go hurtling into the air, and break up into fragments as they come down, one big tree after another is lifted up out of the ground and then collapses flat, smashing down others in its fall.'[16]

Six German divisions, led by the Alpine Corps, had been ordered to take the high ground and open a route to the coast. They swarmed forward at 6 a.m. and were soon running into crowds of blue-grey Frenchmen, their hands in the air, dazed by the ferocity of the shelling. The defenders, part of General de Mitry's detachment, had only recently taken over the line, but quickly found themselves 'nailed to the spot' by the shellfire. Massed above the battlefield was the German Air Force, the 'uncontested master of the air' (as one authority put it), which 'attacked from a low height', firing on any 'pockets of resistance' and harassing any troops moving up to the battlefield.[17] News of the fall of Kemmel Hill buoyed the mood at OHL, which had been downcast after the death of Manfred von Richthofen, Germany's celebrated 'red baron', killed on 21 April, after coming down in a hail of ground fire near Sailly-le-Sec on the River Somme. With the heaviest guns now being able to reach Calais and Boulogne, another push might cause the whole Allied position in the north to collapse. Fritz von Lossberg, Chief of Staff at Fourth Army, wanted to press on and informed OHL of his plans to exploit the advance, moving up supporting divisions and artillery as quickly as possible, only for Ludendorff – being unusually cautious – to warn him against counter-attacks. They should dig in and wait for their artillery to move up before trying again the following morning. It was only later on that German commanders realized how close the Allied line had come to total collapse on 25 April. Only three French battalions held a crucial four-kilometre section of the front, and had German divisions pressed their advantage and pushed on, they might have broken through.[18]

Foch acted with a greater sense of urgency. He telephoned Haig to tell him that withdrawing behind Ypres 'must not be contemplated' and that he was ordering more artillery and aircraft to Flanders.[19] Counter-attacks were thrown in as soon as forces could be gathered, with British, Belgian and French troops fighting together as they had done at Ypres in 1914. Fierce battles were also fought in the air as aircraft flew low over the battlefield strafing anything that moved, before coming under ground fire. Ten German aircraft were shot down that day, and the newly formed Royal Air Force was ordered to mount heavy attacks on railway stations and approach routes behind the line despite the poor visibility across much of the front.[20] The fighting around Kemmel was extraordinarily intense. One French soldier remembered marching past a battery of howitzers, the gunners 'ramming their shells home like a baker thrusting bread into an oven'. The scene before the French troops almost defied description. The terrain was 'unrecognizable, it is merely holes and muddy quagmires, with wrecked vehicles and a jumble of equipment everywhere: devastation, abominable desolation'. They relieved a battalion in the line and found 'nothing but scared soldiers, huddled in shell-holes'.[21]

It rained heavily overnight and the ground quickly became waterlogged, increasing the misery on both sides of the line as long columns of reinforcements trudged up towards the blasted hill, still shrouded in smoke like a ruptured volcano. German troops had been ordered to restart their advance at 8 a.m., but, before they could do so, a scattered series of counter-attacks broke out in the early hours, with British troops entering Kemmel village, but everywhere else finding progress hard going: the ground was sodden, the creeping barrage was thin and flanking fire meant that the attack went to ground.[22] Exhaustion was also beginning to take its toll on the harassed German forces, which had been under spasmodic artillery fire since the previous morning. Bringing up enough ammunition over the shell-pitted ground took time (and the presence of cloying mustard gas did not help), and it was not until 29 April that the German offensive could be restarted. Once again, a furious *Feuerwalze* preceded the attack, but this time Allied batteries were able to reply with significant counter-battery fire, which blunted the main assault. With little chance for further gains, OHL ordered Fourth Army to go on to the defensive on 1 May. If there had ever been a moment for decisive success at Kemmel Hill, it had now passed.

Whether through ignorance or wilful blindness, the duo who had led Germany's war effort since September 1916 still believed that they held the strategic advantage. Following the failure of *Georgette*, Colonel Albrecht von Thaer, a staff officer with IX Reserve Corps, travelled to Avesnes, convinced that the High Command – the 'demigods' as he called them – were not being given the correct information about the degree to which German troops were 'more or less exhausted'. Progress in Flanders had been impressive to begin with, but when attacking divisions were replaced by reserve units, particularly those that had already been in action in March, progress rapidly tailed off. Hindenburg listened 'patiently' to these concerns before replying in a 'deep, soothing voice' that Thaer was mistaken, that he only saw a part of the picture:

> I have daily reports from everywhere, both about the tactical situation and about the mood of the troops. The latter is good everywhere, even brilliant, but that of the enemy is really bad according to our intelligence. Look, in Russia it didn't take one attempt for the colossus to fall. We repeated our attacks, here and there, and all of a sudden it was done. It will go the same way in the west. Look, thank God, we still have another five months ahead of us before winter sets in; so we can still give them a whole series of offensives – an attack here, an attack there, an attack here, an attack there . . .

When Thaer managed to see Ludendorff, he found a man who was visibly under pressure, his 'inner agitation' noticeable by the increasing movement of his finger tapping on a pencil. When Thaer tried to explain the situation, Ludendorff suddenly let loose a furious tirade:

'What's with all this complaining? What do you want from me? Should I be making peace at all costs? If the troops are getting worse, if their discipline is weakening, then it's your fault, the fault of all the commanders who are not seizing the opportunity. How else would it be possible for whole divisions to have filled their stomachs with food and drink in captured enemy supply dumps without pushing the attack forward? That is of course the reason that the great March offensive and now *Georgette* did not make it any further!'[23]

Opinions differed about what should be done. On 19 April, Georg Wetzell authored a memorandum on the situation and – much as he had done since November 1917 – argued for an attack against the French. With Allied troops now massed in the north, Wetzell did not think a success in Flanders was possible. Instead they should look to bring together about 25–30 divisions for a 'strong surprise attack' along the Chemin des Dames in mid-May, which offered the prospect of 'profound political consequences'.[24] Wetzell knew that this contradicted a central tenet of Ludendorff's plans for 1918, which had been based upon destroying the BEF (with any attacks against the French being merely diversions), but he saw few opportunities elsewhere. Although Ludendorff still hoped for something to turn up at the front, such as a sudden Allied collapse, the Crown Prince was ordered to begin planning for a thrust across the Chemin des Dames, codenamed Operation *Blücher*. This was scheduled for 20 May and would then be followed up by another strike by Eighteenth Army between Montdidier and Lassigny (Operation *Gneisenau*). Wetzell trusted that any attack across the Aisne would so frighten the French that they would pour in reinforcements, thus weakening the junction with the British, which could then be broken through. 'Decisive results can only be achieved in the near future on the Montdidier–Reims front,' he wrote, 'and there we must strive for victory on a large scale.'[25]

Ludendorff was struggling to understand a campaign that, according to his own designs, he should already have won. On 4 May, he spoke with Rupprecht at army group headquarters in Tournai and they dwelt on how close the BEF had come to total, irredeemable defeat. Ludendorff insisted that without French assistance the British would have been 'completely beaten'. 'The English do not have the men to replenish their divisions in the short term. If reinforcements had been available, they would already be in France, since there was no doubt that the English expected our attack.' As for the French, they had disbanded over 200 battalions in the past two years and had been capable of only limited offensives. The only hope for the Entente, he admitted, was the Americans, which left the war still finely balanced. 'We have no doubt considerably weakened our forces with the *Georg* and *Michael* battles. We had very heavy casualties. The casualties are why we need to rethink our tactics.' But Ludendorff did not believe that victory was far away. 'After all, it is possible that by the end of May we will have a larger number of divisions in such a battle-ready state that we will be able to strike a new blow!'[26]

The great question remained the employment of the Americans. Pershing had pledged his standard to Foch, but the problem of how to bring a US Army into the field was nowhere near being settled. In late April, an agreement had been reached between London and Washington to prioritize the transportation of infantry, machine-gunners, engineers and signallers of six divisions during the month of May (about 120,000 men).[27] This marked a notable departure from the previous arrangement – when only full divisions would be transported – but, crucially, it would allow American manpower to be built up at a much faster rate. As Tasker Bliss noted in a letter to Peyton C. March, Acting Chief of Staff in Washington, this was the 'quickest and most effective way for us to bring our manpower to bear'. Once in France, these units would be formed into brigades and 'loaned' to the British and French until 'the present emergency is over'. Bliss did not like this any more than Pershing did, but he saw no other way of getting a 'well trained and independent American army' into the field within an acceptable time frame. The alternative, of continuing with the current policy, might mean 'having the war end without our having taken an effective part in it'.[28]

The matter was revisited during a meeting of the Supreme War Council at Abbeville on 1 May, when it was the first item on the agenda. Clemenceau, with his usual biting lack of tact, complained that the French had not been consulted on the 'London Agreement' and that US troops must be allotted to the French Army. He, therefore, had to insist that those soldiers arriving the following month (in June) would be sent to Pétain. Lord Milner tried to smooth over Clemenceau's *amour propre*, arguing that there was never 'any intention of depriving the French of American troops'; indeed, the sole object of the agreement was 'to get their reinforcements over with the least possible delay', but this just opened up a fractious debate about extending the agreement into the summer. Pershing, who was looking on in silence, must have found the sight of the British and French squabbling over his men deeply troubling. He had originally planned to transport the remaining artillery and auxiliary units in June, which would bring the six divisions up to full strength, but this might not now be possible. He rose above the fray and refused to be railroaded, saying that he 'looked forward to a time when the United States would have its own army' that would be 'complete, homogenous, and under its own supreme command'.[29]

The battle was resumed the following day. Foch began by outlining the gravity of what they were facing. With German troops threatening both Paris and the Channel ports, 'it was essential that at least 120,000 infantry and machine-gun units should, during the months of May, June, and July, be given priority of transportation from America over other arms'. He understood Pershing's objections – that this would delay the formation of an independent army – but appealed to him 'at this grave hour to think solely of their common duty to the cause they served'. Lloyd George then added another thick layer of persuasion. 'We had now reached the stage where our resources were exhausted', he warned. They had taken 'boys of 18' and 'men of 50' and there was now a risk that both Britain and France would 'go under'. However, were this to happen, it would be 'an honourable defeat, because each had put the very last man into the army, whereas the United States would go under after putting in only as many men as had the Belgians . . .'[30]

Pershing did not flinch as the British Prime Minister issued his wounding comparison. In private, he would complain bitterly about the attitude of his allies, but in front of the Supreme War Council he was his rigid, inscrutable best. He understood the 'seriousness of the situation' and spoke for the American people in their 'earnest desire to take their full part in this battle', but he only differed in the 'methods of attaining that desire'. He reminded everyone that the United States was 'an independent power' and the morale of her troops 'depended on their fighting under their own flag'. At one point, a flash of anger crossed Foch's gaze:

'You are willing to risk our being driven back to the Loire?'

'Yes I am willing to take the risk,' responded Pershing, who made it clear that the war could not be won by 'feeding untrained American recruits into the Allied armies'.[31]

With Pershing going about as far as he could, it was arranged to continue the 'London Agreement' into June, after which it would be revisited. The divisions would be sent to the British and French armies for 'training and service' until such time as they were withdrawn by Pershing (after consultation with Foch). In the meantime, Lloyd George pulled as many men as he could out of Palestine and Italy, while emptying the depots in England of all who could be spared. Clemenceau acted with the same tenacity, calling up the class of 1919 in April and exploring methods of drawing more indigenous troops from France's colonies in Africa.[32] Substituting technology – tanks, aeroplanes, poison gas – for manpower was another possibility, but whatever was tried, sooner or later, the Allies would have to return to the offensive.

Foch issued 'General Directive No. 3' on 20 May, which outlined his plan for the campaign. 'After an effort without precedent against the whole of the battlefront the enemy has halted; for three weeks he has not attacked anywhere in force.' The Germans could not 'remain inactive' without admitting that their great gamble had failed, hence it was likely that their operations would continue for some time to come. Nevertheless Foch was determined to remain active and sought two important results: to free the Amiens area, including the Amiens–Paris railway, from enemy interference; and to push the Germans back from their recent gains in Flanders.[33] Accordingly orders were issued to General Fayolle (through Pétain) to begin drawing up plans for an attack in the Amiens–Montdidier sector, which inevitably provoked further controversy. 'There is always disagreement between Pétain and Foch', complained Fayolle. 'The latter would like to attack, the former would not. Pétain exaggerates the power of the Boche, Foch does not appreciate its true value. They are both right and wrong. If the two were combined, they would create a true and complete leader.'[34]

The squabbles between the two men were abruptly halted by the news that another great attack (Operation *Blücher*) had been launched on the Chemin des Dames. At 1 a.m. on 27 May, over 4,000 guns opened fire along a twenty-four-mile front between Chauvigny and Berry-au-Bac, with the shelling reaching up to twelve miles behind the line, concentrating on road junctions, railway stations, headquarters and known battery positions.[35] 'There are flashes, hisses, cracks and fizzles from thousands of mortars and guns of all calibres in the direction of the enemy', recalled one German soldier of peering into no-man's-land. 'The hills in the distance become ablaze, flares spring up from the enemy in a wide arc . . . and then fall in the appalling smoke. The hurricane of fire raises a storm. Ear-piercing, nerve-wracking droning fills the air; the earth shakes from the powerful blows. It is impossible to make oneself understood with words. The handles of the sweating gunners and engineers fly mechanically into one another with impressive speed.'[36] The aim of the attack was to seize the ridge as quickly as possible, including the shell-battered ruins of La Malmaison, before driving down to the Aisne and then, if possible, reaching the Vesle 'in one go'.[37]

Ever since the fighting of late 1917, the pockmarked heights north of the Aisne had been a quiet place, used, by both sides, as a 'nursery' where inexperienced or shattered units could stay. Four British divisions had been sent there in early May as part of Foch's policy of *roulement* (whereby some of Haig's tired divisions were moved to quiet French sectors), only to find themselves in an unfortunate position – a situation worsened by a growing disagreement with the local French Army commander, General Denis Auguste Duchêne, an abrasive and petulant 55-year-old who had been Foch's Chief of Staff in 1914. Duchêne opted to hold his front line in strength, deploying his divisions along the ridgeline, which he believed offered the best place to defeat any German attack. He was also aware that retreating from ground that had been conquered at such cost would make 'a most unfortunate impression on public opinion'. When Franchet d'Espèrey – his superior – heard of this, he argued that Duchêne should thin his manpower out and fight in the manner that had been laid down by GQG in a series of instructions in December 1917, that of defence-in-depth. But Duchêne would not budge and Pétain let the general have his way, concerned about the effect of relieving him at such a crucial time and believing in the merits of allowing his subordinates freedom of action in how they deployed their troops.[38]

The difficulty for Duchêne was that as more French troops were shifted north, there were fewer and fewer units to form an adequate reserve in the centre, and he found his command being stretched to breaking point. His Sixth Army held a fifty-five-mile sector of front from Reims to Noyon, which meant that each division held about 3.5 miles – an even longer frontage than had been allocated to the ill-fated British Fifth Army on 21 March.[39] Duchêne was also unhappy that his right flank was held by four exhausted and under-strength British divisions as part of Lieutenant-General Sir Alexander Hamilton-Gordon's IX Corps. None of the British commanders thought Duchêne was doing the right thing, and during a fraught conference on 15 May they all argued that they should thin out the Forward Zone and mount their main defence south of the Aisne river, which would give them a better chance of surviving any German assault. But Duchêne was not persuaded.

'It is quite simple,' he told the assembled officers. 'One remains where one is. One does not go back.'[40]

Scattered intelligence had been coming into GQG of German activity behind the lines for some time, but the full scale of Ludendorff's assault only became clear when it was too late. Against Duchêne, General Max von Boehn's Seventh Army massed thirteen divisions in the first wave, with four in support, against just four French and British divisions, in places outnumbering their opponents by more than 4:1. With the forward positions isolated, German guns then began to concentrate on neutralizing French artillery. Only 20 per cent of the shells fired in the counter-battery phase of the bombardment were high explosive – the rest were a mixture of 'blue cross' and 'green cross': the first to act as a 'mask breaker' that would irritate the victim and make it impossible to put on a gas mask; followed by the pulmonary agents (usually a mixture of chlorine, phosgene or diphosgene) intended to affect the lungs.[41] The results were terrifying. French artillery, which should have opened fire as soon as the German attack started, was silent, drowning under an exploding rain of gas: men ripping off their masks, vomiting and struggling to breathe, then choking on the secondary gases that lay in wait.

Zero Hour was at 3.40 a.m. In the flickering darkness, German stormtroopers, with their unearthly gas-masked appearance, haversacks bulging with grenades, rifles on their shoulders, crossed the Ailette on makeshift bridges, before clambering up the slopes towards the ridgeline. The struggle in the forward zones was over very quickly. One French officer grimly recorded how each enemy infantry regiment was accompanied by a company of flamethrowers, extra machine-gunners and a battery of artillery. 'It's a wave that submerges everything. This mass rushes forward . . . subdividing into thousands of small columns that infiltrate through all the pathways, bypassing machine-guns everywhere and following a very formidable rolling barrage, shooting while marching.' In the centre, the French 21st and 22nd Divisions were rapidly overcome, their men dying where they stood or being rounded up in shocked, stumbling groups and taken prisoner. Five out of their six colonels were 'buried in their command posts' and all battalion commanders became casualties. That day 21st Division lost 160 officers and 6,000 men and only 1,200 men of 157th Division, in support, survived.[42]

By 5.30 a.m., most of the ridge had fallen and a yawning gap had opened in the French line. Fighting on both flanks had been tougher, but in the centre the attackers surged down towards the Aisne. Duchêne had issued orders for the demolition of the bridges, but not all could be blown in time, and by nightfall the Germans had advanced twelve miles, crossing the Aisne and even reaching the Vesle. 'It was just as at manoeuvres', reminisced the Crown Prince years later. 'The headquarters flag fluttered in the wind; runners and motor-cyclists came and went, and the telephone worked at high pressure.'[43] What was left of the French Sixth Army stumbled back from the front in small groups, mixed-up battalions and regiments, with an air of haunted desperation on their faces. Despite making a series of courageous stands, 8th and 50th Divisions of Hamilton-Gordon's IX Corps had 'ceased to exist as organized bodies'.[44] Duchêne ordered up all the reserves he had, but they could not stop Boehn from making further sizeable advances on succeeding days. German troops crossed the Vesle on 28 May, entered Soissons and pushed on about five miles, buoyed by a growing sense that the great moment had finally arrived.

Pétain knew that they must hold the Marne and bar the way to Paris. He ordered his dwindling reserves to be put on to trains and hurried up in an increasingly desperate attempt to plug the gap. By the end of May, thirty-two French divisions, seventeen of which were 'completely' worn out, had been drawn into the fighting, alongside five British ones. Another five divisions would arrive over the next few days, but Pétain warned Foch that the French were reaching the limits of their resources: 'It is impossible to take more divisions from other parts of the front.' Along quiet sectors of the line, some divisions were holding as many as eight miles of trenches with no reserves behind them.[45] Foch was not minded to give in to thoughts of defeat, even if news of the Chemin des Dames was an enormous strain upon him. On 28 May, he warned Haig that the amount of French reserves available to intervene on his front would now be 'strongly reduced'. For the time being, the British would have to rely on their own divisions to counter any German attack. When Haig saw Foch several days later, he thought the Frenchman 'looked more anxious than I have ever seen him', complaining how his men were 'not fighting well' and that his reserves had 'melted away very quickly'.[46] Pétain had concentrated on sending reinforcements to hold the flanks of the great bulge now torn in his front, at Soissons and Reims, which meant that German troops continued to push south, reaching the Marne by the fourth day of operations, having taken 42,000 prisoners and 400 guns, and 'exceeding all expectations' of the German High Command.[47]

Fortunately Allied troops were now pouring into the breach,

including – finally – the Americans. As part of Pershing's agreement with Foch, US divisions were now moving into quiet sectors of the line to complete their training. By the end of May, the total strength of the AEF was just over 600,000 men, but not all were ready to go into battle.[48] By this point Pershing's most experienced and well-trained formation was 1st Division – the 'Big Red One' – which had gone into the line on the night of 20/21 April, coming under the orders of the French VI Corps northwest of Montdidier near the village of Cantigny. This was certainly greatly appreciated by Foch, but both US and French commanders wanted to do more: they wanted to prove that the Americans could fight. Soon plans were hatched for 1st Division to take and hold the village. The divisional commander, Major-General Robert Lee Bullard, was a 57-year-old Alabaman who spoke fluent French and who was determined to follow French guidance to the letter. Each battalion was equipped with a machine-gun company, mortars and 37 mm quick-firing cannon. The French also provided air cover and dedicated flamethrower teams, alongside twelve Schneider tanks. Artillery support was formidable: 234 guns were to support the attack of a single regiment, which produced an intensity of fire that could hardly be improved.[49]

The attack went ahead at 6.45 a.m. on 28 May after an hour's preliminary bombardment. 'It was a remarkable sight', noted a staff officer observing the attack through his field glasses; 'great clouds of smoke rolling up from the shelled districts, against which the flashes of bursting shells stood out.' Pershing would have approved of the way his men went over, crossing the long expanse of no-man's-land 'in two lines of two waves each . . .' going forward 'as if it were at inspection – really splendid – lines straight'.[50] Elements of two German regiments were in the village, but they were either killed or wounded by the shelling or taken prisoner after stumbling out of their dugouts and cellars, covered in dust. Within half an hour, the Americans had captured the village and held on despite six separate attempts to retake it over the next two days. 'While relatively small, the affair at Cantigny on the 28th was well planned and splendidly executed', Pershing cabled Washington. 'It was important in this first attack that we should succeed and that we should hold our ground, especially as the French had previously taken Cantigny twice and had each time been driven out by the Germans . . . It is my firm conviction that our troops are the best in Europe and our staffs are the equals of any.'[51]

As the German advance pressed upon the high ground north of the Marne, Pershing ordered two more divisions (2nd and 3rd) to deploy immediately into the line, with the doughboys clambering on to trucks and being driven, as quickly as possible, through the verdant June countryside towards the firing line – notable for the sausage-shaped German observation balloons in the sky. By 2 June, 2nd Division was barring the Château-Thierry to Paris highway opposite a 'heavy, menacing frown in the landscape' known as Belleau Wood, having been ordered to 'hold the line at all hazards'.[52] The Germans came in that afternoon, unaware that they were facing fresh troops. 'It wasn't the mass formation I had expected to see after what I had heard of German attacks', noted a US Marine, who lay crouched in a newly dug rifle pit. 'Those lines were well extended. At least six or seven paces of open space were between the men . . . They wore the "coal-scuttle" helmet. Their rifles, bayonets fixed, were at the ready. They advanced slowly and steadily.' Steeled by their training and confident in their weaponry, the Americans opened fire at 100 yards. 'Up and down the line I could see my men working their rifle bolts. I looked for the front line of the Germans. There wasn't any! Killed and wounded, they had crumpled and vanished in the grain.'[53]

Not content with just holding the line, 2nd Division went on to the offensive on 6 June, launching a series of attacks into the broken, trench-lined wood that had been turned into a fortress by the defenders. Both sides were determined to demonstrate their martial prowess and it took almost three weeks for the Americans, with French support, to clear the wood. Fighting was savage. Doughboys went into the battle relying on their rifles, but quickly found that in the thick undergrowth much more was needed to take on entrenched defenders, including heavy-artillery support, mortars and endless amounts of grenades. By 16 June, 2nd Division had sustained over 4,300 casualties, including many suffering from mustard gas poisoning, but they had taken the wood. After the war, James Harbord, Pershing's former Chief of Staff who commanded a brigade during the battle, remarked that more was at stake at Belleau Wood than simply 'standing between the invader and fair Paris'. 'It was a struggle for psychological mastery . . . The odds in experience, in terrain and in prestige were with the German; the honours at the end lay with the American.'[54]

22. 'It will be a glorious day'

The battlefields of the Western Front may have been bathed in warm summer sunshine, but shadows were beginning to lengthen across Imperial Germany. Her troops were now within thirty-six miles of Paris, yet their offensive power was already waning and their morale was increasingly fragile. By May, ominous reports were circulating about the looting of German supply dumps – now that Allied ones were more difficult to come by – as well as the spread of small-scale mutinies and a rising trickle of desertions. It was not uncommon for German units to arrive at the front missing a fifth of their man-power, with soldiers trying their luck jumping off trains or vanishing behind the lines at railway stations. Even Ludendorff sensed that something else was needed to break the deadlock. On 8 June, he wrote to the Chancellor, Georg von Hertling, about the need to undertake a 'political offensive' in between the periods of fighting which would 'provide the opportunity to exploit the success of our military victories'.[1]

Coordinating military and political activity was a sound idea, but it was already too late. A week before Ludendorff had raised the prospect of his 'political offensive', Rupprecht informed Hertling that they must initiate peace negotiations immediately – including making an announcement on the status of Belgium. 'We will be in a position to deal our enemies in the west a few more heavy blows, but barely enough to cause them a decisive defeat', with the stalemate ('depressing static warfare') likely to continue for the foreseeable future. In such a situation, the Allies would be better off thanks to American aid, leaving Germany in an unenviable position. 'We are currently still holding a few trump cards – such as the threat of new attacks . . . General Ludendorff is of the same view, that in all probability a decisive victory, which would destroy our enemies, is no longer possible, but he is nevertheless hoping for the saving grace of a

Deus ex machina, namely the sudden internal collapse of one of the Western powers along the lines of the collapse of the Russian Empire.' But Rupprecht was sceptical. 'East and West are entirely different, and none of the Western states is as brittle as the Russian Empire was even before the war.'[2]

In the absence of anything else, Ludendorff looked to another strike on the Western Front. With too many British and French divisions still north of the Oise, he needed to move them out of position before a final attack could be launched in Flanders some time in July. This was provisionally codenamed Operation *Hagen* and would, in Ludendorff's words, 'bring about the decision'. Two further attacks were authorized in the meantime: Eighteenth Army pushing south towards Compiègne (*Gneisenau*) and Seventh Army striking due west towards Villers-Cotterêts (*Hammerschlag*). Both operations were intended to straighten out the great salient that the Germans had gouged out of the French line and allow them to free up the lateral railway lines that were vital for the movement of guns and supplies around the front.[3] Once again, Ludendorff's siege train of artillery was shunted up and the tons of shells stockpiled, following the methods of attack that had now been perfected: a short and intensive bombardment in the early hours, including extensive gas shelling of enemy batteries, designed to shock and disorientate the defenders, before the infantry went forward.

Only something was different this time: the French knew they were coming. Aerial reconnaissance had already revealed 'increased activity' around Péronne, Chaulnes, Roye and Montdidier, with observers spotting the movement of heavy artillery and the glow of campfires at night. Deserters were also coming in, eager to reveal that an offensive was imminent.[4] Indeed, so obvious were German preparations that French intelligence even asked whether they should be regarded as a ruse, intended to draw their attention away from another sector. But when new German wireless codes were broken on 2 June, their suspicions were confirmed. On the afternoon of 8 June, just hours before the attack was scheduled to take place, General Georges Humbert, Third Army commander, ordered his batteries to commence a careful programme of 'counter-preparation': firing 'massive but short' bombardments on

suspected assembly areas before unleashing shelling at 'maximum intensity' at 11.50 p.m. – just ten minutes before Zero Hour.[5]

The way the French would hold their lines was also evolving.
Pétain had originally called for the construction of an intricate system of defence-in-depth in this sector, but there had not been the
men or the time to build one, leaving Humbert holding the front
position in strength, much as Duchêne had done on the Aisne. As
German activity became more noticeable, both Pétain and the army
group commander, Fayolle, insisted that this was a mistake. On 4
June, Fayolle ordered Humbert to make his main stand in his second
position, between two and four miles further to the rear, while thin-
ning out the front lines that would be subjected to the worst
Minenwerfer fire: 'The mission of the army, as previously defined, is to
ensure the integrity of the first position. However, what we've learnt
from recent events is that it is necessary to preserve as much as possible from the effects of the intense enemy bombardments . . . As a
consequence, the main line of resistance will be pulled back as far as
possible to the line of support or the line of the redoubts.'[6]

Humbert's plans were meticulous and imaginative, but he was
unfortunate that German artillery preparation began earlier than he
had been led to believe, which reduced the effectiveness of his 'counter-
preparation' on the morning of 9 June. General Hutier's Eighteenth
Army had massed fifteen divisions in the first wave (against nine French
ones) and swept forward at 4.20 a.m., its assault troops utilizing an
array of weaponry – trench mortars and flamethrowers, light machine-
guns and grenades – allowing them to quickly carve open Humbert's
forward positions and round up scattered groups of French infantry
still sheltering in their dugouts. By the end of the day, Eighteenth
Army had gained about six miles and taken 8,000 prisoners – encouraging enough, but nowhere near the scale of the victory on 27 May.
Numerous problems had also been encountered during the day: mist
and fog that prevented observation; the difficulty in keeping the creeping barrage moving smoothly across a broken landscape of small hills
and woods; a lack of ammunition; shortages of telephone cable; and
strengthening enemy artillery fire, which rose in violence during the
afternoon.[7]

The attack continued on 10 June, a cool and hazy day of 'changeable battles and counter-attacks', with Hutier gaining several more miles, but there was no wild rout from the field; instead Humbert was orchestrating an orderly withdrawal that sapped German strength and allowed him time to bring up his reserves.[8] Foch had been kept informed of the course of the battle by regular telephone calls and was encouraged by what he had heard, but he was already thinking about counter-attacking. That day, General Charles Mangin, the craggy-faced 'butcher' who had been in restless exile since the collapse of the Nivelle offensive the previous year, was summoned to meet Fayolle, who told him that he was being given command of Tenth Army. However, before he could take up his position, he was needed to lead an immediate counter-attack into the enemy's flank and he would have five divisions to do it:

'When can you attack?' Fayolle asked. 'We must leave as soon as possible.'

'Certainly', Mangin replied. 'But where are the Boches?'

'That way, this morning they were going towards this line', Fayolle said, pointing out positions on a map spread out on his desk. 'Now we aren't too sure.'

'Ah! And the attack divisions?'

'Two have arrived, one is arriving, two are on their way; we don't really know where.'

'Ah! I am going to speak with your Chief of Staff and then I will tell you when I will be able to attack.'

Mangin was then ushered in to see Foch.

'You will attack?'

'Yes, General.'

'Tomorrow morning?'

'I cannot set the hour of attack yet. But I will see my five divisions . . . at six o'clock and they will leave at seven o'clock in a hurry.'

Foch and Fayolle then burst out laughing, leaving Mangin with a surprised look upon his face. Foch told him that they had been having a conversation about how soon Mangin would be able to get his divisions moving. When Foch said that the attack needed to go in the following day, Fayolle had insisted that it was 'absolutely impossible'.

'Well! You'll see!' Foch replied.[9]

Mangin was as good as his word. He rushed off to the front and somehow managed to get his forces assembled and ready to counter-attack – doing in a matter of hours what would have previously taken days. Supported by four *groupements* of tanks (both Schneiders and Saint-Chamonds), Mangin was to eject the Germans from the Matz valley, striking east into the German right flank around the villages of Méry and Cuvilly – flat open ground that would be ideal for tank action. Mangin's orders made it clear that there would be no further retreats: 'Tomorrow's operation must be the end of the defensive bat-tle that we have been waging for nearly two months; it must mark the end of the Germans, the resumption of the offensive, and result in success. Everyone must understand.'[10] One French officer remem-bered watching the tanks moving up in the final moments before the assault. They were like 'monsters coming out of the woods and gain-ing on us, they glide through the night like a herd of hippos, an armoured squadron slowly splitting the green wheat, and leaving behind a large trail of beautiful Saint-Chamond tanks, heavy as fort-resses, the spur, the cannon at the front, the traps, the spiky caterpillar tracks and all the pieces from the fighting armour'.[11]

The attack went in at 11 a.m., following a short thirty-minute bombardment that engulfed the German positions in clouds of smoke, dust and fragments of shell. Mangin visited the leading lines before the assault and was radiant to be back at the front among his men: 'Never', he told an aide, 'have they been so beautiful and so full of energy.'[12] The defenders had not been expecting such a furious assault and fell back in shock and surprise when they saw the tanks moving up through the wheat fields, crushing everything before them. Mangin's divisions gained between two and three kilometres and took 1,000 prisoners, but came to a standstill about 4 p.m. – the men exhausted and the tank force neutralized. Of 144 vehicles deployed that day, sixty-nine were put out of action, mostly by light artillery that was able to engage them over open sights, their shells punching through the thin armour with sickening effect.[13] Yet the ferocity of the assault made a deep impression upon OHL, which had not believed the French were still capable of putting up such a fight.

Ludendorff's second phase of the attack, Operation *Hammerschlag*, broke down even sooner than *Gneisenau* had. Two corps attacked on 12 June, only to find that the French, having been forewarned, had already evacuated their forward positions. The preliminary bombardment was only ninety minutes long and lacked the ferocity of earlier attacks. 'It bangs and thunders away, as is our custom in our repeated offensives,' noted one German observer, 'but it isn't the same as it was on 21 March or 27 May.' He also noticed how the attacking infantry 'don't get off the ground after the creeping barrage' and complained that 'our men don't get into a proper fighting mood'.[14] French infantry disputed their progress step by step, launching swift counter-attacks and fighting stubbornly for every piece of ground. That evening Army Group Wilhelm bluntly informed OHL that enemy resistance was 'so strong and organized' that any advantages gained would be 'disproportionate to their own losses' and recommended that the attack be stopped.[15]

Even the thick veil of secrecy that OHL kept over the Western Front could not prevent rumours from spreading that things were not going well. On 24 June, Richard von Kühlmann gave a speech in which he cast doubt on whether an 'absolute end' to the war could be expected 'through purely military means alone, without any diplomatic negotiations'. He hoped the Entente understood that victory against Germany was 'a dream and an illusion' and that they would 'find a way to approach us with peace offers which correspond to the situation and satisfy German vital needs'.[16] When the duo at OHL read the speech, they were furious, complaining that Kühlmann's speech had revealed the 'weakness' of Germany's situation to their enemies. The following day they fired off a telegram to Hertling accusing the Foreign Secretary of having 'a devastating effect' on the army and that they could no longer work with him. The Kaiser, saddened and subdued, summoned Kühlmann and told him that he must resign, 'not because he did not have the crown's confidence but

because he lacked Ludendorff and Hindenburg's'. Admiral Paul von
Hintze, an ambitious naval officer and courtier who was serving as
Minister to Norway, was appointed as Kühlmann's replacement.[17]

Yet again the duo at OHL had got their way, forcing out a political figure who did not share their uncompromising view of the war.
Ludendorff maintained, at least in public, that the Allies had been
terribly wounded by the fighting so far and were close to the end. For
some time, he had been thinking about an operation to take Reims,
which would allow the crucial Laon–Soissons lateral railway line to
be reopened, as well as forcing the Allies to move their reserves out
of position, before Operation *Hagen* could deliver the final blow.
Writing long after the war, Ludendorff summed up the decision he
was now facing:

> What to do? Should we lower our offensive weapon, surrender to the
> enemy's gleaming blade of retaliation? That would mean forgoing
> military victory. How do we define great commanders? The power
> of one-sidedness, the quashing of all doubt or faintheartedness in
> one's own chest, the steadfast adherence to one great decision, which
> strengthens the soul. Marshal Foch is right when he describes the
> willpower of the leader, which even in desperate situations does not
> shake his belief in ultimate victory, to be the most striking character-
> istic of the general. In this difficult war, I had already so often turned
> desperate situations into good ones with steadfastness and firm
> trust. Our situation this time was far from desperate. For me, there-
> fore, there was also no doubt. It was necessary to dictate to the enemy
> by mobilizing extreme force.[18]

His opponent, Foch, was determined to see out whatever Ludendorff had in store. In 'Directive No. 4', issued on 1 July, the Allied
Generalissimo outlined the great dangers that a renewed German
attack could pose. The enemy were just eighteen miles from Dunkirk,
thirty-six miles from Calais and thirty-six miles from Paris. 'An
advance of 24 miles towards Abbeville would cut the communications with the north of France, and separate the British and French
Armies – a result of considerable military importance for the issue of
the war. An even smaller advance towards Paris – although this

advance would not have any marked influence on the military operations and thereby lead to a decision – would make a profound impression on public opinion, cause the evacuation of the capital under the menace of bombardment, and doubtless hamper the hands of the Government, whose free action is so indispensable for the conduct of the war.' Therefore, Foch wanted to 'focus their activity' along the central section of the front, from Château-Thierry to Lens, which would allow them to cover the vital centres of both Paris and Abbeville while reacting quickly to any diversionary effort in either Flanders or Champagne.[19]

Pétain remained a sullen figure, annoyed by what he believed to be Foch's over-indulgence of the British and highly sensitive to any interference in his own command responsibilities. Fayolle, who worked closely with him throughout this period, recorded how Pétain was 'hopeless because of his lack of confidence' and complained that 'When you shield yourself without being able to fight back, the danger only grows with time because of wear and tear . . .'[20] Pétain was particularly unhappy after Foch ordered him to relieve one of the British divisions in his sector and send further artillery to support General de Mitry's detachment in Flanders – complaining that he 'refused' to give Ypres 'the same value as Paris'. He was also disappointed by sniping criticism from the Senate Army Commission, which was busy investigating the collapse on 27 May – what was being dubbed 'France's Caporetto'. Pétain survived – Clemenceau still retained faith in him – but Duchêne and Franchet d'Espèrey were both fired and Pétain lost his Chief of Staff, Paul Anthoine, deemed too pessimistic by Foch, who took the opportunity to move him on.[21]

Haig was in a better mood and had recovered from his darkest hour in April 1918, even taking a week's leave on 6 July. The focus of German attacks in May and June on the French Army gave the BEF a much-needed respite and he was able to rebuild his divisions – now that a steady stream of manpower was arriving in France. Between 21 March and the end of August, over half a million men were shipped across the English Channel, after the minimum age for overseas service was lowered and workers were combed out of munitions factories.[22] Yet Haig was still concerned about the potential for an attack in the north and kept a close watch upon the number of reserve divisions available to Rupprecht (which he estimated at twenty-five). When Foch directed him to release two corps to move to Champagne, where German activity had picked up, Haig refused, arguing that this was merely a diversion and that the British front was as threatened as ever. 'On the whole, then,' he wrote on 14 July, 'the enemy's intentions do not appear to me to be very clearly defined, and I adhere to my previous opinion that the most effective course for him to pursue is to undertake minor offensive operations in Champagne and Flanders with a view to dispersing and absorbing the Allies' reserves, and subsequently delivering his main blow in the centre.'[23]

Haig underestimated Ludendorff's recklessness. Operation *Marneschutz–Reims* opened the following day, 15 July, along a seventy-mile front between Château-Thierry in the west, past Reims (which would be outflanked), and then running eastwards along the old battlefields of Champagne to Massiges and Cernay. Seventh Army would make a hazardous crossing of the Marne and then drive south-east towards Épernay, hopefully linking up with the First and Third Armies as they moved south towards Châlons. Operation orders stressed the importance of speed – with commanders being warned that they needed to overrun the enemy's gun line and beat their reserves on the first day. Again, it looked to be another breathtakingly powerful enterprise: forty-eight divisions, 6,353 guns, 2,000 trench mortars and 900 aircraft were assembled, giving the attackers an almost 2:1 advantage in men and guns.[24]

Throughout the planning stages of the Reims attack, Ludendorff's mood was one of confidence and determination, but behind the massive array of force, the German Army was rusting away, its battalions hollowed out by the heavy losses of recent months and losing more men every day to a dangerous influenza pandemic that was spreading across Europe. In Army Group Crown Prince, almost every division suffered from influenza, with Third Army recording a 'significant reduction' in fighting power.[25] At Crown Prince Wilhelm's headquarters, 'a certain mental depression' was noticeable as they planned the attack. OHL's focus on delivering a final blow in Flanders seemed 'right in theory', the Crown Prince admitted, but he wondered whether they had enough troops and guns to mount the preliminary operation at Reims as well. 'For the supply of men from home was dropping off rapidly,' he admitted, 'and such as came were, generally speaking, no longer of the best stamp.' The attack at Reims was 'probably the last great offensive effort of which we were capable'.[26]

Surprise was essential, but never likely. Allied intelligence now had a deep understanding of German offensive tactics, and operational intelligence had also been uncharacteristically lax, giving the French a priceless advantage. Prisoners had been dribbling in for weeks, all eager to divulge what was going on, while a spy in the Crown Prince's staff reported that an offensive in Champagne was imminent.[27] Foch concentrated fighter strength in the Marne area, including both British and American squadrons, and they quickly gained air superiority over the battlefield. Daily sorties were made looking for the characteristic indications of enemy troop movements, accompanied by clouds of dust, which were impossible to prevent in the long summer days. Although Germany had introduced a new fighter in May, the Fokker D.VII, which had excellent performance, it could not be produced in sufficient numbers to provide the aerial cover that Ludendorff's armies desperately needed. About half of Germany's pursuit squadrons had been brought in to support the offensive, but they were still outnumbered by the combined French, British and American forces massed against them (900 to 1,800 fighters), which set the scene for some of the biggest aerial duels of the war.[28]

As Ludendorff prepared to strike Reims, French plans were already well advanced to attack the west face of the Marne pocket on 18 July, led by Mangin's Tenth Army advancing towards Fère-en-Tardenois with its right flank covered by General Jean-Marie Degoutte's Sixth Army. This would be the 'double battle' of the Marne that had been meticulously arranged by Foch and Pétain. Weygand noted how, in the days leading up to the battle, Foch stayed in 'constant liaison' with Pétain. 'He put everything in place to help him to organize, consolidate the defence and counter-attack as best as possible. But he stuck especially to being in perfect agreement with him on leading the battle.' French reserves, including over 2,000 guns and 500 tanks, were being concentrated for the counter-offensive, and Foch would not let them be dispersed under any circumstances. 'Mangin and Degoutte were like two impatient racehorses,' Weygand added, 'with their eyes fixed on the starter's flag.'[29]

15 July was overcast, the sky troubled by dark clouds. A thick mist was clinging to the waters of the Marne when Boehn's Seventh Army launched its assault at 3.50 a.m. The bombardment had wiped out the forward positions and, under the cover of smoke shells, the attackers were able to cross the river on boats or pontoons and secure a bridge-head about five kilometres deep on either side of the village of Dormans.[30] From there they tried to push on through the wooded hills on the far shore, but ran into tough resistance and could make little further progress. The Allied defence was simply too strong and well organized to be breached as easily as it had been on 27 May. There were moments of concern at GQG, which feared its line would give way, but German strength began to ebb as the day wore on. 'The striking in the forest is terrible, nerve-racking', remembered one German soldier who had watched his platoon get caught in heavy shellfire. 'The clearing . . . is caught every five minutes by a light battery and in a short time is a black crater . . . Our men run aimlessly hither and thither; no cover!'[31] Reinforcements were ordered forward, but they struggled to reach the battlefield, which was under heavy attack. By nightfall, the German lines were littered with 'chaotic piles of dead and wounded men and horses, as well as destroyed vehicles, which impeded every forward movement'.[32]

Progress was even more disappointing in Champagne. The French Fourth Army was in the line, commanded by General Henri Gouraud, a flamboyant fifty-year-old Parisian who had lost his right arm at Gallipoli. Like Mangin, he was tried and tested in the fire of combat and looked to the day of battle with a glowing sense of certainty and excitement. 'The bombardment will be terrible', he told his men before the attack. 'You will endure it without weakness . . . The strong and brave hearts of free men beat in your breasts. None will look behind, none will give way . . . And therefore your General tells you it will be a glorious day.'[33] He followed Pétain's instructions on defence-in-depth closely and placed his men in the second position, about 2,000 yards behind the front line, which sheltered them from the worst of the bombardment. The forward trenches were taken quickly, but the attack faltered everywhere it reached the main line of resistance. The French positions were intact and well defended, with observers sighting columns of German troops and guns, which were then targeted by accurate salvos of shellfire. That evening OHL gloomily recorded that the 'overall impression was that the enemy was expecting our attack'.[34]

Ludendorff was rapidly losing control of the situation. The attacks in Champagne were hastily shut down, with hopes resting on a sudden collapse of the French line south of Reims. On the evening of the second day (16 July), Hermann von Kuhl telephoned Ludendorff, finding him 'very sad', and urged him to continue the assault. Kuhl cited the experience of 21 March, when they had not achieved as much as they would have liked, only for the enemy to collapse on subsequent days. But Ludendorff would not agree. Further attacks would have to wait; they 'could not risk the losses involved'.[35] Desperate fighting took place along the banks of the Marne on 16 and 17 July as the Germans tried to enlarge their bridgehead, only to come under sustained air attack. Germany could not prevent Allied aircraft from making hundreds of low-level sorties over the river, machine-gunning columns of troops and trying to destroy the pontoon bridges. The RAF lost fifteen machines over the Marne in three days, but helped to pin back the enemy advance, and, on 17 July, Colonel Reinhardt, Chief of Staff at Seventh Army, reported that the bombing and shelling against the Marne bridges were so heavy 'that demolition is at present greater than construction', with 70 per cent of all bridge trains being destroyed.[36]

Faced with the imminent ruin of his plans, Ludendorff grew increasingly restive and gloomy. A staff officer at OHL complained that 'serious questions' needed to be asked about the First Quartermaster-General and his 'incoherence'. 'His Excellency is working himself ragged, is getting too bogged down in the details. The situation is really serious.'[37] On the evening of 17 July, he left Avesnes and travelled north to Tournai, from where he would direct Operation *Hagen* (once enough artillery had been redeployed), although this was now more in hope than in expectation. As Ludendorff abandoned the battle on the Marne, the final elements of Mangin's counter-attack were coming together. Huge numbers of troops, guns and tanks were moving into position, concealed from the air by the deep woodland of Villers-Cotterêts – in spite of a last-minute wobble from Pétain. On the morning of 15 July, as German troops crossed the Marne, he ordered preparations for Mangin's offensive to be suspended, hoping to redeploy French and American forces, but Foch overruled him. Taking a calculated risk that the line could hold without endangering the counter-attack, Foch insisted that it continue. 'Please understand that, until you inform me of some fresh crisis,' Foch wired later that day, 'there can be no question of slowing down in any way, still less of stopping, Mangin's preparations.'[38]

On the morning of 18 July, amid fierce thunderstorms and downpours of rain, Mangin's counter-attack broke against the German lines south of Soissons. In Tenth Army, the crucial northern part of the salient was held by XX Corps, commanded by General Pierre Berdoulat, who had ordered the Moroccan Division, alongside both 1st and 2nd US Divisions, to spearhead the attack. There would be no artillery preparation. As the British had demonstrated at Cambrai, by conducting artillery registration before the battle, it was possible to fire an accurate creeping barrage at the moment of assault, thus preserving the element of surprise. The offensive would also rely on extensive armoured support: 240 medium tanks (either Saint-Chamonds or Schneiders) and 540 Renault FT-17s. The Renault was a revolutionary light tank with a two-man crew, noticeable for its fully rotating turret, which mounted either a machine-gun or a 37 mm cannon. It had first gone into battle in late May, but 18 July was the first time that it would play a major role in an offensive – helping to neutralize machine-gun positions and strongpoints ahead of the infantry.[39]

With eighteen divisions in the first wave (against just ten under-strength divisions from Boehn's Seventh Army), Tenth and Sixth Armies greatly overmatched their opponent, but would have to progress against defences of considerable strength. The ground was rolling, but interrupted by a series of wooded defiles, and with enemy machine-gunners hidden in thick, swaying fields of ripening grain or

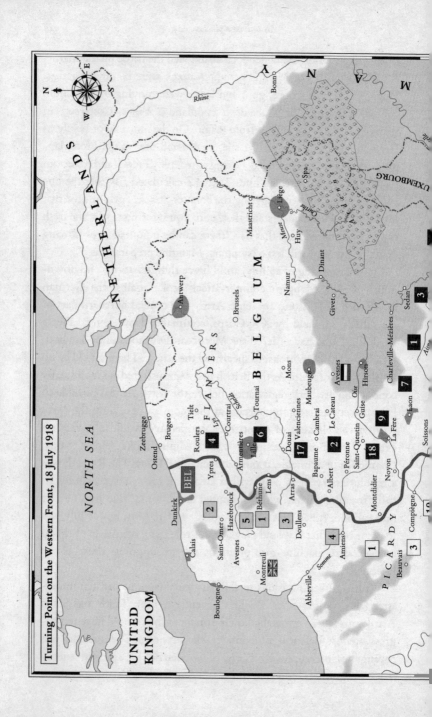

Turning Point on the Western Front, 18 July 1918

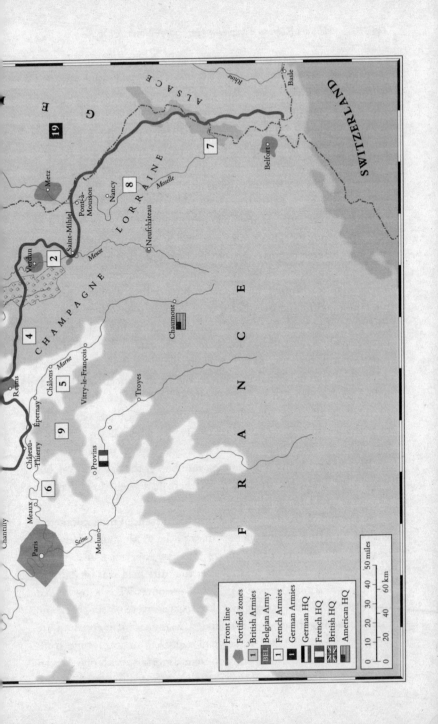

located in fortified farm buildings. In many cases, American troops (making up about a third of the attacking infantry) only arrived at their jumping-off positions with moments to spare – leaving them to advance across unknown territory in darkness – a great test for even experienced troops. But this ensured the attack gained complete surprise, and when the creeping barrage roared into life at 4.35 a.m., covering the battlefield in thick, white smoke, the attacking troops had little choice but to move out as quickly as possible into the flare-ridden darkness.

Progress was swift. Individual German machine-gunners tried to hold up the advance, but most were swiftly overrun, crushed by the tanks or the creeping barrage, or shot or bayonetted by the infantry that came in their wake. One doughboy remembered how it was 'every man for himself, an irregular, broken line, clawing through the tangles, climbing over fallen trees, plunging heavily into Boche rifle-pits. Here and there a well-fought Maxim gun held its front until somebody – officer, non-com, or private – got a few men together and, crawling to left or right, gained a flank and silenced it.'[40] When tougher defences were encountered, officers quickly signalled to the tanks to try to help them, and the Renaults proved particularly effective, providing what one report called 'a great deal of assistance' in helping battalions to advance when they came across especially stubborn machine-gun nests. Mechanical breakdown and artillery fire gradually reduced their numbers as the day wore on, but when they had been used in mass, there had been little that the defenders could do against them.[41]

By the end of the day, Tenth Army had advanced nine kilometres with Sixth Army, extending the attack to the south, gaining five kilometres. 'As evening came on,' recalled an American soldier, 'the fumes of burned cordite settling over the battlefield was [sic] almost choking and stung the eyes. Groups of prisoners were being herded to the rear by armed guards, and litter bearers were passing back and forth collecting the dead and wounded. Many German corpses were scattered about.'[42] Allied forces had captured an impressive haul: 20,000 prisoners, 518 guns and 300 trench mortars, with one American regiment taking 3,000 Germans from five different divisions.

Mangin dashed off a suitably gushing order thanking the Americans for their 'magnificent courage' and 'indomitable tenacity', which 'completely routed a surprised enemy' and 'checked the counter-attacks of his fresh divisions'. He was 'proud to have commanded you during such days and to have fought with you for the deliverance of the world'.[43]

The shock was equally profound on the other side of the line. Years later Ludendorff would insist that Operation *Marneschutz–Reims* had been based on 'sound military principles', but it was a desperate gamble, coming at the end of a long losing streak.[44] He knew that he could not stop attacking without admitting that the war was lost. To do so would hand the initiative over to the enemy with their 'vast resources in war material'. So he continued pinning his hopes on a climactic battle in Flanders that would never take place. But others, lower down the chain of command, knew immediately what Mangin's counter-attack signified. 'In a certain sense the enemy had succeeded in effecting a strategic surprise', recorded Army Group Crown Prince in its war diary that evening. It had been assumed that 'our own offensive would overrun a surprised and weak enemy in an irresistible drive', producing a 'catastrophe' around Reims that would draw in Allied reserves, but this had not happened. 'The enemy early had gained exact knowledge of the preparations for the attacks against Reims and Châlons and thus was able to prepare himself for the defence.' More worrying was the method by which the Allies were now able to launch offensives. 'The tanks, employed in numbers never known before and much better developed technically, rolled ahead of the infantry in long, connected lines. Our defence was not adapted to this mass employment on a wide front and was effective only in spots.' The events of 18 July were 'a turning point in the history of the World War'.[45]

'There was a pronounced air of good feeling and confidence' on 24 July as Allied commanders gathered at Foch's headquarters, now located at Bombon, a short drive from GQG at Provins.[46] Like Joffre after the First Battle of the Marne, Foch wanted to keep the enemy moving. 'The moment had arrived to abandon the generally defensive attitude forced on us hitherto by numerical inferiority,' he announced, 'and to pass to the offensive.' He wanted to undertake a series of attacks across the front 'intended to free railways of vital importance' at Amiens, Château-Thierry and the salient at Saint-Mihiel, southeast of Verdun (which was close to the Paris–Avricourt railway line). 'How long these different operations will take and how far they will carry us cannot be determined now.' Although it was still anticipated that victory would come in 1919 rather than 1918, he hoped that it might be possible to launch a new offensive in the late summer or early autumn that would, as he put it, 'increase our advantages and leave no respite to the enemy'.[47]

Of the four generals at Bombon, Pétain was the most cautious, wary about over-committing their forces and telling Foch that 'The French Army, after four years of war and the severest trials, is at present worn out, bled white, anaemic.'[48] He had already tired of Mangin's endless demands for reinforcements and kept a jealous grasp on his reserves – worried that continual bloodletting would leave his forces in no position to continue the war into 1919 and, accordingly, he requested more time to consider the proposals. Haig and Pershing were more upbeat and agreed with Foch that they had to take advantage of their present superiority in manpower, tanks and aircraft to press the enemy hard. That day, Pershing issued orders for the formation of the US First Army, which would become operational on 10 August and was tasked with reducing the salient at Saint-Mihiel. It was not clear when this operation could take place, or indeed how soon American divisions could be redeployed and concentrated in Lorraine, but Pershing was happy that an independent American Army was now finally in sight.

Strung along in dusty, dispirited columns, German troops were already evacuating the Marne pocket at speed, retreating back to the line of the Vesle and abandoning Soissons, which was recaptured on 6 August. This meant that the first of Foch's proposed operations – to clear Château-Thierry – was now almost completed. With that in mind, Foch visited Haig on 26 July and they discussed the projected attack at Amiens, which would be entrusted to General Rawlinson, commander of the reconstituted Fourth Army. Henry Rawlinson was glad to be back in the field. He had endured a frustrating eighteen months since the final attacks on the Somme, being sidelined for the operation at Ypres and only returning after General Gough had been relieved of command in late March, but he was determined to make up for lost time. The attack at Amiens would employ all the techniques that were now well established in Allied armies: extensive deception efforts; no preliminary bombardment; the mass employment of tanks; and extensive air cover. Australian and Canadian troops were massed together for the operation, having escaped significant fighting all year, which meant they were refreshed and ready to go. In contrast to his worries before the attack on 1 July 1916, Rawlinson was confident that things were now different. 'There is nothing to show that the Boche knows what is coming south of the Somme', he wrote on the eve of the attack. 'We shall have eight excellent divisions and three hundred and fifty tanks against him on this part of the battle-front, in a perfect tank country; and three cavalry divisions ready to press through any hole that is made. I have great hopes that we shall win a great success.'[49]

The attack was originally scheduled for 10 August, but Foch – worried lest the enemy withdraw from their exposed positions – spoke to Haig and they agreed to move it forward by forty-eight hours. This added an extra burden of staff work on Rawlinson, but fortunately resulted in no great harm. By the evening of 7 August, fourteen British, Australian, Canadian and French divisions – perhaps upwards of 100,000 men – were drawn up behind the front, unsuspected by the enemy. They were supported by more than 2,000 guns and 530 tanks, all covered over by camouflage netting or hidden behind canvas screens, awaiting the moment to go forward.[50] When the bombardment opened at 4.20 a.m., the sky briefly flashed white before a crashing series of explosions broke out along the German front line, still hidden in the early-morning mist. Gaining complete surprise, Allied troops were able to burst through the thin screen of defences in a welter of fire and steel. Men of the German Second Army, strung out in small machine-gun teams or squads occupying thinly scraped rifle pits, could only respond fitfully as they were swamped by the oncoming infantry, supported by tanks zigzagging across the battlefield, correcting their course every now and then, crushing any barbed wire and opening fire on anything that moved.

By the time the mist had burnt off, the German forward defences along a twenty-kilometre front (between Morlancourt on the Ancre and Moreuil north of the Avre) had been overrun and reserve troops were 'leapfrogging' on to their final objectives. 'It was like the old open warfare we used to read about', a Canadian battalion commander noted. Orders were now given verbally: 'the brigade staff was a group of officers on the side of the road, with the brigade pennant sticking up. Officers commanding battalions would send forth at a gallop, get instructions to take some region and one to take another and it looked like a north-country lake scattered with islands, it was open country with villages all heavily wooded scattered around on it . . .'[51] Rawlinson pushed forward his cavalry while also unleashing his light tanks, Medium Mark As (known as 'Whippets'), which were able to wreak havoc in the German rear, while British and French aircraft wheeled over the battlefield bombing and machine-gunning long columns of retreating infantry that would scatter at their approach.

German casualties had been catastrophic; and the bloodied columns of wounded, limping soldiers leaving the battlefield told a desperate story. Official figures for the German Army were as high as 36,500 men, including 27,500 missing or taken prisoner, with the loss of 400 guns.[52] The attackers had advanced between six and eight miles, completely unhinging the German defences and forcing a significant redeployment of both Second and Eighteenth Armies. When Rupprecht went to a briefing on the morning of 9 August, he was told that there was 'no other option but to fall back behind the Somme'. He recognized this was inevitable, only for Ludendorff to ring up and – when he was speaking to Kuhl – demand that Second Army 'hold its position'. He was sending the Alpine Corps as reinforcements and wanted 'to plan every move of the newly arrived battalions'. Kuhl tried to mollify Ludendorff as best he could, nodding and continually saying 'yes' or 'we cannot yet predict how this will turn out, everything depends on how circumstances develop'. Rupprecht could only watch in horror. 'The miserable fact that our troops are doing so badly can be variously attributed to: exhaustion, their inferior organization (compared to how it was earlier) and despondency over events . . .'[53]

There seemed no way out of Germany's bind. At a Crown Council meeting at Spa on 14 August, Kühlmann emphasized the darkening scene. 'At the moment the enemy's determination and confidence in victory were greater than ever. To a certain extent this was explained by their recent military successes in the west, but the main reason was their original and ever-growing conviction that the Allies, with their comparatively inexhaustible reserves of men, raw material and manufactures, must in time overthrow the allied Central Powers.' Austria had now confirmed that 'she has reached the end of the resources' and could not 'hold out after the winter'. Even Hindenburg, whose robust self-confidence had always seen him through bad times, had to admit that they could 'no longer hope to break the will of our enemies by military operations' and that they must adopt a 'strategic defensive'.[54] The shattering realization that the war was lost hit the Supreme War Lord hardest of all. 'The Kaiser maintained an outward calm,' recorded one account, 'but anyone looking into his face saw in the tense features and deep furrows an emotional suffering and, in his flaming eyes, the overwhelming inner agitation, which sought a solution.'

'I realize that we have to take stock', he said wearily. 'We have reached the limits of our capabilities. The war must be ended.'[55]

23. 'Keep steady'

'With regard to the present military situation, the essential facts are well known', announced David Lloyd George before the House of Commons on Wednesday, 7 August 1918 – just before the parliamentary recess and a day before Rawlinson would strike at Amiens (an operation the Prime Minister was unaware of). 'There has been four and a half months of such fighting as has never been seen on the face of this globe. The magnitude of the armies, the ferocity of the conflict, the losses inflicted and sustained, the valour displayed by the men who took part in the contest – such fighting has never been witnessed on the face of this globe – and not merely in all that, but in the issues which hung in the balance of that fighting.' There had been, he admitted, 'very very anxious moments, and those who knew the most were the most anxious. The losses were considerable in men, especially in the numbers of prisoners captured, I regret to say, and in material . . .' But Lloyd George was confident that those deficits had been paid off: reinforcements had been sent to France and every gun that was lost, and more, had been replaced with deliveries from home.[1]

'The House seemed rather tired, and members were not so responsive as usual to the Prime Minister's buoyant eloquence', reported a journalist from *The Times* sent to cover the speech. 'There were many gaps on the green benches', including his predecessor, Herbert Asquith, even if the galleries were 'crowded with eager listeners'.[2] Lloyd George cautioned that the war was far from over, but explained that the Germans had miscalculated how quickly the Allies would respond to their offensives, particularly the speed with which losses had been made up (which Lloyd George would surely draw most of the credit for), the increased rapidity with which American troops were transported to France, and also the 'first experiment in unity of command', which had 'achieved great results'. He waved away the controversies over Foch's position and insisted that he was not Generalissimo 'in the real full sense of the term'. 'What has been established has been unity of strategic command, and that has answered every purpose, as the Germans know too well, and to their cost.'

Despite the optimistic sounds emanating from the Prime Minister, he remained concerned at the direction the war was taking. Suspecting the French Government of using Foch to preserve their own manpower at the expense of their coalition partners, he worried about the effect that continued heavy fighting would have on Britain's position in the alliance. He did not want (as he explained before a meeting of his closest advisers) 'the British Army to be so reduced that next year we should find ourselves the third Military Power on the Western Front'.[3] He had sent feelers out about moving Haig on and believed that General Plumer would be a possible replacement, but struggled to gain traction when the war seemed to be at such a moment of balance. News about Amiens briefly cheered him, and at a luncheon at Newport Town Hall he paid tribute to 'the brilliant qualities of our troops, and of the French troops', as well as to 'the very courageous leadership of Sir Douglas Haig and General Rawlinson'. He also warned against complacency. 'Still I want to say again,' he added finally, 'it is not over . . . Do not get too excited over it. Keep steady.'[4]

'Keeping steady' was exactly what Foch was trying to do. With Amiens safe, French and British forces mounted a series of further attacks in late August, extending the fighting north and south in an ever-widening cascade of operations. Tenth Army attacked towards Chauny on 20 August and quickly punched another hole in the German line, gaining 3–4 kilometres and taking 8,000 prisoners and 100 guns.[5] Mangin was doing exactly what was expected of him: hitting the Germans hard, forcing them to yield ground, though without suffering too greatly in the process. *But the horse was still straining at the bit* and he grumbled about not being able to exploit the attack as much as he would have liked, sensing that the enemy was beginning to crumble. Pétain again refused to release more reserves to Tenth Army, leaving Mangin twisting in the wind. 'One must manoeuvre', Mangin wrote home on 22 August. 'I think they should feel sorry for not giving me most of what I asked for.'[6]

General Sir Julian Byng, Third Army commander, opened his own offensive on 21 August, advancing eastwards over the old Somme battlefield towards Bapaume. Unlike Mangin, Byng advanced cautiously and was well aware of the care that needed to be taken with his men. At least 50 per cent of the infantry of his thirteen divisions were described as 'boys', later known as the 'men of 18 in 1918', who had been rushed to the front in the frantic days after the March offensive.[7] Byng took the first German position, his troops advancing in widely spaced 'worms' behind a heavy barrage, marked by smoke. Considerable difficulty was encountered in crossing the muddy wastes of the Ancre, which had been pulverized in the fighting of 1916, and because of this Byng opted not to continue the attack until Fourth Army had come up on his right and taken Albert. As soon as one offensive began to slow down, another attack would be launched. Fourth Army resumed its own forward movement on 22 August and General Sir Henry Horne's First Army pushed off four days later, engaging German troops across the front and preventing any concentrated enemy response.

This sequence of attacks, which continually expanded in width, bore little resemblance to the kind of operations that had been fought, by both sides, since 1915. Instead of getting bogged down in a narrow pocket and having to bring up men and supplies over badly torn-up ground, as the Germans were now having to do, Foch continually enlarged his battle by constant attacks on each flank. 'Once again he is not searching for the breakthrough, but the general battle', noted Weygand years later. 'It is applying the principles that he has not ceased to advocate since 9 May 1915', but which hitherto had not been possible because he lacked the means to do so.[8]

Saint-Mihiel would be the next part of this 'general battle'. Ever since he had chosen Lorraine as the likely deployment area for his expeditionary force, Pershing had seen Saint-Mihiel as a useful laboratory that could be used to blood the Americans and test their military organization. As soon as the decision had been reached on the Marne, Pershing began withdrawing divisions from the front and concentrating them in the new American sector in the Woëvre. On 16 August, the objectives for the attack were finalized. Fourteen divisions of the US First Army would 'undertake the reduction of the

Saint-Mihiel salient' with the 'minimum result' being the 'reopening of the Paris–Nancy Railroad in the vicinity of Commercy'. Pershing, with his eyes on Metz and the Longwy–Briey iron region, hoped that a breakthrough at Saint-Mihiel would be a rapier thrust, ending the war. The bulk of US forces would be deployed along the southern face of the salient, with subsidiary units on the west face, and together they would cause the collapse of the entire German position. It was hoped to launch the attack on 11 September.[9]

Just as Pershing was settling into First Army headquarters at Ligny-en-Barrois, there was a sudden change of plan, due, in part, to Haig, who was convinced that a decision was now finally in sight. On 27 August, he wrote to Foch explaining that 'In order to exploit the present favourable situation I am strongly of opinion that it is very desirable that American Divisions should take an active share in the battle without delay, and I beg to submit for your consideration that they should be so distributed as to admit of a concentric movement being made on Cambrai, on Saint-Quentin, and from the south upon Mézières.'[10] Earlier that month, Haig had been dismayed when Pershing had asked for the five American divisions in training with the BEF to be returned to his command as soon as possible. Although it was agreed that two would stay with Haig's forces, the British Commander-in-Chief regarded the American concentration at Saint-Mihiel as an 'eccentric' act that would, as he explained in a letter to Henry Wilson, 'lead to nothing'. American divisions should be 'distributed' among British and French forces 'to enable a concentric movement being begun without delay'.[11]

Foch immediately saw the value of Haig's proposal and travelled to Ligny on 30 August to put it to Pershing. As soon as they had exchanged greetings, Foch unrolled a map of the front and explained that 'the German armies were in more or less disorder' and that they 'must not allow them to reorganize'. He now wanted the objectives for Saint-Mihiel to be curtailed. Instead, the Americans would mount a new attack alongside the French Fourth Army west of Verdun between the Meuse and the Argonne forest, from where they would drive north towards Mézières and Sedan, not Metz as originally understood. Pershing could barely believe what he was hearing.

'Well, Marshal, this is a very sudden change', he admitted, taking all his legendary self-control not to lose his temper. 'We are going forward as already recommended to you and approved by you, and I cannot understand why you want these changes.'

'That is true,' Foch replied, 'but the fate of the 1918 campaign will be decided in the Aisne region and I wish to limit the Woëvre (Saint-Mihiel) attack so that the Americans can participate in the Meuse offensive, which will produce still greater results.'

'Marshal Foch . . . This virtually destroys the American army that we have been trying for so long to form.'

The two men argued for some time, moving around the table (where Foch's map was laid) and pointing out different objectives, different routes, different ways to deliver the final blow. Pershing claimed that Foch's proposals would 'prevent, or at least seriously delay, the formation of a distinctive American army' and reiterated that US forces would only fight together as an independent army and not be parcelled out across the front. Foch's argument was that they needed to act quickly and put all their resources together in a concentric attack, the British driving east and the French and Americans moving north, crushing Ludendorff's armies in a vice. This was a logical assessment, but when Foch insisted that American forces be split between the French Fourth and Second Armies, it opened up all the old wounds of 'amalgamation'. Pershing blanched white at what he felt was another attempt to steal his manpower to bolster the broken French Army and he refused. Foch left Ligny looking 'very pale and apparently exhausted'.[12]

Foch's decision to reorient US forces to face north and not northeast would be the cause of much later inquiry and debate, between those who claimed it was logical and correct, allowing Pershing to directly aid British and French forces elsewhere on the front, and those who rued the missed opportunities of a drive on Metz and cursed the disorganization and dislocation that the change produced in the Argonne. Pershing wrote a long letter to Foch the following day in which he agreed that it was necessary to exploit the unexpectedly favourable situation, but made it clear that he would 'no longer agree to any plan which involves a dispersion of our units'. American soldiers were 'no longer willing to be incorporated in other armies' and it was, to Pershing at least, 'impracticable' to conduct the attack at Saint-Mihiel and then assemble between twelve and sixteen divisions within a matter of days to strike north in the Argonne (which lay sixty miles away). Therefore, either Saint-Mihiel was abandoned or the attack on Mézières postponed.[13]

With American troops already training for the attack, it was essential to make a decision one way or another. Whatever their frustrations, both men recognized that they were dependent on each other: Foch for American manpower that would tip the scales of war; and Pershing for the artillery, tanks, air power and logistical support provided by Paris. The American travelled up to Bombon on 2 September to meet Foch and Pétain, where they agreed to limit the attack at Saint-Mihiel to just the elimination of the salient and then begin a new attack west of the Meuse with American troops, supported on their left by Gouraud's Fourth Army. Foch issued General Instructions the following day: 'At present the Allied offensive is developing successfully from the Scarpe to the Aisne, forcing the enemy to retire all along that front. In order to expand and intensify this offensive, it is important that all the Allied forces engage in the battle without delay and operate in convergent directions against all favourable parts of the front.' The British and the French left would continue to attack towards Cambrai and Saint-Quentin, the French centre would drive the enemy back beyond the Aisne and Ailette, and, once the Saint-Mihiel attack had taken place, Pershing would lead an assault in the 'general direction' of Mézières 'to be launched no later than September 20 to 25'.[14]

The Kaiser's announcement of 14 August that the war must be ended had not resulted in any specific, concrete moves for peace. Paul von Hintze assured him that recent defeats were no more than 'little setbacks', and once the enemy had been halted, they would be able to enter into peace negotiations.[15] He retreated to his summer residence at Schloss Wilhelmshöhe near Kassel, where he went for walks, received guests and spent time with his wife, Dona, who had suffered a heart attack. With the *Kaiserin* confined to her bed, Wilhelm grew increasingly unstable, his mood depressed by the course the war was taking.

'The campaign is lost', he whispered to his aides on 2 September. 'Our troops have been retreating ever since the 18th July. We are exhausted. I don't know what they are doing at Avesnes. When the offensive on the Marne began on July 15th I was assured that the French had no more than 8 divisions in reserve and the English perhaps 13. Instead, the enemy assembled a number of divisions unobserved by us in the Villers-Cotterêts forest, attacked and forced us to retire after piercing our right flank. Since then we have suffered defeat after defeat.'[16]

This was an accurate summary of the events of the last six weeks, but the Kaiser could not bring himself to move against the generals at OHL. He remained cocooned in his cosseted isolation, comforted by his staff and, with Berg-Markienen overseeing his Civil Cabinet, under the influence of a hardliner who was dedicated to protecting the monarchy at all costs. When Albert Ballin, head of the Hamburg–Amerika Line and an old friend of the Kaiser's, asked for a private audience, Berg insisted on accompanying them. Strolling through the grounds of the Wilhelmshöhe, Ballin tried to tell Wilhelm to open negotiations with President Wilson and to 'modernise' the 'political structure' of the Reich before it was too late, but he struggled to cut through the constant interruptions of Berg. It seemed to Ballin, he later confessed, 'quite impossible to spell out, or even to intimate, the seriousness and the frightful danger in which Germany found itself. My determination collapsed.'[17]

The realization that Germany was losing the war was even becoming evident at the Supreme Command. On 2 September, Mertz von Quirnheim, a section chief at OHL, spoke to Ludendorff, who received him in a 'most serious mood'. Going over the situation map, lying across his desk, Ludendorff 'openly admitted that he did not know how to continue the fight'. When Quirnheim asked him whether he had informed Hintze about the 'serious situation', Ludendorff shook his head. 'He said he had not, adding that it was too difficult for him to report the real situation to the Foreign Office without making it too frightening . . .'[18] That day reports arrived that renewed British attacks along the Arras–Cambrai road had forced Seventeenth Army to fall back. Fighting tenaciously, Horne's First Army, spearheaded by the Canadian Corps, had broken through a northern extension to the Hindenburg Line (known as the Drocourt–Quéant Line). Georg Wetzell thought the situation was 'extremely serious' and that Ludendorff was 'completely exhausted'. When the duo chaired a meeting of army group Chiefs of Staff at Avesnes on 6 September, there was no answer to the Allied attacks, only excuses. Hindenburg insisted that there had not been any 'operational mistakes'. On the contrary, the causes of the 'unfavourable situation' were 'great indiscretion', which had allowed word to leak out about *Marneschutz–Reims*, and surprise at Mangin's counter-attack near Soissons. Poor performance was also to blame in Second Army. Even Otto von Below, the victor of Caporetto, was not spared criticism – his leadership at Seventeenth Army had 'not been up to par'.[19]

Ludendorff's demeanour shocked those present at Avesnes. He stood behind Hindenburg, leaving most of the talking to the Field Marshal. 'Ludendorff gave the impression of being ill', noted Kuhl. Fritz von Lossberg was also unimpressed. He had been assigned to a new army group led by the former commander of Seventh Army, Max von Boehn, and found Ludendorff 'very nervous', which was 'a drastic change from his usually firm personality'. When he did speak, he refused to accept that poor strategy or operational decision-making was at fault for their perilous situation. 'He had quite a few critical things to say about the troops', remembered Lossberg. 'He blamed the soldiers and their leaders for the recent events, without acknowledging that his own misguided leadership was in large part the reason for the failures.'[20] Although Ludendorff promised to get better at telephoning subordinates directly and not interfering in their duties, few believed him. Wetzell, who had served at OHL for over two years, resigned three days later, complaining about Ludendorff's habit of bypassing the chain of command and of not listening to anything he had to say.

Ludendorff's state of nervousness and high tension had been noted for some time. Dr Münter, Hindenburg's personal physician, reported on his behaviour and told him that he needed more relaxation, sleep and physical activity. The 'enormous daily workload and responsibility' on his shoulders had 'resulted in a state of nervous overload, which manifested itself in exhaustion, irritability and inner unrest'. Münter recommended that an old friend and former medical officer, Dr Hochheimer, be brought in to consult on Ludendorff's condition, which he agreed to. Hochheimer gave Ludendorff an exact daily programme to follow and carefully observed his moods. 'His sleep at night is geared to events at the front, to which he is always listening with half an ear; he sleeps from 12 midnight to 5 a.m., sometimes even less! Then the thoughts – strategic, tactical, political, economic – start to order themselves again . . . The man is completely alone, he is married to his work.'[21]

Already German intelligence had picked up alarming signs of American activity around Saint-Mihiel. On 3 September, the local commander, General Gallwitz, asked OHL whether 'in the event of a hostile attack' he should hold on or withdraw to a rearward line known as the Michel Position. It was only on 10 September that Ludendorff confirmed that they were to abandon the salient.[22] But it was already too late. The US First Army attacked on the morning of 12 September, crushing German troops who were in the process of evacuating their positions and scoring a first, definitive victory. Pershing ensured that they attacked with overwhelming force: nine full-strength American divisions (including his most experienced units), supported by the elite II Colonial Corps (assigned to the attack by Pétain), overmatched their opponent with three times as many infantry; five or six times as many guns; and over seven times as many aircraft. It was, as one doughboy wrote, 'the easiest day the battalion has ever had. I hope to have more like it, but I doubt it.'[23]

The defeat at Saint-Mihiel was followed in quick succession by a further series of damaging events. Austria formally communicated peace proposals to the United States (through the Legation of Sweden) on 16 September, which was followed soon afterwards by the collapse of Bulgarian troops on the Salonika Front, uncovering the southern flank of the Central Powers. In turn, Bulgaria requested the cessation of hostilities on 24 September and signed an armistice five days later. There was little that could be done to prevent this sudden splintering of the alliance. Hindenburg issued a defiant decree to the army urging his troops to keep fighting: 'The readiness for peace does not contradict the spirit that we are leading the fight for our homeland.' He looked back to the peace offers of December 1916 and stressed that 'the enemy had answered every previous statement of readiness for peace with derision and mockery'. It was, therefore, 'necessary that the army continues to fight . . . It is only in this way that we will contribute towards breaking the enemy's will to annihilate.'[24]

By the second week of September, the *Westheer* had fallen back to the Hindenburg Line, abandoning all the ground it had gained between the Scarpe and the Vesle, fighting tenaciously all the way, but unable to stem the Allied advance for more than a day or two. The army had mustered over 200 divisions in March 1918 – but by the end of September it had shrunk to just 125, with only forty-seven of these deemed 'fit for combat'. Losses had been catastrophic, reaching over 230,000 per month in August and September, with the 'particularly alarming' fact that about half of these were classed as missing – a firm indication that all was not well.[25] Harassed by influenza, conscious of heavy losses, and no longer believing that victory was possible, German soldiers underwent a crisis of morale in the late summer and early autumn. 'From mid-1918 onwards it was over', recalled one veteran from Thuringia; 'everyone was completely shattered and tried as hard as possible to save his life after the long ordeal. Troops were hardly ever replaced, the artillery became more terrifying by the minute, and the aircraft squadrons arrived in their droves.' Men became desperate to go home. 'The long suffering of the war', he noted, 'brought the men to despair and it was said many times that we would be willing to walk home even half naked if the war would finish at long last.'[26]

OHL left Avesnes soon after the conference on 6 September and moved back to Spa. Much now depended upon whether the Hindenburg Line would keep the enemy at bay, conserve Germany's declining manpower and then bring coalition forces to the negotiating table. Fritz von Lossberg, who had recently looked over the main sections of the Siegfried Line, was not optimistic, telling Ludendorff that 'no long-term resistance was likely' upon it. They should, in his opinion, make an immediate withdrawal to a rear position that was then being sketched out (the Antwerp–Meuse Line), while destroying everything in their path – a sort of grand version of the retreat of 1917. But Ludendorff would not have it. They would stand and fight. In contrast to the elastic form of defence-in-depth that the German Army had practised so successfully since 1915, they were now to follow a strict policy of holding the main line at all costs. Everything had come full circle.[27]

Foch spent his time at Bombon, finalizing the arrangements for the concentric attack that would strike the German Army before the arrival of bad weather. The Franco-American attack in the Meuse–Argonne would begin on 26 September, with the British First and Third Armies going into battle the following day. A breakout in Flanders would then take place on 28 September, before the British Fourth and French First Armies joined the attack a day or so later.[28] 'The operations which will follow take on a particular type of nervous, vigorous and wonderfully precise activity', recorded one of Foch's admirers. 'The Marshal will finally prove by action that the principles of war are unchangeable; that the basis of his teaching at the École de Guerre has not lost any of its value; that the Napoleonic concept, clear and flexible, has kept all its strength, despite the formidable creations of the German industrial war machine.'[29]

How much success would greet this assault was the great imponderable. On 8 September, Pétain had sent Foch a long draft of 'The Battle of 1919', a thirty-five-page assessment, filled with annexes, that described the likely characteristics of war into the following year and the resources that France would be able to muster. Pétain claimed that a series of preliminary actions should be conducted (to fix German reserves) before a main operation achieved a decisive victory.[30] This narrative had been heard before, and Foch was no longer interested. He was confident the enemy were on the run and needed only further encouragement to keep them going. On 25 September, he took up his command post in the forest of Trois-Fontaines (just north of Saint-Dizier on the Marne) and issued a final directive, underlining the importance of what was about to happen. The Americans must 'push as far and as fast as possible' towards Buzancy, with French troops alongside them advancing with the same 'speed, decision and initiative'.[31]

Haig was also convinced that risks could now be taken freely and, unlike Pétain, found himself urging his commanders to act as aggressively as possible. When Henry Wilson had circulated a memorandum on 'British Military Policy 1918–1919' in late July that claimed the 'decisive struggle' on the Western Front would not begin until the following summer, the British Commander-in-Chief was unimpressed. 'Words! Words! Words! Lots of words! And little else!' he scribbled upon his copy. On 10 September, he visited the War Office for an interview with Lord Milner, and was eager to explain just how much had changed at the front. 'Within the last four weeks we had captured 77,000 prisoners and nearly 800 guns! There has never been such a victory in the annals of Britain, and its effects are not yet apparent.' Haig then predicted that the 'discipline of the German Army is quickly going, and the German officer is no longer what he was. It seems to me to be the beginning of the end.'[32]

Haig was more right than many suspected. The first thunderous blow was landed on Thursday, 26 September, with Franco-American forces striking north into the Meuse–Argonne. The ground was difficult: an attackers' nightmare of thickly wooded hillsides, broken by steep defiles and riddled with trenches and machine-gun posts. Pershing attacked with three large corps, about 330,000 assault troops against 61,000 Germans; intending to bludgeon his way through with overwhelming force.[33] They attacked in the half-light of morning after a three-hour bombardment, making good progress (at the deepest point going up to four miles), but then becoming strung out and pinned down against a series of tough positions, particularly at Montfaucon, a hilltop village that commanded the battlefield and was soon given the nickname of 'Little Gibraltar'. 'It is impossible to recount that raging battle in minute detail', noted one of the attacking infantrymen. 'We were hammering at dozens of machine-gun nests at a time and as fast as we reduced them, and, scratched and bleeding, plunged through the bushes to further our advance, we found ourselves up against an equal or greater number. We out-flanked them, or took them by frontal attack, aided by one-pounders and machine-guns. Daring men sneaked upon them through the brush, and silenced them with hand grenades.'[34]

Progress slowed to a crawl over the next few days, with the Germans throwing in more divisions and fighting bravely for every inch of ground. Anxiously awaiting news in his headquarters, Pershing bristled with impatience. On the morning of the second day, he ordered divisional and brigade commanders to move as far forward as possible and prosecute the attack with 'energy and rapidity': 'Corps and division commanders will not hesitate to relieve on the spot any officer of whatever rank who fails to show in this emergency those qualities of leadership required to accomplish the task that confronts us.'[35] Pershing's wish to push on was understandable, but, in the thick woods of the Argonne forest, combat devolved into a savage, close-quarter melee, and American battalions, unused to the intensity of fighting, began to lose cohesion. A whole host of problems emerged: poor liaison between units; shortages of vital supplies; and lack of proper fire support. Once the creeping barrage had run out, the doughboys had almost no artillery preparation and had to make their way forward unsupported, and do so day after day until they were relieved. One young American remembered coming across a piece of open ground, which was littered with 'dead men in olive drab and feld grau, scattered equipment, and cripples . . . They'd pushed in with the same esprit as Pickett's brigade at Gettysburg and with about the same results.'[36] Within four days the AEF had sustained 45,000 casualties and, amid growing disorganization, Pershing had no choice but to suspend the offensive.[37]

The frustrations that Pershing encountered in the Meuse–Argonne were not unexpected for an inexperienced army in tough conditions, but they gave greater weight to those who suggested that the sudden move from Saint-Mihiel had been a dangerous error. Pershing had deployed his best-trained and most experienced divisions at Saint-Mihiel (including 1st, 2nd and 42nd Divisions), which meant those units that opened the great attack on 26 September were much less seasoned – and the shock of combat was brutal. They did not lack for bravery and aggressive spirit; only the organization and skill that prolonged fighting helped to create. Pershing put a brave face on it, writing to Newton Baker on 2 October that the 'operations here have gone very well, but, due to the rains and the conditions of the roads, have not gone forward as rapidly nor as far as I had hoped. But this terrain over which we now operate is the most difficult on the Western Front. Our losses so far have been moderate. I have taken out three of the newest divisions and replaced them by older ones. We shall be prepared to advance again in a day or two more.'[38]

Better results were obtained further north, where the ground was more favourable and the men were less green. The British First and Third Armies launched a succession of attacks on 27 September, with the Canadian Corps crossing the Canal du Nord and opening the way to the capture of Cambrai and Douai. The fighting then flowed north, where a combined British–Belgian army group (under the command of King Albert) broke out of the narrow salient around Ypres, which had been quiet since the final attacks on the Lys had petered out in late April. In his desperation to protect other vital sectors of the front, Ludendorff had moved troops out of Flanders, leaving just five divisions to hold the seventeen miles of front between Diksmuide and Voormezeele (four miles south of Ypres), praying that the wet weather and swampy ground would prevent any Allied breakthrough.[39] German forces, outnumbered two to one, had already made plans to withdraw to the Passchendaele Ridge, but found themselves isolated and overrun when the attack was launched in the early hours of 28 September. There was the usual clatter of machine-gun fire from stubborn detachments that had be to winkled out one by one, but there was little artillery support – most of the German batteries having been silenced by a concentrated series of barrages at Zero Hour. In a single day, the attackers managed to seize almost the whole of the Houthulst forest (at the northern edge of the salient) and the crucial villages of Broodseinde and Gheluvelt.

The final part of Foch's series of attacks opened on 29 September with the assault on the main Hindenburg system along the Saint-Quentin Canal. Unlike the Canal du Nord, which had never been

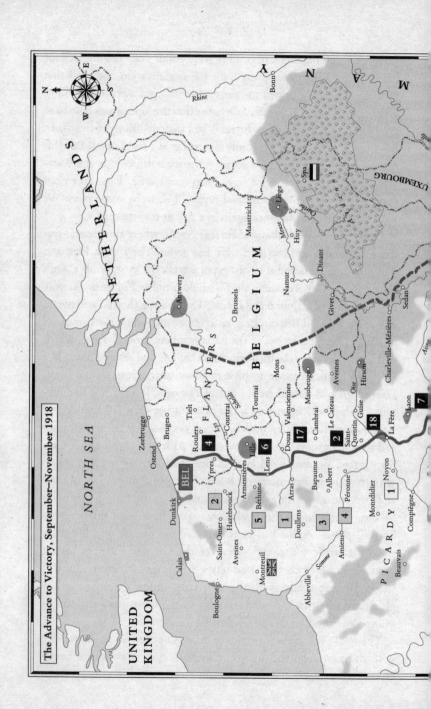

The Advance to Victory, September–November 1918

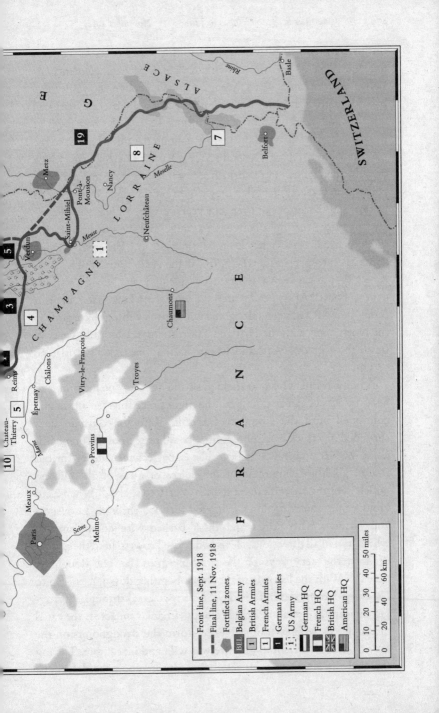

Front line, Sept. 1918
Final line, 11 Nov. 1918
Fortified zones
BEL Belgian Army
1 British Armies
1 French Armies
1 German Armies
1 US Army
German HQ
French HQ
British HQ
American HQ

0 10 20 30 40 50 miles
0   20   40   60 km

FRANCE

SWITZERLAND

Paris
Meaux
Seine
Melun
Provins
Troyes
Vitry-le-François
Châlons
Épernay
Marne
Château-Thierry
Reims
Chaumont
Neufchâteau
Verdun
Saint-Mihiel
Meuse
Pont-à-Mousson
Nancy
Moselle
Metz

CHAMPAGNE
LORRAINE
ALSACE

Belfort
Basle
Rhine

1
10
5
3
4
5
1
7
8
19

finished, the Saint-Quentin was a daunting water obstacle – thirty-five feet wide – and strung with barbed-wire entanglements. At Bellicourt, the canal passed through a tunnel, about 6,000 yards long, but this sector was protected by multiple lines of trenches, hardened dugouts and machine-gun nests positioned along the best fields of fire. Rawlinson entrusted the main assault on the tunnel sector to the two divisions of Major-General Herbert Read's II US Corps, which Pershing had let stay in the British sector. Despite their inexperience, Rawlinson was confident that they would get through. 'Under Foch's tuition and the lessons of over four years of war, we are really learning,' he wrote the night before the assault, 'and the synchronization of the various attacks has been admirable . . . I feel pretty happy about the prospects as a whole, for, if the Americans are inexperienced, they are as keen as mustard and splendid men.' Haig also came over to Fourth Army headquarters to wish them luck. 'He is in great form,' noted Rawlinson, 'delighted with the way things have gone in the North, and with the First and Third Armies. He thinks we shall finish the war this year, and I hope he may be right, but it is no certainty.'[40]

A bombardment by 1,000 field guns and another 600 medium and heavy pieces began at 10.30 p.m. the night preceding the attack and continued until the moment of assault. With the German lines shrouded in a thick bank of fog, little could be seen of the bombardment, but its power was inescapable: 'a perfect tornado of furious sound, a hellish compound of the voices of guns of all calibres', which 'rent the air and caused the very earth to shake'.[41] When Zero Hour came, the doughboys struggled forward through an outpost zone strewn with mines and thick barbed-wire entanglements, which 'ran in all directions, cleverly disposed so as to herd the attackers into the very jaws of the machine-guns' (as one doughboy noted).[42] With the left side of the attack bogging down, it was up to IX Corps, to the south, to make the decisive breakthrough. Springing forward at 5.50 a.m., British troops either swam across the canal or ran across wobbly footbridges to storm the strongpoints on the far side. Enemy machine-gun fire was wild and inaccurate. The fog shielded the attackers until they were almost upon the defenders, who were then dealt with in brutal, slashing combat. By the time the fog had cleared, it was evident that the German hold on the canal had been broken. 'Suddenly the mist rose, and the sun of our "Austerlitz" appeared, strong and refulgent', observed a British officer who had survived the assault. 'Over the brow of the rise opposite to us came a great grey column. Never had we seen such a thing; we counted the files; there were nearly a thousand prisoners in the column. Half an hour later a similar column appeared, and then another and another – we had broken the Hindenburg Line, and 4,200 prisoners, 70 cannon and more than 1,000 machine guns were the trophies of the fight gathered by our single division.'[43]

Ludendorff had seen enough. On the evening of 28 September, at six o'clock – with the sun trailing in a pink sky – he had gone to see Hindenburg and told him that even if they, somehow, managed to hold on in the west, their position 'could only grow worse'. He had, therefore, come to a fateful decision: they needed to ask for an armistice. 'The Field Marshal listened to me with emotion', he remembered. 'He answered that he had intended to say the same to me in the evening, that he had considered the whole situation carefully, and thought the step necessary.' They must request conditions that would allow for an 'orderly evacuation' of France and Belgium 'and the resumption of hostilities on our own borders'. The two men then parted, shaking hands, before returning to their own rooms, alone; their thoughts heavy with the stark realization that all they had worked for and sacrificed was now within an ace of vanishing for ever.[44]

The duo took their proposals to Paul von Hintze the following morning. Hintze, who had travelled up to Spa with the Kaiser and the Chancellor, found himself describing the latest situation with their allies: Bulgaria had 'fallen away'; Austria–Hungary would do so imminently; and Turkey was now only a burden on German resources. Ludendorff then took over, telling him that the 'situation of the army' required an 'immediate armistice to prevent a catastrophe'.[45] Hintze struggled to take in what the generals were saying, but admitted that, if it were true, then there were only three options left: a dictatorship; what he termed 'a revolution from above'; or an appeal to President

Wilson for an immediate ceasefire based upon the 'high ideals' enshrined in his 'Fourteen Points' (which had been published in January 1918 and set out a programme for 'open covenants of peace', freedom of navigation on the seas, the self-determination of peoples and the formation of a 'general association of nations' – what would become the League of Nations).[46] The idea of a dictatorship was swiftly discarded, which only left the possibility of moving towards a more democratic system of parliamentary government – an option that both Hindenburg and Ludendorff agreed was necessary, even if they worried that it might delay any request for negotiations.

The Kaiser now entered the picture. Looking frailer than ever (he had endured a recent bout of sciatica, which left him hobbling about on a cane), the Supreme War Lord received the news that the army 'was at the end of its resistance . . . with the utmost calm'.[47] Hintze explained what had been said that morning and Colonel Wilhelm Heye (Ludendorff's new Chief of Operations) gave a briefing on the dire state of the Army. Arguments went back and forth. Count von Hertling dismissed Hintze's call for a parliamentary democracy and refused to believe that the situation was as bad as the duo seemed to believe. Hintze refused to back down and managed to convince the Kaiser to begin immediate negotiations, while also firing the starting gun on essential political reform, signing the paperwork on expanding the franchise in Prussia and promising further steps in this direction. Wilhelm emerged from the meeting shaken and despairing. Hertling had rejected any further measures and resigned, leaving Wilhelm to look, once again, for a new Chancellor. 'God has not permitted us to achieve the aim for which we hoped but rather has elected for us the way of suffering and misery', he wrote to the *Kaiserin*. He departed for Potsdam the following day, having instructed Berg-Markienen to begin the search for a new Chancellor who could lead them into a future that, in his own words, appeared 'difficult and incomprehensibly dark'.[48]

The man who was eventually drafted in to replace Hertling was Prince Maximilian, the 51-year-old heir to the Grand Duchy of Baden. Having spent most of the war on prisoner relief work with

29. General John Pershing lands at Boulogne, 13 June 1917. Pershing fought hard against Allied demands for US troops to be 'amalgamated' into British and French divisions and was determined to build an independent American army with its own sector of the front.

30. American troops marching through Paris, June 1917. The joyous reception from Parisians was a reflection of how exhausted the French nation had become by this stage of the war.

31. 13/Durham Light Infantry in their forward trenches during the Third Battle of Ypres, 20 September 1917. Despite its infamous reputation, the battle took a heavy toll on the German defenders and underlined the effectiveness of 'bite and hold', set-piece attacks.

32. German soldiers pose with a knocked-out British tank during the Battle of Cambrai. The mass use of tanks on 20 November 1917 marked a new phase of manoeuvre and surprise on the Western Front.

33. German stormtroopers move forward during the spring offensive. By combining new infiltration tactics with short, intensive bombardments, German units were able to make stunning gains in March and April 1918.

34. Appointed Generalissimo in April 1918, Marshal Ferdinand Foch led the Allies to victory with his characteristic mix of optimism and determination: 'He appears to me to be exceptionally alert in body and mind,' wrote a British liaison officer, 'and to be of a masterful and determined character. He knows what he wants and gets it done.'

35. German infantry cross the Ailette river during the Third Battle of the Aisne, 27 May 1918. German troops advanced more than twelve miles in a matter of hours, sparking fears that the advance on Paris was about to resume.

36. An aerial duel between a Sopwith Camel and a group of Albatros fighters. By 1918 the Allies had regained control of the air over the Western Front.

37. Often maligned, General Charles Mangin was a born survivor, abrasive and petulant, but there were few better fighting generals of the war. He led the counter-attacks at the Matz and the Marne in June and July 1918 that finally wrested the initiative away from the German Army.

38. A Schneider CA1 tank leads the way during an attack on the Marne, July 1918.

39. British Mark V tanks move forward during the attack at Amiens, 10 August 1918. The combination of Allied armour, air power and artillery had become devastating by the final months of the war.

40. US troops struggle forward at Hill 240 during the Meuse–Argonne offensive. 'The line was not a line at all,' wrote one doughboy, 'but an irregular series of shell holes occupied by small groups twenty-five yards or more apart, in bush and thickets so dense that one group at times could not see its neighbours.'

41. Ferdinand Foch (*second from right*) standing outside his personal railway carriage in the siding at Compiègne shortly after the armistice terms had been signed. When he was asked whether he was happy with the conditions, he replied that he was 'quite satisfied'. 'After all, why does one make war? It is to enforce one's policy.'

the German Red Cross, he could plausibly pose as the kind of 'moderate' figure to oversee the transformation of the Government, even if he was privately unconvinced that democracy would suit the Reich. He met Colonel Hans von Haeften, the head of the Foreign Section of the High Command, on 1 October and was given the unvarnished truth about the state of the Army, which left him speechless. When he had recovered sufficiently, he asked whether they might not delay an announcement, perhaps until November, only to be told that this was not possible. Hindenburg wrote to him on 3 October insisting that 'a peace offer to our enemies be issued at once' and 'the situation daily becomes more critical'. When Max complained to Berg that the armistice was a 'fatal mistake' and he would have no part in it, Berg shrugged.

'You were certainly not my candidate, but I have no other.'

Max gave in, asserting to the end that he had been coerced into issuing the note, but cognisant of the fact that it would be sent with or without his approval. He was sworn in as Chancellor on 4 October and began forming a new government, with crucial positions reserved for the Majority Socialists, who were committed to further constitutional reform and would do anything to end the war.[49]

It was late on the afternoon of 6 October that the Swiss *Chargé d'Affaires* in Washington transmitted Germany's request for an armistice to President Wilson. Germany accepted Wilson's programme as laid down on 8 January (the 'Fourteen Points') and, in order to 'avoid further bloodshed', asked for a 'general armistice on land, on water, and in the air'.[50] When the officers at OHL were told the news there was stunned silence, which then turned to 'soft moans and sobs'. The staff officer Albrecht von Thaer always remembered Ludendorff addressing them, 'his face filled with the deepest sorrow, pale, but with his head held high. A genuinely handsome heroic German figure! I had to think of Siegfried with the deadly wound in the back from Hagen's spear.' Ludendorff admitted what had been known for weeks now: that Germany's allies were deserting her and the war could no longer be won.

'Since 8 August, things have gone downhill rapidly', he admitted:

Some units continued to be so unreliable that they had to be pulled out of the front at an accelerated rate. If they were replaced by troops still willing to fight, they were met with calls of 'scab' and demands that they no longer fight . . . It is therefore to be expected that, with the help of the battling Americans, in the not too distant future the enemy will achieve a great victory, a breakthrough on a grand scale. Then the *Westheer* will lose its last foothold and will retreat back over the Rhine to carry the revolution back to Germany.

With that Ludendorff bowed his head, turned and left the room.[51]

24. 'The full measure of victory'

For all of Woodrow Wilson's eloquence and rhetorical skill, he was initially lost for words when presented with Prince Max's telegram. He immediately sent for his closest adviser, Edward Mandell House – 'Colonel' House as he was known – who was then in New York. 'I would suggest making no direct reply to the German note', House wired back. 'A statement from the White House saying, quote, The President will at once confer with the Allies regarding the communication received from the German Government, unquote, should be sufficient.'[1] House arrived in Washington the following afternoon and together with Robert Lansing, the Secretary of State, they discussed the possible ramifications of the note. Were the Germans really ready to surrender? How could the Allies agree to an armistice without guarantees that the German Army would respect their terms? A draft had been prepared, but Wilson was unsatisfied with it and worked hard on putting down something that would maintain Allied military superiority but also not spurn the chance of a settlement.

It took two days to finalize the response, which was sent on 8 October. Wilson did not reject German overtures out of hand, but requested further clarification before negotiations could begin: 'Before making reply to the request of the Imperial German Government, and in order that that reply shall be as candid and straightforward as the momentous interests involved require, the President of the United States deems it necessary to assure himself of the exact meaning of the note of the Imperial Chancellor.' Did the Chancellor accept the 'Fourteen Points' and were subsequent discussions merely 'to agree upon the practical details of their application'? Moreover, the President did not 'feel at liberty' to propose an armistice when the armies of the Central Powers were occupying the soil of the Associated Powers. Germany had to 'withdraw their forces everywhere from invaded territory' and the President also wished to know 'whether the Imperial Chancellor is speaking merely for the constituted authorities of the Empire who have so far conducted the war'.[2]

Allied governments reacted to news of the German offer with a strange mixture of trepidation and delight. Studying Wilson's response carefully, Lloyd George spotted that there had been no specific mention of Alsace–Lorraine, while the old bugbears about the 'Fourteen Points' were never far beneath the surface, with 'absolute freedom of navigation upon the seas' being something that the British Government could never accept.[3] In Paris, the German note sparked off a bitter row between Poincaré and Clemenceau, who were soon at odds over whether an armistice should be granted. When the French President wrote that nothing could be considered until German troops were no longer on French soil and that they should then march on to Berlin, Clemenceau snapped back, offering his resignation (unless Poincaré withdrew his comments) and accusing the President of trying to institute 'personal rule'. 'At the first request for an armistice, I nearly went mad, mad with joy', Clemenceau later told a friend. 'It was finished. I had seen too much of the front, too many of those water-filled holes where men had lived for four years . . .'[4]

Poincaré disliked the old senator, but could not dispense with his services in this great hour of decision, which demanded cool heads. A meeting of the Supreme War Council was held on 7 October, with Lloyd George, Clemenceau and Vittorio Orlando (the Italian Prime Minister) agreeing to consider an armistice with Germany if the following conditions were fulfilled: the evacuation of France, Alsace–Lorraine, Belgium, Luxembourg and Italy; the German Army to retire behind the Rhine; the withdrawal of Central Powers' forces from the Trentino and Istria, Serbia and Montenegro; the immediate restoration of all territory held by Russia and Romania before the war; and the cessation of submarine warfare. This was communicated to Tasker Bliss, the US representative – who could not attend, having come down with influenza – but he refused to sign the resolution without instructions from Washington.[5]

Concerns that the Americans would sign a peace treaty with Germany over the heads of the Allies began to heat up as the discussions continued. On the evening of 9 October, just hours after Wilson's response had been sent, the three Prime Ministers addressed a joint telegram to the President calling for 'an American representative possessing the full confidence of the United States Government' to be sent to France to keep them 'fully informed' of US policy at all times.[6] This was combined with furious behind-the-scenes lobbying to warn the Americans against making a separate peace. On 15 October, Irwin Laughlin, the US *Chargé d'Affaires* in London, reported to Lansing 'a fear that the President may go farther along the road towards a final solution without consulting with and considering the particular wishes of his cobelligerents . . . Even should the danger of a premature armistice be avoided it is feared that we may be tricked by this hypocritical waving of a white flag into concluding a peace which will be but the shadow and not the substance of the complete victory which is within sight, and a peace which will provide Germany with undeserved opportunities for future mischief-making.'[7]

The danger of getting sucked into negotiations that would allow Germany desperately needed breathing space soon became evident. Ludendorff was summoned to see Prince Max on 9 October after being presented with a series of questions about how long the Army could hold out. Max was under pressure from every side, including from those who wanted all contact with the Allies to be broken off and the demand for evacuation to be rejected. Ludendorff was more bullish than he had been for weeks, admitting that the Supreme Command 'felt less nervous' than they had been at the beginning of the month – a response to the gradual slowing down of Allied efforts since the heavy attacks in the last week of September. But he nevertheless believed that negotiations could not be broken off. 'The army needs rest,' he told Max, hoping that some respite could be found to allow his men to recover and then make a stand along the German border.[8] A further note was issued on 12 October, which accepted the President's terms with the assumption that the other powers associated with the United States did the same. Germany was now 'absolutely ready to comply with the parts of the President's note regarding evacuation' and she recommended that Wilson convene a 'mixed commission' to 'make the necessary arrangements'. The Chancellor also wished to reassure Washington that the 'present German Government' was supported by a 'large majority' in the Reichstag and that Prince Max 'speaks in the name of the German Government and of the German people'.[9]

By the time the second German note was published, the mood in Washington was hardening. On 10 October, the British passenger liner RMS *Leinster* had been sunk outside Dublin Bay with the loss of over 500 lives – sparking anger at Germany's continued prosecution of the submarine campaign. After further discussions involving House, Lansing and Baker, the second note was sent on the afternoon of 14 October. Neither the United States Government nor the Allied powers would 'consent to consider an armistice as long as the armed forces of Germany continue the illegal and inhuman processes which they still persist in'. Not only were German submarines 'sinking passenger ships at sea', the retreating armies on the Western Front were also 'pursuing a course of wanton destruction which has always been regarded as being in direct violation of the rules and practices of civilized warfare'. Therefore no arrangements would be accepted unless they provided 'absolutely satisfactory safeguards and guarantees of the maintenance of the present military supremacy of the armies of the United States, and of the Allies in the field'.[10]

By the beginning of October the Allied advance had come to a standstill; the inevitable result of heavy fighting on the Hindenburg Line, worsening weather and all-consuming exhaustion. Surveying the disappointing situation along the old battlefields of Champagne, where the advance of Gouraud's Fourth Army had congealed, Foch was insistent that they get moving. 'After eight days of continuous combat, Fourth Army has obtained honourable results undoubtedly, but certainly inferior to those that had been expected against an adversary seized on all sides and that only resists at certain points with worn out, heterogeneous units, hurriedly formed . . .' He reminded Pétain that each senior officer 'must take the battle in his own hands and lead it himself with his last ounce of energy'.[11] Pétain did as he was told, ordering his commanders to forget their tiredness and to act with more energy. 'In a big battle like the one which is currently taking place,' he wrote, victory would come to the most tenacious; 'one must soak up this conviction and share it with your subordinates'.[12]

Pershing renewed his attack towards the rolling heights of Romagne and Cunel at 5.30 a.m. on 4 October. Special instructions had been issued 'regarding flanking manoeuvres, mixing of units, and close cooperation between commanders' – areas that had been particularly lacking on 26 September.[13] Pershing also insisted that his men be assigned 'successive objectives', which would 'allow the green troops to reform now and then before continuing the advance' – a belated recognition of the need for more order and method in their attacks. They were now closing with the Kriemhilde *Stellung*, a section of the Hindenburg Line that ran down to the Meuse. This was an objective that should have fallen on the first day, but was now defended stoutly. German reinforcements had been pouring into the Meuse for weeks, and by the time Pershing could restart the offensive he was facing twenty-seven divisions in the line with another seventeen in reserve (against thirty divisions in total on 26 September).[14] Pershing was resigned, his earlier aggression replaced by a realization that this was how the war was fought in France. 'Attack was resumed at 5:25 this morning. Met considerable resistance; advance very slow', he recorded in his diary. 'Cannot say that it is due to the fault of anyone, but is a natural result of [a] very stubborn defence by the Germans. Our men have had to fight for every 100 yards they have gained, and it looks as though we will have a slow, hard advance . . . There is no course except to fight it out, taking the best possible advantage of the ground which now lays to the advantage of the Germans.'[15]

It took a week of hard fighting for the Americans to clear the Argonne. Time and again, US battalions found their cohesion melting away in the broken woodland, getting strung out into smaller and smaller units against an enemy that could not be seen, let alone destroyed, while the difficulties of supply, in getting enough food, ammunition and water up to the forward positions, caused First Army staff officers endless worry. 'The line was not a line at all, but an irregular series of shell holes occupied by small groups twenty-five yards or more apart, in bush and thickets so dense that one group at times could not see its neighbours', wrote one doughboy about the fighting at this time. 'Three to four men in a hole was the usual garrison. The Boche line was apparently just as uncertain and flexible, some fifty to one hundred yards away. Each side would sneak up now and then and throw grenades. The only way to feed the men was at night when a small detail would dash to a hole, throw in rations, and run. The Boche was nervous and at the least sign of movement opened up with machine guns, followed by potato mashers [stick grenades].'[16]

Further north, Haig's armies had also resumed their advance despite heavy rain on 7 October, which then turned into a persistent drizzle. Cambrai was abandoned on the night of 8/9 October with Canadian soldiers spreading out into the city trying to extinguish the fires that had been started by the retreating Germans. After the set-piece battles of late September, the course of the fighting was now more fluid, less predictable, and demanded a different set of skills to those of trench warfare. German rearguards occupied the best defensive positions and kept British and French advanced patrols at bay for long enough to escape into the night. Booby-traps and delayed-action mines were commonplace, alongside the ever-present problems of torn-up railways, blown bridges and damaged roads. Heavy gas shelling also caused a continuous trickle of casualties as the advance went on. One British soldier, in action at Wambaix, southeast of Cambrai, described an attack on 9 October. 'Apart from the noise of the barrage, we might have been performing an exercise in field-training. The country was open, nearly level fields with a few trees here and there, and there were no trenches – it was a real "war of movement" at last. The wall of bursting shells in front, with the smoke of the explosions drifting away on a light breeze, and following the barrage an unbroken line of men at intervals of about ten feet from each other, moving forward with fixed bayonets and rifles at the trail . . .'[17]

Haig met Foch on 10 October. The Generalissimo was 'in very good spirits', Haig recorded, 'and highly complimentary at what [the] British Army had done.'[18] Foch had just issued a new directive, which described the three 'convergent' attacks that the Allies were now embarked upon: towards Belgium; Solesmes and Wassigny; and the Aisne and the Meuse. 'The most profitable to exploit, thanks to the success of the British Armies, is that of Solesmes–Wassigny', it read. 'It is therefore to be pursued in the greatest possible strength, in order to develop it at the same time as progress is made towards Avesnes–Mons'. There would also be an operation to free up the area around Lille with

British forces moving northeastwards between the Scheldt and Sambre rivers.[19] When this had been explained, Haig handed the directive to his Chief of Staff, Herbert Lawrence. 'Lawrence has a cold and so is looking at things in a gloomy way tonight', Haig noted. Lawrence 'foresaw many dangers ahead', telling Haig that 'the British Army is doing all the fighting, the French will do nothing, and the American Army is quite incapable of doing anything'. Haig brushed off such pessimism. 'I think the situation highly satisfactory, and the results of our victories will be *very far reaching* . . .'[20]

King Albert's army group pushed forward in Flanders on the chilly morning of 14 October. Conscious that the German Fourth Army was already in the process of evacuating as many men and as much material as it could, there was a desire to get moving again as soon as possible. French and Belgian troops would press on towards Tielt and Ghent, while General Plumer's Second Army guarded their right flank by advancing on Courtrai. Despite the numerous pillboxes and machine-gun nests that lay across the muddied ground, the Germans did not make a general stand, but began moving out as soon as the creeping barrage was fired. The Belgians advanced eight kilometres, with over 10,000 prisoners being taken. Roulers was abandoned at nightfall and two of Plumer's corps reached the northern outskirts of Menin. 'The Franco-Belgian attack that day', recorded Lieutenant-General Cyriaque Gillain, Chief of the General Staff of the Belgian Army, 'completely broke down the defensive organization of the enemy, who no longer has any defensive works behind him. For the most part, the enemy's front-line divisions may be considered out of the picture', with the other divisions encountered only being of poor quality or thoroughly exhausted.[21]

By mid-October, the British Fourth Army had reached Le Cateau and the valley of the River Selle. The river itself was only a thin stream, eighteen feet wide, but excellent observation on the east bank made it a more difficult proposition and Rawlinson's troops would have to fight their way through a series of orchards and water meadows, criss-crossed with hedgerows.[22] Resisting the temptation to try to rush through, Rawlinson waited several days for his guns to be brought up and then ordered a forty-eight-hour preliminary bombardment, which opened on 15 October. With over 1,300 guns, Fourth Army fired almost as much weight of shell as had been used at Amiens back in August, pulverizing the defending divisions, now little more than a collection of weak battalions.[23] When the attack went in on the morning of 17 October, engineers had bridges across the Selle in a matter of minutes and, covered by the barrage and a thick, lying mist, the infantry were able to cross without difficulty. 'Promptly at 7 our bombardment started up and the guns put up a perfect barrage – a real wall of fire – just ahead', remembered a British junior officer. Thankfully, 'the guns had done their work and only a few Germans popped up here and there out of shell holes and dugouts. If they seemed prepared to put up a fight our fellows gave them three rounds "rapid" – most of them just put up their hands and surrendered, crying "*Kamerad!*"'[24]

Ludendorff arrived in Berlin on 17 October to deliver a military report to the Chancellor. In spite of the terrible reverse across the front, he had 'no fear of a military collapse' and was confident that the army would retreat 'in good order'. Various schemes were dusted off for reinforcing the *Westheer*, such as moving even more divisions from the east and combing out industry for a 'single strong reinforcement' of 600,000 men – an offer that Ludendorff grasped with alacrity, saying that if he had the men he could 'face the future with confidence'.[25] But even if these reserves could be mustered, the question of how to respond to Wilson's reply was pressing. Hindenburg issued his own 'estimate' of the situation the following day, which drew attention to what was believed to be the 'great contrast' between Wilson and Foch. 'Wilson wants to have a just peace of reconciliation and understanding. Foch wants a complete humiliation of Germany and satisfaction of French vanity.' Whichever one won out, he believed, 'will depend solely on the attitude of Germany'. If the front could be held, then Wilson would prevail; on the other hand, any weakening would allow Foch to triumph. 'A yielding to Foch's demands will mean the annihilation of Germany and the shattering of every prospect of peace.'[26]

For Rupprecht, who had now lapsed into a deep depression, there was only one thing they could do: retreat behind the Meuse immediately to allow their men time to regroup. 'The Supreme Command is still of the opinion that it might be possible to balance out localized setbacks by quickly throwing in reserves, but the fact is that we do not have any reserves left that are fit for action, and the constant redeployment of divisions, as was previously so popular with OHL, made our troops so tired that their performance was significantly impaired.'[27] The idea of a sudden withdrawal all the way to the Meuse had been raised before, but Ludendorff could not countenance such a bold redeployment – convinced that it was impracticable as well as likely to weaken Germany's position in the negotiations with Wilson. On 19 October, he issued a directive to his commanders warning them that because the Antwerp–Meuse Line was unfinished, it was necessary to gain as much time as possible to allow work to continue.[28] Moreover, Germany should only accept armistice conditions that allowed for the 'orderly evacuation' of France and Belgium. Anything less than two or three months should be rejected. Nor should they 'accept anything that makes it impossible for us to renew hostilities'. He did not wish to break faith with Wilson, he told his staff, but they could not possibly do anything 'inconsistent' with 'national honour'.[29]

Prince Max had been considering the response to Wilson's note of 14 October for several days. It was, he wrote, a 'terrible document' that 'altered the situation in Germany fundamentally', causing a great wave of disappointment to wash across the country 'like the bursting of a dam'.[30] After the War Cabinet meeting of 17 October and further discussions in the Reichstag, it was agreed that negotiations must continue. The Kaiser prohibited all attacks on passenger steamers, but refused to resign. A reply was sent on 21 October reassuring Wilson that the German Empire had now undergone an 'essential change' in its political structure. 'The actual Government has been formed in complete accord with the desires of popular representation as a result of a vote, equal, general, secret and direct.' In future no government could stay in power unless it had a majority in the Reichstag. Therefore, Germany had confidence that the President of the United States would not 'approve any requirement irreconcilable with the honour of the German people and the preparation of a just peace'.[31]

In Washington, Wilson was without his adviser, House, who was on his way to France to act as the President's personal representative, but he did not lack for decision. He was in no mood to trust the earnest proclamations from Berlin, and his third note, sent on 24 October, reiterated that the only armistice he would accept 'would be one which should leave the United States and the Powers associated with her, in a position to enforce any arrangement that may be entered into to make a renewal of hostilities on the part of Germany impossible'. He was not impressed by the political changes that had taken place in Germany and noted that the German people 'had no means of commanding the acquiescence of the military authorities of the Empire in the popular will', with the power of the 'King of Prussia' currently 'unimpaired'. If the United States had to deal with the 'military master and the monarchical autocrats of Germany', then she would 'demand not peace negotiations but surrender'.[32] As an editorial in *The New York Times* put it, 'It is believed here there can be no possible misconstruction of these words, and the President is known to be a most careful measurer of the language he employs. If this sort of an armistice is granted, and no other kind is thought possible of being made with the sanction of Marshal Foch and the other Allied military advisers, it will involve nothing less than complete surrender by the German military forces . . .'[33]

The Kaiser remained in Berlin for most of the month, lost in his thoughts, signing whatever paperwork Max put in front of him. When Wilson's third note arrived, with its unmistakeable demand for further political reform, a look of great sadness washed over his face. 'With every note more is demanded', he complained. 'Wilson wants to prescribe what sort of Constitution Germany should adopt and wants to complete the subjection and abdication of the German federal princes. I'm not going.'[34] It was enough to spark a full-scale revolt from the duo at OHL, who were now faced, squarely, with the logical result of their demand for an armistice. Hindenburg was furious, warning his army group commanders (in a telegram transmitted on 24 October) that because Wilson 'demands military capitulation', it was 'unacceptable for us soldiers' and their only reply would be 'to continue our resistance with might and main'.[35] This, in turn, sparked off Prince Max's refusal to continue unless the generals were reined in. Hindenburg's defiant communication was 'a piece of unwarranted interference' that completely undermined the new government's attempt to prove its independence of the High Command at a moment of grave importance. Max did not want to move against Hindenburg – admitting that it might be wise to keep him in place ('to avoid alarming army and people unnecessarily') – but demanded that Ludendorff be sacked or he would resign.[36]

The showdown between the Kaiser and his generals took place on 26 October. Ludendorff had already prepared his resignation letter that morning, but Hindenburg pleaded with him 'not to desert the Emperor and the army at this time' and to try to see Prince Max. But with the Chancellor confined to his bed with influenza, which left him feverish and troubled, they were called to see the Kaiser at the Bellevue Palace instead. Ludendorff was as irascible as ever, launching into a series of angry warnings about the threat to the Fatherland and how Wilson's note had to be rejected, but the Kaiser was not interested. He made it clear that Hindenburg's communication of 24 October, which had undermined both his and the Chancellor's authority, was unacceptable. Ludendorff then said that because he no longer had the confidence of His Majesty, he wished to resign.

'Good,' the Kaiser replied, 'then you can have it.'[37]

Hindenburg, who had said little, also offered to resign, but this was refused.

'You stay' was all the Kaiser said to him before they were dismissed. Hans von Plessen, standing silently by the side, found it 'a very difficult, very sad meeting'. The Kaiser was 'quite passive' throughout.[38]

The Central Powers were now breaking apart. On 24 October – the anniversary of Caporetto – Italian forces mounted their final offensive at Vittorio and caused the collapse of Austrian forces along the Piave. After several days of hard fighting, Austrian troops refused to go into the line and began drifting away from the battlefield or surrendering in large numbers. The empire finally sued for peace five days later. After Bulgaria and Austria, Turkey was the next to fall, agreeing armistice conditions on 30 October. Only Germany remained in the war. From his sickbed, Prince Max helped draft Germany's final reply to Wilson.

With speculation now widespread that the Kaiser was going to abdicate and that peace would be signed within hours, there was no appetite for breaking off negotiations. In a short statement, Max reaffirmed the 'far-reaching changes' that had taken place in 'German constitutional existence' and that the 'military powers' were now subordinate to the Government. Accordingly, Germany 'now awaits the proposals for an armistice'.[39]

Lieutenant-General Wilhelm Groener was the man chosen as Ludendorff's successor. There were plenty of other officers who were considered, including Kuhl and Lossberg, but Groener was preferred because of the need for someone 'whose abilities went beyond the purely military'. After leaving the War Ministry in August 1917, Groener had been transferred to an army group in Ukraine (as Chief of Staff) and thus had extensive experience of the sinews of the German war effort. He took up his new position with little joy, only an overwhelming feeling of loss as the German war effort began to crumble. He would rather have rejected the offer, telling a friend that he would become a scapegoat for Germany's failure. 'Honour cannot come from this vocation.'[40]

Groener arrived at Spa on 30 October, where Hindenburg briefed him on the situation, telling him that Ludendorff was to blame for his own dismissal and that 'the difficulties with the Chancellor had now been overcome'. No sooner had Groener seen Hindenburg than he was faced with the dreadful reality of the situation. The day before, a whole *Landwehr* division, which had been serving on the Eastern Front (and contained a number of Alsatians and Poles in its ranks), had refused to enter the line. Even though the 'strictest measures' would be taken against the mutineers, Groener knew that this would not have much effect on the 'wavering spirit' of the army.[41] He set off to visit the army groups and gain a greater appreciation of what was happening out at the front – but each hour brought more depressing news. That day (1 November) a renewed assault along the Meuse finally broke through the thin German lines, with American troops seizing Barricourt and Buzancy, and drawing closer to the crucial rail links that sustained the Army in the west. Georg Wetzell, now serving as Chief of Staff at Fifth Army, wired that the Americans were 'attacking in mass formations in the general direction of Stenay' and 'that the troops are fighting courageously but just cannot do anything', and it was, therefore, imperative to retreat behind the Meuse immediately.[42]

Soon after arriving at Spa, Groener had ordered a staff officer, Captain Loose, to tour the front and gather information on the morale of the Army. Loose reported on 3 November that commanders and their staff were united in their belief that morale was poor everywhere. Many soldiers were suffering from nervous exhaustion or mental breakdown. Portraits of the Kaiser, Hindenburg and Ludendorff were being taken down from mess halls everywhere: 'The men want peace at any price.'[43] The following morning, Groener ordered the immediate withdrawal to the Antwerp–Meuse Line, a sensible decision, but it was already too late. Outbreaks of disorder were now spreading across Germany. On 4 November, mutiny broke out in the High Seas Fleet at Kiel, where poor conditions, boredom and the lure of socialist propaganda had eaten away at discipline for months. When rumours spread that the Kaiser was planning to deploy his fleet in one final sally out to meet the Royal Navy – a 'death cruise' – sailors began to refuse orders, electing their own councils and marching through the streets. The authorities tried to contain the situation, but failed. By 6 November, when Groener was urgently recalled to Berlin, other coastal towns were falling under the control of revolutionaries demanding 'peace and bread'.

Back in the capital, Groener met Prince Max in the garden of the Reich Chancellor's Palace and told him that they needed an armistice within a matter of days. When Max suggested waiting perhaps a week, Groener shook his head.

'Even that is too long to wait . . . I too had hoped we should be able to wait eight or ten days till we have taken up our position on the [Antwerp–Meuse] line . . . I have come to the conclusion, that, painful as it is, we must take the step of asking Foch.'[44]

The end began to draw near, but its exact outlines remained indistinct. Foch had moved his headquarters to Senlis, thirty miles north of Paris, in mid-October and spent most of his time sketching out a possible armistice agreement with Germany. On 19 October, he issued his final directive, in which he ordered King Albert's army group to liberate Brussels; the rest of the British Army to 'throw the enemy back upon the almost impenetrable *massif* of the Ardennes'; and the French and Americans to drive towards La Capelle and Chimay, Mézières and Sedan.[45] Foch continued to push his commanders on, urging them to act with energy despite mounting exhaustion. Haig was now 'tired and rather irritable' – suddenly seeming to lose his nerve, his solid confidence and optimism beginning to waver in the final moments as he contemplated another year of fighting. Pétain also became increasingly withdrawn. 'He preferred rather to flee from it and to isolate himself' was the verdict of one staff officer at GQG. Even Pershing had reached a point of near-collapse by the final weeks of the war and was observed in his staff car, sobbing by the side of the road, calling out for his late wife.[46]

All were present at a military conference at Senlis on 25 October. Foch began by stating that he had been 'entrusted by the Allied Governments with the care of drafting the general lines of an eventual armistice with Germany' and he wanted to know what those terms should be. Haig believed that 'a very great part of the German forces had been beaten', but not 'disintegrated', and that they were, in his opinion, 'still capable of withdrawing to a shorter front and of making a very effective stand there against equal or even superior forces'. On the other hand, they were 'pretty well exhausted', with the British and French Armies suffering from a shortage of infantry and the Americans requiring 'time to get in shape'. Therefore they should demand the immediate evacuation of Belgium and France; the occupation of Alsace–Lorraine, Metz and Strasbourg; 'restitution' of all rolling stock seized by Germany; and the repatriation of their inhabitants. These conditions would 'place us on the German frontier in case of a resumption of hostilities'.[47]

Foch found Haig's uncharacteristic pessimism hard to fathom. They were 'dealing with an army that has been beaten every day for three months, an army that is now losing on a front of four hundred kilometres: that has, since July 15, lost more than 250,000 prisoners and 4,000 guns; an army that is, physically and morally, thoroughly beaten'. Moreover, now was the time to keep up the pressure. 'When one hunts a wild beast and finally comes upon him at bay, he then comes in the face of greater danger, but it is not the time to stop, it is time to redouble his blows without paying attention to the ones he himself receives.' As for Pétain, any conditions should allow for the possibility of resuming hostilities under 'favourable conditions' and he recommended the occupation of the entire line of the Rhine. Pershing agreed. If the German Government was serious about peace, then it should not object to 'strict conditions'. Therefore France and Belgium should be evacuated within thirty days; German troops should withdraw east of the Rhine and allow the Allies to seize whatever bridgeheads they should demand; there should be no interference in the transportation of Americans across the seas; and all U-boats and their bases should be surrendered to a neutral power until further notice.

On 26 October – the day of Ludendorff's dismissal – Foch wrote up the terms they had agreed upon. Firstly, Germany must evacuate all occupied territory within two weeks (Foch calculated that this would force them to leave behind much of their war materiel, including most of their heavy guns). The left bank of the Rhine must be demilitarized, with the Allies occupying four strategically vital bridgeheads at Mainz, Koblenz, Cologne and Strasbourg. Germany was also required to surrender 5,000 locomotives, 150,000 railway wagons and 150 submarines; disclose the location of all minefields, both on land and at sea; and remove her naval fleet to the Baltic. Whether Foch expected the Germans to sign was never clear. It was probable that he took a calculated risk, offering terms that were severe, but which fell short of unconditional surrender. If the Germans signed, then so be it; if they did not, then they would carry on and, in all likelihood, a revolution would break out in the homeland.[48]

Amid the rain and cold, the advance continued throughout October and into November. While the British marched eastwards and the Americans drove north, the French were left to move up in the centre. Progress was steady, if not spectacular, leading to a growing sense of frustration. General Mangin had dragged his army forward, often through sheer force of will, but had to be content with following up the enemy without landing the decisive blow that he had long sought. Pétain had always been reluctant to give him enough reserves and now, with the end in sight, he cut a frustrated figure. The sight of French towns ablaze, their roads torn up, brought back memories from the German retreat of 1917 and he demanded that no German prisoners be returned home until the damage had been rectified, but this was never approved.[49] In November, Margin was transferred to Nancy, where he was given orders to plan for a major Franco-American thrust into Lorraine. He was confident that the attack would be devastating. 'Collapse is certain, inevitable; and retreat is impossible', he wrote, realizing that an advance in this sector would force the enemy into an ever-narrowing gap between the southern point of Holland and the Saarland. 'The Battle of Lorraine was set for 14 November. But on the 11th, the armistice was signed; by surrendering in open country, the German armies escaped disaster.'[50]

Pershing was also having doubts about whether the Allies should stop fighting. On 30 October, he wrote to the Supreme War Council on the subject of 'complete victory' and argued that the balance of forces was now moving so clearly in their direction that they should refrain from granting Germany anything short of unconditional surrender. An armistice, he predicted, would 'revivify the low spirits of the German army and enable it to reorganize and resist later on, and would deprive the Allies of the full measure of victory by failing to press their present advantage to its complete military end'. He warned that it would be difficult, if not impossible, to resume hostilities if a peace conference failed.[51] Such a bullish attitude stemmed, in part, from his natural aggression, but also from a growing recognition of the fighting power of the US Army. Pershing had always considered his soldiers and officers to be superior to their allies and now he had real grounds for believing so. The attack on 1 November, which captured the Barricourt Ridge and forced the Germans into a full retreat across the Meuse, had shown just how effective the AEF had become.

They were veterans at last, no longer unused to the rhythms and demands of the Western Front. Now split into two armies, First and Second, the AEF had finally grown to rival the size of European forces. They were also becoming just as skilful. General Hunter Liggett, commanding First Army (with Pershing becoming a de-facto army group commander), executed the attack utilizing every weapon at his disposal. The whole front was photographed and mapped from the air up to three miles in; 600 guns were available – one for every twenty yards of front; while, overhead, American pilots bombed and strafed ground targets or chased away the few enemy fighters still left airborne.[52] A two-hour preliminary bombardment began at 3.30 a.m. on 1 November, before merging into a furious, layered creeping barrage, gas and high explosive, thickened up with machine-gun and mortar fire. 'The sky behind us was a flickering, gleaming red', recalled one attacker as he readied to go over the top. 'The roar was as of myriad drums rolling almost in unison, and the air overhead seemed almost alive with whistling visiting cards to the departing Jerry . . . After the firing had ceased there was extreme quietness . . .'[53]

The doughboys advanced six miles against trifling, broken opposition, securing their objectives by the afternoon. There was an occasional rifle pit or machine-gun team that needed clearing out at the point of the bayonet, but the bombardment was so heavy as to prevent any significant resistance and American troops were able to march forward on to the Barricourt Heights, placing their heavy guns within range of Sedan and the Metz railway line. 'In the closing battle we had an American Army in the full sense of the word for the first time in the war', noted Liggett. 'In the past, French artillery, aviation and other technical troops had made up our deficiencies . . . Here we were at home on the front of the attack, and Americans manned the communications, the telegraph lines, water supply, ammunition and supply dumps, and virtually all the services, while other Americans planned the battle and others fought it.' As Pershing wrote in his diary that evening, 'Everyone knew his task and did it well.'[54]

By the final days of the war, the Allied armies had made impressive gains since their nadir in the spring. Now the front line ran from Ghent through Mons and Maubeuge, down to Mézières and Stenay along the Meuse. German soldiers were surrendering in impressive numbers, dribbling into the Allied lines in ever-larger groups. Between the Soissons counter-attack on 18 July and the armistice, 385,000 Germans surrendered, alongside the capture of 6,615 guns – allowing most soldiers a glimpse of large numbers of the enemy that had hitherto only been seen in small groups.[55] 'At last the weather broke and as November approached, grew bitterly cold; snow fell and froze, movement became hazardous, cover was difficult, and the tempo of the advance slackened', noted one British veteran. 'We were then so far ahead of artillery and supplies that it was becoming more or less a self-contained effort; fortunately resistance was by that time mediocre, and prisoners surrendered in droves. We gazed curiously at these shabby, grey-clad figures, mostly too old or too young, as they shuffled past so listlessly with glazed and expressionless eyes; surely these were not the Jerries who had exacted such a terrible toll from us, all the way from Albert?'[56] The German Army was beaten; there now only remained the final settling of accounts.

The German armistice delegation left Spa at midday on 7 November and were driven down towards the front lines at Guise. There were eight men in total: Matthias Erzberger, author of the Peace Resolution of July 1917 and now drafted in to act as Chairman; Count Alfred von Oberndorff (Ambassador to Bulgaria); Major-General Detlof von Winterfeldt (a former Military Attaché in Paris); Captain Ernst Vanselow (representing the Imperial Navy); and an interpreter, a captain and two secretaries. The journey took hours. At Chauny, 'not a single house was still standing; one ruin lined up next to another', recalled Erzberger. 'The ghostly vestiges loomed in the air in the moonlight; there were no signs of life.' At 4 a.m. they reached the railway station at Tergnier and were put on board a special train. Cognac was passed around and they set off. 'We were not told of the destination, only commanded not to open the windows during the journey.'[57]

They were going to Rethondes in the forest of Compiègne, where Foch's personal railway carriage was situated. At nine o'clock on the morning of 8 November, they were escorted along duckboard tracks through a small dripping wood to where the Generalissimo was waiting for them. 'His face was serious, his words cold and without arrogance', wrote Weygand, who handed out copies of Foch's terms and announced that they had seventy-two hours to sign. Hostilities would continue until they did so.[58] The response from the German delegation was one of shock and horror. Winterfeldt, the most senior

German soldier present, turned pale and Erzberger asked whether military operations could be terminated immediately, citing the growth of revolutionary spirit in Germany. Foch brushed this away (stating that such a situation was 'the usual disease prevailing in beaten armies') and reiterated that he would not stop his armies until Germany signed. Suitably chastened, Erzberger drafted a telegram to Prince Max requesting further instructions.[59]

It would be another thirty-six hours before Erzberger received authorization. In Berlin, the Government was beginning to fracture. The Social Democrats had already issued an ultimatum demanding the abdication of the Kaiser, and revolutionary groups were seizing power across the country. By 7 November, red flags were flying over Brunswick and Cologne, and a republic had even been proclaimed in Munich, causing the King, Ludwig III, to flee. The Kaiser had left the capital for Spa, where he remained huddled with his closest advisers. Prince Max tried his best to make him 'realize the truth', as he put it. On the evening of 8 November, he telephoned Spa and explained that abdication 'has become necessary to save Germany from civil war'.[60] But Wilhelm refused to consider this possibility, claiming that if he did so there would be chaos in Germany and the Army would disintegrate. He was considering leading the still-loyal elements of the Army back home to restore order and was confident that the people would rally to his standard.

This was a comforting, if vain, illusion. A group of fifty army officers had been invited to Spa to report on the morale of the *Westheer*, but only thirty-nine had been able to make it. When they had assembled, Hindenburg explained that revolution had broken out in Germany and that the Kaiser was being asked to renounce his throne. OHL would do all it could to prevent this from happening, but needed to know whether it could command the support of the Army to march back home and put down the unrest. After taking a series of votes, Colonel Heye took the news to the Kaiser, telling him bluntly that the men were exhausted and an armistice was urgently required.

'The troops remain loyal to His Majesty, but they are tired and indifferent and want nothing except rest and peace. At the present moment, they would not march against Germany, even with Your

Majesty at their head. They would not march against Bolshevism. They want one thing only – an armistice at the earliest possible moment.'[61]

It was left to Groener to deliver the final blow. 'The army will march back home in good order under its leaders and commanding generals, but not under the leadership of Your Majesty.'

The Kaiser's face flickered with anger – 'his emaciated and sallowed face twitched and winced'. Shortly afterwards, he agreed to renounce the imperial throne and go into exile in Holland.[62]

At Rethondes, Foch's terms were signed at 5.15 a.m. on 11 November with hostilities to cease in just under six hours' time. After the documentation had been completed and the paper stamped, Erzberger and his team prepared to return to a Fatherland already torn apart by revolution and chaos, pausing for a moment to issue a short note protesting about the terms imposed upon them, which they regarded as impossible to fulfil and likely to 'precipitate the German people into anarchy and famine'. Erzberger then added a final sentence, poignant and searching: 'The German people who during 50 months have struggled against a world of enemies, in spite of all violence, preserve their liberty and unity. A people of 70 million suffers, but does not perish.'[63] Foch, who had remained standing throughout, refused to shake hands with any member of the German delegation and watched, impassively, as they left. Then, with a brief sigh, he looked up at the assorted staff officers who clustered around him, including Weygand and the British representative, Sir Rosslyn Wemyss.

'Well, gentlemen,' he said, 'it's over. Go.'

Epilogue

There were no furnished railway carriages to take the German generals back home. In Brussels, Rupprecht was exhausted and weak from influenza when he received news of the outbreak of revolution in Bavaria. He issued a proclamation to his troops calling for a vote on the future relationship between the people and the crown and then burnt his papers, taking refuge in the Spanish Embassy. From there he was given a false name ('Mr Landsberg') and crossed the border into the Netherlands a day after the armistice had been signed.[1] His fellow army group commander the Crown Prince did the same, albeit after a short delay. After watching his father go into exile, he drove to his headquarters, intending to lead his men back home. This was rudely shattered on the morning of 11 November when he received a letter from the new government informing him that it had no further use for him. Worried that he would become embroiled in a civil war, he crossed the border into Holland several days later. The Dutch Government sent him to the Isle of Wieringen, on the chilly, fog-bound Zuider Zee. 'Stiff with cold we are,' he later wrote, 'wretched at heart and rootless on foreign soil . . . Days and weeks ensue that are so cheerless and leaden as to be almost unbearable.'[2]

In Berlin, Hindenburg agreed to remain as Chief of the General Staff and work towards the suppression of the revolution and the rehabilitation of the army. OHL moved to Wilhelmshöhe on 15 November, with Groener arranging the retreat of the *Westheer*. Foch had given Germany two weeks to evacuate France (including Alsace–Lorraine), Belgium and Luxembourg, with a further seventeen days to cross the Rhine and move through what would now become the Allied occupation zones on the west bank. Such a massive redeployment, three million men plus scores of wounded, was an enormous undertaking, but by late November most of the army had re-entered Germany – the result of impressive staff work alongside the threat of being taken prisoner, which forced a quick pace along the rutted roads, now lined with abandoned equipment and stores.[3]

The campaign on the Western Front had left 1,493,000 Germans dead, with another three million wounded, and a Fatherland bereft and bewildered at the sudden and catastrophic collapse of the *Westheer*.[4] Germany was now engulfed in violent street fighting between communists and right-wing paramilitary groups as the newly installed government of Friedrich Ebert tried to suppress a series of left-wing uprisings across the country. The realization that Germany's struggle – 'against a world of enemies', as Erzberger put it – had been in vain produced a shattering, visceral reaction. Some could never accept that she had been defeated and, instead, blamed an unholy alliance of cowardly politicians, Bolsheviks and Jews for undermining the army and weakening her will to fight. Had the Germany Army not been victorious in Russia? Had her enemies not bled themselves white in vain efforts to break her lines in the west? Were German troops still not everywhere on foreign soil? This would eventually become the *Dolchstosslegende*, the 'stab in the back' myth, that would help lay the groundwork for the seizure of power by Adolf Hitler and the National Socialists, who vowed to avenge the defeat of 1918 and bury for ever the memory of the 'November criminals'.

The claim that the German Army had not been defeated in 1918 was readily grasped by those who had been raised on the invincibility of Prussian arms and who still retained faith in its commanders at OHL. But by the final months of the war the German Army had become exhausted, morally and physically, and unable to do more than stop the Allied assaults for a day or two before resuming its painful, stumbling retreat. The adoption of short, hurricane bombardments, gas shelling and stormtrooper tactics had produced breakthroughs, sometimes spectacular ones, in the spring and summer of 1918, but decisive victory had still eluded the German Army. Against them was a grand coalition, battered but still capable, and now able to draw on the inexhaustible strength of America. It was in those final months that the long struggle for advantage on the battlefield, for a tactical edge that would somehow break the deadlock, became irresistible – sweeping away what remained of the *Westheer* and ushering in a new age of combined arms warfare: aircraft, tanks, infantry and artillery, brought together in ever more sophisticated ways.

For the man who had led this coalition, the armistice was a triumph. Sir John Du Cane, Haig's liaison officer, visited Foch at seven o'clock on the evening of 11 November to find the Generalissimo alone, sitting in his chair, smoking. His usual companion, Weygand, had gone to bed (having been up all night finalizing the arrangements), and they talked for an hour, discussing how the negotiations had gone. Du Cane then asked if Foch was not, perhaps, a little disappointed that the war had ended too soon, thinking of Mangin's attack into Lorraine, scheduled in three days' time.

'No,' Foch replied. 'I am quite satisfied with the conditions of the armistice. They give us all we want. After all, why does one make war? It is to enforce one's policy. What is our policy? To clear the Germans out of France and Belgium, to make it impossible for them to continue the war, and finally to dictate peace. We shall do all that quicker than if we went on fighting, and, what is more, without any further sacrifice of life. No, I am quite satisfied.'[5]

Not all Foch's commanders shared this satisfaction. In the final weeks of the war, Pétain suddenly grew uneasy. As he contemplated the signing of the armistice without a decisive *French* victory, he could not help but wonder if the negotiations were premature. On 9 November, he wrote to Foch on the 'immense difference there would be between an agreement at our present positions and a brilliant, clearly French, victory over Germany'.[6] Foch was not minded to keep fighting for a day longer than necessary, but Pétain could not help dwelling on the enormous, almost unimaginably high, cost of bringing Germany to terms. French war dead amounted to 1,383,000, with four million wounded, including almost a million severely wounded or permanently disabled.[7] With France's northeastern border region devastated by the fighting and the thorough destruction meted out to it by the German Army, it would take decades for her to recover, and for Pétain the danger of not crushing Germany now, while she still had the chance, would always rankle with him. For the first time in his professional career, he wept.

Pershing understood Pétain's frustrations. At Chaumont, the

American General spent armistice morning in his office, standing in front of a large wall map, his hands folded as he watched the hands of the clock sweep towards 11 a.m.

'I suppose our campaigns are ended,' he said, 'but what an enormous difference a few days more would have made.'[8]

Like Pétain, he would have preferred to see the German Army completely crushed, but there was little chance of that. President Wilson had gone to war with 'no selfish ends to serve', disdainful of the traditional theories of the balance of power and committed to a principled treatment of Germany without retribution.[9] This sense of magnanimity was easier for the Americans. The American Expeditionary Force had lost just 117,000 dead – a fraction of the blood cost that France or Britain had paid – and by the armistice it had become bigger than the BEF and almost as large as the French Army.[10] Arguments would later be made about how important the Americans were to the victory of 1918; after all, they had reached Sedan and severed Hindenburg's jugular vein, the Mézières–Montmédy railway line that supplied much of the Western Front. This was a source of justifiable pride, but most doughboys would have admitted how much they were assisted by the sustained pressure on other parts of the front, reaping the harvest made by the long, bloody and seemingly fruitless efforts of the British and French since 1914.

The price of defeating the German Army was never cheap. British losses between August and November 1918 were just shy of 300,000, one of the worst periods of the war and a vivid reminder of how much hard fighting the BEF had been through since the opening day at Amiens.[11] Even so, there was little feeling of frustration or unease at British GHQ, only a sense of fulfilment and gratitude. Haig's staunch character, his imperturbability in most situations, had brought him through the great trial intact. The Reverend George Duncan, a close personal friend, saw the British Commander-in-Chief several days after the armistice and noticed how he was largely unchanged by the rigours of the war. 'As we sat there I noted how fresh he looked, thinner perhaps and less broad shouldered than he once was, yet still lithe and vigorous, and I reflected how well he had stood up to the strain of those terrible years.' When Duncan asked whether he had thought about following the enemy into Germany, Haig was not interested. 'We have beaten them in a fair fight,' he replied, 'and that is enough for me.' Duncan saw that there was 'no exaltation, no bitterness' and 'no trace of hate' in Haig's character, only a growing sympathy for Germany's plight. 'Personally, I would have let them off more easily', Haig said as he contemplated the prospect of peace.[12]

The men who had defeated the German Empire now receded into the background as the leaders of the victorious powers – the 'Big Four' of Wilson, Clemenceau, Lloyd George and Orlando – tried to turn the armistice into a permanent reordering of Europe at a peace conference in Paris. But to bring some order and normality to a world that had been shattered by war was a thankless, impossible task. Already, across most of what had been the former Austro-Hungarian, Russian and Ottoman Empires, a series of revolutions and internecine conflicts had broken out as ethnic and national groups revived historical claims and fought for the establishment of independent states. This arc of violence stretched north to the Baltics and down to the Middle East; lands that lay, for the most part, beyond the reach of the Allied powers in the west.

Of the political figures in 1919, none would be more important than Woodrow Wilson, the bookish former President of Princeton University, who stood at the apex of his power as leader of the most powerful country in the world. Declaring that he must attend the peace conference, Wilson departed New York on 4 December, arriving in Brest nine days later. He was met by an enthusiastic welcoming reception from the local Mayor, who saluted him as 'the messenger of justice and peace'. 'Long live President Wilson!' he declared. 'Long live the champion and apostle of international justice!' The President was then driven to the station, his route lined by masses of bunting, cheering crowds, and thousands of American and French soldiers. One waiting journalist breathlessly reported that the 'splendid display' had been 'a demonstration of popular enthusiasm and national sympathy such as rarely, if ever . . . has been accorded the head of a foreign Government visiting France'.[13]

Apart from one short return to Washington, Wilson would remain in Europe until the conference concluded in the summer. It opened on 18 January 1919 in the Palace of Versailles with a stirring speech by Clemenceau, demanding justice for his country, which, 'still more than any others, has endured the sufferings of war, of which entire provinces, transformed into vast battlefields, have been systematically wasted by the invader, and which has paid the heaviest tribute to death'. Moreover, it was clear who was to blame for this cataclysm. 'The truth, bathed in blood, has already escaped from the Imperial archives ... In the hope of conquering, first, the hegemony of Europe, and next the mastery of the world, the Central Empires, bound together by a secret plot found the most abominable pretexts for trying to crush Serbia and force their way to the East. At the same time, they disowned the most solemn undertakings in order to crush Belgium and force their way into the heart of France.'[14]

The conference continued, in fits and starts, until the formal signing on 28 June. The 'Big Four' met regularly to thrash out common positions, but the task soon proved intractable as the war aims and territorial claims that Britain, France and Italy had won at such cost were balanced alongside the concept of self-determination that Wilson was still committed to. Orlando, the leader of the weakest power, stormed out of the conference in April over the refusal of the major powers to give the port of Fiume, on the Adriatic coast, to Italy – a prize that had been promised in the Treaty of London in 1915. There were also disagreements over how hard Germany should be punished, with Lloyd George and Wilson growing uneasy at the French insistence on the weakening of Germany, fearing that further punishment would only stimulate demands for revenge and imperil future trading relations. As for Wilson, he soon tired of the exhausting schedule of discussions and meetings that went on day after day. It is possible that in late April he suffered some kind of 'cardiovascular accident' – a minor stroke that left him struggling to read and write.[15]

The final terms were presented to the German delegation on 7 May. Germany would accept responsibility for starting the war ('the war guilt clause'). Her army would be reduced to a 'permanent police force' of no more than 100,000 men, without tanks, gas, heavy artillery or aircraft. The Great General Staff would be dissolved and compulsory military service abolished. Her fleet would be limited to six battleships and she was prohibited from acquiring submarines – with all other vessels being surrendered to the Allied powers. There would also be significant territorial adjustment of her borders. The Rhineland would be demilitarized and the left bank occupied by Allied or associated forces for fifteen years. Alsace–Lorraine would be restored to France; West Prussia and Posen to Poland (thus separating East Prussia from Germany); and Danzig would become a 'free city' under the control of the League of Nations. Germany's colonies, seized by the Allies during the war, would be administered under 'mandates' supervised by the United Kingdom or France. Germany would also have to agree a process by which reparations would be paid to the Allied powers – a sum that had yet to be determined.[16]

In Germany's formal response, communicated on 29 May, the Secretary for Foreign Affairs, Count Ulrich von Brockdorff-Rantzau, expressed a sense of disappointment and anger that he struggled to contain. 'We hoped for the peace of justice which had been promised to us', he told Clemenceau. 'We were aghast when we read in that document the demands made upon us by the victorious violence of our enemies.' The treaty would be 'more than the German people can bear' and he denounced what he saw as the contradictions between the earlier assurances of Allied statesmen and the terms that had been offered to them.[17] A series of 'counter-proposals' were then offered, essentially trying to lessen the terms, but these were brushed aside with a stark rejoinder that they must be accepted or rejected. If Germany did not sign the treaty, the armistice agreement would be terminated 'and the Allied and Associated Powers will take such steps as they think needful to enforce their terms'.[18]

With the threat of war hanging over their heads, the German delegation returned to Versailles on 28 June to sign the treaty. Clemenceau had insisted that it take place in the Hall of Mirrors – the same gilded room where the German Empire had been proclaimed in triumph after the Franco-Prussian War – and arranged for the Germans to march past a line of disfigured French veterans, 'living reminders of the damage inflicted by Germany'.[19] The justice or not of Versailles would long be debated, but for the time being there was only joy as the long shadow of war over Europe lifted. 'When the first boom of cannon at 4.30 told that Peace at last was an accomplished fact, Paris was already in the street', reported an English journalist. 'Before 6 o'clock the crowds had become so dense that all traffic was suspended in the principal thoroughfares . . . Indeed, Paris has perhaps never given itself up so fully to a demonstration of pure joy as to-night. It seems as if an immense weight had been lifted off the shoulders of the city.'[20] The leaders of the victorious powers then went their separate ways: Clemenceau to Paris; Lloyd George on a steamer bound for Dover; and Wilson to Brest, from where he would return home, only partially recovered from the seizure that had nearly incapacitated him over recent weeks.

In Holland, beyond the reach of the Allies, was the ex-Kaiser; who took up his exile in a manor house on the outskirts of the town of Doorn, east of Utrecht. The Allies had periodically called for him to be tried and punished, but it never came to anything. The former Supreme War Lord was left to ponder on what might have been, publishing his memoirs in 1922, in which he defended his actions and dismissed his critics. 'I do not care what my foes say about me', he wrote bitterly. 'I do not recognize them as my judges.'[21] He lingered on until June 1941, the month that Nazi Germany invaded the Soviet Union. His death went un-mourned: 'a half-forgotten fugitive in a foreign land'.[22] By then the Great War had become a byword for slaughter and futility, a meaningless exercise that accomplished nothing but the murder of an entire generation; and the peace that it produced sowed the seeds for the Second World War. The victory that the remarkable fellowship of Joffre, Foch, Pétain, Haig and Pershing had won on the Western Front was overshadowed: merely the first act of a great tragedy.

Cast of Characters

ALBERT I, King of the Belgians (1875–1934): Assumed command of the Belgian Army in August 1914 and spent the remainder of the war with his men in a small lodgement behind the Yser river.

ALLENBY, General Sir Edmund Henry Hynman (1861–1936): Commanded the British Cavalry Division in 1914 before taking charge of Third Army (1915–17). Transferred to the Egyptian Expeditionary Force in June 1917.

ASQUITH, Herbert Henry (1852–1928): Liberal Party politician and Prime Minister of the United Kingdom (1908–16).

BADEN, Prince Maximilian Alexander Friedrich Wilhelm von (1867–1929): Honorary President of the Baden branch of the German Red Cross who was appointed Imperial Chancellor on 3 October 1918.

BAKER, Newton Diehl (1871–1937): US Secretary of War (1916–21).

BALFOUR, Arthur James, 1st Earl of Balfour (1848–1930): Conservative politician who was appointed First Lord of the Admiralty in May 1915 and Foreign Secretary the following year.

BAUER, Colonel Max Hermann (1869–1929): Artillery expert who served throughout the war in the Operations Section of the German Supreme Command.

BAYERN, Crown Prince Rupprecht Maria Luitpold Ferdinand von (1869–1955): Heir to the throne of Bavaria. Commanded the German Sixth Army (1914–16) and Army Group Rupprecht (1916–18).

BELOW, General Fritz Wilhelm Theodor Karl von (1853–1918): Replaced Karl von Bülow at the German Second Army in 1915 until he moved to command First Army in 1916. Appointed to Ninth Army in June 1918.

BELOW, General Otto Ernst Vinzent Leo von (1857–1944): Served on the Eastern Front, in the Balkans and on the Italian Front between 1914 and 1917. Brought back to the Western Front in February 1918 (after his time in Italy) to take charge of the German Seventeenth Army.

BERG-MARKIENEN, Friedrich Wilhelm Bernard von (1866–1939): President of East Prussia who was appointed Chief of the Kaiser's Civil Cabinet in January 1918.

BETHMANN HOLLWEG, Theobald Theodor Friedrich Alfred von (1856–1921): German Imperial Chancellor (1909–17).

BLISS, General Tasker Howard (1853–1930): Chief of Staff of the United States Army (1917–18). Assigned to the Supreme War Council as American Permanent Military Representative in November 1917.

BOEHN, General Max Ferdinand Karl von (1850–1921): Commander of the German Seventh Army (1915–18). Promoted to army group command in August 1918.

BRIAND, Aristide Pierre Henri (1862–1932): French statesman and politician who served as Prime Minister between October 1915 and March 1917.

BÜLOW, Field Marshal Karl Wilhelm Paul von (1846–1921): Commander of the German Second Army (1914–15) who was briefly tasked with coordinating First and Third Armies in August 1914. Suffered a heart attack in March 1915.

BYNG, General Hon. Sir Julian Hedworth George (1862–1935): Commander of the British Third Army (1917–18).

CASTELNAU, General Noël Édouard Marie Joseph Curières de (1851–1944): Commander of the French Second Army (1914–15) and Army Group Centre (1915). Recalled from retirement in December 1916 to command Army Group East.

CHURCHILL, Winston Leonard Spencer (1874–1965): First Lord of the Admiralty (1911–15) who resigned from government in October 1915. Served as Minister of Munitions (1917–18).

CLEMENCEAU, Georges Eugène Benjamin (1841–1929): French senator and member of the Senate Army Commission who was appointed Prime Minister on 16 November 1917.

CONRAD VON HÖTZENDORF, Field Marshal Franz Xaver Josef Graf (1852–1925): Chief of the General Staff of the Austro-Hungarian Army and Navy (1906–17).

CURZON, Lord George Nathaniel, 1st Marquess Curzon of Kedleston (1859–1925): British statesman and former Viceroy of India (1898–1905) who served as Lord Privy Seal (1915–16) and Leader of the House of Lords (1916–24).

DE MITRY, General Antoine (1857–1924): French cavalry officer who commanded a 'Northern Army Detachment' in Flanders in April and May 1918.

DUBAIL, General Augustin Yvon Edmond (1851–1934): Commander of the French First Army (1914) and Army Group East (1915–16).

DUCHÊNE, General Denis Auguste (1862–1950): Commander of the French Tenth Army (1916–17) and Sixth Army (1917–18). Relieved of command in June 1918.

D'URBAL, General Victor Louis Lucien (1858–1943): Cavalry officer who commanded the French Eighth Army (1914–15) and Tenth Army (1915–16).

EINEM, General Karl Wilhelm Georg August von (1853–1934): Commander of the German Third Army between September 1914 and November 1918.

EMMICH, General Albert Theodor Otto von (1848–1915): Led a task force that captured Liège in August 1914.

ERZBERGER, Matthias (1875–1921): German Catholic Centre Party politician who was part of the first parliamentary government formed in October 1918. Led the armistice delegation at Compiègne.

FALKENHAUSEN, General Ludwig Alexander Friedrich August Philipp von (1844–1936): Commander of the German Sixth Army (1916–17). Appointed Governor-General of Belgium in April 1917.

FALKENHAYN, General Erich Georg Sebastian Anton (1861–1922): Prussian Minister of War (1913–15) and Chief of the General Staff (1914–16). After being relieved of command in August 1916 he was appointed commander of Ninth Army in Romania and led Army Group 'F' in Turkey.

FAYOLLE, General Marie Émile (1852–1928): Recalled from retirement in 1914 to divisional command before replacing Pétain at XXXIII Corps in 1915. Served as commander of Sixth Army (1916) and First Army (1916–17). Took charge of Reserve Army Group in March 1918.

FERRY, Abel Jules Édouard (1881–1918): French politician and soldier. Became Under-Secretary for Foreign Affairs in 1914 before serving at the front with his regiment in 1914–15. Mortally wounded by shellfire in September 1918 while inspecting the front.

FOCH, Marshal Ferdinand (1851–1929): Led the French XX Corps in August 1914 and was quickly promoted to Ninth Army (1914) and Army Group North (1915–16). Appointed Army Chief of Staff (May 1917) and Supreme Allied Commander (April 1918).

FRANCHET D'ESPÈREY, General Louis Félix Marie François Franchet (1856–1942): Commander of the French I Corps (1914) and took charge of Fifth Army before the Battle of the Marne. Served as commander of Army Group East (1916) and Army Group North (1916–18).

FRENCH, Field Marshal Sir John Denton Pinkstone (1852–1925): Commander-in-Chief of the British Expeditionary Force (1914–15). Returned home in December 1915 to take charge of Home Forces. Served as Lord-Lieutenant of Ireland (1918–21).

GALLIÉNI, General Joseph Simon (1849–1916): Decorated colonial soldier recalled from retirement in 1914 to become Military Governor of Paris. Served as Minister of War between October 1915 and March 1916.

GALLWITZ, General Max Karl Wilhelm von (1852–1937): Appointed commander of the German Second Army on the Somme in July 1916, while also taking charge of Army Group Gallwitz. Subsequently commanded Fifth Army (1916–18).

GOUGH, General Sir Hubert de la Poer (1870–1963): Commander of the British Reserve Army – later renamed Fifth Army (1916–18). Dismissed after the collapse of Fifth Army on 27 March 1918.

GOURAUD, General Henri Joseph Eugène (1867–1946): Commander of the French Expeditionary Corps at the Dardanelles, where he was wounded and had to have his right arm amputated. Commander of the French Fourth Army (1917–18).

GROENER, General Karl Eduard Wilhelm (1867–1939): Head of the Railway Section of the German General Staff in 1914 before moving to the War Ministry in 1916. Replaced Ludendorff as First Quartermaster-General in October 1918.

HAIG, Field Marshal Sir Douglas (1861–1928): Went to war with the British I Corps, later taking charge of First Army (1915). Replaced Sir John French as Commander-in-Chief of the British Expeditionary Force in December 1915.

HANKEY, Maurice Pascal Alers (1877–1963): Secretary of the Committee of Imperial Defence who served, successively, as Secretary to the Dardanelles Committee, War Committee and War Cabinet between 1914 and 1918.

HARBORD, Brigadier-General James Guthrie (1866–1947): Appointed Chief of Staff to General Pershing in April 1917. Took charge of US 4 Marine Brigade in June 1918.

HAUSEN, General Max Clemens Lothar Freiherr von (1846–1922): Commanded the Royal Saxon Army (Third Army) on the outbreak of war. Relieved from duty in September 1914 owing to illness.

HERTLING, Georg, Graf von (1843–1919): Delegate for the Catholic Centre Party in the Reichstag. Appointed Imperial Chancellor and Prime Minister of Prussia on 1 November 1917. Resigned on 3 October 1918.

HINDENBURG, Paul Ludwig Hans Anton von Beneckendorff und von (1847–1934): Brought out of retirement in August 1914 to take charge of the German Eighth Army in East Prussia. Replaced Falkenhayn as Chief of the General Staff in August 1916.

HINTZE, Paul von (1864–1941): Former German naval officer and diplomat who served as Ambassador to China (1914) and Norway (1917) before being appointed Foreign Secretary in July 1918.

HOHENZOLLERN, Crown Prince Friedrich Wilhelm Victor August Ernst (1882–1951): Eldest son of the Kaiser. Took charge of the German Fifth Army in August 1914 before commanding Army Group Crown Prince (1917–18).

HOHENZOLLERN, Kaiser Friedrich Wilhelm Viktor Albert ('Wilhelm II') (1859–1941): German Emperor, King of Prussia, who reigned from 1888 to 1918. Abdicated on 9 November 1918.

HOLTZENDORFF, Admiral Henning Rudolf Adolf Karl von (1853–1919): Uncompromising proponent of unrestricted submarine warfare and Chief of the Admiralty General Staff (1915–18).

HOUSE, 'Colonel' Edward Mandell (1858–1938): Adviser to President Wilson who travelled to France in October 1918 as the President's personal representative.

HUTIER, General Oskar Emil von (1857–1934): After serving on the Eastern Front, he was brought to France to command the newly formed Eighteenth Army for the spring offensive (1918).

JELLICOE, Admiral of the Fleet Sir John Rushworth (1859–1935): Appointed commander of the Royal Navy's Grand Fleet on the outbreak of war and led it at its most significant engagement at Jutland in May–June 1916. Served as First Sea Lord (1916–17).

JOFFRE, Marshal Joseph Jacques Césaire (1852–1931): Appointed Chief of the French General Staff in 1911 and Commander-in-Chief on the outbreak of war. He resigned in December 1916 and led the French Military Mission to the United States the following year.

KITCHENER, Field Marshal Lord Horatio Herbert (1850–1916): British Secretary of State for War (1914–16). Lost in the sinking of HMS *Hampshire* in June 1916.

KLUCK, General Alexander Heinrich Rudolph von (1846–1934): Commanded the German First Army (1914–15). Retired from active service in March 1915 after being wounded by shrapnel.

KNOBELSDORF, Konstantin Schmidt von (1860–1936): Chief of Staff of the German Fifth Army (1914–16).

KUHL, Lieutenant-General Hermann Josef von (1856–1958): Served in a variety of staff positions, including Chief of Staff of the German First Army (1914), Twelfth Army and Sixth Army (1915). Assigned to Army Group Rupprecht as Chief of Staff (1916–18).

KÜHLMANN, Richard von (1873–1948): German Ambassador at Constantinople (1916–17) and Foreign Secretary (1917–18).

LANGLE DE CARY, General Fernand Louis Armand Marie de (1849–1927): Commander of the French Fourth Army (1914–1915) and Army Group Centre (1915–16).

LANREZAC, General Charles Louis Marie (1852–1925): Commander of the French Fifth Army in 1914. Sacked on the eve of the Battle of the Marne (5 September 1914).

LANSING, Robert (1864–1928): US Secretary of State (1915–20).

LEMAN, General Gérard Mathieu Joseph Georges (1851–1920): Commander of the fortifications surrounding Liège and 3rd Belgian Division. Taken prisoner at Fort de Loncin and held in captivity until 1917, when he was repatriated to Switzerland because of poor health.

LIGGETT, General Hunter (1857–1935): Commander of US I Corps at the Second Battle of the Marne and Saint-Mihiel. Appointed commander of US First Army in October 1918.

LLOYD GEORGE, David (1863–1945): Liberal politician who was put in charge of the Ministry of Munitions in May 1915. Appointed Secretary of State for War after Kitchener's death in June 1916. Replaced Asquith as British Prime Minister in December 1916.

LOSSBERG, Colonel Friedrich Karl 'Fritz' von (1868–1942): German defensive expert who served in a variety of staff positions, including Chief of Staff at Third Army (1915), First Army (1916), Sixth Army (1917), Fourth Army (1917–18) and Army Groups Boehn and Duke Albrecht (1918). Known as the 'Lion of the Defensive'.

LUDENDORFF, General Erich Friedrich Wilhelm (1865–1937): Served with the German Second Army in 1914 before being transferred to Eighth Army in East Prussia. Appointed First Quartermaster-General in August 1916. Resigned on 26 October 1918.

LYAUTEY, Marshal Louis Hubert (1854–1834): French Resident-General of Morocco (1912–16) who was appointed Minister of War in December 1916. Resigned in March 1917.

MAISTRE, General Paul André Marie (1858–1922): Appointed commander of the French Sixth Army in May 1917. After briefly commanding French troops in Italy, he returned to the Western Front in 1918 to command Tenth Army and (from July) Army Group Centre.

MANGIN, General Charles Emmanuel Marie (1866–1925): Colonial soldier who moved from divisional and corps command (1914–16) to take charge of the French Sixth Army in 1917. Dismissed after the Nivelle offensive, he returned to command Tenth Army in June 1918 and led the counter-attacks at the Matz and the Marne.

MARWITZ, General Georg Cornelius Adalbert von der (1856–1929): Cavalry officer who was appointed commander of the German Second Army in December 1916. Moved to command Fifth Army in the Argonne in October 1918.

MAUD'HUY, General Louis Ernest de (1857–1921): Commander of the French Tenth Army (1914–15) and Seventh Army (1915). Demoted to corps commander before being relieved in June 1918.

MAUNOURY, General Michel Joseph (1847–1923): Commander of the French Sixth Army (1914–15). Retired from active service in March 1915 after being severely wounded by a sniper.

MICHAELIS, Georg Max Ludwig (1857–1936): Served as Imperial Chancellor and Prime Minister of Prussia between July and November 1917.

MICHELER, General Joseph Alfred (1861–1931): Commander of the French Tenth Army (1916) before being appointed to Reserve Army Group for the Nivelle offensive.

MILLERAND, Étienne Alexandre (1859–1943): French Minister of War (1914–15).

MILNER, Alfred, Viscount (1854–1925): Colonial administrator and member of the War Cabinet (1916–18). Appointed Secretary of State for War in April 1918.

MOLTKE, Colonel-General Helmuth Johannes Ludwig von (1848–1916): Chief of the General Staff (1906–14) and one of the architects of the German war plan of 1914. Replaced on 14 September 1914 by Falkenhayn.

NIVELLE, General Robert Georges (1856–1924): Artillery officer who was appointed commander of the French Second Army at Verdun in May 1916. Succeeded Joffre as Commander-in-Chief and masterminded the Nivelle offensive in the spring of 1917. Dismissed on 15 May 1917.

PAINLEVÉ, Paul (1863–1933): Respected mathematician who was head of the Inventions Committee at the French Ministry of War. Appointed Minister of War in March 1917 and formed a government between September and November 1917.

PERSHING, General John Joseph (1860–1948): Commander-in-Chief of the American Expeditionary Force.

PÉTAIN, Marshal Henri Philippe Benoni Omer (1856–1951): Commander of the French XXXIII Corps during the fighting in Artois (1915) and appointed to Second Army in July 1915. Promoted to Army Group Centre in May 1916. Succeeded Nivelle as Commander-in-Chief in May 1917.

PLESSEN, General Hans Georg Hermann von (1841–1929): Close friend of and adviser to the Kaiser. Served as Commandant of OHL and His Majesty's Adjutant-General (1914–18).

PLUMER, General Sir Herbert Charles Onslow (1857–1932): Commander of the British Second Army (1915–18).

POINCARÉ, Raymond Nicolas Landry (1860–1934): President of the French Republic (1913–20).

RAWLINSON, General Sir Henry Seymour (1864–1925): Commander of the British Fourth Army (1916–18).

RIBOT, Alexandre Félix Joseph (1842–1923): French Finance Minister (1914–17) who formed a short-lived government between March and September 1917.

RICHTHOFEN, Captain Manfred Albrecht Freiherr von (1892–1918): Renowned German fighter pilot and leader of Jagdgeschwader II. Shot down and killed in action on 21 April 1918.

ROBERTSON, General Sir William Robert (1860–1933): Quartermaster-General and Chief of Staff to the British Expeditionary Force (1914–15). Served as Chief of the Imperial General Staff (1915–18).

ROQUES, General Pierre Auguste (1856–1920): French Minister of War between March and December 1916.

SCHULENBURG, General Friedrich Bernhard Karl Gustav Ulrich Erich Graf von der (1865–1939): Cavalry officer who was appointed Chief of Staff to Army Group Crown Prince in October 1916.

SMITH-DORRIEN, General Sir Horace Lockwood (1858–1930): Commander of the British II Corps and Second Army (1914–15). Relieved of command on 6 May 1915.

SMUTS, Field Marshal Jan Christiaan (1870–1950): South African statesman and military officer. Member of the Imperial War Cabinet and War Policy Committee (1917–18).

STANLEY, Edward George Villiers, 17th Earl of Derby (1865–1948): British diplomat and soldier. Appointed Secretary of State for War in December 1916. Served as Ambassador to France (1918–20).

TAPPEN, General Dietrich Gerhard Emil Theodor (1866–1953): Chief of Operations at OHL (1914–16).

TIRPITZ, Grand Admiral Alfred Peter Friedrich von (1849–1930): Secretary of State for the Imperial German Navy (1897–1916).

VALLIÈRES, General Pierre des (1868–1918): Chief of the French Mission to the British Army (1915–17). Killed in action at Juvigny on 28 May 1918.

VIVIANI, René Jean Raphaël Adrien (1863–1925): French Prime Minister between May 1914 and October 1915.

WETZELL, Lieutenant-Colonel Georg (1869–1947): Chief of Operations at OHL (1916–18).

WEYGAND, General Maxime (1867–1965): Served throughout most of the war as Foch's Chief of Staff. Appointed French Permanent Military Representative on the Supreme War Council between December 1917 and April 1918, after which he returned to Foch's staff.

WILSON, Lieutenant-General Sir Henry Hughes (1864–1922): Former Director of Military Operations at the War Office who was appointed Sub-Chief of Staff to Sir John French in 1914. He served as Britain's Permanent Military Representative on the Supreme War Council before replacing Robertson as CIGS in February 1918.

WILSON, Thomas Woodrow (1856–1924): 28th President of the United States (1913–21).

WÜRTTEMBERG, Albrecht, Duke of (1865–1939): Commander of the German Fourth Army (1914–17) and Army Group Duke Albrecht (1917–18).

Abbreviations

AEF: American Expeditionary Force
AFGG: *Les Armées françaises dans la Grande guerre*
ANZAC: Australian and New Zealand Army Corps
AWM: Australian War Memorial, Canberra
BA-MA: Bundesarchiv-Militärarchiv, Freiburg
BEF: British Expeditionary Force
BLO: Bodleian Library, Oxford
CAB: Cabinet Office files
CIGS: Chief of the Imperial General Staff
GHQ: General Headquarters (British Expeditionary Force)
GQG: *Grand Quartier Général* (French High Command)
IWM: Imperial War Museum, London
LAC: Library & Archives Canada, Ottawa
LOC: Library of Congress, Washington DC
MHI: Military History Institute, Carlisle, Pennsylvania
NCO: Non-commissioned officer
OHL: *Oberste Heeresleitung* (German Supreme Army Command)
RAF: Royal Air Force
RFC: Royal Flying Corps
TNA: The National Archives, Kew
USAWW: *United States Army in the World War, 1917–1919*
VC: Victoria Cross
WO: War Office files

References

Preface

1 AWM: 3DRL/2206, A. G. Thomas diary, 21 July 1916.
2 *Statistics of the Military Effort of the British Empire during the Great War. 1914–1920* (London: HMSO, 1922), p. 243.
3 J. B. A. Bailey, 'The First World War and the Birth of Modern Warfare', in M. Knox and W. Murray (eds.), *The Dynamics of Military Revolution, 1300–2050* (Cambridge: Cambridge University Press, 2001), pp. 132–53.

Prologue: 'An act of hostility'

1 'Imperial German Legation in Belgium-Brussels, 2 August 1914', in A. Mombauer (ed. and trans.), *The Origins of the First World War. Diplomatic and Military Documents* (Manchester: Manchester University Press, 2013), pp. 532–3.
2 'The Austro-Hungarian Ultimatum to Serbia', and 'Serbia's Reply to the Austro-Hungarian Ultimatum', in ibid., pp. 291–5, 352–6.
3 E. J. Galet, *Albert, King of the Belgians in the Great War. His Military Activities Set Down with His Approval*, trans. E. Swinton (London: Putnam, 1931), pp. 46, 49–50.
4 '4 August: Bethmann Hollweg's Reichstag Speech', in Mombauer (ed. and trans.), *The Origins of the First World War*, pp. 571–2.
5 'Message from M. Poincaré', Appendix II, in R. Poincaré, *The Memoirs of Raymond Poincaré (1913–1914)*, trans. G. Arthur (London: William Heinemann, 1928), pp. 309–10.
6 B. Whitlock, *Belgium. A Personal Narrative* (New York: D. Appleton and Company, 1919), p. 63.

Part 1: 'War is not like manoeuvres'

1 'A vision of Attila'

1 F. Fischer, *Germany's Aims in the First World War* (New York: W. W. Norton & Co., 1967; first publ. 1961), p. 50.

2 'Comments by Moltke on the Memorandum, c. 1911', in R. T. Foley (trans. and ed.), *Alfred von Schlieffen's Military Writings* (London: Frank Cass, 2003), p. 179.

3 E. J. Galet, *Albert, King of the Belgians in the Great War. His Military Activities Set Down with His Approval*, trans. E. Swinton (London: Putnam, 1931), pp. 73–4.

4 J. Lipkes, *Rehearsals. The German Army in Belgium, August 1914* (Leuven: Leuven University Press, 2007), p. 39.

5 M. O. Humphries and J. Maker (eds.), *Germany's Western Front. Translations from the German Official History of the Great War. 1914, Part 1* (Waterloo, Ont.: Wilfrid Laurier Press, 2013), p. 104.

6 Galet, *Albert, King of the Belgians*, p. 56; and Commander-in-Chief of the Belgian Army, *The War of 1914. Military Operations of Belgium in Defence of the Country to Uphold Her Neutrality* (London: W. H. & L. Collingridge, 1915), pp. 11–13.

7 E. Ludendorff, *My War Memories 1914–1918* (2 vols., London: Hutchinson & Co., 1919), I, pp. 32–6.

8 Galet, *Albert, King of the Belgians*, p. 80.

9 C. Donnell, *Breaking the Fortress Line 1914* (Barnsley: Pen & Sword, 2013), pp. 60–62.

10 E. and L. Klekowski, *Americans in Occupied Belgium, 1914–1918. Accounts of the War from Journalists, Tourists, Troops and Medical Staff* (Jefferson, NC: McFarland & Company, 2014), p. 14.

11 'German Letter from an Officer in the Assault', in C. F. Horne (ed.), *Source Records of the Great War* (7 vols., USA: National Alumni, 1923), II, pp. 47–8.

12 'A French Gunner', *General Joffre* (London: Simpkin, Marshall, Hamilton, Kent & Co., n.d.), pp. 13–14.

13 'The French Plan of Campaign', Appendix 9, in Sir J. Edmonds, *Military Operations. France and Belgium, 1914* (2 vols., London: Macmillan and Co., 1933), I, pp. 445–9.

14 Lanrezac to Joffre, 14 August 1914, in Ministère de la Guerre, *Les Armées françaises dans la Grande guerre* (Paris: Imprimerie Nationale, 1922–39) [hereafter *AFGG*], Book 1/1 – *Annexes*, Vol. 1, No. 283, pp. 290–91.

15 Joffre to Lanrezac, 14 August 1914, in *AFGG*, Book 1/1 – *Annexes*, Vol. 1, No. 270, p. 280.

16 'General Instructions No. 1', 8 August 1914, Appendix IV, in S. Tyng, *The Campaign of the Marne 1914* (London: Humphrey Milford, 1935), pp. 362–4.

17 'Note du général commandant l'armée au sujet de l'attitude à tenir pour attaquer des organisations défensives', 15 August 1914, in *AFGG*, Book 1/1 – *Annexes*, Vol. 1, No. 319, p. 317.

18 R. A. Doughty, *Pyrrhic Victory. French Strategy and Operations in the Great War* (London and Cambridge, Mass.: Harvard University Press, 2005), p. 61.

19 J. Boff, *Haig's Enemy. Crown Prince Rupprecht and Germany's War on the Western Front* (Oxford: Oxford University Press, 2018), p. 23.

20 R. Poincaré, *The Memoirs of Raymond Poincaré 1914*, trans. G. Arthur (London: William Heinemann, 1929), p. 51.

21 J. C. Joffre, *The Memoirs of Marshal Joffre*, trans. T. Bentley Mott (2 vols., London: Geoffrey Bles, 1932), I, pp. 161–2.

22 '6 August: Minutes of British War Council Meeting', in A. Mombauer (ed. and trans.), *The Origins of the First World War. Diplomatic and Military Documents* (Manchester: Manchester University Press, 2013), pp. 587–90.

23 'Instructions to Sir John French from Lord Kitchener August 1914', Appendix 8, in Edmonds, *Military Operations. 1914*, I, pp. 499–500.

24 W. J. Philpott, 'Gone Fishing? Sir John French's Meeting with General Lanrezac, 17 August 1914', *Journal of the Society for Army Historical Research*, Vol. 84, No. 339 (Autumn 2006), pp. 254–9.

25 Humphries and Maker (eds.), *Germany's Western Front. 1914, Part 1*, p. 81.

26 BA-MA: RH 61/1235, Moltke to Bülow, 11 August 1914.

27 I. Senior, *Invasion 1914. The Schlieffen Plan to the Battle of the Marne* (Oxford: Osprey, 2012), p. 366.

28 A. von Kluck, *The March on Paris and the Battle of the Marne 1914* (London: Edward Arnold, 1920), p. 9.

29 A. Mombauer, *Helmuth von Moltke and the Origins of the First World War* (Cambridge: Cambridge University Press, 2001), pp. 232–4; and Kaiser Wilhelm II quoted in S. McMeekin, *July 1914. Countdown to War* (London: Icon Books, 2013), p. 343.

30 W. Bloem, *The Advance from Mons 1914* (London: Peter Davis, 1930), p. 38.

31 BA-MA: N550/1, 'Die Operationen der 1 Armee bis zum Eintreffen in der Aisne–Stellung (vom 9 August bis zum 12 September 1914)', p. 6.

32 H. H. Herwig, *The Marne, 1914. The Opening of World War I and the Battle That Changed the World* (New York: Random House, 2011; first publ. 2009), pp. 171–2.

33 A. Kramer, *Dynamic of Destruction. Culture and Mass Killing in the First World War* (Oxford: Oxford University Press, 2007), p. 8.

34 J. Horne and A. Kramer, *German Atrocities, 1914. A History of Denial* (New Haven, Conn., and London: Yale University Press, 2001), pp. 24, 26, 43.

35 Tyng, *Marne*, pp. 79–80; E. D. Brose, *The Kaiser's Army. The Politics of Military Technology in Germany during the Machine Age, 1870–1918* (Oxford: Oxford University Press, 2001), p. 196; and C. Delvert, *From the Marne to Verdun. The War Diary of Captain Charles Delvert, 101st Infantry, 1914–1916*, trans. I. Sumner (Barnsley: Pen & Sword, 2016), p. 36.

36 P. Lintier, *My Seventy-Five. Journal of a French Gunner (August–September 1914)* (London: Peter Davis, 1929), p. 55.

37 H. Strachan, *The First World War. I. To Arms* (Oxford: Oxford University Press, 2003; first publ. 2001), p. 218.

38 H. Contamine, *9 Septembre 1914. La Victoire de la Marne* (Paris: Éditions Gallimard, 1970), p. 120.

39 A. Grasset, *La Guerre en action. Surprise d'une Division: Rossignol–Saint-Vincent* (Nancy: Éditions Berger-Levrault, 1932), p. 76.

40 E. Greenhalgh, *The French Army and the First World War* (Cambridge: Cambridge University Press, 2014), p. 41.

41 F. de Langle de Cary, *Souvenirs de commandement 1914–1916* (Paris: Payot, 1935), pp. 136–7.

42 Ruffey to GQG, 23 August 1914, in *AFGG*, Book 1/1 – *Annexes*, Vol. 1, No. 1088, p. 865.

43 Strachan, *The First World War*. I. *To Arms*, p. 207; and R. A. Prete, *Strategy and Command. The Anglo-French Coalition on the Western Front, 1914* (Montreal: McGill–Queen's University Press, 2009), pp. 27–8.

44 Tyng, *Marne*, p. 102.

45 Sir E. Spears, *Liaison 1914. A Narrative of the Great Retreat* (London: Eyre & Spottiswoode, 1968; first publ. 1930), p. 110.

46 Edmonds, *Military Operations. 1914*, I, p. 68.

47 IWM: Documents 2304, 'Anonymous Account of the Battle of Mons, August 1914'.

48 Sir H. Smith-Dorrien, *Memories of Forty-Eight Years' Service* (London: John Murray, 1925), pp. 385–6.

49 F. Engerand, *Lanrezac* (Paris: Éditions Bossard, 1926), p. 40.

50 Humphries and Maker (eds.), *Germany's Western Front. 1914, Part 1*, pp. 239, 241.

2 'To the last extremity'

1 Sir E. Spears, *Liaison 1914. A Narrative of the Great Retreat* (London: Eyre & Spottiswoode, 1968; first publ. 1930), p. 192.

2 'The G.Q.G.'s Instructions on Tactics', 24 August 1914, Appendix XXII, in Spears, *Liaison 1914*, pp. 517–18.

3 R. Recouly, *Joffre* (London and New York: D. Appleton & Company, 1931), p. 92.

4 'General Instructions No. 2', 25 August 1914, Appendix VII, in S. Tyng, *The Campaign of the Marne 1914* (London: Humphrey Milford, 1935), pp. 369–71.

5 Sir J. E. Edmonds, *Military Operations. France and Belgium, 1914* (2 vols., London: Macmillan and Co., 1933), I, pp. 140–41.

6 Sir H. Smith-Dorrien, *Memories of Forty-Eight Years' Service* (London: John Murray, 1925), pp. 386, 411.

7 M. von Poseck, *The German Cavalry. 1914 in Belgium and France* (Berlin: E. S. Mittler & Sohn, 1923), p. 65.

8 Ministère de la Guerre, *Les Armées françaises dans la Grande guerre* (Paris: Imprimerie Nationale, 1922–39) [hereafter *AFGG*], Book 1/2, p. 121.

9 L.-E. Mangin, *Le Général Mangin 1866–1925* (Paris: Éditions Fernand Lanore, 1986), pp. 149–50.

10 Letter, 29 August 1914, in H. von Moltke, *Erinnerungen. Briefe. Dokumente 1877–1916* (Stuttgart: Der Kommende Tag A.G. Verlag, 1922), p. 382.

11 'Von Moltke's General Directive to the German Armies after the Battle of the Frontiers', 27 August 1914, Appendix VIII, in Tyng, *Marne*, pp. 371–4.

12 'Memorandum of 1905', in R. T. Foley (trans. and ed.), *Alfred von Schlieffen's Military Writings* (London: Frank Cass, 2003), p. 172.

13 A. Mombauer, *Helmuth von Moltke and the Origins of the First World War* (Cambridge: Cambridge University Press, 2001), p. 243.

14 A. von Kluck, *The March on Paris and the Battle of the Marne 1914* (London: Edward Arnold, 1920), pp. 69, 164.

15 Ibid., p. 83.

16 Ibid., p. 94.

17 BA-MA: N550/1, 'Die Operationen der 1 Armee bis zum Eintreffen in der Aisne–Stellung (vom 9 August bis zum 12 September 1914)', p. 31.

18 Tyng, *Marne*, p. 200. Emphasis added.

19 J. C. Joffre, *The Memoirs of Marshal Joffre*, trans. T. Bentley Mott (2 vols., London: Geoffrey Bles, 1932), I, pp. 220–21, 236–8.

20 Spears, *Liaison 1914*, p. 322; and R. A. Prete, *Strategy and Command. The Anglo-French Coalition on the Western Front, 1914* (Montreal: McGill–Queen's University Press, 2009), p. 107.

21 French to Kitchener, 30 August 1914, in Sir G. Arthur, *Life of Lord Kitchener* (3 vols., London: Macmillan and Co., 1920), III, p. 47.

22 French to Kitchener, 31 August 1914, in R. Holmes, *The Little Field Marshal. A Life of Sir John French* (London: Cassell, 2005; first publ. 1981), p. 231.

23 Kitchener to French, 31 August 1914, in G. H. Cassar, *Kitchener. Architect of Victory* (London: William Kimber, 1977), p. 235.

24 'General Joffre's Instruction for the Battle of the Marne', 4 September 1914, Appendix 30, in Edmonds, *Military Operations. 1914*, I, pp. 543–4.

25 Joffre, *Memoirs*, I, p. 255.

26 E. Herbillon, *Souvenirs d'un officier de liaison pendant la Guerre mondiale. Du général en chef au gouvernement* (2 vols., Paris: Jules Tallandier, 1930), I, p. 27 (entry, 6 September 1914).

27 H. H. Herwig, *The Marne, 1914. The Opening of World War I and the Battle That Changed the World* (New York: Random House, 2011; first publ. 2009), pp. 240–42.

28 R. Dahlmann, *Die Schlacht vor Paris. Das Marnedrama 1914, Part 4* (Berlin: Gerhard Stalling, 1928), p. 49.

29 C. Mallet, *Impressions and Experiences of a French Trooper, 1914–15* (New York: E. P. Dutton & Company, 1916), pp. 43–4.

30 Herwig, *The Marne, 1914*, p. 311.

31 T. von Bose, *Das Marnedrama 1914. Die Kämpfe des Gardekorps und des rechten Flügels der 3. Armee von 5. bis 8. September* (Berlin: Gerhard Stalling, 1928), p. 157.

32 Herwig, *The Marne, 1914*, pp. 217–18.

33 J. de Pierrefeu, *French Headquarters 1915–1918*, trans. Major C. J. C. Street (London: Geoffrey Bles, 1924), p. 43.

34 Joffre, *Memoirs*, I, p. 254.

35 Edmonds, *Military Operations. 1914*, I, p. 343.

36 K. von Bülow, *Mein Bericht zur Marneschlacht* (Berlin: A. Scherl, 1919), p. 60.

37 Letter, 8 September 1914, in Moltke, *Erinnerungen*, p. 384.

38 BA-MA: RH 61/986, Tappen diary, 8 September 1914.

39 Reichsarchiv, *Der Weltkrieg 1914 bis 1918*. IV. *Der Marne-Feldzug. Die Schlacht* (Berlin: E. S. Mittler & Sohn, 1926), p. 23.

40 Herwig, *The Marne, 1914*, p. 274.

41 Reichsarchiv, *Der Weltkrieg*. IV. *Der Marne-Feldzug. Die Schlacht*, p. 31.

42 H. von Kuhl, *Der Marnefeldzug 1914* (Berlin: E. S. Mittler & Sohn, 1921), p. 219.

43 Recouly, *Joffre*, p. 183.

44 Spears, *Liaison 1914*, p. 446.

45 'Communication du général commandant la IXe armée aux troupes', 9 September 1914, in *AFGG*, Book 1/3 – *Annexes*, Vol. 2, No. 2121, p. 547.

46 R. Poincaré, *The Memoirs of Raymond Poincaré 1914*, trans. G. Arthur (London: William Heinemann, 1929), p. 156.

47 'Radio Allemande intercepté à Belfort', 30 August 1914, in *AFGG*, Book 1/2 – *Annexes*, Vol. 2, No. 1396, p. 7.

48 BA-MA: RH 61/1235, Bülow to his wife, Molly, 16 September 1914.

49 W. Bloem, *The Advance from Mons 1914* (London: Peter Davis, 1930), p. 167.

50 P. Maze, *A Frenchman in Khaki* (London: William Heinemann, 1934), p. 62.

51 État numérique des pertes pendant le mois de septembre 1914', in *AFGG*, Book 1/3 – *Annexes*, Vol. 4, No. 5296, p. 845; and Herwig, *The Marne, 1914*, p. 315.

52 BA-MA: N550/1, 'Die Operationen der 1 Armee bis zum Eintreffen in der Aisne–Stellung (vom 9 August bis zum 12 September 1914)', p. 44.

53 Edmonds, *Military Operations. 1914*, I, pp. 419–20.

54 M. Bauer, *Der große Krieg in Feld und Heimat. Erinnerungen und Betrachtungen* (Tübingen: Oslander'sche Buchhandlung, 1922), p. 58.

3 'Men of real worth'

1 Sir H. Smith-Dorrien, *Memories of Forty-Eight Years' Service* (London: John Murray, 1925), p. 435.

2 Joffre to Millerand, 18 September 1914, in Ministère de la Guerre, *Les Armées françaises dans la Grande guerre* (Paris: Imprimerie Nationale, 1922–39) [hereafter *AFGG*], Book 1/4 – *Annexes*, Vol. 1, No. 394, p. 368.

3 Joffre to Millerand, 20 September 1914, in *AFGG*, Book 2 – *Annexes*, Vol. 1, No. 19, pp. 12–13.

4 L. Cecil, *Wilhelm II. 2. Emperor and Exile, 1900–1941* (Chapel Hill, NC: University of North Carolina Press, 1996), p. 216.

5 S. Tyng, *The Campaign of the Marne 1914* (London: Humphrey Milford, 1935), p. 170.

6 E. von Falkenhayn, *General Headquarters 1914–1916 and Its Critical Decisions* (London: Hutchinson & Co., 1919), p. 22.

7 *AFGG*, Book 1/2, p. 477.

8 BA-MA: RH 61/986, Tappen diary, 16 September 1914.

9 Reichsarchiv, *Der Weltkrieg 1914 bis 1918*. V. *Der Herbst-Feldzug 1914*, Part 1: *Im Westen bis zum Stellungskrieg, im Osten bis zum Rückzug* (Berlin: E. S. Mittler & Sohn, 1929), p. 63.

10 M. Gilbert, *Winston S. Churchill*. III. *1914–1916* (London: Heinemann, 1971), p. 98.

11 W. S. Churchill, *The World Crisis 1911–1918. Abridged and Revised Edition* (London: Macmillan and Co., 1943), pp. 205, 212.

12 E. J. Galet, *Albert, King of the Belgians in the Great War. His Military Activities Set Down with His Approval* (London: Putnam, 1931), p. 263.

13 M. Jauneaud, 'Souvenirs de la bataille d'Arras (Octobre 1914)', *Revue des Deux Mondes*, Vol. 58 (August 1920), p. 574.

14 J. C. Joffre, *The Memoirs of Marshal Joffre*, trans. T. Bentley Mott (2 vols., London: Geoffrey Bles, 1932), I, p. 295.

15 A. Grasset, *Le Maréchal Foch* (Nancy: Berget-Levrault, 1919), p. 3.

16 F. Foch, *The Memoirs of Marshal Foch*, trans. T. Bentley Mott (London: William Heinemann, 1931), pp. 127, 135.

17 Jauneaud, 'Souvenirs de la bataille d'Arras (Octobre 1914)', p. 577.

18 Ibid., p. 588.

19 M. Jauneaud, 'Souvenirs de la bataille d'Arras: II', *Revue des Deux Mondes*, Vol. 58 (August 1920), p. 835.

20 Viscount French, *1914* (London: Constable, 1919), p. 166.

21 Crown Prince R. von Bayern, *Mein Kriegstagebuch* (3 vols., Berlin: E. S. Mittler, 1929), I, p. 203 (entry, 13 October 1914).

22 Reichsarchiv, *Der Weltkrieg*. V. *Der Herbst-Feldzug 1914*, Part 1, pp. 282–3.

23 *AFGG*, Book 1/4, p. 307.

24 Foch, *Memoirs*, pp. 168, 169.

25 G. Sheffield and J. Bourne (eds.), *Douglas Haig. War Diaries and Letters 1914–1918* (London: Weidenfeld & Nicolson, 2005), p. 73 (entries, 16 and 19 October 1914).

26 Ibid., p. 74 (entry, 21 October 1914).

27 G. von der Marwitz, *Weltkriegsbriefe*, ed. E. von Tschischwitz (Berlin: Steiniger-Verlage, 1940), p. 53.

28 Reichsarchiv, *Der Weltkrieg*. V. *Der Herbst-Feldzug 1914*, Part 1, pp. 304–5.

29 O. Schwink, *Ypres 1914. An Official Account Published by Order of the German General Staff*, trans. G.C.W. (London: Constable, 1919), pp. 36, 42.

30 French, *1914*, p. 228.

31 G. H. Cassar, *The Tragedy of Sir John French* (London and Toronto: Associated University Presses, 1985), p. 164.

32 Sir J. E. Edmonds, *Military Operations. France and Belgium, 1914* (2 vols., London: Macmillan and Co., 1933), II, p. 192.

33 Ibid., pp. 222, 241.

34 Ibid., p. 282.

35 M. von Poseck, *The German Cavalry. 1914 in Belgium and France* (Berlin: E. S. Mittler & Sohn, 1923), p. 215.

36 Sir J. Marshall-Cornwall, *Foch as Military Commander* (London: B. T. Batsford, 1972), p. 139.

37 Lord Loch (liaison officer at GHQ) quoted in K. Jeffery, *Field Marshal Sir Henry Wilson. A Political Soldier* (Oxford: Oxford University Press, 2006), p. 138.

38 H. F. Stacke, *The Worcestershire Regiment in the Great War* (2 vols., Uckfield: Naval & Military Press, 2002; first publ. 1928), I, pp. 33–4.

39 Schwink, *Ypres 1914*, p. x.

40 P. Witkop (ed.), *German Students' War Letters*, trans. A. F. Wedd (Philadelphia, Pa.: First Pine Street Books, 2002; first publ. 1929), p. 123.

41 Edmonds, *Military Operations. 1914*, II, pp. 467–8.

42 H. H. Herwig, *The First World War. Germany and Austria–Hungary 1914–1918* (London: Arnold, 1997), p. 119.

43 BA-MA: RH 61/933, Plessen diary, 25 December 1914.

44 French, *1914*, p. 237.

45 Edmonds, *Military Operations. 1914*, II, pp. 466–7.

46 Foch to Joffre, 13 November 1914, in *AFGG*, Book 1/4 – *Annexes*, Vol. 4, No. 4252, pp. 893–6.

47 R. T. Foley, *German Strategy and the Path to Verdun. Erich von Falkenhayn and the Development of Attrition, 1870–1916* (Cambridge: Cambridge University Press, 2005), p. 112 n. 15.

48 Reichsarchiv, *Der Weltkrieg. VI. Der Herbst-Feldzug 1914*, Part 2: *Der Abschluß der Operationen im Westen und Osten* (Berlin: E. S. Mittler & Sohn, 1929), pp. 406–7.

49 F. Fischer, *Germany's Aims in the First World War* (New York: W. W. Norton & Co., 1967; first publ. 1961), pp. 103–4.

50 W. Görlitz (ed.), *The Kaiser and His Court. The Diaries, Note Books and Letters of Admiral Georg Alexander von Müller, Chief of the Naval Cabinet, 1914–1918* (London: Macdonald & Co., 1961; first publ. 1959), p. 47 (entry, 1 December 1914).

4 'New conditions'

1 R. Poincaré, *The Memoirs of Raymond Poincaré 1914*, trans. G. Arthur (London: William Heinemann, 1929), p. 222.

2 F. Foch, *The Memoirs of Marshal Foch*, trans. T. Bentley Mott (London: William Heinemann, 1931), pp. 183–4.

3 Poincaré, *Memoirs 1914*, pp. 225–6.

4 P. Simkins, *Kitchener's Army. The Raising of the New Armies, 1914–16* (Manchester: Manchester University Press, 1988), p. 41.

5 I. Beckett, T. Bowman and M. Connelly, *The British Army and the First World War* (Cambridge: Cambridge University Press, 2017), p. 94.

6 G. H. Cassar, *Kitchener. Architect of Victory* (London: William Kimber, 1977), pp. 249–50.

7 R. Holmes, *The Little Field Marshal. A Life of Sir John French* (London: Cassell, 2005; first publ. 1981), p. 254.

8 Foch to Joffre, 9 November 1914, in J. C. Joffre, *The Memoirs of Marshal Joffre*, trans. T. Bentley Mott (2 vols., London: Geoffrey Bles, 1932), I, p. 319.

9 R. A. Prete, *Strategy and Command. The Anglo-French Coalition on the Western Front, 1914* (Montreal: McGill–Queen's University Press, 2009), pp. 173–4.

10 'Instruction générale no. 8 pour les généraux commandant les armées', 8 December 1914, in Ministère de la Guerre, *Les Armées françaises dans la Grande guerre* (Paris: Imprimerie Nationale, 1922–39) [hereafter *AFGG*], Book 2 – *Annexes*, Vol. 1, No. 280, pp. 375–7.

11 Foch to Joffre, 14 December 1914, in *AFGG*, Book 2 – *Annexes*, Vol. 1, No. 341, p. 473.

12 'Note pour les corps d'armée', 14 December 1914, in *AFGG*, Book 2 – *Annexes*, Vol. 1, No. 345, p. 476.

13 E. Fayolle, *Cahiers secrets de la Grande guerre*, ed. H. Contamine (Paris: Plon, 1964), p. 65 (entry, 18 December 1914).

14 Langle de Cary to Joffre, 13 January 1915, in *AFGG*, Book 2 – *Annexes*, Vol. 1, No. 607, pp. 869–70.

15 'Note au sujet de la conduite des attaques (suite à la note no. 923 du 2 janvier)', 15 January 1915, in *AFGG*, Book 2 – *Annexes*, Vol. 1, No. 631, pp. 910–11.

16 Hindenburg to Wilhelm II, 9 January 1915, in M. O. Humphries and J. Maker (eds.), *Germany's Western Front. Translations from the German Official History of the Great War.* II. *1915* (Waterloo, Ont.: Wilfrid Laurier Press, 2009), p. 16.

17 P. von Hindenburg, *Out of My Life*, trans. F. A. Holt (London: Cassell and Company, 1920), p. 132.

18 E. von Falkenhayn, *General Headquarters 1914–1916 and Its Critical Decisions* (London: Hutchinson & Co., 1919), p. 56.

19 R. Foley, 'East or West? Erich von Falkenhayn and German Strategy, 1914–1915', in M. Hughes and M. Seligmann (eds.), *Leadership in Conflict 1914–1918* (London: Leo Cooper, 2000), p. 127.

20 BA-MA: RH 61/933, Plessen diary, 24 October 1914.

21 A. Mombauer, *Helmuth von Moltke and the Origins of the First World War* (Cambridge: Cambridge University Press, 2001), p. 276.

22 W. Görlitz (ed.), *The Kaiser and His Court. The Diaries, Note Books and Letters of Admiral Georg Alexander von Müller, Chief of the Naval Cabinet, 1914–1918* (London: Macdonald & Co., 1961; first publ. 1959), p. 40 (entry, 26 October 1914).

23 C. Clark, *Kaiser Wilhelm II* (Harlow: Pearson Education, 2000), p. 227; and letter, 2 January 1915, in Grand Admiral von Tirpitz, *My Memoirs* (2 vols., New York: Dodd, Mead and Company, 1919), II, p. 282.

24 L. Sondhaus, *The Great War at Sea. A Naval History of the First World War* (Cambridge: Cambridge University Press, 2014), p. 139.

25 'The German Declaration of a Naval War Zone (February 4, 1915)', in J. V. Fuller (ed.), *Papers Relating to the Foreign Relations of the United States, 1915, Supplement, The World War* (Washington: Government Printing Office, 1928), Document 123.

26 J. P. Guéno and Y. Laplume (eds.), *Paroles de poilus. Lettres et carnets du front 1914–1918* (Paris: Radio France, 1998), p. 90.

27 Foch to Joffre, 1 January 1915, in *AFGG*, Book 2 – *Annexes*, Vol. 1, No. 526, pp. 742–3.

28 E. Greenhalgh, *The French Army and the First World War* (Cambridge: Cambridge University Press, 2014), p. 96.

29 Ibid., p. 81; and G. E. Torrey, '*L'Affaire de Soissons*, January 1915', *War in History*, Vol. 4, No. 4 (October 1997), pp. 398–410.

30 Joffre, *Memoirs*, I, p. 323.

31 Kitchener to French, 2 January 1915, in G. H. Cassar, *The Tragedy of Sir John French* (London and Toronto: Associated University Presses, 1985), p. 197. Original emphasis.

32 Cassar, *Kitchener*, p. 268.

33 French to Kitchener, 3 January 1915, in Cassar, *The Tragedy of Sir John French*, p. 198.

34 Viscount French, *1914* (London: Constable, 1919), pp. 308–10.

35 French to Joffre, 18 February 1915, and Joffre to French, 19 February 1915, in *AFGG*, Book 2 – *Annexes*, Vol. 2, Nos. 917 and 927, pp. 235–7, 247–8.

36 D. R. Stone, *The Russian Army in the Great War. The Eastern Front, 1914–1917* (Lawrence, Kan.: University Press of Kansas, 2015), p. 137.

37 Humphries and Maker (eds.), *Germany's Western Front*. II. *1915*, p. 25.

38 *AFGG*, Book 2, p. 425.

39 Joffre, *Memoirs*, II, p. 339.

40 A. von Kirchbach, *Kämpfe in der Champagne (Winter 1914–Herbst 1915)* (Oldenburg: Gerhard Stalling, 1919), p. 11.

41 J. Alter (ed.), *Ein Armeeführer erlebt den Weltkrieg. Persönliche Aufzeichnungen des Generalobersten v. Einem* (Leipzig: v. Hase & Koehler, 1938), p. 98.

42 BA-MA: RH 61/986, Tappen diary, 20 February 1915.

43 Humphries and Maker (eds.), *Germany's Western Front*. II. *1915*, pp. 35–7.

44 R. A. Doughty, *Pyrrhic Victory. French Strategy and Operations in the Great War* (London and Cambridge, Mass.: Harvard University Press, 2005), p. 143. Losses for the German Third Army were 1,100 officers and 45,000 other ranks. Reichsarchiv, *Der Weltkrieg 1914 bis 1918*. VII. *Die Operationen des Jahres 1915, Part 1: Die Ereignisse im Winter und Frühjahr* (Berlin: E. S. Mittler & Sohn, 1931), p. 53.

45 'Compte rendu des opérations du 18 mars', 18 March 1915, in *AFGG*, Book 2 – *Annexes*, Vol. 2, No. 1223, pp. 671–2.

46 Kirchbach, *Kämpfe in der Champagne*, p. 48.

5 'A real bad business'

1 H. Domelier, *Behind the Scenes at German Headquarters* (London: Hurst and Blackett, 1919), pp. 17–23, 36.

2 Grand Admiral von Tirpitz, *My Memoirs* (2 vols., New York: Dodd, Mead and Company, 1919), II, pp. 468–70 (letters, 28 and 29 September 1914).

3 F. von Lossberg, *Lossberg's War. The World War I Memoirs of a German Chief of Staff*, trans. D. T. Zabecki and D. J. Biedekarken (Lexington, Ky.: University of Kentucky Press, 2017), p. 126.

4 Domelier, *Behind the Scenes*, p. 120.

5 M. O. Humphries and J. Maker (eds.), *Germany's Western Front. Translations from the German Official History of the Great War.* II. *1915* (Waterloo, Ont.: Wilfrid Laurier Press, 2009), pp. 85, 89–91.

6 Ibid., pp. 92–3.

7 R. T. Foley, *German Strategy and the Path to Verdun. Erich von Falkenhayn and the Development of Attrition, 1870–1916* (Cambridge: Cambridge University Press, 2005), pp. 157–63.

8 R. L. DiNardo, *Breakthrough. The Gorlice–Tarnow Campaign, 1915* (Santa Barbara, Calif.: Praeger, 2010), p. 25; and Foley, *German Strategy*, pp. 128–9.

9 Falkenhayn to Conrad, 13 April 1915, and Conrad to Falkenhayn, 13 April 1915, in E. von Falkenhayn, *General Headquarters 1914–1916 and Its Critical Decisions* (London: Hutchinson & Co., 1919), pp. 83–4.

10 J. B. Scott (ed.), *The Proceedings of the Hague Peace Conferences. Translation of the Official Texts. The Conference of 1899* (New York: Oxford University Press, 1920), pp. 266, 438.

11 M. Bauer, *Der große Krieg in Feld und Heimat. Erinnerungen und Betrachtungen* (Tübingen: Oslander'sche Buchhandlung, 1922), p. 67.

12 U. Trumpener, 'The Road to Ypres: The Beginnings of Gas Warfare in World War I', *Journal of Modern History*, Vol. 47, No. 3 (September 1975), pp. 466–7, 472–3.

13 D. Preston, *A Higher Form of Killing. Six Weeks in World War I That Forever Changed the Nature of Warfare* (London and New York: Bloomsbury, 2015), p. 87.

14 L. F. Haber, *The Poisonous Cloud. Chemical Warfare in the First World War* (Oxford: Oxford University Press, 1986), p. 31.

15 R. Recouly, *Joffre* (London and New York: D. Appleton & Company, 1931), pp. 231–3.

16 A. Bourachot, *Marshal Joffre. The Triumphs, Failures and Controversies of France's Commander-in-Chief in the Great War*, trans. A. Uffindell (Barnsley: Pen & Sword, 2014), p. 148.

17 Kitchener to French, 3 March 1915, and French to Kitchener, 7 March 1915, in R. Holmes, *The Little Field Marshal. A Life of Sir John French* (London: Cassell, 2005; first publ. 1981), pp. 270–71.

18 French to Winifred Bennett, 5 March 1915, in Holmes, *The Little Field Marshal*, p. 277. Original emphasis.

19 Sir J. E. Edmonds and G. C. Wynne, *Military Operations. France and Belgium, 1915* (2 vols., London: Macmillan and Co., 1927), I, p. 151; and G. French (ed.), *Some War Diaries, Addresses, and Correspondence of Field Marshal the Right Honble. The Earl of Ypres* (London: Herbert Jenkins, 1937), pp. 183–4 (entries, 11 and 14 March 1915). French was being overoptimistic. German losses were around 10,000 (not the 17,000–18,000 that he predicted). Humphries and Maker (eds.), *Germany's Western Front*. II. *1915*, p. 67.

20 Edmonds and Wynne, *Military Operations. 1915*, I, pp. 154–5.

21 'Extrait du procès-verbal de la conférence du 27 mars [sic] entre lord Kitchener et le maréchal French d'une part, M. le ministre de la Guerre et le général en chef d'autre part', 30 March 1915, in Ministère de la Guerre, *Les Armées françaises dans la Grande guerre* (Paris: Imprimerie Nationale, 1922–39) [hereafter *AFGG*], Book 3 – *Annexes*, Vol. 1, No. 23, pp. 38–9.

22 French (ed.), *Some War Diaries*, p. 188 (entry, 31 March 1915).

23 H. von Kuhl, *Der Weltkrieg 1914–1918. Dem deutschen Volke dargestellt* (Berlin: Verlag Tradition Wilhelm Kolk, 1929), pp. 194–5.

24 J. Mordacq, *Le Drame de l'Yser. La Surprise des gaz (Avril 1915)* (Paris: Éditions des Portiques, 1933), pp. 62, 64–5.

25 Humphries and Maker (eds.), *Germany's Western Front*. II. *1915*, p. 165.

26 Foch to Joffre, 23 April 1915, in *AFGG*, Book 2 – *Annexes*, Vol. 2, No. 1422, pp. 983–4.

27 Kitchener to French, 24 April 1915, in Sir G. Arthur, *Life of Lord Kitchener* (3 vols., London: Macmillan and Co., 1920), III, p. 234.

28 H. Matthews quoted in G. H. Cassar, *Hell in Flanders Fields. Canadians at the Second Battle of Ypres* (Toronto: Dundurn Press, 2010), pp. 182–3.

29 French to Kitchener, 24 April 1915, in Arthur, *Lord Kitchener*, III, p. 233.

30 Holmes, *The Little Field Marshal*, p. 284.

31 Sir C. E. Callwell, *Field-Marshal Sir Henry Wilson. His Life and Diaries* (2 vols., London: Cassell and Company, 1927), I, p. 224.

32 Kuhl, *Der Weltkrieg 1914–1918*, p. 195.

33 Lossberg, *Lossberg's War*, pp. 144–6.

34 'Note du général Foch', March 1915, in *AFGG*, Book 3 – *Annexes*, Vol. 1, No. 24, p. 40. Original emphasis.

35 'Note', 14 February 1915, in *AFGG*, Book 2 – *Annexes*, Vol. 2, No. 874, pp. 163–4.

36 *AFGG*, Book 3, pp. 27, 34.

37 S. Ryan, *Pétain the Soldier* (South Brunswick, NJ, and New York: A. S. Barnes, 1969), p. 17.

38 P. Guedalla, *The Two Marshals. Bazaine. Pétain* (London: Hodder and Stoughton, 1943), p. 282.

39 C. Williams, *Pétain* (London: Little, Brown, 2005), p. 109.

40 D'Urbal to Foch, 8 May 1915, in *AFGG*, Book 3 – *Annexes*, Vol. 1, No. 143, p. 224.

41 *Pages de gloire de la Division Marocaine* (Paris: Primerie et Librairie Militaire, n.d.), p. 22; and J. Krause, *Early Trench Tactics in the French Army. The Second Battle of Artois, May–June 1915* (Farnham: Ashgate, 2013), p. 70.

42 M. Daille, *Histoire de la Guerre mondiale. Joffre et la guerre d'usure 1915–1916* (Paris: Payot, 1936), p. 115.

43 Crown Prince R. von Bayern, *Mein Kriegstagebuch* (3 vols., Berlin: E. S. Mittler, 1929), I, pp. 336–8 (entry, 9 May 1915).

44 Lossberg, *Lossberg's War*, p. 147.

45 'Note pour les généraux commandants de C. A., au général commandant l'artillerie', 10 May 1915, in *AFGG*, Book 3 – *Annexes*, Vol. 1, No. 184, pp. 269–70.

46 Krause, *Early Trench Tactics*, p. 79.

47 Reichsarchiv, *Der Weltkrieg 1914 bis 1918*. VIII. *Die Operationen des Jahres 1915*, Part 2: *Die Ereignisse im Westen im Frühjahr und Sommer, im Osten vom Frühjahr bis zum Jahreschluß* (Berlin: E. S. Mittler & Sohn, 1932), p. 66.

48 W. Beumelburg, *Schlachten des Weltkrieges*. 17. *Loretto* (Berlin: Gerhard Stalling, 1927), p. 151.

49 R. von Bayern, *Mein Kriegstagebuch*, I, p. 338 (entry, 9 May 1915).

6 'Only inaction is shameful'

1 House of Commons Debates, 15 June 1915, Vol. 72, cc. 559–60.

2 'The Prime Minister's Speech', *The Times*, 16 June 1915.

3 Sir J. E. Edmonds, *Military Operations. France and Belgium, 1915* (2 vols., London: Macmillan and Co., 1928), II, p. 39 n. 3.

4 G. H. Cassar, *The Tragedy of Sir John French* (London and Toronto: Associated University Presses, 1985), p. 238; and Viscount French, *1914* (London: Constable, 1919), p. 357.

5 'Need for Shells', *The Times*, 14 May 1915.

6 G. H. Cassar, *Kitchener. Architect of Victory* (London: William Kimber, 1977), p. 356.

7 Edmonds, *Military Operations. 1915*, II, p. 41.

8 R. Poincaré, *The Memoirs of Raymond Poincaré 1915*, trans. G. Arthur (London: William Heinemann, 1930), p. 120.

9 Ibid., pp. 93–5, 120.

10 A. Ferry, *La Guerre vue d'en bas et d'en haut (Lettres, notes, discours et rapports)* (Nancy: Bernard Grasset, 1920), p. 35–6. Original emphasis.

11 Poincaré, *Memoirs 1915*, p. 141.

12 M. M. Farrar, 'Politics Versus Patriotism: Alexandre Millerand as French Minister of War', *French Historical Studies*, Vol. 11, No. 4 (Autumn 1980), pp. 597–8; and E. Greenhalgh, *The French Army and the First World War* (Cambridge: Cambridge University Press, 2014), p. 100.

13 N. Stone, *The Eastern Front 1914–1917* (New York: Charles Scribner's Sons, 1975), pp. 136, 139; and R. L. DiNardo, *Breakthrough. The Gorlice–Tarnow Campaign, 1915* (Santa Barbara, Calif.: Praeger, 2010), p. 99.

14 Crown Prince R. von Bayern, *Mein Kriegstagebuch* (3 vols., Berlin: E. S. Mittler, 1929), I, p. 365 (entry, 7 June 1915).

15 M. O. Humphries and J. Maker (eds.), *Germany's Western Front. Translations from the German Official History of the Great War*. II. *1915* (Waterloo, Ont.: Wilfrid Laurier Press, 2009), pp. 187–8.

16 J. Boff, *Haig's Enemy. Crown Prince Rupprecht and Germany's War on the Western Front* (Oxford: Oxford University Press, 2018), pp. 76–7.

17 W. Groener, *Lebenserinnerungen. Jugend. Generalstab. Weltkrieg* (Göttingen: Vandenhoeck & Ruprecht, 1957), p. 245.

18 TNA: WO 32/5323, 'Proposals for the Technical Methods to be Adopted in an Attempt to Break through a Strongly Fortified Position, Based on the Knowledge Acquired from the Errors Which Appear to Have been Committed by the French during the Winter Campaign in Champagne'.

19 TNA: WO 32/5323, 'Experiences Gained in the Winter Battle in Champagne from the Point of View of the Organization of the Enemy's Line of Defences and the Means of Combating an Attempt to Pierce Our Line'.

20 R. T. Foley, *German Strategy and the Path to Verdun. Erich von Falkenhayn and the Development of Attrition, 1870–1916* (Cambridge: Cambridge University Press, 2005), p. 164.

21 M. Bauer, *Der große Krieg in Feld und Heimat. Erinnerungen und Betrachtungen* (Tübingen: Oslander'sche Buchhandlung, 1922), p. 86.

22 P. Witkop (ed.), *German Students' War Letters*, trans. A. F. Wedd (Philadelphia, Pa.: First Pine Street Books, 2002; first publ. 1929), pp. 224–5.

23 D'Urbal to Joffre, 19 May 1915, in Ministère de la Guerre, *Les Armées françaises dans la Grande guerre* (Paris: Imprimerie Nationale, 1922–39) [hereafter *AFGG*], Book 3 – *Annexes*, Vol. 1, No. 291, pp. 389–92.

24 J. Krause, *Early Trench Tactics in the French Army. The Second Battle of Artois, May–June 1915* (Farnham: Ashgate, 2013), p. 134.

25 *AFGG*, Book 3, pp. 92, 96; and 'Note au sujet de l'emploi du canon de 75', 19 June 1915, in *AFGG*, Book 3 – *Annexes*, Vol. 1, No. 676, pp. 864–5.

26 M. Daille, *Histoire de la Guerre mondiale. Joffre et la guerre d'usure 1915–1916* (Paris: Payot, 1936), p. 123.

27 E. Fayolle, *Cahiers secrets de la Grande guerre*, ed. H. Contamine (Paris: Plon, 1964), p. 112 (entry, 17 June 1915).

28 'Instruction pour le général Foch', 12 July 1915, and 'Instruction pour le général de Castelnau', 12 July 1915, in *AFGG*, Book 3 – *Annexes*, Vol. 2, Nos. 896 and 897, pp. 147–8, 150–52.

29 TNA: WO 159/4/6, 'An Appreciation of the Military Situation in the Future', 26 June 1915.

30 Lord Hankey, *The Supreme Command 1914–1918* (2 vols., London: George Allen and Unwin, 1961), I, p. 349.

31 P. Guinn, *British Strategy and Politics 1914 to 1918* (Oxford: Clarendon Press, 1965), p. 90.

32 'Procès-verbal de la conférence des représentants des différentes armées alliées tenue à Chantilly, le 7 juillet 1915', in *AFGG*, Book 3 – *Annexes*, Vol. 2, No. 860, pp. 75–84.

33 Stone, *The Eastern Front*, pp. 182–3.

34 E. von Falkenhayn, *General Headquarters 1914–1916 and Its Critical Decisions* (London: Hutchinson & Co., 1919), pp. 126–7.

35 Humphries and Maker (eds.), *Germany's Western Front. II. 1915*, pp. 217–18.

36 F. von Lossberg, *Lossberg's War. The World War I Memoirs of a German Chief of Staff*, trans. D. T. Zabecki and D. J. Biedekarken (Lexington, Ky.: University of Kentucky Press, 2017), p. 158.

37 J. Alter (ed.), *Ein Armeeführer erlebt den Weltkrieg. Persönliche Aufzeichnungen des Generalobersten v. Einem* (Leipzig: v. Hase & Koehler, 1938), p. 131.

38 N. Lloyd, *Loos 1915* (Stroud: Tempus, 2006), pp. 34–5.

39 TNA: WO 158/13, French to Joffre, 10 August 1915, and Joffre to French, 12 August 1915.

40 Lloyd, *Loos 1915*, pp. 39–40; and TNA: CAB 22/2, Minutes of Dardanelles Committee Meeting, 20 August 1915. Original emphasis.

41 BLO: MS. Asquith 8, Asquith to King George V, 20 August 1915.

42 TNA: CAB 22/2, Minutes of Dardanelles Committee Meeting, 3 September 1915; and Cassar, *Kitchener*, p. 389.

43 Poincaré, *Memoirs 1915*, p. 197.

44 'Réunion des commandants de groupe d'armées du 11 juillet [sic]', in *AFGG*, Book 3 – *Annexes*, Vol. 2, No. 1150, pp. 554–8.

45 E. Greenhalgh, *Foch in Command. The Forging of a First World War General* (Cambridge: Cambridge University Press, 2011), p. 126.

46 Edmonds, *Military Operations. 1915*, II, pp. 151–2.

47 TNA: WO 95/158, 'IV Corps Proposals for an Attack on Loos and Hill 70', 22 August 1915.

7 'No getting through'

1 B. Serrigny, *Trente ans avec Pétain* (Paris: Librairie Plon, 1959), p. 33.

2 'Projet d'opérations en Champagne', 21 July 1915, in Ministère de la Guerre, *Les Armées françaises dans la Grande guerre* (Paris: Imprimerie Nationale, 1922–39) [hereafter *AFGG*], Book 3 – *Annexes*, Vol. 2, No. 981, p. 277.

3 *AFGG*, Book 3, pp. 535–6; and Sir J. E. Edmonds, *Military Operations. France and Belgium, 1915* (2 vols., London: Macmillan and Co., 1928), II, pp. 163, 177.

4 M. Daille, *Histoire de la Guerre mondiale. Joffre et la guerre d'usure 1915–1916* (Paris: Payot, 1936), pp. 186–7.

5 'Instruction préparatoire aux attaques', 5 September 1915, in *AFGG*, Book 3 – *Annexes*, Vol. 2, No. 1335, pp. 803–7.

6 A. von Kirchbach, *Kämpfe in der Champagne (Winter 1914–Herbst 1915)* (Oldenburg: Gerhard Stalling, 1919), p. 75.

7 J. Alter (ed.), *Ein Armeeführer erlebt den Weltkrieg. Persönliche Aufzeichnungen des Generalobersten v. Einem* (Leipzig: v. Hase & Koehler, 1938), pp. 149–50.

8 Ibid., p. 150.

9 TNA: WO 95/158, GHQ to Haig, 18 September 1915.

10 N. Lloyd, *Loos 1915* (Stroud: Tempus, 2006), pp. 125–6.

11 'Instruction personnelle et secrète à Messieurs les généraux commandants de corps d'armée', 1 September 1915, and 'Instruction personnelle et secrète pour MM. les généraux commandants de corps d'armée', 4 September 1915, in *AFGG*, Book 3 – *Annexes*, Vol. 2, Nos. 1315 and 1332, pp. 772, 798.

12 IWM: Documents 6874, Major P. H. Pilditch, 'The War Diary of an Artillery Officer 1914–1918', p. 158.

13 T. Cook, *No Place to Run. The Canadian Corps and Gas Warfare in the First World War* (Vancouver: UBC Press, 1999), p. 77.

14 Lloyd, *Loos 1915*, pp. 131, 158.

15 Crown Prince R. von Bayern, *Mein Kriegstagebuch* (3 vols., Berlin: E. S. Mittler, 1929), I, pp. 382–4 (entry, 25 September 1915).

16 Reichsarchiv, *Der Weltkrieg 1914 bis 1918*. IX. *Die Operationen des Jahres 1915*, Part 3: *Die Ereignisse im Westen und auf dem Balkan vom Sommer bis zum Jahresschluß* (Berlin: E. S. Mittler & Sohn, 1933), p. 54.

17 M. O. Humphries and J. Maker (eds.), *Germany's Western Front. Translations from the German Official History of the Great War*. II. *1915* (Waterloo, Ont.: Wilfrid Laurier Press, 2009), p. 294.

18 *AFGG*, Book 3, p. 372; and 'Message téléphoné', 25 September 1915, in *AFGG*, Book 3 – *Annexes*, Vol. 3, No. 1739, p. 107.

19 'Compte rendu des opérations du 14e corps d'armée pendant les journées des 25 au 30 septembre 1915', in *AFGG*, Book 3 – *Annexes*, Vol. 3, No. 2513, p. 746; and *AFGG*, Book 3, p. 369.

20 R. Christian-Frogé, *La Grande guerre vécue, racontée, illustrée par les combattants* (2 vols., Paris: Aristide Quillet, 1922), I, p. 259.

21 'Ordre annexe à l'ordre d'opérations pour la journée du 26 septembre', in *AFGG*, Book 3 – *Annexes*, Vol. 3, No. 1645, p. 41.

22 Alter (ed.), *Ein Armeeführer*, pp. 150–51.

23 BA-MA: RH 61/1495, 'Die Leitung des deutschen Westheeres im September und Oktober 1915 seit dem Beginn der Herbstschlacht in der Champagne und im Artois', pp. 12, 14–15.

24 F. von Lossberg, *Lossberg's War. The World War I Memoirs of a German Chief of Staff*, trans. D. T. Zabecki and D. J. Biedekarken (Lexington, Ky.: University of Kentucky Press, 2017), pp. 163–73.

25 Humphries and Maker (eds.), *Germany's Western Front*. II. *1915*, p. 304.

26 TNA: CAB 45/121, Account of Major J. Buckley, 1 January 1927.

27 TNA: CAB 45/120, Account of Lieutenant L. G. Duke, 20 November 1918.

28 Edmonds, *Military Operations. 1915*, II, p. 342 n. 1.

29 *AFGG*, Book 3, pp. 444–5.

30 I. Sumner, *They Shall Not Pass. The French Army on the Western Front 1914–1918* (Barnsley: Pen & Sword, 2012), p. 59.

31 Pétain to Castelnau, 28 September 1915, in *AFGG*, Book 3 – *Annexes*, Vol. 3, No. 2109, p. 404.

32 BA-MA: RH 61/1495, 'Die Leitung des deutschen Westheeres . . .', p. 27.

33 Lossberg, *Lossberg's War*, pp. 173–4.

34 TNA: PRO 30/57/53, Haig to Kitchener, 29 September 1915.

35 Lloyd, *Loos 1915*, pp. 63–7.

36 G. Sheffield and J. Bourne (eds.), *Douglas Haig. War Diaries and Letters 1914–1918* (London: Weidenfeld & Nicolson, 2005), p. 159 (entry, 28 September 1915).

37 French to Winifred Bennett, 27 September and 2 October 1915, in R. Holmes, *The Little Field Marshal. A Life of Sir John French* (London: Cassell, 2005; first publ. 1981), p. 305. Original emphasis.

38 Y. Gras, *Castelnau ou l'art de commander 1851–1944* (Paris: Éditions Denoël, 1990), p. 251; and C. Baussan, 'General de Castelnau', *Studies. An Irish Quarterly Review*, Vol. 6, No. 24 (December 1917), p. 597.

39 Lossberg, *Lossberg's War*, p. 175.

40 BA-MA: RH 61/1495, 'Die Leitung des deutschen Westheeres . . .', p. 47.

41 Humphries and Maker (eds.), *Germany's Western Front*. II. *1915*, p. 323.

42 H. Ludwig quoted in J. Sheldon, *The German Army on the Western Front 1915* (Barnsley: Pen & Sword, 2012), pp. 278–80.

43 Alter (ed.), *Ein Armeeführer*, p. 167.

44 *AFGG*, Book 3, p. 489.

45 R. Poincaré, *The Memoirs of Raymond Poincaré 1915*, trans. G. Arthur (London: William Heinemann, 1930), pp. 253–4.

46 *AFGG*, Book 3, pp. 537–40; and Edmonds, *Military Operations. 1915*, II, p. 391.

47 'Rapport sur les opérations de la Xe armée pendant la période du 25 septembre au 11 octobre 1915', in *AFGG*, Book 3 – *Annexes*, Vol. 4, No. 3050, pp. 193–4.

48 'Rapport sur les opérations de la IIe armée en Champagne et enseignements à en tirer', 1 November 1915, in *AFGG*, Book 3 – *Annexes*, Vol. 4, No. 3042, p. 168. Original emphasis.

49 E. von Falkenhayn, *General Headquarters 1914–1916 and Its Critical Decisions* (London: Hutchinson & Co., 1919), p. 172.

50 J. Boff, *Haig's Enemy. Crown Prince Rupprecht and Germany's War on the Western Front* (Oxford: Oxford University Press, 2018), p. 90.

51 Reichsarchiv, *Der Weltkrieg*. IX. *Die Operationen des Jahres 1915*, Part 3, pp. 89, 97.

52 Bernstorff to Lansing, 1 September 1915, in J. V. Fuller (ed.), *Papers Relating to the Foreign Relations of the United States, 1915, Supplement, The World War* (Washington: Government Printing Office, 1928), Document 767.

53 A. Watson, *Ring of Steel. Germany and Austria–Hungary at War, 1914–1918* (London: Allen Lane, 2015; first publ. 2014), p. 240.

54 'Through German Eyes', *The Times*, 12 October 1915.

55 O. Johnson, 'Père Joffre', *The Times*, 21 October 1915.

56 'Note sur l'emploi des forces anglaises pendant la campagne d'hiver 1915–1916', 7 October 1915, in *AFGG*, Book 3 – *Annexes*, Vol. 3, No. 2792, pp. 1023–4.

Part 2: 'Scales of fate'

8 'A place of execution'

1 J. Charteris, *At G.H.Q.* (London: Cassell and Company, 1931), p. 121.

2 Haig to Leopold Rothschild, 9 December 1915, in G. Sheffield and J. Bourne (eds.), *Douglas Haig. War Diaries and Letters 1914–1918* (London: Weidenfeld & Nicolson, 2005), p. 172.

3 J. C. Joffre, *The Memoirs of Marshal Joffre*, trans. T. Bentley Mott (2 vols., London: Geoffrey Bles, 1932), II, pp. 415–16.

4 W. S. Churchill, *The World Crisis 1911–1918 Abridged and Revised Edition* (London: Macmillan and Co., 1943), p. 640.

5 J. Charteris, *Field-Marshal Earl Haig* (New York: Charles Scribner's Sons, 1929), p. 70; and Sheffield and Bourne (eds.), *Douglas Haig*, p. 173 (entry, 14 December 1915).

6 'Instructions for General Sir D. Haig', Appendix 5, in Sir J. E. Edmonds et al., *Military Operations. France and Belgium, 1916. Appendices* (2 vols., London: Macmillan and Co., 1932–8), I, pp. 40–41.

7 Ministère de la Guerre, *Les Armées françaises dans la Grande guerre* (Paris: Imprimerie Nationale, 1922–39) [hereafter *AFGG*], Book 4/1, pp. 11–16.

8 Vallières to Joffre, Report No. 125, 1 January 1916, in E. Greenhalgh (ed. and trans.), *Liaison. General Pierre des Vallières at British General Headquarters, January 1916 to May 1917* (Stroud: History Press, 2016), pp. 47–8.

9 J. K. Tanenbaum, *General Maurice Sarrail 1856–1929. The French Army and Left-Wing Politics* (Chapel Hill, NC: University of North Carolina Press, 1974), pp. 53–4.

10 Joffre, *Memoirs*, II, pp. 401–2.

11 J. de Pierrefeu, *French Headquarters 1915–1918*, trans. Major C. J. C. Street (London: Geoffrey Bles, 1924), pp. 47–8.

12 Lord Hankey, *The Supreme Command 1914–1918* (2 vols., London: George Allen and Unwin, 1961), I, p. 424.

13 J. Grigg, *Lloyd George. From Peace to War 1912–1916* (London: Penguin Books, 2002; first publ. 1985), p. 313.

14 G. H. Cassar, *Kitchener. Architect of Victory* (London: William Kimber, 1977), p. 429.

15 G. H. Cassar, *Asquith as War Leader* (London: Hambledon, 1994), pp. 136–7, 145; and Sir G. Arthur, *Life of Lord Kitchener* (3 vols., London: Macmillan and Co., 1920), III, p. 185.

16 TNA: CAB 24/1, No. 33, 'Memorandum on the Conduct of the War', 8 November 1915.

17 'The Worn Kaiser', *The Times*, 26 January 1916.

18 Reichsarchiv, *Der Weltkrieg 1914 bis 1918. X. Die Operationen des Jahres 1916. Bis zum Wechsel in der Obersten Heeresleitung* (Berlin: E. S. Mittler & Sohn, 1936), pp. 1–2.

19 Ibid., pp. 5–6.

20 E. von Falkenhayn, *General Headquarters 1914–1916 and Its Critical Decisions* (London: Hutchinson & Co., 1919), pp. 209–18.

21 R. T. Foley, *German Strategy and the Path to Verdun. Erich von Falkenhayn and the Development of Attrition, 1870–1916* (Cambridge: Cambridge University Press, 2005), p. 189.

22 'Le général de division Dubail, commandant le groupe d'armées de l'Est, à Monsieur le général commandant la Ire armée, la région fortifiée de Verdun', 9 August 1915, in *AFGG*, Book 3 – *Annexes*, Vol. 2, No. 1135, pp. 533–4.

23 Foley, *German Strategy*, pp. 190–91.

24 Reichsarchiv, *Der Weltkrieg. X. Die Operationen des Jahres 1916*, p. 27.

25 M. Bauer, *Der große Krieg in Feld und Heimat. Erinnerungen und Betrachtungen* (Tübingen: Oslander'sche Buchhandlung, 1922), p. 101.

26 Reichsarchiv, *Der Weltkrieg. X. Die Operationen des Jahres 1916*, p. 27.

27 F. von Lossberg, *Lossberg's War. The World War I Memoirs of a German Chief of Staff*, trans. D. T. Zabecki and D. J. Biedekarken (Lexington, Ky.: University of Kentucky Press, 2017), p. 195.

28 Crown Prince Wilhelm, *My War Experiences* (London: Hurst and Blackett, n.d.), p. 166.

29 Foley, *German Strategy*, p. 215 and n. 26; and Crown Prince Wilhelm, *My War Experiences*, pp. 170–71.

30 R. G. Head, *Oswald Boelcke. Germany's First Fighter Ace and Father of Air Combat* (London: Grub Street, 2016), p. 87; and E. W. von Hoeppner, *Germany's War in the Air. The Development and Operations of German Military Aviation in the World War*, trans. J. Hawley Larned (Nashville, Tenn. Battery Press, 1994; first publ. 1921), p. 49.

31 Crown Prince Wilhelm, *My War Experiences*, pp. 178–9.

32 W. Groener, *Lebenserinnerungen. Jugend. Generalstab. Weltkrieg* (Göttingen: Vandenhoeck & Ruprecht, 1957), p. 291.

33 R. A. Doughty, *Pyrrhic Victory. French Strategy and Operations in the Great War* (London and Cambridge, Mass.: Harvard University Press, 2005), pp. 267–9.

34 Crown Prince Wilhelm, *My War Experiences*, p. 180.

35 BA-MA: RH 61/986, Tappen diary, 21 February 1916.

36 *AFGG*, Book 4/1, p. 218.

37 I. Ousby *The Road to Verdun. France, Nationalism and the First World War* (London: Jonathan Cape, 2002), p. 69.

38 Reichsarchiv, *Der Weltkrieg. X. Die Operationen des Jahres 1916*, p. 83.

39 H. Wendt, *Verdun 1916. Die Angriffe Falkenhayns im Maasgebiet mit Richtung auf Verdun als strategisches Problem* (Berlin: Mittler & Sohn, 1931), p. 74; and A. Horne, *The Price of Glory. Verdun 1916* (Harmondsworth: Penguin, 1964; first publ. 1962), p. 111.

40 Langle de Cary to Herr, 23 February 1916, in *AFGG*, Book 4/1 – *Annexes*, Vol. 1, No. 511, p. 674. Emphasis added.

41 Joffre, *Memoirs*, II, pp. 439–40.

42 Ibid., p. 444.

43 'Message téléphoné', in *AFGG*, Book 4/1 – *Annexes*, Vol. 1, No. 681, p. 781.

44 B. Serrigny, *Trente ans avec Pétain* (Paris: Librairie Plon, 1959), p. 46.

45 Ibid., pp. 48–9.

46 'The First Attack, February 21st, described by a French Staff Officer', in C. F. Horne (ed.), *Source Records of the Great War* (7 vols., USA: National Alumni, 1923), IV, p. 54.

47 H. Bordeaux quoted in D. Mason, *Verdun* (Moreton-in-Marsh: Windrush Press, 2000), p. 73.

48 H. P. Pétain, *Verdun*, trans. M. Mac Veagh (New York: The Dial Press, 1930), pp. 78–9, 84–7.

9 'Costly and fatal toils'

1 W. Groener, *Lebenserinnerungen. Jugend. Generalstab. Weltkrieg* (Göttingen: Vandenhoeck & Ruprecht, 1957), p. 295.

2 Crown Prince Wilhelm, *My War Experiences* (London: Hurst and Blackett, n.d.), p. 185.

3 E. von Falkenhayn, *General Headquarters 1914–1916 and Its Critical Decisions* (London: Hutchinson & Co., 1919), p. 234; and R. T. Foley, *German Strategy and the Path to Verdun. Erich von Falkenhayn and the Development of Attrition, 1870–1916* (Cambridge: Cambridge University Press, 2005), p. 224.

4 I. Sumner, *They Shall Not Pass. The French Army on the Western Front 1914–1918* (Barnsley: Pen & Sword, 2012), p. 104.

5 E. Greenhalgh, *The French Army and the First World War* (Cambridge: Cambridge University Press, 2014), p. 141.

6 H. P. Pétain, *Verdun*, trans. M. Mac Veagh (New York: The Dial Press, 1930), p. 123.

7 M. Daille, *Histoire de la Guerre mondiale. Joffre et la guerre d'usure 1915–1916* (Paris: Payot, 1936), p. 321.

8 I. Sumner, *Kings of the Air. French Aces and Airmen of the Great War* (Barnsley: Pen & Sword, 2015), p. 71.

9 H. M. Mason, Jr, *High Flew the Falcons. The French Aces of World War I* (Philadelphia and New York: J. B. Lippincott, 1965), pp. 67, 71–2.

10 A. Schwencke, *Die Tragödie von Verdun 1916*, Part 2. *Das Ringen um Fort Vaux* (Berlin: Gerhard Stalling, 1928), pp. 17–18.

11 L. Loiseau and G. Bénech (eds.), *Carnets de Verdun* (Paris: Librio, 2006), p. 29.

12 Crown Prince Wilhelm, *My War Experiences*, p. 189.

13 Reichsarchiv, *Der Weltkrieg 1914 bis 1918*. X. *Die Operationen des Jahres 1916. Bis zum Wechsel der Obersten Heeresleitung* (Berlin: E. S. Mittler & Sohn, 1936), p. 213; and L. Gold, *Die Tragödie von Verdun 1916*, Parts 3 and 4. *Die Zermürbungsschlacht* (Berlin: Gerhard Stalling, 1929), p. 18.

14 W. Görlitz (ed.), *The Kaiser and His Court. The Diaries, Note Books and Letters of Admiral Georg Alexander von Müller, Chief of the Naval Cabinet, 1914–1918* (London: Macdonald & Co., 1961; first publ. 1959), p. 140 (entry, 2 March 1916).

15 Falkenhayn, *General Headquarters*, pp. 214–15.

16 Görlitz (ed.), *The Kaiser and His Court*, p. 145 (entry, 10 March 1916).

17 Grand Admiral von Tirpitz, *My Memoirs* (2 vols., New York: Dodd, Mead and Company, 1919), II, pp. 419–20.

18 H. Wendt, *Verdun 1916. Die Angriffe Falkenhayns im Maasgebiet mit Richtung auf Verdun als strategisches Problem* (Berlin: Mittler & Sohn, 1931), p. 243.

19 P. Simkins, *Kitchener's Army. The Raising of the New Armies, 1914–16* (Manchester: Manchester University Press, 1988), pp. 156–7.

20 'Resources of The Allies', *The Times*, 22 February 1916.

21 TNA: CAB 42/12/5, Sir W. Robertson, 'Future Military Operations', 31 March 1916.

22 J. Grigg, *Lloyd George. From Peace to War 1912–1916* (London: Penguin Books, 2002; first publ. 1985), p. 377.

23 G. Sheffield and J. Bourne (eds.), *Douglas Haig. War Diaries and Letters 1914–1918* (London: Weidenfeld & Nicolson, 2005), p. 183 (entry, 29 March 1916).

24 TNA: CAB 42/12/5, 'Minutes of the Eightieth Meeting of the War Committee', 7 April 1916.

25 Sheffield and Bourne (eds.), *Douglas Haig*, p. 183 (entry, 29 March 1916).

26 Joffre to Haig, 27 March 1916, in Ministère de la Guerre, *Les Armées françaises dans la Grande guerre* (Paris: Imprimerie Nationale, 1922–39) [hereafter *AFGG*], Book 4/1 – *Annexes*, Vol. 2, No. 1553, pp. 775–7.

27 Haig to Joffre, 10 April 1916, in *AFGG*, Book 4/1 – *Annexes*, Vol. 3, No. 1926, pp. 319–22.

28 Rawlinson quoted in R. Prior and T. Wilson, *Command on the Western Front. The Military Career of Sir Henry Rawlinson 1914–18* (Barnsley: Pen & Sword, 2004; first publ. 1992), p. 139.

29 TNA: WO 158/233, 'Plans for Offensive by Fourth Army', 3 April 1916.

30 Rawlinson quoted in Prior and Wilson, *Command on the Western Front*, p. 141.

31 N. Lloyd, '"With Faith and Without Fear": Sir Douglas Haig's Command of First Army during 1915', *Journal of Military History*, Vol. 71, No. 4 (October 2007), pp. 1051–76; and S. Marble, 'General Haig Dismisses Attritional Warfare, January 1916', *Journal of Military History*, Vol. 65, No. 4 (October 2001), pp. 1061–5.

32 TNA: WO 256/9, Haig diary, 5 April 1916.

33 TNA: WO 158/233, Lieutenant-General Sir L. E. Kiggell (Haig's Chief of Staff) to Rawlinson, 13 April 1916.

34 TNA: WO 158/233, Rawlinson to Kiggell, 19 April 1916, and Kiggell to Rawlinson, 16 May 1916.

35 H. Afflerbach, *Falkenhayn. Politisches Denken und Handeln im Kaiserreich* (Munich: Oldenbourg, 1994), pp. 374–5.

36 Groener, *Lebenserinnerungen*, p. 305.

37 Foley, *German Strategy*, pp. 240–41.

38 Rupprecht quoted in J. Boff, *Haig's Enemy. Crown Prince Rupprecht and Germany's War on the Western Front* (Oxford: Oxford University Press, 2018), p. 95.

39 BA-MA: RH 61/986, Tappen diary, 28 April 1916.

40 'The American Note of April 18, 1916 on the "Sussex"' and 'German Reply of May 4, 1916', in J. V. Fuller (ed.), *Papers Relating to the Foreign Relations of the United States, 1916, Supplement, The World War* (Washington: Government Printing Office, 1929), Documents 308, 337. 'Visit and search' referred to the right of warships to board merchant vessels to ascertain their status and cargo.

41 Wendt, *Verdun 1916*, pp. 128–9. After despatching this letter, General Mudra was summarily dismissed and sent to the Argonne.

42 Crown Prince Wilhelm, *My War Experiences*, pp. 194–5, 199, 200.

43 Joffre to Pétain, 2 April 1916, in *AFGG*, Book 4/1 – *Annexes*, Vol. 3, No. 1672, pp. 28–9.

44 E. Greenhalgh, *Victory Through Coalition. Britain and France during the First World War* (Cambridge: Cambridge University Press, 2005), p. 47.

45 E. Greenhalgh, *Foch in Command. The Forging of a First World War General* (Cambridge: Cambridge University Press, 2011), p. 154.

46 R. A. Doughty, *Pyrrhic Victory. French Strategy and Operations in the Great War* (London and Cambridge, Mass.: Harvard University Press, 2005), pp. 284–5.

47 J. C. Joffre, *The Memoirs of Marshal Joffre*, trans. T. Bentley Mott (2 vols., London: Geoffrey Bles, 1932), II, p. 451.

48 C. Mangin, *Lettres de Guerre 1914–1918* (Paris: Librairie Arthème Fayard, 1950), p. 111.

49 'L'attaque du plateau de Douaumont par la 5e division d'infanterie', 31 May 1916, in *AFGG*, Book 4/2 – *Annexes*, Vol. 1, No. 748, p. 1072.

50 *Historique du 43e Régiment d'Artillerie de Campagne* (Paris: Henri Charles-Lavauzelle, 1920), p. 19.

51 'Message téléphoné', 22 May 1916, in *AFGG*, Book 4/2 – *Annexes*, Vol. 1, No. 468, p. 687; and A. Horne, *The Price of Glory. Verdun 1916* (Harmondsworth: Penguin, 1964; first publ. 1962), pp. 235–6.

10 'Hunted on all sides'

1 L. V. Smith, *Between Mutiny and Obedience. The Case of the French Fifth Infantry Division during World War I* (Princeton, NJ: Princeton University Press, 1994), p. 144.

2 'L'attaque du plateau de Douaumont par la 5e division d'infanterie', 31 May 1916, in Ministère de la Guerre, *Les Armées françaises dans la Grande guerre* (Paris: Imprimerie Nationale, 1922–39) [hereafter *AFGG*], Book 4/2 – *Annexes*, Vol. 1, No. 748, p. 1078.

3 Nivelle to Pétain, 25 May 1916, in *AFGG*, Book 4/2 – *Annexes*, Vol. 1, No. 582, p. 808.

4 C. Delvert, *From the Marne to Verdun. The War Diary of Captain Charles Delvert, 101st Infantry, 1914–1916*, trans. I. Sumner (Barnsley: Pen & Sword, 2016), p. 159.

5 L. Gold, *Die Tragödie von Verdun 1916*, Parts 3 and 4. *Die Zermürbungsschlacht* (Berlin: Gerhard Stalling, 1929), p. 115.

6 A. H. Boer, *The Great War from the German Trenches. A Sapper's Memoir, 1914–1918*, trans. and ed. B. van Boer and M. L. Fast (Jefferson, NC: McFarland & Co., 2016), pp. 114–15.

7 *Journal du Commandant Raynal. Le Fort de Vaux* (Paris: Albin Michel, 1919), pp. 95, 102; and Crown Prince Wilhelm, *My War Experiences* (London: Hurst and Blackett, n.d.), p. 213.

8 Pétain to Joffre, 11 June 1916, in *AFGG*, Book 4/2 – *Annexes*, Vol. 2, No. 1153, pp. 12–13.

9 J. C. Joffre, *The Memoirs of Marshal Joffre*, trans. T. Bentley Mott (2 vols., London: Geoffrey Bles, 1932), II, p. 456.

10 Joffre to Pétain, 12 June 1916, in *AFGG*, Book 4/2 – *Annexes*, Vol. 2, No. 1183, pp. 49–50.

11 S. Lauzanne, 'A French Statesman, Aristide Briand', *North American Review*, Vol. 214, No. 790 (September 1921), p. 289.

12 'Comité secret du 16 juin 1916', in Assemblée Nationale, *Journal officiel de la République française. Débats parlementaires. Chambre des députés: compte rendu in-extenso* (Paris: Journal officiel, 1919), pp. 1–3.

13 Ibid., '"(suite)". 19 juin 1916', pp. 63, 65.

14 R. Poincaré, *Au service de la France*. VIII. *Verdun 1916* (Paris: Librairie Plon, 1931), pp. 274–7; and J. C. King, *Generals and Politicians. Conflict between France's High Command, Parliament and Government, 1914–1918* (Berkeley and Los Angeles: University of California Press, 1951), p. 122.

15 N. Stone, *The Eastern Front 1914–1917* (New York: Charles Scribner's Sons, 1975), pp. 249, 254.

16 Reichsarchiv, *Der Weltkrieg 1914 bis 1918*. X. *Die Operationen des Jahres 1916. Bis zum Wechsel der Obersten Heeresleitung* (Berlin: E. S. Mittler & Sohn, 1936), pp. 320–21.

17 Ibid., p. 192; and Crown Prince Wilhelm, *My War Experiences*, p. 218.

18 L. Madelin, *Verdun* (Paris: Librairie Félix Alcan, 1920), p. 101.

19 A. Horne, *The Price of Glory. Verdun 1916* (Harmondsworth: Penguin Books, 1964; first publ. 1962), p. 289.

20 L. Loiseau and G. Bénech (eds.), *Carnets de Verdun* (Paris: Librio, 2006), p. 66.

21 Reichsarchiv, *Der Weltkrieg*. X. *Die Operationen des Jahres 1916*, p. 193.

22 'Aux soldats de l'armée de Verdun', 23 June 1916, in *AFGG*, Book 4/2 – *Annexes*, Vol. 2, No. 1472, p. 403.

23 H. P. Pétain, *Verdun*, trans. M. Mac Veagh (New York: The Dial Press, 1930), p. 179.

24 Reichsarchiv, *Der Weltkrieg*. X. *Die Operationen des Jahres 1916*, p. 195; Crown Prince Wilhelm, *My War Experiences*, p. 219; and Knobelsdorf to OHL, 27 June 1916, in H. Wendt, *Verdun 1916. Die Angriffe Falkenhayns im Maasgebiet mit Richtung auf Verdun als strategisches Problem* (Berlin: Mittler & Sohn, 1931), p. 170.

25 R. T. Foley, *German Strategy and the Path to Verdun. Erich von Falkenhayn and the Development of Attrition, 1870–1916* (Cambridge: Cambridge University Press, 2005), pp. 253, 254 n. 72.

26 'Great Naval Battle', *The Times*, 3 June 1916.

27 J. Pollock, *Kitchener. Comprising the Road to Omdurman and Saviour of the Nation* (London: Constable, 2001; first publ. 1998), pp. 482–3.

28 'The Man and the Soldier', *The Times*, 7 June 1916.

29 J. Charteris, *At G.H.Q.* (London: Cassell and Company, 1931), p. 146.

30 Rawlinson quoted in Pollock, *Kitchener*, p. 487.

31 Sir J. E. Edmonds, *Military Operations. France and Belgium, 1916* (2 vols., London: Macmillan and Co., 1933), I, pp. 300–301.

32 J. H. Morrow, Jr., *The Great War in the Air. Military Aviation from 1909 to 1921* (Tuscaloosa, Ala.: University of Alabama Press, 2009; first publ. 1993), p. 170.

33 TNA: WO 256/10, Haig diary, 30 June 1916.

34 Edmonds, *Military Operations. 1916*, I, pp. 313–14.

35 R. Atwood, *General Lord Rawlinson. From Tragedy to Triumph* (London: Bloomsbury Academic, 2018), p. 142.

36 IWM: Documents 22872, Memoir of Lieutenant W. V. C. Lake.

37 A. J. Evans cited in M. Mace and J. Grehan (eds.), *Slaughter on the Somme 1 July 1916. The Complete War Diaries of the British Army's Worst Day* (Barnsley: Pen & Sword, 2013), p. 54.

38 'General Sir Walter Congreve, V.C.', *The Times*, 1 March 1927.

39 Second Lieutenant K. Macardle quoted in H. Sebag-Montefiore, *Somme. Into the Breach* (London: Viking, 2016), p. 204.

40 E. Fayolle, *Cahiers secrets de la Grande guerre*, ed. H. Contamine (Paris: Plon, 1964), p. 165 (entry, 1 July 1916).

41 Captain de Suzannet and Major Héring quoted in E. Greenhalgh (ed. and trans.), *Liaison. General Pierre des Vallières at British General Headquarters, January 1916 to May 1917* (Stroud: History Press, 2016), pp. 119, 121–3.

42 TNA: WO 256/11, Haig diary, 2 and 5 July 1916.

43 Lloyd George quoted in J. P. Harris, *Douglas Haig and the First World War* (Cambridge: Cambridge University Press, 2008), p. 242.

44 W. Langford, *Somme Intelligence. Fourth Army HQ 1916. Prisoner Interrogations and Captured Documents* (Barnsley: Pen & Sword, 2013),

p. 31; and Reichsarchiv, *Der Weltkrieg. X. Die Operationen des Jahres 1916*, p. 352.

45 W. Miles, *Military Operations. France and Belgium, 1916* (2 vols., London: Macmillan and Co., 1938), II, p. 27; and Reichsarchiv, *Der Weltkrieg. X. Die Operationen des Jahres 1916*, p. 355.

46 F. von Lossberg, *Lossberg's War. The World War I Memoirs of a German Chief of Staff*, trans. D. T. Zabecki and D. J. Biedekarken (Lexington, Ky.: University of Kentucky Press, 2017), p. 212.

47 J. Sheldon, *The German Army on the Somme 1914–1916* (Barnsley: Pen & Sword, 2012; first publ. 2005), p. 179.

48 Reichsarchiv, *Der Weltkrieg. X. Die Operationen des Jahres 1916*, p. 321.

49 TNA: WO 256/11, Haig diary, 11 July 1916, original emphasis; and WO 158/234, 'Note of discussion as to attack on LONGUEVAL plateau and the C-in-C's decision thereon'.

50 Miles, *Military Operations. 1916*, II, pp. 67–82.

51 Reichsarchiv, *Der Weltkrieg. X. Die Operationen des Jahres 1916*, p. 414.

52 M. von Gallwitz, *Erleben im Westen 1916–1918* (Berlin: E. S. Mittler & Sohn, 1932), p. 60.

11 'The future is darker than ever'

1 M. von Gallwitz, *Erleben im Westen 1916–1918* (Berlin: E. S. Mittler & Sohn, 1932), p. 61.

2 Reichsarchiv, *Der Weltkrieg 1914 bis 1918. X. Die Operationen des Jahres 1916. Bis zum Wechsel der Obersten Heeresleitung* (Berlin: E. S. Mittler & Sohn, 1936), p. 366.

3 Gallwitz, *Erleben im Westen*, p. 80.

4 Reichsarchiv, *Der Weltkrieg. X. Die Operationen des Jahres 1916*, pp. 349, 371, 375.

5 F. von Below, 'Experience of the German 1st Army in the Somme Battle' (General Staff (Intelligence), General Headquarters, 3 May 1917), p. 5.

6 Ibid., p. 6. Original emphasis.

7 É. Fayolle, *Cahiers secrets de la Grande guerre*, ed. H. Contamine (Paris: Plon, 1964), p. 168 (entry, 16 July 1916).

8 Sir H. Gough, *The Fifth Army* (London: Hodder and Stoughton, 1931), p. 139.

9 AWM: 2DRL/0547, Captain H. S. Davis, letter, 3 September 1916.

10 A. von Stosch, *Somme-Nord*, Part II. *Die Brennpunkte der Schlacht im Juli 1916* (Berlin: Gerhard Stalling, 1927), p. 81.

11 Ibid., p. 88.

12 W. Miles, *Military Operations. France and Belgium, 1916* (2 vols., London: Macmillan and Co., 1938), II, p. 108 n. 2.

13 E. Greenhalgh, *Foch in Command. The Forging of a First World War General* (Cambridge: Cambridge University Press, 2011), p. 174; and 'Note. Remise au général Sir Douglas Haig', 19 July 1916, in Ministère de la Guerre, *Les Armées françaises dans la Grande guerre* (Paris: Imprimerie Nationale, 1922–39) [hereafter *AFGG*], Book 4/2 – *Annexes*, Vol. 3, No. 2491, pp. 106–7.

14 C. Duffy, *Through German Eyes. The British and the Somme 1916* (London: Phoenix, 2007; first publ. 2006), p. 193.

15 S. Robbins (ed.), *The First World War Letters of General Lord Horne* (Stroud: History Press for the Army Records Society, 2009), p. 182 (letter, 23 July 1916).

16 'The Valiant Soldiers of France', *The Times*, 2 August 1916.

17 'Mémorandum pour la réunion des commandants de groupes d'armées', 20 August 1916, in *AFGG*, Book 5/1 – *Annexes*, Vol. 1, No. 2, pp. 9, 22.

18 TNA: WO 256/11, Haig diary, 3 July 1916. Original emphasis.

19 'Journal de marche de Joffre', 11 August 1916, in E. Greenhalgh (ed. and trans.), *Liaison. General Pierre des Vallières at British General Headquarters, January 1916 to May 1917* (Stroud: History Press, 2016), pp. 150–51.

20 Miles, *Military Operations. 1916*, II, pp. 196–7.

21 J. Charteris, *Field-Marshal Earl Haig* (New York: Charles Scribner's Sons, 1929), p. 196; and J. Beach, *Haig's Intelligence. GHQ and the German Army, 1916–1918* (Cambridge: Cambridge University Press, 2013), p. 207.

22 G. Sheffield and J. Bourne (eds.), *Douglas Haig. War Diaries and Letters 1914–1918* (London: Weidenfeld & Nicolson, 2005), p. 213 (entry, 1 August 1916). Original emphasis.

23 Robertson to Kiggell, 5 July 1916, in D. R. Woodward (ed.), *The Military Correspondence of Field-Marshal Sir William Robertson, Chief of the*

Imperial General Staff, December 1915–February 1918 (London: Bodley Head for the Army Records Society, 1989), pp. 64–6.

24 Sheffield and Bourne (eds.), *Douglas Haig*, pp. 213–14 (entry, 1 August 1916).

25 TNA: WO 158/235, Kiggell to Rawlinson and Gough, 2 August 1916.

26 'The King's Visit to France', *The Times*, 17 August 1916.

27 G. H. Cassar, *Asquith as War Leader* (London: Hambledon Press, 1994), p. 194.

28 Lloyd George to Maurice, 2 September 1916, in J. Grigg, *Lloyd George. From Peace to War 1912–1916* (London: Penguin, 2002; first publ. 1985), p. 387; and D. R. Woodward, *Field Marshal Sir William Robertson. Chief of the Imperial General Staff in the Great War* (Westport, Conn.: Praeger, 1998), p. 62.

29 TNA: WO 256/13, Haig diary, 17 September 1916.

30 Crown Prince Wilhelm, *My War Experiences* (London: Hurst and Blackett, n.d.), pp. 228–9.

31 Ibid., pp. 229–30.

32 H. Afflerbach, *Falkenhayn. Politisches Denken und Handeln im Kaiserreich* (Munich: Oldenbourg, 1994), pp. 437–42.

33 E. von Falkenhayn, *General Headquarters 1914–1916 and Its Critical Decisions* (London: Hutchinson & Co., 1919), p. 324.

34 Gallwitz, *Erleben im Westen*, p. 57.

35 W. Groener, *Lebenserinnerungen. Jugend. Generalstab. Weltkrieg* (Göttingen: Vandenhoeck & Ruprecht, 1957), p. 317.

36 Afflerbach, *Falkenhayn*, p. 450.

37 W. Görlitz (ed.), *The Kaiser and His Court. The Diaries, Note Books and Letters of Admiral Georg Alexander von Müller, Chief of the Naval Cabinet, 1914–1918* (London: Macdonald & Co., 1961; first publ. 1959), p. 199 (entry, 30 August 1916).

38 Reichsarchiv, *Der Weltkrieg 1914 bis 1918. XI. Die Kriegführung im Herbst 1916 und im Winter 1916/17. Vom Wechsel in der Obersten Heeresleitung bis zum Entschluß zur Rückzug in die Siegfried-Stellung* (Berlin: E. S. Mittler & Sohn, 1938), p. 3.

39 Ibid., p. 20.

40 Ibid., pp. 32–5.

41 F. von Lossberg, *Lossberg's War. The World War I Memoirs of a German Chief of Staff*, trans. D. T. Zabecki and D. J. Biedekarken (Lexington, Ky: University of Kentucky Press, 2017), p. 242.

42 Rupprecht quoted in J. Boff, *Haig's Enemy. Crown Prince Rupprecht and Germany's War on the Western Front* (Oxford: Oxford University Press, 2018), p. 125.

43 M. Bauer, *Der große Krieg in Feld und Heimat. Erinnerungen und Betrachtungen* (Tübingen: Oslander'sche Buchhandlung, 1922), p. 107.

44 Boff, *Haig's Enemy*, pp. 122–4.

45 J. H. Morrow, Jr., *The Great War in the Air. Military Aviation from 1909 to 1921* (Tuscaloosa, Ala.: University of Alabama Press, 2009; first publ. 1993), p. 151.

46 Gallwitz, *Erleben im Westen*, pp. 95, 111.

47 Ibid., pp. 109–10.

12 'The face of a general in victory'

1 TNA: WO 158/235, 'Preliminary Notes on Tactical Employment of Tanks'.

2 Rawlinson quoted in R. Prior and T. Wilson, *Command on the Western Front. The Military Career of Sir Henry Rawlinson 1914–18* (Barnsley: Pen & Sword, 2004; first publ. 1992), p. 229.

3 Ibid., pp. 227–35.

4 C. Duffy, *Through German Eyes. The British and the Somme 1916* (London: Phoenix, 2007; first publ. 2006), pp. 212–14.

5 W. Miles, *Military Operations. France and Belgium, 1916* (2 vols., London: Macmillan and Co., 1938), II, p. 364.

6 Ibid., p. 293 n. 1.

7 C. Headlam, *History of the Guards Division in the Great War 1915–1918* (3 vols., London: John Murray, 1924), I, p. 165 n.

8 Rupprecht quoted in Duffy, *Through German Eyes*, pp. 230–31.

9 F. von Lossberg, *Lossberg's War. The World War I Memoirs of a German Chief of Staff*, trans. D. T. Zabecki and D. J. Biedekarken (Lexington, Ky.: University of Kentucky Press, 2017), p. 246.

10 Hans Frimmel quoted in A. Watson, *Enduring the Great War. Combat, Morale and Collapse in the German and British Armies, 1914–1918* (Cambridge: Cambridge University Press, 2008), p. 167.

11 Miles, *Military Operations. 1916*, II, p. 344.

12 R. Prior and T. Wilson, *The Somme* (New Haven, Conn., and London: Yale University Press, 2005), p. 244.

13 Haig to King George V, 5 October 1916, in G. Sheffield and J. Bourne (eds.), *Douglas Haig. War Diaries and Letters 1914–1918* (London: Weidenfeld & Nicolson, 2005), p. 236.

14 TNA: WO 256/13, Haig diary, 5 October 1916.

15 TNA: CAB 42/21/3, Haig to Robertson, 7 October 1916.

16 TNA: WO 158/236, Note, A. A. Montgomery, 13 October 1916.

17 Reichsarchiv, *Der Weltkrieg 1914 bis 1918. XI. Die Kriegführung im Herbst 1916 und im Winter 1916/17. Vom Wechsel der Obersten Heeresleitung bis zum Entschluß zum Rückzug in die Siegfried-Stellung* (Berlin: E. S. Mittler & Sohn, 1938), pp. 77, 78.

18 Crown Prince R. von Bayern, *Mein Kriegstagebuch* (3 vols., Berlin: E. S. Mittler, 1929), II, p. 34 (entry, 27 September 1916).

19 J. Boff, *Haig's Enemy. Crown Prince Rupprecht and Germany's War on the Western Front* (Oxford: Oxford University Press, 2018), p. 129.

20 M. von Gallwitz, *Erleben im Westen 1916–1918* (Berlin: E. S. Mittler & Sohn, 1932), p. 117; and R. von Bayern, *Mein Kriegstagebuch*, II, pp. 26–7 (entry, 19 September 1916).

21 W. Jürgensen, *Das Füsilier-Regiment 'Königin' Nr. 86 im Weltkriege* (Berlin: Gerhard Stalling, 1925), p. 132; and *Histories of Two Hundred and Fifty-One Divisions of the German Army Which Participated in the War (1914–1918)* (Washington DC: Government Printing Office, 1920), pp. 19, 56, 366.

22 A. Watson, *Ring of Steel. Germany and Austria–Hungary at War, 1914–1918* (London: Allen Lane, 2015; first publ. 2014), pp. 325–6; and G. Hirschfeld et al., *Die Deutschen an der Somme 1914–1918. Krieg, Besatzung, Verbrannte Erde* (Essen: Klartext Verlag, 2006), p. 147.

23 Gallwitz, *Erleben im Westen*, pp. 114, 127; and R. von Bayern, *Mein Kriegstagebuch*, II, p. 39 (entry, 4 October 1916).

24 Reichsarchiv, *Der Weltkrieg. XI. Die Kriegführung im Herbst 1916 und im Winter 1916/17* pp. 77–8.

25 H. von Kuhl, *Der Weltkrieg 1914–1918. Dem deutschen Volke dargestellt* (Berlin: Verlag Tradition Wilhelm Kolk, 1929), p. 527.

26 Duffy, *Through German Eyes*, p. 310.

27 J. Werner, *Knight of Germany. Oswald Boelcke, German Ace*, trans. C. W. Sykes (Havertown, Pa: Casemate, 2009; first publ. 1985), p. 4.

28 H. A. Jones, *The War in the Air. Being the Story of the Part Played in the Great War by the Royal Air Force* (6 vols., Oxford: Clarendon Press, 1922–37), II, pp. 296–7.

29 Miles, *Military Operations. 1916*, II, p. 459.

30 E. Greenhalgh (ed. and trans.), *Liaison. General Pierre des Vallières at British General Headquarters, January 1916 to May 1917* (Stroud: History Press, 2016), pp. 184–5 (entry, 24 October 1916).

31 J. C. King, *Generals and Politicians. Conflict between France's High Command, Parliament and Government, 1914–1918* (Berkeley and Los Angeles: University of California Press, 1951), p. 130.

32 R. Poincaré, *Au service de la France. VIII. Verdun 1916* (Paris: Librairie Plon, 1931), p. 337.

33 Ministère de la Guerre, *Les Armées françaises dans la Grande guerre* (Paris: Imprimerie Nationale, 1922–39) [hereafter *AFGG*], Book 4/3, p. 383.

34 'Note', 17 October 1916, in ibid., *Annexes*, Vol. 1/2, No. 1076, p. 1601.

35 Reichsarchiv, *Der Weltkrieg. XI. Die Kriegführung im Herbst 1916 und im Winter 1916/17*, p. 139.

36 'Traduction d'un message trouvé sur un pigeon voyageur allemand', 24 October 1916, in *AFGG*, Book 4/3 – *Annexes*, Vol. 2/1, No. 1227, p. 198.

37 L. Madelin, *Verdun* (Paris: Librairie Félix Alcan, 1920), p. 134; and 'Compte rendu des opérations exécutées par la 38e division du 23 octobre (inclus) au 30 octobre (inclus)', in *AFGG*, Book 4/3 – *Annexes*, Vol. 2/1, No. 1508, p. 658.

38 J. C. Joffre, *The Memoirs of Marshal Joffre*, trans. T. Bentley Mott (2 vols., London: Geoffrey Bles, 1932), II, p. 494.

39 *Le Matin*, 26 October 1916.

40 Henry Bordeaux quoted in L.-E. Mangin, *Le Général Mangin 1866–1925* (Paris: Éditions Fernand Lanore, 1986), p. 244.

41 Nivelle to Joffre, 11 November 1916, in *AFGG*, Book 4/3 – *Annexes*, Vol. 2/1, No. 1587, pp. 788–90.

42 Prior and Wilson, *The Somme*, pp. 271–2.

43 TNA: WO 158/236, Haig to his army commanders, 29 October 1916, and Rawlinson to Haig, 7 November 1916.

44 TNA: WO 256/14, Haig diary, 13 November 1916.

45 'Décisions prises par les généraux en chef des armées alliées ou leurs représentants accrédités, à l'issue de la conférence, tenue à Chantilly les 15 et 16 novembre 1916', in *AFGG*, Book 5/1 – *Annexes*, Vol. 1, No. 119, pp. 217–19.

46 J. H. Boraston (ed.), *Sir Douglas Haig's Despatches (December 1915–April 1919)* (London: J. M. Dent & Sons, 1919), p. 58.

47 Miles, *Military Operations. 1916*, II, p. xvi.

48 TNA: CAB 37/159/32, Lansdowne Memorandum, 13 November 1916.

49 Watson, *Ring of Steel*, p. 324.

50 R. von Bayern, *Mein Kriegstagebuch*, II, p. 63 (entry, 10 November 1916).

51 R. B. Talbot Kelly, *A Subaltern's Odyssey. Memoirs of the Great War 1915–1917* (London: William Kimber, 1980), p. 118.

13 *'A very serious decision'*

1 W. Görlitz (ed.), *The Kaiser and His Court. The Diaries, Note Books and Letters of Admiral Georg Alexander von Müller, Chief of the Naval Cabinet, 1914–1918* (London: Macdonald & Co., 1961; first publ. 1959), p. 222 (entry, 6 December 1916); and F. von Lossberg, *Lossberg's War. The World War I Memoirs of a German Chief of Staff*, trans. D. T. Zabecki and D. J. Biedekarken (Lexington, Ky.: University of Kentucky Press, 2017), p. 262.

2 A. Watson, *Ring of Steel. Germany and Austria–Hungary at War, 1914–1918* (London: Allen Lane, 2015; first publ. 2014), pp. 332–3; and 'Ten Months in Germany', *The Times*, 8 December 1916.

3 'Proposals for Peace Negotiations Made by Germany, 12 December 1916', and 'Note of President Wilson', 18 December 1916, in J. B. Scott (ed.), *Official Statements of War Aims and Peace Proposals. December 1916 to November 1918* (Washington DC: Carnegie Endowment for International Peace, 1921), pp. 2–3, 13.

4 'Entente Reply to German Proposals', 29 December 1916, in ibid., p. 27.

5 D. Steffen, 'The Holtzendorff Memorandum of 22 December 1916 and Germany's Declaration of Unrestricted U-Boat Warfare', *Journal of Military History*, Vol. 68, No. 1 (January 2004), pp. 215–24.

6 Hindenburg to Bethmann Hollweg, 23 December 1916, in E. Ludendorff, *The General Staff and Its Problems*, trans. F. A. Holt (2 vols., London: Hutchinson & Co., 1920), I, pp. 293–4. Original emphasis.

7 Bethmann Hollweg to Hindenburg, 24 December 1916, in ibid., I, pp. 295–7.

8 Hindenburg to Bethmann Hollweg, 26 December 1916, in ibid., I, pp. 298–9.

9 'Notes of the Conference between the Imperial Chancellor, Field-Marshal von Hindenburg and General Ludendorff at Pless at 11.15 a.m. on January 1, 1917', in ibid., I, pp. 304–6.

10 Watson, *Ring of Steel*, p. 422; and Görlitz (ed.), *The Kaiser and His Court*, p. 230 (entry, 9 January 1917).

11 Ministère de la Guerre, *Les Armées françaises dans la Grande guerre* (Paris: Imprimerie Nationale, 1922–39) [hereafter *AFGG*], Book 4/3, p. 477.

12 'Ordre général no. 189', 18 December 1916, in *AFGG*, Book 4/3 – *Annexes*, Vol. 2/2, No. 1930, p. 1484.

13 R. Poincaré, *Au service de la France*. IX. *L'Année trouble 1917* (Paris: Librairie Plon, 1932), p. 14.

14 A. G. Lennox (ed.), *The Diary of Lord Bertie of Thame 1914–1918* (2 vols., London: Hodder and Stoughton, 1924), II, p. 85 (entry, 18 December 1916).

15 J. C. Joffre, *The Memoirs of Marshal Joffre*, trans. T. Bentley Mott (2 vols., London: Geoffrey Bles, 1932), II, p. 536.

16 E. L. Spears, *Prelude to Victory* (London: Jonathan Cape, 1939), p. 31.

17 'Gen. Nivelle's Parting Blow', *The Times*, 18 December 1916. Original emphasis.

18 J. de Pierrefeu, *French Headquarters 1915–1918*, trans. Major C. J. C. Street (London: Geoffrey Bles, 1924), p. 120; and 'Le Général Nivelle', *L'Écho de Paris*, 13 December 1916.

19 E. Greenhalgh, *Foch in Command. The Forging of a First World War General* (Cambridge: Cambridge University Press, 2011), pp. 201–2; and

Nivelle to Foch, 16 December 1916, and Minister of War to Nivelle, 20 December 1916, in *AFGG*, Book 5/1 – *Annexes*, Vol. 1, Nos. 298 and 324, pp. 518, 549.

20 B. H. Liddell Hart, *Foch. The Man of Orleans* (London: Eyre & Spottiswoode, 1933), p. 233.

21 R. Recouly, *Joffre* (London and New York: D. Appleton & Company, 1931), pp. 336–7.

22 E. Greenhalgh (ed. and trans.), *Liaison. General Pierre des Vallières at British General Headquarters, January 1916 to May 1917* (Stroud: History Press, 2016), p. 194.

23 J. Grigg, *Lloyd George. From Peace to War 1912–1916* (London: Penguin Books, 2002; first publ. 1985), pp. 450–51.

24 The Earl of Crawford (President of the Board of Agriculture and Fisheries) quoted in ibid., p. 438.

25 C. Clifford, *The Asquiths* (London: John Murray, 2003; first publ. 2002), pp. 367–8.

26 Lord Hankey, *The Supreme Command 1914–1918* (2 vols., London: George Allen and Unwin, 1961), II, p. 573.

27 House of Commons Debates, 19 December 1916, Vol. 88, cc. 1333–9.

28 D. French, *The Strategy of the Lloyd George Coalition, 1916–1918* (Oxford: Clarendon Press, 1995), p. 14.

29 TNA: CAB 28/2, 'The Conference of the Allies at Rome on January 5, 6, and 7, 1917'.

30 French, *Lloyd George Coalition*, pp. 50–51.

31 TNA: WO 256/14, Haig diary, 15 December 1916.

32 Nivelle to Haig, 21 December 1916, Appendix 2, in Sir J. E. Edmonds et al., *Military Operations. France and Belgium, 1917. Appendices* (London: Macmillan and Co., 1940), pp. 4–6.

33 'Conférence du 15 janvier 1917 (à la Trésorerie, Downing Street)', in *AFGG*, Book 5/1 – *Annexes*, Vol. 1, No. 447, pp. 777–84.

34 Ibid. Original emphasis.

35 Ibid.

36 Ibid., *Annexes*, Vol. 1, No. 456, p. 808.

37 A. J. P. Taylor (ed.), *Lloyd George. A Diary by Frances Stevenson* (London: Hutchinson & Co., 1971), pp. 138–9 (entry, 15 January 1917).

38 Bernstorff to Lansing, 31 January 1917, in J. V. Fuller (ed.), *Papers Relat-ing to the Foreign Relations of the United States, 1917, Supplement 1, The World War* (Washington DC: United States Government Printing Office, 1931), Document 92.

39 Lossberg, *Lossberg's War*, p. 265.

40 G. P. Neumann, *The German Air Force in the Great War*, trans. J. E. Gurdon (London: Hodder and Stoughton, 1921), pp. 223–4; and Reichsarchiv, *Der Weltkrieg 1914 bis 1918. XI. Die Kriegführung im Herbst 1916 und im Winter 1916/17. Vom Wechsel in der Obersten Heeresleitung bis zum Entschluß zum Rückzug in die Siegfried-Stellung* (Berlin: E. S. Mittler & Sohn, 1938), p. 510.

41 Crown Prince R. von Bayern, *Mein Kriegstagebuch* (3 vols., Berlin: E. S. Mittler, 1929), II, p. 85 (entry, 17 January 1917).

42 *Grundsätze für die Führung in der Abwehrschlacht im Stellungskriege vom 1 Dezember 1916* (Berlin: Reichsdruckerei, 1916), pp. 9–10; and TNA: WO 157/22, 'German Instructions for a Counter-Attack Organized in Depth', in GHQ Summary of Information, 29 July 1917.

43 E. Ludendorff, *My War Memories 1914–1918* (2 vols., London: Hutchin-son & Co., 1919), I, p. 308; and G. C. Wynne, *If Germany Attacks. The Battle in Depth in the West* (London: Faber & Faber, 1939), p. 138.

44 Reichsarchiv, *Der Weltkrieg. XI. Die Kriegführung im Herbst 1916 und im Winter 1916/17*, pp. 511–12.

45 Ibid., pp. 513, 514–16.

46 'Address of the President of the United States to Congress', 3 February 1917, in Fuller (ed.), *Foreign Relations, 1917, Supplement 1*, Document 100.

14 *'An entirely new situation'*

1 J. de Pierrefeu, *French Headquarters 1915–1918*, trans. Major C. J. C. Street (London: Geoffrey Bles, 1924), p. 131.

2 'Plan d'opérations pour 1917', 25 January 1917, in Ministère de la Guerre, *Les Armées françaises dans la Grande guerre* (Paris: Imprimerie Nationale, 1922–39) [hereafter *AFGG*], Book 5/1 – *Annexes*, Vol. 2, No. 518, pp. 947–51.

3 132 Schneider CA1 tanks were deployed on 16 April 1917. T. Gale, *The French Army's Tank Force and Armoured Warfare in the Great War. The Artil-lerie Spéciale* (Farnham: Ashgate, 2013), p. 42.

4 D. Rolland, *Nivelle. L'Inconnu du Chemin des Dames* (Paris: Imago, 2012), pp. 83–4.

5 E. L. Spears, *Prelude to Victory* (London: Jonathan Cape, 1939), p. 66.

6 C. Falls, *Military Operations. France and Belgium, 1917* (3 vols., London: Macmillan and Co., 1940), I, p. 53; and Nivelle to Haig, 26 January 1917, in *AFGG*, Book 5/1 – *Annexes*, Vol. 2, No. 523, p. 961.

7 Vallières to Nivelle, 26 January 1917, in E. Greenhalgh (ed. and trans.), *Liaison. General Pierre des Vallières at British General Headquarters, January 1916 to May 1917* (Stroud: History Press, 2016), p. 221.

8 *AFGG*, Book 5/1, pp. 223, 234 n. 1; and 'Proposed Organization of Unified Command on the Western Front, 26th February 1917', Appendix 18, in Sir J.E. Edmonds et al., *Military Operations. France and Belgium, 1917. Appendices* (London: Macmillan and Co., 1940), p. 62.

9 Falls, *Military Operations. 1917*, I, p. 536 n. 1.

10 J. Grigg, *Lloyd George. War Leader 1916–1918* (London: Penguin Books, 2003; first publ. 2002), p. 41.

11 Lord Hankey, *The Supreme Command 1914–1918* (2 vols., London: George Allen and Unwin, 1961), II, p. 616; and 'Agreement Signed at Anglo-French Conference Held at Calais, 26th/27th February 1917', Appendix 19, in Edmonds et al., *Military Operations. 1917. Appendices*, pp. 64–5.

12 D. R. Woodward, *Lloyd George and the Generals* (London and Toronto: Associated University Presses, 1983), p. 150.

13 TNA: CAB 24/6, GT 93, 'Note by the Chief of the Imperial General Staff Regarding the Calais Agreement of 27th February 1917.'

14 S. McMeekin, *The Russian Revolution. A New History* (New York: Basic Books, 2017), pp. 95–100; and 'Abdication Proclamation of March 14, 1917', in C. F. Horne (ed.), *Source Records of the Great War* (7 vols., USA: National Alumni, 1923), V, p. 85.

15 Page to Lansing, 24 February 1917, in J. V. Fuller (ed.), *Papers Relating to the Foreign Relations of the United States, 1917, Supplement 1, The World War* (Washington DC: US Government Printing Office, 1931), Document 158.

16 'Acting Secretary of State to the Diplomatic Representatives in All Countries', 26 February 1917, in Fuller (ed.), *Foreign Relations, 1917, Supplement 1*, Document 162.

17 'President Sounds Warlike Note in Inaugural', *Washington Times*, 5 March 1917.

18 F. von Lossberg, *Lossberg's War. The World War I Memoirs of a German Chief of Staff*, trans. D. T. Zabecki and D. J. Biedekarken (Lexington, Ky.: University of Kentucky Press, 2017), p. 269; and E. Ludendorff, *My War Memories 1914–1918* (2 vols., London: Hutchinson & Co., 1919), II, p. 405.

19 Ludendorff, *My War Memories*, I, p. 333; and A. Watson, *Ring of Steel. Germany and Austria–Hungary at War, 1914–1918* (London: Allen Lane, 2015; first publ. 2014), pp. 378–84.

20 Hindenburg to Lyncker, 27 March 1917, in H. Michaelis, E. Schraepler and G. Scheel (eds.), *Ursachen und Folgen. Vom deutschen Zusammenbruch 1918 und 1945 bis zur staatlichen Neuordnung Deutschlands in der Gegenwart: Die Wende des ersten Weltkrieges und der Beginn der innenpolitischen Wandlung 1916/1917* (Berlin: Herbert Wendler & Co., 1958), p. 196.

21 'Aus einem Feldpostbrief', in ibid., p. 191.

22 'Erlaß Hindenburgs zur Ernährungslage', 23 March 1917, in ibid., p. 194.

23 *Frightfulness in Retreat* (London: Hodder & Stoughton, 1917), p. 12.

24 J. Boff, *Haig's Enemy. Crown Prince Rupprecht and Germany's War on the Western Front* (Oxford: Oxford University Press, 2018), pp. 150–51; and Crown Prince R. von Bayern, *Mein Kriegstagebuch* (3 vols., Berlin: E. S. Mittler, 1929), II, p. 116 (entry, 15 March 1917).

25 G. von der Marwitz, *Weltkriegsbriefe*, ed. E. von Tschischwitz (Berlin: Steiniger-Verlage, 1940), p. 218.

26 Reichsarchiv, *Der Weltkrieg 1914 bis 1918*. XII. *Die Kriegführung im Frühjahr 1917* (Berlin: E. S. Mittler & Sohn, 1939), pp. 137, 145.

27 D. French, 'Failures of Intelligence: The Retreat to the Hindenburg Line and the March 1918 Offensive', in M. Dockrill and D. French (eds.), *Strategy and Intelligence. British Policy during the First World War* (London: Hambledon Press, 1996), pp. 77–84.

28 É. Fayolle, *Cahiers secrets de la Grande guerre*, ed. H. Contamine (Paris: Plon, 1964), pp. 205–6 (entry, 9 March 1917).

29 Spears, *Prelude to Victory*, pp. 209–10.

30 J. C. King, *Generals and Politicians. Conflict between France's High Command, Parliament and Government, 1914–1918* (Berkeley and Los Angeles: University of California Press, 1951), pp. 147–8.

31 R. Poincaré, *Au service de la France*. IX. *L'Année trouble 1917* (Paris: Librairie Plon, 1932), pp. 75, 77.

32 'More Evidence of German Infamy', *The Times*, 22 March 1917.

33 'Bulletin de renseignements No. 65', 23 March 1917, in *AFGG*, Book 5/1 – *Annexes*, Vol. 3, No. 1008, p. 214; and Fayolle, *Cahiers secrets*, p. 207 (entry, 21 March 1917).

34 P. Painlevé, *Comment j'ai nommé Foch et Pétain. La Politique de guerre de 1917: Le Commandement unique interallié* (Paris: Librairie Félix Alcan, 1923), pp. 42–3.

35 Micheler to Nivelle, 22 March 1917, in *AFGG*, Book 5/1 – *Annexes*, Vol. 3, No. 994, pp. 193–5.

36 'Directive pour les armées britanniques, l'armée belge et les groupes d'armées françaises', 4 April 1917, in *AFGG*, Book 5/1 – *Annexes*, Vol. 3, No. 1167, pp. 547–9. Original emphasis.

37 Spears, *Prelude to Victory*, p. 356.

38 Poincaré, *Au service de la France*. IX, p. 97.

39 Ibid., p. 107; and Rolland, *Nivelle*, p. 155.

40 Painlevé, *Comment j'ai nommé Foch et Pétain*, pp. 53–4; and R. A. Doughty, *Pyrrhic Victory. French Strategy and Operations in the Great War* (London and Cambridge, Mass.: Harvard University Press, 2005), p. 344.

41 Painlevé, *Comment j'ai nommé Foch et Pétain*, p. 54.

15 'Tortured ground'

1 L. James, *Imperial Warrior. The Life and Times of Field-Marshal Viscount Allenby* (London: Weidenfeld & Nicolson, 1993), p. 92.

2 M. Bechthold, 'Bloody April Revisited: The Royal Flying Corps at the Battle of Arras, 1917', *British Journal of Military History*, Vol. 4, No. 2 (February 2018), pp. 50–69.

3 C. Falls, *Military Operations. France and Belgium, 1917* (3 vols., London: Macmillan and Co., 1940), I, p. 182.

4 R. MacLeod, 'Sight and Sound on the Western Front: Surveyors, Scientists, and the "Battlefield Laboratory", 1915–1918', *War & Society*, Vol.

18, No. 1 (May 2000), pp. 34–7; and B. Rawling, *Surviving Trench Warfare. Technology and the Canadian Corps, 1914–1918* (Toronto: University of Toronto Press, 2014; first publ. 1992), p. 111.

5 J. Boff, *Haig's Enemy. Crown Prince Rupprecht and Germany's War on the Western Front* (Oxford: Oxford University Press, 2018), p. 157.

6 A. Dieterich, 'The German 79th Reserve Infantry Division in the Battle of Vimy Ridge, April 1917', *Canadian Military History*, Vol. 15, No. 1 (April 2012), p. 76.

7 G. W. L. Nicholson, *Official History of the Canadian Army in the First World War. Canadian Expeditionary Force 1914–1919* (Ottawa: Queen's Printer, 1962), pp. 253–4.

8 Falls, *Military Operations. 1917*, I, pp. 179–80.

9 Captain R. Monypenny quoted in J. Nicholls, *Cheerful Sacrifice. The Battle of Arras 1917* (Barnsley: Pen & Sword, 2013; first publ. 1990), p. 125.

10 Falls, *Military Operations. 1917*, I, p. 231.

11 F. von Lossberg, *Lossberg's War. The World War I Memoirs of a German Chief of Staff*, trans. D. T. Zabecki and D. J. Biedekarken (Lexington, Ky.: University of Kentucky Press, 2017), pp. 273–5.

12 TNA: WO 158/37, Haig to Nivelle, 12 April 1917.

13 Haig to King George V, 9 April 1917, in G. Sheffield and J. Bourne (eds.), *Douglas Haig. War Diaries and Letters 1914–1918* (London: Weidenfeld & Nicolson, 2005), p. 278. Original emphasis.

14 R. A. Doughty, *Pyrrhic Victory. French Strategy and Operations in the Great War* (London and Cambridge, Mass.: Harvard University Press, 2005), p. 349.

15 T. Gale, *The French Army's Tank Force and Armoured Warfare in the Great War. The Artillerie Spéciale* (Farnham: Ashgate, 2013), pp. 38–9.

16 'Plan de défense', 12 February 1917, and 'Étude des organisations défensives allemandes sur le front du CA', 14 February 1917, in Ministère de la Guerre, *Les Armées françaises dans la Grande guerre* (Paris: Imprimerie Nationale, 1922–39) [hereafter *AFGG*], Book 5/1 – *Annexes,* Vol. 2, Nos. 664 and 680, pp. 1204–9, 1238.

17 'Rapport sur les conditions dans lesquelles s'est effectuée la préparation d'artillerie pour l'attaque du 16 avril', 7 May 1917, in *AFGG*, Book 5/1, *Annexes,* Vol. 4, No. 1883, pp. 1484–6.

18 Reichsarchiv, *Der Weltkrieg 1914 bis 1918*. XII. *Die Kriegführung im Frühjahr 1917* (Berlin: E. S. Mittler & Sohn, 1939), pp. 290–91.

19 Ibid., p. 295.

20 Doughty, *Pyrrhic Victory*, p. 345.

21 J.-Y. Le Naour, *1917. La Paix impossible* (Paris: Perrin, 2015), pp. 90–92.

22 E. L. Spears, *Prelude to Victory* (London: Jonathan Cape, 1939), p. 487.

23 *AFGG*, Book 5/1, p. 637.

24 N. Offenstadt (ed.), *Le Chemin des Dames. De l'évènement à la mémoire* (Paris: Stock, 2004), pp. 160–61.

25 'Compte rendu des évènements du 16 avril (nuit du 15 au 16)', in *AFGG*, Book 5/1 – *Annexes*, Vol. 4, No. 1462, pp. 965–6.

26 Gale, *The French Army's Tank Force*, p. 50.

27 J. de Pierrefeu, *French Headquarters 1915–1918*, trans. Major C. J. C. Street (London: Geoffrey Bles, 1924), p. 152.

28 'Compte rendu du commandant Tournès, officier de liaison à la VIe armée', 16 April 1917, in *AFGG*, Book 5/1 – *Annexes*, Vol. 3, No. 1359, p. 878.

29 'Compte rendu de fin de journée', 16 April 1917, and 'Le général Guérin, commandant la 15e division d'infanterie coloniale, à M. le général commandant le 2e corps d'armée colonial', 16 April 1917, in *AFGG*, Book 5/1 – *Annexes*, Vol. 3, Nos. 1413 and 1414, pp. 924, 925.

30 R. Poincaré, *Au service de la France*. IX. *L'Année trouble 1917* (Paris: Librairie Plon, 1932), pp. 114, 118.

31 'Die Schlacht an der Aisne', *Berliner Tageblatt*, 17 April 1917.

32 BA-MA: PH 5-I/8, 'Bisherige Erfahrungen aus den Kämpfen im April', 25 April 1917.

33 BA-MA: PH 5-I/11, 'Erfahrungen aus den Kämpfen im Ap. 1917 u.a. bei Arras.'

34 E. Ludendorff, *My War Memories 1914–1918* (2 vols., London: Hutchinson & Co., 1919), II, p. 430; and Boff, *Haig's Enemy*, p. 160.

35 Crown Prince R. von Bayern, *Mein Kriegstagebuch* (3 vols., Berlin: E. S. Mittler, 1929), II, p. 136 (entry, 9 April 1917).

36 Reichsarchiv, *Der Weltkrieg*. XII. *Die Kriegführung im Frühjahr 1917*, p. 543.

37 Falls, *Military Operations. 1917*, I, p. 556; and Reichsarchiv, *Der Weltkrieg*. XII. *Die Kriegführung im Frühjahr 1917*, pp. 410, 546.

38 '250,000 Strikers in Berlin', *The Times*, 20 April 1917; and A. Watson, *Ring of Steel. Germany and Austria–Hungary at War, 1914–1918* (London: Allen Lane, 2015; first publ. 2014), p. 479.

39 I. V. Hull, *The Entourage of Kaiser Wilhelm II 1888–1918* (Cambridge: Cambridge University Press, 1982), p. 284. The three-class franchise grouped voters into different classes and gave greater weight to those that paid more in taxation.

40 'Die kaiserliche Osterbotschaft', 7 April 1917, in H. Michaelis, E. Schraepler and G. Scheel (eds.), *Ursachen und Folgen. Vom deutschen Zusammenbruch 1918 und 1945 bis zur staatlichen Neuordnung Deutschlands in der Gegenwart: Die Wende des ersten Weltkrieges und der Beginn der innenpolitischen Wandlung 1916/1917* (Berlin: Herbert Wendler & Co., 1958), p. 319.

41 J. C. G. Röhl, *Wilhelm II. Into the Abyss of War and Exile, 1900–1941*, trans. S. de Bellaigue and R. Bridge (Cambridge: Cambridge University Press, 2014), p. 1166.

42 W. Görlitz (ed.), *The Kaiser and His Court. The Diaries, Note Books and Letters of Admiral Georg Alexander von Müller, Chief of the Naval Cabinet, 1914–1918* (London: Macdonald & Co., 1961; first publ. 1959), pp. 260–61 (entry, 23 April 1917).

43 H. H. Herwig, *The First World War. Germany and Austria–Hungary 1914–1918* (London: Arnold, 1997), p. 318.

44 Reichsarchiv, *Der Weltkrieg. XII. Die Kriegführung im Frühjahr 1917*, p. 549.

45 Doughty, *Pyrrhic Victory*, p. 354.

46 Sir J. Davidson, *Haig. Master of the Field* (London: Peter Nevill, 1953), p. 14.

47 E. Greenhalgh (ed. and trans.), *Liaison. General Pierre des Vallières at British General Headquarters, January 1916 to May 1917* (Stroud: History Press, 2016), p. 252 (entry, 24 April 1917).

48 E. Greenhalgh, *The French Army and the First World War* (Cambridge: Cambridge University Press, 2014), pp. 194–5.

49 Micheler to Nivelle, 29 April 1917, in E. Herbillon, *Le Général Alfred Micheler (1914–1918)* (Paris: Librairie Plon, 1933), p. 186.

50 TNA: CAB 45/201, Major-General G. S. Clive diary, 28 April 1917. Original emphasis.

51 D. Rolland, *Nivelle. L'Inconnu du Chemin des Dames* (Paris: Imago, 2012), p. 201.

52 B. Serrigny, *Trente ans avec Pétain* (Paris: Librairie Plon, 1959), p. 85.

53 'Directive No. 1', 19 May 1917, in *United States Army in the World War, 1917–1919* (17 vols., Washington DC: US Government Printing Office, 1948), II, pp. 1–2.

Part 3: 'A matter of command'

16 'Patience and tenacity'

1 LOC: Pershing diary, 13 June 1917.

2 *Le Matin*, 14 June 1917.

3 J. J. Pershing, *My Experiences in the World War* (2 vols., New York: Frederick A. Stokes, 1931), I, pp. 58–9.

4 S. L. A. Marshall, *World War I* (Boston and New York: Houghton Mifflin, 2001; first publ. 1964), p. 279.

5 R. O'Connor, *Black Jack Pershing* (New York: Doubleday & Co., 1961), p. 13.

6 D. F. Trask, *The AEF and Coalition Warmaking, 1917–1918* (Lawrence, Kan.: University Press of Kansas, 1993), p. 12.

7 R. B. Bruce, *A Fraternity of Arms. America and France in the Great War* (Lawrence, Kan.: University Press of Kansas, 2003), p. 98.

8 Joffre to Painlevé, 20 May 1917, in Ministère de la Guerre, *Les Armées françaises dans la Grande guerre* (Paris: Imprimerie Nationale, 1922–39) [hereafter *AFGG*], Book 5/2 – *Annexes*, Vol. 1, No. 249, p. 427.

9 *United States Army in the World War, 1917–1919* (17 vols., Washington DC: US Government Printing Office, 1948), I, p. 3.

10 Pershing, *My Experiences*, I, p. 63.

11 J. G. Harbord, *Leaves from a War Diary* (New York: Dodd, Mead and Company, 1925), p. 49.

12 Pershing to Baker, 9 July 1917, in A. S. Link (ed.), *The Papers of Woodrow Wilson* (69 vols., Princeton, NJ: Princeton University Press, 1966–94), Vol. 43, pp. 262–4.

13 *AFGG*, Book 5/2, p. 193.

14 E. Greenhalgh, *The French Army and the First World War* (Cambridge: Cambridge University Press, 2014), pp. 211–12. Soldiers' pay was increased in March 1917 with a franc a day combat allowance (for each day spent in the front line), as well as a further long-service allowance of 0.2 francs a day for those who had served two years beyond their obligation.

15 'Rapport', 30 May 1917, and Maistre to Franchet d'Espèrey, 28 May 1917, in *AFGG*, Book 5/2 – *Annexes*, Vol. 1, Nos. 372 and 354, pp. 591, 616.

16 *AFGG*, Book 5/2, p. 195.

17 'Général commandant en chef à toutes autorités', in *AFGG*, Book 5/2 – *Annexes*, Vol. 1, No. 459, pp. 766–7.

18 Greenhalgh, *French Army*, pp. 208–11.

19 'Pourquoi nous nous battons', *L'Écho de Paris*, 27 June 1917.

20 'Directive No. 2', 20 June 1917, in *AFGG*, Book 5/2 – *Annexes*, Vol. 1, No. 542, pp. 906–7.

21 'Directive No. 3', 4 July 1917, in *AFGG*, Book 5/2 – *Annexes*, Vol. 1, No. 629, pp. 1055–64.

22 'Note sur la situation actuelle', 5 June 1917, in *AFGG*, Book 5/2 – *Annexes*, Vol. 1, No. 426, p. 719.

23 Sir J. E. Edmonds, *Military Operations. France and Belgium, 1917* (3 vols., London: HMSO, 1948), II, p. 54 n. 2.

24 Ibid., pp. 35–8.

25 IWM: 95/16/1, 'Recollections by A. Sambrook', p. 58.

26 Sir C. Harington, *Plumer of Messines* (London: John Murray, 1935), pp. 97–8.

27 'Compte rendu d'opération de la journée du 7 juin', in *AFGG*, Book 5/2 – *Annexes*, Vol. 1, No. 456, pp. 762–4.

28 Harington, *Plumer*, p. 101.

29 S. Marble, *British Artillery on the Western Front in the First World War. 'The Infantry cannot do with a gun less'* (Farnham: Ashgate, 2013), p. 185.

30 D. French, *The Strategy of the Lloyd George Coalition, 1916–1918* (Oxford: Clarendon Press, 1995), pp. 67, 74.

31 D. R. Woodward (ed.), *The Military Correspondence of Field-Marshal Sir William Robertson, Chief of the Imperial General Staff, December 1915– February 1918* (London: Bodley Head for the Army Records Society, 1989), p. 193.

32 Robertson to Haig, 13 June 1917, in R. Blake (ed.), *The Private Papers of Douglas Haig, 1914–1919* (London: Eyre & Spottiswoode, 1952), p. 239. Original emphasis.

33 Ibid., pp. 238, 240 (entries, 12 and 19 June 1917).

34 TNA: CAB 27/6, 'Cabinet Committee on War Policy', 19 June 1917.

35 Ibid., 21 June 1917.

36 French, *Lloyd George Coalition*, p. 113; and D. Lloyd George, *War Memoirs of David Lloyd George* (2 vols., London: Odhams Press, 1933–6), II, p. 1292.

37 Reichsarchiv, *Der Weltkrieg 1914 bis 1918*. XII. *Die Kriegführung im Frühjahr 1917* (Berlin: E. S. Mittler & Sohn, 1939), p. 554.

38 Reichsarchiv, *Der Weltkrieg 1914 bis 1918*. XIII. *Die Kriegführung im Sommer und Herbst 1917. Die Ereignisse außerhalb der Westfront bis November 1918* (Berlin: E. S. Mittler & Sohn, 1942), pp. 2–3.

39 Hindenburg to Bethmann Hollweg, 19 June 1917, in E. Ludendorff, *The General Staff and Its Problems*, trans. F. A. Holt (2 vols., London: Hutchinson & Co., 1920), II, p. 448.

40 Reichsarchiv, *Der Weltkrieg*. XIII. *Die Kriegführung im Sommer und Herbst 1917*, p. 7.

41 'Events in the Reichstag', *The Times*, 10 July 1917; and 'Resolution on Peace Terms Passed by the Reichstag', in J. B. Scott (ed.), *Official Statements of War Aims and Peace Proposals. December 1916 to November 1918* (Washington DC: Carnegie Endowment for International Peace, 1921), pp. 114–15.

42 Hindenburg to the Kaiser and Ludendorff to the Kaiser, 12 July 1917, in Ludendorff, *The General Staff*, II, pp. 461, 462.

43 K. H. Jarausch, *The Enigmatic Chancellor. Bethmann Hollweg and the Hubris of Imperial Germany* (New Haven, Conn., and London: Yale University Press, 1973), pp. 346–7, 372.

44 J. Sheldon, *The German Army at Passchendaele* (Barnsley: Pen & Sword, 2007), p. 315.

45 Edmonds, *Military Operations. 1917*, II, p. 72 n. 2.

46 P. Hart, *Bloody April. Slaughter in the Skies over Arras, 1917* (London: Cassell, 2006; first publ. 2005), p. 11.

47 J. H. Morrow, Jr, *The Great War in the Air. Military Aviation from 1909 to 1921* (Tuscaloosa, Ala.: University of Alabama Press, 2009; first publ. 1993), p. 216.

48 V. M. Yeates, *Winged Victory* (London: Grub Street, 2010; first publ. 1934), p. 31.

49 J. H. Morrow, Jr, *German Air Power in World War I* (Lincoln, Neb.: University of Nebraska Press, 1982), pp. 95–6, 109.

50 F. von Lossberg, *Lossberg's War. The World War I Memoirs of a German Chief of Staff*, trans. D. T. Zabecki and D. J. Biedekarken (Lexington, Ky.: University of Kentucky Press, 2017), pp. 287–8; and Crown Prince R. von Bayern, *Mein Kriegstagebuch* (3 vols., Berlin: E. S. Mittler, 1929), II, p. 232 (entry, 31 July 1917).

17 'Terrible butchery'

1 Robertson to Haig, 18 July 1917, and Haig to Robertson, 21 July 1917, in D. R. Woodward (ed.), *The Military Correspondence of Field-Marshal Sir William Robertson, Chief of the Imperial General Staff, December 1915–February 1918* (London: Bodley Head for the Army Records Society, 1989), pp. 203–6.

2 Robertson to Haig, 21 July 1917, in ibid., pp. 206–7.

3 TNA: CAB 24/21, GT 1532, 'War Cabinet. Allied Conference at Paris 25th–26th July 1917. Future Military Policy'; and Robertson to Haig, 14 April 1917, in Woodward (ed.), *Military Correspondence*, p. 171.

4 Sir J. E. Edmonds, *Military Operations. France and Belgium, 1917* (3 vols., London: HMSO, 1948), II, p. 138 n. 2; and H. A. Jones, *The War in the Air. Being the Story of the Part Played in the Great War by the Royal Air Force* (6 vols., Oxford: Clarendon Press, 1922–37), IV, pp. 142–3.

5 Sir H. Gough, *The Fifth Army* (London: Hodder and Stoughton, 1931), p. 192; and N. Lloyd, *Passchendaele. A New History* (London: Viking, 2017), pp. 39–42, 75–6.

6 IWM: Documents 20504, W. B. St Leger diary, 31 July 1917.

7 E. Greenhalgh, *The French Army and the First World War* (Cambridge: Cambridge University Press, 2014), p. 233.

8 TNA: WO 95/642, 'Narrative of Operations on July 31st, 1917 by II Corps', p. 4.

9 I. Verrinder, *Tank Action in the Great War. B Battalion's Experiences 1917* (Barnsley: Pen & Sword, 2009), p. 77.

10 J. Sheldon, *The German Army at Passchendaele* (Barnsley: Pen & Sword, 2007), pp. 81–2.

11 Edmonds, *Military Operations. 1917*, II, pp. 178 n. 1, 179 n. 1.

12 Gough, *The Fifth Army*, p. 201.

13 TNA: WO 256/21, Haig diary, 1 August 1917.

14 E. Ludendorff, *My War Memories 1914–1918* (2 vols., London: Hutchinson & Co., 1919), II, p. 478.

15 Ludendorff to higher commanders, 31 July 1917, in H. Michaelis, E. Schraepler and G. Scheel (eds.), *Ursachen und Folgen. Vom deutschen Zusammenbruch 1918 und 1945 bis zur staatlichen Neuordnung Deutschlands in der Gegenwart: Die Wende des ersten Weltkrieges und der Beginn der innenpolitischen Wandlung 1916/1917* (Berlin: Herbert Wendler & Co., 1958), pp. 224–5.

16 P. von Hindenburg, *Out of My Life*, trans. F. A. Holt (London: Cassell and Company, 1920), p. 312.

17 L. Cecil, *Wilhelm II. 2. Emperor and Exile, 1900–1941* (Chapel Hill, NC: University of North Carolina Press, 1996), p. 252; F. Fischer, *Germany's Aims in the First World War* (New York: W. W. Norton & Co., 1967; first publ. 1961), p. 401; and D. Stevenson, *1917. War, Peace, and Revolution* (Oxford: Oxford University Press, 2017), p. 250.

18 'Peace Proposal of Pope Benedict XV', 1 August 1917, in J. B. Scott (ed.), *Official Statements of War Aims and Peace Proposals. December 1916 to November 1918* (Washington DC: Carnegie Endowment for International Peace, 1921), pp. 129–31.

19 Reichsarchiv, *Der Weltkrieg 1914 bis 1918*. XIII. *Die Kriegführung im Sommer und Herbst 1917. Die Ereignisse außerhalb der Westfront bis November 1918* (Berlin: E. S. Mittler & Sohn, 1942), pp. 15–16.

20 'Statement of Premier Painlevé in the Chamber of Deputies in Paris on Peace Terms: Alsace–Lorraine', 18 September 1917, and 'Address of Chancellor Michaelis to the Main Committee of the Reichstag', 28 September 1917, in Scott (ed.), *Official Statements*, pp. 136, 147.

21 D. French, *The Strategy of the Lloyd George Coalition, 1916–1918* (Oxford: Clarendon Press, 1995), pp. 144–7.

22 M. Thompson, *The White War. Life and Death on the Italian Front 1915–1919* (London: Faber & Faber, 2008), p. 279.

23 M. von Gallwitz, *Erleben im Westen 1916–1918* (Berlin: E. S. Mittler & Sohn, 1932), p. 220.

24 R. A. Doughty, *Pyrrhic Victory. French Strategy and Operations in the Great War* (London and Cambridge, Mass.: Harvard University Press, 2005), p. 380; and Reichsarchiv, *Der Weltkrieg*. XIII. *Die Kriegführung im Sommer und Herbst 1917*, p. 104.

25 Ministère de la Guerre, *Les Armées françaises dans la Grande guerre* (Paris: Imprimerie Nationale, 1922–39) [hereafter *AFGG*], Book 5/2, p. 829; and R. Christian-Frogé, *La Grande guerre vécue, racontée, illustrée par les combattants* (2 vols., Paris: Aristide Quillet, 1922), II, p. 82.

26 Christian-Frogé, *La Grande guerre*, II, p. 81.

27 Greenhalgh, *French Army*, pp. 239, 240.

28 Reichsarchiv, *Der Weltkrieg*. XIII. *Die Kriegführung im Sommer und Herbst 1917*, pp. 107, 108.

29 R. McLeod and C. Fox, 'The Battles in Flanders during the Summer and Autumn of 1917 from General von Kuhl's *Der Weltkrieg 1914–18*', *British Army Review*, No. 116 (August 1997), p. 82.

30 T. Cook, *No Place to Run. The Canadian Corps and Gas Warfare in the First World War* (Vancouver: UBC Press, 1999), p. 120.

31 McLeod and Fox, 'The Battles in Flanders', p. 87.

32 Crown Prince R. von Bayern, *Mein Kriegstagebuch* (3 vols., Berlin: E. S. Mittler, 1929), II, p. 247 (entry, 20 August 1917).

33 TNA: CAB 24/24/GT1814, 'Report on Operations in Flanders from 4th August to 20th August, 1917.'

34 Lord Hankey, *The Supreme Command 1914–1918* (2 vols., London: George Allen and Unwin, 1961), II, p. 693.

35 Lloyd George to Robertson, 26 August 1917, in Woodward (ed.), *Military Correspondence*, p. 220; and TNA: CAB 23/13, 'War Cabinet 225 A', 28 August 1917.

36 'Second Army's Notes on Training and Preparation for Offensive Operations', 31 August 1917, Appendix XXV, in Edmonds, *Military Operations. 1917*, II, p. 459.

37 Edmonds, *Military Operations. 1917*, II, p. 238.

38 AWM: 3DRL/1465, Account of A. D. Hollyhoke, pp. 2–3.

39 Lloyd, *Passchendaele*, pp. 179–83.

40 AWM: 2DRL/0277, S. E. Hunt, 'The Operation at Polygon Wood', pp. 7, 9–10.

41 Reichsarchiv, *Der Weltkrieg*. XIII. *Die Kriegführung im Sommer und Herbst 1917*, p. 77 n. 1.

42 McLeod and Fox, 'The Battles in Flanders', pp. 85, 86. Original emphasis.

43 A. von Thaer, *Generalstabsdienst an der Front und in der O.H.L.* (Göttingen: Vandenhoeck & Ruprecht, 1958), p. 140 (entry, 28 September 1917).

44 Sheldon, *The German Army at Passchendaele*, p. 185; and J. Boff, *Haig's Enemy. Crown Prince Rupprecht and Germany's War on the Western Front* (Oxford: Oxford University Press, 2018), p. 180.

45 Reichsarchiv, *Der Weltkrieg*. XIII. *Die Kriegführung im Sommer und Herbst 1917*, p. 79 n. 1.

46 G. Sheffield and J. Bourne (eds.), *Douglas Haig. War Diaries and Letters 1914–1918* (London: Weidenfeld & Nicolson, 2005), p. 332 (entry, 4 October 1917).

47 Ibid., pp. 331–2 (entry, 3 October 1917).

48 TNA: CAB 24/28/GT2243, Haig to Robertson, 8 October 1917.

49 TNA: CAB 27/6, 'Eighteenth Meeting of the Cabinet Committee on War Policy', 3 October 1917.

50 Hankey quoted in French, *Lloyd George Coalition*, p. 157. Original emphasis.

51 TNA: CAB 24/28/GT2242, 'Future Military Policy', 9 October 1917.

52 Robertson to Haig, 6 October 1917, in Woodward (ed.), *Military Correspondence*, pp. 233–4.

18 'Nothing but the war'

1 J. G. Harbord, *The American Army in France 1917–1919* (Boston: Little, Brown, and Company, 1936), pp. 134, 153.

2 J. J. Pershing, *My Experiences in the World War* (2 vols., New York: Frederick A. Stokes, 1931), I, pp. 80–84.

3 Harbord, *The American Army*, p. 152.

4 M. E. Grotelueschen, *The AEF Way of War. The American Army and Combat in World War I* (New York: Cambridge University Press, 2007), pp. 27–8.

5 Pershing, *My Experiences*, I, p. 150.

6 US Department of the Army, *Final Report of Gen. John J. Pershing. Commander-in-Chief American Expeditionary Forces* (Washington DC: Government Printing Office, 1919), pp. 14–15.

7 Grotelueschen, *The AEF Way of War*, pp. 28–9.

8 *History of the First Division during the World War, 1917–1919* (Philadelphia, Pa.: John C. Winston, 1922), pp. 19–21; and R. B. Bruce, *A Fraternity of Arms. America and France in the Great War* (Lawrence, Kan.: University Press of Kansas, 2003), pp. 118–19.

9 IWM: Documents 22753, Captain G. N. Rawlence diary, 12 October 1917.

10 TNA: WO 256/23, Haig diary, 13 and 18 October 1917. Original emphasis.

11 E. Greenhalgh (ed. and trans.), *Liaison. General Pierre des Vallières at British General Headquarters, January 1916 to May 1917* (Stroud: History Press, 2016), pp. 258, 268 (entries, early May 1917 and 18 May 1917); and G. Sheffield and J. Bourne (eds.), *Douglas Haig. War Diaries and Letters 1914–1918* (London: Weidenfeld & Nicolson, 2005), p. 294 (entry, 18 May 1917).

12 Reichsarchiv, *Der Weltkrieg 1914 bis 1918*. XIII. *Die Kriegführung im Sommer und Herbst 1917. Die Ereignisse außerhalb der Westfront bis November 1918* (Berlin: E. S. Mittler & Sohn, 1942), p. 194; and S. McMeekin, *The Russian Revolution. A New History* (New York: Basic Books, 2017), p. 196.

13 D. Stevenson, *1917. War, Peace, and Revolution* (Oxford: Oxford University Press, 2017), p. 226; and V. Wilcox, 'Generalship and Mass Surrender during the Italian Defeat at Caporetto', in I. F. W. Beckett (ed.), *1917. Beyond the Western Front* (Leiden and Boston: Brill, 2009), p. 30.

14 A. Bostrom, 'The Influence of Industry on the Use and Development of Artillery', in J. Krause (ed.), *The Greater War. Other Combatants and Other Fronts, 1914–1918* (Basingstoke: Palgrave Macmillan, 2014), pp. 56–7.

15 G. Gras, *Malmaison. 23 Octobre 1917* (Paris: Imprimeries Vieillemard, 1934), p. 69.

16 T. Gale, *The French Army's Tank Force and Armoured Warfare in the Great War. The Artillerie Spéciale* (Farnham: Ashgate, 2013), pp. 27–8.

17 Ibid., pp. 103–4; and H. Desagneaux, *A French Soldier's War Diary 1914–1918*, trans. G. J. Adams (Barnsley: Pen & Sword, 2014; first publ. 1975), p. 55.

18 Ministère de la Guerre, *Les Armées françaises dans la Grande guerre* (Paris: Imprimerie Nationale, 1922–39) [hereafter *AFGG*], Book 5/2, p. 1106.

19 *AFGG*, Book 5/2, p. 1110.

20 'The French Victory on the Aisne', *The Times*, 25 October 1917.

21 J. de Pierrefeu, *French Headquarters 1915–1918*, trans. Major C. J. C. Street (London: Geoffrey Bles, 1924), p. 187.

22 N. Lloyd, *Passchendaele. A New History* (London: Viking, 2017), p. 254. Original emphasis.

23 G. W. L. Nicholson, *Official History of the Canadian Army in the First World War. Canadian Expeditionary Force 1914–1919* (Ottawa: Queen's Printer, 1962), p. 313.

24 Lloyd, *Passchendaele*, p. 280.

25 W. Rutherford, *The Tsar's War 1914–1917. The Story of the Imperial Russian Army in the First World War* (Cambridge: Ian Faulkner, 1992), p. 277.

26 L. M. Easton (ed. and trans.), *Journey to the Abyss. The Diaries of Count Harry Kessler, 1880–1918* (New York: Alfred A. Knopf, 2011), pp. 781–4 (entry, 3 October 1917).

27 L. Cecil, *Wilhelm II. 2. Emperor and Exile, 1900–1941* (Chapel Hill, NC: University of North Carolina Press, 1996), pp. 258–61.

28 Reichsarchiv, *Der Weltkrieg 1914 bis 1918. XIV. Die Kriegführung an der Westfront im Jahre 1918* (Berlin: E. S. Mittler & Sohn, 1944), pp. 52–3.

29 Ibid., pp. 53–4.

30 C. Ernest Fayle, *Seaborne Trade. III. The Period of Unrestricted Submarine Warfare* (New York: Longmans, Green & Co., 1924), pp. 182, 187.

31 A. Watson, *Ring of Steel. Germany and Austria–Hungary at War, 1914–1918* (London: Allen Lane, 2015; first publ. 2014), p. 351; and Reichsarchiv, *Der Weltkrieg. XIV. Die Kriegführung an der Westfront im Jahre 1918*, p. 10.

32 G. Strutz, *Schlachten des Weltkrieges. 31. Die Tankschlacht bei Cambrai* (Berlin: Gerhard Stalling, 1929), p. 18.

33 H. A. Jones, *The War in the Air. Being the Story of the Part Played in the Great War by the Royal Air Force* (6 vols., Oxford: Clarendon Press, 1922–37), IV, pp. 236–7.

34 W. Miles, *Military Operations. France and Belgium, 1917* (3 vols., London: HMSO, 1948), III, p. 90 n. 1.

35 Ibid., pp. 140, 149.

36 Strutz, *Tankschlacht bei Cambrai*, p. 171. The quote is from C. von Clausewitz, *On War*, ed. and trans. M. Howard and P. Paret (Princeton, NJ: Princeton University Press, 1984; first publ. 1976), p. 370.

37 P. Gibbs, *Now It Can be Told* (New York and London: Harper & Brothers, 1920), p. 491.

38 Miles, *Military Operations. 1917*, III, p. 273; and Reichsarchiv, *Der Weltkrieg*. XIII. *Die Kriegführung im Sommer und Herbst 1917*, p. 143.

39 Miles, *Military Operations. 1917*, III, p. 227; and Reichsarchiv, *Der Weltkrieg*. XIII. *Die Kriegführung im Sommer und Herbst 1917*, p. 144.

40 Reichsarchiv, *Der Weltkrieg*. XIV. *Die Kriegführung an der Westfront im Jahre 1918*, p. 59 n. 1.

41 D. French, *The Strategy of the Lloyd George Coalition, 1916–1918* (Oxford: Clarendon Press, 1995), p. 167; and G. Mead, *The Good Soldier. The Biography of Douglas Haig* (London: Atlantic Books, 2014; first publ. 2007), pp. 309–10.

42 Sir J. E. Edmonds, *Military Operations. France and Belgium, 1918* (5 vols., London: Macmillan and Co., 1935), I, p. 32.

43 W. S. Churchill, *Great Contemporaries* (London: Odhams Press, 1949; first publ. 1937), p. 244.

44 J. C. King, *Generals and Politicians. Conflict between France's High Command, Parliament and Government, 1914–1918* (Berkeley and Los Angeles: University of California Press, 1951), p. 195; and D. R. Watson, *Georges Clemenceau. A Political Biography* (London: Eyre Methuen, 1974), p. 271.

19 'The greatest effort we have made'

1 E. Ludendorff, *My War Memories 1914–1918* (2 vols., London: Hutchinson & Co., 1919), II, p. 553.

2 H. H. Herwig, *The First World War. Germany and Austria–Hungary 1914–1918* (London: Arnold, 1997), p. 384; and 'Aus einer Rede des Grafen Westarp im Reichstag am 19. März 1918', in H. Michaelis, E. Schraepler and G. Scheel (eds.), *Ursachen und Folgen. Vom deutschen Zusammenbruch 1918 und 1945 bis zur staatlichen Neuordnung Deutschlands in der Gegenwart:*

Der militärische Zusammenbruch und das Ende des Kaiserreichs (Berlin: Herbert Wendler & Co., n.d.), p. 183.

3 L. Cecil, *Wilhelm II. 2. Emperor and Exile, 1900–1941* (Chapel Hill, NC: University of North Carolina Press, 1996), pp. 264–5.

4 Hindenburg to the Kaiser, 7 January 1918, in Michaelis, Schraepler and Scheel (eds.), *Ursachen und Folgen*, pp. 133–5.

5 The Kaiser to Hindenburg, January 1918, in E. Ludendorff, *The General Staff and Its Problems*, trans. F. A. Holt (2 vols., London: Hutchinson & Co., 1920), II, pp. 531–2.

6 W. Görlitz (ed.), *The Kaiser and His Court. The Diaries, Note Books and Letters of Admiral Georg Alexander von Müller, Chief of the Naval Cabinet, 1914–1918* (London: Macdonald & Co., 1961; first publ. 1959), pp. 324–5 (entries, 16–17 January 1918).

7 I. V. Hull, *The Entourage of Kaiser Wilhelm II 1888–1918* (Cambridge: Cambridge University Press, 1982), p. 288.

8 Hindenburg to the Kaiser, 7 January 1918, in Michaelis, Schraepler and Scheel (eds.), *Ursachen und Folgen*, p. 135.

9 Reichsarchiv, *Der Weltkrieg 1914 bis 1918*. XIV. *Die Kriegführung an der Westfront im Jahre 1918* (Berlin: E. S. Mittler & Sohn, 1944), p. 16; and D. T. Zabecki, *The German 1918 Offensives. A Case Study in the Operational Level of War* (London and New York: Routledge, 2006), p. 107.

10 Reichsarchiv, *Der Weltkrieg*. XIV. *Die Kriegführung an der Westfront im Jahre 1918*, p. 75.

11 Ibid.

12 Ludendorff, *My War Memories*, II, p. 590.

13 Reichsarchiv, *Der Weltkrieg*. XIV. *Die Kriegführung an der Westfront im Jahre 1918*, p. 77 n. 3.

14 Crown Prince R. von Bayern, *Mein Kriegstagebuch* (3 vols., Berlin: E. S. Mittler, 1929), II, p. 322 (entry, 21 January 1918); and Zabecki, *The German 1918 Offensives*, p. 109.

15 F. von Lossberg, *Lossberg's War. The World War I Memoirs of a German Chief of Staff*, trans. D. T. Zabecki and D. J. Biedekarken (Lexington, Ky.: University of Kentucky Press, 2017), pp. 311–18.

16 Zabecki, *The German 1918 Offensives*, p. 115; and Ludendorff, *My War Memories*, II, pp. 587–8.

17 'British War Aims', *The Times*, 7 January 1918.

18 K. Grieves, *The Politics of Manpower, 1914–18* (Manchester: Manchester University Press, 1988), p. 166.

19 TNA: CAB 24/4, G185, 'War Cabinet. Cabinet Committee of Man-Power. Draft Report.'

20 R. Blake (ed.), *The Private Papers of Douglas Haig, 1914–1919* (London: Eyre & Spottiswoode, 1952), pp. 277–8 (entry, 7 January 1918). Original emphasis.

21 Sir J. E. Edmonds, *Military Operations. France and Belgium, 1918* (5 vols., London: Macmillan and Co., 1935), I, pp. 54–5.

22 R. A. Doughty, *Pyrrhic Victory. French Strategy and Operations in the Great War* (London and Cambridge, Mass.: Harvard University Press, 2005), p. 416.

23 'Directive no. 4 pour les groupes d'armées et les armées', 22 December 1917, in Ministère de la Guerre, *Les Armées françaises dans la Grande guerre* (Paris: Imprimerie Nationale, 1922–39) [hereafter *AFGG*], Book 6/1 – *Annexes*, Vol. 1, No. 202, p. 359.

24 D. F. Trask, *The AEF and Coalition Warmaking, 1917–1918* (Lawrence, Kan.: University Press of Kansas, 1993), p. 24.

25 J. J. Pershing, *My Experiences in the World War* (2 vols., New York: Frederick A. Stokes, 1931), I, p. 272.

26 Pershing to Pétain, 6 January 1918, in *United States Army in the World War, 1917–1919* (17 vols., Washington DC: US Government Printing Office, 1948) [hereafter *USAWW*], III, p. 262.

27 Bliss to Pershing, 2 January 1918, and Pershing to Bliss, 8 January 1918, in ibid., III, pp. 259, 264.

28 Robertson to Pershing, 10 January 1918, and Pershing to Robertson, 15 January 1918, in ibid., III, pp. 11–13, 18–19.

29 'Conference Held at Trianon Palace, Versailles', 29 January 1918, in ibid., III, pp. 29–31.

30 GHQ, AEF War Diary, 11 January 1918, in ibid., III, p. 268.

31 'Joint Note No. 12', Appendix 9, in *Military Operations. France and Belgium, 1918. Appendices* (London: Macmillan and Co., 1935), pp. 37–42.

32 Robertson to Derby, 2 February 1918, in D. R. Woodward (ed.), *The Military Correspondence of Field-Marshal Sir William Robertson, Chief of the Imperial General Staff, December 1915–February 1918* (London: Bodley Head for the Army Records Society, 1989), p. 280.

33 D. R. Woodward, *Lloyd George and the Generals* (London and Toronto: Associated University Presses, 1983), pp. 258–9.

34 Lloyd George quoted in T. H. Bliss, 'The Evolution of the Unified Command', *Foreign Affairs*, Vol. 1, No. 2 (15 December 1922), p. 16.

35 P. E. Wright, *At the Supreme War Council* (New York and London: G. P. Putnam's Sons, 1921), p. 65.

36 Robertson to Haig, 24 January 1918, and Robertson to Lord Derby, 2 February 1918, in Woodward (ed.), *Military Correspondence*, pp. 274, 280.

37 Bliss, 'The Evolution of the Unified Command', p. 30.

38 P. Maze, *A Frenchman in Khaki* (London: William Heinemann, 1934), pp. 267–8.

39 Gough to GHQ, 1 February 1918, Appendix 11, and GHQ Instructions, 9 February 1918, Appendix 13, in Sir J. E. Edmonds et al., *Military Operations. France and Belgium, 1918. Appendices*, pp. 46, 51.

40 M. Middlebrook, *The Kaiser's Battle* (London: Penguin, 2000; first publ. 1978), p. 71; and G. Sheffield and J. Bourne (eds.), *Douglas Haig. War Diaries and Letters 1914–1918* (London: Weidenfeld & Nicolson, 2005), p. 385 (entry, 2 March 1918).

41 P. von Hindenburg, *Out of My Life*, trans. F. A. Holt (London: Cassell and Company, 1920), p. 341.

42 G. Fong, 'The Movement of German Divisions to the Western Front, Winter 1917–1918', *War in History*, Vol. 7, No. 2 (April 2000), pp. 229, 232.

43 Reichsarchiv, *Der Weltkrieg*. XIV. *Die Kriegführung an der Westfront im Jahre 1918*, p. 101; and Zabecki, *The German 1918 Offensives*, p. 125.

44 Edmonds, *Military Operations. 1918*, I, p. 147.

45 E. Jünger, *Storm of Steel*, trans. M. Hofmann (London: Penguin Books, 2003; first publ. 1920), p. 231.

46 Thaer quoted in Herwig, *The First World War*, p. 394.

20 'I fear it means disaster'

1 E. Ludendorff, *My War Memories 1914–1918* (2 vols., London: Hutchinson & Co., 1919), II, pp. 597–8.

2 P. C. Ettighoffer, *Sturm 1918. Sieben Tage deutsches Schicksal* (Gütersloh: Bertelsmann, 1938), p. 110.

3 Reichsarchiv, *Der Weltkrieg 1914 bis 1918*. XIV. *Die Kriegführung an der Westfront im Jahre 1918* (Berlin: E. S. Mittler & Sohn, 1944), p. 110.

4 H. von Wolff, *Kriegsgeschichte des Jäger-Bataillon von Neumann (1. Schles.) Nr. 5, 1914–1918* (Zeulenroda: Bernhard Sporn, 1930), p. 217; and Reichsarchiv, *Der Weltkrieg*. XIV. *Die Kriegführung an der Westfront im Jahre 1918*, p. 111.

5 Reichsarchiv, *Der Weltkrieg*. XIV. *Die Kriegführung an der Westfront im Jahre 1918*, p. 125.

6 D. Stevenson, *With Our Backs to the Wall. Victory and Defeat in 1918* (London: Penguin Books, 2012; first publ. 2011), p. 54

7 Sir H. Gough, *The Fifth Army* (London: Hodder and Stoughton, 1931), p. 266.

8 M. Middlebrook, *The Kaiser's Battle* (London: Penguin Books, 2000; first publ. 1978), p. 322; and Sir J. E. Edmonds, *Military Operations. France and Belgium, 1918* (5 vols., London: Macmillan and Co., 1935), I, p. 254.

9 J. H. Morrow, Jr, *The Great War in the Air. Military Aviation from 1909 to 1921* (Tuscaloosa, Ala.: University of Alabama Press, 2009; first publ. 1993), p. 297.

10 Edmonds, *Military Operations. 1918*, I, pp. 164–5; and G. Sheffield and J. Bourne (eds.), *Douglas Haig. War Diaries and Letters 1914–1918* (London: Weidenfeld & Nicolson, 2005), pp. 389–90 (entry, 21 March 1918).

11 Edmonds, *Military Operations. 1918*, I, p. 102; and Ministère de la Guerre, *Les Armées françaises dans la Grande guerre* (Paris: Imprimerie Nationale, 1922–39) [hereafter *AFGG*], Book 6/1, p. 237.

12 *AFGG*, Book 6/1, p. 236.

13 E. Herbillon, *Souvenirs d'un officier de liaison pendant la Guerre mondiale. Du général en chef au gouvernement* (2 vols., Paris: Jules Tallandier, 1930), II, p. 227 (entry, 21 March 1918).

14 Reichsarchiv, *Der Weltkrieg*. XIV. *Die Kriegführung an der Westfront im Jahre 1918*, pp. 111, 121–2; Edmonds, *Military Operations. 1918*, I, p. 260; and Crown Prince R. von Bayern, *Mein Kriegstagebuch* (3 vols., Berlin: E. S. Mittler, 1929), II, p. 345 (entry, 21 March 1918).

15 Reichsarchiv, *Der Weltkrieg*. XIV, p. 133; and D. T. Zabecki, *The German 1918 Offensives. A Case Study in the Operational Level of War* (London and New York: Routledge, 2006), p. 141.

16 Crown Prince Wilhelm, *My War Experiences* (London: Hurst and Blackett, n.d.), p. 303.

17 Reichsarchiv, *Der Weltkrieg*. XIV. *Die Kriegführung an der Westfront im Jahre 1918*, p. 166.

18 Gough, *The Fifth Army*, p. 281.

19 Reichsarchiv, *Der Weltkrieg*. XIV. *Die Kriegführung an der Westfront im Jahre 1918*, p. 167.

20 H. von Kuhl, *Genesis, Execution and Collapse of the German Offensive in 1918*. Part Two. *The Execution and Failure of the Offensive*, trans. H. Hossfeld (Washington DC: US Army War College, 1934), pp. 37–8.

21 IWM: 89/21/1, Account of Captain J. E. March, p. 41.

22 P. Maze, *A Frenchman in Khaki* (London: William Heinemann, 1934), p. 291.

23 TNA: WO 158/28, 'Conference at Dury at 11 p.m., Sunday, March 24th, 1918'; and Edmonds, *Military Operations. 1918*, I, p. 392.

24 Wilson quoted in E. Greenhalgh, 'Myth and Memory: Sir Douglas Haig and the Imposition of Allied Unified Command in March 1918', *Journal of Military History*, Vol. 68, No. 3 (July 2004), pp. 800–801.

25 G. A. Riddell, *Lord Riddell's War Diary 1914–1918* (London: Ivor Nicholson & Watson, 1933), p. 320 (entry, 23 March 1918).

26 TNA: WO 158/28, 'Record of Third Conference held at DOULLENS at 12 noon, 26th March, 1918.' Original emphasis.

27 R. Poincaré, *Au service de la France*. X. *Victoire et armistice 1918* (Paris: Librairie Plon, 1933), pp. 87–8.

28 Edmonds, *Military Operations. 1918*, I, p. 542; and F. Foch, *The Memoirs of Marshal Foch*, trans. T. Bentley Mott (London: William Heinemann, 1931), pp. 301–3.

29 Sheffield and Bourne (eds.), *Douglas Haig*, p. 392 n. 1 (24 March 1918); and J. de Pierrefeu, *French Headquarters 1915–1918*, trans. Major C. J. C. Street (London: Geoffrey Bles, 1924), p. 235.

30 R. Binding, *A Fatalist at War*, trans. I. F. D. Morrow (Boston and New York: Houghton Mifflin, 1929), p. 207.

31 G. von der Marwitz, *Weltkriegsbriefe*, ed. E. von Tschischwitz (Berlin: Steiniger-Verlage, 1940), pp. 285–6.

32 Reichsarchiv, *Der Weltkrieg*. XIV. *Die Kriegführung an der Westfront im Jahre 1918*, p. 133.

33 Marwitz, *Weltkriegsbriefe*, pp. 284–5.

34 M. Kitchen, *The German Offensives of 1918* (Stroud: Tempus, 2005; first publ. 2001), p. 99.

35 Reichsarchiv, *Der Weltkrieg*. XIV. *Die Kriegführung an der Westfront im Jahre 1918*, p. 255 n. 1.

36 Zabecki, *The German 1918 Offensives*, p. 151.

37 'The German 24th Division in the Offensive of March, 1918', *Royal United Services Institution. Journal*, Vol. 69, No. 474 (1924), p. 346.

38 H. A. Jones, *The War in the Air. Being the Story of the Part Played in the Great War by the Royal Air Force* (6 vols., Oxford: Clarendon Press, 1922–37), IV, p. 316.

39 R. von Bayern, *Mein Kriegstagebuch*, II, p. 357 (entry, 26 March 1918).

40 Wilhelm Ritter von Leeb quoted in J. Boff, *Haig's Enemy. Crown Prince Rupprecht and Germany's War on the Western Front* (Oxford: Oxford University Press, 2018), p. 217.

41 Reichsarchiv, *Der Weltkrieg*. XIV. *Die Kriegführung an der Westfront im Jahre 1918*, pp. 219, 220.

42 J. J. Pershing, *My Experiences in the World War* (2 vols., New York: Frederick A. Stokes, 1931), I, pp. 364–5.

43 Edmonds, *Military Operations. 1918*, p. 115.

44 E. Fayolle, *Cahiers secrets de la Grande guerre*, ed. H. Contamine (Paris: Plon, 1964), p. 265 (entry, 28 March 1918).

45 Edmonds, *Military Operations. 1918*, II, pp. 153–5; and Reichsarchiv, *Der Weltkrieg*. XIV. *Die Kriegführung an der Westfront im Jahre 1918*, p. 266.

46 R. A. Pereira, *A Batalha do Lys a 9 de Abril de 1918 e A Acção Notavel das Tropas Portuguêsas na Mesma Batalha* (Porto: Fernando d'Alcantara, 1930), p. 20.

47 F. E. Whitton, *History of the 40th Division* (Uckfield: Naval & Military Press, 2004; first publ. 1926), p. 210.

48 Sheffield and Bourne (eds.), *Douglas Haig*, p. 400 (entry, 9 April 1918); and 'Note', 10 April 1918, in *AFGG*, Book 6/1 – *Annexes*, Vol. 3, No. 1579, p. 314.

49 Edmonds, *Military Operations. 1918*, II, p. 490.

50 'Special Order of the Day', 11 April 1918, Appendix 10, in Edmonds, *Military Operations. 1918*, II, p. 512.

51 Stevenson, *With Our Backs to the Wall*, p. 75.

21 'Hold the line at all hazards'

1 M. Weygand, *Mémoires. Idéal vécu* (Paris: Ernest Flammarion, 1953), p. 505.

2 Sir J. P. Du Cane, *Marshal Foch* (privately printed, 1920), pp. 1–2, 5.

3 Sir J. E. Edmonds, *Military Operations. France and Belgium, 1918* (5 vols., London: Macmillan and Co., 1937), II, p. 315.

4 F. Foch, *The Memoirs of Marshal Foch*, trans. T. Bentley Mott (London: William Heinemann, 1931), pp. 319–20.

5 Edmonds, *Military Operations. 1918*, II, pp. 313–14.

6 Du Cane, *Marshal Foch*, pp. 11–13.

7 G. Sheffield and J. Bourne (eds.), *Douglas Haig. War Diaries and Letters 1914–1918* (London: Weidenfeld & Nicolson, 2005), p. 404 (entry, 14 April 1918).

8 Haig to Foch, 18 April 1918, in *United States Army in the World War, 1917–1919* (17 vols., Washington DC: US Government Printing Office, 1948) [hereafter *USAWW*], II, p. 328.

9 K. Jeffery, *Field Marshal Sir Henry Wilson. A Political Soldier* (Oxford: Oxford University Press, 2006), p. 224; and Foch, *Memoirs*, pp. 335–7.

10 Pétain to Foch, 24 April 1918, in *USAWW*, II, pp. 345–8.

11 E. Greenhalgh, *Foch in Command. The Forging of a First World War General* (Cambridge: Cambridge University Press, 2011), p. 319; and 'Note by the General-in-Chief of the Allied Armies in France', 19 April 1918, Appendix 16, in Edmonds, *Military Operations. 1918*, II, pp. 519–20. Original emphasis.

12 R. Poincaré, *Au service de la France. X. Victoire et armistice 1918* (Paris: Librairie Plon, 1933), p. 123.

13 D. T. Zabecki, *The German 1918 Offensives. A Case Study in the Operational Level of War* (London and New York: Routledge, 2006), p. 202.

14 Crown Prince R. von Bayern, *Mein Kriegstagebuch* (3 vols., Berlin: E. S. Mittler, 1929), II, p. 387 (entry, 19 April 1918).

15 C. E. W. Bean, *The Official History of Australia in the War of 1914–1918* (13 vols., Sydney: Angus & Robertson, 1941–2), V, p. 552; and D. R. Higgins, *Mark IV vs A7V: Villers-Bretonneux 1918* (Oxford: Osprey, 2012), pp. 63–4.

16 'The Loss of Mount Kemmel, 25th April, 1918', *Royal United Services Institution. Journal*, Vol. 66, No. 461 (1921), p. 129.

17 Ministère de la Guerre, *Les Armées françaises dans la Grande guerre* (Paris: Imprimerie Nationale, 1922–39) [hereafter *AFGG*], Book 6/1, p. 499.

18 Edmonds, *Military Operations. 1918*, II, pp. 428–9; and Reichsarchiv, *Der Weltkrieg 1914 bis 1918*. XIV. *Die Kriegführung an der Westfront im Jahre 1918* (Berlin: E. S. Mittler & Sohn, 1944), p. 297.

19 Edmonds, *Military Operations. 1918*, II, p. 437.

20 H. A. Jones, *The War in the Air. Being the Story of the Part Played in the Great War by the Royal Air Force* (6 vols., Oxford: Clarendon Press, 1922–37), IV, p. 398.

21 H. Desagneaux, *A French Soldier's War Diary 1914–1918*, trans. G. J. Adams (Barnsley: Pen & Sword, 2014; first publ. 1975), p. 59.

22 Edmonds, *Military Operations. 1918*, II, pp. 432–3.

23 'Aus den Tagebuchaufzeichnungen des Obersten im Generalstabe von Thaer vom 26/27 April und 2 Mai 1918', in H. Michaelis, E. Schraepler and G. Scheel (eds.), *Ursachen und Folgen. Vom deutschen Zusammenbruch 1918 und 1945 bis zur staatlichen Neuordnung Deutschlands in der Gegenwart: Der militärische Zusammenbruch und das Ende des Kaiserreichs* (Berlin: Herbert Wendler & Co., n.d.), pp. 255–8.

24 Reichsarchiv, *Der Weltkrieg*. XIV. *Die Kriegführung an der Westfront im Jahre 1918*, pp. 312–13.

25 Zabecki, *The German 1918 Offensives*, p. 210.

26 Reichsarchiv, *Der Weltkrieg*. XIV. *Die Kriegführung an der Westfront im Jahre 1918*, pp. 314–15.

27 'London Agreement', 24 April 1918, in *USAWW*, II, pp. 342–4.

28 Bliss to March, 20 April 1918, in ibid., p. 333.

29 First Meeting, 5th Session, Supreme War Council, 1 May 1918, in ibid., pp. 360–65.

30 Third Meeting, 5th Session, Supreme War Council, 2 May 1918, in ibid., pp. 366–71.

31 J. J. Pershing, *My Experiences in the World War* (2 vols., New York: Frederick A. Stokes, 1931), II, pp. 28–9.

32 E. Greenhalgh, *The French Army and the First World War* (Cambridge: Cambridge University Press, 2014), pp. 287–9.

33 'General Directive No. 3', 20 May 1918, Appendix II, in Edmonds, *Military Operations. 1918*, III, pp. 339–41.

34 E. Fayolle, *Cahiers secrets de la Grande guerre*, ed. H. Contamine (Paris: Plon, 1964), p. 274 (entry, 19 May 1918).

35 Edmonds, *Military Operations. 1918*, III, p. 47.

36 T. von Bose, *Schlachten des Weltkrieges. 32. Deutsche Siege 1918* (Berlin: Gerhard Stalling, 1929), p. 29.

37 Reichsarchiv, *Der Weltkrieg. XIV. Die Kriegführung an der Westfront im Jahre 1918*, p. 339.

38 Duchêne to Franchet d'Espèrey, 28 April 1918, in *AFGG*, Book 6/2 – *Annexes*, Vol. 1, No. 68, p. 162; and R. A. Doughty, *Pyrrhic Victory. French Strategy and Operations in the Great War* (London and Cambridge, Mass.: Harvard University Press, 2005), pp. 449–50.

39 Edmonds, *Military Operations. 1918*, III, p. 32.

40 T. Travers, *How the War was Won. Command and Technology in the British Army on the Western Front, 1917–1918* (Barnsley, Pen & Sword, 2005; first publ. 10 1992), p. 101.

41 Edmonds, *Military Operations. 1918*, III, p. 50; and Greenhalgh, *French Army*, p. 294.

42 R. Christian-Frogé, *La Grande guerre vécue, racontée, illustrée par les combattants* (2 vols., Paris: Aristide Quillet, 1922), II, pp. 130–32.

43 Crown Prince Wilhelm, *My War Experiences* (London: Hurst and Blackett, n.d.), p. 320.

44 Edmonds, *Military Operations. 1918*, III, p. 82.

45 Ibid., pp. 147–8.

46 Foch to Haig, 28 May 1918, in *AFGG*, Book 6/2 – *Annexes*, Vol. 1, No. 505, pp. 659–60; and Sheffield and Bourne (eds.), *Douglas Haig*, p. 416 (entry, 31 May 1918).

47 Reichsarchiv, *Der Weltkrieg. XIV. Die Kriegführung an der Westfront im Jahre 1918*, p. 363.

48 Pershing to Peyton C. March (US Chief of Staff), 1 June 1918, in *USAWW*, II, p. 434.

49 M. E. Grotelueschen, *The AEF Way of War. The American Army and Combat in World War I* (New York: Cambridge University Press, 2007), pp. 75–6.

50 'Account by an Eye-Witness of the Attack on Cantigny', 29 May 1918, in *USAWW*, IV, pp. 321–2.

51 Pershing to March and Newton, 1 June 1918, in ibid., II, p. 434.

52 J. H. Hallas (ed.), *Doughboy War. The American Expeditionary Force in World War I* (Boulder, Colo.: Lynne Rienner, 2000), p. 85; and J. G. Harbord, *The American Army in France 1917–1919* (Boston: Little, Brown, and Company, 1936), p. 283.

53 F. M. Wise, *A Marine Tells It to You* (New York: J. H. Sears & Co., 1929), p. 203.

54 E. G. Lengel, *Thunder and Flames. Americans in the Crucible of Combat, 1917–1918* (Lawrence, Kan.: University Press of Kansas, 2015), p. 169; and Harbord, *The American Army*, p. 300.

22 'It will be a glorious day'

1 A. Watson, *Ring of Steel. Germany and Austria–Hungary at War, 1914–1918* (London: Allen Lane, 2015; first publ. 2014), p. 525; and Ludendorff to Hertling, 8 June 1918, in H. Michaelis, E. Schraepler and G. Scheel (eds.), *Ursachen und Folgen. Vom deutschen Zusammenbruch 1918 und 1945 bis zur staatlichen Neuordnung Deutschlands in der Gegenwart: Der militärische Zusammenbruch und das Ende des Kaiserreichs* (Berlin: Herbert Wendler & Co., n.d.), p. 262.

2 Rupprecht to Hertling, 1 June 1918, in Michaelis, Schraepler and Scheel (eds.), *Ursachen und Folgen*, p. 260.

3 Reichsarchiv, *Der Weltkrieg 1914 bis 1918*. XIV. *Die Kriegführung an der Westfront im Jahre 1918* (Berlin: E. S. Mittler & Sohn, 1944), p. 415; and D. T. Zabecki, *The German 1918 Offensives. A Case Study in the Operational Level of War* (London and New York: Routledge, 2006), p. 233.

4 Ministère de la Guerre, *Les Armées françaises dans la Grande guerre* (Paris: Imprimerie Nationale, 1922–39) [hereafter *AFGG*], Book 6/2, pp. 262–4.

5 R. A. Doughty, *Pyrrhic Victory. French Strategy and Operations in the Great War* (London and Cambridge, Mass.: Harvard University Press, 2005), p. 456; and 'Ordre particulier no. 1285', 8 June 1918, in *AFGG*, Book 6/2 – *Annexes*, Vol. 2, No. 1277, p. 461.

6 *AFGG*, Book 6/2, p. 281.

7 Sir J. E. Edmonds, *Military Operations. France and Belgium, 1918* (5 vols., London: Macmillan and Co., 1939), III, p. 179; and Reichsarchiv, *Der Weltkrieg*. XIV. *Die Kriegführung an der Westfront im Jahre 1918*, pp. 398–9.

8 Reichsarchiv, *Der Weltkrieg. XIV. Die Kriegführung an der Westfront im Jahre 1918*, p. 401.

9 C. Mangin, *Lettres de Guerre 1914–1918* (Paris: Librairie Arthème Fayard, 1950), pp. 268–9.

10 *AFGG*, Book 6/2, p. 322.

11 R. Christian-Frogé, *La Grande guerre vécue, racontée, illustrée par les combattants* (2 vols., Paris: Aristide Quillet, 1922), II, p. 144.

12 'Compte rendu', 11 June 1918, in *AFGG*, Book 6/2 – *Annexes*, Vol. 2, No. 1436, p. 619.

13 R. G. Tindall, 'Tanks at Cantigny and in the Mangin Counterattack of 11 June 1918', *Command and General Staff School Quarterly*, Vol. XVIII, No. 69 (June 1938), p. 96.

14 H. Sulzbach, *With the German Guns. Four Years on the Western Front 1914–1918*, trans. R. Thonger (London: Leo Cooper, 1973), p. 192.

15 Reichsarchiv, *Der Weltkrieg. XIV. Die Kriegführung an der Westfront im Jahre 1918*, p. 385.

16 'German War Aims. Von Kühlmann's Declaration', *The Times*, 26 June 1918.

17 Reichsarchiv, *Der Weltkrieg. XIV. Die Kriegführung an der Westfront im Jahre 1918*, p. 511; and L. Cecil, *Wilhelm II. 2. Emperor and Exile, 1900–1941* (Chapel Hill, NC: University of North Carolina Press, 1996), p. 271.

18 Ludendorff quoted in W. Foerster, *Der Feldherr Ludendorff im Unglück* (Wiesbaden: Limes Verlag, 1952), p. 13.

19 Edmonds, *Military Operations. 1918*, III, pp. 217–18.

20 E. Fayolle, *Cahiers secrets de la Grande guerre*, ed. H. Contamine (Paris: Plon, 1964), p. 283 (entry, 12 June 1918).

21 Doughty, *Pyrrhic Victory*, p. 459; and E. Greenhalgh, *The French Army and the First World War* (Cambridge: Cambridge University Press, 2014), p. 300.

22 D. Stevenson, *With Our Backs to the Wall. Victory and Defeat in 1918* (London: Penguin Books, 2012; first publ. 2011), p. 66.

23 TNA: WO 158/29, Haig to Foch, 14 July 1918.

24 Reichsarchiv, *Der Weltkrieg. XIV. Die Kriegführung an der Westfront im Jahre 1918*, p. 437; and Zabecki, *The German 1918 Offensives*, pp. 257–9.

25 Reichsarchiv, *Der Weltkrieg*. XIV. *Die Kriegführung an der Westfront im Jahre 1918*, p. 441 n. 1.

26 Crown Prince Wilhelm, *My War Experiences* (London: Hurst and Blackett, n.d.), p. 330.

27 E. Greenhalgh, *Foch in Command. The Forging of a First World War General* (Cambridge: Cambridge University Press, 2011), pp. 388–9.

28 E. R. Hooton, *War over the Trenches. Air Power and the Western Front Campaigns 1916–1918* (Hersham: Ian Allen, 2010), p. 229.

29 M. Weygand, *Mémoires. Idéal vécu* (Paris: Ernest Flammarion, 1953), p. 564.

30 *AFGG*, Book 6/2, p. 499.

31 'The Marne-Drama of July 15th, 1918' in C. F. Horne (ed.), *Source Records of the Great War* (7 vols., USA: National Alumni, 1923), VI, p. 253.

32 W. Beumelburg, *Schlachten des Weltkrieges. 34. Der letzte deutsche Angriff, Reims 1918* (Berlin: Gerhard Stalling, 1930), p. 72.

33 'By General Gouraud', in Horne (ed.), *Source Records*, VI, pp. 243–4.

34 Reichsarchiv, *Der Weltkrieg*. XIV. *Die Kriegführung an der Westfront im Jahre 1918*, p. 451.

35 Ibid., p. 451 n. 2.

36 'Colonel Reinhardt's Report on the Situation South of the Marne', 17 July 1918, in *United States Army in the World War, 1917–1919* (17 vols., Washington DC: US Government Printing Office, 1948) [hereafter *USAWW*], V, p. 183.

37 Foerster, *Der Feldherr Ludendorff im Unglück*, p. 28.

38 Foch quoted in Edmonds, *Military Operations. 1918*, III, p. 234.

39 T. Gale, *The French Army's Tank Force and Armoured Warfare in the Great War. The Artillerie Spéciale* (Farnham: Ashgate, 2013), p. 166.

40 J. W. Thomason, Jr, *Fix Bayonets!* (New York and London: Charles Scribner's Sons, 1927), pp. 98–101.

41 Gale, *The French Army's Tank Force*, pp. 175–6.

42 MHI: WW1 2487, 'My Memories of World War I', by Captain M. B. Helm, pp. 16–17.

43 M. S. Neiberg, *The Second Battle of the Marne* (Bloomington, Ind.: Indiana University Press, 2008), p. 130; and Mangin quoted in J. J. Pershing,

My Experiences in the World War (2 vols., New York: Frederick A. Stokes, 1931), II, pp. 161–2.

44 E. Ludendorff, *My War Memories 1914–1918* (2 vols., London: Hutchinson & Co., 1919), II, p. 640.

45 War Diary, Army Group German Crown Prince, 18 July 1918, in *USAWW*, V, pp. 678–80.

46 Pershing, *My Experiences*, II, p. 171.

47 'Memorandum by General Foch', 24 July 1918, Appendix XX, in Edmonds, *Military Operations. 1918*, III, pp. 367–70.

48 Pétain quoted in F. Foch, *The Memoirs of Marshal Foch*, trans. T. Bentley Mott (London: William Heinemann, 1931), p. 430.

49 Sir F. Maurice (ed.), *The Life of General Lord Rawlinson of Trent* (London: Cassell and Company, 1926), p. 227.

50 Edmonds, *Military Operations. 1918*, IV, pp. 23, 24.

51 LAC: RG41, Vol. 7, Account of Colonel D. H. C. Mason.

52 Reichsarchiv, *Der Weltkrieg. XIV. Die Kriegführung an der Westfront im Jahre 1918*, p. 567.

53 Crown Prince R. von Bayern, *Mein Kriegstagebuch* (3 vols., Berlin: E. S. Mittler, 1929), II, p. 435 (entry, 9 August 1918).

54 'Signed Minutes of the Conference at General Headquarters on August 14, 1918', in E. Ludendorff, *The General Staff and Its Problems*, trans. F. A. Holt (2 vols., London: Hutchinson & Co., 1920), II, pp. 580–83.

55 A. Niemann, *Kaiser und Revolution. Die entscheidenden Ereignisse im Großen Hauptquartier* (Berlin: August Scherl, 1922), p. 43.

23 'Keep steady'

1 House of Commons Debates, 7 August 1918, Vol. 109, cc. 1412–28.

2 'British War Effort. Prime Minister's Review', *The Times*, 8 August 1918.

3 D. French, *The Strategy of the Lloyd George Coalition, 1916–1918* (Oxford: Clarendon Press, 1995), p. 272.

4 'Mr Lloyd George on the Battle', *The Times*, 12 August 1918.

5 Ministère de la Guerre, *Les Armées françaises dans la Grande guerre* (Paris: Imprimerie Nationale, 1922–39) [hereafter *AFGG*], Book 7/1, p. 228.

6 C. Mangin, *Lettres de Guerre 1914–1918* (Paris: Librairie Arthème Fayard, 1950), p. 299.

7 Sir J. E. Edmonds, *Military Operations. France and Belgium, 1918* (5 vols., London: Macmillan and Co., 1947), IV, p. 181.

8 M. Weygand, *Mémoires. Idéal vécu* (Paris: Ernest Flammarion, 1953), p. 595.

9 'Reduction of St-Mihiel Salient', 16 August 1918, in *United States Army in the World War, 1917–1919* (17 vols., Washington DC: US Government Printing Office, 1948) [hereafter *USAWW*], VIII, pp. 129–30.

10 TNA: WO 158/29, Haig to Foch, 27 August 1918.

11 Haig to Wilson, 27 August 1918, in G. Sheffield and J. Bourne (eds.), *Douglas Haig. War Diaries and Letters 1914–1918* (London: Weidenfeld & Nicolson, 2005), p. 450.

12 J. J. Pershing, *My Experiences in the World War* (2 vols., New York: Frederick A. Stokes, 1931), II, pp. 243–7.

13 Ibid., pp. 248–50.

14 'Conference of September 2' and 'Plan for Converging Attack by Combined Allied Forces on the Western Front', 3 September 1918, in *USAWW*, VIII, pp. 47, 50.

15 L. Cecil, *Wilhelm II. 2. Emperor and Exile, 1900–1941* (Chapel Hill, NC: University of North Carolina Press, 1996), p. 274.

16 W. Görlitz (ed.), *The Kaiser and His Court. The Diaries, Note Books and Letters of Admiral Georg Alexander von Müller, Chief of the Naval Cabinet, 1914–1918* (London: Macdonald & Co., 1961; first publ. 1959), p. 383 (entry, 2 September 1918).

17 Ibid., pp. 384–5 (entry, 4 September 1918); and L. Cecil, *Albert Ballin. Business and Politics in Imperial Germany, 1888–1918* (Princeton, NJ: Princeton University Press, 1967), p. 338.

18 'Niederschrift des Obersten und Abteilungschefs in der Obersten Heeresleitung, Mertz von Quirnheim', in H. Michaelis, E. Schraepler and G. Scheel (eds.), *Ursachen und Folgen. Vom deutschen Zusammenbruch 1918 und 1945 bis zur staatlichen Neuordnung Deutschlands in der Gegenwart: Der militärische Zusammenbruch und das Ende des Kaiserreichs* (Berlin: Herbert Wendler & Co., n.d.), pp. 292–3.

19 'Aus dem privaten Kriegstagebuch des Generals von Kuhl', in ibid., p. 304.

20 F. von Lossberg, *Lossberg's War. The World War I Memoirs of a German Chief of Staff*, trans. D. T. Zabecki and D. J. Biedekarken (Lexington, Ky.: University of Kentucky Press, 2017), p. 356.

21 W. Foerster, *Der Feldherr Ludendorff im Unglück* (Wiesbaden: Limes Verlag, 1952), pp. 72–3; and Hochheimer quoted in N. Lloyd, *Hundred Days. The End of the Great War* (London: Viking, 2013), p. 141.

22 Gallwitz to Supreme Command, 3 September 1918, and reply, 10 September 1918, in *USAWW*, VIII, pp. 289–90, 294–5.

23 Reichsarchiv, *Der Weltkrieg 1914 bis 1918*. XIV. *Die Kriegführung an der Westfront im Jahre 1918* (Berlin: E. S. Mittler & Sohn, 1944), pp. 601; and MHI: WWI 146, J. E. Ausland, 'The Last Kilometer. Saint-Mihiel' (entry, 12 September 1918).

24 Reichsarchiv, *Der Weltkrieg*. XIV. *Die Kriegführung an der Westfront im Jahre 1918*, p. 628.

25 H. H. Herwig, *The First World War. Germany and Austria–Hungary 1914–1918* (London: Arnold, 1997), p. 424; and Reichsarchiv, *Der Weltkrieg*. XIV. *Die Kriegführung an der Westfront im Jahre 1918*, p. 621.

26 B. Ziemann, *Violence and the German Soldier in the Great War. Killing, Dying, Surviving*, trans. A. Evans (London: Bloomsbury Academic, 2017), p. 152.

27 Lossberg, *Lossberg's War*, p. 357; and J. Boff, *Haig's Enemy. Crown Prince Rupprecht and Germany's War on the Western Front* (Oxford: Oxford University Press, 2018), p. 238.

28 'Note', 23 September 1918, in *AFGG*, Book 7/1 – *Annexes*, Vol. 2, No. 1257, p. 624.

29 A. Grasset, *Le Maréchal Foch* (Nancy: Berger-Levrault, 1919), p. 82.

30 E. Greenhalgh, *The French Army and the First World War* (Cambridge: Cambridge University Press, 2014), pp. 336–7.

31 'Note', 25 September 1918, in *AFGG*, Book 7/1 – *Annexes*, Vol. 2, No. 1286, pp. 665–6.

32 Sheffield and Bourne (eds.), *Douglas Haig*, pp. 434, 458 (entry, 10 September 1918).

33 G. Wawro, *Sons of Freedom. The Forgotten American Soldiers Who Defeated Germany in World War I* (New York: Basic Books, 2018), p. 307.

34 R. N. Johnson, *Heaven, Hell, or Hoboken* (Cleveland, O.: O. S. Hubbell, 1919), pp. 95–6.

35 H. Drum (Chief of Staff, First Army) to I, III, IV and V Corps, 27 September 1918, in *USAWW*, IX, pp. 138–40.

36 W. S. Triplet, *A Youth in the Meuse–Argonne. A Memoir, 1917–1918*, ed. R. Ferrell (Columbia, Mo.: University of Missouri Press, 2000), p. 171.

37 G. Mead, *Doughboys. America and the First World War* (London: Penguin Books, 2000), p. 307.

38 Pershing to Baker, 2 October 1918, in Pershing, *My Experiences*, II, p. 312.

39 Sir F. Maurice, *The Last Four Months. The End of the War in the West* (London: Cassell and Company, 1919), p. 158.

40 Sir F. Maurice (ed.), *The Life of General Lord Rawlinson of Trent* (London: Cassell and Company, 1926), p. 238.

41 R. E. Priestley, *Breaking the Hindenburg Line. The Story of the 46th (North Midland) Division* (London: T. Fisher Unwin, 1919), p. 49.

42 MHI: WWI 1827, Account of W. J. Strauss, p. 57.

43 IWM: 84/11/2, Account of Major H. J. C. Marshall, p. 9.

44 E. Ludendorff, *My War Memories 1914–1918* (2 vols., London: Hutchinson & Co., 1919), II, p. 721.

45 'Staatssekretär von Hintze über die Vorgänge im Großen Hauptquartier in Spa am 29. September 1918', in Michaelis, Schraepler and Scheel (eds.), *Ursachen und Folgen*, pp. 319–20; and Ludendorff, *My War Memories*, II, pp. 722–3.

46 'Address to Congress Stating the Peace Terms of the United States, 8 January 1918, in *America Joins the World. Selections From the Speeches and State Papers of President Wilson, 1914–1918* (New York: Association Press, 1919), pp. 70–79.

47 Görlitz (ed.), *The Kaiser and His Court*, p. 397 (entry, 29 September 1918).

48 Cecil, *Wilhelm II. 2. Emperor and Exile*, p. 279.

49 Prince M. von Baden, *The Memoirs of Prince Max of Baden*, trans. W. M. Calder and C. W. H. Sutton (2 vols., London: Constable & Co., 1928), II, pp. 3–23.

50 'German Request for an Armistice', 6 October 1918, in J. B. Scott (ed.), *Official Statements of War Aims and Peace Proposals. December 1916 to November 1918* (Washington DC: Carnegie Endowment for International Peace, 1921), p. 415.

51 'Auszug aus den Tagebuchnotizen des Obersten von Thaer vom 30. September und 1. Oktober 1918', in Michaelis, Schraepler and Scheel (eds.), *Ursachen und Folgen*, pp. 322–3.

24 'The full measure of victory'

1 House to Wilson, 6 October 1918, in A. S. Link (ed.), *The Papers of Woodrow Wilson* (69 vols., Princeton, NJ: Princeton University Press, 1966–94), Vol. 51, p. 254.

2 'Answer to German Peace Proposal', 8 October 1918, in *United States Army in the World War, 1917–1919* (17 vols., Washington DC: US Government Printing Office, 1948) [hereafter *USAWW*], X, pp. 7–8.

3 J. Grigg, *Lloyd George. War Leader 1916–1918* (London: Penguin Books, 2003; first publ. 2002), p. 625.

4 D. R. Watson, *Georges Clemenceau. A Political Biography* (London: Eyre Methuen, 1974), p. 326.

5 'Armistice Terms', 7 October 1918, in *USAWW*, X, pp. 4–5; and D. F. Trask, *The United States in the Supreme War Council. American War Aims and Inter-Allied Strategy, 1917–1918* (Westport, Conn.: Greenwood Press, 1978; first publ. 1961), p. 154.

6 Diplomatic Liaison Officer with the Supreme War Council to the Secretary of State, 9 October 1918, in J. V. Fuller (ed.), *Papers Relating to the Foreign Relations of the United States, 1918, Supplement 1, The World War*. 1 (Washington: Government Printing Office, 1933), Document 295.

7 Laughlin to Lansing, 15 October 1918, in ibid., Document 312.

8 Prince M. von Baden, *The Memoirs of Prince Max of Baden*, trans. W. M. Calder and C. W. H. Sutton (2 vols., London: Constable & Co., 1928), II, pp. 66–9.

9 'German Reply to President Wilson's Note', 12 October 1918, in *USAWW*, X, p. 9.

10 'President Wilson's Reply to the German Note of October 12, 1918', 14 October 1918, in *USAWW*, X, p. 10.

11 Foch to Pétain, 4 October 1918, in Ministère de la Guerre, *Les Armées françaises dans la Grande guerre* (Paris: Imprimerie Nationale, 1922–39) [hereafter *AFGG*], Book 7/2 – *Annexes*, Vol. 1, No. 137, p. 214.

12 Pétain to Maistre, 4 October 1918, in *AFGG*, Book 7/2 – *Annexes*, Vol. I, No. 139, p. 216.

13 'Operations Report, October 1–6, 1918', in *USAWW*, IX, p. 228.

14 J. J. Pershing, *My Experiences in the World War* (2 vols., New York: Frederick A. Stokes, 1931), II, pp. 290, 324.

15 LOC: Pershing diary, 4 October 1918.

16 MHI: WWO 6855, Account of Major S. W. Fleming, p. 64.

17 F. E. Noakes, *The Distant Drum. A Memoir of a Guardsman in the Great War* (London: Frontline Books, 2010; first publ. 1952), p. 183.

18 G. Sheffield and J. Bourne (eds.), *Douglas Haig. War Diaries and Letters 1914–1918* (London: Weidenfeld & Nicolson, 2005), pp. 471–2 (entry, 10 October 1918).

19 Sir J. E. Edmonds and R. Maxwell-Hyslop, *Military Operations. France and Belgium, 1918* (5 vols., London: HMSO, 1947), V, pp. 232–3.

20 Sheffield and Bourne (eds.), *Douglas Haig*, p. 472 (entry, 10 October 1918). Original emphasis.

21 *AFGG*, Book 7/2, pp. 130–31.

22 Sir A. Montgomery, *The Story of the Fourth Army in the Battles of the Hundred Days, August 8th to November 11th, 1918* (London: Hodder and Stoughton, 1920), p. 204.

23 R. Prior and T. Wilson, *Command on the Western Front. The Military Career of Sir Henry Rawlinson 1914–18* (Barnsley: Pen & Sword, 2004; first publ. 1992), p. 383.

24 Second Lieutenant C. Carter quoted in M. Brown, *The Imperial War Museum Book of 1918. Year of Victory* (London: Pan, 1999; first publ. 1998), pp. 264–5.

25 Baden, *Memoirs*, II, pp. 99, 109.

26 'Estimate of Political Situation', 18 October 1918, in *USAWW*, X, pp. 12–13.

27 Crown Prince R. von Bayern, *Mein Kriegstagebuch* (3 vols., Berlin: E. S. Mittler, 1929), II, p. 463 (entry, 18 October 1918).

28 Reichsarchiv, *Der Weltkrieg 1914 bis 1918*. XIV. *Die Kriegführung an der Westfront im Jahre 1918* (Berlin: E. S. Mittler & Sohn, 1944), pp. 656–7.

29 E. Ludendorff, *My War Memories 1914–1918* (2 vols., London: Hutchinson & Co., 1919), II, p. 754.

30 Baden, *Memoirs*, II, p. 89.

31 'The German Reply to President Wilson's Note of October 14, 1918', 21 October 1918, in *USAWW*, X, pp. 15–16.

32 'President Wilson's Reply to the German Note of October 21, 1918', 24 October 1918, in *USAWW*, X, pp. 17–18.

33 'Calls for Dictated Peace', *The New York Times*, 24 October 1918.

34 L. Cecil, *Wilhelm II. 2. Emperor and Exile, 1900–1941* (Chapel Hill, NC: University of North Carolina Press, 1996), pp. 281, 283.

35 Hindenburg to Army Group Gallwitz, 24 October 1918, in *USAWW*, X, p. 19.

36 Baden, *Memoirs*, II, pp. 195–7.

37 Ludendorff, *My War Memories*, II, p. 763; and N. Lloyd, *Hundred Days. The End of the Great War* (London: Viking, 2013), pp. 234–5.

38 Plessen quoted in W. Foerster, *Der Feldherr Ludendorff im Unglück* (Wiesbaden: Limes Verlag, 1952), pp. 116–17; and Cecil, *Wilhelm II. 2. Emperor and Exile*, p. 285.

39 'German Reply to President Wilson's Note of October 24, 1918', 27 October 1918, in *USAWW*, X, p. 24.

40 G. W. Rakenius, *Wilhelm Groener als Erster Generalquartiermeister. Die Politik der Obersten Heeresleitung 1918/19* (Boppard am Rhein: Harald Boldt, 1977), p. 16.

41 W. Groener, *Lebenserinnerungen. Jugend. Generalstab. Weltkrieg* (Göttingen: Vandenhoeck & Ruprecht, 1957), pp. 440–43.

42 Group of Armies Gallwitz, War Diary, 2 November 1918, in *USAWW*, IX, p. 576.

43 S. Stephenson, *The Final Battle. Soldiers of the Western Front and the German Revolution of 1918* (Cambridge: Cambridge University Press, 2009), p. 73.

44 Baden, *Memoirs*, II, pp. 300–301.

45 F. Foch, *The Memoirs of Marshal Foch*, trans. T. Bentley Mott (London: William Heinemann, 1931), pp. 501–2.

46 D. Dutton (ed.), *Paris 1918. The War Diary of the British Ambassador, the 17th Earl of Derby* (Liverpool: Liverpool University Press, 2001), p. 295 (entry, 26 October 1918); J. de Pierrefeu, *French Headquarters 1915–1918*, trans. Major C. J. C. Street (London: Geoffrey Bles, 1924), pp. 298–9; and W. T. Walker, *Betrayal at Little Gibraltar. A German Fortress, a Treacherous*

American General, and the Battle to End World War I (New York: Simon & Schuster, 2016), p. 237.

47 'Proceedings of Military Conference at Senlis', 25 October 1918, in *USAWW*, X, pp. 19–23.

48 E. Greenhalgh, *Foch in Command. The Forging of a First World War General* (Cambridge: Cambridge University Press, 2011), pp. 474–5.

49 Lloyd, *Hundred Days*, p. 209.

50 C. Mangin, *Comment finit la Guerre* (Paris: Librairie Plon, 1920), p. 215.

51 Pershing to the Supreme War Council, 30 October 1918, in *USAWW*, X, pp. 28–30.

52 G. Wawro, *Sons of Freedom. The Forgotten American Soldiers Who Defeated Germany in World War I* (New York: Basic Books, 2018), pp. 446–7.

53 B. A. Colonna, *The History of Company B, 311th Infantry in the World War* (Freehold, NJ: Transcript Printing House, 1922), pp. 70–71.

54 H. Liggett, *A.E.F. Ten Years Ago in France* (New York: Dodd, Mead and Company, 1928), p. 224; and LOC: Pershing diary, 1 November 1918.

55 Edmonds and Maxwell-Hyslop, *Military Operations. 1918*, V, p. 557.

56 IWM: 81/21/1, Account of A. J. Turner, p. 53.

57 'Aus einem Bericht Erzbergers über seine Fahrt nach Compiègne am 7. November 1918', in H. Michaelis, E. Schraepler and G. Scheel (eds.), *Ursachen und Folgen. Vom deutschen Zusammenbruch 1918 und 1945 bis zur staatlichen Neuordnung Deutschlands in der Gegenwart: Der militärische Zusammenbruch und das Ende des Kaiserreichs* (Berlin: Herbert Wendler & Co., n.d.), p. 475.

58 M. Weygand, *Mémoires. Idéal vécu* (Paris: Ernest Flammarion, 1953), p. 639.

59 Foch, *Memoirs*, pp. 549–52.

60 Baden, *Memoirs*, II, pp. 336, 341.

61 M. Baumont, *The Fall of the Kaiser*, trans. E. I. James (London: George Allen and Unwin, 1931), p. 111.

62 Crown Prince Wilhelm, *Memoirs of the Crown Prince of Germany* (New York: Charles Scribner's Sons, 1922), pp. 290, 294.

63 'German Declaration at Signature of Armistice', 11 November 1918, in *USAWW*, X, p. 51.

Epilogue

1 J. Boff, *Haig's Enemy. Crown Prince Rupprecht and Germany's War on the Western Front* (Oxford: Oxford University Press, 2018), pp. 245–7.

2 Crown Prince Wilhelm, *Memoirs of the Crown Prince of Germany* (New York: Charles Scribner's Sons, 1922), pp. 352, 358.

3 S. Stephenson, *The Final Battle. Soldiers of the Western Front and the German Revolution of 1918* (Cambridge: Cambridge University Press, 2009), pp. 154–5.

4 W. S. Churchill, *The World Crisis 1911–1918. Abridged and Revised Edition* (London: Macmillan and Co., 1943), p. 823.

5 Sir J. P. Du Cane, *Marshal Foch* (privately printed, 1920), pp. 81–2.

6 R. Griffiths, *Marshal Pétain* (London: Constable, 1970), p. 85.

7 E. Greenhalgh, *The French Army and the First World War* (Cambridge: Cambridge University Press, 2014), p. 377; and R. A. Doughty, *Pyrrhic Victory. French Strategy and Operations in the Great War* (London and Cambridge, Mass.: Harvard University Press, 2005), p. 508.

8 D. Smythe, *Pershing: General of the Armies* (Bloomington and Indianapolis, Ind.: Indiana University Press, 2007; first publ. 1986), p. 232.

9 R. H. Zieger, *America's Great War. World War I and the American Experience* (Lanham, Md.: Rowman & Littlefield, 2000), p. 174.

10 G. Wawro, *Sons of Freedom. The Forgotten American Soldiers Who Defeated Germany in World War I* (New York: Basic Books, 2018), pp. 482, 507.

11 Sir J. E. Edmonds and R. Maxwell-Hyslop, *Military Operations. France and Belgium, 1918* (5 vols., London: HMSO, 1947), V, p. 562.

12 G. S. Duncan, *Douglas Haig As I Knew Him* (London: George Allen and Unwin, 1966), p. 91.

13 'Greeted by High Officials', *The New York Times*, 14 December 1918.

14 'Preliminary Peace Conference, Protocol No. 1, Session of January 18, 1919', in J. V. Fuller (ed.), *Papers Relating to the Foreign Relations of the United States, The Paris Peace Conference, 1919*. III (Washington: Government Printing Office, 1943), Document 3.

15 A. Scott Berg, *Wilson* (New York: Berkley Books 2013), p. 586.

16 'Preliminary Peace Conference, Protocol No. 6, Plenary Session of May 6, 1919', in Fuller (ed.), *Foreign Relations, 1919*. III, Document 8.

17 Brockdorff-Rantzau to Clemenceau, 29 May 1919, in J. V. Fuller (ed.), *Papers Relating to the Foreign Relations of the United States, The Paris Peace Conference, 1919*. VI, Document 89.

18 Clemenceau to Brockdorff-Rantzau, 16 June 1919, in Fuller (ed.), *Foreign Relations, 1919*. VI, Document 93.

19 R. Gerwath, *The Vanquished. Why the First World War Failed to End, 1917–1923* (London: Penguin Books, 2017; first publ. 2016), p. 199.

20 'Peace with Germany', *The Times*, 30 June 1919.

21 Wilhelm II, *The Kaiser's Memoirs*, trans T. R. Ybarra (New York and London: Harper & Brothers, 1922), p. 337.

22 'Ex-Kaiser William II', *The Times*, 5 June 1941.

Select Bibliography

Afflerbach, H., *Falkenhayn. Politisches Denken und Handeln im Kaiserreich* (Munich: Oldenbourg, 1994)

Alter, J. (ed.), *Ein Armeeführer erlebt den Weltkrieg. Persönliche Aufzeichnungen des Generalobersten v. Einem* (Leipzig: v. Hase & Koehler, 1938)

Arthur, Sir G., *Life of Lord Kitchener* (3 vols., London: Macmillan and Co., 1920)

Atwood, R., *General Lord Rawlinson. From Tragedy to Triumph* (London: Bloomsbury Academic, 2018)

Baden, Prince M. von, *The Memoirs of Prince Max of Baden*, trans. W. M. Calder and C. W. H. Sutton (2 vols., London: Constable & Co., 1928)

Bailey, J. B. A., 'The First World War and the Birth of Modern Warfare', in M. Knox and W. Murray (eds.), *The Dynamics of Military Revolution, 1300–2050* (Cambridge: Cambridge University Press, 2001), pp. 132–53

Bauer, M., *Der große Krieg in Feld und Heimat. Erinnerungen und Betrachtungen* (Tübingen: Oslander'sche Buchhandlung, 1922)

Baumont, M., *The Fall of the Kaiser*, trans. E. I. James (London: George Allen and Unwin, 1931)

Bayern, Crown Prince R. von, *Mein Kriegstagebuch* (3 vols., Berlin: E. S. Mittler, 1929)

Beach, J., *Haig's Intelligence. GHQ and the German Army, 1916–1918* (Cambridge: Cambridge University Press, 2013)

Bean, C. E. W., *The Official History of Australia in the War of 1914–1918* (13 vols., Sydney: Angus & Robertson, 1941–2)

Bechthold, M., 'Bloody April Revisited: The Royal Flying Corps at the Battle of Arras, 1917', *British Journal of Military History*, Vol. 4, No. 2 (February 2018), pp. 50–69

Beckett, I. F. W., T. Bowman and M. Connelly, *The British Army and the First World War* (Cambridge: Cambridge University Press, 2017)

Beumelburg, W., *Schlachten des Weltkrieges. 34. Der letzte deutsche Angriff, Reims 1918* (Berlin: Gerhard Stalling, 1930)

Binding, R., *A Fatalist at War*, trans. I. F. D. Morrow (Boston and New York: Houghton Mifflin, 1929)

Blake, R. (ed.), *The Private Papers of Douglas Haig, 1914–1919* (London: Eyre & Spottiswoode, 1952)

Bliss, T. H., 'The Evolution of the Unified Command', *Foreign Affairs*, Vol. 1, No. 2 (15 December 1922), pp. 1–30.

Bloem, W., *The Advance from Mons 1914* (London: Peter Davis, 1930)

Boff, J., *Winning and Losing on the Western Front. The British Third Army and the Defeat of Germany in 1918* (Cambridge: Cambridge University Press, 2012)

———, *Haig's Enemy. Crown Prince Rupprecht and Germany's War on the Western Front* (Oxford: Oxford University Press, 2018)

Boraston, J. H. (ed.), *Sir Douglas Haig's Despatches (December 1915–April 1919)* (London: J. M. Dent & Sons, 1919)

Bose, T. von, *Das Marnedrama 1914. Die Kämpfe des Gardekorps und des rechten Flügels der 3. Armee vom 5. bis 8. September* (Berlin: Gerhard Stalling, 1928)

———, *Schlachten des Weltkrieges. 32. Deutsche Siege 1918* (Berlin: Gerhard Stalling, 1929)

Bourachot, A., *Marshal Joffre. The Triumphs, Failures and Controversies of France's Commander-in-Chief in the Great War*, trans. A. Uffindell (Barnsley: Pen & Sword, 2014)

Brose, E. D., *The Kaiser's Army. The Politics of Military Technology in Germany during the Machine Age, 1870–1918* (Oxford: Oxford University Press, 2001)

Bruce, R. B., *A Fraternity of Arms. America and France in the Great War* (Lawrence, Kan.: University Press of Kansas, 2003)

Bülow, K. von, *Mein Bericht zur Marneschlacht* (Berlin: A. Scherl, 1919)

Callwell, Sir C. E., *Field-Marshal Sir Henry Wilson. His Life and Diaries* (2 vols., London: Cassell and Company, 1927)

Cassar, G. H., *Kitchener. Architect of Victory* (London: William Kimber, 1977)

———, *The Tragedy of Sir John French* (London and Toronto: Associated University Presses, 1985)

———, *Asquith as War Leader* (London: Hambledon, 1994)

———, *Hell in Flanders Fields. Canadians at the Second Battle of Ypres* (Toronto: Dundurn Press, 2010)

Cecil, H. and P. H. Liddle (eds.), *Facing Armageddon. The First World War Experienced* (Barnsley: Leo Cooper, 1996)

Cecil, L., *Wilhelm II. 2. Emperor and Exile, 1900–1941* (Chapel Hill, NC: University of North Carolina Press, 1996)

Charteris, J., *Field-Marshal Earl Haig* (New York: Charles Scribner's Sons, 1929)

——, *At G.H.Q.* (London: Cassell and Company, 1931)

Christian-Frogé, R., *La Grande Guerre vécue, racontée, illustrée par les combattants* (2 vols., Paris: Aristide Quillet, 1922)

Churchill, W. S., *The World Crisis, 1911–1918. Abridged and Revised Edition* (London: Macmillan and Co., 1943)

Clark, C., *Kaiser Wilhelm II* (Harlow: Pearson Education, 2000)

——, *The Sleepwalkers. How Europe Went to War in 1914* (London: Penguin Books, 2013; first publ. 2012)

Clifford, C., *The Asquiths* (London: John Murray, 2003; first publ. 2002)

Contamine, H., *9 Septembre 1914. La Victoire de la Marne* (Paris: Éditions Gallimard, 1970)

Cook, T., *No Place to Run. The Canadian Corps and Gas Warfare in the First World War* (Vancouver: UBC Press, 1999)

Dahlman, R., *Die Schlacht vor Paris. Das Marnedrama 1914,* Part 4 (Berlin: Gerhard Stalling, 1928)

Daille, M., *Histoire de la Guerre mondiale. Joffre et la guerre d'usure 1915–1916* (Paris: Payot, 1936)

Davidson, Sir J., *Haig. Master of the Field* (London: Peter Nevill, 1953)

Delvert, C., *From the Marne to Verdun. The War Diary of Captain Charles Delvert, 101st Infantry, 1914–1916*, trans. I. Sumner (Barnsley: Pen & Sword, 2016)

Desagneaux, H., *A French Soldier's War Diary 1914–1918*, trans. G. J. Adams (Barnsley: Pen & Sword, 2014; first publ. 1975)

Domelier, H., *Behind the Scenes at German Headquarters* (London: Hurst and Blackett, 1919)

Donnell, C., *Breaking the Fortress Line 1914* (Barnsley: Pen & Sword, 2013)

Doughty, R. A., *Pyrrhic Victory. French Strategy and Operations in the Great War* (London and Cambridge, Mass.: Harvard University Press, 2005)

Du Cane, Sir J. P., *Marshal Foch* (privately printed, 1920)

Duffy, C., *Through German Eyes. The British and the Somme 1916* (London: Phoenix, 2007; first publ. 2006)

Duncan, G. S., *Douglas Haig As I Knew Him* (London: George Allen and Unwin, 1966)

Dutton, D. (ed.), *Paris 1918. The War Diary of the British Ambassador, the 17th Earl of Derby* (Liverpool: Liverpool University Press, 2001)

Easton, L. M. (ed. and trans.), *Journey to the Abyss. The Diaries of Count Harry Kessler, 1880–1918* (New York: Alfred A. Knopf, 2011)

Edmonds, Sir J. E., et al., *Military Operations. France and Belgium*, 14 vols. (London: Macmillan and Co., 1922–48)

Engerand, F., *Lanrezac* (Paris: Éditions Bossard, 1926)

Ettighoffer, P. C., *Sturm 1918. Sieben Tage deutsches Schicksal* (Gütersloh: Bertelsmann, 1938)

Falkenhayn, E. von, *General Headquarters 1914–1916 and Its Critical Decisions* (London: Hutchinson & Co., 1919)

Fayolle, E., *Cahiers secrets de la Grande guerre*, ed. H. Contamine (Paris: Plon, 1964)

Ferry, A., *La Guerre vue d'en bas et d'en haut (lettres, notes, discours et rapports)* (Paris: Bernard Grasset, 1920)

Fischer, F., *Germany's Aims in the First World War* (New York: W. W. Norton & Co., 1967; first publ. 1961)

Foch, F., *The Memoirs of Marshal Foch*, trans. T. Bentley Mott (London: William Heinemann, 1931)

Foerster, W., *Der Feldherr Ludendorff im Unglück* (Wiesbaden: Limes Verlag, 1952)

Foley, R. T., 'East or West? General Erich von Falkenhayn and German Strategy, 1914–15', in M. Hughes and M. Seligmann (eds.), *Leadership in Conflict, 1914–1918* (Barnsley: Leo Cooper, 2000), pp. 117–37

——, *German Strategy and the Path to Verdun. Erich von Falkenhayn and the Development of Attrition, 1870–1916* (Cambridge: Cambridge University Press, 2005)

Foley, R. T. (trans. and ed.), *Alfred von Schlieffen's Military Writings* (London: Frank Cass, 2003)

Fong, G., 'The Movement of German Divisions to the Western Front, Winter 1917–1918', *War in History*, Vol. 7, No. 2 (April 2000), pp. 225–35

French, D., *British Strategy and War Aims 1914–16* (London: Allen and Unwin, 1986)

——, *The Strategy of the Lloyd George Coalition, 1916–1918* (Oxford: Clarendon Press, 1995)

French, G. (ed.), *Some War Diaries, Addresses, and Correspondence of Field Marshal the Right Honble. The Earl of Ypres* (London: Herbert Jenkins, 1937)

French, Sir J. D. P., *1914* (London: Constable, 1919)

Gale, T., *The French Army's Tank Force and Armoured Warfare in the Great War. The Artillerie Spéciale* (Farnham: Ashgate, 2013)

Galet, E. J., *Albert King of the Belgians in the Great War. His Military Activities Set Down with His Approval* (London: Putnam, 1931)

Gallwitz, M. von, *Erleben im Westen 1916–1918* (Berlin: E. S. Mittler & Sohn, 1932)

Gibbs, P., *Now It Can be Told* (New York and London: Harper & Brothers, 1920)

Gilbert, M., *Winston S. Churchill*. III. *1914–1916* (London: Heinemann, 1971)

Gold, L., *Die Tragödie von Verdun 1916*, Parts 3 and 4. *Die Zermürbungsschlacht* (Berlin: Gerhard Stalling, 1929)

Görlitz, W. (ed.), *The Kaiser and His Court. The Diaries, Note Books and Letters of Admiral Georg Alexander von Müller, Chief of the Naval Cabinet, 1914–1918* (London: Macdonald & Co., 1961; first publ. 1959)

Gough, Sir H., *The Fifth Army* (London: Hodder and Stoughton, 1931)

Goya, M., *La Chair et l'acier. L'Armée française et l'invention de la guerre moderne (1914–1918)* (Paris: Tallandier, 2004)

Gras, G., *Malmaison. 23 Octobre 1917* (Paris: Imprimeries Vieillemard, 1934)

Gras, Y., *Castelnau, ou l'art de commander 1851–1944* (Paris: Éditions Denoël, 1990)

Grasset, A., *Le Maréchal Foch* (Nancy: Berger-Levrault, 1919)

——, *La Guerre en action. Surprise d'une Division: Rossignol–Saint-Vincent* (Paris: Éditions Berger-Levrault, 1932)

Greenhalgh, E., 'Myth and Memory: Sir Douglas Haig and the Imposition of Allied Unified Command in March 1918', *Journal of Military History*, Vol. 68, No. 3 (July 2004), pp. 771–820

——, *Victory Through Coalition. Britain and France during the First World War* (Cambridge: Cambridge University Press, 2005)

——, *Foch in Command. The Forging of a First World War General* (Cambridge: Cambridge University Press, 2011)

——, *The French Army and the First World War* (Cambridge: Cambridge University Press, 2014)

Greenhalgh, E. (ed. and trans.), *Liaison. General Pierre des Vallières at British General Headquarters, January 1916 to May 1917* (Stroud: History Press, 2016)

Grieves, K., *The Politics of Manpower, 1914–18* (Manchester: Manchester University Press, 1988)

Griffiths, R., *Marshal Pétain* (London: Constable, 1970)

Grigg, J., *Lloyd George. From Peace to War 1912–1916* (London: Penguin Books, 2002; first publ. 1985)

——, *Lloyd George. War Leader 1916–1918* (London: Penguin Books, 2003; first publ. 2002)

Groener, W., *Lebenserinnerungen. Jugend. Generalstab. Weltkrieg* (Göttingen: Vandenhoeck & Ruprecht, 1957)

Grotelueschen, M. E., *The AEF Way of War. The American Army and Combat in World War I* (New York: Cambridge University Press, 2007)

Guéno, J. P. and Y. Laplume (eds.), *Paroles de poilus. Lettres et carnets du front 1914–1918* (Paris: Radio France, 1998)

Guinn, P., *British Strategy and Politics 1914 to 1918* (Oxford: Clarendon Press, 1965)

Haber, L. F., *The Poisonous Cloud. Chemical Warfare in the First World War* (Oxford: Oxford University Press, 1986)

Hallas, J. H. (ed.), *Doughboy War. The American Expeditionary Force in World War I* (Boulder, Colo.: Lynne Rienner, 2000)

Hankey, Lord, *The Supreme Command 1914–1918* (2 vols., London: George Allen and Unwin, 1961)

Harbord, J. G., *Leaves from a War Diary* (New York: Dodd, Mead and Company, 1925)

——, *The American Army in France 1917–1919* (Boston: Little, Brown, and Company, 1936)

Harington, Sir C., *Plumer of Messines* (London: John Murray, 1935)

Harris, J. P., *Douglas Haig and the First World War* (Cambridge: Cambridge University Press, 2008)

Hart, P., *Bloody April. Slaughter in the Skies over Arras, 1917* (London: Cassell, 2006; first publ. 2005)

Head, R. G., *Oswald Boelcke. Germany's First Fighter Ace and Father of Air Combat* (London: Grub Street, 2016)

Herbillon, E., *Souvenirs d'un officier de liaison pendant la Guerre mondiale. Du général en chef au gouvernement* (2 vols., Paris: Jules Tallandier, 1930)

——, *Le Général Alfred Micheler (1914–1918)* (Paris: Librairie Plon, 1933)

Herwig, H. H., *The First World War. Germany and Austria–Hungary 1914–1918* (London: Arnold, 1997)

——, *The Marne, 1914. The Opening of World War I and the Battle That Changed the World* (New York: Random House, 2011; first publ. 2009)

Hindenburg, P. von, *Out of My Life*, trans. F. A. Holt (London: Cassell and Company, 1920)

Hoeppner, E. W. von, *Germany's War in the Air. The Development and Operations of German Military Aviation in the World War*, trans. J. Hawley Larned (Nashville, Tenn.: Battery Press, 1994; first publ. 1921)

Holmes, R., *The Little Field Marshal. A Life of Sir John French* (London: Cassell, 2005; first publ. 1981)

Hooton, E. R., *War over the Trenches. Air Power and the Western Front Campaigns 1916–1918* (Hersham: Ian Allen, 2010)

Horne, A., *The Price of Glory. Verdun 1916* (Harmondsworth: Penguin Books, 1964; first publ. 1962)

Horne, C. F. (ed.), *Source Records of the Great War* (7 vols., USA: National Alumni, 1923)

Horne, J. and A. Kramer, *German Atrocities, 1914. A History of Denial* (New Haven, Conn., and London: Yale University Press, 2001),

House, E. M., *The Intimate Papers of Colonel House*, ed. C. Seymour (4 vols., London: Ernest Benn, 1926–8)

Hull, I. V., *The Entourage of Kaiser Wilhelm II 1888–1918* (Cambridge: Cambridge University Press, 1982)

Humphries, M. O. and J. Maker (eds.), *Germany's Western Front. Translations from the German Official History of the Great War. II. 1915* (Waterloo, Ont.: Wilfrid Laurier Press, 2009)

——, *Germany's Western Front. Translations from the German Official History of the Great War. 1914, Part 1* (Waterloo, Ont.: Wilfrid Laurier Press, 2013)

Jarausch, K. H., *The Enigmatic Chancellor. Bethmann Hollweg and the Hubris of Imperial Germany* (New Haven, Conn., and London: Yale University Press, 1973)

Jauneaud, M., 'Souvenirs de la bataille d'Arras (Octobre 1914)', *Revue des Deux Mondes*, Vol. 58 (August 1920), pp. 571–98

——, 'Souvenirs de la bataille d'Arras: II', *Revue des Deux Mondes*, Vol. 58 (August 1920), pp. 825–56

Jeffery, K., *Field Marshal Sir Henry Wilson. A Political Soldier* (Oxford: Oxford University Press, 2006)

Joffre, J. C., *The Memoirs of Marshal Joffre*, trans. T. Bentley Mott (2 vols., London: Geoffrey Bles, 1932)

Johnson, R. N., *Heaven, Hell, or Hoboken* (Cleveland, O.: O. S. Hubbell, 1919)

Jones, H. A., *The War in the Air. Being the Story of the Part Played in the Great War by the Royal Air Force* (6 vols., Oxford: Clarendon Press, 1922–37)

Jünger, E., *Storm of Steel*, trans. M. Hofmann (London: Penguin Books, 2003; first publ. 1920)

King, J. C., *Generals and Politicians. Conflict between France's High Command, Parliament and Government, 1914–1918* (Berkeley and Los Angeles: University of California Press, 1951)

Kirchbach, A. von, *Kämpfe in der Champagne (Winter 1914–Herbst 1915)* (Oldenburg: Gerhard Stalling, 1919)

Kitchen, M., *The German Offensives of 1918* (Stroud: Tempus, 2005; first publ. 2001)

Kluck, A. von, *The March on Paris and the Battle of the Marne 1914* (London: Edward Arnold, 1920)

Krause, J., *Early Trench Tactics in the French Army. The Second Battle of Artois, May–June 1915* (Farnham: Ashgate, 2013)

Krause, J. (ed.), *The Greater War. Other Combatants and Other Fronts, 1914–1918* (Basingstoke: Palgrave Macmillan, 2014)

Kuhl, H. von, *Der Marnefeldzug 1914* (Berlin: E.S. Mittler & Sohn, 1921)

——, *Der Weltkrieg 1914–1918. Dem deutschen Volke dargestellt* (Berlin: Verlag Tradition Wilhelm Kolk, 1929)

——, *Genesis, Execution and Collapse of the German Offensive in 1918*. Part Two. *The Execution and Failure of the Offensive*, trans. H. Hossfeld (Washington DC: US Army War College, 1934)

Langle de Cary, F. de, *Souvenirs de commandement 1914–1916* (Paris: Payot, 1935)

Le Naour, J.-Y., *1917. La Paix Impossible* (Paris: Perrin, 2015)

Lengel, E. G., *Thunder and Flames. Americans in the Crucible of Combat, 1917–1918* (Lawrence, Kan.: University Press of Kansas, 2015)

Lennox, A. G. (ed.), *The Diary of Lord Bertie of Thame 1914–1918* (2 vols., London: Hodder and Stoughton, 1924)

Liddell Hart, B., *Foch, the Man of Orleans* (Westport, Conn.: Greenwood Press, 1980; first publ. 1931)

Liggett, H., *A.E.F. Ten Years Ago in France* (New York: Dodd, Mead and Company, 1928)

Link, A. S. (ed.), *The Papers of Woodrow Wilson* (69 vols., Princeton, NJ: Princeton University Press, 1966–94)

Lintier, P., *My Seventy-Five. Journal of a French Gunner (August–September 1914)* (London: Peter Davis, 1929)

Lipkes, J., *Rehearsals. The German Army in Belgium, August 1914* (Leuven: Leuven University Press, 2007)

Lloyd, N., 'Lord Kitchener and "the Russian News": Reconsidering the Origins of the Battle of Loos', *Defence Studies*, Vol. 5, No. 3 (September 2005), pp. 346–65

——, *Loos 1915* (Stroud: Tempus, 2006)

——, '"With Faith and Without Fear": Sir Douglas Haig's Command of First Army during 1915', *Journal of Military History*, Vol. 71, No. 4 (October 2007), pp. 1051–76

——, 'Allied Operational Art in the Hundred Days 1918', *British Army Review*, No. 156 (Winter 2012–13), pp. 116–25

——, *Hundred Days. The End of the Great War* (London: Viking, 2013)

——, *Passchendaele. A New History* (London: Viking, 2017)

Lloyd George, D., *War Memoirs of David Lloyd George* (2 vols., London: Odhams Press, 1933–6)

Loiseau, L. and G. Bénech (eds.), *Carnets de Verdun* (Paris: Librio, 2006)

Lossberg, F. von, *Lossberg's War. The World War I Memoirs of a German Chief of Staff*, trans. D. T. Zabecki and D. J. Biedekarken (Lexington, Ky.: University of Kentucky Press, 2017)

Ludendorff, E., *My War Memories 1914–1918* (2 vols., London: Hutchinson & Co., 1919)

——, *The General Staff and Its Problems*, trans. F. A. Holt (2 vols., London: Hutchinson & Co., 1920)

Madelin, L., *Verdun* (Paris: Librairie Félix Alcan, 1920)

Mallet, C., *Impressions and Experiences of a French Trooper, 1914–15* (New York: E. P. Dutton & Company, 1916)

Mangin, C., *Comment finit la Guerre* (Paris: Librairie Plon, 1920)

——, *Lettres de Guerre 1914–1918* (Paris: Librairie Arthème Fayard, 1950)

Mangin, L.-E., *Le Général Mangin 1866–1925* (Paris: Éditions Fernand Lanore, 1986)

Marshall-Cornwall, Sir J., *Foch as Military Commander* (London: B. T. Batsford, 1972)

Marwitz, G. von der, *Weltkriegsbriefe*, ed. E. von Tschischwitz (Berlin: Steiniger-Verlage, 1940)

Mason, D., *Verdun* (Moreton-in-Marsh: Windrush Press, 2000)

Mason, Jr, H. M., *High Flew the Falcons. The French Aces of World War I* (Philadelphia and New York: J. B. Lippincott, 1965)

Maurice, Sir F., *The Last Four Months. The End of the War in the West* (London: Cassell and Company, 1919)

—— (ed.), *The Life of Lord Rawlinson of Trent* (London: Cassell and Company, 1926)

Maze, P., *A Frenchman in Khaki* (London: William Heinemann, 1934)

McLeod, R. and C. Fox, 'The Battles in Flanders during the Summer and Autumn of 1917 from General von Kuhl's *Der Weltkrieg 1914–18*', *British Army Review*, No. 116 (August 1997), pp. 78–88

McMeekin, S., *July 1914. Countdown to War* (London: Icon Books, 2013)

——, *The Russian Revolution. A New History* (New York: Basic Books, 2017)

Mead, G., *Doughboys. America and the First World War* (London: Penguin Books, 2000)

——, *The Good Soldier. The Biography of Sir Douglas Haig* (London: Atlantic Books, 2014; first publ. 2007)

Michaelis, H., E. Schraepler and G. Scheel (eds.), *Ursachen und Folgen. Vom deutschen Zusammenbruch 1918 und 1945 bis zur staatlichen Neuordnung Deutschlands in der Gegenwart. Die Wende des ersten Weltkrieges und der Beginn der innenpolitischen Wandlung 1916/1917* (Berlin: Herbert Wendler & Co., 1958)

——, *Ursachen und Folgen. Vom deutschen Zusammenbruch 1918 und 1945 bis zur staatlichen Neuordnung Deutschlands in der Gegenwart. Der militärische Zusammenbruch und das Ende des Kaiserreichs* (Berlin: Herbert Wendler & Co., n.d.)

Middlebrook, M., *The First Day on the Somme. 1 July 1916* (London: Penguin Books, 1984; first publ. 1971)

——, *The Kaiser's Battle* (London: Penguin Books, 2000; first publ. 1978)

Ministère de la Guerre, *Les Armées françaises dans la Grande guerre* (Paris: Imprimerie Nationale, 1922–39)

Moltke, H. von, *Erinnerungen. Briefe Dokumente 1877–1916* (Stuttgart: Der Kommende Tag A.G. Verlag, 1922)

Mombauer, A., *Helmuth von Moltke and the Origins of the First World War* (Cambridge: Cambridge University Press, 2001)

Mombauer, A. (ed. and trans.), *The Origins of the First World War. Diplomatic and Military Documents* (Manchester: Manchester University Press, 2013)

Montgomery, Sir A., *The Story of Fourth Army in the Battles of the Hundred Days, August 8th to November 11th, 1918* (London: Hodder and Stoughton, 1920)

Mordacq, J., *Le Drame de l'Yser. La Surprise des gaz (Avril 1915)* (Paris: Éditions des Portiques, 1933)

Morrow, Jr, J. H., *German Air Power in World War I* (Lincoln, Nebr.: University of Nebraska Press, 1982)

——, *The Great War in the Air. Military Aviation from 1909 to 1921* (Tuscaloosa, Ala.: University of Alabama Press, 2009; first publ. 1993)

Nebelin, M., *Ludendorff. Diktator im Ersten Weltkrieg* (Munich: Siedler Verlag, 2010)

Neiberg, M. S., *The Second Battle of the Marne* (Bloomington, Ind.: Indiana University Press, 2008)

Neumann, P., *The German Air Force in the Great War*, trans. J. E. Gurdon (London: Hodder and Stoughton, 1921)

Nicholls, J., *Cheerful Sacrifice. The Battle of Arras 1917* (Barnsley: Pen & Sword, 2003; first publ. 1990)

Nicholson, G. W. L., *Official History of the Canadian Army in the First World War. Canadian Expeditionary Force 1914–1919* (Ottawa: Queen's Printer, 1962)

Niemann, A., *Kaiser und Revolution. Die entscheidenden Ereignisse im Großen Hauptquartier* (Berlin: August Scherl, 1922)

Noakes, F. E., *The Distant Drum. A Memoir of a Guardsman in the Great War* (London: Frontline Books, 2010; first publ. 1952)

O'Connor, R., *Black Jack Pershing* (New York: Doubleday & Co., 1961)

Offenstadt, N. (ed.), *Le Chemin des Dames. De l'évènement à la mémoire* (Paris: Stock, 2004)

Ousby, I., *The Road to Verdun. France, Nationalism and the First World War* (London: Jonathan Cape, 2002)

Painlevé, P., *Comment j'ai nommé Foch et Pétain. La politique de guerre de 1917: Le commandement unique interallié* (Paris: Librairie Félix Alcan, 1923)

Passingham, I., *Pillars of Fire. The Battle of Messines Ridge, June 1917* (Stroud: Sutton, 1998)

Pershing, J. J., *My Experiences in the World War* (2 vols., New York: Frederick A. Stokes, 1931)

Pétain, H. P., *Verdun*, trans. M. Mac Veagh (New York: The Dial Press, 1930)

Philpott, W. J., *Anglo-French Relations and Strategy on the Western Front, 1914–18* (London: Macmillan, 1996)

——, 'Gone Fishing? Sir John French's Meeting with General Lanrezac, 17 August 1914', *Journal of the Society for Army Historical Research*, Vol. 84, No. 339 (Autumn 2006), pp. 254–9

——, *Bloody Victory. The Sacrifice on the Somme and the Making of the Twentieth Century* (London: Little, Brown, 2009)

Pierrefeu, J. de, *L'Offensive du 16 Avril. La Vérité sur l'affaire Nivelle* (Paris: Renaissance du Livre, 1919)

——, *French Headquarters 1915–1918*, trans. Major C. J. C. Street (London: Geoffrey Bles, 1924)

Poincaré, R., *Au service de la France* (10 vols., Paris: Librairie Plon, 1926–33)

——, *The Memoirs of Raymond Poincaré (1913–1914)*, trans. G. Arthur (London: William Heinemann, 1928)

——, *The Memoirs of Raymond Poincaré 1914*, trans. G. Arthur (London: William Heinemann, 1929)

——, *The Memoirs of Raymond Poincaré 1915*, trans. G. Arthur (London: William Heinemann, 1930)

Pollock, J., *Kitchener. Comprising the Road to Omdurman and Saviour of the Nation* (London: Constable, 2001; first publ. 1998)

Porch, D., *The March to the Marne. The French Army 1871–1914* (Cambridge: Cambridge University Press, 1981)

Poseck, M. von, *The German Cavalry. 1914 in Belgium and France* (Berlin: E. S. Mittler & Sohn, 1923)

Prete, R. A., *Strategy and Command. The Anglo-French Coalition on the Western Front, 1914* (Montreal: McGill–Queen's University Press, 2009)

Priestley, R. E., *Breaking the Hindenburg Line. The Story of the 46th (North Midland) Division* (London: T. Fisher Unwin, 1919)

Prior, R. and T. Wilson, *Command on the Western Front. The Military Career of Sir Henry Rawlinson, 1914–1918* (Barnsley: Pen & Sword, 2004; first publ. 1992)

——, *Passchendaele. The Untold Story* (New Haven, Conn., and London: Yale University Press, 2002; first publ. 1996)

——, *The Somme* (New Haven, Conn, and London: Yale University Press, 2005)

Rakenius, G. W., *Wilhelm Groener als Erster Generalquartiermeister. Die Politik der Obersten Heeresleitung 1918/19* (Boppard am Rhein: Harald Boldt, 1977)

Rawling, B., *Surviving Trench Warfare. Technology and the Canadian Corps, 1914–1918* (Toronto: University of Toronto Press, 2014; first publ. 1992)

Recouly, R., *Joffre* (London and New York: D. Appleton & Company, 1931)

Reichsarchiv, *Der Weltkrieg 1914 bis 1918* (15 vols., Berlin: E. S. Mittler & Sohn, 1925–44)

Richthofen, M. von, *The Red Baron* (Barnsley: Pen & Sword, 2009; first publ. 1994)

Riddell, G. A., *Lord Riddell's War Diary 1914–1918* (London: Ivor Nicholson & Watson, 1933)

Röhl, J. C. G., *Wilhelm II. Into the Abyss of War and Exile, 1900–1941*, trans. S. de Bellaigue and R. Bridge (Cambridge: Cambridge University Press, 2014)

Rolland, D., *Nivelle. L'Inconnu du Chemin des Dames* (Paris: Imago, 2012)

Ryan, S., *Pétain the Soldier* (South Brunswick, NJ, and New York: A. S. Barnes, 1969)

Schwink, O., *Ypres 1914. An Official Account Published by Order of the German General Staff*, trans G.C.W. (London: Constable, 1919)

Scott, J. B. (ed.), *Official Statements of War Aims and Peace Proposals. December 1916 to November 1918* (Washington DC: Carnegie Endowment for International Peace, 1921)

Serrigny, B., *Trente ans avec Pétain* (Paris: Librairie Plon, 1959)

Sheffield, G., *Forgotten Victory. The First World War: Myths and Realities* (London: Headline, 2001)

——, *The Somme* (London: Cassell, 2003)

——, *The Chief. Douglas Haig and the British Army* (London: Aurum Press, 2011)

Sheffield, G. and J. Bourne (eds.), *Douglas Haig. War Diaries and Letters 1914–1918* (London: Weidenfeld & Nicolson, 2005)

Sheldon, J., *The German Army at Passchendaele* (Barnsley: Pen & Sword, 2007) Simkins, P., *Kitchener's Army. The Raising of the New Armies, 1914–16* (Manchester: Manchester University Press, 1988)

——, *The German Army on the Somme 1914–1916* (Barnsley: Pen & Sword, 2012; first publ. 2005)

Smith, L. V., *Between Mutiny and Obedience. The Case of the French Fifth Infantry Division during World War I* (Princeton, NJ: Princeton University Press, 1994)

Smith-Dorrien, Sir H., *Memories of Forty-Eight Years' Service* (London: John Murray, 1925)

Smythe, D., *Pershing. General of the Armies* (Bloomington and Indianapolis, Ind.: Indiana University Press, 2007; first publ. 1986)

Sondhaus, L., *The Great War at Sea. A Naval History of the First World War* (Cambridge: Cambridge University Press, 2014)

Spears, Sir E. L., *Liaison 1914. A Narrative of the Great Retreat* (London: Eyre & Spottiswoode, 1968; first publ. 1930)

——, *Prelude to Victory* (London: Jonathan Cape, 1939)

Statistics of the Military Effort of the British Empire during the Great War. 1914–1920 (London: HMSO, 1922)

Steffen, D., 'The Holtzendorff Memorandum of 22 December 1916 and Germany's Declaration of Unrestricted U-Boat Warfare', *Journal of Military History*, Vol. 68, No. 1 (January 2004), pp. 215–24

Stephenson, S., *The Final Battle. Soldiers of the Western Front and the German Revolution of 1918* (Cambridge: Cambridge University Press, 2009)

Stevenson, D., *1914–1918. The History of the First World War* (London: Penguin Books, 2005; first publ. 2004)

——, *With Our Backs to the Wall. Victory and Defeat in 1918* (London: Penguin Books, 2012; first publ. 2011)

——, *1917. War, Peace, and Revolution* (Oxford: Oxford University Press, 2017)

Stone, N., *The Eastern Front 1914–1917* (New York: Charles Scribner's Sons, 1975)

Stosch, A. von, *Somme-Nord*. Part II. *Die Brennpunkte der Schlacht im Juli 1916* (Berlin: Gerhard Stalling, 1927)

Strachan, H., *The First World War*. I. *To Arms* (Oxford: Oxford University Press, 2003; first publ. 2001)

Strutz, G., *Schlachten des Weltkrieges*. 31. *Die Tankschlacht bei Cambrai* (Berlin: Gerhard Stalling, 1929)

Sulzbach, H., *With the German Guns. Four Years on the Western Front 1914–1918*, trans. R. Thonger (London: Leo Cooper, 1973)

Sumner, I., *They Shall Not Pass. The French Army on the Western Front 1914–1918* (Barnsley: Pen & Sword, 2012)

——, *Kings of the Air. French Aces and Airmen of the Great War* (Barnsley: Pen & Sword, 2015)

Talbot Kelly, R. B., *A Subaltern's Odyssey. Memoirs of the Great War 1915–1917* (London: William Kimber, 1980)

Tanenbaum, J. K., *General Maurice Sarrail 1856–1929. The French Army and Left-Wing Politics* (Chapel Hill, NC: University of North Carolina Press, 1974)

Taylor, A. J. P. (ed.), *Lloyd George. A Diary by Frances Stevenson* (London: Hutchinson & Co., 1971)

Thaer, A. von, *Generalstabsdienst an der Front und in der O.H.L.* (Göttingen: Vandenhoeck & Ruprecht, 1958)

Thomason, Jr, J. W., *Fix Bayonets!* (New York and London: Charles Scribner's Sons, 1927)

Tirpitz, Grand Admiral von, *My Memoirs* (2 vols., New York: Dodd, Mead and Company, 1919)

Torrey, G. E., '*L'Affaire de Soissons*, January 1915', *War in History*, Vol. 4, No. 4 (October 1997), pp. 398–410

Trask, D. F., *The United States in the Supreme War Council. American War Aims and Inter-Allied Strategy, 1917–1918* (Westport, Conn.: Greenwood Press, 1978; first publ. 1961)

——, *The AEF and Coalition Warmaking, 1917–1918* (Lawrence, Kan.: University Press of Kansas, 1993)

Travers, T., *The Killing Ground. The British Army, the Western Front and the Emergence of Modern Warfare 1900–1918* (Barnsley: Pen & Sword, 2003; first publ. 1987)

——, *How the War was Won. Command and Technology in the British Army on the Western Front, 1917–1918* (Barnsley: Pen & Sword, 2005; first publ. 1992)

Triplet, W. S., *A Youth in the Meuse–Argonne. A Memoir, 1917–1918*, ed. R. Ferrell (Columbia, Mo.: University of Missouri Press, 2000)

Trumpener, U., 'The Road to Ypres: The Beginnings of Gas Warfare in World War I', *Journal of Modern History*, Vol. 47, No. 3 (September 1975), pp. 460–80

Tyng, S., *The Campaign of the Marne 1914* (London: Humphrey Milford, 1935)

United States Army in the World War, 1917–1919 (17 vols., Washington DC: US Government Printing Office, 1948)

US Department of the Army, *Final Report of Gen. John J. Pershing. Commander-in-Chief American Expeditionary Forces* (Washington DC: Government Printing Office, 1919)

Watson, A., *Enduring the Great War. Combat, Morale and Collapse in the German and British Armies, 1914–1918* (Cambridge: Cambridge University Press, 2008)

——, *Ring of Steel. Germany and Austria–Hungary at War, 1914–1918* (London: Allen Lane, 2015; first publ. 2014)

Watson, D. R., *Georges Clemenceau. A Political Biography* (London: Eyre Methuen, 1974)

Wawro, G., *Sons of Freedom. The Forgotten American Soldiers Who Defeated Germany in World War I* (New York: Basic Books, 2018)

Wendt, H., *Verdun 1916. Die Angriffe Falkenhayns im Maasgebiet mit Richtung auf Verdun als strategisches Problem* (Berlin: Mittler & Sohn, 1931)

Werner, J., *Knight of Germany. Oswald Boelcke, German Ace*, trans. C. W. Sykes (Havertown, Pa.: Casemate, 2009; first publ. 1985)

Weygand, M., *Mémoires. Idéal vécu* (Paris: Ernest Flammarion, 1953)

Wilhelm II, *The Kaiser's Memoirs*, trans T. R. Ybarra (New York and London: Harper & Brothers, 1922)

Wilhelm, Crown Prince of Germany, *Memoirs of the Crown Prince of Germany* (New York: Charles Scribner's Sons, 1922)

——, *My War Experiences* (London: Hurst and Blackett, n.d.)

Williams, C., *Pétain* (London: Little, Brown, 2005)

Wise, F. M., *A Marine Tells It to You* (New York: J. H. Sears & Co., 1929)

Woodward, D. R., *Lloyd George and the Generals* (London and Toronto: Associated University Presses, 1983)

Woodward, D. R. (ed.), *The Military Correspondence of Field-Marshal Sir William Robertson, Chief of the Imperial General Staff, December 1915–February 1918* (London: Bodley Head for the Army Records Society, 1989)

Zabecki, D. T., *The German 1918 Offensives. A Case Study in the Operational Level of War* (London and New York: Routledge, 2006)

Zwehl, H. von, *Maubeuge, Aisne–Verdun. Das VII. Reserve-Korps im Weltkriege von seinem Beginn bis Ende 1916* (Berlin: Karl Curtius, 1921)

Index